FUTURES AND OPTIONS

McGraw-Hill Series in Finance

Consulting Editor

Charles A. D'Ambrosio, *University of Washington*

FUTURES AND OPTIONS

Franklin R. Edwards

Columbia University

Cindy W. Ma

Metallgesellschaft

McGraw-Hill, Inc.

New York   St. Louis   San Francisco   Auckland   Bogotá
Caracas   Lisbon   London   Madrid   Mexico   Milan
Montreal   New Delhi   Paris   San Juan   Singapore
Sydney   Tokyo   Toronto

This book was set in Times Roman by Publication Services.
The editors were Kenneth A. MacLeod and Peitr Bohen;
the production supervisor was Friederich W. Schulte.
The cover was designed by Circa '86.
Project supervision was done by Publication Services.
R. R. Donnelley & Sons Company was printer and binder.

FUTURES AND OPTIONS

Acknowledgments appear on pages 633–636, and on this page by reference.

2 3 4 5 6 7 8 9 0 DOC DOC 9 0 9 8 7 6 5 4 3 2

ISBN 0-07-019441-6

Library of Congress Cataloging-in-Publication Data

Edwards, Frankin R., (date).
    Futures and options / Franklin R. Edwards, Cindy W. Ma.
       p.   cm. — (McGraw-Hill series in finance)
    Includes bibliographical references and index.
    ISBN 0-07-019441-6
    1. Futures market.   2. Hedging (Finance)   3. Options (Finance)
4. Futures.   I. Ma, Cindy W.   II. Title.   III. Series.
HG6024.A3E38   1992
332.64'5—dc20   91-37802

ABOUT THE AUTHORS

Franklin R. Edwards is a member of the Business School faculty at Columbia University and Director of the Center for the Study of Futures Markets at Columbia. As Director of the Futures Center, he is responsible for the management of the center and for its programs. He has held this position since 1980.

Professor Edwards, a member of the faculty of the Columbia Business School since 1966, holds the Arthur F. Burns Chair in Free and Competitive Enterprise. He also served the school as Vice Dean from 1979 to 1981, a role in which he was responsible for all faculty and academic affairs as well as the institution's strategic planning. He holds a Ph.D. from Harvard University and a J.D. from the New York University Law School.

His major areas of research and expertise are futures, securities, and commodity markets, and the regulation of these markets, and banking regulation. He teaches courses dealing with all of these areas at the Columbia Business School. Professor Edwards has published more than 70 articles and is a frequent speaker before university and business groups. He has also testified before Congressional committees, and he has organized and run major conferences on banking and futures markets.

Professor Edwards served as a Public Director on the Futures Industry Association Board of Directors from 1982 to 1987, and as a member of the Nominating Committee of the American Stock Exchange from 1988 to 1990. He is presently a member of the Shadow Financial Regulatory Committee and the New York Mercantile Exchange's Business Conduct Committee.

Prior to joining Columbia University, Professor Edwards held positions at the Federal Reserve Board and at the Office of the Comptroller of the Currency in Washington, D.C. He has been a consultant to regulatory agencies, financial institutions, and law firms on issues related to futures and option markets and to regulatory matters in general.

Cindy W. Ma is the Vice President of MG Futures Inc., a derivative products unit of Metallgesellschaft AG in Germany. She is responsible for proprietary trading in energy futures, developing risk management programs, derivative product research, and the marketing of derivative products to institutional clients.

She received a Ph.D. in money and financial markets from Columbia University in 1988 and a B.S. in accounting from Indiana University in 1982. Prior to joining Metallgesellschaft, she was an associate at the Center for the Study of Futures Markets at Columbia University. She was also an adjunct instructor in a banking management training course for various major commercial banks in New York City. After Indiana University, she worked as a CPA with Arthur Andersen & Co. for two years.

Over the past 10 years, she has received a number of scholarships, fellowships, and awards. She has published several articles dealing with futures markets, and she currently serves on the New Product Committee of the New York Mercantile Exchange.

CONTENTS

PREFACE

During the past five years the authors collaborated in teaching futures and commodity options at Columbia University's Graduate School of Business. At Columbia they were also associated with the Center for the Study of Futures Markets, the leading academic center for research on futures and commodity option markets. For the past three years Cindy has also worked as a trader and research analyst for Metallgesellschaft, a large internationally diversified commodity and industrial firm. In these capacities the authors have been able to view from all angles the rapid and unprecedented expansion of futures and option markets, and have interacted extensively with students, traders, large commercial hedgers, exchange officials, brokerage firms, regulators, legislators and academics.

The perspectives of these respective players are often quite different. Practitioners are interested primarily in how markets can be used either to make money by trading or to reduce risk by using futures and options to hedge existing price risks. Traders seek to understand why futures and option prices do what they do, the reasons for the price relationships that commonly exist, and to identify trading strategies that work. Hedgers want to know how to construct and manage an effective hedging strategy.

Government regulators and legislators, in contrast, are concerned about whether futures and option markets operate efficiently and in the public interest. They want to be certain that customers are not taken advantage of, that speculative excesses do not occur, and that prices in these markets accurately reflect underlying market demand and supply conditions. They also seek to understand the effect that various institutional arrangements have on the performance of the markets.

Students at universities generally wish to acquire a comprehensive understanding of these markets. They want to know everything that practitioners know, but also to understand why these markets exist, how they developed, how they operate, why there is controversy about them, and why government regulation is necessary.

In putting together a course on futures and commodity option markets the authors became aware that there did not exist a textbook which provided the kind of comprehensive treatment of these markets that the authors sought. One reason for this deficiency is that futures and option markets, as well as academic research on these markets, have been undergoing rapid transformation, and it has been difficult for potential authors to keep abreast of developments. The need for an up-to-date and comprehensive textbook was further driven home to the authors by Cindy's experience as a trader.

Our objective at the outset was to write a book that would not be so abstract and complicated that only academics would read it, but would nevertheless be up-to-date enough to reflect the current state of academic research. We have, consequently, tried to keep mathematics and abstract formulas to a minimum, and to utilize whenever possible examples based on real data to illustrate complex ideas. The book also makes extensive use of graphs to show price relationships that exist among futures and option contracts. We strongly believe that these relationships are much easier to comprehend when they can be seen in a visual context. Finally, we provide dozens of hedging examples using different kinds of futures and option contracts so that students can see the nuances of the various hedging strategies. These examples, rather than ignoring the potential pitfalls of hedging as do many discussions of hedging, alert readers to possible problems so that they can make informed decisions.

We have designed this book primarily for use in undergraduate and MBA courses on futures and commodity option markets. No prior knowledge of these markets is necessary to follow the discussion in the book—we start at the beginning. Many instructors, however, may feel that the book can be easily adapted to graduate level courses by supplementing it with material dealing with the derivation of key mathematical formulas and by the inclusion of a reading list containing the primary academic articles that underlie discussion in the text. In addition, students wishing to pass the requisite licensing examinations in order to work in the futures industry will find that most of the required information is contained in the book.

While the main focus of the book is on futures markets, the book includes three comprehensive chapters dealing with option markets. We have not, however, tried to provide a comprehensive treatment of traditional stock option markets, since to do so would make the book unmanageably long. Instructors, nevertheless, will be hard pressed to cover all of the material now included in the text in a one-semester course.

The book can be viewed as being organized into five distinct sections. Section 1, consisting of Chapters 1 through 6, covers the fundamentals of futures markets. It encompasses the growth of these markets in the United States and abroad, the trading that currently takes place in different futures contracts, the reasons for trading futures, the structure and operation of the markets, the institutions and institutional arrangements that underpin these markets, pricing fundamentals, and how futures are used to hedge risks associated with price fluctuations.

The six chapters in this section provide an overview of futures markets that by itself is sufficient for readers wishing only to understand why futures markets exist, what they are, and how they function. Readers who want to know about specific futures contracts, and in particular about financial futures, will need to read additional chapters in the book.

The second section of the book consists of Chapters 7 through 9. These chapters discuss the social benefits of futures markets, the role of speculators, why regulation of futures markets is considered necessary, the goals and structure of regulation, and how the public interest is related to the various types of regulation. The section concludes with a discussion of the key regulatory issues that are currently being debated. These chapters are included in the book because we believe that a full understanding of futures markets is not possible without understanding the regulatory structure that governs them.

The third section of the book, consisting of Chapters 10 through 15, is an in-depth examination of particular types of futures contracts. The first four chapters cover financial futures. Chapter 15 examines commodity futures.

Financial futures are classified and discussed according to the kinds of financial instruments on which the futures are traded. In particular, Chapters 10 and 11 discuss stock index futures; Chapter 12 looks at short-term interest rate futures; Chapter 13 examines long-term interest rate futures; and Chapter 14 covers foreign currency futures. Together these chapters provide a comprehensive treatment of financial futures: what they are, what kinds of contracts are traded, how they are priced, and how they are used by speculators and hedgers.

Chapter 15 covers commodity futures markets, and includes discussions of futures on agricultural commodities, energy products, and precious and industrial metals. These markets are covered in a single chapter, in contrast to the five chapters devoted to financial futures, because much of the general discussion in the first six chapters is directly applicable to commodity futures. In addition, most of the examples contained in the earlier chapters use commodity futures contracts rather than financial futures contracts.

The fourth section of the book, Chapters 16 and 17, discusses how futures contracts are traded and who makes and who loses money. Chapter 16 examines the two basic approaches used by traders: fundamental and technical analysis. The discussion covers the most popular technical trading methodologies, and concludes with some suggested procedures that traders can use to develop their own trading strategies. Chapter 17 surveys the research which has been done on the question of who makes and who loses money by trading futures. The chapter also contains a comprehensive analysis of commodity funds: what they are, how they operate, and what their historical performance has been compared to alternative investments, like stocks and bonds.

The fifth and final section of the book, consisting of Chapters 18, 19, and 20, provides an overview of option markets, and, in particular, of options on futures contracts. These chapters provide a comprehensive treatment of the fundamentals of option markets and of how options are used by both speculators and hedgers. An important objective of these chapters is to describe how commodity options and futures options differ from futures contracts, and to discuss the advantages and the disadvantages of the different instruments when used for speculative and hedging purposes.

Instructors can choose to use the book as we have organized it, or they can omit some chapters in order to spend more time on others or to emphasize particular aspects of futures or option markets. For example, instructors wishing to emphasize only financial futures can combine the first four chapters of the book with Chapters 10 through 14, and possibly Chapter 7. Instructors wishing to stress commodity futures can use the first seven chapters together with Chapter 15. Or, a shorter but still comprehensive course on futures and options can utilize Chapters 1 through 7, Chapters 18, 19, and 20, and one or two of the financial futures chapters, such as Chapters 10 and 13. A course emphasizing speculative trading can use Chapters 1, 2, 4, 7, 16, and 17; and, if option trading is included, Chapters 18, 19, and 20 can be utilized as well. Such a course should probably also include a "trading game" so that students can obtain a "hands-on" feel for the markets. We have generally used such a trading game in the courses we have taught. Finally, some instructors may want to introduce options earlier in the course, which can be done by assigning some or all of Chapter 18 sooner.

ACKNOWLEDGMENTS

We have used several earlier versions of this book in classes at Columbia over the past two years, and would like to thank our students for their patience in putting up with the many errors and omissions that crept into the early manuscripts. Hopefully, we have discovered and corrected most of these. The book is stronger, of course, because of the opportunity we have had to experiment with different versions of it in a classroom setting and because of the feedback received from students.

We could not have written this book without the supportive environments provided by the Columbia Business School and Metallgesellschaft. We were given the opportunity to explore various subjects in depth and to utilize the extensive research facilities and resources of our two institutions, including the opportunity to discuss ideas with many knowledgeable and stimulating colleagues.

Many people helped with the preparation of this book during the past two years. We were fortunate to be able to discuss questions we had with a number of experts in the field. In particular, Stefan Judisch, Art Benson, and Bill Benson of Metallgesellschaft, patiently explained to us the many nuances of futures and option markets. At Columbia University, Mary Hennion cheerfully and efficiently typed several versions of many chapters, and Hong Choi, Meng Tan, and Ahmet Kocagil provided research assistance when needed. We want to thank the Chicago Mercantile Exchange (CME) and the photographer, Mark Segal, for allowing us to use the excellent photograph of the CME trading floor shown on the cover of the book.

We also wish to acknowledge the many helpful comments made by the reviewers of the book, including Esther Ancel, University of Wisconsin–Milwaukee; Robert Brooks, University of Alabama at Tuscaloosa; Peggy Fletcher, Northeastern University; Shantaram Hegde, University of Connecticut; Joel Morse, University of Baltimore; Hun Park, University of Illinois; Lakshmi Shyam-Sunder, Dartmouth College; John Thatcher, University of Wisconsin at Whitewater; and William Welch, Florida International University.

Finally, we wish to express our appreciation to our respective families for providing the environment and encouragement necessary to support the many long and late hours that were required for us to complete the book. We are grateful for their understanding and patience.

Franklin R. Edwards
Cindy W. Ma

ABBREVIATIONS OF INSTITUTIONS

AMEX	American Stock Exchange
BM&F	Bolsa Mercandil y De Futuros
BOTCC	Board of Trade Clearing Corp.
CBOE	Chicago Board Options Exchange
CBOT	Chicago Board of Trade
CFTC	Commodity Futures Trading Commission
CME	Chicago Mercantile Exchange
COMEX	Commodity Exchange
CRCE	Chicago Rice & Cotton Exchange
CSCE	Coffee, Sugar & Cocoa Exchange
DTB	Deutsche Terminborse
EMS	European Monetary System
EOE	European Options Exchange
FDIC	Federal Deposit Insurance Corporation
FOX	London Futures and Options Exchange
GNMA	Government National Mortgage Association
ICC	Intermarket Clearing Corp.
ICCH	International Commodities Clearing House Limited
IMM	International Monetary Exchange
IPE	International Petroleum Exchange
KCBOT	Kansas City Board of Trade
LIFFE	London International Financial Futures Exchange
LME	London Metal Exchange
MATIF	Le Marché à Terme des Instruments Financiers
MGE	Minneapolis Grain Exchange

MidAM	Mid-America Commodity Exchange
NFA	National Futures Association
NYCE	New York Cotton Exchange
NYFE	New York Futures Exchange
NYMEX	New York Mercantile Exchange
NYSE	New York Stock Exchange
OCC	Options Clearing Corp.
OPEC	Organization of Petroleum Exporting Countries
OSE	Osaka Securities Exchange
PHLX	Philadelphia Stock Exchange
SEC	Securities and Exchange Commission
SIMEX	Singapore International Mercantile Exchange
SOFFEX	Swedish Options and Financial Futures Exchange
SOM	Stockholm Options Market
TIFFE	Tokyo International Financial Futures Exchange
TSE	Tokyo Stock Exchange

CHAPTER

1

AN INTRODUCTION TO FUTURES MARKETS

1.1 INTRODUCTION

In 1960 four million futures contracts changed hands during the year on all futures exchanges in the United States. In 1990 nearly 280 million contracts were traded— more each week than in all of 1960. In the last decade alone trading jumped from 98 million to over 276 million contracts. Figure 1-1 depicts this phenomenal growth.

The commodities that are traded today have changed dramatically from those of the past. Thirty years ago most of the trading was in agricultural products, such as corn and soybeans. Today more than half of all futures trading is in financial instruments, such as bonds, stocks, and foreign currencies. Table 1.1 shows the volume of total trading, by type of commodity, for the years 1960 and 1990. In 1960 agricultural products accounted for 78 percent of all trading. In 1990 such trading was less than 21 percent of total futures trading volume. Today (1990), more than 70 percent of trading is done in commodities for which there was *no* futures trading in 1960.

Table 1.2 lists the 10 futures contracts that were the most actively traded in 1960 and 1990, respectively, with the date at which trading in each contract began. Taken together, the 10 most active contracts represented 85.15 percent of total trading in 1960, and 72.56 percent in 1990. In 1960 the nine most actively

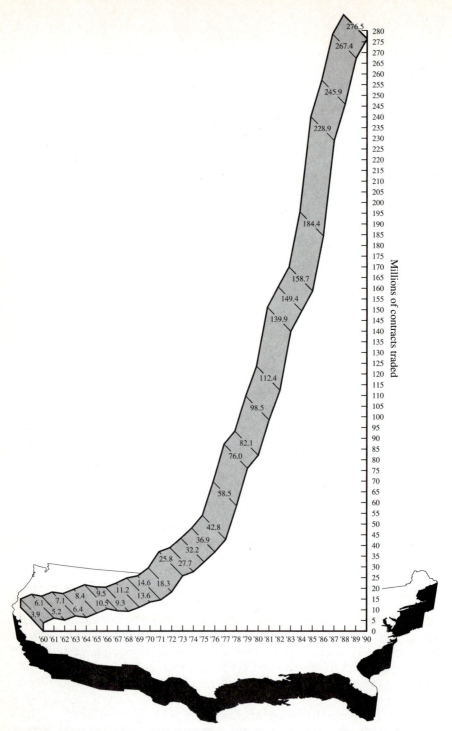

FIGURE 1-1
Volume of futures trading, 1960 through 1990. (Futures Industry Association, Inc.)

TABLE 1.1
Futures contracts traded by commodity group

	1990		1960	
	Contracts	**Percentage**	**Contracts**	**Percentage**
1. Interest rates	123,419,532	44.63	—	—
2. Agriculturals	57,088,348	20.64	3,021,844	77.92
3. Energy products	35,441,295	12.82	—	—
4. Foreign currencies	28,880,894	10.44	—	—
5. Precious metals	14,812,847	5.36	454	0.00
6. Equity indices	14,767,090	5.34	—	—
7. Non-precious metals	1,853,281	0.67	80,341	2.08
8. Others	272,217	0.10	775,512	20.00
Total	276,535,504	100.00	3,878,151	100.00

Source: Futures Industry Association, Inc.

TABLE 1.2
Ten most actively traded futures contracts

Commodity	Date started	1990			1960		
		Rank	**Contracts**	**%**	**Rank**	**Contracts**	**%**
T-bonds	1977	1	75,499,257	27.30	—	—	—
Eurodollars	1981	2	34,695,625	12.55	—	—	—
Crude oil	1983	3	23,686,897	8.57	—	—	—
S&P 500	1982	4	12,139,209	4.39	—	—	—
Corn	1921	5	11,423,027	4.13	4	316,843	8.17
Soybeans	1937	6	10,301,905	3.73	1	1,165,464	30.05
Gold	1975	7	9,730,041	3.52	—	—	—
Deutschemark	1972	8	9,169,230	3.32	—	—	—
Japanese yen	1972	9	7,437,235	2.69	—	—	—
Swiss franc	1972	10	6,524,893	2.36	—	—	—
Eggs*	1919	—	—	—	2	491,319	12.67
Wheat	1921	—	—	—	3	394,186	10.16
Potatoes*	1931	—	—	—	5	255,559	6.59
Soybean oil	1941	—	—	—	6	212,118	5.47
Soybean meal	1940	—	—	—	7	149,190	3.85
Oats	1921	—	—	—	8	145,407	3.75
Rye*	1921	—	—	—	9	96,189	2.48
Copper	1947	—	—	—	10	76,125	1.96
Total			200,607,319	72.56		3,302,400	85.15

*No longer traded.

Source: Futures Industry Association, Inc.

traded contracts were on agricultural commodities. Today six of the ten most active contracts are financial futures, with U.S. Treasury bonds by far the most active, accounting for over 27 percent of total trading. Finally, of the ten most active contracts in 1960, only two are among the ten most active today: soybeans and corn.

These changes have taken place largely in the last decade. Although trading in foreign currencies began in 1972, and in T-bonds in 1977, it was not until the late 1970s that trading in financial instruments took off. The introduction of stock index futures in 1982 and oil futures in the early 1980s completed the transformation.

The changing nature of futures has meant new types of market participants. Today the largest and most prestigious financial institutions use futures—banks, pension funds, insurance companies, investment companies, and university endowment funds. Futures markets have become an integral part of how these institutions manage their risks and their portfolios of assets.

1.2 WHAT ARE FUTURES CONTRACTS?

A futures contract is an agreement between a seller and a buyer that calls for the seller (called the *short*) to deliver to the buyer (called the *long*) a specified quantity and grade of an identified commodity, at a fixed time in the future, and at a price agreed to when the contract is first entered into. Further, the law requires that all futures contracts be bought and sold on *designated contract markets*, commonly known as commodity or futures exchanges. It is permissible under the law for a futures contract to be written and traded on any *commodity*. The only question is: what is a *commodity?*

The Commodity Exchange Act, which is the body of federal laws that governs futures markets, originally defined a commodity as including a number of agricultural products, such as wheat, cotton, wool, eggs, soybeans, frozen concentrated orange juice, and so forth. This list, however, was repeatedly revised to reflect what exchanges wished to trade.

In 1974 Congress adopted an entirely different approach by expanding the definition of a commodity to include "all other goods and articles, except onions as provided in Public Law 85-839, and all services, rights and interests in which contracts for future delivery are presently or in the future dealt in." Under this definition of a commodity, futures contracts now can be traded on everything except onions. (Onions are excluded because Congress passed a law specifically banning the trading of futures contracts on onions, accomplishing this by declaring that onions are not a legally recognized commodity.) Today, the term commodity includes T-bonds, the S&P stock index, bank deposits, foreign currencies, and even price indexes that reflect inflation rates. There is no way of predicting what kinds of futures contracts will be traded in future years.

Futures contracts must be bought or sold on *designated contract markets*. A designated contract market is an organized commodities (or futures) exchange that has been so designated under the provisions of the Commodity Exchange

TABLE 1.3
Futures exchanges in the United States

Exchange	1990 Trading volume	
	Contracts	Percentage
1. Chicago Board of Trade (CBOT)	120,769,784	43.67
2. Chicago Mercantile Exchange (CME)	84,837,757	30.68
3. New York Mercantile Exchange (NYMEX)	36,357,871	13.15
4. Commodity Exchange (COMEX)	15,496,931	5.60
5. Coffee, Sugar & Cocoa Exchange (CSCE)	8,973,911	3.25
6. Mid-America Commodity Exchange (MidAM)	3,975,528	1.44
7. New York Cotton Exchange (NYCE)	2,746,209	0.99
8. New York Futures Exchange (NYFE)	1,656,968	0.60
9. Kansas City Board of Trade (KCBOT)	1,187,083	0.43
10. Minneapolis Grain Exchange (MGE)	478,077	0.17
11. Chicago Rice & Cotton Exchange (CRCE)	55,385	0.02
Total	276,535,504	100.00

Source: Futures Industry Association, Inc.

Act. Table 1.3 lists 11 futures exchanges that have received such designation in the United States, and the volume of trading on each exchange. Table 1.4 lists the specific futures contracts traded on each exchange in 1990. The two largest exchanges, the Chicago Board of Trade and the Chicago Mercantile Exchange, alone account for nearly 75 percent of total trading.

1.3 FORWARD MARKETS AS FORERUNNERS OF FUTURES MARKETS

Historically, the development of futures markets followed the development of *forward* markets. In earlier years, transporting goods from where they were produced to where they were sold often took many months. In the 1800s, for example, grain produced in England and shipped to the United States took months to reach market. During this time events often occurred that drastically changed the price of the grain. If prices fell significantly, the grain might even have to be sold at a loss, bringing ruin to the producer of the grain.

Producers, therefore, sought to avoid this price risk by selling their grain *forward* (or on a "to arrive" basis), even at prices somewhat lower than they expected to receive by waiting until the grain arrived at market months later. If, for example, they thought they could get $2.00 a bushel six months from now when the grain arrived at market, they might still be willing to sell it forward for $1.90 a bushel in order to lock in a certain selling price. The 10 cent price differential might be viewed as simply the cost of insurance: the *insurance fee* paid to guarantee a fixed (and profitable) selling price. When a producer voluntarily pays this *fee,* he obviously views selling forward as a superior alternative to bearing the *price risk* himself.

TABLE 1.4
Commodity futures contracts traded in 1990

	1990 Trading volume*
Chicago Board of Trade	
T-bonds	75,499,257
Corn	11,423,027
Soybeans	10,301,905
T-notes ($6\frac{1}{2}$ to 10 years)	6,054,222
Soybean meal	4,904,471
Soybean oil	4,658,302
Wheat	2,876,270
T-notes (5 years)	2,532,828
MMI Maxi	951,325
Municipal Bond Index	696,861
Oats	433,567
Silver	181,057
T-notes (2 years)	110,789
30-day interest rate	81,300
Gold	44,463
Mortgage backed	16,848
Japanese government bonds	3,062
TOPIX	230
	120,769,784
Chicago Mercantile Exchange	
Eurodollar	34,695,625
S&P 500 Stock Index	12,139,209
Deutschemark	9,169,230
Japanese yen	7,437,235
Swiss franc	6,524,893
Live cattle	3,797,376
British pound	3,410,333
Live hogs	2,241,272
T-bills	1,869,610
Canadian dollar	1,408,799
Pork bellies	1,303,129
Feeder cattle	391,308
Lumber	201,984
Australian dollar	105,241
One-month LIBOR	84,148
Nikkei 225	52,046
Dollar/yen difference	3,727
Dollar/mark difference	1,478
Dollar/pound difference	1,064
French franc	50
	84,837,757

(continued)

TABLE 1.4 — cont'd.

	1990 Trading volume*
New York Mercantile Exchange	
Crude oil	23,686,897
Heating oil	6,376,871
Unleaded gasoline	5,205,995
Platinum	820,934
Natural gas	132,820
Palladium	95,642
Propane	38,636
Residual fuel oil	76
	36,357,871
Commodity Exchange	
Gold	9,730,041
Silver	3,913,609
High grade copper	1,853,185
Aluminum	96
	15,496,931
Coffee, Sugar & Cocoa Exchange	
Sugar #11	5,424,801
Coffee C	1,774,050
Cocoa	1,635,917
Sugar #14	139,143
	8,973,911
Mid-America Commodity Exchange	
Soybeans	1,565,641
T-bonds	1,461,046
Corn	455,289
Wheat	147,033
Deutschemark	82,534
Swiss franc	75,819
Japanese yen	54,283
Live hogs	29,533
British pound	25,846
Live cattle	19,284
New York gold	15,084
Oats	13,502
New York silver	11,005
Canadian dollar	9,287
Soybean meal	5,437
T-bills	3,884
Platinum	1,012
T-notes	9
	3,975,528

(continued)

TABLE 1.4 — cont'd.

	1990 Trading volume*
New York Cotton Exchange	
Cotton #2	1,534,611
U.S. Dollar Index	565,194
Frozen concentrated orange juice	342,574
5-year T-notes	222,271
2-year T-notes	69,409
European Currency Unit	12,150
	2,746,209
New York Futures Exchange	
NYSE Composite Index	1,574,641
CRB Index	70,233
T-bond (30-year)	12,094
	1,656,968
Kansas City Board of Trade	
Wheat	1,136,234
Value Line Index	35,558
Mini Value Line	14,081
Grain sorghum	1,210
	1,187,083
Minneapolis Grain Exchange	
Wheat	477,043
White wheat	1,014
Oats	20
	478,077
Chicago Rice & Cotton Exchange	
Rice, rough new	55,385

*The number of futures contracts bought (or sold) during the year.
Source: Futures Industry Association, Inc.

But who would be willing to take the other side of the producer's forward contract? Who would the purchaser (or long) be? It could be either a speculator or another commercial firm seeking to offset (or hedge) still another price risk. A miller, for example, might need to purchase grain in six months to fulfill a future commitment he has to deliver flour at an already agreed-upon price. To protect his profit margin, the miller could purchase grain forward, locking in the price of the grain as well as a source of supply. He could achieve this by taking the long side of the producer's forward contract.

In this example the grain producer's and the miller's needs happened to coincide. If they knew of each other's existence, they could quickly reach a forward agreement that was mutually beneficial. Indeed, if both agreed on what they expected the price of grain to be in the future, they would also be happy to contract for future delivery at that price. If, for example, both thought the price in six months would be $2.00 a bushel, they would both be happy to enter into a forward agreement now to deal at $2.00 a bushel in six months. Both would get what they wanted—price certainty—and neither would have to pay a fee for this certainty: they would sell and buy at a price exactly equal to the price they anticipated getting had they waited until later to buy and sell. By contracting forward, therefore, they would receive their anticipated price and eliminate all price uncertainty.

This ideal state of affairs seldom exists. More likely, grain producers and millers do not know of each others' existence. In most markets a *middleman* is required to bring producers (or sellers) and consumers (or buyers) together. Automobile dealers, grocery stores, real estate brokers, bond dealers, and securities brokers are all examples of *middlemen*. The middleman or dealer matches buyers and sellers and receives a fee for doing so.

In the case of forward markets, a dealer will simultaneously enter into forward contracts with both the grain producer and the miller. The dealer will be the long to the grain producer (the short) and the short to the miller (the long). If the two contracts are identical, the dealer will have no price risk. If the contracts are different, perhaps because the quantities contracted for are different, because the type of grain is different, or because the maturity dates are different, the dealer will have to bear the remaining price risk. *[margin note: Dealer]* *[margin note: Unhedged Price Risk]*

In addition, the dealer will have to bear the risk of a default by a contracting party (and *vice versa*), even if the forward contracts are perfectly matched. For example, if the grain producer were to fail to deliver grain at the contractual price, the dealer would nevertheless still have to supply grain to the miller at the agreed-upon price. Thus, dealers in forward contracts must be compensated for both the price and credit risks they bear. *[margin note: Default Risk]*

Further, to the extent that there is a net imbalance of hedgers, dealers may become the counterparty to the excess hedging—or they may become speculators. For example, if there is a surplus of short hedgers, the dealer may assume a long speculative position. Once again, the dealer will have to be compensated for bearing the resulting price risk.

Forward markets have existed and flourished for centuries because they provide a useful way to manage price uncertainty. In the United States forward contracting was used extensively in the nineteenth century by participants in the grain trade. At that time grain prices were subject to large seasonal price changes. Subsequent to harvest, farmers would flood the market with grain, causing prices to collapse. Later, shortages would develop and grain prices would soar. To avoid these cyclical price extremes, buyers and sellers of grain turned to forward contracting as an alternative way to meet their needs. In the nineteenth century this activity was centered in Chicago, which was the grain marketing center in the United States. The initiation of organized futures trading in 1848 at the Chicago Board of Trade was a natural outgrowth of the active forward market in grain that existed at that time.

1.4 STANDARDIZATION AS A KEY CHARACTERISTIC OF A FUTURES CONTRACT

A key distinction between futures and forward contracts is that the terms of a futures contract are standardized. Buyers or sellers of a gold futures contract cannot individually negotiate about how much gold must be delivered, the form and quality of the gold that will have to be delivered, and where delivery must take place. Indeed, a COMEX gold futures contract requires the delivery of 100 ounces of gold bullion with a fineness of 0.999 at only exchange-approved warehouses in New York City. The parties to an analogous forward contract would customarily negotiate each of these terms.

Although highly standardized, a number of futures contracts with different delivery dates are commonly traded on a particular commodity at any moment in time. There may, for example, be as many as thirteen different gold futures contracts traded, each with a different delivery date, starting from the current month and going out two years into the future. Thus, traders can choose among several futures contracts which differ only by their delivery dates.

The one feature of a futures contract that changes constantly—every trading day, every minute, and possibly every trade—is the *contract's unit price,* or the anticipated future value of the underlying commodity. When a trader buys or sells a futures contract, he agrees at that time on a price at which he will either buy or sell a unit of the underlying commodity at some agreed-upon time in the future. For example, if at 11:00 A.M. on April 11, 1989, you purchased a December 89 silver futures contract, you would have agreed to buy silver at 624.5 cents per ounce at the contract's expiration in December of 1989. This price is the market assessment, at 11:00 A.M. on April 11, 1989, of what silver bullion is likely to be worth in December 1989. On the next day, or even one or two minutes later, that assessment may change, perhaps because of new information or changes in expectations about future market conditions.

Once having bought or sold a futures contract, you are locked into the price at which you bought or sold. Changes in futures prices will result in holders' making profits or incurring losses. This will become clear later as we work through some examples.

The purpose of standardizing futures contracts is to create an instrument that reduces to a minimum the transaction costs associated with trading a deferred delivery instrument. If all terms of a futures contract had to be individually negotiated by the parties to the contract, as they are in a forward contract, the costs would be much higher. Further, by permitting trading in a contract with a limited number of designated delivery dates, trading is concentrated in relatively few discrete time intervals so that liquidity is enhanced.

1.4.1 An Example

Suppose that on April 11, 1989, I buy one December 89 silver futures contract, at 624.1 cents per ounce. As a buyer of a December 89 futures contract, I agree to take delivery and pay for 5000 ounces of silver bullion in December 1989 at a price of 624.1 cents an ounce. If the prevailing price of silver happens to be only 550 cents an ounce when December 1989 arrives, I may feel bad, but there is nothing I can do. If I had known that the price of silver would be so low in December 1989, of course, I would not have agreed to pay 624.1 cents in April 1989. The seller, on the other hand, is not the least bit unhappy: he is getting to sell December silver at a higher price than had he waited until December 1989 to sell. He made the right decision to agree to sell it in advance at the higher price!

1.5 WHO TRADES FUTURES CONTRACTS AND WHY

Futures contracts are bought and sold by a large number of individuals and businesses, and for a variety of purposes. Most individuals buy and sell futures because they wish to speculate about future price levels of the commodity that underlies a futures contract, whether it is silver, gold, corn, T-bonds, or crude oil. Businesses usually buy and sell futures for the opposite reason: to eliminate (or hedge) their risk exposure due to changes in the price of a commodity. Managers of large pools of money, such as pension funds or mutual funds, may also use futures as a less costly way of achieving their portfolio goals. The various objectives and trading strategies associated with using futures markets are the subject of later chapters in the book. At this point we will demonstrate in a very simple context the activities of speculators and hedgers.

1.5.1 Speculation

Speculators buy and sell futures contracts with the expectation of profiting from changes in the price of the underlying commodity. A speculator who believes that *cash* silver prices will be higher in the future may buy silver now and hold it until a future time when he can sell it at the higher price. This is something not everyone may be willing to do, since it involves taking delivery of silver bullion and storing it. Another alternative is for speculators to buy a futures contract that permits them to take delivery of silver at some time in the future, presumably at a time when the price of silver is higher. Of course, for this strategy to be profitable, the futures price that a speculator pays now will have to be less than the price he will be able to sell the silver for after he takes delivery. Assuming that current futures prices are below what our speculator thinks cash silver prices will be in the future, he will buy a futures contract today, plan to take delivery (or otherwise *offset* his delivery obligation) of the silver at some point in the future, and then sell the silver at the later time for a profit. If he is wrong, and silver prices do not rise but in fact fall, the speculator will lose money. Thus, trading futures is an easy and low-cost way for speculators to make bets on the future prices of various commodities.

1.5.2 Hedging

Hedgers seek to protect themselves against price changes in a commodity in which they have an interest. They assume a futures position with the objective of reducing their risk. Speculators, in contrast, willingly take on additional risk with the objective of profiting from price changes.

Take the simple case of a farmer, who has planted her corn crop and is waiting to harvest it. She already knows with reasonable certainty what this crop is going to cost her: the cost of the seed, fertilizer, time and effort, and so forth. She does not, of course, know how much corn she will harvest. It will depend on the weather. If the weather is favorable, she will have a lot of corn; if unfavorable, there will be less corn. She also does not know the price at which she will be able to sell the corn once it is harvested. Suppose that it is now April and that our farmer anticipates that she will be ready to sell her corn by next September, six months from today. Although the current price of corn is known, no one knows what the price of corn will be in six months—it might be higher or lower.

The farmer is exposed to two types of risk: the possibility that her corn crop will be of a lower quantity than she hopes; and the possibility that, even if her crop yield is good, the price of corn will fall significantly before she has a chance to bring the corn to market and sell it. The first of these is often referred to as *quantity risk,* and the second as *price risk.*

Futures markets enable the farmer to hedge (or reduce) her price risk. She can accomplish this by selling her corn now, for future delivery: by simply selling (or shorting) September corn futures contracts, for example, she can agree now, in April, to sell (or deliver) her corn in September when she harvests it, at a price that she agrees to now (in April).

The price that the farmer will have agreed to sell corn for in September is the current price that is quoted for the September corn futures contract. This price reflects the market's *best guess* as to what the price of corn will be next September. This guess, of course, could turn out to be wrong: the price might be much higher or lower than everybody now thinks it will be. Many things can happen between April and September. For example, the weather may be very dry, making crop yields low. This would cause a sharp rise in prices. Or the opposite could occur. Whatever happens, our farmer, by shorting futures contracts, is protected. She has locked in her selling price. She no longer has any price risk. If she had not hedged, on the other hand, lower prices might have significantly reduced her income. Her earnings may even have fallen short of the cost of growing and delivering the corn.

One of the drawbacks of hedging, it should be recognized, is that by hedging the farmer gives up the possibility of reaping a windfall gain from a sharp rise in the price of corn. If she did nothing, for example, and waited until September to sell her corn and the price of corn rose, she could have benefited handsomely by selling her corn at the higher price. But if the price of corn had gone down instead of up, she would have lost money. Thus, by not hedging, the farmer might have made higher or lower profits than she anticipated, depending on how lucky she was. By hedging, she can eliminate that part of her fate dependent upon the price of corn in the future. Not hedging, therefore, is tantamount to making a bet (or speculating) on the price of corn in the future.

It should be obvious that futures markets do not enable hedgers to insulate themselves from quantity risk but only from price risk. For example, if crop yields are lower than expected, the farmer will have less corn to sell (or deliver) in September and will therefore have lower revenue. Hedgers can lock in only the price at which they will be able to sell in the future; they cannot lock in future revenue.

1.6 SOCIAL BENEFITS OF FUTURES MARKETS

Futures markets provide two important social benefits: risk management through hedging, and price discovery.

Hedgers use futures to shift unwanted price risk to others, usually specula-tors, who willingly assume the risk in the hope of making profits. In the absence of futures markets, this risk could not be managed as efficiently: the cost-of-risk to society would be higher, and we would all be worse-off.

A second benefit of futures market is *price discovery,* or the market's ability to "discover" true equilibrium prices. Futures markets provide centralized trading where information about fundamental supply and demand conditions for a com-modity is efficiently assimilated and acted on and, as a consequence, equilibrium prices determined.

The economic benefits of having more accurate prices are well-known. More accurate prices result in a superior allocation of resources because both consumers and producers make better decisions about which commodities to consume, which to produce, how to produce them, and how much to produce and consume in the present versus the future.

The way in which hedgers and speculators interact in futures markets to produce these social benefits is the subject of Chapter 7.

1.7 TRADING STATISTICS

Two kinds of trading statistics are reported daily by exchanges: *volume* and *open interest*. Volume is a measure of trading activity during a selected period of time, such as a day. It refers to the number of futures contracts that are either bought or sold during that period (for example, a day). For every contract that is bought, there is a contract sold. Thus, to arrive at daily volume we count the number of contracts that are bought during the day (which is the same as the number that is sold). Similarly, volume for a month is the number of contracts bought during the month, and volume for a year is the number of contracts bought during the entire year. As such, volume measures the trading activity that occurs during a certain period of time.

Open interest is an entirely different concept. It measures the number of futures contracts that remain "open" at a particular point in time, usually at the close of trading. If a trader buys a contract in the morning and sells it in the afternoon of the same day to the same trader that he bought it from, volume for the day will be two contracts, but the number of contracts open at day's end (open interest) will be zero. Volume is two contracts because there were two contracts bought (or sold) during the day: one when the buyer initiated his position and one when he sold his position. There will be no open interest at day's end because no trader will have an outstanding obligation at that time.

At any moment open interest can be determined by looking at the books of the clearing house. The number of long (or short) positions at the clearing house measures the existing open interest. Open interest is like a snapshot photograph; volume is like a motion picture, which runs for a certain amount of time.

These statistics can be useful in assessing the liquidity of a market. Everything else equal, liquidity is usually greater in markets with more participants and more trading. High volume indicates the presence of currently active buyers and sellers; high open interest indicates the presence of traders already holding positions and therefore assures that there will be buyers and sellers in the future.

Table 1.5 shows the volume and open interest statistics for crude oil futures contracts. Both daily volume and open interest are shown for all crude oil contracts being traded on three separate dates in March of 1989. March 21 is the last trading day for the April 89 contract. Two features are immediately obvious. First, the

TABLE 1.5
Volume and open interest: Crude oil futures contracts

Date	Contract	Daily volume	Closing open interest
Mar 2, 1989	Apr 89	43,729	81,780
	May 89	24,513	56,551
	Jun 89	11,449	30,497
	Jul 89	4,869	18,807
	Aug 89	2,426	11,368
	Sep 89	1,068	7,981
	Oct 89	1,732	8,203
	Nov 89	110	1,593
Mar 20, 1989	Apr 89	26,525	6,290
	May 89	44,298	85,738
	Jun 89	15,812	43,848
	Jul 89	4,520	26,825
	Aug 89	1,500	14,713
	Sep 89	1,069	10,976
	Oct 89	1,461	10,540
	Nov 89	208	5,310
Mar 21, 1989	Apr 89	5,389	1,211
	May 89	48,870	87,951
	Jun 89	25,535	45,577
	Jul 89	9,588	28,676
	Aug 89	3,407	15,409
	Sep 89	2,786	9,804
	Oct 89	2,532	10,402
	Nov 89	2,339	6,619

volume of trading and the open interest in contracts with different delivery dates are markedly different. Both volume and open interest are usually greater in nearby contracts than in contracts calling for delivery at more distant dates. Second, as a contract moves toward its delivery date, volume and open interest tend to rise and then fall sharply before the delivery date occurs, as traders exit the market to avoid having to make or take delivery (see April 89 contract). Thus, the liquidity of more distant contracts is usually less than in nearby contracts and, immediately prior to delivery, liquidity falls considerably.

1.8 STATISTICS ON HEDGING AND SPECULATION

The only data that provide some insight into the relative volume of hedging and speculative trading in futures markets are the "Commitments of Traders" data compiled by the Commodity Futures Trading Commission (CFTC). The CFTC is the federal agency charged with regulating futures markets in the United States. The regulation of futures markets is examined in depth in chapters 8 and 9.

The CFTC requires that *large traders* report their futures positions at the close of trading each day. *Large traders* are those holding an aggregate futures position in a commodity equal to or greater than that designated by the CFTC. The *reportable* position size differs by commodity and may be changed by the CFTC at any time. Traders holding smaller positions do not have to report their positions. The reportable position in heating oil futures in October, 1990, for example, was 100 contracts.

All traders in futures markets also are required to declare themselves to be either *commercial* or *non-commercial* traders. *Commercial* traders use futures contracts for hedging purposes and normally carry on an active business in the cash markets underlying the futures markets in which they hold positions. All positions held by commercial traders are assumed to be hedging positions. Similarly, the futures positions held by *non-commercial* traders are assumed to be speculative positions.

Table 1.6 is an example of the trader data that is made public by the CFTC at the end of each month for each futures market. It shows reportable commercial and non-commercial positions in crude oil futures as of May 31, 1990, broken out by long and short positions. (Longs are buyers; shorts are sellers.) *Non-reportable* long and short positions are derived by subtracting the respective total long and short reportable positions from total open interest. Non-reportable positions are commonly assumed to be speculative positions.

If the above assumptions are made for the data in Table 1.6, the following conclusions can be drawn (using the "All" row statistics):

- Reportable positions account for 72.7 and 67.6 percent of the total long and short open interest respectively.
- Hedgers account for 62.8 percent of total long positions and 51.6 percent of total short positions; and therefore speculators account for about 37.2 and 48.4 percent of total long and short positions respectively.

TABLE 1.6
Crude oil, light 'sweet'—New York Mercantile Exchange commitments of traders in all futures combined and indicated futures, May 31, 1990

(CONTRACTS OF 1,000 BARRELS)

FUTURES	TOTAL OPEN INTEREST	REPORTABLE POSITIONS								NONREPORTABLE POSITIONS	
		NON-COMMERCIAL				COMMERCIAL		TOTAL			
		LONG OR SHORT ONLY		LONG AND SHORT (SPREADING)							
		LONG	SHORT	LONG	SHORT	LONG	SHORT	LONG	SHORT	LONG	SHORT
ALL	281,615	7,690	24,845	20,183	20,183	176,723	145,414	204,596	190,442	77,019	91,173
OLD	218,786	5,937	18,822	10,780	10,780	140,221	119,509	156,938	149,111	61,848	69,675
OTHER	62,829	3,891	8,161	7,265	7,265	36,502	25,905	47,658	41,331	15,171	21,498

CHANGES IN COMMITMENTS FROM APRIL 30, 1990

ALL	3,220	-135	-2,550	-7,110	-7,110	16,421	15,047	9,176	5,387	-5,956	-2,167

PERCENT OF OPEN INTEREST REPRESENTED BY EACH CATEGORY OF TRADERS:

ALL	100.0%	2.7	8.8	7.2	7.2	62.8	51.6	72.7	67.6	27.3	32.4
OLD	100.0%	2.7	8.6	4.9	4.9	64.1	54.6	71.7	68.2	28.3	31.8
OTHER	100.0%	6.2	13.0	11.6	11.6	58.1	41.2	75.9	65.8	24.1	34.2

NUMBER OF TRADERS IN EACH CATEGORY

NUMBER OF TRADERS:											
ALL	160	19	31	14	14	80	78	107	116		
OLD	148	18	25	10	10	75	70	98	100		
OTHER	43	3	13	4	4	15	21	22	34		

CONCENTRATION RATIOS
PERCENT OF OPEN INTEREST HELD BY THE INDICATED NUMBER OF LARGEST TRADERS

	BY GROSS POSITION				BY NET POSITION			
	4 OR LESS TRADERS		8 OR LESS TRADERS		4 OR LESS TRADERS		8 OR LESS TRADERS	
	LONG	SHORT	LONG	SHORT	LONG	SHORT	LONG	SHORT
ALL	19.1	17.0	31.5	24.6	14.9	7.3	22.0	12.3
OLD	19.7	17.4	30.0	25.7	16.4	14.2	24.8	20.0
OTHER	42.8	28.4	59.1	39.9	38.5	19.0	47.7	25.1

Source: Commodity Futures Trading Commission.

- There is a *net long* hedger imbalance of 31,309 $(176,723 - 145,414)$ contracts; and a corresponding *net short* speculative position of 31,309 $(24,845 + 91,173 - 7690 - 77,019)$ contracts.
- A substantial portion of both the long and short speculative positions are held by small (non-reporting) traders: 90.92% $(\frac{77,019}{7,690+77,019} \times 100\%)$ and 78.59% $(\frac{91,173}{24,845+91,173} \times 100\%)$ respectively.

While these statistics are helpful in understanding futures markets, they do not tell the whole story. First, they are for only one day each month. We do not know what happens on other days. Second, they tell us nothing about the volume of trading. For example, trading by day-traders, who do not hold positions overnight, is not reported. Since such trading is probably speculative, volume figures for speculation and hedging, were they available, would no doubt show speculation to be more important than the open interest data indicates. Third, it may not be correct to treat all commercial positions as hedging positions and all non-reportable positions as speculative positions. At least some commercial traders hold speculative positions from time-to-time, and some non-reporting traders may be hedgers. These issues are discussed in Chapter 17, where the activities of speculators are examined in greater detail.

1.9 OTHER DEFERRED DELIVERY CONTRACTS

Futures are only one type of *deferred delivery* instrument. Forward contracts and option contracts also involve taking or making delivery of a commodity at some date in the future. There are large markets for both of these instruments, just as for futures contracts. In addition, in recent years a number of hybrid "derivative-market" instruments have been developed that employ various combinations of futures, forwards, and options.

1.9.1 Option Contracts

An option contract, unlike a futures contract, imposes an obligation on only one party. The contract gives one party (the buyer) the *right*, but not the *obligation*, to purchase or sell a stated quantity and quality of the underlying commodity (or asset) at some point in the future, at a price agreed to when the contract is first entered into. If the buyer chooses to exercise this right, the seller of the option is then obligated to perform—that is, either to purchase or to sell the commodity.

When the purchaser (or holder) of an option exercises the option, or invokes his rights, he either pays the agreed-upon price (the *strike* price) and receives delivery of the commodity (a *call* option) or delivers the commodity and receives payment (a *put* option). In contrast, the seller of the option (or the *writer* of the option) is obligated to make or receive delivery, depending upon whether he wrote a call or a put. In either case, the writer of the option has no ability to determine whether, or at what point, the option will be exercised. This right resides only with the purchaser of the option.

For this right the purchaser pays a one-time, non-refundable fee (known as the *premium*) to the writer of the option. After paying the premium, the purchaser is not liable for any additional payments as a result of his option position. The writer of the option, in contrast, is exposed to unlimited liability: the price of the commodity in question may change substantially between the time he has written (sold) the option contract to the time when the holder (buyer) chooses to exercise it. He must be prepared to make delivery or to receive delivery at the agreed-upon price, notwithstanding any change in the market price that may have occurred.

Similar to futures contracts, commodity options are also traded for hedging or speculative purposes. In our earlier example, the farmer who hedged her corn crop by assuming a short position in corn futures contracts could instead have purchased a put option on corn. This would have given her the right, but not the obligation, to sell her corn to the writer of the put for a fixed price stated in the option contract. This would protect her against a fall in the price of corn, just as her short futures position would. The put option, however, gives the farmer an additional benefit: if the price of corn *were* to rise rather than fall, she could simply allow the option contract to lapse unexercised and sell her crop at the higher price. She thus is protected against a fall in price, but she can still benefit from an increase in the price.

These rights and potential benefits do not come free: the purchaser must pay a premium for the option, which may be substantial. When deciding between options or futures, therefore, an important consideration is the relative costs of using each.

Options can also be used for speculative purposes. If a speculator believes that prices will rise in the future, he can buy a call option; if he believes they will fall in the future, he can acquire put options. The premium he pays for each option, of course, will reflect the market consensus about the prospects for such an increase or decrease in prices. Whether it is worthwhile for the speculator to purchase an option depends upon whether he thinks the market consensus is accurate: whether prices will change by enough to make his profits greater than the option premium. Chapters 18, 19, and 20 discuss the fundamentals of options and how they are used in greater detail.

1.9.2   Forward Contracts

Forward contracts are very similar to futures contracts. The contractual provisions and obligations of purchasers and sellers of forward contracts closely resemble those found in futures contracts. A critical distinction is that futures contracts can be traded only on organized exchanges, whereas forward contracts are traded off-exchange. As we shall discuss later, this distinction is important because it changes the nature of the contracting parties' obligations and risks. To be more specific, a person who is long a forward contract has an obligation to purchase at some date in the future a particular commodity at a price agreed to when he entered into the contract, and a person who is short has an obligation to sell or deliver a particular commodity at a price agreed to when she entered into the contract. However, the quantity and the quality of the commodity to be delivered in accordance with a forward contract is usually not standardized, but is negotiated between the parties at the time they contract. This gives forward contracts a certain flexibility that futures contracts do not have: they can be tailored precisely to the needs of the parties. The parties can also agree on specific delivery requirements and procedures that best suit their needs. However, it is possible that the terms of a forward contract can be standardized in ways quite similar to a futures contract. In recent years, in fact, brokerage firms have been offering such forward contracts, raising the issue of whether these contracts constitute illegal off-exchange dealing in futures contracts.

At present the law distinguishes between a forward and a futures contract on the basis of delivery. If delivery is intended and regularly occurs under a certain type of contractual arrangement, the instrument is likely to be considered a forward and not a futures contract. This criterion is consistent with Congress's desire to permit off-exchange transactions between persons involved in a commercial cash commodity business, where deferred delivery of a commodity is a natural part of doing business.

In addition, by virtue of a special amendment in 1974 to the Commodity Exchange Act (the so-called Treasury Amendment), deferred delivery contracts written on various financial instruments, and the trading of such instruments, are permitted off-exchange. While the interpretation of this Amendment is in dispute, it has been interpreted as sanctioning the trading of forward contracts on such items as foreign currencies, Treasury securities, Government National Mortgage Association Certificates, and so forth.

Historically, the parties involved in forward markets have been large and sophisticated: banks, institutional investors, large corporations, and brokerage firms. The two largest forward markets today are *swaps* and foreign currency markets.[1] It has been estimated that more than 500 billion dollars of both swaps and foreign currency forward contracts are written each year.

The chief reason that forward markets are restricted to large participants is that all forward contracts entail significant credit risks to the contracting parties: the risk that one of the contracting parties will default on his obligation either to make or take delivery. In this event the non-defaulting party may suffer substantial losses. To minimize this risk, contracting parties usually deal only with others who enjoy a high credit standing, such as large banks and corporations. This way of handling credit risk also eliminates the need to use the kind of mark-to-the-market margining system employed for futures markets (discussed in Chapter 2).

In contrast to forward markets, the parties involved in futures markets need not have a universally recognized high credit standing because of the role of the clearing association in futures markets. It is common, therefore, for participants

---

[1] A *swap* involves two parties exchanging, or swapping, forward obligations. For example, in an *interest rate* swap one party swaps fixed-rate interest payments for the other party's floating-rate interest payments.

in futures markets to be smaller than in forward markets. It should be recognized, however, that the same participants can, and often do, trade in both forward and futures markets. Large banks, for example, deal in both forward and futures foreign currency markets, so that these markets are closely related and are linked by the arbitrage conducted by traders common to both markets.

Thus, for many parties forward and futures markets are substitutes for one another. They are alternative instruments which can be used either to speculate or to hedge. At a specific time, however, the relative costs, liquidity, and convenience of using one market versus the other will differ.

1.10   GROWTH OF FOREIGN FUTURES MARKETS

The explosive growth of futures and options markets during the 1980s was not confined to the United States. Sensing the potential in these markets, exchanges in foreign countries quickly introduced additional and competing contracts. In Japan, the United Kingdom, and France, futures markets have grown at an even faster pace than in the United States.

In 1985, just five years ago, U.S. futures exchanges accounted for 83 percent of futures trading in the entire world. Today (1990) the U.S. accounts for only 61 percent, a loss in market share of 22 percent (see Figure 1-2). Five years ago all 10 of the most actively traded futures in the world were U.S. exchange-traded contracts. Today that number is six (see Table 1.7). Futures on Japanese and French government bonds, Euroyen, and the Nikkei 225 stock index have moved into the top 10 in the world.

Table 1.8 also shows the intensity and directness of foreign competition: *Knockoffs* eight of the top 10 U.S. futures contracts currently traded on U.S. exchanges are now traded on foreign exchanges — exact "knockoffs." With the increasing globalization of financial markets, and the coming screen-based trading system, competition between U.S. and foreign exchanges will become even more intense in the future.

In 1990 there were more than 39 foreign futures and commodity options exchanges. Table 1.9 lists these foreign exchanges together with their 1990 trading volumes.

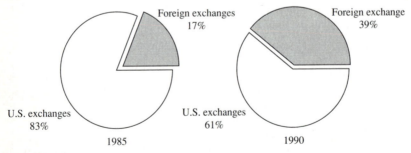

FIGURE 1-2
World market share: Futures trading volume.

TABLE 1.7
Ten most actively traded futures in the world: 1985 & 1990

1985		1990
Contract (exchange)		Contract (exchange)
Treasury bonds (CBOT)	1	Treasury bonds (CBOT)
S&P 500 (CME)	2	Eurodollars (CME)
Eurodollars (CME)	3	Crude oil (NYMEX)
Gold 100 oz (COMEX)	4	Japanese government bonds (TSE)
Soybeans (CBOT)	5	French government bonds (MATIF)
Deutschemarks (CME)	6	Euroyen (TSE)
Corn (CBOT)	7	NIKKEI 225 (OSE)
Silver 5000 oz (COMEX)	8	S&P 500 (CME)
Swiss francs (CME)	9	Corn (CBOT)
Live cattle (CME)	10	Soybeans (CBOT)

CBOT	Chicago Board of Trade
CME	Chicago Mercantile Exchange
COMEX	Commodity Exchange
MATIF	Le Marché à Terme des Instruments Financiers
NYMEX	New York Mercantile Exchange
OSE	Osaka Securities Exchange
TSE	Tokyo Stock Exchange

TABLE 1.8
Ten most actively traded U.S. futures: (1990)

		Exchange traded	
Rank	Contracts (exchange)	U.S. 1990	Foreign 1990
1	Treasury bonds (CBOT)	X	X
2	Eurodollars (CME)	X	X
3	Crude oil (NYMEX)	X	X
4	S&P 500 (CME)	X	
5	Corn (CBOT)	X	
6	Soybeans (CBOT)	X	X
7	Gold 100 oz (COMEX)	X	X
8	Deutschemarks (CME)	X	X
9	Japanese yen (CME)	X	X
10	Swiss francs (CME)	X	X

CBOT	Chicago Board of Trade
CME	Chicago Mercantile Exchange
COMEX	Commodity Exchange ot New York
NYMEX	New York Mercantile Exchange

TABLE 1.9
Foreign futures and commodity options exchanges

	1990 Trading volume* (number of contracts)
London International Financial Futures Exchange, U.K.	34,169,805
Le Marché à Terme des Instruments Financiers, France	28,587,734
Osaka Securities Exchange, Japan	22,776,790
Tokyo Stock Exchange, Japan	21,623,268
Tokyo Commodity Exchange, Japan	14,839,637
Tokyo International Financial Futures Exchange, Japan	14,450,989
London Metal Exchange, U.K.	13,352,954
Sydney Futures Exchange, Australia	11,562,582
Bolsa Mercandil y De Futuros, Brazil	9,875,196
Tokyo Grain Exchange, Japan	7,144,758
International Petroleum Exchange, U.K.	6,946,173
Tokyo Sugar Exchange, Japan	6,378,228
Singapore Monetary Exchange, Singapore	5,720,610
Stockholm Options Exchange, Sweden	5,196,372
SOFFEX, Switzerland	4,655,114
London Futures and Options Exchange, U.K.	4,416,857
Osaka Grain Exchange, Japan	3,351,462
European Options Exchange, Netherlands	2,895,989
Osaka Sugar Exchange, Japan	2,840,713
Osaka Textile Exchange, Japan	1,726,279
Kobe Rubber Exchange, Japan	1,383,394
Toyahashi Dried Cocoon Exchange, Japan	1,328,122
Nagoyo Textile Exchange, Japan	1,273,746
Maebashi Dried Cocoon Exchange, Japan	1,159,978
Winnipeg Commodity Exchange, Canada	1,100,361
Nagoyo Grain & Sugar Exchange, Japan	918,526
Toronto Futures Exchange, Canada	751,543
Montreal Exchange, Canada	680,790
New Zealand Futures Exchange, New Zealand	623,439
Kanmon Commodity Exchange, Japan	573,750
Financial Futures Market, Netherlands	532,899
Hong Kong Futures Exchange, Hong Kong	507,534
Hokkaido Grain Exchange, Japan	476,801
Yokohama Raw Silk Exchange, Japan	433,371
Kobe Raw Silk Exchange, Japan	387,611
Kobe Grain Exchange, Japan	387,066
Kuala Lumpur Commodity Exchange, Malaysia	263,525
Baltic Futures Exchange, U.K.	165,063
Deutsche Terminborse, Germany	111,028

*The trading volume figure includes both futures and options contracts.

Source: Futures Industry Association, Inc.

CONCLUSION

This chapter has introduced futures markets by briefly describing what futures contracts are, why they are traded, who trades them, and how they differ from other deferred delivery contracts, such as options. The chapter has described the phenomenal growth in futures markets in recent years and has provided information about the kinds of futures contracts that are traded. In addition, it has discussed the respective roles of speculators and hedgers, and the social benefits that flow from futures markets. Finally, the chapter has concluded by showing that futures markets are expanding rapidly in foreign countries as well as in the United States.

Several of the topics touched upon in this chapter are revisited and discussed more extensively in later chapters of the book. In Chapters 2 and 3, to which we now turn, the institutional structure and operational mechanics of futures markets are examined in depth. Later, in Chapters 4, 5, and 6, pricing and hedging fundamentals of futures are covered; and, in Chapter 7, armed with the knowledge contained in the earlier chapters, the social benefits of futures markets are revisited with greater analytical vigor.

QUESTIONS

1. Why are some futures contracts successful while others fail?

2. What is the key difference between a speculator and a hedger?

3. What is the difference between open interest and trading volume?

4. Explain the designations *reportable positions, commercial positions,* and *noncommercial positions* in Table 1.6.

5. What is meant by the term *net hedger imbalance*? How is it measured?

6. What do you think the term *spreading* in Table 1.6 means?

7. What is the difference between a forward and a futures contract?

8. What is the legal distinction between a forward contract and a futures contract?

9. Why should there be more small traders in futures markets than in forward markets?

10. How do options contracts differ from both futures and forward contracts?

11. What social benefits do futures markets provide?

SUGGESTED READING

Black, D. "Success and Failure of Futures Contracts: Theory and Empirical Evidence." Salomon Brothers Center for the Study of Financial Institutions Monograph Series in Finance and Economics, New York University, 1986.

Carlton, D. "Futures Markets: Their Purpose, Their History, Their Growth, Their Successes and Failures." *The Journal of Futures Markets,* Fall 1984, pp. 237–272.

Miller, M. "Financial Innovation: The Last Twenty Years and the Next." *Journal of Financial and Quantitative Analysis,* December 1986, pp. 459–471.

Silber, W. "Innovation, Competition, and New Contract Design in Futures Markets." *The Journal of Futures Markets,* Summer 1981, pp. 123–156; "Comments," by Gary Seevers, pp. 157–160, and by Kurt Dew, pp. 161–168.

Telser, L. G. "Why Are There Organized Futures Markets?" *Journal of Law and Economics,* Vol. 24 (1981), pp.1–22.

Telser, L. G. and H. N. Higinbotham. "Organized Futures Markets: Cost and Benefits." *Journal of Political Economy,* Vol. 85 (1977), pp. 969–1000.

Williams, J. "The Origin of Futures Markets." *Agricultural History,* January 1982, pp. 206–216.

CHAPTER
2

MECHANICS
OF BUYING
AND SELLING
FUTURES

This chapter describes the institutions and the procedures that are fundamental to buying and selling futures contracts. It discusses futures commission merchants (FCMs), exchanges, clearing associations, the order flow, various types of customer orders, the margin system, physical delivery, and alternative ways that a futures position can be liquidated (or closed out).

2.1 FUTURES COMMISSION MERCHANTS

Note

The futures commission merchant is a central institution in the futures industry. Commonly referred to as an FCM (an abbreviation that will be used throughout the book), it performs functions similar to a *brokerage house* in the securities industry. A person wishing to buy or sell futures will first have to open an account at an FCM. Customers give their trading orders to an account executive employed at the FCM, who in turn sees that this order is executed on the floor of a *contract market* (or an exchange). The FCM collects margin balances from customers, maintains customer money balances, and records and reports all trading activity of its customers. It customarily provides customers with monthly statements reporting all trading activity and end-of-month account balances.

FCMs are regulated by the Commodity Futures Trading Commission (CFTC) under the Commodity Exchange Act (CEA), and are required to register with the CFTC. Under the CEA, an FCM is defined as any person or entity that solicits or accepts orders for futures contracts and accepts money or other assets in support of the trades that may result from those orders.

It is also possible for persons to submit orders to *agents* of FCMs—persons who solicit or accept orders for futures contracts but who do not accept money or assets in connection with such trades. Such entities, therefore, are not FCMs, but are considered to be *introducing brokers*. They will, of course, have to be associated with an FCM in order to attend to all of a customer's needs.

As of May 31, 1989, there were 329 FCMs registered with the CFTC, and 1690 introducing brokers. The lion's share of futures business, however, is done by a handful of large FCMs.

2.2 EXCHANGES

In order to execute a customer order, FCMs must transmit such orders to an exchange (or a *contract market*) where the particular futures contract is traded. As we saw in Chapter 1, there are 11 such exchanges in the United States, and many others in foreign countries.

Note

Exchanges perform three functions: (1) provide and maintain a physical marketplace (often called the *floor*) where futures contracts can be bought and sold by members of the exchange; (2) police and enforce ethical and financial standards applicable to the futures trading conducted on the exchange; and (3) promote the business interests of members. Exchanges do not themselves engage in trading futures but only provide the facilities for others to do so.

Exchanges are usually membership organizations whose members can be either individuals or business organizations. Membership is limited to a specified number of seats. In return for agreeing to abide by the various exchange rules, members receive the right to trade on the floor of the exchange. Table 2.1 shows the number of members which belong to the major U.S. exchanges and the price of a full membership (or seat) as of March 31, 1991.

There are two basic reasons to buy a seat on an exchange: to engage in *floor trading* activities, and to acquire the right to execute futures trades without having to pay FCM commissions. For example, a large commercial firm that does a large amount of hedging may find it cost-effective to become an exchange member: by doing so it can avoid costly commission fees.

It is also possible that someone may buy a seat on an exchange as an investment. Generally, the value of an exchange membership rises as the volume of trading on that exchange increases. Thus, if an exchange is fortunate enough to initiate trading in futures contracts that speculators and hedgers find desirable, seat prices may rise along with trading volume. If, of course, an exchange loses volume, seat prices will fall.

TABLE 2.1
U.S. futures exchanges: Memberships and seat prices as of March 31, 1991

Exchanges	Memberships Full	Others*	Seat prices
Chicago Board of Trade	1,402	748	$340,000
Chicago Mercantile Exchange	625	2,099	$400,000
New York Mercantile Exchange	765	—	$305,140
Commodity Exchange	618	264	$78,000
Coffee, Cocoa & Sugar Exchange	527	118	$70,000
Mid-America Commodity Exchange	1,205	—	$5,250
New York Cotton Exchange	450	104	$48,000
New York Futures Exchange	619	—	$100
Kansas City Board of Trade	192	45	$30,000

*Others include memberships other than full members, such as associate members, and licensees.

2.3   CLEARINGHOUSES

Every futures exchange has a clearinghouse associated with it which *clears* all transactions on that exchange. The clearing house may be part of the exchange's own organization or may be an entirely separate entity.

The term *clearing* is used to describe several functions performed by the clearinghouse. First, members of an exchange provide daily reports to the associated clearinghouse containing the details of all futures trades, which the clearinghouse then matches (shorts against longs) in order to provide a daily reconciliation. This requires exchange members to confirm all trades they have made during the day. Once this is done, the clearinghouse *accepts* the trades and is legally substituted as both buyer and seller on the contract trades.

Second, as we will see later, buying and selling futures contracts requires daily collections and payments of funds to parties of futures transactions. The clearinghouse computes daily for each clearing member the net gain or loss on the member's futures positions (both its customers and its proprietary account) due to price movements during the day. It then collects the amount of the net losses from clearing members and pays them over to clearing members with a net gain for the day.

The clearinghouse performs other functions which are vital to futures markets as well. Because of the critical importance of these institutions, we defer further discussion of them to the next chapter, where an extensive examination of clearing associations is undertaken.

2.4   FLOOR BROKERS

All futures transactions must be executed on the floor of an exchange. It is the floor brokers who take responsibility for executing the orders to trade futures contracts that are accepted by FCMs.

Floor brokers are generally self-employed individual members of the exchange who act as agents for FCMs and other exchange members in executing futures transactions. Floor traders may trade for their own accounts as well as for customer accounts. This practice is known as *dual* trading, and is discussed in Chapter 9. Floor trading procedures and ethical codes of conduct are specified and policed by exchanges. Floor traders are also subject to CFTC regulations.

Dual trading

Finally, exchange floors are organized into several different *pits* (or physical locations), where different futures contracts are traded. Thus, floor traders usually specialize in particular commodities (such as silver and gold) since it is physically impossible to be everywhere at the same time.

pits

2.5 THE ORDER FLOW: INITIATING A TRADE

Figure 2-1 depicts the order flow that accompanies all futures trades—in this case an order to buy or sell one futures contract. Buyers and sellers begin by contacting their FCM, which in turn directs the customer's order to a floor broker on the exchange floor who executes the trade. Not every FCM needs to be a member of the exchange. If it is not, it must place its customers' orders (as well as its own) through another FCM which is a member of an exchange. All orders are executed on the floor of the exchange according to exchange rules. An important aspect of these rules is that they require all bids and offers to be exposed to other traders in the pit in order to assure execution of orders at open and competitive prices. (This is called the open outcry system.) The prices at which trades are made are recorded and electronically disseminated throughout the world in seconds.

Note Open outcry system.

After orders are executed, buying and selling floor brokers report all trades to the clearinghouse and confirm them as to their specifics. If there is a disagreement as to exactly who executed which order at which price, this is called an out-trade. Such errors are immediately brought before an exchange committee which decides how to resolve them. Once confirmed by the respective floor brokers, the trades are reported back to the initiating FCMs. The FCM then reports to the buyer or seller in writing that the trade he has requested has been made and at what price.

Note

Figure 2-1 shows the results of a one-contract trade: the clearinghouse will have on its books two contractual obligations—one long and one short. These trade obligations will run to the respective clearing members (such as Merrill Lynch and Shearson Lehman), and not to the initiating customers of the FCMs. The names of the initiating buyers and sellers will appear only on the books of FCMs, as obligations of the FCMs. In other words, only clearing members have accounts at clearinghouses; public traders have accounts at FCMs.

At all times the books of the clearinghouse must be balanced: there must be the same number of short and long contractual positions. For every contract traded there must be both a buyer and a seller. This is not true of FCMs. They may have either a net long or short customer position, depending upon the demands of their customers. If, for example, Merrill Lynch's customers bought 500 gold futures contracts, while the customers of Shearson Lehman sold 500 gold futures contracts, Merrill Lynch would have a net long position of 500 gold contracts and Shearson Lehman

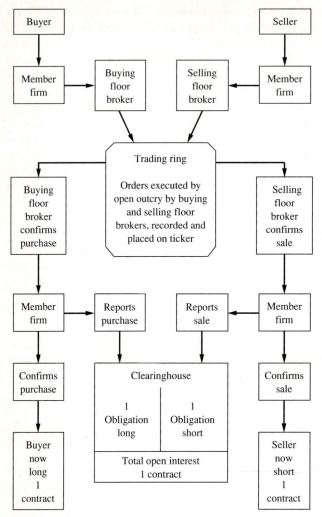

FIGURE 2-1
Initiating trades and accompanying order flow for futures contracts.

would have a net short position of 500 gold contracts. The clearinghouse, of course, would still have a balanced position: 500 short and 500 long gold futures contracts.

2.6   LIQUIDATING OR SETTLING A FUTURES POSITION

Once having established a futures position, traders have an obligation under the terms of the futures contract either to take delivery (a long position) or to make delivery (a short position) of the underlying commodity. However, as we shall see, making or taking *physical* delivery is only one of several ways that futures contracts can be settled. There are three common ways of liquidating a futures position: physical delivery; by making an offsetting futures transaction (called *offsetting*); and by engaging in an *exchange for physicals* (called an EFP). In addition, as a variant of physical delivery, some futures contracts permit settlement by *cash delivery*.

2.6.1 Physical Delivery

Note

Liquidating a futures position by making or taking physical delivery is usually the most cumbersome way to fulfill contractual obligations. It requires actually purchasing or selling a commodity, something traders would normally not want to do unless they had a particular need for the commodity (and in the large amounts required). A commercial firm, which deals in commodities, might very well wish to settle by physical delivery. In addition, at certain times it might be financially desirable to settle by physical delivery, even if it is inconvenient.

To see how physical delivery works, let us take a particular futures contract: silver traded on COMEX. A trader who is short one silver futures contract is required to make delivery of 5000 troy ounces (6 percent more or less) of refined silver in bars cast in weights of 1000 to 1100 ounces each. The silver must be assayed at not less than 0.999 fineness, and must bear the serial number and identifying stamp of a refiner approved and listed by COMEX. (*Approved silver bullion bars are bars that carry the stamp of an exchange-approved silver refiner.*) This guarantees that the bars will meet the exchange's weight and fineness standards. In addition, the exchange requires that the silver must be delivered at one of several exchange-approved warehouses in the New York area. Since traders often store silver bullion in exchange-approved warehouses, making a delivery can mean simply transferring ownership of a stock of silver bullion in a warehouse from one owner to another.

The operational procedure for making physical delivery on silver futures is as follows (procedures may differ by the type of futures contract). At the beginning of the delivery month on the exchange-designated *notice* days, let us say for the December 89 contract, exchange rules require that *all* traders having open positions in the December 89 contract notify their respective FCMs that they intend to make or take delivery during December, and when and in what quantities such deliveries are desired. The FCMs in turn must notify the clearinghouse of their customers' intentions. After this *nomination* process is complete, the clearinghouse matches longs and shorts, usually by matching the oldest short position to the oldest long position until all short quantities are matched with a long. Delivery notices are then sent, via the customer's FCM, to all parties, indicating to whom their delivery obligation runs and when, where, and in what quantities delivery is to be made. Exchange rules provide for substantial default penalties in the event that a party fails to perform. When delivery is satisfactorily made, the clearinghouse is notified and extinguishes on its books the obligations of the respective clearing FCMs. These FCMs in turn extinguish the corresponding customer obligations to them.

Physical delivery imposes obvious costs on traders: warehouse expenses, insurance costs, possibly shipping costs, and brokerage fees. In addition, if a long does not need the commodity for commercial purposes, he or she will have to re-sell it at an additional cost. Similarly, the short may have to purchase the commodity before he or she can make delivery. As we will see later, there are alternative ways of liquidating futures obligations which avoid these costs.

How common is physical delivery? The answer to this question depends on how delivery is viewed. The answer will also vary by commodity and by individual contract. For example, physical delivery as a percentage of the total (cumulative) trading volume in a contract is almost always very small: on the order of one percent (or less). However, delivery can be a significant percentage of open futures positions (or open interest). In the delivery month, or right before the delivery month, for example, most open positions will be settled by physical delivery. Further, even when compared to peak open interest in a contract, physical delivery may still be significant.

Another important aspect of physical delivery is its relationship to the *deliverable stock* of a commodity. By *deliverable stock* of a commodity is commonly meant the amount of a commodity that meets exchange-specified quality standards and is available for delivery at exchange-specified locations (such as warehouses). Deliverable stocks, of course, may (and usually do) constitute far less of a commodity's stock than actually exists, in the United States and the rest of the world. Since it may sometimes be difficult to bring such stocks into *deliverable position*, however, the concept of a deliverable stock is relevant.

Tables 2.2 and 2.3 show that for some gold and copper futures contracts traded on the COMEX, physical delivery has been a substantial percentage of deliverable stocks—sometimes greater than 100 percent. Thus, when deciding whether to make physical delivery, it is important for shorts, if they do not already own the commodity in question, to realize that it may not always be easy (or inexpensive) to purchase the commodity with which to make delivery. Having to pay a premium to purchase the physical commodity may be a hidden cost to liquidating a short contractual obligation by physical delivery.

2.6.2 Offsetting

The most common way of liquidating an open futures position is to effect an offsetting futures transaction—in effect, to reverse the initial transaction which established the futures position (shown earlier in Figure 2-1). Figure 2-2 shows the order flow that would accompany such an offsetting transaction. The initial buyer (long) liquidates his position by selling (or going short) an identical futures contract (same commodity and same delivery month). Similarly, the initial seller (short) liquidates his position by buying (going long) an identical contract. After these trades are executed and reported to the clearinghouse, both traders' obligations are extinguished on the books of the clearinghouse and on the FCMs.

Figure 2-2 assumes that the same two traders who initiated positions in Figure 2-1 also liquidated them in Figure 2-2. This need not be the case. If, for example, only the initial long (short) wished to liquidate his position, he would have to find another buyer (seller) for his position. To do this he might have to be willing to sell (buy) his futures contract at a lower (higher) price. When the initial long (short) finds another buyer (seller) for his position, this new long (short) is substituted

TABLE 2.2
Deliveries on COMEX gold futures contracts, 1977 to 1985

Year	Deliveries (in contracts)	Deliveries as a percentage of certified stocks near the start of the month	Deliveries as a percentage of open interest four months before delivery month
		December contracts	
1977	9,257	51.8	92.6
1979	9,042	39.7	23.4
1980	31,589	62.5	107.1
1981	11,406	44.8	33.2
1982	13,215	62.3	32.8
1983	17,174	69.1	43.8
1984	17,096	72.4	49.5
1985	16,401	77.9	46.8
		February contracts	
1978	5,526	26.5	171.3
1979	4,474	17.4	45.5
1980	16,076	65.7	80.9
1981	16,553	36.2	70.4
1982	25,752	110.4	129.8
1983	19,387	74.0	82.7
1984	9,479	38.5	62.1
1985	10,915	47.3	39.9

TABLE 2.3
Deliveries on COMEX copper futures contracts, 1977 to 1985

Year	Deliveries (in contracts)	Deliveries as a percentage of certified stocks near the start of the month	Deliveries as a percentage of open interest four months before delivery month
		December contracts	
1977	4,215	27.9	33.7
1978	6,561	44.3	36.5
1979	5,837	101.2	41.8
1980	4,411	32.2	32.8
1981	8,201	58.0	36.0
1982	9,346	47.0	39.1
1983	18,919	58.5	52.9
1984	5,881	25.7	23.3
1985	2,329	23.5	11.1
		February contracts	
1977	6,306	37.3	47.2
1978	6,506	44.6	52.5
1979	4,850	38.8	27.8
1980	7,705	71.5	40.6
1981	9,679	68.4	53.6
1982	9,872	63.9	53.4
1983	11,799	50.0	53.2
1984	12,432	38.0	42.2
1985	5,962	31.2	21.1

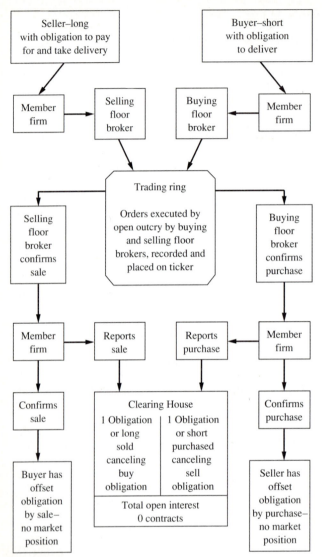

FIGURE 2-2
Liquidating trades and accompanying order flow for futures contracts.

for the initial long (short) on the books of the clearinghouse. Thus, in these circumstances, in contrast to what appears in Figure 2-2, the clearinghouse will
continue to show on its books one long and one short obligation, and total open
interest will still be one contract. The clearinghouse obviously plays a vital role
in facilitating settlement by offset. This function is discussed in depth in Chapter 3.

In comparison to making or taking physical delivery, settlement by offset is
relatively simple. It requires only a liquid futures market to facilitate offsetting
trades, and entails only the usual brokerage costs.

2.6.3   Exchange of Futures for Physicals

Note

Exchange of futures for physicals (called an EFP) is a form of physical delivery. EFPs may occur *prior* to the time when delivery is called for under exchange rules. For example, if a short can identify someone with a corresponding long futures position, he can approach this long and attempt to strike an agreement with him for fulfilling his obligation. In particular, if the long agrees, the short can make physical delivery to the long immediately, rather than wait until the contract ceases trading. Thus, an EFP transaction involves the sale of a commodity off the exchange by the holder of short contracts to the holder of long contracts, at mutually agreed-upon terms and at a mutually agreed-upon price.

EFPs are an exception to the general requirement that all offsetting transactions in futures occur through the competitive execution of orders on an exchange trading floor. Both the short and the long in an EFP transaction, however, must notify the exchange and the clearinghouse of the agreement and transaction so that the clearinghouse can make the proper book entries to extinguish the respective short and long positions on its books.

Why would anyone do an EFP, as opposed to make delivery under the usual delivery mechanism established by an exchange? Because it permits more flexibility than do exchange delivery rules. The long and short may agree to delivery at a different location or at a different time than is permissible under the formal delivery rules, and may even agree to settle their contractual obligations with the delivery of something entirely different from the commodity on which their futures obligations are based. Most often, however, this means delivery of a close substitute for the specified commodity, but which is still not permitted under the strict exchange delivery rules. For example, a long silver trader may agree to permit a trader who is short silver contracts to fulfill her obligation by delivering silver coins instead of the silver bullion that is specified in the futures contract.

Thus, EFPs are a way to give futures traders greater flexibility in settling their contractual obligations, and of making physical delivery more attractive. To the extent that they occur, EFPs are obviously beneficial to both shorts and longs; otherwise either the short or the long would not agree to participate.

Table 2.4 provides a detailed description of the way in which physical deliveries took place on the New York Mercantile's heating oil futures contracts from 1983 to 1988. Almost all physical deliveries in 1983 were done under standard exchange delivery rules (columns A and E). However, in 1984 and subsequent years, EFP transactions became the dominant form of physical settlement in heating oil futures (as well as other petroleum futures). In 1988 EFPs accounted for 90 percent of all heating oil deliveries. Thus, EFPs are becoming an increasingly popular physical delivery alternative to the standard exchange delivery procedures.

Another variation of physical delivery is the ADP (alternative delivery procedure). An ADP transaction is performed *after* the end of trading in a contract and *after* longs and shorts have been matched by the clearinghouse. In such a transaction a long and a short agree to effect delivery under terms or conditions that are different from those prescribed by exchange rules. Parties to an ADP must notify the clearinghouse that an ADP transaction has taken place so that the clearinghouse can extinguish the parties' respective futures obligations.

Note

TABLE 2.4
Types of physical delivery—heating oil futures contracts, January 1983 to December 1988

Contract	Contracts delivered				Percentage of total			Total volume H	Maximum open interest I	J (A/I)
	Standard A	ADP B	EFP C	Total D	Standard E (A/D)	ADP F (B/D)	EFP G (C/D)			
8301	620	401	—	1,021	60.72	39.28	0.00	155,000	8,710	7.12
8302	859	188	—	1,047	82.04	17.96	0.00	200,000	11,100	7.74
8303	324	129	—	453	71.52	28.48	0.00	167,000	9,720	3.33
8304	290	56	—	346	83.82	16.18	0.00	109,000	9,010	3.22
8305	315	137	—	452	69.69	30.31	0.00	126,000	7,720	4.08
8306	317	118	—	435	72.87	27.13	0.00	117,000	7,950	3.99
8307	261	381	—	642	40.65	59.35	0.00	157,000	11,000	2.35
8308	256	657	—	913	28.04	71.96	0.00	134,000	11,000	2.33
8309	92	1,188	—	1,280	7.19	92.81	0.00	125,000	11,100	0.83
8310	352	410	—	762	46.19	53.81	0.00	138,000	11,300	3.12
8311	292	548	—	840	34.76	65.24	0.00	95,000	8,320	3.51
8312	687	992	—	1,679	40.92	59.08	0.00	311,000	11,900	5.77
8401	766	1,063	1,177	3,006	25.48	35.36	39.16	182,425	11,600	6.60
8402	397	617	990	2,004	19.81	30.79	49.40	196,967	11,200	3.54
8403	326	582	1,111	2,019	16.15	28.83	55.03	300,212	11,900	2.74
8404	320	821	1,520	2,661	12.03	30.85	57.12	180,228	9,950	3.22
8405	293	564	272	1,129	25.95	49.96	24.09	165,355	9,480	3.09
8406	764	587	581	1,932	39.54	30.38	30.07	144,911	8,450	9.04
8407	330	494	890	1,714	19.25	28.82	51.93	141,182	9,210	3.58
8408	192	354	1,578	2,124	9.04	16.67	74.29	124,781	8,920	2.15
8409	603	326	1,604	2,533	23.81	12.87	63.32	134,955	8,980	6.71
8410	1,465	452	1,167	3,084	47.50	14.66	37.84	137,359	9,600	15.26
8411	687	422	2,462	3,571	19.24	11.82	68.94	139,462	11,200	6.13
8412	943	693	1,359	2,995	31.49	23.14	45.38	260,122	11,500	8.20

8501	966	1,319	3,193	5,478	17.63	24.08	58.29	209,869	11,400	8.47
8502	988	501	1,338	2,827	34.95	17.72	47.33	253,140	11,600	8.52
8503	459	190	563	1,212	37.87	15.68	46.45	210,209	12,000	3.83
8504	421	587	249	1,257	33.49	46.70	19.81	161,501	9,630	4.37
8505	152	269	844	1,265	12.02	21.26	66.72	150,677	9,230	1.65
8506	453	161	829	1,443	31.39	11.16	57.45	126,903	8,950	5.06
8507	466	86	583	1,135	41.06	7.58	51.37	118,138	8,930	5.22
8508	112	780	1,435	2,327	4.81	33.52	61.67	110,877	8,380	1.34
8509	303	254	2,850	3,407	8.89	7.46	83.65	150,439	11,000	2.75
8510	217	151	2,124	2,492	8.71	6.06	85.23	155,967	9,870	2.20
8511	376	404	1,652	2,432	15.46	16.61	67.93	151,340	9,610	3.91
8512	852	553	3,181	4,586	18.58	12.06	69.36	270,841	11,400	7.47
8601	958	1,080	2,594	4,632	20.68	23.32	56.00	259,776	11,700	8.19
8602	501	615	2,008	3,124	16.04	19.69	64.28	293,796	11,500	4.36
8603	195	391	1,840	2,426	8.04	16.12	75.85	256,184	11,300	1.73
8604	370	655	2,921	3,946	9.38	16.60	74.02	197,972	11,300	3.27
8605	306	365	1,247	1,918	15.95	19.03	65.02	195,789	11,200	2.73
8606	544	170	1,104	1,818	29.92	9.35	60.73	178,112	11,100	4.90
8607	270	213	2,086	2,569	10.51	8.29	81.20	207,431	11,500	2.35
8608	475	218	5,004	5,697	8.34	3.83	87.84	228,591	11,900	3.99
8609	734	385	3,117	4,236	17.33	9.09	73.58	274,115	12,000	6.12
8610	616	226	3,234	4,076	15.11	5.54	79.34	239,713	11,800	5.22
8611	585	866	4,724	6,175	9.47	14.02	76.50	215,800	11,700	5.00
8612	724	777	6,098	7,599	9.53	10.23	80.25	487,622	13,200	5.48

(continued)

TABLE 2.4—cont'd.

| Contract | Contracts delivered | | | | Percentage of total | | | Total volume H | Maximum interest I | J (A/I) |
	Standard A	ADP B	EFP C	Total D	Standard E (A/D)	ADP F (B/D)	EFP G (C/D)			
8701	369	913	7,541	8,823	4.18	10.35	85.47	333,675	13,700	2.69
8702	1,048	1,000	6,150	8,198	12.78	12.20	75.02	405,107	13,200	7.94
8703	1,132	110	4,380	5,622	20.14	1.96	77.91	399,663	12,900	8.78
8704	441	188	4,180	4,809	9.17	3.91	86.92	367,102	12,100	3.64
8705	386	135	2,214	2,735	14.11	4.94	80.95	303,675	12,200	3.16
8706	319	112	2,780	3,211	9.93	3.49	86.58	286,742	11,800	2.70
8707	417	531	4,195	5,143	8.11	10.32	81.57	232,880	11,900	3.50
8708	423	80	6,024	6,527	6.48	1.23	92.29	247,291	11,800	3.58
8709	57	569	4,949	5,575	1.02	10.21	88.77	294,114	12,400	0.46
8710	659	188	6,369	7,216	9.13	2.61	88.26	334,327	12,500	5.27
8711	379	217	7,771	8,367	4.53	2.59	92.88	297,022	13,100	2.89
8712	232	535	12,817	13,584	1.71	3.94	94.35	519,643	13,600	1.71
8801	1,231	504	20,768	22,503	5.47	2.24	92.29	531,055	13,500	9.12
8802	490	1,804	16,297	18,591	2.64	9.70	87.66	561,541	12,700	3.86
8803	355	314	15,513	16,182	2.19	1.94	95.87	459,742	12,200	2.91
8804	309	315	13,970	14,594	2.12	2.16	95.72	380,559	12,000	2.58
8805	177	277	8,621	9,075	1.95	3.05	95.00	337,805	12,100	1.46
8806	396	159	9,621	10,176	3.89	1.56	94.55	298,859	11,800	3.36
8807	577	299	6,758	7,634	7.56	3.92	88.53	264,736	25,900	2.23
8808	570	266	8,748	9,584	5.95	2.78	91.28	329,744	22,300	2.56
8809	367	264	6,359	6,990	5.25	3.78	90.97	341,122	29,500	1.24
8810	286	214	8,620	9,120	3.14	2.35	94.52	416,088	25,700	1.11
8811	1,352	248	10,548	12,148	11.13	2.04	86.83	376,385	36,600	3.69
8812	817	423	19,717	20,957	3.90	2.02	94.08	625,707	32,200	2.54

Source: New York Mercantile Exchange.

TABLE 2.5
Physical deliveries of NYMEX energy futures contracts, 1984 to 1988 (in contracts)

	1988	1987	1986	1985	1984
Crude oil					
Trading volume	18,858,948	14,581,614	8,313,529	3,980,867	1,840,342
Total deliveries	612,282	434,012	276,127	157,991	66,780
1. Standard procedures	6,702	13,748	17,683	23,966	15,596
2. Alternative procedures	2,435	2,929	2,868	1,863	1,669
3. EFPs	603,145	417,335	255,576	132,162	49,515
Heating oil					
Trading volume	4,935,015	4,293,395	3,275,044	2,207,733	2,091,541
Total deliveries	157,554	79,810	48,216	29,861	28,772
1. Standard procedures	6,927	5,862	6,278	5,765	7,086
2. Alternative procedures	5,087	4,578	5,961	5,255	6,975
3. EFPs	145,540	69,370	35,977	18,841	14,711
Unleaded gasoline					
Trading volume	3,292,055	2,056,238	439,352	132,611	—
Total deliveries	127,558	52,645	14,068	20,637	—
1. Standard procedures	8,052	10,635	2,863	6,880	—
2. Alternative procedures	2,942	2,032	2,125	3,487	—
3. EFPs	116,564	39,978	9,080	10,270	—

Source: New York Mercantile Exchange.

Finally, Table 2.5 provides annual summaries of all physical deliveries for crude oil, heating oil, and unleaded gasoline futures contracts for all contracts taken together. It is clear that while physical deliveries are a small fraction of total trading volume, EFPs constitute a large percentage of such deliveries.

2.6.4   Cash Delivery

A relatively new procedure for settling futures obligations is cash delivery. This procedure is a substitute for physical delivery and completely eliminates having to make or take physical delivery. It is available only for futures contracts that specifically designate cash delivery as the settlement procedure. Physical delivery is not permitted on these contracts. Contracts as diverse as stock index futures and feeder cattle today use cash delivery to settle contracts. Table 2.6 lists the contracts which currently employ cash delivery.

Note

The mechanics of cash delivery are simple: the price of the relevant futures contract, at the close of trading in that contract, is set equal to the cash price of the underlying commodity at that time. Any moneys owing to either the short or the long at that time, because of setting the futures price equal to the cash price, is transferred (via the clearinghouse and FCMs) from the party who owes the money to the party who is owed the money. (This mechanism will become clearer when the operation of variation margins is discussed in the next section of this chapter.) This procedure is obviously much simpler than making and taking physical delivery, since it avoids having to handle the physical commodity at all. It also

TABLE 2.6
**Futures contracts employing cash settlement,
as of February 1991**

1. Chicago Board of Trade
   - MMI MAXI
   - Municipal Bond Index
   - 30-day Interest Rate
   - Mortgage-Back
2. Chicago Mercantile Exchange
   - S&P 500 Index
   - 3-month Eurodollar
   - Feeder Cattle
   - Eurorate Differential
   - Nikkei 225
3. New York Cotton Exchange
   - U.S. Dollar Index
4. New York Futures Exchange
   - CRB Index
   - NYSE Composite Index

means, however, that a buyer can no longer use a futures contract to acquire the physical commodity. He will have to buy the commodity elsewhere, if that is what he wants.

Note

Exchanges have adopted cash delivery as an alternative to physical delivery for two reasons. First, the nature of the underlying commodity may not permit feasible physical delivery. For example, stock index futures would require physical delivery of hundreds or thousands of shares of stock in finely calculated proportions, requiring a cumbersome and costly delivery procedure. Second, cash delivery avoids the problem that it may be difficult for traders to acquire the physical commodity at the time of delivery because of a temporary shortage of supply. Cash delivery also makes it difficult for traders to *manipulate* or influence futures prices by causing an artificial shortage of the underlying commodity.

The popularity of cash delivery has grown substantially in recent years, and has enabled exchanges to offer futures contracts that would not have been feasible without such a delivery mechanism. The second and fourth most active futures contracts in 1990 were cash delivery contracts (i.e., Eurodollars and the S&P 500 index respectively).

2.7 INITIAL MARGINS

Note

Buyers and sellers of futures contracts must post margin funds with their FCMs. Although futures contracts are deferred delivery (and therefore deferred payment) contracts, buyers and sellers must nevertheless pay over funds to their FCMs to meet initial margin requirements (in contrast to most forward contracts). The minimum level of margin requirements is set by exchanges: FCMs must collect from customers at least this amount and hold the funds in segregated accounts. It is common, however, for FCMs to require that customers post more than the minimum required by exchanges.

Note

The purpose of margin deposits is to assure performance: to guarantee that both longs and shorts ultimately meet their contractual obligations. Margin deposits, therefore, are similar to posting a performance bond. In particular, if, in purchasing a futures contract, a long has agreed to pay $400 an ounce for gold, but the market price falls to $350 an ounce, it will not be advantageous for the long to fulfill his $400 contractual obligation. He may even consider defaulting, in which event the defaulting customer's FCM would incur his obligation to purchase the gold at $400 an ounce. To protect themselves, FCMs require customers to post with them initial margin funds sufficient to cover possible customer losses due to changes in the price of the underlying commodity (and therefore in the futures price).

The level of the initial margin is different for different futures contracts. In general, it is directly related to the price volatility of the commodity that underlies the futures contract: the greater the price volatility, the higher is the initial margin requirement. More specifically, exchanges commonly set initial minimum margin levels equal to $\mu + 3\sigma$, where μ is the average of the daily absolute changes in the dollar value of a futures contract and σ is the standard deviation of these daily changes, measured over some time period in the recent past.

Note

Let us take gold futures contracts as an example. Each gold futures contract is for 100 ounces of gold. Let us assume that the current market price of gold is $400 an ounce, and that the average daily absolute price change is $10 an ounce. Further, assume that the standard deviation of the distribution of recent absolute daily price changes is $3 an ounce. Thus, μ is equal to 10×100 ounces, or $1000; σ is equal to 3×100 ounces, or $300; and $\mu + 3\sigma = \$1000 + \$900$, or $1900. This would be the initial margin requirement on a gold futures contract. (Table 16.3 in Chapter 16 contains similar statistical information for other futures contracts.)

The logic behind such a margin formula is that exchanges and FCMs want initial margins to cover all likely daily changes in the value of a futures contract, and therefore to cover all likely customer losses.[1] Exceptionally large price movements will not be covered. In this case, FCMs must hope that traders make good their losses and continue to honor their obligations.[2]

Table 2.7 shows the initial and maintenance margin requirements specified by various exchanges for the top 10 futures contracts in the United States. Since futures prices for near-month contracts are generally more volatile than prices for more distant contracts, exchanges often require higher margins for positions in

---

[1] A normal distribution is completely defined by its mean, μ, and its standard deviation, σ. It is the most frequently used probability model in economic and business decisions. The mean plus and minus a given number of standard deviations will include a precise proportion of the number of observations in the normal distribution. The following relationships may be expected to hold approximately: i). $\mu + \sigma$ includes about 68% of the observations; ii). $\mu + 2\sigma$ includes about 95% of the observations; and iii). $\mu + 3\sigma$ includes about 99.7% of the observations. Therefore, if changes in futures prices are assumed to be normally distributed, there is only a small probability that daily price changes will occur that are less than $\mu - 3\sigma$ or greater than $\mu + 3\sigma$.

[2] Daily price limits are sometimes used by exchanges to keep prices from changing by more than a specified amount during the day. The pros and cons of price limits are discussed in Section 3.4.3 in Chapter 3.

TABLE 2.7
Minimum margin requirements specified by exchanges: Ten most actively traded futures contracts as of March 31, 1989

| Futures | Exchange | Spot month* | | | | | | Non-spot month | | | | | |
| | | Speculator | | Hedger | | | | Speculator | | Hedger | | | |
		Initial	Maintenance	Initial	Maintenance			Initial	Maintenance	Initial	Maintenance		
T-bonds	CBOT	2,500	2,000	2,000	2,000			2,500	2,000	2,000	2,000		
Eurodollars	CME	800	500	800	500			800	500	800	500		
Crude oil	NYMEX	3,000	2,100	3,000	2,100			2,000	1,400	2,000	1,400		
S&P 500	CME	15,000	4,000	4,000	4,000			15,000	4,000	4,000	4,000		
Corn	CBOT	600	400	400	400			600	400	400	400		
Soybeans	CBOT	1,500	1,250	1,250	1,250			1,500	1,250	1,250	1,250		
Gold	COMEX	1,300	975	1,000	750			1,300	975	1,000	750		
Deutschemark	CME	1,700	1,300	1,300	1,300			1,700	1,300	1,300	1,300		
Japanese yen	CME	2,000	1,500	2,000	1,500			2,000	1,500	2,000	1,500		
Swiss franc	CME	2,000	1,500	2,000	1,500			2,000	1,500	2,000	1,500		

* The term *spot month* is commonly used to refer to the futures contract that calls for immediate delivery, or the contract that is closest (nearest) to delivery.

near-month contracts. Hedger margins also are considerably lower than specula-tive margins. The likelihood of a hedger incurring serious (net) losses is much less, since hedgers typically hold both long and short positions in a commodity simultaneously. Thus, the risk of a hedging customer defaulting because of a se-rious loss caused by a price change is less than the risk of a speculative customer defaulting. Finally, while not shown in Table 2.7, margins on *spread* positions (two or more offsetting futures positions) are much lower than speculative mar-gins for the same reason: a lower likelihood of the trader incurring significant net losses. As stated earlier, FCMs, in order to obtain even greater protection, often impose higher initial margins than those required by exchanges, depending on the particular customer's credit-standing.

2.8   VARIATION MARGINS

To maintain customer deposits at the level of the initial margin (or at the *main-tenance margin* level), it is necessary for FCMs to make daily adjustments to customer accounts in response to changes in the value of customer positions.[3] As discussed in the last section, changes in futures prices change the value of futures contracts. To maintain initial or specified maintenance margin levels, therefore, FCMs require customers to make daily payments to them equal to the losses on their futures positions, while FCMs in turn pay to customers the gains on their po-sitions. These daily payments are calculated by *marking to the market* customer accounts—revaluing accounts based on daily (futures) settlement prices. The daily payments are called *variation margins,* and must generally be made before the mar-ket opens on the next trading day. The mechanics for the collection and payment of variation margins involves the clearinghouse and is discussed in the next chapter.

2.9   AN EXAMPLE OF MARGIN CALCULATIONS AND PAYMENTS

This example uses the hypothetical trading activity of a customer to demonstrate the margin payments that would typically be incurred in trading futures. As part of the example we also show how to calculate daily trading gains and losses, daily account equity, and the cumulative net profits or losses from the trades made. The hypothetical trades are in unleaded gasoline futures during April 1989, and the futures prices used to make all of the calculations shown in Tables 2.8 and 2.9 are the actual prices that occurred in April of 1989. The trades are

1. April 3: bought 2 May 89 contracts at 67.85 cents per gallon
2. April 12: sold 2 May 89 contracts at 70.11 cents per gallon
3. April 18: sold 4 June 89 contracts at 69.33 cents per gallon
4. April 21: bought 4 June 89 contracts at 71.18 cents per gallon

---

[3]The maintenance margin is the minimum amount per contract that a customer must keep on deposit at all times. It often is somewhat lower than the initial margin level.

TABLE 2.8
Daily gains and losses and cumulative trading profits and losses—unleaded gasoline, April 3, 1989 to April 28, 1989

	May contract (spot month)		June contract (non-spot month)		Marked to market cash flows	Cumulative profit/loss	
	Trade price	Settlement price	Trade price	Settlement price		Unrealized	Realized
	cent/gallon	cent/gallon	cent/gallon	cent/gallon	$	$	$
3	67.85	67.85		65.00	—	—	—
4		69.46		65.93	+1,352.40	+1,352.40	—
5		66.43		63.93	−2,545.20	−1,192.80	—
6		64.55		62.46	−1,579.20	−2,772.00	—
7		64.95		62.89	+336.00	−2,436.00	—
10		67.29		64.41	+1,965.60	−470.40	—
11		69.00		65.91	+1,436.40	+966.00	—
12	70.11	70.11		66.84	+932.40	—	+1,898.40
13		68.81		65.81	—	—	+1,898.40
14		70.02		66.54	—	—	+1,898.40
17		72.08		68.21	—	—	+1,898.40
18		73.86	69.33	69.33	—	—	+1,898.40
19		74.62		70.23	−1,512.00	−1,512.00	+1,898.40
20		74.65	71.18	71.36	−1,898.40	−3,410.40	+1,898.40
21		74.16		71.18	+302.40	—	−1,209.60
24		72.23		69.18	—	—	−1,209.60
25		76.16		71.38	—	—	−1,209.60
26		78.12		72.33	—	—	−1,209.60
27		78.12		72.27	—	—	−1,209.60
28		74.12		71.22	—	—	−1,209.60

TABLE 2.9
Margin account and account equity—unleaded gasoline, April 3, 1989 to April 24, 1989

April	Transactions	Equity			Margin account		
		Beginning $	Cash flow* $	Ending $	Margin call $	Deficiency $	Excess $
3	Deposit $5,000	0	+5,000	5,000.00	—	—	5,000.00
4	Bought 2 May	5,000.00	—	5,000.00	1,000.00	1,000.00	—
5	Deposit $1,000	6,000.00	+1,352.40	7,352.40	—	—	1,352.40
6		7,352.40	-2,545.20	4,807.20	—	—	—
7	Deposit $2,772	4,807.20	-1,579.20	3,228.00	2,772.00	2,772.00	—
10		6,000.00	+336.00	6,336.00	—	—	336.00
11	Withdraw $2,301.60	6,336.00	+1,965.60	8,301.60	—	—	2,301.60
12	Sold 2 May	6,000.00	+1,436.40	7,436.40	—	—	1,436.40
13	Withdraw $3,368.80	7,436.40	+932.40	8,368.80	—	—	8,368.80
14		5,000.00	—	5,000.00	—	—	5,000.00
17		5,000.00	—	5,000.00	—	—	5,000.00
18	Sold 4 June	5,000.00	—	5,000.00	3,000.00	3,000.00	—
19	Deposit $3,000	8,000.00	-1,512.00	6,488.00	—	—	—
20		6,488.00	-1,898.40	4,589.60	—	3,410.40	—
21	Bought 4 June	4,589.60	+302.40	4,892.00	—	—	4,892.00
24	Withdraw $4,892	0	—	0	—	—	—

* Marked to market cash flows from Table 2.8.

All purchases and sales are assumed, for simplicity, to take place at the settlement price on the day of the trade.[4] The required initial and maintenance margins per contract are as follows:

	Spot-month	Non-spot month
Initial	$3,000	$2,000
Maintenance	$2,100	$1,400

Table 2.8 shows the daily settlement prices for the May and June futures contracts, and computes the daily gains and losses on the customer's futures positions. These gains and losses are both *realized* and *unrealized*. Realized gains and losses are those resulting from actual purchases and sales. Unrealized gains and losses are incurred because the account is revalued every day, or marked to market prices each day. (Readers should be able to calculate these losses and gains. Hint: each futures contract requires the delivery of 42,000 gallons of gasoline.)

Table 2.9 shows the customer's daily margin account. It assumes that the account is opened on April 3 with a deposit of $5000, in anticipation of making future trades, and it provides the daily transactions made in the margin account, from April 3 through April 24, because of the following transactions:

- April 3
  Customer purchases 2 May contracts resulting in an initial margin call for $1000, which is the difference between the customer's $5000 deposit on the previous day and the initial margin requirement of $6000 ($3000 × 2 = $6000).
- April 4
  Customer responds to the margin call and deposits $1000. His account experiences an unrealized gain of $1352.40 during the day, bringing his equity to $7352.40. Since the equity is above the initial margin requirement, the customer is entitled to withdraw cash if he wishes, but he does not.
- April 5
  A substantial drop in gasoline prices results in an unrealized loss of $2545.20. The equity falls to $4807.20. Since total equity is still above the $4200 ($2100 × 2) maintenance margin level, no margin call is issued.
- April 6
  Gasoline prices continue to decline, resulting in another loss of $1579.20, further reducing equity to $3228.00. Since equity is now less than the required maintenance margin of $4200, a variation margin call is issued for $2772 ($6000 − $3228 = $2772), bringing the equity in the account back to the initial $6000 required margin level.

---

[4]The settlement price is determined by the exchange and is based on the range of prices near the close of trading. It is not necessarily the last-trade price of the day.

- April 7
  Customer answers the margin call by depositing $2772. Gasoline prices make a slight recovery. Equity rises to $6336.
- April 10
  The price of gasoline continues to rise. The customer's equity increases to $8301.60. He requests that the broker pay him the excess in his margin account, which is $2301.60 (the difference between the initial required margin of $6000 and the current equity of $8301.60).
- April 11
  Gasoline prices increase. The customer has an unrealized gain of $1436.40, bringing the equity in the account to $7436.40.
- April 12
  The customer liquidates his position by selling 2 May contracts at 70.11 cents per gallon, realizing a gain for that day of $932.40. His equity rises to $8368.80. The columns on the right side of Table 2.8 show his cumulative performance up to this date: he has a net profit of $1898.40.
- April 13
  The customer withdraws $3368.80 from his account, leaving only the $5000 he originally used to open his account.
- April 18
  Customer sells 4 June contracts, requiring an initial margin of $8000 ($2000×4). Hence, a margin call of $3000 is issued ($8000 − $5000 = $3000).
- April 19
  Customer meets his margin call by depositing $3000. An increase in gasoline prices results in an unrealized loss of $1512.00. The account equity is still above the required $5600 ($1400×4) maintenance level, so no margin call is issued.
- April 20
  Gasoline prices continue to surge, causing a further loss of $1898.40. Equity falls to $4589.60, resulting in the broker issuing a margin call for $3410.40 to restore the account equity to the initial required margin level of $8000 ($8000 − $4589.60 = $3410.40).
- April 21
  The customer cannot meet the margin call and decides to offset his position by buying 4 June contracts at 71.18 cents per gallon, for a gain of $302.40. His remaining equity is $4892, which he requests be paid to him. For the entire month, the customer's trading activity has resulted in a net loss of $1209.60.

2.10 TYPES OF ORDERS

When trading futures it is important to understand the various types of orders that can be used. Up to now we have discussed trading futures as if there were only one type of order: a *market order* to buy or sell. A market order instructs

Note

a broker to execute an order immediately, at the best available market price. There are, however, more complex types of orders that traders commonly employ. This section describes the most frequently used orders.

In general, a *futures order* refers to a set of instructions given to a broker (FCM) by a customer requesting that the broker take certain actions in the futures market on behalf of the customer. Figure 2-3 displays a typical order form used by a brokerage firm. Order forms usually include the following information:

1. The commodity to be traded.
2. Quantity of contracts to be bought or sold.
3. The futures contract month and year.
4. The futures exchange on which the futures contract is traded.
5. The price at which the trade is to be executed.
6. Name of the customer and his commodity account number.
7. Date of the order.
8. Length of time the order is valid. Generally, orders are good only for the day they are entered, unless the order is marked *good till canceled* (GTC).

The discussion which follows describes the various types of orders and gives an example of each. These examples use actual minute-by-minute transaction prices for the June 89 crude oil futures contract, during May 16, 1980.[5] These prices are shown in Table 2.10. Prices for crude oil are quoted in dollars per barrel.

1. Market Order (MKT)
   Example: "BUY 1 June 89 Crude MKT"
   An order placed to buy or sell *at the market* means that the order should be executed at the best possible price immediately following the time it is received by a floor broker on the trading floor. The customer, in this case, is less concerned with the price he will receive than with the speed of execution. He wants to be in or out of the market immediately. For example, if a market order is placed at 11:00 A.M., on May 16, 1989, and the market is currently being bid at $20.90 and offered at $20.92, the order will probably be filled immediately at the price of $20.92 per barrel.

2. Limit Order
   Examples: "BUY 1 June 89 Crude 20.90"
   "SELL 1 June 89 Crude 20.96"
   A *limit order* is used when the customer wants to buy (sell) at a specified price below (above) the current market price. The order must be filled either

---

[5]Crude oil futures are traded on the New York Mercantile Exchange, between 9:45 A.M. to 3:10 P.M., New York time.

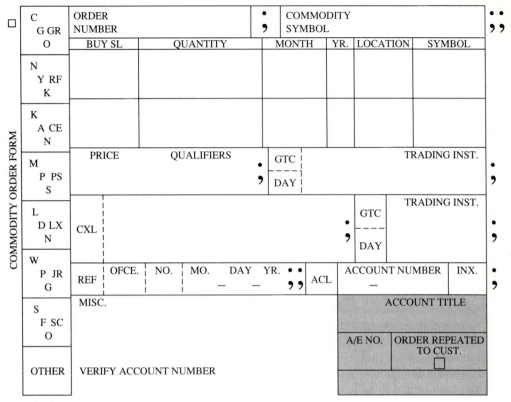

FIGURE 2-3
Futures order form.

at the price specified on the order or at a better price. For the above orders the buy-limit order may only be filled at the limit price (20.90) or below, and the sell-limit order may be filled only at 20.96 or above. Assuming the two limit orders are placed at 11:00 A.M., when the market is at 20.92, neither of these orders can be executed immediately. The buy-limit order will be filled at 11:10 A.M. at the specified price of 20.90, while the sell-limit order will be executed at 11:15 A.M., at the price of 20.97.

The advantage of a limit order is that a trader knows the worst price he will receive if his order is executed. However, he is not assured of execution, as with a market order: the market must pass through the customer's designated limit in order for him to obtain execution.

3. Market If Touched (MIT) Order
   Example: "SELL 1 June 89 Crude 21.05 MIT"
   When the market reaches the specified limit price, an *MIT order* becomes a market order for immediate execution. The actual execution may or may not be at the limit price. An MIT buy order is placed at a price below the current market price. An MIT sell order is placed at a price above the current mar-

TABLE 2.10
Intra-day prices for June 89 crude oil futures contract,
May 16, 1989, dollars per barrel

Time	Price	Time	Price	Time	Price
11:00am	20.92	12:24pm	20.93	1:52pm	21.06
11:01am	20.94	12:25pm	20.92	1:53pm	21.07
11:02am	20.96	12:26pm	20.90	1:54pm	21.10
11:03am	20.93	12:27pm	20.93	1:55pm	21.10
11:04am	20.92	12:28pm	20.93	1:56pm	21.12
11:05am	20.93	12:29pm	20.92	1:57pm	21.12
11:06am	20.95	12:30pm	20.91	1:58pm	21.08
11:07am	20.95	12:32pm	20.93	1:59pm	21.06
11:08am	20.94	12:33pm	20.94	2:00pm	21.05
11:09am	20.95	12:34pm	20.92	2:01pm	21.06
11:10am	20.90	12:35pm	20.95	2:02pm	21.05
11:11am	20.90	12:37pm	20.95	2:03pm	21.05
11:12am	20.91	12:40pm	20.93	2:04pm	21.04
11:13am	20.91	12:46pm	20.95	2:05pm	21.07
11:14am	20.94	12:47pm	20.96	2:06pm	21.05
11:15am	20.97	12:48pm	20.95	2:07pm	21.08
11:16am	21.00	12:51pm	20.95	2:08pm	21.07
11:17am	21.02	12:53pm	20.96	2:09pm	21.08
11:18am	21.04	12:54pm	20.97	2:10pm	21.08
11:19am	21.02	12:56pm	20.98	2:12pm	21.10
11:20am	21.04	12:58pm	20.98	2:13pm	21.10
11:21am	21.02	12:59pm	20.95	2:14pm	21.11
11:22am	21.05	1:00pm	20.96	2:16pm	21.08
11:23am	21.03	1:03pm	20.97	2:17pm	21.10
11:24am	21.03	1:04pm	20.98	2:19pm	21.07
11:25am	21.02	1:05pm	21.02	2:20pm	21.05
11:27am	21.03	1:06pm	21.02	2:21pm	21.05
11:29am	21.04	1:07pm	21.05	2:22pm	21.04
11:31am	21.03	1:08pm	21.07	2:23pm	21.05
11:34am	21.05	1:09pm	21.07	2:25pm	21.06
11:35am	21.03	1:10pm	21.08	2:26pm	21.04
11:36am	21.02	1:11pm	21.06	2:27pm	21.05
11:37am	21.03	1:12pm	21.08	2:28pm	21.02
11:38am	21.02	1:13pm	21.08	2:29pm	20.98
11:39am	21.04	1:14pm	21.10	2:30pm	20.97
11:42am	21.03	1:15pm	21.10	2:31pm	20.98
11:43am	21.01	1:16pm	21.07	2:32pm	21.00
11:44am	20.98	1:17pm	21.07	2:33pm	21.01
11:45am	20.98	1:18pm	21.08	2:34pm	21.02
11:46am	20.97	1:19pm	21.12	2:35pm	21.01
11:47am	20.99	1:20pm	21.11	2:37pm	20.97
11:48am	21.01	1:21pm	21.13	2:38pm	20.92
11:49am	20.99	1:22pm	21.13	2:39pm	20.92
11:50am	21.00	1:23pm	21.13	2:40pm	20.89
11:51am	20.98	1:24pm	21.14	2:41pm	20.93
11:52am	20.98	1:25pm	21.15	2:42pm	20.93
11:53am	20.95	1:26pm	21.18	2:43pm	20.95
11:54am	20.95	1:27pm	21.16	2:44pm	20.90
11:55am	20.95	1:28pm	21.16	2:45pm	20.89
11:56am	20.94	1:29pm	21.13	2:46pm	20.91
11:57am	20.93	1:30pm	21.12	2:48pm	20.90
11:58am	20.94	1:31pm	21.13	2:49pm	20.86
11:59am	20.97	1:32pm	21.12	2:50pm	20.84
12:00pm	20.98	1:33pm	21.15	2:51pm	20.82
12:01pm	20.96	1:34pm	21.13	2:52pm	20.77
12:02pm	20.97	1:35pm	21.15	2:53pm	20.77
12:04pm	20.96	1:36pm	21.16	2:54pm	20.78
12:06pm	20.94	1:37pm	21.17	2:55pm	20.83
12:08pm	20.93	1:38pm	21.16	2:57pm	20.84
12:09pm	20.92	1:39pm	21.18	2:58pm	20.81
12:10pm	20.94	1:40pm	21.17	2:59pm	20.80
12:11pm	20.92	1:41pm	21.15	3:00pm	20.79
12:12pm	20.92	1:42pm	21.12	3:01pm	20.81
12:13pm	20.90	1:43pm	21.11	3:02pm	20.82
12:15pm	20.90	1:44pm	21.12	3:03pm	20.81
12:16pm	20.92	1:45pm	21.12	3:04pm	20.80
12:17pm	20.91	1:46pm	21.09	3:05pm	20.77
12:19pm	20.90	1:47pm	21.10	3:06pm	20.73
12:20pm	20.90	1:48pm	21.09	3:07pm	20.71
12:21pm	20.90	1:49pm	21.11	3:08pm	20.70
12:22pm	20.88	1:50pm	21.07	3:09pm	20.69
12:23pm	20.90	1:51pm	21.08	3:10pm	20.67

ket price. If the above MIT sell order is placed with the broker at 11:00 A.M., it will not become a market order until 11:22 A.M., when the market hits 21.05. The order may then be filled immediately, or at any subsequent price. If, for example, the sell order is not filled until 11:23 A.M., the seller will receive 21.03 which is below his limit price. MIT orders are used by traders who want to ensure that they receive an execution if the market reaches their designated limit prices.

4. Market-On-Close (MOC) Order

Example: "BUY 3 June 89 Crude MOC"

A *Market-On-Close order* instructs the floor broker to buy or sell for the customer at the market during the official closing period for that contract. The actual execution price need not be the last sale price which occurred, but it must fall within the range of prices traded during the official close of the contract month on the exchange that day. In this example, the given order has to be executed between 3:09–3:10 P.M., the 2-minute official closing trading period for crude oil futures.

5. Stop Order   *Stop (Loss) Order*

Examples: "BUY 2 June 89 Crude 21.15 stop"
                "SELL 2 June 89 Crude 20.75 stop"

In contrast to limit orders, a *buy-stop order* is placed at a price *above* the present market price, and a *sell-stop order* is placed at a price *below* the present market price. Stop orders become market orders when the designated price limit is reached. The execution of simple stop orders, however, is not restricted to the designated limit price. They may be executed at any price subsequent to the designated stop-order price being touched. Thus, the execution price may be either above or below the designated stop-price. Assume that both of the above stop orders are placed at 11:00 A.M., when the market is at 20.92. The buy-stop order cannot be processed until 1:25 P.M. when the stop-price of 21.15 is first touched. If the order can be executed immediately, it will be filled at 1:25 P.M., at the price of 21.15. If it cannot be executed until 1:26 P.M., it will be filled at 21.18, and so forth. Similarly, the sell-stop order will be executed at 3:06 P.M. at 20.73.

Stop orders are often used to limit losses on open futures positions: a sell-stop order to limit losses on an open long position, and a buy-stop order to limit losses on an open short position. Stop orders are also used by technical traders to initiate new positions when market prices penetrate what they believe are key *support* or *resistance* price levels. In Chapter 16, technical trading techniques and terminologies are discussed in greater detail.

6. Stop-Limit Order

Examples: "BUY 2 June 89 Crude 21.15 stop limit"
                "SELL 2 June 89 Crude 20.75 stop limit"

A *stop-limit order* is similar to a regular stop order except that its execution is restricted to the specified limit price or "better." To see the difference between the two types of orders, assume, in contrast to the previous example, that when the market first touches 21.15 at 1:25 P.M., the above stop-limit buy-order does not get filled at that price because of market conditions (more buyers than seller in the pit). With a *stop-limit buy* order, the floor broker must try to buy 2 June crude at 21.15 or *less*. Hence, the order will not be executed until 1:29 P.M., at a price of 21.13. In the case of the *stop-limit sell* order, if the market moves quickly from 20.77 (3:05 P.M.) to 20.73 (3:06 P.M.), so that the broker has no chance to execute at 20.75 or better, the order will not be filled at all that day because prices fall continuously until the close of trading. He is obliged to fill it at 20.75 or higher, which he cannot do.

Thus, a broker may not be able to execute a stop-limit order in a *fast* market because of the restrictions placed on the execution price. Since stop-limit orders do not guarantee an execution, they are not recommended for use in limiting losses on open positions.

7. **Exchange for Physical (EFP) Order**
   Example: "SELL 2 June 89 Crude 21.10 EFP to XYZ Co."
   EFP orders are also referred to as *Against Actual, Versus Cash,* or *Ex-Pit* orders. EFPs permit the exchange of a futures position for a physical position. The parties to an EFP privately negotiate the terms of the EFP, including cash and futures prices as well as delivery terms. Once agreed upon, the EFP is communicated to the exchange. The transaction, therefore, is completed outside the exchange trading floor, and is considered an off-exchange transaction.

8. **Discretionary Order**
   Example: "BUY 2 June 89 Crude 20.92 with 1 Point Disc"
   A *discretionary order* gives a specific amount of discretion to a broker. For example, a broker may be given discretion to buy when prices exceed the limit price, and to sell when prices go below the limit price. Assume that such a buy order is placed at 11:01 A.M., when the market is at 20.94. The order cannot be filled immediately. The floor broker, however, is given the discretion to pay up to 20.93 (an extra one point) to get the order executed.

9. **Not Held Order**
   Example: "BUY 2 June 89 Crude 20.92 Not Held"
   Although similar to the discretionary order, the *not held order* gives the floor broker additional discretion. If, for example, the market is trading close to 20.92 at 11:00 A.M. but looks weak, a customer may decide to submit this type of order. It gives the floor broker the option either to wait for a lower price than 20.92 or to execute immediately. In the event that the broker does so unwisely and fails to execute at all, he cannot be held liable for failing to execute at 20.92 when he had the opportunity to do so.
   This type of order relies on the floor broker's market judgment in determining when to buy or sell. A good understanding between customer, salesperson, and floor broker is a necessary element when using such discretionary orders.

10. **Spread Order**
    Example: "Spread BUY 2 June 89 Crude SELL 2 July 89 Crude, June 90 cents premium"
    "Spread BUY 3 August 89 Heating Oil SELL 3 July 89 Heating Oil, August 20 Pts or less premium"

"Spread BUY 4 December 89 Heating Oil SELL 4 December 89 Crude MKT"
"Spread BUY 4 December 89 Heat Crack, Product $4.00 premium"
In addition to outright positions, markets are made in *spread prices*: relative prices between one delivery month and another within the same commodity or between different commodities. A *spread order* directs the broker to buy and sell simultaneously two different futures contracts, either at the *market* or at a specified *spread premium*. The first two examples represent *intra-market* spreads: both ends of the spread are in the same commodity. Intra-market spreads are the most popular type of spread. The last two examples are *inter-commodity* spreads: they involve different commodities.

Like orders for outright futures positions, spread orders can be placed at specified limit prices or at the market. To avoid errors, it is customary to write the BUY side of each spread order first. Since spread orders on most exchanges qualify for lower commission rates and lower margin requirements, it is necessary to precede the command portion of such orders with the word "spread."

Finally, although the foregoing types of orders are the most commonly used, it should be recognized that a trader can vary the price limits, time limits, or other variables of an order to suit his needs.

CONCLUSION

Chapters 1 and 2 have covered the institutional details that participants in futures markets need to know. Clearinghouses are key institutions and a thorough underl-standing of what they do and how they do it is vital to understanding how futures markets operate. While clearinghouses have been touched upon at several points in the discussion in this chapter, we have deferred a thorough examination of their operations to Chapter 3, to which we now turn.

QUESTIONS

1. What is a seat on an exchange? Why would someone buy a seat on an exchange? What factors determine the value of a seat?
2. What is an FCM? How does an FCM differ from an introducing broker?
3. What functions are performed by a futures exchange?
4. What does a clearing association do?
5. What is a pit?
6. In what ways can the holder of a futures position satisfy (or settle) his obligations?
7. What is meant by *deliverable stock*?
8. What is a floor trader? Do floor traders have an advantage over other traders?
9. What is dual trading?
10. What is an out-trade?
11. Why has the frequency of EFPs been increasing in some futures markets?
12. What is an ADP transaction?

13. What is meant by *cash settlement*? What kinds of commodities are suitable for cash settlement?

14. Why do FCMs impose margins on their customers? How do they determine margin levels? What is a safe level? (See Table 2.7)

15. Why do exchanges have mandatory minimum margins?

16. What is meant by *marking-to-the-market* a customer's account? What is a variation margin payment?

17. Explain the calculations in Table 2.8. What is the difference between realized and unrealized gains and losses?

18. Calculate the trader's profits for the month of April in Table 2.8 by summing all equity infusions and withdrawals made by the trader. Compare this to the "cumulative realized profit/loss" column in Table 2.8. What is the difference?

SUGGESTED READING

Figlewski S. "Margins and Market Integrity: Margin Setting for Stock Index Futures and Options." *The Journal of Futures Markets,* Fall 1984, pp. 385–416.

Garbade, K. and W. Silber. "Cash Settlement of Futures Contracts: An Economic Analysis." *The Journal of Futures Markets,* Winter 1983, pp. 451–472.

Hartzmark, M. "The Effects of Changing Margin Levels on Futures Market Activity, the Composition of Traders in the Market, and Price Performance." *Journal of Business,* April 1986, pp. 147–180.

Tomek, W. "Margins on Futures Contracts: Their Economic Roles and Regulation." in *Futures Markets: Regulatory Issues,* ed. by A. Peck. American Enterprise Institute for Public Policy Research, Washington DC, 1985, pp. 143–210.

CHAPTER
3

THE CLEARINGHOUSE

Clearinghouses are key institutions in futures markets. They are the institutional bedrock foundation upon which futures markets are built. Clearinghouses perform two critical functions: they assure the financial integrity of futures transactions by guaranteeing obligations among clearing members, and they enable customer *offset* as a simple and convenient mechanism for settling futures contract obligations. In addition, clearinghouses have a number of important operational functions. They enter and record trades made on associated exchanges, match all trades, and assure that the parties to these trades agree on the terms of the trade. They then *clear* the trades. In clearing a trade the clearinghouse registers the trade, combines new trades with the existing open positions held by clearing members, and calculates new open positions for all clearing members. When a trade is registered, the clearinghouse becomes the *opposite party* to every trade, making it directly responsible to clearing members. If a clearing member were to fail, therefore, its obligations would be met by the clearinghouse itself.

The role of the clearinghouse in futures markets is different from that of clearing associations in banking and securities markets. Although both kinds of institutions perform a banking function by facilitating the transfer of funds between contracting parties and their agents, clearing associations in banking and securities markets do not become legal parties to transactions, do not act as guarantors, and do not operate as a pervasive self-regulatory institution. Nor are they involved in facilitating settlement by delivery. In futures markets clearing associations are not a mere processing convenience; they are an integral component of these markets. In essence, they convert a forward contractual obligation into a futures obligation.

3.1 STRUCTURE

All organized futures exchanges in the United States have an affiliated clearing-house which clears futures trades made on that exchange. There are 14 futures exchanges and 9 clearinghouses in the United States (see the appendix to this chapter). Six of these are organized as separate not-for-profit corporations, where membership is limited to members of the affiliated exchange. Three are departments within an exchange. All clearinghouses organized as separate corporations refund or rebate excessive income (or clearance fees) to their members prior to the end of their respective fiscal years, so that they do not have substantial annual retained earnings. In all cases, firms approved to clear trades (or clearing members) must meet financial requirements that are more onerous than the membership requirements of the affiliated exchanges.

Membership in a clearing association may be attractive for two reasons: it is prestigious, and it may be profitable. Since all trades on an organized futures market must be cleared, exchange members who are not members of a clearing association must clear through a clearing member. Thus, in clearing for non-clearing exchange members, clearing members obtain certain benefits: direct fee income; the avoidance of having to pay clearing fees themselves; complete anonymity for their trading activities; and, very often, the investment income on the margin deposits posted by non-clearing members' customers. Against these benefits the clearing member must weigh the costs of membership, of which the major ones are the financial and reporting obligations and the restrictive regulations that go with membership.

In general, the clearinghouse is managed by officers independent from the affiliated exchange. However, this management is responsible to a clearing corporation Board of Directors, elected by the members of the clearinghouse. The members of the Board usually reflect, either formally or informally, the diverse interests of the related exchange—clearing floor brokers or traders, commission houses, trade hedgers, and so forth. It is the Board's responsibility to set the policies and procedures of the clearinghouse; it is the management's responsibility to implement those policies.

3.2 THE CLEARINGHOUSE IN OPERATION: AN EXAMPLE

The best way to understand the role of clearing associations is to work through a simple hypothetical example. While many such examples are possible, the one discussed below is sufficiently rich to elucidate the critical function of the clearinghouse.

The hypothetical example depicted in Figure 3-1 has nine parties: a clearinghouse, two clearing member FCMs (Futures Commission Merchants), a non-clearing FCM, and five individual customers (or traders), of whom two are customers of the non-clearing FCM and three are customers of the two clearing FCMs. For simplicity, all transactions are assumed to be in the same futures contract.

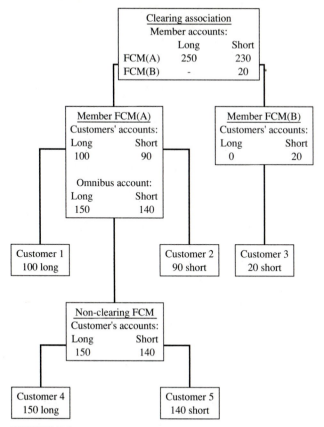

FIGURE 3-1
The clearinghouse in operation. (*The Journal of Futures Markets*,
Vol. 3, #4, 1983, p. 372.)

The various positions of each party are assumed to be the following. With respect to the two customers of the non-clearing FCM, one is long 150 contracts and the other is short 140 contracts. Thus, the non-clearing FCM, which must clear through a clearing member FCM (assumed to be Firm A), has a net long position of 10 contracts with FCM(A), on an *omnibus basis*.[1]

In addition, besides having the non-clearing FCM as a customer, FCM(A) has two other individuals as customers: one has a long position of 100 contracts, and the other a short position of 90 contracts. Thus, in clearing (or recording) these transactions with the clearing association, FCM(A) ends up with a net long position of 20 contracts with the clearing association (10 in its omnibus account).

---

[1]The account is carried in the name of the originating FCM; the underlying customers are unknown to the receiving or clearing FCM.

Clearing member FCM(B) has only one customer, who has a short position of 20 contracts. FCM(B), therefore, has a net short position of 20 contracts with the clearing association.

It should be noted that in becoming the opposite legal party to all futures transactions, the clearinghouse always has a balanced position — an equal number of long and short contracts in all contracts traded on the affiliated exchange. (In most cases, of course, FCMs and customers will not hold balanced positions.) In addition, it is important to recognize that clearing associations deal only with their members, and not with non-member FCMs or other traders. Thus, clearing association obligations extend only to clearing members.

A central activity of the clearinghouse is to collect security deposits (or margins) on the futures contracts that it clears. The purpose of these deposits is to assure that clearing members will be able to fulfill their obligations. While this procedure may be implemented in different ways, for the purposes of this example we make the following assumptions:

- The clearinghouse collects margin deposits from members on a *net* basis.

- Clearing FCMs collect margins from their customers on a *gross* basis.

- The current value of a futures contract in this hypothetical example is $10 (value of a futures contract equals price per unit times number of commodity units, such as gallons or ounces, in a contract).

- The initial minimum margin required by the clearinghouse for each contract is $1 (which in this case is 10 percent of the contract's current value).

- The initial minimum margin required by member FCMs of their customers also is $1 per contract, but may be higher at the discretion of the FCM.[2]

- All contracts are marked-to-the-market daily, and variation margins are paid in (or withdrawn) the next morning, both by FCMs vis-a-vis clearing associations and by customers vis-a-vis FCMs.

- There is a daily price limit of $1 in either direction.[3]

---

[2]Exchanges require that exchange members impose minimum margins on their customers. Clearing associations establish them for clearing members. FCMs are free to impose margins on their customers higher than the exchange minimum. In addition, the Commodity Futures Trading Commission's (CFTC) Regulation Section 1.58 requires an FCM which maintains an omnibus account at another FCM to collect initial and maintenance margin on a level no less than that established for customer accounts by the rules of the applicable contract market. In our hypothetical example, there is no distinction between original (or initial) margins and maintenance margins.

[3]Daily price limits set an upper and lower limit for how much a futures price can change on a given day. Minimum initial margins are often set in a way that reflects daily price limits, but there is no necessary relationship. The use of daily price limits, and their relationship to initial margins, is discussed later in the chapter.

Given these assumptions, we can see that in our hypothetical example, FCM(A) collects at least $480 of margin deposits — $250 from the longs and $230 from the shorts. A gross margining system requires that margins be posted on all long and short positions. The non-clearing FCM must post margin with the clearing FCM on a gross basis (CFTC Regulation Section 1.58). In addition, FCM(B) collects $20 of margin deposits from its customer.

It is quite possible, and even likely, that the two clearing FCMs may demand more customer margin deposits than the required minimum of $500 (i.e., 480 for FCM(A) and 20 for FCM(B)). The amount they require will depend on the financial characteristics of the customer and is a matter of negotiation between the FCM and its customer.

The clearinghouse usually collects margins on the net position of each clearing member: the net position is 20 contracts long for FCM(A) and 20 contracts short for FCM(B). Thus, the clearing association collects from clearing members a total of $40. Of the total customer margin deposits of $500, therefore, the clearing association holds $40 and the two member FCMs hold the remaining $460. (If the clearing association were to require gross margining, it would hold the entire $500.)

Now let us suppose that the value of the futures contract increases by $1, or changes from $10 to $11 during the day, due to an increase in the futures price. The longs will have profits of $1 on each contract, and the shorts a $1 loss on each contract. Thus, FCMs will require a variation margin of $1 from each of their customers holding short positions: FCM(A) will require additional total margin of $230, and FCM(B) an additional $20. These funds will be passed through to customers holding long positions, who may wish to withdraw their profits by receiving payment of $250 from FCM(A).

FCMs, therefore, perform a banking function by effecting a transfer of funds from some customers (the shorts) to others (the longs), while at the same time continuing to maintain the original level of total margin deposits. Similarly, the clearing association, by requiring FCM(B) to post additional (or variation) margin of $20 and by transferring this amount to FCM(A), performs a banking function between clearing members.

The extent to which clearing associations perform a guarantor function can now be seen more clearly. In particular, as long as the magnitude of the daily changes in the value of a futures contract does not exceed the amount of the initial margin deposits, the margin deposits held by the clearing association *and* its clearing members are sufficient to meet the financial obligations of both buyers and sellers of futures contracts. In our hypothetical example, for instance, even if the shorts failed to meet their variation margin calls because they were bankrupt, the profits of the longs ($250) could still be paid to them out of the margins already posted by the shorts. Thus, the profits of either the shorts or the longs are *bonded* up to the amount of the margin posted. Further, at the instant of default, the clearing association and its clearing members will customarily liquidate the shorts' position by entering into an offsetting transaction, eliminating any further liability.

To summarize the implications of our hypothetical example thus far, both buyers and sellers of futures contracts are protected against the nonperformance of the other party by a procedure whereby each of them posts initial margin deposits with an FCM and agrees to pay or receive on a daily basis from that FCM any losses or gains occurring as a result of changes in the market value of the futures contract. Similarly, clearing FCMs post initial margins with their own clearing associations and pay in or receive daily losses or gains. The amount of customer margin deposits held by clearing FCMs as opposed to the clearing association depends upon the type of margining system in use: net or gross. In all cases, however, when there is a default, customers with profits look to their respective FCMs to obtain what they are owed, and clearing FCMs look to clearing associations to obtain any profits that they are owed on their *net* position with other clearing members. Thus, in our hypothetical example, where there was a default by the shorts, the clearing association would guarantee only the 20 contracts that constituted FCM(A)'s net long position with it. FCM(A) itself would be the guarantor on the other 250 long customer contracts.

The fact that the clearing association guarantee extends only to clearing members and only to the net position of clearing members is not always well understood. In the hypothetical example, the counterpart of FCM(A)'s net long position of 20 contracts is held by FCM(B). FCM(A) has no way of knowing whether FCM(B) is conducting its business in a prudent manner: collecting customer margins in a timely way, not taking excessively risky positions, and so forth. The clearing association, in guaranteeing all clearing members, removes the necessity for each member to know and investigate other members. Consequently, the clearing association necessarily becomes the regulator and monitor of all clearing members so that it can protect itself and fulfill its guarantor obligations.

If clearing associations were to guarantee all futures contracts, rather than only the net open positions of their clearing members, there would no longer be a market incentive for customers to evaluate the financial integrity of the FCMs they choose to deal with. Indeed, customers would probably look only for the "cheapest" FCM, and not worry about the ability of the FCM to meet its financial obligations, since they could rely on the clearing association guarantee. The result could very well be a general dilution in the credit-worthiness of FCMs and an increase in the cost to the industry of assuring the financial integrity of futures markets.[4]

Thus, in futures markets there are really two guarantors: clearing associations and clearing FCMs. The solvency of both is essential to the stability and integrity of futures markets. A key function of the clearinghouse, therefore, is to regulate clearing members in order to assure their solvency.

---

[4]An instructive parallel may be the Federal Deposit Insurance Corporation (FDIC) guaranteeing commercial bank deposits. In our case, the clearing association would be in the role of the FDIC. The effect of FDIC deposit insurance on diluting the soundness of banks is well understood. See, for example, Sam Peltzman, "Capital Investment in Commercial Banking and Its Relationship to Portfolio Regulation," *Journal of Political Economy*, 78(1):3 January, 1970.

3.3 SOME POTENTIAL PITFALLS

The margining system described above may not be adequate to protect customers if certain circumstances and conditions occur. To begin with, if FCMs do not keep customer margin deposits "paid up" on a daily basis (which is required by exchange rules), such deposits may not be sufficient to cover default losses.

Second, in the event of either a sharp run-up in price or a sharp sell-off in the market (as occurred on October 19, 1987), it may be difficult or even impossible to liquidate defaulting customers' positions. In such circumstances ultimate losses may not only exceed customer margin deposits but might conceivably be so large as to trigger the bankruptcy of a clearing FCM itself, and possibly the clearing association itself. While no U.S. clearing association has ever failed, in 1974 the Bourse de Commerce de Paris, the clearing organization for the Paris futures markets, did default. The new French clearing organization, the Banque Centrale de Compensation, is now backed by large banks.

To protect traders against situations where losses exceed margin deposits, clearing associations have adopted a host of self-insurance devices to guarantee performance. They have guarantee and/or capital funds, and have erected elaborate procedures for assessing solvent members to cover the obligations of insolvent members.[5]

3.4 A COMPARISON OF THE MAJOR CLEARINGHOUSES: STRUCTURE AND REGULATORY FRAMEWORK

Table 3.1 provides a summary comparison of six major futures clearinghouses.[6] Five are in the United States; the sixth, the International Commodities Clearing House Limited (ICCH), is in London. The five U.S. clearing associations together clear more than 96 percent of all futures trades in the United States, while the ICCH clears for many of the major futures exchanges outside of the United States.[7]

---

[5]Non-clearing FCMs are not regulated by clearing associations. However, non-clearing FCMs, which are contract market members, are subject to regulation by the relevant exchange, and FCMs which are not members of any contract market are regulated by the National Futures Association (NFA). The CFTC also has jurisdiction over all FCMs and exercises oversight authority.

[6]See Appendix 3-1 for a complete listing of all existing clearinghouses.

[7]The ICCH provides services to the London Metal Exchange, The London International Financial Futures Exchange, The London Potato Futures Association Limited, The International Petroleum Exchange of London Limited, The GAFTA Soyabean Meal Futures Association Limited, The London Meat Futures Exchange Limited, and The London Vegetable Futures Exchange. It also provides clearing services to all market associations on the London FOX (The Futures and Options Exchange): The London Cocoa Terminal Market Association Limited, The London Vegetable Oil Terminal Market Association Limited, and the London Wool Terminal Market Association Limited. Through its subsidiaries, the ICCH also clears for The Hong Kong Futures Exchange, the Kuala Lumpur Commodity Exchange, and exchanges in Australia, New Zealand, France, Brazil, and Bermuda.

TABLE 3.1
Comparative analysis of futures clearing associations

Organizational structure and solvency regulation	Commodity Exchange	Chicago Mercantile Exchange	Chicago Board of Trade	Coffee, Sugar and Cocoa Exchange	New York Mercantile Exchange	International Commodity Clearing House
Organizational structure	Separate affiliated corporation	Clearing association is part of Exchange	Separate affiliated corporation	Separate affiliated corporation	Clearing association is part of Exchange	Separate corporation owned by six banks
Minimum capital requirement for membership — firm:	$2.0 million	$1.5 million	$1.5–3.5 million	$2.0 million	$0.5 million	£100,000 to £1 million, depending on the commodity
Individual:	$0.5 million	n.a.	$0.5 million	n.a.	$0.25 million	
Financial reporting requirements	In compliance with CFTC	In compliance with CFTC	In compliance with CFTC	In compliance with CFTC	In compliance with CFTC	Annual reports, quarterly net worth
Guarantee fund requirements:	$200,000 to $2 million based upon net worth	$50,000	none	$100,000 to $500,000 based on net capital	$50,000	none
Primary assets used by members to fulfill contribution to guarantee fund	U.S. Government securities and bank letters of credit	U.S. Government securities and negotiable CDs of accepted banks	n.a.	U.S. Government securities and bank letters of credit	U.S. Government securities	n.a.

Margin requirements:						
1. Calculation	Net	Gross	Net	Combination of net and gross*	Gross	Net on larger side of a position
2. Original margin	Increases with position size	Constant for all position sizes	Constant with all position sizes	Increases with position size	Increases with position size	May change with position size, at discretion of ICCH
3. Payment form	Cash, U.S. Government securities, letters of credit	Cash only on CME; also letters of credit on IMM and IOM	Cash, U.S. Government securities, letters of credit	Cash, U.S. Government securities, letters of credit	Cash, U.S. Government securities	Cash, foreign currency, U.S. Treasury bills, letters of credit
4. Investment of margin funds	Interest accrues to clearing association	Interest accrues to clearing members†	Interest accrues to clearing members	Interest accrues to clearing association	Interest accrues to clearing members	Interest accrues to ICCH
5. Variation margin payment form	Cash only	Cash only	Cash only	Cash only	Cash only	Same assets acceptable for initial margin
Position limits	Yes Tied to net capital	Yes Clearing committee may require more capital the larger the position at its discretion	Yes Clearing association may impose them on individual members at its discretion	Yes Tied to net capital	Yes At the discretion of the ICCH	Yes

(continued)

61

TABLE 3.1—cont'd.

Organizational structure and solvency regulation	Commodity Exchange	Chicago Mercantile Exchange	Chicago Board of Trade	Coffee, Sugar and Cocoa Exchange	New York Mercantile Exchange	International Commodity Clearing House
Daily Price limits‡	Yes	Yes	Yes	Yes	Yes	Depends on specific exchange#
Procedure in event of default:						
Attachable assets	CM assets; Association's Guarantee Fund; Association's surplus funds	CM assets; Exchange Guarantee Fund; Exchange's surplus funds; Exchange's trust fund	CM assets; Association's surplus funds	CM assets; Association's Guarantee Fund; Association's surplus funds	CM assets; Association's Guarantee Fund; Exchange's surplus funds	CM assets; ICCH capital
Assessment procedure	Pro rata assessment on CM's cleared trades; limited to lower of 25% of CM's net capital or $10 million; not more than one assessment every ten days§	Unlimited pro rata on net capital, cleared trades, and open interest	No assessment of members permitted	Pro rata assessment on CM's cleared trades and open interest; limited to lower of 25% of net capital or $10 million	Unlimited, shared equally by all members of Exchange	

	$75 million	$200 million	$184 million	$25 million	$98 million	£16 to 20 million
Guarantee and clearinghouse capital/lines of credit (1/1/89)						
Contract volume 1990††	15,496,931	84,837,757	120,769,784	8,973,911	36,357,871	59,050,852**
Percentage of total U.S. futures trading in 1990	5.60	30.68	43.67	3.25	13.15	—

n.a.: not applicable.

CM: Clearing member.

* Net on FCM proprietary accounts; net plus the smaller side of gross on FCM customer accounts.

† Except for investment of discount on U.S. Treasury Bills, interest on which accrues to clearing association.

‡ Limits are set by respective exchanges, are different for different commodities, and are usually not imposed in delivery month.

\# Most exchanges have intra-day price limits: when they are hit the market closes for 30 minutes, after which trading is resumed.

§ A clearing member has the option of resigning from Clearing Association in periods.

†† Does not include options volume cleared.

** Estimate only.

The following discusses the information presented in Table 3.1 and some key issues related to clearinghouses.[8]

3.4.1   Organizational Structure

Of the five U.S. clearing operations studied, three are organized as separate, not-for-profit, clearing corporations, and two are part of an associated futures exchange (the Chicago Mercantile Exchange and the New York Mercantile Exchange). Those organized as separate corporations are run by independent managers responsible to a Board of Directors made up of elected members of the clearing corporation. When the clearing function is part of the exchange itself, it is managed by exchange officers responsible to the Board of Directors of the exchange. When the clearing operation is organized as a separate corporation, exchange members are insulated from the obligations of the corporation and its clearing members; otherwise, they are not. The ICCH is organized quite differently: it is owned and controlled by six major British banks, none of which are members of an organized futures exchange. It is a profit-making enterprise: the owners put their capital at risk in the expectation of earning a profitable return.

All clearinghouses are, to a greater or lesser extent, sensitive to developments taking place on associated futures exchanges. When the clearing operation is part of an exchange itself, the relationship is obvious. When it is organized as a separate corporation, its policies are still established by members of the affiliated exchange, who usually control its Board. Finally, in the case of the ICCH, while the controlling banks are not directly involved in the management of futures exchanges, they nevertheless lend substantial amounts of money to exchange members.

3.4.2   Margins

There are significant differences in the margining systems used by clearing associations. Some collect initial margins on a gross basis (or according to the total number of contracts held by clearing members), and others on a net basis only (or on the difference between the total long and total short contracts). Also, the Coffee, Sugar and Cocoa Clearing Corporation collects members' customer-margins on a *net plus a smaller side* basis (net plus the total number of contracts on the smaller of the long or short positions). All of them require lower margins on the various straddle positions, for which the expected volatility (and potential loss) is less. There also are differences with respect to the kinds of assets that can be used by members to satisfy initial margin requirements. Almost all clearing associations accept only cash or U.S. government securities. Some, however, accept letters of credit to meet variation margin calls (the ICCH).

---

[8]This information was compiled from clearing association rulebooks and publications, and through personal interviews with the managements of the associations covered in Table 3-1.

Lastly, members can withdraw their excess margins (or profits) from all of the clearing associations. On U.S. clearing associations such withdrawals are automatic; on the ICCH they are not. The ICCH specifically requires its members to make written requests to withdraw their profits, and approval of such requests is not automatic. This provision probably accounts for ICCH's willingness to accept bank guarantees and letters of credit to meet variation margin calls.

There is considerable debate about whether a gross margin system is superior to a net margin system. Under either system, it should be noted, the total amount of (minimum) margin deposits collected from the *customers* of member FCMs is identical. However, with a net system clearing members hold most of these funds; with a gross system the clearing association holds all of the funds (assuming that clearing margins are equal to customer margins). If all clearing members properly segregate customer funds (as required by law) and collect variation margins in a timely fashion (as required by exchange rules), there is no meaningful difference between a gross and a net system, at least with respect to the security provided by customer margin deposits.[9] An argument that clearing associations should collect margin funds on a gross basis, therefore, is essentially an argument that clearing members cannot be fully relied on to collect and safeguard customers' funds. There is no evidence to support this concern.

3.4.3   Other Solvency Regulations

There are four additional regulations imposed by clearing associations and exchanges that are directed at keeping clearing members solvent. Most clearing associations impose minimum capital requirements and position limits on members, and exchanges often set daily price limits on futures prices and establish minimum *customer* margins that all exchange members must observe. Each of these is discussed below.

MINIMUM CAPITAL REQUIREMENTS. Minimum capital requirements have the obvious purpose of restricting clearing membership to the more financially substantive firms and, as a consequence, of reducing the probability of member insolvency. Everything else being equal, the greater a member's capital, the greater the loss (or variance of return) he can withstand. The higher the capital requirements, however, the fewer clearing members there will be, and the less the competition. At present, existing capital requirements do not seem to be unduly restricting competition.

POSITION LIMITS. Position limits (or limiting the size of a *clearing member's* net position) are directed at limiting the risk that any single clearing member can

---

[9]Clearinghouses, notwithstanding the margin system they are using, may impose similar initial margin requirements by adjusting the level of the margin requirement. For example, margin levels tend to be lower when margin is collected on a gross basis than on a net basis.

assume and, therefore, at limiting the risk exposure of the clearing association. They are essentially a requirement that risk be diversified. Some clearing associations have formal restrictions that are enunciated in their rulebooks; others have informal policies that are applied to members at the discretion of the clearing association management.

In general, position limits are tied to a member's capital: the greater his capital, the larger the position he can take. Larger positions increase the variance of a member's earnings distribution and therefore increase the probability of his insolvency (everything else being equal). A requirement of greater capital counteracts this effect: it reduces the probability of bankruptcy, everything else being equal.

DAILY PRICE LIMITS.   These regulations are supplemented by exchange regulations that are indirectly related to solvency: daily price limits and minimum customer margin requirements. Daily price limits set an upper and lower limit on how much futures prices can change on a given day. When these limits are "hit," all trading usually ceases for the remainder of the day.

The benefits and costs associated with price limits are more indefinite than proponents and critics of them would have us believe. Two benefits are commonly cited. First, it is argued that price limits impose on markets a "cooling-off" period, during which more rational traders will come to dominate. Without price limits, "excessive" speculative activity may result in an increase in the volatility of futures prices, which might result in more customer defaults. The imposition of daily price limits is premised on the assumption that, at least over short periods of time, speculative activity is destabilizing: it increases the variance of futures prices. There is little evidence to support this contention.

The second benefit cited is that price limits enable traders to better respond to variation margin calls by giving them additional time to raise funds, and by making more predictable the amount of cash they may need during any given period of time. Limits also give clearing associations time to collect member margins, and FCMs time to collect customer margins.

Against these potential benefits must be weighed the temporary market illiquidity that price limits may cause. When price limits are hit, markets close, and the liquidity of futures contracts evaporates. The magnitude and incidence of the losses associated with this locked-in effect are difficult to assess.

MANDATORY MINIMUM CUSTOMER MARGIN REQUIREMENTS.   The last related solvency regulation is mandatory minimum customer margin requirements imposed by futures exchanges on exchange members (of which a subset are members of the affiliated clearing association). These requirements are presumably directed at keeping competition among FCMs from pushing initial customer margins to too low a level: to levels at which customer defaults would be unacceptably high.

The rationale for mandatory minimum customer margins may be the interdependencies that exist in futures markets. If customer defaults are not covered by margin deposits, FCMs may sustain losses that could threaten their viability. And if some FCMs were to default, it could threaten other FCMs, undermining confidence in futures markets. The result could be less trading and less market liquidity.

All FCMs, both clearing and non-clearing, enjoy the fruits that stem from public confidence in the integrity of futures markets. While the clearing association lies at the heart of this confidence, the soundness of FCMs is, as we have seen, equally important. Non-clearing FCMs, which are not subject to the regulations of clearing associations, may have some incentive to take excessively high risks for the sake of short-run gains. Specifically, by requiring very low margins from customers such an FCM may seek to increase customer demand for its services in order to increase its current fee income. However, when customers fail to meet their margin calls, the FCM may default rather than meet its obligations. If this were to happen all FCMs would suffer the consequences of a reduction in public confidence. Stated in other terms, there are negative *externalities* associated with the insolvency of even non-clearing FCMs. Thus, exchange-imposed minimum customer margins, which apply to all members, are intended to reduce the likelihood of such insolvencies, or to keep them at an acceptable level.

3.4.4 Self-Insurance Arrangements

Many clearing associations have self-insurance arrangements to meet losses that may occur if some of their members do become insolvent. Four of the six clearing associations surveyed have either funded or unfunded schemes (or both). Two have no self-insurance arrangement: the Chicago Board of Trade and the ICCH. By *funded* is meant the existence of guarantee funds and trust funds, where clearing members have already paid-in assets or obtained independent bank guarantees. Unfunded programs are the various ex-post assessment schemes that permit associations to assess members to make up default losses. The advantage of the former, of course, is that it leaves no doubt about the willingness and ability of members to meet their obligations when default occurs, at least to the extent of the guarantee fund's coverage. There is no historical evidence to suggest, however, that members would not meet ex post assessments. In addition, all clearinghouses have capital that could be used to meet losses.

In recent years clearinghouses have increased their guarantee funds and have moved to limit members' liability by restricting ex post assessments (replacing the traditional "good-to-the-last-drop" assessment systems). Members also have limited their liability by forming separate corporate affiliates for the sole purpose of clearing.

3.5 UNRESOLVED ISSUES

There are a number of important unresolved issues related to clearing associations. Some of these involve questions about the role of government regulation; others are industry matters.

3.5.1 Consolidation of Clearing Associations

In the United States there are nine clearinghouses, all operating independently of one another, each with different rules and regulations. In England, there is one clearing association that serves many different futures exchanges. Should U.S. associations be consolidated into a few, or even a single, clearing corporation?

The possible benefits of consolidation are reasonably clear. First, there may be cost efficiencies related to a larger scale of operation (or economies of scale), but just how much is unknown. Second, to the extent that clearing membership is expanded, risks can be further diversified. This benefit should not be exaggerated, however, since most large clearing firms are already members of all of the major clearing associations. Third, because many clearing firms are members of more than one clearing association, consolidation can eliminate costly duplication in surveillance and auditing functions.[10] Fourth, it will result in better information about members' aggregate positions. At present, there is little exchange of information among clearing associations. Fifth, there are interdependencies among clearing associations that would be better appreciated and perhaps better handled if they were consolidated. Specifically, margin calls made by one clearing association on its members may have adverse effects on other clearing associations. Lastly, consolidation would result in uniform rules that would reduce information and transaction costs for clearing members now trading on many exchanges.

There may also be drawbacks associated with consolidation. First, consolidation may reduce competition. It will obviously reduce the number of clearing associations and will probably reduce the number of clearing FCMs. To take a worst-case scenario, if there were only one clearing association, its members could set monopoly clearing prices that would be passed through to non-clearing firms and traders, and ultimately to customers. Under the existing institutional arrangement of many clearing associations, clearing costs (and therefore trading costs) are one factor that potential users of futures markets take into consideration when deciding which exchange to trade on.

Second, while consolidation may spread risks, it may arguably make the entire futures industry vulnerable to a catastrophic event in a single commodity. Such an event might now bankrupt only one clearing association; with a single (or consolidated) clearing association, it may bring down everyone.

In view of these competing considerations, one solution may be partial consolidation: consolidation into not one but two or three clearing corporations. This may capture most of the benefits of consolidation but still preserve a sufficient degree of diversity and competition. Alternatively, partial consolidation (or cooperation) along certain functional or operational lines (such as data processing) may be feasible, although it clearly will not capture all of the potential benefits.

---

[10]There exists an agreement among New York clearing associations that accomplishes this for firms dealing on the New York Exchanges.

Risk-sharing via a pooled industry guarantee fund might also result in reduced costs as well as greater protection for everyone. All of this, however, abstracts from the many historical, political, and human obstacles to consolidation.

3.5.2 Limited versus Unlimited Liability of Clearing Members

The soundness of a clearing association necessarily rests with its managers and the governing clearing members. It is essential that these responsible parties have incentives consistent with the welfare of both the industry and the public. A traditional device that has been employed in the past to assure that the proper incentives are present is to make clearing members unlimitedly liable for all losses that may occur because of a default by any member.

In recent years there has been a trend towards limiting member liability. This is happening in two ways: by changes in membership rules that directly limit member liability to specific amounts, and by the growing use by members of lower-capitalized clearing affiliates. This trend bears careful watching, since it may undercut the economic incentives of members to monitor, police, and enforce clearing associations' rules and regulations.[11]

3.5.3 Explicit versus Discretionary Rules

There are two distinct regulatory systems used by clearing associations. Some, particularly those in New York, have adopted quite formal and explicit rules and regulations; others, especially in Chicago, have retained the traditional discretionary philosophy.

An example of this difference is their disparate approaches to position limits. The New York associations have established position limits that are explicitly related to a member's capital. Clearing members know at the outset that if they want to hold positions greater than those specified in the rules they will have to increase the amount of their capital (or reduce the size of some of their positions). In contrast, the Chicago associations frequently have no fixed position limits, or none that are set forth in the association's rules and that are applied indiscriminately to all members. The imposition of such limits is left to the discretion of the clearing association (or to the clearing management or to a clearing committee), and depends upon the general circumstances and perhaps a particular trader's situation.

The pros and cons of these alternative approaches are fairly clear. On the one hand, formal and explicit rules give clearing members (and their customers)

---

[11] An argument against unlimited liability is that it imposes unacceptable costs on clearing members, and may as a consequence reduce the number of members, as well as cause them to limit their liability in other ways.

more predictability: they know at the beginning what the rules are and therefore what can be demanded of them. This minimizes regulatory uncertainty, and should lower transaction costs. (However, on occasion, formal rules may increase such costs by requiring that unnecessary or even counter-productive rules be imposed.) On the other hand, discretionary rules give clearing associations greater latitude to protect members and can be tailored to suit the circumstances. Thus, the gain in customer predictability is at the cost of clearing association flexibility.

Exactly where the balance should be struck is difficult to judge. However, one thing is certain: the growing differences in regulatory philosophy and approach among clearing associations are and will continue to be a source of confusion, both to member firms and to their customers.

3.6   WHAT IS THE ROLE OF GOVERNMENT?

Aside from having general oversight responsibility, government regulation presently plays no role in assuring the solvency of clearing associations. Should it?

Clearing members have a direct and obvious stake in the soundness of their associations. They have significant personal liability in the event of a default, and their entire livelihood depends on the prosperity of futures markets, of which public confidence is a key ingredient. They also are in the best position to evaluate the costs of additional rules to increase soundness, and to appraise the effects of these costs on the users of futures markets. If public confidence in futures markets is less than optimal, it would seem to be in the interest of clearing members to establish rules that increase it. Thus, there is no reason to suspect that clearing associations will adopt a standard of soundness inconsistent with public welfare. Alternatively stated, there do not appear to be any significant externalities.

Nevertheless, government has, at least implicitly, a *lender-of-last-resort* responsibility. An unusual and unanticipated event or an occasional episode of speculative excesses (not unknown in the history of financial markets) could threaten the viability of clearing associations, and perhaps even the entire financial system. In such circumstances, government, and the Federal Reserve in particular, must be prepared to step in and provide the necessary liquidity in order to diffuse the crisis. The Federal Reserve did in fact do this in October, 1987, when the stock market suffered an unprecedented decline.

CONCLUSION

Recognizing that the operation of clearing associations is not central in the thinking of most futures market participants, we have nevertheless included this chapter in our book for two reasons. First, the welfare of all futures traders is dependent on the ability of FCMs and clearing associations to meet their obligations. It is important, therefore, that traders understand the underlying clearing mechanisms so that they can evaluate the viability and the potential exposure they have to default. Second, understanding the clearing mechanisms and the associated institutions makes clear why traders need to exercise care in choosing an FCM to handle their accounts.

Although the clearing mechanisms underlying futures markets in the United States have worked well, this has not always been true in other countries. In 1987 a major clearing association default occurred in Hong Kong, in London the 1985 "Tin Crisis" very nearly toppled the London Metal Exchange, and in the 1970s the major French clearing association in Paris collapsed. The 1987 Stock Market Crash also severely tested the clearing mechanism in the United States. Although some problems did occur, the system functioned well, given the stressful conditions that existed at that time.

We have now completed our discussion of the institutional and operational aspects of futures markets. In Chapter 4, we turn to a completely different subject: the pricing of futures contracts.

QUESTIONS

1. Does a clearing association always have an equal number of long and short contracts on its books?
2. Does an FCM always have an equal number of long and short contracts on its books?
3. Do customers of an FCM look to their FCM to make good on their net trading profits or do they look to a clearing association?
4. What are the main functions of clearing associations? Do they guarantee all futures contracts in the event of customer default?
5. What is the obligation of a clearing member for the debts of other members of the clearing association?
6. If a customer defaults and does not pay to his or her FCM the variation margin that is due, who is obligated to fulfill that customer's futures obligations?
7. What would happen if a clearing association failed to make good on its obligations?
8. What membership requirements (or qualifications) do you think clearing members should have?
9. Why would a firm want to be a clearing member?
10. Why are there so many futures clearing associations in the United States?
11. What are the guarantee funds of clearing associations?
12. What function do the position limits of clearing associations serve?
13. What role should the federal government have in regulating clearing associations and in guaranteeing futures contracts against default?

SUGGESTED READING

Edwards, F. R. "The Clearing Association in Futures Markets: Guarantor and Regulator." *The Journal of Futures Markets*, Winter 1983, pp. 369–392.

Jordan, J. and G. Morgan. "Default Risk in Futures Markets: The Customer-Broker Relationship." *Journal of Finance,* Vol. 45 (July 1990), pp. 909–933.

APPENDIX: EXCHANGES AND CLEARINGHOUSES

Futures exchanges	Clearinghouses
Chicago Board of Trade (CBOT)	Board of Trade Clearing Corp. (BOTCC)
Chicago Mercantile Exchange (CME)	CME Clearinghouse Division*
New York Mercantile Exchange (NYMEX)	NYMEX Clearinghouse Division*
Commodity Exchange, Inc. (COMEX)	COMEX Clearing Association
Coffee, Sugar & Cocoa Exchange (CSCE)	CSC Clearing Corporation
New York Cotton Exchange (NYCE)	Commodity Clearing Corp.
New York Futures Exchange (NYFE)	Intermarket Clearing Corp. (ICC)
Mid-America Commodity Exchange (MidAm)	BOTCC
Kansas City Board of Trade (KCBOT)	KCBOT Clearing Corp.
Minneapolis Grain Exchange (MGE)	MGE Clearinghouse Division*
Chicago Rice & Cotton Exchange (CRCE)	BOTCC
AMEX Commodities Corp. (AMEXCC)	ICC
Philadelphia Board of Trade (PHBOT)	ICC
Pacific Futures Exchange (PFE)	ICC
14 exchanges	9 clearinghouses

Options exchanges	Clearinghouses
Chicago Board Options Exchange (CBOE)	Options Clearing Corp. (OCC)
American Stock Exchange (AMEX)	OCC
Philadelphia Stock Exchange (PHLX)	OCC
New York Stock Exchange (NYSE)	OCC
Pacific Stock Exchange (PSE)	OCC
National Association of Securities Dealers (NASD)	OCC

*Clearinghouse is a department within the exchange. All other clearinghouses are separately incorporated and independent from the exchange.

CHAPTER
4

FUTURES
PRICES

Understanding futures prices, and the relationships between the prices of futures contracts with different delivery dates, is essential to using futures markets. Futures prices can be confusing to the uninitiated because of the many different ways that prices are quoted. Once these pricing conventions are mastered, however, there is an obvious economic logic to the structure of futures prices.

This chapter describes the various pricing conventions and explains the economic rationale underlying futures prices. In particular, it describes the way in which futures prices are reported, the relationship between futures prices and the price of the underlying cash commodity, the arbitrage logic underlying the standard of *cost-of-carry* price relationship, and why futures prices sometimes diverge from the cost-of-carry relationship. In addition, key pricing concepts, such as *contango, backwardation, convenience yield,* and *basis* are defined and explained. Finally, intra-commodity, inter-commodity, and inter-market price spreads are examined and explained.

4.1 READING THE NEWSPAPER

Table 4.1 reproduces a typical daily futures price quotation table found in newspapers around the country. Futures prices are continuously available during trading hours on computer screens throughout the world. Each price change is disseminated almost instantaneously by information services like those provided by Reuters and Telerate. For our purposes, however, it will be sufficient to examine daily price quotations, such as those in Table 4.1.

Pricing conventions differ by commodity. The prices of silver futures are quoted in cents per troy ounce of silver bullion. Other futures contracts are quoted

TABLE 4.1
Price quotations for futures contracts

COMMODITY FUTURES PRICES

Tuesday, April 11, 1989.

Open Interest Reflects Previous Trading Day.

	Open	High	Low	Settle	Change	Lifetime High	Low	Open Interest

COPPER-STANDARD (CMX) – 25,000 lbs.; cents per lb.

	Open	High	Low	Settle	Change	Lifetime High	Low	Open Interest
Apr	143.80	144.20	141.00	141.00	– .50	144.20	125.00	211
May	140.80	143.90	139.35	140.00	– .45	146.00	73.15	19,379
July	133.20	135.70	132.30	132.30	– .90	138.50	76.00	10,547
Sept	128.00	130.00	127.00	126.40	– 1.30	131.50	76.00	2,436
Dec	123.00	124.00	121.90	120.50	– 1.70	126.00	77.45	2,258

Est vol 16,000; vol Mon 21,946; open int 34,831, +2,061.

SILVER (CMX) – 5,000 troy oz.; cents per troy oz.

	Open	High	Low	Settle	Change	Lifetime High	Low	Open Interest
Apr	....	....	....	583.4	+ 1.3	618.5	572.0	4
May	585.5	588.0	584.6	586.3	+ 1.3	965.0	576.0	47,110
July	597.0	599.0	595.5	597.3	+ 1.3	985.0	586.5	19,250
Sept	606.5	609.5	606.5	608.3	+ 1.3	861.0	598.0	7,648
Dec	624.0	625.5	623.0	624.1	+ 1.3	886.0	614.0	10,203
Mr90	640.2	641.0	640.2	639.9	+ 1.3	910.0	630.0	6,521
May	....	....	....	650.6	+ 1.3	910.0	642.0	3,642
July	....	....	....	661.6	+ 1.3	761.5	652.0	2,455
Sept	....	....	....	672.9	+ 1.3	760.0	665.0	774
Dec	....	....	....	689.1	+ 1.3	742.0	683.0	502

Est vol 10,000; vol Mon 15,638; open int 98,133, –456.

SOYBEANS (CBT) 5,000 bu.; cents per bu.

	Open	High	Low	Settle	Change	Lifetime High	Low	Open Interest
May	718	722	717¼	720½	+ 1½	1003	647	36,155
July	732½	733	728¾	732¼	+ 1½	986	684	28,886
Aug	732	733	729½	732½	+ 1	951	712¾	6,085
Sept	721¼	722	719	721	....	835	695¼	4,705
Nov	719	721½	716½	717¾	– 1¾	793	663	23,237
Ja90	729	730	726	727½	– 1¾	767	684	2,701
Mar	739	739	734	736½	– 2½	774	711	760
May	745½	745½	742	744	....	778	711	226

Est vol 32,000; vol Mon 49,449; open int 102,824, +488.

SOYBEAN MEAL (CBT) 100 tons; $ per ton.

	Open	High	Low	Settle	Change	Lifetime High	Low	Open Interest
May	221.50	222.90	221.30	222.10	+ .20	304.00	200.50	24,953
July	220.80	221.80	220.40	221.10	+ .30	300.00	215.90	15,855
Aug	219.50	220.30	219.00	219.50	– .20	298.00	214.00	4,948
Sept	218.50	218.50	217.50	218.00	....	270.00	210.50	3,931
Oct	215.00	216.30	215.00	215.80	+ .10	237.00	203.00	2,418
Dec	215.00	216.00	214.20	214.60	+ .10	270.00	199.50	5,403
Ja90	215.00	215.80	214.50	214.50	– .50	230.00	207.00	580
Mar	215.50	215.50	214.50	214.50	– .20	230.50	208.00	267
May	....	....	....	214.20	– .80	230.50	209.00	358

Est vol 13,000; vol Mon 22,824; open int 58,713, –2,414.

CRUDE OIL, Light Sweet (NYM) 1,000 bbls.; $ per bbl.

	Open	High	Low	Settle	Change	Lifetime High	Low	Open Interest
May	20.70	20.89	20.56	20.63	+ .04	21.48	12.52	64,533
June	19.80	20.00	19.68	19.74	+ .02	20.66	12.60	73,542
July	19.21	19.36	19.04	19.08	– .02	20.10	12.65	35,135
Aug	18.74	18.85	18.48	18.54	– .04	19.63	12.60	25,041
Sept	18.25	18.44	18.10	18.14	– .10	19.28	12.68	12,910
Oct	18.06	18.18	17.80	17.83	– .13	18.93	12.75	13,147
Nov	17.84	17.90	17.67	17.58	– .15	18.67	15.00	9,546
Dec	17.70	17.74	17.45	17.37	– .18	18.50	12.87	10,190
Ja90	17.48	17.52	17.40	17.17	– .21	18.10	15.67	3,296
Feb	17.38	17.40	17.30	17.02	– .22	17.95	15.74	1,345
Mar	17.20	17.20	17.20	16.87	– .23	17.80	16.10	869
Apr	....	....	....	16.72	– .24	17.35	16.70	160
May	16.95	16.95	16.95	16.57	– .25	18.17	16.25	298

Est vol 81,442; vol Mon 101,668; open int 250,013, –9,084.

HEATING OIL NO. 2 (NYM) 42,000 gal.; $ per gal.

	Open	High	Low	Settle	Change	Lifetime High	Low	Open Interest
May	.5375	.5430	.5300	.5323	– .0022	.5650	.3520	18,913
June	.5190	.5225	.5110	.5121	– .0006	.5475	.3465	16,887
July	.5100	.5125	.5015	.5027	– .0010	.5380	.4575	7,752
Aug	.5130	.5130	.5030	.5052	– .0015	.5400	.3545	6,218
Sept	.5170	.5180	.5080	.5102	– .0018	.5450	.3640	3,181
Oct	.5245	.5245	.5160	.5157	– .0021	.5490	.3720	2,421
Nov	.5280	.5280	.5220	.5212	– .0024	.5550	.3800	1,688
Dec	.5350	.5350	.5285	.5267	– .0029	.5605	.3785	1,004

Est vol 17,583; vol Mon 16,896; open int 58,106, +942.

(continued)

TABLE 4.1—cont'd.

INTEREST RATE INSTRUMENTS

TREASURY BONDS (CBT) —$100,000; pts. 32nds of 100%

	Open	High	Low	Settle	Chg	Yield Settle	Chg	Open Interest
June	88-10	88-17	88-08	88-10	− 2	9.297 +	.007	246,220
Sept	88-10	88-16	88-08	88-10	− 2	9.297 +	.007	36,756
Dec	88-10	88-17	88-09	88-10	− 2	9.297 +	.007	13,583
Mr90	88-16	88-17	88-10	88-11	− 2	9.294 +	.008	5,262
June	88-14	88-17	88-10	88-11	− 2	9.294 +	.008	3,030
Sept	....	....	....	88-09	− 2	9.301 +	.007	298
Dec	....	....	....	88-07	− 2	9.309 +	.008	281
Mr91	....	....	....	88-04	− 2	9.320 +	.007	97
June	....	....	....	88-00	− 2	9.336 +	.008	196

Est vol 95,000; vol Mon 110,900; op int 305,731, −2,296.

EURODOLLAR (IMM) —$1 million; pts. of 100%

	Open	High	Low	Settle	Chg	Yield Settle	Chg	Open Interest
June	89.49	89.52	89.47	89.48	− .02	10.52 +	.02	277,343
Sept	89.34	89.36	89.31	89.32	− .02	10.68 +	.02	162,555
Dec	89.29	89.32	89.27	89.27	− .03	10.73 +	.03	103,906
Mr90	89.65	89.69	89.63	89.63	− .03	10.37 +	.03	64,889
June	89.91	89.94	89.87	89.88	− .03	10.12 +	.03	32,762
Sept	90.07	90.10	90.03	90.04	− .03	9.96 +	.03	26,300
Dec	90.08	90.11	90.04	90.05	− .03	9.95 +	.03	24,456
Mr91	90.22	90.25	90.20	90.19	− .03	9.81 +	.03	13,030
June	90.32	90.35	90.28	90.27	− .03	9.73 +	.03	10,290
Sept	90.36	90.39	90.32	90.31	− .03	9.69 +	.03	20,914
Dec	90.37	90.40	90.31	90.32	− .03	9.68 +	.03	11,139
Mr92	90.43	90.46	90.38	90.37	− .03	9.63 +	.03	2,853

Est vol 100,769; vol Mon 114,751; open int 750,437, +399.

TREASURY BILLS (IMM) —$1 mil.; pts. of 100%

	Open	High	Low	Settle	Chg	Discount Settle	Chg	Open Interest
June	91.16	91.19	91.15	91.15	− .01	8.85 +	.01	14,142
Sept	91.03	91.05	91.01	91.02	....	8.98		3,799
Dec	90.95	90.97	90.95	90.95	+ .01	9.05 −	.01	1,311
Mr90	....	....	....	91.23		8.77		334

Est vol 2,231; vol Mon 2,525; open int 19,608, −496.

CURRENCY

JAPANESE YEN (IMM) 12.5 million yen; $ per yen (.00)

	Open	High	Low	Settle	Change	Lifetime High	Low	Open Interest
June	.7618	.7626	.7610	.7617	+ .0006	.8485	.7500	47,231
Sept	.7723	.7730	.7715	.7722	+ .0005	.8580	.7690	1,609
Dec	.7830	.7835	.7830	.7827	+ .0004	.8635	.7735	326

Est vol 12,922; vol Mon 18,418; open int 49,249, −2,049.

W. GERMAN MARK (IMM) —125,000 marks; $ per mark

	Open	High	Low	Settle	Change	Lifetime High	Low	Open Interest
June	.5350	.5355	.5335	.5341	− .0007	.5975	.5317	45,078
Sept	.5398	.5403	.5383	.5389	− .0007	.5977	.5366	924
Dec	.5442	.5442	.5428	.5438	− .0008	.5895	.5430	204

Est vol 14,079; vol Mon 23,768; open int 46,206, +1,199.

CANADIAN DOLLAR (IMM) —100,000 dlrs.; $ per Can $

	Open	High	Low	Settle	Change	Lifetime High	Low	Open Interest
June	.8379	.8382	.8371	.8373	− .0002	.8433	.7670	17,931
Sept	.8341	.8341	.8333	.8335	− .0002	.8385	.7990	1,058
Dec	.8306	.8306	.8306	.8299	− .0002	.8370	.7920	240

Est vol 1,764; vol Mon 3,123; open int 19,280, −285.

BRITISH POUND (IMM) —62,500 pds.; $ per pound

	Open	High	Low	Settle	Change	Lifetime High	Low	Open Interest
June	1.6898	1.6916	1.6790	1.6812	− .0056	1.8370	1.6200	21,856
Sept	1.6800	1.6810	1.6680	1.6704	− .0058	1.8030	1.6580	498
Dec	1.6740	1.6750	1.6626	1.6648	− .0056	1.7450	1.6540	115

Est vol 6,431; vol Mon 5,627; open int 22,619, +542.

SWISS FRANC (IMM) —125,000 francs-$ per franc

	Open	High	Low	Settle	Change	Lifetime High	Low	Open Interest
June	.6070	.6080	.6046	.6057	− .0011	.7145	.6046	33,184
Sept	.6134	.6140	.6108	.6117	− .0012	.7210	.6108	578
Dec	.6178	.6205	.6175	.6182	− .0018	.6653	.6175	153

Est vol 12,675; vol Mon 21,581; open int 33,915, +1,841.

S&P 500 INDEX (CME) 500 times index

	Open	High	Low	Settle	Chg	High	Low	Open Interest
June	300.40	302.20	300.20	301.95	+ 1.70	306.20	263.80	131,224
Sept	304.90	306.50	304.70	306.35	+ 1.75	309.70	271.50	2,147
Dec	....	....	....	310.70	+ 1.70	313.20	298.90	930

Est vol 30,133; vol Mon 24,342; open int 134,301, −1,464.
Indx prelim High 298.87; Low 297.12; Close 298.49 +1.38

Source: *The Wall Street Journal*, April 12, 1989.

differently. For example, copper is quoted in cents per pound, soybeans and grains in cents per bushel, soybean meal in terms of dollars per ton, heating oil as cents per gallon, and crude oil in terms of dollars per barrel.

Financial futures are more complicated. Foreign currency futures are quoted as U.S. dollars per one unit of the underlying foreign currency; T-bills, Eurodollars and Certificate of Deposit (CD) futures are quoted on the basis of an index equal to 100 minus the relevant interest rate on these instruments; T-bonds are listed as a percentage (and thirty-seconds of a percentage point) of the underlying bond's par value; and stock index futures are quoted in index points where each point is worth so many dollars. Mastering the different pricing conventions is like learning a foreign language: you have to remember it. (We will describe in detail in later chapters the pricing conventions for specific futures contracts.)

Table 4.1, which appeared in the *Wall Street Journal* on April 12, 1989, shows the trading statistics for the *previous* day, April 11. Take silver futures as an example. There are nine columns. All but the first and last columns contain price quotations. The table also has 10 rows, each beginning with a different month in either 1989 or 1990. This indicates that on April 11 there were 10 silver futures contracts traded or listed on the Commodity Exchange (COMEX), each with a different delivery date. The month shown in a particular row of the table signifies the delivery month of that contract. For example, December 89 refers to the contract requiring delivery during the month of December, 1989. As can be seen from the table, there are price quotations for each futures contract listed. The following explains the quotations that appear in each column in Table 4.1:

- **Open.** The price for the day's first trade that occurs during the time period designated as the opening of the market (or the opening call).
- **High.** The highest price of a trade recorded during the day.
- **Low.** The lowest price of a trade recorded during the day.
- **Settle.** The settlement price is usually determined by formula using the range of prices recorded within the closing period (such as the last minute of trading). It is determined by the exchange's settlement committee and is intended to indicate the fair value of the futures contract at the close of trading. As such, the settlement price is not usually the last trading price of the day, and sometimes may not even be within the day's price range (see December 89 crude oil futures contract in Table 4.1).
- **Change.** The price change that occurred from yesterday's close to today's close. More precisely, it is today's settlement price minus yesterday's settlement price. This change can, of course, be either positive or negative.
- **Lifetime High or Low.** The highest or lowest price ever recorded during the entire life of the contract that is being quoted. For example, if a contract is traded for 24 months prior to its delivery month, this is the highest or lowest price recorded during that 24-month period up to the day of the quotation (April 11, 1989, in Table 4.1).

- **Open Interest.** This refers to the number of futures contracts that are open (or being held) at the close of the previous day's trading. In Table 4.1, the May 89 silver futures contract shows an open interest of 47,110 contracts at the close of trading on April 10, while open interest for all 10 contract months on April 10 is 98,133 contracts.

- **Volume.** Volume is the total number of futures contracts that are traded during the day. Volume by individual contract is not reported in Table 4.1, but estimated volume for all silver futures contracts on April 11, 1989 is reported as 10,000 contracts, while the actual volume for the previous day, April 10, 1989, is 15,638 contracts.

The actual figures for open interest and trading volume usually lag price quotations by one day. Although on this particular day total open interest exceeded total trading volume, there is no necessary relationship between them. Both change every day, and on any given day volume can be greater or less than open interest in a commodity.

4.2 PRICE CHARACTERISTICS

In Table 4.1 futures prices for the May 89 silver contract opened at 585.5 cents, hit a high of 588.0 cents during the day, fell to a low of 584.6 cents, and settled at 586.3 cents. If you had bought at the opening price of 585.5 cents, you would have been obligated to accept delivery (or buy) silver in May of 1989 at a price of 585.5 cents per ounce, whatever the actual price of silver might be in May of 1989. Further, since each silver contract calls for the delivery of 5000 ounces of silver, each contract you buy (or are long) would obligate you to purchase $29,275 worth of silver bullion (5000 × $5.855).

In silver, as opposed to some other futures, futures trading continues during the delivery month. This is why there are, on April 11, price quotations for the April 1989 contract. At the end of April, when trading in the April contract ceases, some contracts will be settled by delivery. But before that time some may be offset and others may be satisfied by EFPs. In contrast, heating oil futures contracts stop trading at the end of the month *preceding* the delivery month. Thus, in April there are no price quotations for the April heating oil contract; trading has already ended.

It is notable that the only price quotations which appear in April for the May 90, July 90, September 90, and December 90 silver contracts are the settlement prices. This means that there was no trading during the day in any of these contracts. The settlement price is determined by the exchange using a standard formula that infers what the price of these contracts would have been had they been traded. Such a price is obviously not a market-determined price, and for some commodities may not be a good representation of the price at which you could buy or sell the contract. The inferred settlement price, however, is used by exchanges and clearinghouses to determine variation margins calls.

Finally, an examination of the settlement prices of the silver contracts listed shows that futures prices rise as the date of delivery is more distant. For example, on April 11, 1989, the settlement price is 583.4 cents for the April 89 contract, 586.3 cents for the May 89 contract, 661.6 cents for the July 90 contract, and so on up to 689.1 cents for the December 90 contract. Thus, between the December 90 and the April 89 contracts there is a price difference of 105.7 cents. This orderly price progression is not due to chance but to a well-known pricing relationship commonly referred to as *cost-of-carry*. We will have more to say about this relationship later in the chapter.

4.3   CASH PRICES VERSUS FUTURES PRICES

4.3.1   The Relationship between Cash and Futures Prices

Every commodity has a *spot,* or cash, price. This is the prevailing market price of the commodity for immediate delivery. When we go to a wine store and buy a bottle of wine, we pay the spot price for the wine. Similarly, silver bullion can be purchased in the cash market for immediate delivery, or for delivery at some date in the future with a futures contract.

There may be more than one cash price for a commodity at a moment in time. Heating oil, for example, is quoted by region of the country. The cash market for oil is geographically segmented because of the time and the costs associated with transporting oil from one part of the country to another. Similarly, the cash price of oil in Europe is different from the cash price of oil in the United States. When immediate delivery is required, the price in any local market is determined solely by local demand and supply conditions. There is no time to bring in the commodity from outside the area. Table 4.2 shows a variety of cash price quotations for heating oil existing in the United States on April 11, 1989.

The relevant cash price with which to compare futures prices is determined by the delivery requirements of the futures contract. For example, the heating oil futures contract calls for delivery of No.2 heating oil at designated terminals located in the New York Harbor area. The cash price that will be most comparable

TABLE 4.2
Heating oil: Cash price quotations on April 11, 1989 (cents per gallon)

	Low	High
New York Cargo	53.50	54.00
New York Barge	54.50	55.00
Boston Cargo	54.50	55.25
Gulf Coast Waterborne	53.25	55.00
Gulf Coast Pipeline	52.75	54.25
Los Angeles Pipeline	62.00	63.00
San Francisco Pipeline	64.00	65.00
Seattle Pipeline	65.00	66.00

Source: Platt's Oilgram Price Report, April 12, 1989.

to the heating oil futures prices, therefore, is the cash price for heating oil in the New York area. If you were short a futures contract and chose to deliver oil, you would generally purchase oil located in New York and deliver it to fulfill your contract obligation. By buying oil in New York, you avoid the cost of transporting oil from some other region of the country to the New York Harbor area.

The market for silver bullion is different. Silver is traded worldwide. Silver bullion can be quickly transported from one country to another—usually between London, New York, or Zurich—if even small price differentials occur. In addition, much of the world's known privately-held silver bullion is held in exchange-approved warehouses in London and New York—some 200 million ounces. Thus, the relevant cash price for silver is the one that best reflects the demand and supply of silver bullion in a worldwide market. Table 4.3 shows the usual cash price quotations for silver that appear daily in newspapers. The cash price that is commonly referred to is the *London silver fixing*. This is the price at which silver bullion can be bought or sold for immediate delivery in London. It also reflects what silver bullion can be bought and sold for in New York and in most other countries.

In Table 4.3 the London silver fixing price for April 11, 1989, is quoted as £3.428 (U.S. dollar equivalent 582.4 cents), while the Handy & Harman silver base price for New York is 582.5 cents. Compare these prices to the price of the near month (May 89) silver futures contract in New York, which is 586.3 cents. While these prices are very close, they are not identical.

TABLE 4.3
Cash prices for precious metals

CASH PRICES

Tuesday, April 11, 1989.
(Quotations as of 4 p.m. Eastern time)

	Tues	Mon	Yr.Ago
PRECIOUS METALS			
Gold, troy oz			
Engelhard indust bullion	386.30	382.80	452.22
Engelhard fabric prods	405.62	401.94	474.83
Handy & Harman base price	385.00	381.50	450.80
London fixing AM 384.75 PM ...	385.00	381.50	450.80
Krugerrand, whol	a387.00	386.00	450.20
Maple Leaf, troy oz.	a398.50	398.00	464.50
American Eagle, troy oz.	a398.50	398.50	464.50
Platinum, (Free Mkt.)	529.00	524.75	533.50
Platinum, indust (Engelhard)	532.00	519.00	537.75
Platinum, fabric prd (Engelhard)	632.00	619.00	637.75
Palladium, indust (Engelhard) ...	166.00	163.00	123.50
Palladium, fabrc prd (Englhard)	181.00	178.00	138.50
Silver, troy ounce			
Engelhard indust bullion	5.855	5.865	6.420
Engelhard fabric prods	6.265	6.276	6.829
Handy & Harman base price	5.825	5.810	6.425
London Fixing (in pounds)			
Spot (U.S. equiv. $5.824)	3.4280	3.3980	3.4775
3 months	3.5385	3.5080	3.5455
6 months	3.6505	3.6210	3.6190
1 year	3.8905	3.8540	3.7870
Coins, whol $1,000 face val	a4,240	4,225	5.080

Source: The Wall Street Journal, April 12, 1989.

Note: Prices shown above are dealers' ask prices.

Should they be identical? If the futures price were higher than the cash price, an easy arbitrage would be to purchase cash silver and simultaneously sell silver futures at the higher price, and then deliver the physical silver to fulfill the futures contractual obligation. The profit on this transaction would be the difference between the selling and buying prices minus any costs that might be associated with either the transaction or with making delivery. Similarly, if the futures price were lower than the cash price, one could purchase futures contracts and simultaneously borrow physical silver and sell it short in the cash market. After taking delivery on the futures, one would then return the physical silver to the party from whom it was borrowed, and pocket the difference between the higher cash price and the lower futures price.

Traders who take advantage of these so-called *cash-futures* arbitrage opportunities, therefore, assure that cash and futures prices will normally have a well-defined relationship to one another. In particular, cash and near month futures prices should differ only by the transaction costs associated with doing a cash-futures arbitrage. (We will have more to say about the role of arbitrage in determining prices later in the chapter.)

A difference between the quoted near month futures price in Table 4.1 and the quoted cash or spot price in Table 4.3 may also occur because of reporting differences. First, the time of the day for which prices are reported may be different. An observed price difference might not exist if prices were quoted at exactly the same time of day. Second, the futures settlement price is a *constructed price,* and may not represent a price at which one could actually buy or sell. Thus, the existence of small differences in quoted prices may not mean that there exist *real* differences, or that profitable cash-futures arbitrage opportunities exist. *Real* price quotations must come from dealers or traders with whom one can trade.

Figure 4-1 shows the actual relationship between daily cash and near month futures prices of silver during 1988. The cash price is the Handy & Harman quotation for New York, and the futures price is based on the near month (or next-expiring) contract on the same day. In other words, to construct this graph we used the prices of successive expiring futures contracts. For example, during March we used the futures prices for the April contract, during May we used the July futures prices, and so on, constructing a continuous time series of near month futures prices. It is clear from Figure 4-1 that cash and near month silver futures prices are very closely related, as they should be.

4.3.2 The Cost-of-Carry Relationship

To demonstrate what is commonly known as the *cost-of-carry price relationship,* Figure 4-2 plots for 1988 the same daily cash price shown in Figure 4-1 against the futures price for a single futures contract—the December 88 contract. Figure 4-2 differs from Figure 4-1 because the futures prices plotted in Figure 4-1 are a price series constructed by stringing together prices of consecutive near month futures contracts, while the futures prices shown in Figure 4-2 are for only one futures contract—December 88.

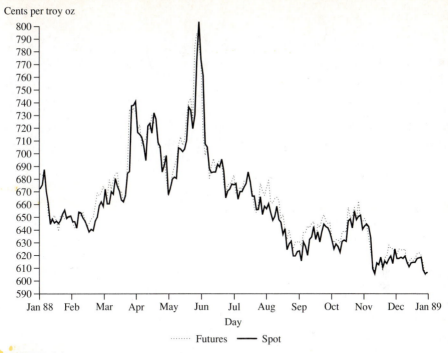

FIGURE 4-1
Daily silver prices: Spot and near month futures, January 4, 1988, to December 30, 1988.

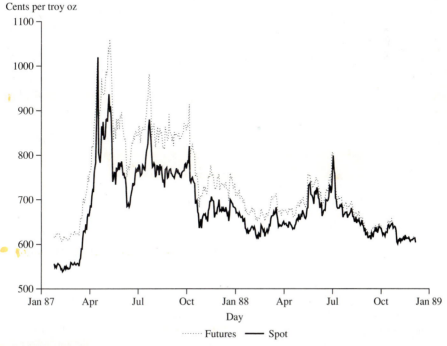

FIGURE 4-2
Daily silver prices: Spot and December 88 futures, February 2, 1987, to December 28, 1988.

The first obvious feature of the price relationship shown in Figure 4-2 is that the December futures price is always above the cash price. Second, the extent to which the December futures price exceeds the cash price is largely determined by the time to delivery. The longer the time period before expiration, the more the futures price exceeds the cash price. Third, as the delivery date approaches, the futures price slowly but inevitably converges to the cash price. The close relationship between the near month futures and cash prices was seen earlier in Figure 4-1. Lastly, all of these price relationships exist no matter what the level of silver cash prices.

The extent to which the December futures price exceeds the cash price at any moment is determined by what is commonly known as the *cost-of-carry*. This term refers to the costs associated with purchasing and carrying (or holding) a commodity for a specified period of time. In theory, at any given time the December silver futures price should equal the cash price of silver plus an allowance for the costs associated with storing (or carrying) the silver until it is time to make delivery on the December futures contract. For example, on April 11, 1989, the price of the December 1989 futures contract should equal the cash price of silver on April 11, 1989, plus the anticipated costs associated with storing the silver until early December, 1989 (when it can be delivered in fulfilment of a short's futures obligation). These costs would include the financing costs associated with purchasing cash silver, storage costs (such as warehouse costs), insurance, shipping costs, and any other costs involved in carrying the cash silver forward in time. A measure of financing costs is the amount of money that would have to be used (or borrowed) to purchase the cash commodity times the relevant interest rate (or financing rate) for the period of time that the commodity is carried (such as three months or a year).

The following formula describes a general cost-of-carry price relationship between the cash (or spot) price and the futures price of any commodity.

Futures price = cash price + financing costs per unit + storage costs per unit

or

$$FP_{t,T} = CP_t + CP_t \times R_{t,T} \times \frac{T-t}{365} + G_{t,T} \qquad (4.1)$$

where $FP_{t,T}$ = the futures price at time t for a futures contract requiring delivery at time T

CP_t = the cash price at time t

$R_{t,T}$ = the annualized riskless interest rate at which funds can be borrowed at time t for period T minus t

$G_{t,T}$ = the costs of storing the physical commodity per unit for the time period from purchase of the commodity (t) to delivery at (T)

This cost-of-carry formula has been simplified because it does not allow for the continuous compounding of interest costs but captures only the simple interest financing cost. A continuous cost-of-carry formulation is shown in the appendix to this chapter.

In addition, the formula assumes the following:

1. There are no information or transaction costs associated with buying or selling either futures or the physical commodity.
2. There is an unlimited ability to borrow or lend money.
3. All borrowing and lending is done at the same interest rate.
4. There is no credit risk associated with buying or selling either the futures contract or a physical commodity (which implies, among other things, that there will be no margins required on futures contracts).
5. Commodities can be stored indefinitely without any change in the characteristics of the commodity (such as its quality).
6. There are no taxes.

Ignoring for the moment the complexities that a relaxation of any of these assumptions might introduce, let us use the above formula to see just how well it describes the price relationships that we observe between cash and futures silver prices. On April 11, 1989, the cash price of silver was 582.5 cents (the Handy & Harman base price). At the close of trading on April 11, the settlement price of the December 89 silver futures contract was 624.1 cents. The time from April 11 to mid-December is approximately eight months. The annualized borrowing rate on April 11, 1989, was about 10.70 percent (the eight-month Eurodollar rate). Finally, the cost of storing silver is negligible and is assumed to be zero. Inserting these numbers into Equation 4.1 above we have

$$582.5 + 582.5 \times 0.1070 \times \tfrac{8}{12} + 0 = 624.05$$

Thus, the simple cost-of-carry formula works quite well in describing the relationship between cash and futures silver prices. However, this may not be true for all commodities at all times, as we will see later.

Another way of looking at the cost-of-carry relationship embodied in Equation 4.1 is that if such a relationship holds, the difference between the futures price and the cash price should equal the cost of carry, or

$$\text{Carry} = FP_{t,T} - CP_t$$

It is also common, in the jargon of the industry, to refer to a futures price that is calculated (or estimated) with the above cost-of-carry formula as a *full-carry* futures price. Figure 4-3 plots two prices: the *actual* market price of the December 88 futures contract, and the *calculated full-carry* price for the same futures contract, using the above cost-of-carry pricing formula. As is evident from the graph, the two prices are closely related. The explanation lies in the role that arbitragers play in futures markets, a subject to which we now turn.

Cents per troy oz

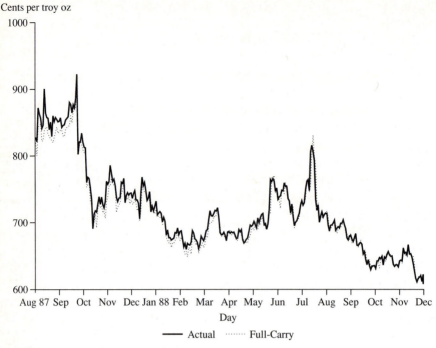

FIGURE 4-3
Silver futures prices: Actual versus full-carry, December 1988 contract.

4.3.3 Cash-Futures Arbitrage

In a simplified world of the kind described by our assumptions (no transaction costs, taxes, and so on), actual futures prices should be exactly equal to cash prices plus the cost-of-carry, or to full-carry futures prices. If actual futures prices were not equal to these constructed full-carry prices, there would exist profitable, no risk cash/futures arbitrage opportunities. Thus, unless there were obstacles to such arbitrage, the activities of arbitragers would cause cash-futures price relationships to conform to that described by the cost-of-carry formula.

To see this, let us suppose that for some unknown reason the observed futures price on, let us say, the December 1989 silver contract is greater than the full-carry price calculated with our formula. In this case we say that the futures price is *rich* to the cash price. On the principle of selling what is overpriced and buying what is underpriced, arbitragers will sell (short) the December 89 futures contract and borrow funds to purchase cash silver, carry the silver until the futures contract expires, and then deliver it in fulfillment of their futures obligations, and use the proceeds to repay their loan. Table 4.4 shows an example of this arbitrage and calculates the profit earned from it.

This arbitrage opportunity exists because the difference between the observed futures and cash prices is too large—it exceeds the cost-of-carry. Such a difference cannot persist in the presence of arbitrage. In the arbitrage transaction described

TABLE 4.4
Cash-and-carry arbitrage example:
Futures are rich to cash

April 11, 1989
- Cash silver = 582.5 cents per ounce
- Eight-month Eurodollar rate = 10.7%
- Full-carry December 89 futures price = 624.1 cents
- December 89 futures now trading at 628.0 cents
- Arbitrage activity: SELL FUTURES, BUY SPOT

Activities	Cash flows
	(Cents)
i. April 11, 1989:	
Sell December futures @ 628 cents	0
Borrow 582.5 cents	+582.5
Buy cash silver @ 582.5	−582.5
ii. December 11, 1989:	
Deliver cash silver against futures	+628.0
Pay back loan	
Principal	−582.5
Interest [$582.5 \times 0.107 \times \frac{8}{12}$]	− 41.6
Net arbitrage profit	+ 3.9

in Table 4.4, futures are sold and the physical commodity is bought. This has the effect of pushing down futures prices by increasing the supply of futures contracts, and of raising cash prices by increasing the immediate demand for the physical commodity. Both effects result in reducing the difference between futures and cash prices. Such arbitrage will continue until the difference between the futures and cash prices narrows to the relevant cost of carry.

The alternative case, where the December 89 futures price is less than the calculated full-carry price (or the futures is *cheap* to the cash) also results in equilibriating arbitrage. Now, however, the difference between the futures and cash prices is too small: it is less than the relevant cost of carry. To profit from this discrepancy arbitragers will buy the futures (because it is cheap relatively) and sell the physical. (If arbitragers do not already own the physical, they can borrow it and short it.) By selling the physical in the cash market arbitragers receive immediate payment. They then loan this amount at the prevailing interest rate for the period of time until delivery is required on the futures contract.[1] Immediately

---

[1]In reality, arbitragers may not have the full proceeds of the short sale available to invest. The lender of the commodity may withhold 10–15 percent of the proceeds as collateral. In this event, the differential between the actual and full carry futures prices will have to be greater to induce arbitrage. While this transaction cost is often present, in the remainder of this book we ignore it for the sake of simplicity.

TABLE 4.5
Reverse cash-and-carry arbitrage example:
Futures are cheap to cash

April 11, 1989
- Cash silver = 582.5 cents per ounce
- Eight-month Eurodollar rate = 10.7%
- Full-carry December 89 futures price = 624.1 cents
- December 89 futures now trading at 620.0 cents
- Arbitrage activity: BUY FUTURES, SELL SPOT

Activities	Cash flows
	(Cents)
i. April 11, 1989:	
Buy December futures @ 620 cents	0
Sell cash @ 582.5 cents	+582.5
Invest proceed @ 10.7%	−582.5
ii. December 11, 1989:	
Take delivery of futures	−620.0
Receive from investment	
Principal	+582.5
Interest [$582.5 \times 0.107 \times \frac{8}{12}$]	+ 41.6
Net arbitrage profit	+ 4.1

prior to delivery, arbitragers will get back the funds they have loaned and use these funds to acquire the physical commodity by accepting delivery on the futures contract. They can now return the physical commodity if they have borrowed it. Table 4.5 provides an example of this *reverse cash-and-carry arbitrage*.

Once again, this arbitrage will correct the price discrepancy between the futures and cash prices. Buying the futures pushes up futures prices. Selling the physical pushes down cash prices. This will continue until the difference between cash and futures prices again widens to equal the cost of carry.

Thus, the rationale which underlies the cost-of-carry pricing relationship is that unlimited cash/futures arbitrage will restore this relationship if it deviates from a full-carry relationship. However, if for any reason this arbitrage cannot take place on an unlimited basis, perhaps because of significant transaction costs associated with such arbitrage, a full-carry pricing relationship may fail to hold. Later in the chapter we describe important departures from this pricing relationship that regularly occur in futures markets.

4.3.4 Basis, Contango, and Backwardation

An important concept in futures market is the *basis*. This term is used to describe the difference between cash and futures prices. Specifically,

$$Basis_{t,T} = cash\ price_t - futures\ price_{t,T}$$

If futures prices are accurately described by a full-carry relationship, the basis is negative, since futures prices are higher than cash prices. This condition is commonly referred to as a *contango* market, meaning that the relationship between futures prices and cash prices is determined solely by the cost-of-carry.

Backwardation is commonly used to refer to a market in which the futures price is less than the cash price. In this case the basis is positive. This condition can occur only if futures prices are determined by considerations other than (or in addition to) cost-of-carry factors. If only cost-of-carry factors determine futures-cash price relationship, the futures price cannot be lower than the cash price.

The term *backwardation* also is sometimes used to refer to a market in which the futures price is *above* the cash price but still *below* the full-carry futures price. In this case the basis is negative, but is less negative than what the full cost-of-carry basis would be.[2]

The terms *contango* and *backwardation* can be used to describe an entire pattern of futures prices, from the price of the nearest month contract to the price of the most distant month contract (or the contract that expires at a time most distant from the present). A contango market is characterized by progressively rising futures prices as the time to delivery becomes more distant, and a backwardation market by progressively lower futures prices as delivery becomes more distant.

A useful way of thinking about these terms is that a contango market is one in which futures prices are reasonably described most of the time by a cost-of-carry pricing relationship, while a backwardation market is one in which futures prices do not fit a full cost-of-carry pricing relationship—and, in particular, in which futures prices are consistently lower than those predicted by the cost-of-carry pricing formula.

On occasion, many futures markets display prices that are in backwardation. The next section describes such markets and explains why backwardation occurs.

4.3.5   Backwardation Markets

Prices for various copper futures contracts on April 11, 1989 are shown in Table 4.1. The near month futures contract, April, has a settlement price of 141 cents per pound. (A copper futures contract calls for delivery of 25,000 pounds of copper.) As can be seen in Table 4.1, the copper settlement prices progressively fall from April 89 to December 89, the most distant contract being traded on April 11, 1989. The December settlement price is 120.50 cents per pound, about 15 percent lower than the April futures price. In addition, the cash copper price on April 11 was 148 cents per pound. This is a classic backwardation market.

---

[2]Another term commonly associated with futures markets is *normal backwardation*. This term is used to refer to a market where futures prices are below *expected* spot prices. In Chapter 7 we discuss the circumstances under which such a market may exist.

TABLE 4.6
Copper futures prices: April 11, 1984

	Open	High	Low	Settle
Apr84	69.70	69.80	69.70	69.10
May84	69.95	70.25	69.40	69.45
July84	71.47	71.65	70.80	70.90
Sept84	72.85	73.05	72.30	72.30
Dec84	74.85	75.05	74.40	74.30

Source: The Wall Street Journal, April 12, 1984.

A market that is in backwardation on one day may not be on another day. For example, on April 11, 1984, copper futures prices looked more like a contango market (see Table 4.6). For some commodities backwardation is rare; for others it is a regular or seasonal occurrence.

Why does backwardation occur? If futures are cheap relative to cash prices (or more distant futures prices are cheap relative to near-month futures prices), it would seem that a simple reverse cash-and-carry arbitrage would provide riskless profits. More specifically, given the April 11 copper prices in Table 4.1, why not buy the July futures contract at 132.3 cents per pound and simultaneously sell copper in the cash market for 148 cents per pound. A firm holding inventories of copper, for example, would have no trouble doing this arbitrage. Even if an arbitrager did not presently own copper, he might borrow it from a firm that was holding copper and sell it short. Later, in July, he could take delivery of copper on his long copper futures position and return the copper to the lending firm.

If this arbitrage could be done on an unlimited basis, demand for July futures contracts would drive up futures prices and selling pressure in the cash market would push down cash prices until the relationship between cash and futures prices returned to the familiar full cost-of-carry relationship. Thus, for backwardation to persist, it must be true that reverse cash-and-carry arbitrage transactions are not generally available to market participants.

A shortage of the physical commodity is the most likely obstacle to such arbitrage. If a shortage of physical copper persists, market participants will not be willing to lend or sell whatever copper they have. Firms holding copper inventories may need the copper to fulfill long-term customer agreements, to use in their own manufacturing processes, and so forth. This makes it impossible to do the reverse cash-and-carry arbitrage described above and it keeps prices from returning to a full-carry relationship.

Is there another arbitrage available that does not require possession of physical copper but would nevertheless return prices to a cost-of-carry relationship? Suppose, for example, that instead of selling copper in the cash market, we were to short the May futures contract while simultaneously buying the July futures contract. Neither transaction, at least initially, involves physical copper. This transaction, however, is not without risk (as was our reverse cash-and-carry arbitrage). Because we do not own physical copper, we will have to buy it at some point in order to deliver copper to fulfill our May futures obligation, and this may be difficult. Alternatively, we will have to offset, prior to delivery, both the short May futures position and the long July position. But we do not know in advance what the prices of the May and July contracts will be when we offset (or what the spread will be). On April 11, 1989, we have no way to predict what May and July futures prices will be a month later. The relationship between the May and July futures prices (commonly known as the May-July spread) can change in unpredictable ways. Thus, this futures spread transaction is really an outright speculation on the spread, and it involves substantial price risk. It is unlikely, therefore, that there will be a large enough volume of this type of arbitrage to return prices to a full-carry relationship.

Another indication that shortages of the physical commodity are the cause of backwardation is that backwardation often occurs at times when cash prices are high and have been rising sharply, a manifestation of a shortage in the physical market. At peaks of business cycles, for example, it is common to find industrial metal futures prices in backwardation.

Figures 4-4 and 4-5 graph futures prices for No.2 heating oil over various time periods in order to show the different price relationships that can exist for the same commodity during different time periods. Figure 4-4 graphs the prices of the September 88, October 88, and November 88 heating oil futures contracts, for the period January 1, 1988, to September 30, 1988. In general, the graph shows that the prices of these contracts are ordered according to time to delivery: the November 88 contract, the most distant one, has the highest price; the October 88 contract has the next highest price; and the September 88 contract, the nearest term contract shown, has the lowest price. This price progression is characterized as a contango market.

Figure 4-5 shows the prices for the December 88, January 89, and March 89 heating oil futures contracts for the period February, 1988 to February, 1989. Here the nearest term contract generally has the highest prices, while the lowest prices are often those for March 89—the most distant contract. This backwardation price relationship is just the opposite from the pattern we saw in Figure 4-4.

The reason the heating oil market is in backwardation during the latter part of 1988, and for the contracts shown, is because at this time of year heating oil is normally in short supply. Thus, it is difficult to do a reverse cost-of-carry arbitrage, which would eliminate the backwardation. Near the end of the winter heating season, when the demand for heating oil is usually high but quite variable, heating oil inventories are at their lowest levels, and suppliers want to avoid having to carry heating oil over the summer. Hence, heating oil is generally not available for arbitragers to borrow.

Finally, it may be useful at this point to ask whether a futures market can display a price pattern where futures prices consistently exhibit prices *higher* than full-carry prices. In other words, could a situation exist where futures prices were consistently rich relative to cash prices?

In this case the arbitrage is to sell futures, buy the physical commodity in the cash market, and carry the commodity forward and use it to make delivery on

Cents per gallon

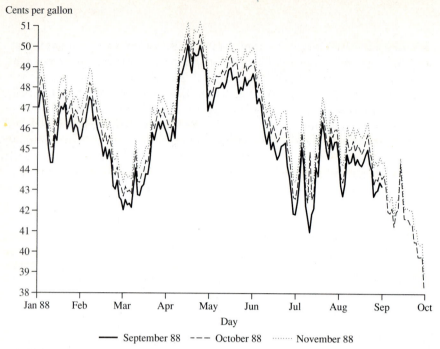

September 88 --- October 88 .... November 88

FIGURE 4-4

Daily heating oil futures prices, January 1, 1988, to September 30, 1988.

Cents per gallon

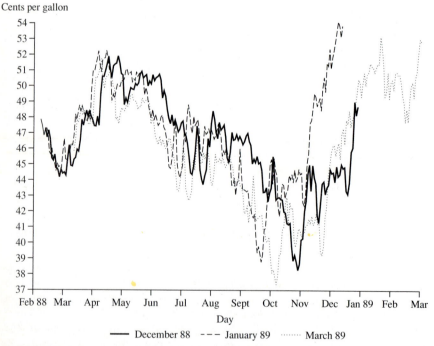

December 88 --- January 89 .... March 89

FIGURE 4-5

Daily heating oil futures prices, February 16, 1988, to February 28, 1989.

the short futures position. (An illustration of such a cash-and-carry arbitrage was given in Table 4.4.) Unless there are obstacles to this arbitrage, or such arbitrage does not occur in sufficiently large volume, it will reduce the difference between cash and futures prices to a level consistent with a full-carry relationship. It is obvious that, in contrast to a reverse cash-and-carry arbitrage, there is nothing to prevent traders from doing this arbitrage: there is no obstacle to buying the cash commodity or to selling futures. Thus, futures prices cannot be persistently higher than cash prices by an amount greater than the costs of carrying the physical commodity forward. When physical shortages exist, however, futures prices can be less than full-carry prices and backwardation can occur.

4.3.6 The Convenience Yield

The concept of a *convenience yield* is another way of viewing markets in backwardation. As explained earlier, the essence of backwardation is a shortage of the available physical commodity. Such a shortage occurs when holders of the physical commodity are unwilling to part with it, even for short periods of time. When this occurs we say that the commodity possesses a convenience yield: there is an implied yield (or return) from simply holding the commodity. This yield need not be a pecuniary return, or a return that is directly measurable. It could, for example, be the implicit return that a firm places on its ability to use its inventory to supply without interruption its longstanding customers—its customer goodwill. While the convenience yield is not directly observable, futures prices allow us to extract an implicit measure of it.

More specifically, the cost-of-carry pricing relationship described by Equation 4.1 above shows that

$$\text{Full-carry } FP_{t,T} - CP_t = CC_{t,T}$$

where $CC_{t,T}$ is the total dollar cost per unit of carrying the commodity from time t to T. If we observe a relationship where the actual futures price ($FP_{t,T}$) is less than $CP_t + CC_{t,T}$, we say that $FP_{t,T}$ contains an implicit convenience yield $Y_{t,T}$. In this case we must restate the above formula as

$$FP_{t,T} - CP_t = CC_{t,T} - Y_{t,T} \tag{4.2}$$

so that

$$(CP_t + CC_{t,T}) - FP_{t,T} = Y_{t,T} \tag{4.3}$$

or

$$\text{Full-carry } FP_{t,T} - FP_{t,T} = Y_{t,T}$$

where $Y_{t,T}$ is the implicit convenience yield for period t to T. In these equations the convenience yield is measured in terms of dollars and cents per unit of the commodity, rather than as a percentage, as is suggested by the term *yield*. To express the convenience yield as an annualized percentage, the usual procedure is to divide the above dollars and cents measure of the convenience yield by the cash price of the commodity and multiply by $(T - t)/365$. Thus, if Equation 4.3 is divided by CP_t and multiplied by $(T - t)/365$, this equation can be rewritten as

$$\left(\frac{CP_t + CC_{t,T} - FP_{t,T}}{CP_t} \right) \frac{365}{T - t} = Y_{t,T}^* \qquad (4.4)$$

where $Y_{t,T}^*$ is the annualized percentage convenience yield.

Observed futures prices together with information about carrying costs can be used to calculate an explicit measure of the convenience yield. For example, on April 11, 1989, the cash price of copper was 141 cents per pound and the price of the December 89 futures contract was 120.5 cents. To calculate the implied convenience yield imbedded in these prices, we can insert these prices together with the appropriate values for the financing and storage costs into Equation 4.4 above and solve for the convenience yield. On April 11, 1989, the relevant annualized financing rate was 12 percent, and the storage cost was a little more than one-half cent per pound per month. Thus, the carrying cost ($CC_{t,T}$) for those 240 days (or approximately eight months) was 15 cents:

$$CC_{t,T} = 141 \times 0.12 \times \frac{240}{365} + 0.5 \times 8 = 15$$

Substituting these values into equation 4.4 reveals an implicit annualized convenience yield of 38.29 percent:

$$\frac{141 + 15 - 120.5}{141} \times \frac{365}{240} = 0.3829$$

Solving for the convenience yield in this manner allows us to state the following principle: the greater the convenience yield, the greater is the backwardation in prices. Thus, a high convenience yield suggests a greater shortage of the physical commodity.

To illustrate the amount of variation in the degree of backwardation that can occur, we have calculated daily convenience yields for No.2 heating oil using cash prices and an approximation to a continuous series of one-month futures prices for the 1987–88 heating season (May 16, 1987, to May 15, 1988). These are graphed in Figure 4-6. As can be seen in this graph, the convenience yield is highest during the early months of 1988. At that time, which is late in the 1987 to 1988 heating season, inventories of fuel oil are low and the demand for heating oil is high and uncertain. Since warm weather could bring a significant fall in the demand for oil, suppliers are deterred from holding large inventories. Alternatively, a sudden cold snap could increase demand for oil sharply, putting significant pressure on available supplies, causing cash prices to rise sharply (albeit temporarily). High convenience yields reflect the temporary supply shortage. Earlier in the heating season, such as in September 1987, large fuel oil inventories are held in anticipation of future heating oil demands, and convenience yields are low.

Cents per gallon

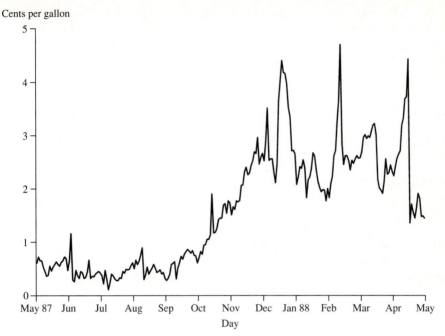

FIGURE 4-6
One-month convenience yields: Heating oil (daily: May 16, 1987, to May 15, 1988).

4.4 SPREADS

In addition to outright long and short positions, traders in futures markets commonly trade *spreads*. A spread position is initiated by the simultaneous purchase and sale of futures contracts on the same commodity but with different delivery months, or by the simultaneous purchase and sale of futures on different commodities for delivery in the same or different months. Since spreads involve holding both long and short positions, price changes in the underlying commodity (or commodities) generally result in simultaneous gains and losses on both sides (or *legs*) of the spread. Spreads are usually put on (or traded) when there is a predictable economic relationship (and therefore price relationship) between the commodities on which the spreads are based. This section describes the types of spreads that are commonly traded and discusses the factors that cause *spread prices* (or the magnitude of the spread) to change over time.

4.4.1 Types of Spreads

INTRA-COMMODITY SPREADS. A spread between different contract months in the same commodity is called an *intra-commodity* spread. An intra-commodity spread is actually a *time* spread. For example, the August–December spread in heating oil refers to the difference between August and December futures prices.

On April 11, 1989, the December 89 futures price was 52.67 cents per gallon, while the August 89 futures price was 51.02 cents per gallon (see Table 4.1). The August-December price spread, therefore, was equal to 1.65 cents a gallon.

Figure 4-7 shows two heating oil price spreads: between the September 88 and November 88 futures contracts (Sep-Nov 88), and between the September 88 and October 88 contracts (Sep-Oct 88). A negative spread indicates a cost-of-carry market: the nearby contract price (Sep) lies below the distant contract price (Oct and Nov). This is illustrated in Figure 4-4. The difference between the spreads in Figure 4-7 represents differences in the expected costs of carrying heating oil for one month versus two months.

INTER-COMMODITY SPREADS. An *inter-commodity* spread is a spread between the prices of two different but related commodities. An example of such a spread is a long December heating oil position and a short December gasoline position. Inter-commodity spreads are generally taken in commodities which have some economic relationship to each other. A special type of inter-commodity spread is the spread between the prices of a commodity and its products (e.g., soybeans and its two products, soybean oil and soybean meal—called the *crush* spread; or crude oil and its two products, heating oil and gasoline—called the *crack*

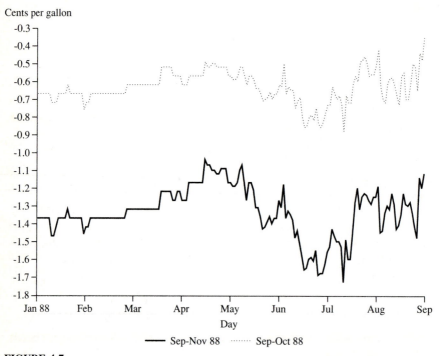

Cents per gallon

FIGURE 4-7
Intra-commodity spreads: Heating oil futures (futures contracts: 8809–8811 and 8809–8810, from January 1, 1988, to August 31, 1988).

spread). Figure 4-8 graphs a one-to-one heating oil crack spread: buying January 89 heating oil and selling January 89 crude oil futures. The crack spread reflects oil refiners' profit margins. Heating oil prices are generally higher during the winter months, rising by more at these times than crude oil prices. Thus, as shown in Figure 4-8, the crack spread increases in value as winter approaches. These spreads are discussed in greater detail in Chapter 15.

INTER-MARKET SPREADS. *Inter-market* price spreads are a variant of inter-commodity spreads. An example is spreading New York heating oil against London gas-oil. Theoretically, regional price differences in a commodity should be equal to transportation costs between the regions. However, variations in regional supply and demand patterns, seasonality, and the availability of transport often result in regional prices differing by more than transportation costs.

Figure 4-9 shows the price patterns of December 88 heating oil futures traded on the New York Mercantile Exchange and on the International Petroleum Exchange (London). Because New York is an oil consumption region (net importer), while the United Kingdom is a producing region (net exporter), heating oil prices in New York are almost always at a premium to those in London. However, if the spread between the two regions exceeds the cost of shipping oil from Europe to New York (which is approximately four cents per gallon), an arbitrage opportunity

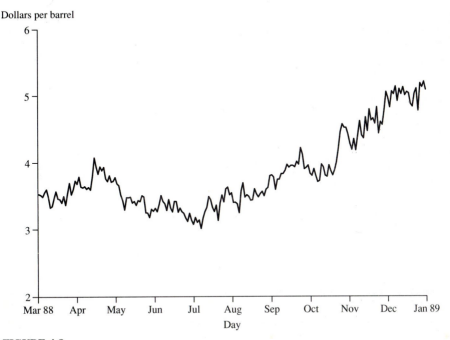

FIGURE 4-8
Inter-commodity spreads: crack spread (futures contracts: Jan 89 heating oil – Jan 89 crude oil from March 1, 1988, to December 19, 1988).

Cents per gallon

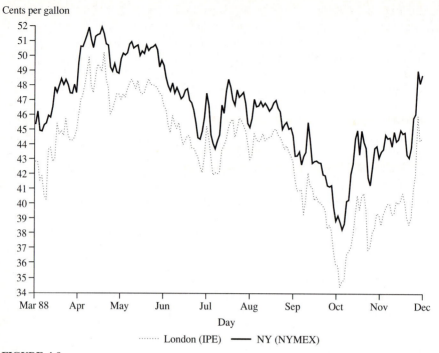

FIGURE 4-9
December 88 heating oil futures prices in New York and London (March 10, 1988, to November 30, 1988).

exists: sell heating oil futures in New York and buy gas-oil in the United Kingdom. As indicated in Figure 4-10, the spreads between New York and London fluctuate between one and four cents most of the time, except during the winter when they can be greater.

4.4.2 Why Trade Spreads

Spread trading has always been important in futures markets. Commercial users frequently trade spreads as a way to move their hedges from one contract month to another. They also trade spreads to recover the costs of storing and financing their inventories.

Spread positions are usually much less volatile than outright positions. For example, on April 11, 1989, May 89 crude oil futures prices increased by 40 cents, whereas the May-June crude oil price spread changed by only 20 cents (see Table 4.1). Hence, because of lower volatility, spread positions are usually considered less risky, and futures exchanges therefore allow traders to post a smaller margin on such positions. The New York Mercantile Exchange requires members to post $3000 as initial margin for outright positions in spot month (or near month) contracts, but requires only $1200 for a related spread position. Thus, trading spreads is often viewed as a more conservative speculative strategy.

Cents per gallon

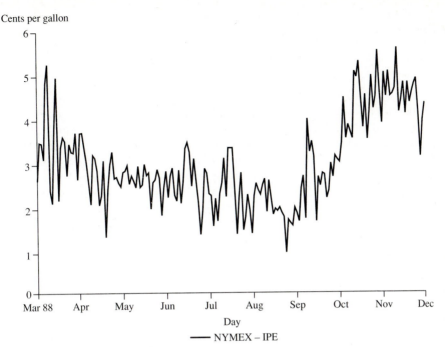

FIGURE 4-10
Inter-market spreads: December 88 heating oil futures in New York and London (March 10, 1988, to November 30, 1988).

4.4.3 Spread Prices

Spread prices are quoted as the difference between the futures prices which form the legs of the spread (see Equation 4.5). What determines the magnitude of a spread at any particular time? The answer is relatively simple for commodities that usually exhibit a full cost-of-carry pricing relationship. For others, such as heating oil, it is considerably more complicated. The discussion in this section focuses on intra-commodity spreads, which are the most commonly traded spreads.

In general, an n-month price spread, at any given time, is measured in dollars and cents per unit of the commodity, and is defined as

$$FP_{t,T+n} - FP_{t,T} = \text{spread}_{t,(T+n,T)} \tag{4.5}$$

where $FP_{t,T}$ and $FP_{t,T+n}$ are, according to Equations 4.1 and 4.2 above, defined as

$$FP_{t,T} = CP_t \times \left(1 + R_{t,T} \times \frac{T-t}{365}\right) + G_{t,T} - Y_{t,T}$$

$$FP_{t,T+n} = CP_t \times \left(1 + R_{t,T+n} \times \frac{T+n-t}{365}\right) + G_{t,T+n} - Y_{t,T+n}$$

Thus, the magnitude of a price spread at a given time depends upon the relevant financing costs, storage costs, and convenience yields:

$$FP_{t,T+n} - FP_{t,T} = \text{difference in financing costs } + \text{ difference in storage costs}$$
$$- \text{ difference in convenience yields}$$

For commodities that have no convenience yield and no storage cost, the inter-month price spread simply reflects the relevant *forward* interest rates (or financing rates) during the time period covered by the spread. For example, Figure 4-11 depicts the three-month price spread between the December 88 and March 89 silver futures contracts traded on the Commodity Exchange, from September, 1987, to August, 1988. These spreads are expressed as annualized percentages (by dividing Equation 4.5 by $FP_{t,T}$, and annualizing).[3] Since there is no convenience yield in silver and the storage cost is minimal, these spreads (expressed as percentages) reflect the implied three-month forward yields from selling March 89 and buying December 88 silver futures. Figure 4-11 shows that, in fact, silver spreads are highly correlated with forward interest rates (which for purposes of Figure 4-11 are deduced from December 88 Eurodollar futures contract traded on the Chicago Mercantile Exchange).

For commodities with convenience yields, spread prices are more complicated. Figure 4-12 shows examples of inter-month price spreads for heating oil futures: between the December 88 and February 89 contracts, and between the December 88 and January 89 contracts, for the period February, 1988, to December, 1988. Prior to November, both spreads are negative, indicating a cost-of-carry market.

The distant month spread (Dec 88–Feb 89) is below the near month spread (Dec 88–Jan 89) until mid-April, after which it increases sharply and goes above the Dec 88–Jan 89 spread. The gap between the two further increases as the spreads become positive in late October (indicating backwardation). (The prices that correspond to these spreads were shown earlier in Figure 4-5.) How can these dramatic shifts in spreads be explained, since both storage costs and interest rates were relatively stable during this period? The answer is that heating oil spreads, such as those depicted in Figure 4-12, are driven largely by changes in convenience yields. In November and December convenience yields in heating oil commonly increase. Thus, in some commodities spread prices reflect relative convenience yields more than anything else.

In summary, spread prices change for a variety of reasons: changes in storage costs, interest rates, convenience yields, and price levels. When trading futures, traders should be aware of what the normal spread relationships are among different commodities and different futures contracts, and should understand why spread prices change.

---

[3]To express the spread in terms of a percentage, one has to divide the spread (in dollar and cents) by the nearby futures price, and then express this percent in an annualized form. Forward interest rates are discussed in Chapter 12.

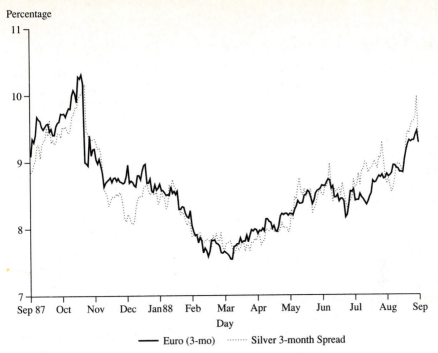

FIGURE 4-11
Intra-commodity spreads versus forward yields: Silver 8812–8903 futures spread versus 3-month Eurodollar rate (from September 1, 1987, to August 31, 1988).

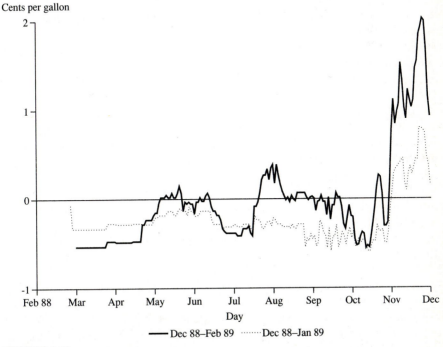

FIGURE 4-12
Intra-commodity spreads: heating oil futures (futures contracts: 8812–8901 and 8812–8902, from February 16, 1988, to November 30, 1988).

CONCLUSION

This chapter has covered the theories and concepts required to understand futures prices. Mastery of these concepts is essential both for developing successful trading strategies and for carrying out effective hedging programs. A discussion of trading strategies is deferred until Chapter 16. In the next two chapters we turn our attention to hedging.

QUESTIONS

1. Using the silver prices in Table 4.1, calculate the full-carry price of the December 89 futures contract.
2. If the futures price is rich to the cash price, explain the arbitrage that will take place. In Table 4.4, what is meant by the full-carry December 89 futures price?
3. If the futures price is cheap to the cash price, explain the arbitrage that will take place.
4. What is the *basis*? What factors determine the magnitude of the basis and variation in the basis?
5. What is backwardation? Why doesn't reverse cash-and-carry arbitrage eliminate backwardation?
6. What is the convenience yield? Why is the convenience yield often high during summer months for gasoline futures?
7. Using the heating oil prices in Tables 4.1 and 4.2, calculate the convenience yields on the May 89 futures contract. (Hint: the relevant cash price is the New York barge price and the full carrying cost for heating oil is 0.80 cents a month.) Can you explain the existence of this convenience yield?
8. Explain the seasonal pattern of heating oil futures prices. In which delivery months does backwardation commonly occur? Why?
9. How can you explain the variations in London–New York heating oil spreads shown in Figures 4-9 and 4-10?
10. Why are spread traders in a full-carry market (such as silver) sometimes called *interest rate* arbitragers?
11. Why would a speculator trade an intra-commodity spread in a commodity like heating oil? What would he or she be speculating on?

SUGGESTED READING

Black, F. "The Pricing of Commodity Contracts." *Journal of Financial Economics*, Vol. 3 (1976), pp. 167–179.

Britto, R. "Simultaneous Determination of Spot and Futures Prices in a Simple Model with Production Risk." *Quarterly Journal of Economics*, May 1984, pp. 351–365.

Carter, C. A., G. C. Rausser, and A. Schmitz. "Efficient Asset Portfolios and the Theory of Normal Backwardation." *Journal of Political Economy*, April 1983, pp. 319–331.

Castelino, M. G. and J. C. Francis. "Basis Speculation in Commodity Futures: The Maturity Effect." *The Journal of Futures Markets*, Summer 1982, pp. 195–206.

Cox, John C., Jonathan E. Ingersoll, Jr., and Stephen A. Ross. "The Relationship between Forward Prices and Futures Prices." *Journal of Financial Economics*, Vol. 9 (1981), pp. 321–346.

Fama, E. and K. French. "Commodity Futures Prices: Some Evidence on Forecast Power, Premiums, and the Theory of Storage." *Journal of Business*, January 1987, pp. 55–73.

Park, H. "Reexamination of Normal Backwardation Hypothesis in Futures Markets." *The Journal of Futures Markets*, Winter 1985, pp. 505–516.

Richard, S. and M. Sundaresan. "A Continuous Time Equilibrium Model of Forward Prices and Futures Prices in a Multigood Economy." *Journal of Financial Economics*, Vol. 9 (December 1981), pp. 347–370.

Stein, J. L. "The Simultaneous Determination of Spot and Futures Prices." *American Economic Review*, Vol. 51 (1961), pp. 1012–1025.

APPENDIX: THE COST-OF-CARRY PRICING FORMULA

The cost-of-carry pricing formula shown in Section 4.2.1 assumes simple interest rates. However, valuation formulas for most derivative securities (e.g., futures and options) are derived using continuously compounded interest rates.

Consider an amount X invested for n years at an interest rate of R per annum. If interest is paid on a simple interest basis, the terminal value of the investment will be $X(1+nR)$. If interest is compounded continuously, the terminal value of the investment becomes Xe^{Rn}. If we assume $X = \$100, R = 10$ percent, and $n = 5$ years, the terminal value of the investment with simple interest will be $\$100(1 + 5 \times 0.1) = \$150$. With continuously compounded interest the terminal value will be $\$100e^{(0.1)(5)} = \$164.87$. The longer the re-investment period (n), the larger will be the difference between the two terminal values. If $n = 1$, the terminal values for the simple interest and continuously compounded cases will be, respectively, $\$110$ and $\$110.56$, a relatively small difference.

Assuming continuously compounded interest rates, Equation 4.1 can be expressed as follows:

$$FP_{t,T} = CP_t e^{(R+G)[(T-t)/365]}$$

This formula can also be modified to reflect the existence of a convenience yield:

$$FP_{t,T} = CP_t e^{(R+G-Y)[(T-t)/365]}$$

where $R, G,$ and Y are, respectively, the financing rate, storage cost, and the convenience yield, all expressed as annualized percentages, $FP_{t,T}$ and CP_t are as defined earlier, and $T - t$ is the fraction of a year until expiration of the futures contract. For short periods of time, the above pricing formula yields futures prices that are very similar to those calculated with Equation 4.1.

CHAPTER
5

HEDGING
FUNDAMENTALS

An important function of futures markets is to permit commercial traders to reduce or control risk by transferring it to others more able or more willing to bear the risk. The activity of trading futures with the objective of reducing or controlling risk is called *hedging.* In contrast, speculative traders willingly assume risk in the hope of making profits from price changes. As we shall see, hedgers willingly give up the chance for additional profits due to favorable price changes in order to reduce their risk exposure.

This chapter covers hedging fundamentals applicable to all types of futures contracts and to all kinds of risk exposures. While the examples in this chapter use specific futures contracts to demonstrate particular hedging concepts, these concepts are general to other futures contracts and other hedging situations.

5.1 RISKS THAT CAN AND CANNOT BE HEDGED

Hedgers seek to eliminate or control the risk exposure that is due to adverse changes in prices. This exposure is called *price risk,* and exists because of uncertainty about future price levels. For example, a farmer who is growing corn and is planning to sell it in six months cannot be certain about what the price of corn will be in six months. It may be lower or higher than he expects—or the price that he anticipated when he planted his corn. If the price turns out to be significantly lower, the farmer may be forced to sell the corn at a price which does not cover production costs. The result may be bankruptcy.

If, on the other hand, the price turns out to be higher, the farmer will have exceptionally high profits.

Alternatively, airlines may wish to set passenger fares that remain fixed for long periods of time. To set profitable fares they must estimate what their costs will be. Once they establish such fares, however, they are subject to the risk that costs may rise unexpectedly, squeezing profit margins. The cost of jet fuel for a typical carrier accounts for about 17 percent of total expenses. A one cent per gallon rise in jet fuel prices, therefore, increases costs substantially and can have a significant effect on earnings per share.

Thus, both the farmer and the airline carrier are exposed to price risk: the farmer to a *sales* (or *output*) price risk, and the airline carrier to a *cost* (or *input*) price risk. Both of these risks, as we shall see, can be reduced or controlled by hedging.

The ultimate goal of any business is, of course, to make profits (the difference between total sales revenue and total costs). Price variation in outputs and inputs is only one source of variation in revenues and costs. Changes in sales revenue can occur either because of changes in prices or because of changes in the quantity sold. Our corn farmer, for example, may have anticipated growing 500,000 bushels of corn, but due to unfavorable weather conditions only managed to harvest 300,000 bushels. Thus, even if he correctly anticipated corn prices (or successfully hedged his price risk), he would still find his sales revenue drastically reduced. Once again, the result could be bankruptcy.

This type of risk we call *quantity* risk: uncertainty about the quantity that will be sold or bought at some future date. It is, unfortunately, not a risk that can be hedged with great precision with futures, options, or any other existing forward instruments. We will, nevertheless, want to keep quantity risk in mind when designing an optimal hedging strategy.

Thus, the focus of any discussion of hedging is on ways to reduce price risk. While reducing or even eliminating price risk may not in all cases be sufficient, in many instances being able to control this risk is the difference between success and failure.

As an operational concept, we view price risk in our subsequent discussion as the variability in a firm's net revenue due to unanticipated changes in the prices of the firm's outputs and/or inputs. The objective of hedging is to eliminate or control this revenue variability.

5.2   THE BASIC LONG AND SHORT HEDGES

Hedging typically involves taking a position in futures that is opposite either to a position that one already has in the cash market or to a future cash obligation that one has or will incur. The latter, for example, may be in the form of a forward contract to buy or sell a commodity. If a futures position is to succeed in reducing price risk, therefore, any gains or losses in the value of the cash position due to changes in the *cash* price will have to be countered by offsetting changes in the value of the futures position due to changes in the *futures* price.

Hedges are basically either short or long. A short hedge, or a *selling hedge,* occurs when a firm which owns or plans to purchase or produce a cash commodity sells futures to hedge this cash position. Here the objective is to protect the value of the cash position against a decline in cash prices. Once the short futures position is established, it is hoped that a decrease (increase) in value of the cash position will be fully or partially offset by a gain (loss) on the short futures position. In the above example of the corn farmer, a short position in corn futures can be used to hedge against a price decline in corn.

A long hedge, or a *buying hedge,* involves a firm purchasing futures to protect itself against a price increase in a commodity prior to purchasing it in either the spot or forward market. It is a way of fixing the cost of raw materials and other inputs, or of establishing an input price against a forward output (short) commitment. The airline carrier in the above example, for instance, might lock-in a future input cost with a long position in futures.

5.3 BASIS FUNDAMENTALS FOR HEDGERS

Understanding *basis risk* is fundamental to hedging. Basis, which is defined as

$$\text{Basis}_{t,T} = \text{Cash Price}_t - \text{Futures Price}_{t,T}$$

is usually quoted as a premium or discount: the cash price as a premium or discount to the futures price. The basis is said to be five cents over (under) futures if the cash price is five cents higher (lower) than the futures price. For example, on July 1, 1988, the New York heating oil cash price was 41 cents per gallon, and the February 89 futures was 44.48 cents. Thus, the New York heating oil basis vis-a-vis the February 89 futures was −3.48 cents. This is commonly quoted as *3.48 under,* since the cash price is 3.48 cents "under" the February 89 futures price.

If futures and cash prices always change by the same amount, the basis will not change. In this case, if the magnitudes (in units) of the cash and futures positions are identical, any loss (gain) in the value of the cash position will be totally offset by a gain (loss) in the value of the futures position. Such a hedge is often called a *perfect* hedge, since it eliminates all price risk. More generally, if the basis does change but the hedger can predict the change accurately, the hedge can also be used to eliminate all price risk. (This will become clear in the subsequent discussion.)

The top part of Figure 5-1 shows the cash and February 89 futures prices for heating oil from March 1, 1988, to January 31, 1989. The corresponding basis is depicted at the bottom of the graph. The graphs indicate that the heating oil market was in backwardation (positive basis) at the end of the 1987–88 heating season (March 88 to mid-May 88), turned into a carry market (negative basis) during the summer months, and returned to an inverted market (positive basis) as the 1988–89 heating season began in late October, 1988.

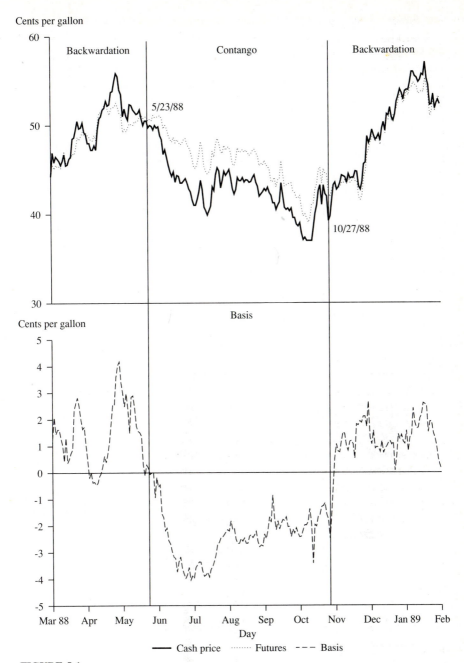

FIGURE 5-1
Heating oil prices: Cash, futures & basis (from March 1, 1988, to January 31, 1989).

Figure 5-1 indicates that the basis is quite volatile, ranging from −4 cents to +4 cents. When the basis moves toward the zero line we say that the basis is *narrowing*: the absolute difference between cash and futures prices becomes smaller. A *widening* of the basis occurs when the basis moves away from the zero line, and the absolute difference between cash and futures prices increases. A narrowing or widening of the basis can result in profits or losses for hedgers, depending on the type of hedge (either a long or short hedge) and on market conditions (a carry-market or an inverted market). A short hedger (a long cash position and a short futures position) is said to be *long the basis,* while a long hedger (a short cash position and a long futures position) is said to be *short the basis*.

It is important not to confuse the concepts of widening and narrowing with the algebraic value of the basis. While the basis has specific algebraic values, these depend on the type of market which exists. In particular, when futures

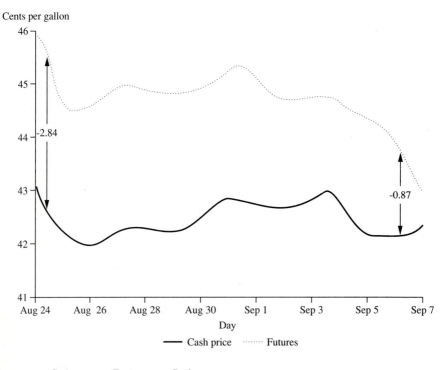

	Cash	Futures	Basis
8/24/88	43.10	45.94	−2.84
9/6/88	42.10	42.97	−0.87
Change	−1.00	−2.97	+1.97

FIGURE 5-2a
Contango market: Prices fall & basis narrows: (heating oil February 89 contract from August 24, 1988, to September 6, 1988).

prices are above cash prices (a contango market), the algebraic value of the basis will decrease (or become more negative) as the basis widens, and will increase (or become less negative) as the basis narrows. However, the reverse is true when futures prices are initially below cash prices, or a backwardation market exists. In this case the algebraic value of the basis increases (becomes more positive) as the basis widens, and decreases (becomes less positive) as the basis narrows. The following examples use actual cash and futures heating oil prices to illustrate these concepts.

1. In a contango market (or a carry market), regardless of the general price trend, a narrowing of the basis benefits the short hedger (he is long the basis), and a widening of the basis benefits the long hedger (he is short the basis).

   • Figure 5-2a illustrates that when both cash and futures markets are in a downtrend, but futures prices are declining faster than cash prices, the basis

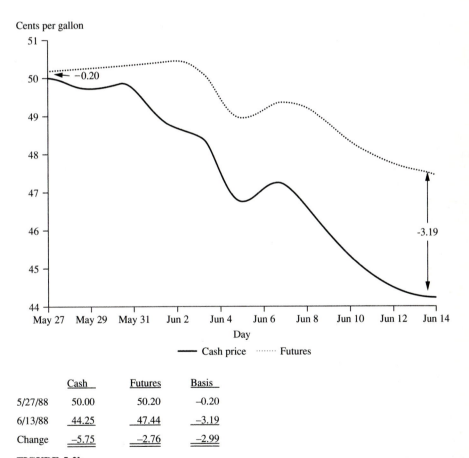

	Cash	Futures	Basis
5/27/88	50.00	50.20	−0.20
6/13/88	44.25	47.44	−3.19
Change	−5.75	−2.76	−2.99

FIGURE 5-2b
Contango market: Prices fall & basis widens (heating oil February 89 contract from May 27, 1988, to June 13, 1988).

Cents per gallon

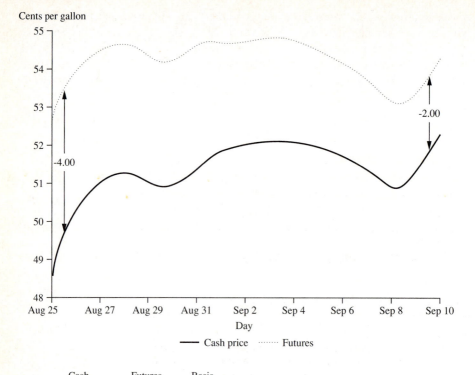

FIGURE 5-2c
Contango market: Prices rise & basis narrows (heating oil February 88 contract from August 26, 1987, to September 9, 1987).

	Cash	Futures	Basis
8/25/87	48.50	52.50	−4.00
9/9/87	52.30	54.30	−2.00
Change	+3.80	+1.80	+2.00

narrows and its algebraic value increases from −2.84 to −0.87 cents per gallon.

- Figure 5-2b illustrates that when both cash and futures markets are in a downtrend, but cash prices are declining faster than futures prices, the basis widens and its algebraic value decreases from −0.20 to −3.19 cents per gallon.
- Figure 5-2c illustrates that when both cash and futures prices are going up but cash prices are rising faster than futures prices, the basis narrows and its algebraic value increases from −4.00 to −2.00 cents per gallon.
- Figure 5-2d illustrates that when both cash and futures prices are going up but futures prices are rising faster than cash prices, the basis widens but its algebraic value decreases from −3.10 to −4.00 cents per gallon.

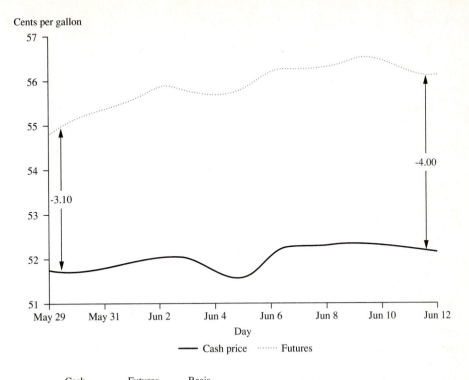

Cents per gallon

	Cash	Futures	Basis
5/29/87	51.75	54.85	–3.10
6/12/87	52.15	56.15	–4.00
Change	+0.40	+1.30	–0.90

FIGURE 5-2d
Contango market: Prices rise & basis widens (heating oil February 88 contract from May 29, 1987, to June 12, 1987).

2. In a backwardation market (or an inverted market), a narrowing of the basis benefits the long hedger, and a widening of the basis benefits the short hedger, just the reverse of what is true for a carry market.
   - Figure 5-3a illustrates that when both cash and futures prices are in a downtrend but cash prices are declining faster than futures prices, the basis narrows and its algebraic value decreases from 4.15 to 1.47 cents per gallon.
   - Figure 5-3b illustrates that when both cash and futures prices are in a downtrend but futures prices are declining faster than cash prices, the basis widens and its algebraic value increases from 1.85 to 3.09 cents per gallon.
   - Figure 5-3c illustrates that when the general price trend is up but futures prices are rising faster than cash prices, the basis narrows and its algebraic value decreases from 2.09 to 0.79 cents per gallon.

Cents per gallon

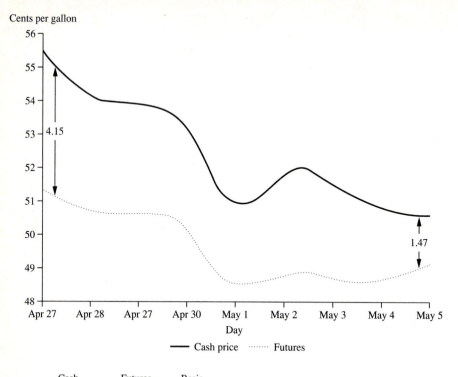

	Cash	Futures	Basis
4/27/88	55.50	51.35	4.15
5/5/88	50.60	49.13	1.47
Change	− 4.90	−2.22	− 2.68

FIGURE 5-3a
Backwardation market: Prices fall & basis narrows (heating oil February 89 contract from April 27, 1988, to May 5, 1988).

- Figure 5-3d illustrates that when the general price trend is up but cash prices are rising faster than futures prices, the basis widens and its algebraic value increases from 0.24 to 4.01 cents per gallon.

3. Seasonality: Variations in basis often follow a seasonal pattern which reflects the changing relationships between supply and demand for a commodity. It is important that hedgers recognize such seasonality. They may be able to benefit when the market switches from backwardation into contango and vice versa, since the change in the basis may be substantial (see, for example, Figure 5-1, on May 23, 1988, and October 27, 1988). Hedgers must be careful not to be caught on the wrong side of a seasonal basis move.

The following sections provide simple examples of both long and short hedging, some with and some without basis risk, in order to illustrate the fun-

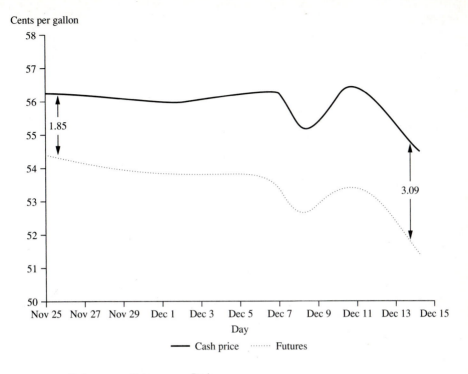

Cents per gallon

	Cash	Futures	Basis
11/25/87	56.25	54.40	1.85
12/14/87	54.50	51.41	3.09
Change	− 1.75	−2.99	+ 1.24

FIGURE 5-3b
Backwardation market: Prices fall & basis widens (heating oil February 88 contract from November 26, 1987, to December 14, 1987).

damentals of hedging. In the next chapter, more sophisticated hedging objectives and strategies are discussed.

5.4   SHORT HEDGE WITH AND WITHOUT BASIS RISK

5.4.1   Short Hedge with Zero Basis Risk

On October 1, 1987, an oil distributor, which presently has a large inventory of heating oil, enters into an agreement to provide 420,000 gallons of heating oil to home owners in the New York area, to be delivered on December 15 at a price equal to the cash price that exists in the New York area on December 15. Thus, the distributor's selling price in December is unknown in October.

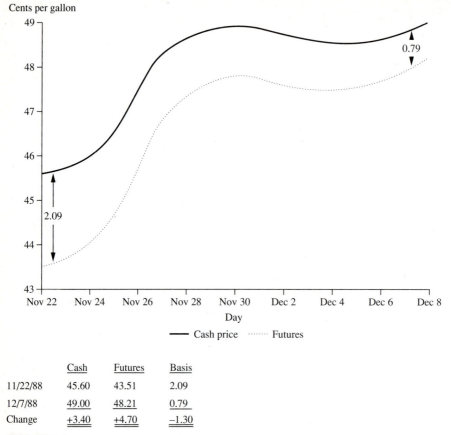

	Cash	Futures	Basis
11/22/88	45.60	43.51	2.09
12/7/88	49.00	48.21	0.79
Change	+3.40	+4.70	−1.30

FIGURE 5-3c

Backwardation market: Prices rise & basis narrows (heating oil February 89 contract from November 22, 1988, to December 7, 1988).

The distributor calculates that, on October 1, the average net cost for the oil in his inventory, which was purchased earlier, is 51 cents per gallon. The cost of carrying the oil until December 15 to fulfill his commitment is approximately 1.87 cents per gallon (0.75 cents per month per gallon, for two and a half months). Thus, on December 15 his cost will be 52.87 cents per gallon.

The distributor expects heating oil prices to be higher in December, as prices generally rise in the winter due to increased demand, but there is no guarantee. The distributor faces price uncertainty. The heating oil cash price on October 1 is 54 cents per gallon. If on December 15 the heating oil cash price were to be 54 cents, the distributor would have a profit of \$4746 [(\$0.5400 − \$0.5287) × 420,000]. However, if the cash price on December 15 turns out to be less than 54 cents, or even less than 52.87 cents, he will have lower profits or even a loss. Given the high volatility of oil prices, the distributor is anxious to lock-in a profit of at least \$4746.

Cents per gallon

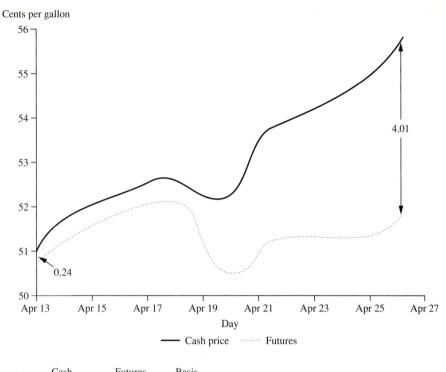

	Cash	Futures	Basis
4/13/88	51.00	50.76	0.24
4/26/88	55.85	51.84	4.01
Change	+ 4.85	+1.08	+ 3.77

FIGURE 5-3d
Backwardation market: Prices rise & basis widens (heating oil February 89 contract from April 13, 1988, to April 26, 1988).

On October 1, the January 89 futures price is 55.87 cents. The basis, therefore, is −1.87. The oil distributor can solve his problem by hedging: specifically, by *shorting* 10 January 89 futures contracts at 55.87 cents a gallon. (The December futures contract ceases trading at the end of November.) Since each contract is for 42,000 gallons, 10 contracts equal 420,000 gallons. By selling futures, the distributor locks-in a forward sales price of 55.87 cents and a profit of $4746.

The following calculates the distributor's net profit under two scenarios in which the basis remains constant: in Case 1, cash prices on December 15 turn out to be higher (56 cents); in Case 2, cash prices turn out to be lower (51 cents). Since the basis is assumed to remain constant, the January 89 futures price on December 15 is simply the cash price on December 15 plus the basis.

Case 1: Prices rise and basis is constant at −1.87 cents

	Oct. 1 ($)	Dec. 15 ($)	Profit (loss)
Cash*:	Long: 0.5100	Short: 0.5600	$21,000
Carry*:			(7,854)
Futures:	Short: 0.5587	Long: 0.5787	(8,400)
Net profit (loss):			$ 4,746

*The cash price shown for October 1 is the distributor's average purchase price per gallon of the oil in his inventory. His cost of carry is $0.0187 × 420,000 gallons. The actual cash price in October was 54 cents

Case 2: Prices fall and basis is constant at −1.87 cents

	Oct. 1 ($)	Dec. 15 ($)	Profit (loss)
Cash*:	Long: 0.5100	Short: 0.5100	$ 0
Carry*:			(7,854)
Futures:	Short: 0.5587	Long: 0.5287	12,600
Net profit (loss):			$ 4,746

*The cash price shown for October 1 is the distributor's average purchase price per gallon of the oil in his inventory. His cost of carry is $0.0187 × 420,000 gallons.

Thus, whether cash prices rise or fall between October 1 and December 15 the distributor's profit margin is protected by the short hedge: the variability of his net revenue is zero.

The key to understanding why this hedge succeeds is to recognize that whatever loss the distributor incurs on his cash position due to a change in cash prices he recoups on the futures position due to a change in futures prices. In the case of a fall in oil prices, while the cash price decreased by three cents below what was expected, the futures price also fell by three cents, so the two positions offset one another perfectly.

In both of the above cases, the basis remained constant, from October 1 to December 15. On October 1 it was −1.87 cents (54.00 − 55.87); and on December 15 it was also −1.87 cents (51.00 − 52.87). When the basis remains unchanged (and consequently the variance of the basis is zero), it is a simple matter to construct a predictable, no-risk hedge. This situation, unfortunately, is not usually the case. The examples in the next section illustrate how a change in the basis can affect the hedging results we obtained in the preceding examples.

5.4.2   Short Hedge with Basis Risk

To demonstrate how the outcomes of the previous hedging examples can change when there is a change in the basis, we have reworked the examples assuming that certain changes in the basis occur.

Case 1 assumes a widening in the basis: between October 1 and December 15 a contango market existed and futures prices increased by more than cash prices. Futures prices rose from 55.87 cents to 58.87 cents, a 3 cent increase, while cash prices rose from 54 to 56 cents, a 2-cent increase. As a consequence of this change in the basis, the hedger incurs a larger loss on his short futures position, which nearly eliminates his entire profit. (Compare to Case 1 in Section 5.4.1.)

Case 1: Prices rise and basis widens, from −1.87 cents to −2.87 cents

	Oct. 1 ($)	Dec. 15 ($)	Profit (loss)
Cash*:	Long: 0.5100	Short: 0.5600	$21,000
Carry*:			(7,854)
Futures:	Short: 0.5587	Long: 0.5887	(12,600)
Net profit (loss):			$ 546

*The cash price shown for October 1 is the distributor's average purchase price per gallon of the oil in his inventory. His cost of carry is $0.0187 × 420,000 gallons.

In Case 2 the basis is assumed to narrow: futures prices fall by more than cash prices. The loss incurred on the distributor's cash position is now more than offset by the profit on the futures position, so that his net profits are considerably higher. (Compare to Case 2 in Section 5.4.1.)

Thus, changes in the basis can dramatically alter hedging results from what they would be in the absence of basis risk. When constructing a hedge, therefore, a common strategy is to minimize basis risk in order to make the outcome of the hedge more predictable.

Case 2: Prices fall and basis narrows, from −1.87 cents to −1.00 cents

	Oct. 1 ($)	Dec. 15 ($)	Profit (loss)
Cash*:	Long: 0.5100	Short: 0.5100	$ 0
Carry*:			(7,854)
Futures:	Short: 0.5587	Long: 0.5200	16,254
Net Profit (loss):			$8,400

*The cash price shown for October 1 is the distributor's average purchase price per gallon of the oil in his inventory. His cost of carry is $0.0187 × 420,000 gallons.

5.5 LONG HEDGE WITH AND WITHOUT BASIS RISK

5.5.1 Long Hedge with Zero Basis Risk

An oil distributor has a long-term supply contract that requires him to deliver 420,000 gallons of heating oil on February 16, 1988, at a price of 55 cents per gallon. On January 4, 1988, the distributor discovers that he does not have enough oil to cover this agreement. It has been a cold winter and increased demand has depleted his inventory. He will, therefore, have to acquire additional oil to meet his supply obligations.

On January 4 the prevailing cash price is 53.50 cents per gallon, and the March 88 futures price is 49.73 cents. (The February 1988 futures contract ceases trading at the end of January.) Since the heating oil market is in backwardation, the expectation is that oil prices will fall between January 4 and February 16.

The distributor is considering several alternative strategies. The first is to purchase oil on January 4 at 53.50 cents, carry it to February 16 at a net cost of 54.70 cents a gallon (53.50 cents plus the one-and-a-half month carrying cost of 1.2 cents per gallon), and deliver it for 55 cents on February 16. In this case his net profit will be $1260[($0.5500 − $0.5470) × 420,000].

The second strategy is premised on the belief that oil prices will fall between January 4 and February 16. In this case he can wait until February, when cash prices are lower, to purchase the oil, which will result in even greater profits. The risk, of course, is that prices will rise instead of fall, in which case he may incur a loss.

The distributor does not want to be exposed to this risk nor does he want to purchase oil now and carry it. He therefore settles on a third strategy: a *long* hedge in heating oil futures.

The following two examples describe the results of such a hedging strategy under the assumption that the basis does *not* change. The basis on January 4 is 3.77 cents: 53.50 − 49.73. In Case 1 cash prices fall to 48.90 cents, whereas in Case 2 they rise to 54.50 cents. In both cases, however, the basis remains constant and the hedge succeeds in locking-in a net profit of $6300.

Case 1: Prices fall and basis is constant at 3.77 cents

	Jan. 4 ($)	Feb. 16 ($)	Profit (loss)
Cash*:	Short: 0.5500	Long: 0.4890	$25,620
Futures:	Long: 0.4973	Short: 0.4513	(19,320)
Net profit (loss):			$ 6,300

*The cash price is the delivery price agreed to by the distributor.

Case 2: Prices rise and basis is constant at 3.77 cents

	Jan. 4 ($)	Feb. 16 ($)	Profit (loss)
Cash*:	Short: 0.5500	Long: 0.5450	$2,100
Futures:	Long: 0.4973	Short: 0.5073	4,200
Net profit (loss):			$6,300

*The cash price is the delivery price agreed to by the distributor.

By using a long hedging strategy the distributor made *greater* profits than had he purchased the oil in the cash market on January 4 and carried it to February 16: $6300 versus $1260. Why? The answer lies in our assumption of no change in the basis. Because the basis remained unchanged, the distributor was able to avoid any carrying costs. In buying spot oil on January 4 and carrying it until February 16, he would have incurred a carrying cost of $5040($0.012 × 420,000), which is exactly equal to the difference between the two profits of $6300 and $1260. Realistically, the distributor could not have expected the basis to remain constant.

5.5.2 Long Hedge with Basis Risk

The next two examples demonstrate how the previous results can change when the assumption of a constant basis is dropped. In the first case, that of falling cash prices, the basis is now assumed to narrow from 3.77 to 2.17; in the second case, that of rising cash prices, the basis is assumed to widen from 3.77 to 7.00.

Case 1: Prices fall and basis narrows, from 3.77 cents to 2.17 cents

	Jan. 4 ($)	Feb. 16 ($)	Profit (loss)
Cash*:	Short: 0.5500	Long: 0.4890	$25,620
Futures:	Long: 0.4973	Short: 0.4673	(12,600)
Net profit (loss):			$13,020

*The cash price is the delivery price agreed to by the distributor.

Case 2: Prices rise and basis widens, from 3.77 cents to 7.00 cents

	Jan. 4 ($)	Feb. 16 ($)	Profit (loss)
Cash*:	Short: 0.5500	Long: 0.5450	$ 2,100
Futures:	Long: 0.4973	Short: 0.4750	(9,366)
Net profit (loss):			$(7,266)

*The cash price is the delivery price agreed to by the distributor.

In Case 1 a narrowing of the basis from 3.77 to 2.17 reduces the distributor's loss on his futures position from $19,320 to $12,600, resulting in an increase in net profits from $6300 to $13,020. In Case 2 a widening of the basis from 3.77 to 7.00 turns a profit of $4200 on the futures position into a loss of $9366, resulting in a net loss of $7266. (Compare with Cases 1 and 2 in Section 5.5.1.)

Thus, unanticipated changes in the basis can cause substantial variation in hedging results, for either long or short hedgers. We will have more to say about managing this risk in Chapter 6. The next section generalizes the concept of basis risk and contrasts this risk with the price risk that would occur in the absence of hedging.

5.6 BASIS RISK VERSUS PRICE RISK

To illustrate the difference between price risk and basis risk in a more general context, let us take the simple example of a copper mining company which has smelt 100,000 pounds of copper ingots and is in the process of shipping it to the buyer. The company and the buyer have already agreed that the sales price will be the market (or cash) price that prevails when the copper is delivered, in three weeks. During this three-week period the mining company is exposed to price risk: if copper prices fall its profits will be reduced or even eliminated.

A standard hedge for this kind of risk is to short (or sell) copper futures—in this case four contracts, since each contract is for 25,000 pounds. The mining company's long cash position of 100,000 pounds will therefore be matched by its short futures position of 100,000 pounds.

Suppose that when copper prices in the cash market change, copper futures prices always change by exactly the same amount: a 10 cent rise (fall) in cash prices is matched by a 10 cent rise (fall) in futures prices. In other words, there is a perfect, one-to-one, correlation between changes in futures and cash prices.[1] Thus, with a short futures position of 100,000 pounds, equal to the company's cash position, a loss in the value of the company's cash position due to a fall in cash copper prices will be exactly offset by an equivalent gain in the value of the company's short futures position (short positions increase in value when prices fall). For example, if both cash and futures copper prices decrease by 10 cents a pound, the gains and losses would be as follows:

Cash position:	$-\$0.10$ per pound $\times$ $100,000$ lbs $=$	$\$(10,000)$
Futures position:	$-\$0.10$ per pound $\times$ $-100,000$ lbs $=$	$10,000$
Net gain (loss)		$\$0$

(The negative sign placed in front of the futures position represents a short position; a number shown in parentheses indicates a loss.)[2]

---

[1] It may be useful to point out that a perfect correlation (or a correlation coefficient of one) can exist between two price series (or other variables) even if those prices do not change by identical magnitudes. For example, if for every $1 increase (decrease) in cash prices, futures prices always increase (decrease) by $0.80 (or perhaps by $1.10), the two price change series will still be perfectly correlated.

[2] It is obvious that a 20 cent rise in both cash and futures prices will also result in a zero net gain or loss, since the gain on the cash position will be balanced by the loss on the futures position.

In this example the mining company succeeded in eliminating all price risk by assuming an equal and offsetting futures position. Hedging is not always this easy or successful. In most cases changes in futures and cash prices will not be identical so we may not want to make the futures and cash positions of equal magnitude. In addition, basis risk will not usually be zero, as was assumed in the above example.

In particular, basis (B) was defined earlier as the difference between the cash price (CP) and the futures price (FP):

$$B_{t,T} = CP_t - FP_{t,T}$$

A change in the basis, therefore, is

$$\Delta B_{t,T} = \Delta CP_t - \Delta FP_{t,T}$$

In the foregoing illustration, all changes in futures and cash copper prices were assumed to be equal. Thus, there could be no change in the basis. If

$$\Delta FP_{t,T} = \Delta CP_t$$

then

$$\Delta B_{t,T} = \Delta CP_t - \Delta FP_{t,T} = 0$$

When changes in futures and cash prices are not equal, which is the usual case, there is *basis risk*. Basis risk is defined as the variance of the basis, or as $\sigma^2(B)_{t,T}$:

$$\sigma^2(B)_{t,T} = \sigma^2(CP_t - FP_{t,T})$$

This can be rewritten as

$$\sigma^2(B)_{t,T} = \sigma^2(CP_t) + \sigma^2(FP_{t,T}) - 2\rho\sigma(CP_t)\sigma(FP_{t,T})$$

where σ^2 is the variance, σ is the standard deviation, and ρ is the correlation coefficient between the futures and cash price series.

This equation reveals that basis risk is zero when the variances of the futures and cash prices are identical and the correlation coefficient between cash and futures prices equals one. For example, if the variances of futures and cash prices are both equal to $4, and there is a perfect correlation between the prices ($\rho = 1$), then

$$\sigma^2(B)_{t,T} = 4 + 4 - 2(1)(2)(2) = 0$$

If, on the other hand, there is not a one-to-one relationship between futures and cash prices, for example, if ρ equals only 0.50, basis risk will not be zero.

$$\sigma^2(B)_{t,T} = 4 + 4 - 2(0.5)(2)(2) = 4$$

Similarly, a difference between the variances of the futures and cash prices will result in some basis risk. In practice, however, the magnitude of the basis risk depends mainly on the degree of correlation between cash and futures prices: the higher the correlation, the less the basis risk.

Since there is never a perfect correlation between cash and futures prices, hedgers always assume some basis risk: to reduce their exposure to price risk (or to the variance of cash prices), they must accept in return an exposure to basis risk. It is obvious, therefore, that for a hedge to be attractive, the basis risk should be significantly less than the hedger's price risk.

5.7 MEASURING THE ANTICIPATED EFFECTIVENESS OF A HEDGE

While the objective of hedging is to reduce exposure to price risk, hedgers, as we have learned, trade price risk for basis risk. One measure of anticipated (or a priori) hedging effectiveness (*HE*) is to compare the basis risk that hedgers expect to assume with the price risk that they expect to eliminate. The smaller the anticipated basis risk is compared to the anticipated price risk, the more effective is the hedge. This measure of effectiveness can be stated formally as

$$HE = 1 - \frac{\sigma^2(B)}{\sigma^2(CP)}$$

or as 1 minus the ratio of the expected variance of the basis to the expected variance of cash prices. The closer *HE* is to one, the more effective the hedge.

Suppose that the airline carrier in our earlier hypothetical example decides to take a long position in futures to hedge against a possible increase in jet fuel cash prices. Since there does not exist a futures contract for jet fuel, the carrier must use one of the other existing petroleum futures contracts: heating oil, gasoline, and crude oil.[3] This strategy is appropriate if some of the demand and supply factors that affect jet fuel prices also affect the prices of the other energy products as well, which is likely since they are petroleum products.

Figures 5-4, 5-5, and 5-6 show the relationships between weekly jet fuel cash prices and weekly near month futures prices for heating oil, crude oil, and gasoline, respectively. The corresponding basis between jet fuel cash prices and each of the different futures prices is depicted at the bottom of the respective graphs. All three futures prices tend to move together with jet fuel cash prices. However, the basis between jet fuel and heating oil is the least volatile, varying within a tighter range. The closeness of the price relationships depicted in these graphs can also be measured by the correlation coefficients shown in Table 5.1. These are estimated using both daily price levels and changes in daily prices for the period July 1986 to December 1988.

The anticipated hedging effectiveness of the three possible cross-hedges—heating oil, gasoline, or crude oil futures—can be determined by calculating the following statistics for each futures:

---

[3]Hedging with these contracts would result in a *cross-hedge*. Cross-hedging is discussed in Section 6.1.1 in Chapter 6.

TABLE 5.1
**Jet fuel cash prices versus near month energy futures prices
(correlation coefficients: daily prices and daily price changes
from July 1986 to December 1988)**

	Heating oil	Gasoline	Crude oil
Jet fuel:			
–Price levels	0.95	0.72	0.83
–Price changes	0.54	0.41	0.45

$$HE^i = 1 - \frac{\sigma^2(B)^i}{\sigma^2(\text{JET})}$$

where   JET = jet fuel cash prices.

   $(B)^i$ = the basis between jet fuel cash prices and the relevant near month futures prices, where i = heating oil, gasoline, or crude oil.

$\sigma^2(\text{JET})$ = the variance of jet fuel cash prices.

   $\sigma^2(B)$ = the variance of the basis, where
   $$\sigma^2(B)^i = \sigma^2(\text{JET}) + \sigma^2(FP)^i - 2\rho^i\sigma(\text{JET})\sigma(FP)^i.$$

   σ = the standard deviation.

   σ^2 = the variance.

   ρ^i = the correlation coefficient between JET fuel cash prices and the prices of commodity i.

The values of the respective HE's are shown in Table 5.2.[4] When the anticipated basis risk (or variance of the basis) is small relative to the expected price risk (or variance of prices), the hedging effectiveness is high. In addition, a low basis risk is usually the result of a high correlation between cash and futures prices. An effective hedge, therefore, occurs when there is a high correlation between cash and futures prices. (The reader can verify this statement by re-computing the equations in Table 5.2 using different correlation coefficients.)[5]

The foregoing measure is not necessarily a good predictor of how a hedge will actually perform. It is only a way of judging how good a particular hedge is likely to be a priori. After the completion of a hedge, its ex post effectiveness might prove to be quite different for several reasons. Ex post hedging effectiveness is discussed in Chapter 6. In addition, the concept of *hedging effectiveness* should not be confused with the concept of an *optimal hedge,* which is also discussed in Chapter 6.

---

[4]The calculations in Table 5-2 assume a one-to-one hedge: the same quantity of heating oil, for example, as jet fuel oil. This need not be true. If it is not, the equations in Table 5.2 would have to be adjusted by weighting the components of the equations to reflect the quantity differences.

[5]The calculations shown in Table 5.2 are designed to expose the components of the variance of the basis. There are more direct ways to compute the variance of the basis.

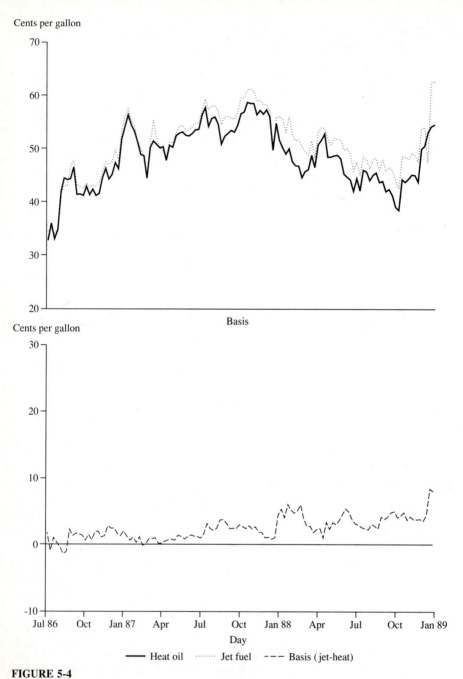

FIGURE 5-4

Jet fuel versus heating oil: Jet fuel cash versus near month heating oil futures prices (weekly from July 1986 to December 1988).

Cents per gallon

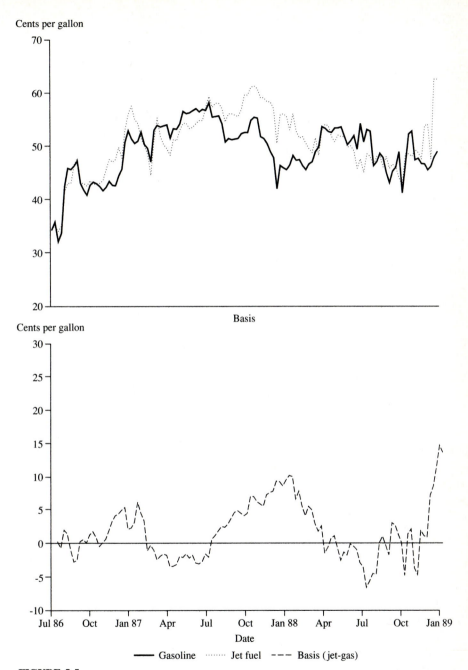

FIGURE 5-5
Jet fuel versus gasoline: Jet fuel cash versus near month gasoline futures prices (weekly from July 1986 to December 1988).

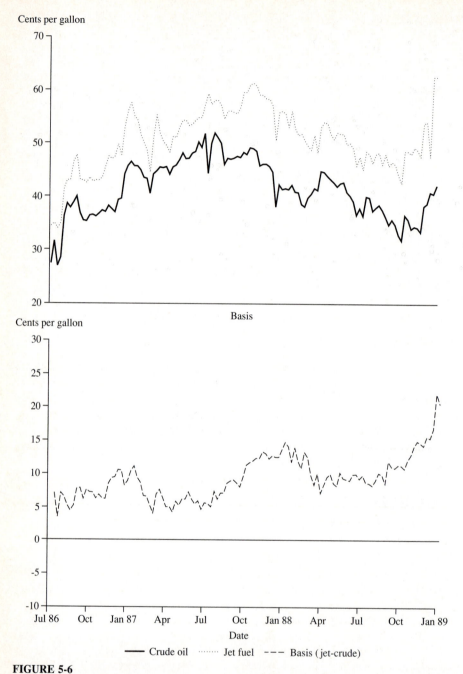

Cents per gallon

Cents per gallon

Basis

Date

——— Crude oil   ········ Jet fuel   – – – Basis (jet-crude)

FIGURE 5-6
Jet fuel versus crude oil: Jet fuel cash versus near month crude oil futures prices (weekly from July 1986 to December 1988).

TABLE 5.2
Measures of anticipated hedging effectiveness:
Jet fuel versus alternative energy futures
(daily prices from July 1986 to December 1988)

1. Hedging with heating oil:
   $\sigma^2(\text{JET}) = 32.58,\ \sigma^2(\text{HEAT}) = 31.22, \rho = 0.95$
   $\sigma(\text{JET}) = 5.71,\ \sigma(\text{HEAT}) = 5.59$
   $\sigma^2(B) = 32.58 + 31.22 - 2 \times 0.95 \times 5.71 \times 5.59 = 3.15$
   $HE = 1 - \frac{3.15}{32.58} = 0.90$

2. Hedging with gasoline:
   $\sigma^2(\text{JET}) = 32.58,\ \sigma^2(\text{GAS}) = 26.55, \rho = 0.72$
   $\sigma(\text{JET}) = 5.71,\ \sigma(\text{GAS}) = 5.15$
   $\sigma^2(B) = 32.58 + 26.55 - 2 \times 0.72 \times 5.71 \times 5.15 = 16.78$
   $HE = 1 - \frac{16.78}{32.58} = 0.48$

3. Hedging with crude oil:
   $\sigma^2(\text{JET}) = 32.58,\ \sigma^2(\text{CRUDE}) = 30.09, \rho = 0.83$
   $\sigma(\text{JET}) = 5.71,\ \sigma(\text{CRUDE}) = 5.49$
   $\sigma^2(B) = 32.58 + 30.09 - 2 \times 0.83 \times 5.71 \times 5.49 = 10.63$
   $HE = 1 - \frac{10.63}{32.58} = 0.67$

CONCLUSION

This chapter examined the fundamental concepts and terminology that underlie hedging with futures contracts. It discussed the risks that can and cannot be hedged with futures, discussed the difference between price risk and basis risk, and provided several examples of how basis changes can undermine a hedging strategy. The chapter concluded with a discussion of how to measure the anticipated effectiveness of various hedging strategies. In the next chapter these concepts are used to develop specific hedging strategies.

QUESTIONS

1. What is meant by *price risk*?
2. What is quantity risk?
3. Why cannot a firm hedge its quantity risk with futures?
4. What is basis risk and why is it fundamental to evaluating a hedging strategy?
5. Why is a short (long) hedger said to be *long (short) the basis*? Relate changes in the algebraic value of the basis to gains and losses incurred by hedgers.
6. Is it true that when the value of the basis rises the basis always widens?
7. Explain the statement: "In general, the magnitude of the basis risk . . . will depend on the degree of correlation between cash and futures prices."
8. In Case 1 in Section 5.4.1, when the hedger shorts January 89 futures at 55.87 cents, why does he not lock-in a profit of $12,600 [($0.5587 − $0.5287) × 420,000]?
9. In the Case 2 in Section 5.5.2, did the long hedger lose money because of being short or long the basis? Explain.

10. Why is it usually true that the anticipated effectiveness of a hedge will be greater the higher the correlation between the price of the commodity being hedged and the price of the futures contract used to hedge the commodity?

11. Explain the statement: "Hedgers are said to be speculators on the basis."

12. You are considering hedging with one of two possible futures contracts, either X or Y. Futures X has a variance of daily prices of nine dollars, almost twice as high as the variance of cash prices, which is five dollars. Futures Y has a price variance of six dollars, much less than X. However, the correlation coefficient between cash prices and the prices of futures X is 0.90, whereas this correlation is only 0.60 with futures Y. Which futures contract, X or Y, would provide a more effective hedge?

SUGGESTED READING

Ederington, L. "The Hedging Performance of the New Futures Market." *Journal of Finance*, Vol. 34 (1979), pp. 157–170.

Kamara, A. and A. Siegal. "Optimal Hedging in Futures Markets with Multiple Delivery Specifications." *Journal of Finance*, September 1987, pp. 1007–1022.

Kawaller, I. "Hedging with Futures Contracts: Going the Extra Mile." *Journal of Cash Management*, July–August 1986, pp. 34–36.

Khoury, N. and P. Yourougou. "The Informational Content of the Basis: Evidence from Canadian Barley, Oats, and Canola Futures Markets." *The Journal of Futures Markets*, February 1991, pp. 69–80.

Toevs, A. and D. Jacob. "Futures and Alternative Hedge Ratio Methodologies." *Journal of Portfolio Management*, Spring 1986, pp. 60–70.

Working, H. "Hedging Reconsidered." *Journal of Farm Economics*, November 1953, pp. 544–561.

6

DEVISING
A HEDGING
STRATEGY

Now that we have covered the fundamentals of hedging, we can turn our attention to the concepts and principles involved in devising a specific hedging strategy. This chapter discusses how to select a futures contract with which to hedge, how to determine and calculate the optimal hedge ratio, and how to design and manage a hedging strategy. Finally, the chapter ends with a brief discussion of the legal and regulatory provisions applicable to hedgers, including the accounting and tax treatment of futures contracts which are part of a hedged position.

6.1 DECIDING ON THE FUTURES CONTRACT

A hedger faces two initial decisions: first, what kind of futures to use and, second, which contract month of that futures to use. Since the hedger will want to maximize hedging effectiveness, this means choosing a futures contract with prices that are highly correlated with the prices of the asset to be hedged (see Chapter 5, Section 5.7).

6.1.1 Which Futures Contract

When hedging an asset on which a futures contract is traded (such as gold or heating oil), it is almost always sensible to hedge with that contract, since futures and cash prices of the same commodity are generally highly correlated.

When hedging an asset on which *no futures contract is traded,* the choice is more difficult. An obvious starting point is to explore using a related commodity on

Cents per gallon

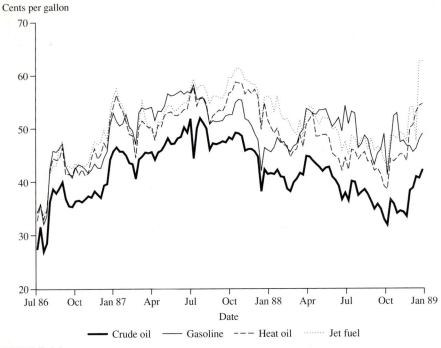

FIGURE 6-1

Jet fuel versus NYMEX energy futures: Jet fuel cash versus near month futures prices (weekly from July 1986 to December 1988).

which a futures is traded. Such a hedge is often referred to as a *cross-hedge.*[1] For example, which futures contract should be used to hedge the price risk associated with jet fuel:[2] heating oil futures, gasoline futures, crude oil futures, or perhaps some other entirely different futures? In general, we will want the past prices of the futures contract chosen not only to be correlated statistically with jet fuel prices but also to have a sensible economic relationship to jet fuel. For example, some of the demand and supply factors that affect jet fuel prices may also affect the prices of heating oil, gasoline, and crude oil—they are all part of the energy complex. In the absence of a rational economic relationship, we cannot have much confidence that a past statistical price relationship will continue into the future.

Figure 6-1 shows the relationships between weekly jet fuel cash prices and the weekly near-month futures prices for heating oil, crude oil, and gasoline.

---

[1]More generally, a *cross-hedge* is when futures on a product other than the deliverable grade of the particular commodity being hedged is used to hedge that commodity's price risk. It might involve a different quality of product, a different delivery location, or a different commodity entirely.

[2]There is no futures contract on jet fuel.

TABLE 6.1
Jet fuel cash prices versus various near month energy futures prices:
Correlations of price changes (daily from July 1986 to December 1988)

	1986–1988	1986	1987	1988
Heating oil futures	0.54	0.76	0.89	0.32
Gasoline futures	0.41	0.74	0.73	0.19
Crude oil futures	0.45	0.70	0.72	0.25

While there is a relationship between jet fuel prices and all three futures prices, the relationship between jet fuel prices and heating oil futures prices is closer than between jet fuel prices and either of the other two futures prices. Table 6.1 provides the respective correlation coefficients among daily prices for the entire period July 1986 to December 1988, as well as for individual years separately. The correlation between changes in jet fuel prices and changes in heating oil futures prices is the highest among the price correlation coefficients. Thus, of these futures contracts, heating oil futures is the best choice with which to cross-hedge jet fuel. (The correlation coefficient of 0.54, however, is not terribly high, and the individual year coefficients are also quite unstable, as the correlation coefficient of 0.32 for 1988 attests.)

6.1.2   Which Contract Month

Suppose that we have decided to hedge a cash heating oil commitment with heating oil futures because of the close relationship between these prices. There is still the question of which heating oil *contract month* to use. Table 6.2 shows correlation coefficients for changes in heating oil cash prices versus changes in the prices of heating oil futures contracts with different delivery dates, estimated with daily data for the entire 1987 year (252 business days). The prices of the near month contract are obviously the most highly correlated with cash prices.

TABLE 6.2
Heating oil prices: Cash versus various
futures contracts (correlations of price
changes and variances of the basis, daily
from January 1987 to December 1987)

	Cash versus futures	
	Correlation of price changes	Variance of basis
Spot month futures	0.89	0.29
Second month futures	0.83	1.17
Third month futures	0.79	3.86
Sixth month futures	0.71	16.94

Thus, using the near month futures contract will reduce basis risk (or the variance of the basis) the most. The basis risk variances associated with the respective contracts are also shown in Table 6.2. The variance of the basis increases as the price correlation between cash and futures prices decreases. Thus, hedging with the near month futures contract is preferrable because it minimizes the basis variation.

The principle of choosing the futures contract with the highest degree of price correlation, however, must be applied in the context of specific hedging situations. Suppose, for example, that an oil distributor enters into a forward agreement on July 6 to deliver oil in exactly six months (on December 6) at the prevailing cash price. An obvious long hedge of this short cash obligation is to purchase a commensurate number of January oil futures contracts, which call for delivery early in December (the first delivery day is in fact the exact date of the forward cash obligation, December 6). Since we can depend on futures and cash prices converging at delivery, there is no uncertainty about what the basis will be on December 6: zero. We also know the basis on July 6, when the hedge is put on. Thus, the basis change between the two dates, July 6 and December 6, is known with absolute certainty. There is, therefore, no basis risk. During this period, the basis may increase or decrease, depending on whether the market on July 6 is in contango or backwardation, but we will be certain about what will happen to the basis by December 6. Thus, *matching* cash and futures obligations in situations like these is another way of eliminating or minimizing basis risk. This strategy, of course, is available only if the duration of a hedger's cash obligations is fixed and known in advance, and there exists a matching future contract.

If there is uncertainty about when the hedger will have to perform his cash obligation (or, say, when his inventory will be sold), he will not be able to pursue a matching strategy but will want to hedge continuously. When hedging a continuous cash obligation for a long period of time, perhaps for several months, it is necessary to decide between two alternatives—hedging with a nearby futures and *rolling the hedge* forward; or hedging with a more distant futures contract, and rolling it less frequently. Using a more distant contract usually increases basis risk, since its price will be less correlated with cash market prices (see Table 6.2). But rolling the hedge often entails greater brokerage costs from having to buy and sell more futures contracts, and greater trading or execution costs from having to buy and sell more frequently. Although a general rule does not exist for deciding between these alternatives, in most cases hedgers prefer to hedge with a futures contract that has a high price correlation—in the above case, either with the near month or the second month contract. This decision minimizes basis risk.

6.2   THE HEDGE RATIO CONCEPT

The next decision for a hedger is to determine the optimal futures position to assume, or to determine the optimal *hedge ratio*. If, for example, the hedger wishes to minimize risk, he must take a futures position (i.e., the number of futures contracts times the quantity represented by each contract) that will result in the maximum possible reduction in the variability of the value of his total (hedged) position.

A general definition of a hedge ratio (HR) is

$$HR = \frac{Q_f}{Q_c}$$

where Q_f is the quantity (or units) of the commodity represented by the futures position, and Q_c is the quantity (or units) of the cash commodity that is being hedged. If, for example, a 300,000 gallon gasoline short futures position is taken to hedge a 400,000 gasoline cash position, the HR equals 0.75.

The hedge ratio that *minimizes risk* (HR^*) is defined as

$$HR^* = \frac{Q_f^*}{Q_c}$$

where Q_f^* is the quantity (or units) of futures that minimizes risk. To understand how the value of this ratio is determined, consider the following:

$$\Delta V_H = \Delta CP \times Q_c - \Delta FP \times Q_f^*$$

where ΔV_H is the change in value of the total hedged position, ΔCP is the change in the cash price, ΔFP is the change in the futures price, Q_c is the cash position, and Q_f^* is the futures position that minimizes risk. Both Q_c and Q_f^* are assumed to be constant for the life of the hedge. If the change in the value of the hedged position is set equal to zero (making variability equal to zero), then

$$\Delta CP \times Q_c = \Delta FP \times Q_f^*$$

and

$$\frac{\Delta CP}{\Delta FP} = \frac{Q_f^*}{Q_c}$$

Thus, since $HR^* = Q_f^*/Q_c$, the value of $HR^* = \Delta CP/\Delta FP$, or is equal to the ratio of the change in the cash price to the change in the futures price. For example, if when cash prices change by \$1, futures prices always change by \$1.25, the minimum-variance hedge ratio will be

$$HR^* = \frac{\$1.00}{\$1.25} = 0.80$$

This ratio can be used to determine the number of futures contracts with which to hedge. Our earlier equation for the minimum-risk hedge ratio (HR^*) can be restated as

$$Q_f^* = Q_c \times \frac{\Delta CP}{\Delta FP}$$

or as

$$Q_f^* = Q_c \times HR^*$$

but

$$Q_f^* = NFC^* \times Q_{fc}$$

where NFC^* is the number of futures contracts that minimizes risk, and Q_{fc} is the quantity (or units) of the commodity represented by each futures contract (for example, 42,000 gallons of heating oil per futures contract). Thus,

$$NFC^* \times Q_{fc} = Q_c \times HR^*$$

and

$$NFC^* = \frac{Q_c}{Q_{fc}} \times HR^*$$

This is the general formula used throughout the book to determine the number of futures contracts with which to hedge in order to achieve the minimum-variance hedge.

To illustrate how this formula is used, consider the example of hedging a long cash position of 420,000 gallons of jet fuel by selling heating oil futures. Assume that for every 50 cent change in the heating oil futures price there is a 35 cent change in the jet fuel cash prices. To establish the minimum-variance hedge, how many futures contracts should be sold? Using the above equations, we know that

$$HR^* = \frac{0.35}{0.50} = 0.70$$

Therefore

$$NFC^* = \frac{420{,}000 \text{ gallons}}{42{,}000 \text{ gallons}} \times 0.70 = 7$$

Thus, the minimum-variance hedge requires selling 7 contracts.

The hedge ratio is a key concept in hedging. Much of the discussion about hedging strategy focuses on how best to estimate and calculate this ratio. As we shall see, there are alternative ways to estimate it, depending on the types of futures contracts used, the particular hedging situation, and the hedger's objectives. These are the subjects of the sections which follow.

6.3   ESTIMATING THE HEDGE RATIO

To determine the number of futures contracts to hedge with, it is necessary to obtain an a priori estimate of the hedge ratio. Alternative methods are used to estimate this ratio, depending on the type of hedge. A discussion of some of these methods must be deferred until later chapters, since they are specific to particular types of futures contracts. For example, the *basis point* and *duration* methods are specific to interest rates futures, and are discussed in Chapters 11 and 12.

In this section two general estimation techniques are discussed which are useful in a wide variety of hedging situations: one is called the *naive* method, and the other is *regression analysis*.

Both procedures use historical price data to estimate the hedge ratio. No one can know with certainty what the relationship will be in the future between the cash and futures prices of the commodity being hedged. We can know only what the cash-futures price relationship has been in the past. Hedgers, therefore, commonly use historical price data to estimate the price relationship (or hedge ratio) that will (hopefully) prevail in the future.

6.3.1   The Naive Method

Let us return for the moment to our earlier example of hedging heating oil with heating oil futures. We selected heating oil futures, and in particular the near month contract, to hedge with because of the high correlation between past heating oil cash and near month futures prices.

Assume that it is now January 1, 1989, and a heating oil distributor in New York is considering hedging his inventory of oil for the next three months by selling near month heating oil futures. He is fearful that a sudden drop in cash prices will occur before he has the opportunity to sell his inventory, or before the end of the cold-weather heating season. He is presently holding an inventory of 2 million gallons of oil. How many futures contracts should he sell to protect fully this cash position?

To answer this question the distributor must estimate the minimum-variance hedge ratio: the value of the ratio of the expected change in the cash price to the expected change in the futures price over the next three months (the life of the hedge).

The distributor has two types of information: knowledge of current market conditions and a forecast of future market conditions; and, knowledge about what the relationship between cash and futures prices has been in the past. In this section we focus on using the latter—past price history—to estimate the cash-futures price relationship in the future.

Table 6.3 provides daily heating oil cash prices (column 1) and heating oil futures prices (column 2) during the last two months of 1988. The ratio of the daily price changes, ΔCash/ΔFutures, is shown in column 3. While this ratio varies from day to day, its mean value is 0.90, suggesting that it may be a reasonable approximation for the oil distributor to use a hedge ratio of one.

If a hedge ratio of one is used, the minimum-variance hedge will be a short position of 48 heating oil futures contracts:

$$\frac{2,000,000 \text{ gallons}}{42,000 \text{ gallons}} \times 1 = 47.6$$

If an exact one-to-one relationship were to occur in the future between cash and futures prices, this hedge would fully protect the distributor against a price decline: any decrease in the value of his cash inventory will be exactly matched by an in-

TABLE 6.3
Daily heating oil price changes: Cash versus near month
(November 2, 1988, to December 30, 1988)

	Cash	Futures	ΔCash/ΔFutures
	Cents per gallon	Cents per gallon	
	(1)	(2)	(3)
881101	43.00	43.17	0.45
881102	43.50	43.35	2.78
881103	44.35	44.32	0.88
881104	44.25	44.08	0.42
881107	44.15	44.13	−2.00
881108	43.50	43.53	1.08
881109	44.50	44.52	1.01
881110	44.00	43.88	0.78
881111	44.10	44.01	0.77
881114	44.10	44.63	0.00
881115	44.80	44.40	−3.04
881116	44.75	44.47	−0.71
881117	43.10	42.97	1.10
881118	42.75	42.76	1.67
881121	43.60	43.47	1.20
881122	45.60	45.44	1.02
881123	45.80	45.72	0.71
881128	48.75	48.65	1.01
881129	48.00	47.79	0.87
881130	48.50	48.32	0.94
881201	49.50	49.18	1.16
881202	48.85	48.96	2.95
881205	48.35	48.36	0.83
881206	48.60	48.60	1.04
881207	49.00	48.89	1.38
881208	48.25	48.08	0.93
881209	49.60	49.50	0.95
881212	50.35	50.20	1.07
881213	49.35	49.27	1.08
881214	51.25	51.13	1.02
881215	51.10	50.94	0.79
881216	52.00	52.02	0.83
881219	50.85	50.75	0.91
881220	50.50	51.47	−0.49
881221	51.25	51.92	1.67
881222	52.65	52.48	2.50
881223	53.25	53.14	0.91
881127	54.05	53.77	1.27
881228	53.62	53.49	1.54
881229	52.85	52.77	1.07
881230	53.85	53.48	1.41
Mean			0.90
Standard deviation			1.03

crease in the value of his futures position. (Readers should experiment with different price changes to verify this statement.)

Since many hedges are done with nearby futures traded on the same commodity that is being hedged, it is often reasonable to assume that the minimum-variance hedge ratio will be equal to one. An assumption that the minimum-variance hedge ratio is equal to one is called the *naive* hedging model. As we will see, however, using a hedge ratio of one can sometimes result in disastrous consequences for hedgers.

6.3.2 Regression Analysis

Another method used to estimate the minimum-variance hedge ratio is *regression analysis*. This technique is specifically constructed to provide the best linear relationship between two price series (or among any statistical series).

More specifically, regression analysis can be used to estimate the following equation for time series of price changes:

$$\Delta CP_t = \alpha + \beta \times \Delta FP_t + \varepsilon_t$$

where ΔCP_t are changes in cash prices, ΔFP_t are changes in futures prices, ε_t is a random error term, and α and β are the estimated coefficients. The statistical procedure used to estimate α and β is such that it guarantees that the sum of the squared error terms $(\Sigma \varepsilon_t^2)$ will be as small as possible (that there is no other linear relationship that can better describe the relationship between ΔCP_t and ΔFP_t).[3] Thus, regression analysis gives us an α and β that best depict the historical linear relationship between ΔCP_t and ΔFP_t. Further, it has been shown that estimates of β provide good approximations of minimum-variance hedge ratios (HR^*).[4]

Returning to our hypothetical heating oil distributor who wishes to hedge his inventory during the first three months of 1989, we estimated the above regression equation using daily cash and near month futures prices for all of 1988 and found

$$\Delta CP_t = 0.0029 + 0.8407 \times \Delta FP_t$$

$$(.025) \quad (.029) \qquad R^2 = 0.77$$

The estimates of α and β are, respectively, 0.0029 and 0.8407. Two commonly used statistical measures in regression analysis, the R^2 and the *standard error of estimate* (in parentheses beneath the estimated coefficients) are also shown.

---

[3]The error term can be restated as

$$\varepsilon_t = \Delta CP_t - (\alpha + \beta \times \Delta FP_t)$$

[4]See Louis Ederington, "The Hedging Performance of the New Futures Market," *Journal of Finance*, March 1979, pp. 157–70. He shows that $HR^* = $ Cov $(\Delta CP, \Delta FP)/\sigma^2(\Delta FP)$, where Cov$(\Delta CP, \Delta FP)$ is the covariance between the cash and futures price changes. This is also the definition of the estimated β in the above regression equation.

R^2 is a measure of the *goodness of fit* of the regression line. It measures the proportion of the total variation in the dependent variable (ΔCP_t) that is explained by movements in the independent variable (ΔFP_t). R^2 has a value between zero and one: an R^2 closer to one denotes a better fit of the regression line. The *standard error of estimate* is used to determine the reliability (or the statistical significance) of the estimated coefficients, by calculating the "*t*-statistic" and determining its significance. In the above equation, the value of α is not statistically different from zero, but the value of β is significantly different from one (as well as from zero).[5] In addition, the R^2 is high, indicating a close relationship between cash and futures prices.[6]

If the estimate of β, 0.84, is taken as the best estimate of HR^*, the distributor's minimum-variance hedge is

$$\frac{2,000,000 \text{ gallons}}{42,000 \text{ gallons}} \times 0.84 = 39.99$$

or about 40 contracts (compared with the 48 contracts calculated using a hedge ratio of 1).

While regression analysis is widely used to estimate HR^*, it must be used with caution. There are often complex statistical issues to be resolved, and there are always important judgements to be made. An extremely important decision involves the choice of data to use in estimating the regression equation. For example, in the foregoing hedging example, should the distributor have used daily oil prices for the entire 1988 year to estimate the regression equation (as we did), or prices for more than one year, or only prices for specific months or seasons? Making these judgements requires knowledge about the particular industry (heating oil in this case). Is there a seasonality in the price relationship? Are price relationships reasonably constant (or predictable) from year to year, month to month, and so on? Do particular market conditions indicate that there will be an unusual price relationship in the future? In sum, statistical analysis must be combined with knowledge of the industry and the markets involved to obtain the best hedging results.

Heating oil provides a good example of how estimates of HR^* can vary when the foregoing regression equation is estimated for different periods. Using data for a longer time period, November 1, 1986, to March 31, 1989, the estimate of β is 0.87, somewhat higher than our previous estimate of 0.84. Further, when the

---

[5]For example, if we want to test the hypothesis that the estimated $\beta(0.8407)$ is equal to the naive hedge ratio of one, the *t*-statistic is derived as:

(estimated coefficient − hypothesized parameter value of one)/ standard error of estimated coefficient

In the above case, $t = (0.8407 - 1)/0.029 = -5.49$. As a rule of thumb, if the computed *t*-statistic is greater than 1.96 or less than −1.96, we can reject the tested hypothesis at a 95% confidence level. Thus, in this case the estimated minimum-variance hedge ratio is not statistically equal to the naive hedge ratio of one. In addition, the estimated β is significantly different from zero. The relevant *t*-statistic is $28.99[(0.8407 - 0)/0.029]$.

[6]Ederington shows that R^2 is also a measure of ex ante hedging effectiveness, which was discussed in Chapter 5, Section 5.7.

equation is estimated for the three separate heating season sub-periods (October 1, 1986 to March 31, 1987; October 1, 1987, to March 31, 1988; and, October 1, 1988, to March 31, 1989), the respective estimated βs are 0.86, 0.92, and 0.90. An average of these three estimates is 0.89. Thus, since the distributor wishes to hedge for January through February (during the heating season), it may be preferable to use a hedge ratio of 0.89 instead of 0.84, in which case he would sell 43 rather than 40 futures contracts. (Readers should verify this calculation.)

6.4 EX ANTE HEDGE RATIOS VERSUS EX POST HEDGING RESULTS: AN EXAMPLE

Assuming we have done our best to predict the hedge ratio for the life of a hedge we are planning (or the ex ante hedge ratio), let us see how actual hedging results using this ratio compare to the results that would have occurred had we not hedged. There is no way to be certain, of course, about how well our hedge will do. Market conditions vary, and unusual events occur. However, in general, we should expect the hedge to reduce the losses we would have suffered had we not hedged.

Consider the following example. On December 1, 1987, an oil distributor enters into a forward contract to deliver 420,000 gallons of heating oil on the sixteenth day of each of the next six months (or, in the event of a holiday, on the next business day of the month after the sixteenth day). The sales price for each delivery that is agreed to is 51.50 cents a gallon. The prevailing cash price is 52.50 cents per gallon.

The distributor believes that cash prices will fall over the next six months, as the weather becomes warmer and demand falls. He therefore plans to buy the oil needed to meet his deliveries immediately before each delivery date, avoiding all storage costs. He will have to pay whatever the cash price happens to be at these times.

To protect himself against the possibility that cash oil prices may rise (instead of fall as he expects), which could impose substantial losses on him, the distributor decides to hedge using heating oil futures. He estimates a regression equation similar to the one reported and discussed earlier, except that he uses daily price data for only the first eleven months of 1987 (since by assumption it is now December 1, 1987). His regression results, let us assume, indicate that the minimum-variance hedge ratio is approximately equal to 1 ($\beta = 1$).

The distributor, therefore, hedges with a long *strip* of futures contracts in the amounts necessary to minimize his risk. Specifically, he immediately takes long futures positions that are synchronized with his forward delivery obligations: 10 January 88 futures contracts at 52.00 cents per gallon to cover the December delivery; 10 February 88 futures at 51.41 cents to cover the January delivery; and 10 March 88 at 48.96 cents, 10 April 88 at 46.83 cents, 10 May 88 at 45.58 cents, and 10 June 88 at 44.58 cents to cover subsequent deliveries—60 contracts overall.

Table 6.4 provides the results of this hedging strategy, along with the results had the distributor not hedged at all. Column 1 is the cash prices of heating

TABLE 6.4
Example of strip hedge using heating oil futures (hedge ratio = 1)

	Cash position				Futures position			Hedged result
	Market price $ (1)	Sales $ (2)	Cost $ (3)	Profit (loss) $ (4)	Entry point $ (5)	Exit point $ (6)	Profit (loss) $ (7)	Profit (loss) $ (8)
Dec 16, 1987	0.5030	216,300	211,260	5,040	0.5200	0.4927	(11,466)	(6,426)
Jan 18, 1988	0.5105	216,300	214,410	1,890	0.5141	0.5071	(2,940)	(1,050)
Feb 16, 1988	0.4790	216,300	201,180	15,120	0.4896	0.4637	(10,878)	4,242
Mar 16, 1988	0.4625	216,300	194,250	22,050	0.4683	0.4408	(11,550)	10,500
Apr 18, 1988	0.5275	216,300	221,550	(5,250)	0.4558	0.5050	20,664	15,414
May 16, 1988	0.5175	216,300	217,350	(1,050)	0.4488	0.4798	13,020	11,970
Mean				6,300				5,775
Standard deviation				9,437				7,653

oil on the respective delivery days, when the distributor actually purchased oil to deliver; column 2 is the total sales revenue from each delivery (for example, $0.5150 \times 420,000$ gallons); column 3 is the total cost of acquiring the oil to deliver [column $1 \times 420,000$ gallons]; and column 4 is the net profit or loss from the delivery, assuming no hedging.

Assuming that he hedges, the results of the distributor's futures transactions can be found in columns 5–7. Column 5 is the respective purchase prices on December 1 for each of the 10-contract futures positions; column 6 is the futures prices prevailing when each of the futures positions is lifted or offset; and column 7 is the profit or loss resulting from these futures transactions. Finally, column 8 is the net profit or loss on the *hedged* position [column 4 + column 7].

Figure 6-2 graphs the monthly cash flows of both the unhedged and hedged positions (columns 4 and 8). It is clear that the cash flows of the hedged position are more stable. The hedge succeeds in reducing variability in cash flow: the standard deviation falls from $9437 to $7653 (see Table 6.4). This is an 18.90 percent reduction in volatility. However, it is equally clear that it does not eliminate all exposure to price risk. Why? Was not the hedge ratio that was used ($\beta = 1$) the minimum-variance hedge ratio?

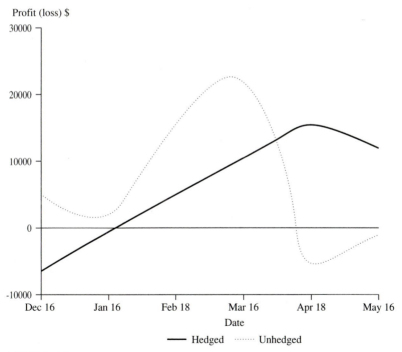

FIGURE 6-2
Monthly cash flows: Strip hedge using heating oil futures (hedge ratio = 1; December 87 to May 88).

The answer to this question is twofold: First, even if the ex ante estimate of β turned out to be exactly equal to the value of β that would be obtained using ex post price data (daily data from December 1, 1987, to May 16, 1988 — the time period of the hedge), putting the hedge on and taking it off on specific days involves basis risk. There is no way to eliminate such risk. Second, the distributor's use of a hedge ratio of one (or the ex ante estimate of $\beta = 1$) was not the best hedge ratio that could have been used to reduce risk had we had perfect foresight.

This is demonstrated in Table 6.5, which shows the different means and standard deviations for the cash flows generated by the hedging example displayed in Table 6.4, assuming *alternative* hedge ratios. In particular, it shows that, ex post, the minimum-variance hedge ratio turned out to be equal to 0.60. If the distributor had used a hedge ratio of 0.60, rather than 1.00, the standard deviation of his net

TABLE 6.5
Extension of hedging results shown in Table 6.4, using alternative hedge ratios

| Hedge ratio | Cash position | | Hedged position | |
	Mean* $	Standard deviation† $	Mean* $	Standard deviation† $
$\beta = 1.10$	6,300	9,437	5,723	8,580
$\beta = 1.05$	6,300	9,437	5,749	8,104
$\beta = 1.00$	6,300	9,437	5,775	7,653
$\beta = 0.95$	6,300	9,437	5,801	7,230
$\beta = 0.90$	6,300	9,437	5,827	6,842
$\beta = 0.85$	6,300	9,437	5,854	6,494
$\beta = 0.80$	6,300	9,437	5,880	6,193
$\beta = 0.75$	6,300	9,437	5,906	5,945
$\beta = 0.70$	6,300	9,437	5,932	5,760
$\beta = 0.65$	6,300	9,437	5,958	5,641
$\beta = 0.60‡$	6,300	9,437	5,985	5,594
$\beta = 0.55$	6,300	9,437	6,011	5,620
$\beta = 0.50$	6,300	9,437	6,037	5,718
$\beta = 0.45$	6,300	9,437	6,064	5,885
$\beta = 0.40$	6,300	9,437	6,090	6,115
$\beta = 0.35$	6,300	9,437	6,116	6,400
$\beta = 0.30$	6,300	9,437	6,143	6,736
$\beta = 0.25$	6,300	9,437	6,168	7,113
$\beta = 0.20$	6,300	9,437	6,195	7,526
$\beta = 0.15$	6,300	9,437	6,221	7,969
$\beta = 0.10$	6,300	9,437	6,248	8,438
$\beta = 0.05$	6,300	9,437	6,274	8,928
$\beta = 0.00$	6,300	9,437	6,300	9,437

* Mean of monthly profits

† Standard deviation of monthly profits

‡ Minimum-variance hedge ratio

cash flows would have been reduced to $5594. This would have been a 40.72 percent reduction in volatility, instead of an 18.90 percent reduction. Even a hedge ratio of 0.60, however, would not have eliminated all variance in net cash flows because of the existence of basis variation.

Table 6.5 also shows what can happen if a position is *over-hedged*: when a hedge ratio greater than the ex post minimun-variance hedge ratio ($\beta = .60$) is used. As the hedge ratio is increased (from 0.60 to 1.10), risk (or the standard deviation) increases (from $5594 to $8580) while average profits fall (from $5985 to $5723). When a position is overhedged, the hedger actually has two positions: a *hedged cash* position, and a *speculative futures* position. The speculative futures position may result in either higher or lower profits, depending upon actual price movements. In this case it results in lower profits. In all cases, however, an overhedged position will result in greater risk.[7]

In summary, careful thought must be given to devising a hedging strategy. A key component is estimating an ex ante minimum-variance hedge ratio that closely approximates the ex post minimum-variance hedge ratio. This requires accurately predicting the relationship between cash and futures prices that will prevail during the life of the hedge.

6.5 HEDGING OBJECTIVES

So far we have discussed hedging strategies that have as their only objective minimizing risk. Hedgers, however, may be willing to assume more risk in order to earn greater profits. Eliminating all price risk often means eliminating all profit, a condition that most businesses cannot tolerate for long. Hedgers, therefore, may want to use a hedge ratio other than the minimum-variance hedge ratio—or consciously to underhedge.

The decision as to how much to hedge will depend upon a hedger's risk preference. The less he hedges the more risk he assumes. In addition, a hedger who has strong beliefs about the future direction of price movements may alter his hedging strategy to reflect those beliefs. (A speculator is someone who holds such beliefs and is unhedged.)

Table 6.5 illustrates the trade-off between profits and risk reduction through hedging. Using the hedging example presented in Table 6.4, Table 6.5 shows the changes in both profits and risk (measured as the standard deviation of cash flows) that are associated with the use of different hedge ratios. A completely unhedged position ($\beta = 0$) results in a profit of $6300 and a standard deviation of $9437. As the hedge is increased, or the hedge ratio is raised from 0 to 0.60 (the ex post minimum-variance hedge ratio), both the standard deviation and profits decrease. Risk is reduced but at the cost of lost profits.

---

[7]Since the volatility of futures prices is often greater than the volatility of cash prices, underhedging is often more efficient than overhedging.

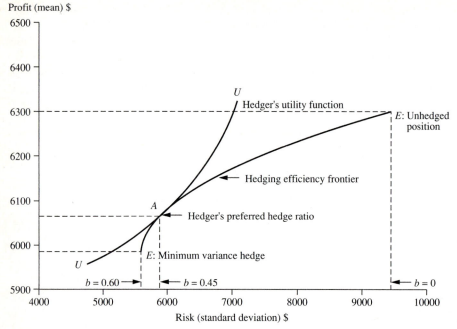

Profit (mean) $

FIGURE 6-3
The optimal hedge ratio.

Thus, a hedger is confronted with a trade-off between risk and return. He must choose the risk and return combination that he most desires (or, in the jargon, that he finds *optimal*). The values he places on changes in risk versus changes in profits will determine his decision. In no case, however, will a hedger knowingly choose a hedge ratio greater than 0.60, since by doing so he will increase risk without any commensurate increase in profits. In Table 6.5, for example, every level of standard deviation (risk) achieved with a hedge ratio between 0.60 and 1.10 can also be achieved with a hedge ratio between 0.05 and 0.60, but with higher profits as well. An obvious pitfall, therefore, is for a hedger to choose a hedge ratio higher than the minimum-variance hedge ratio: to overhedge. This results in a highly speculative futures position having an uncertain outcome.

Figure 6-3 illustrates more generally the hedger's choice of the optimal hedge ratio: the one that maximizes his utility. Line *EE* represents the hedging *efficiency frontier:* the most efficient combinations of risk and return that can be achieved by varying the hedge ratio.[8] Line *UU* represents the highest level of utility that

---

[8]An efficient combination is one with the highest profit for a given risk. In Table 6.5, hedge ratios between 0 and 0.60 are efficient. Diagramatically, the risk-return combinations for hedge ratios between 0.60 and 1.10 would sketch out a line everywhere below EE in Figure 6-3.

the hedger can achieve by hedging (or by being on the efficient frontier *EE*). The slope of *UU* represents how the hedger values changes in risk relative to changes in profits. Point *A*, where *UU* and *EE* touch (or are tangent), indicates the hedger's optimal hedge ratio ($\beta = 0.45$). This hedge strategy yields a profit of $6064 and a standard deviation of $5885, which yields the highest level of utility to the hedger.[9] Thus, either remaining completely unhedged ($\beta = 0$) or adopting the minimum-variance hedge ($\beta = 0.60$) would yield lower utility to this hedger than would a hedge ratio of 0.45.

6.6 IMPROVING PERFORMANCE THROUGH AGGRESSIVE HEDGING STRATEGIES

Previous discussion has shown that primary causes of poor hedging performance are basis risk and instability of the hedge ratio. In this section we discuss hedging strategies that are used to overcome these problems.

6.6.1 Making Use of Basis Relationships

Rather than viewing basis variation as a random and unpredictable variable, we may be able to make use of what is known about basis variation. First, we know that the basis will narrow because of *convergence*. As delivery on a futures contract approaches, the futures price converges to the cash price, narrowing the basis. This was shown in Figure 5-1 for heating oil. Second, given a constant interest rate, there is a negative bound on the basis (Cash − Futures): it is unusual for futures prices to exceed cash prices by more than the cost-of-carry, either for very long or by very much (arbitrage prevents it).[10] Third, there is no upper (or positive) bound on the basis: at times markets can be in substantial backwardation (futures prices are lower than cash prices). Finally, for many commodities there is a seasonal in the basis which, while not totally predictable, can often be utilized in managing basis risk.

Figure 6-4 shows the basis variation for heating oil during the years 1985 to 1989. It is clear that some time in the fall the basis normally turns from negative to positive (although this did not occur in 1986 for the February 87 contract).

---

[9]At point *A* there is also a tangency between *UU* and *EE*: the slopes of the two lines are identical. This means that, with a hedge ratio of 0.45, the marginal rates of substitution between risk and return are identical for both the *UU* and *EE* functions.

[10]If carrying costs were to increase, of course, the basis would become more negative. The major determinant of carrying costs is the interest rate level. If interest rates rise, therefore, the basis will become more negative. However, as we will see later in the book, hedgers can protect against an unexpected rise in interest rates in several ways—by taking a short position in interest rates futures, for example. Thus, the general principles of managing basis discussed here are applicable in a world where interest rates and carrying costs are changing.

Cents per gallon

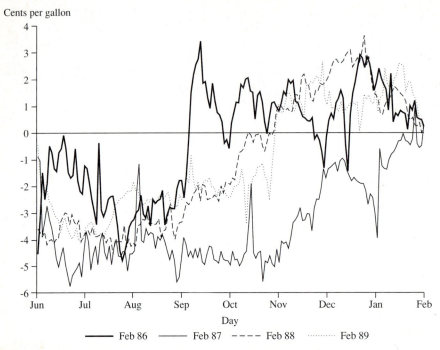

FIGURE 6-4
Basis: February heating oil futures contracts (Feb 86, Feb 87, Feb 88, Feb 89) during the years 1985–86, 1986–87, 1987–88, and 1988–89.

This reflects expectations that, subsequent to the peak demand for heating oil during the winter months, prices will fall toward the end of the cold-weather season as demand slackens. However, the behavior of the February 87 futures basis shows that hedgers still have to monitor market conditions closely and not rely simply on historical price patterns.

How can these basis relationships be used to improve hedging performance? Consider first a short hedge: a short futures position used to hedge a long cash position. Such a hedge will perform better if the basis becomes less negative (Figures 5-2a and 5-2c) or more positive (Figures 5-3b and 5-3d),[11] and will perform worse if the basis becomes more negative (Figures 5-2b and 5-2d) or less positive (Figures 5-3c and 5-3a). The best time to put a short hedge on, therefore, is when futures and cash prices are in a carry relationship (contango), since at that time the basis is negative but is likely to become less negative (or even positive) as price changes occur. (At the very least, the basis will approach zero as the delivery date approaches.)

---

[11]Figures 5-2a to 5-3d provide graphical presentations of these basis relationships.

For a long hedger, who is long futures and effectively short a cash position, the opposite is true. He will benefit if the basis becomes more negative (Figures 5-2b and 5-2d) or less positive (Figures 5-3a and 5-3c), and will suffer if the basis becomes more positive (Figures 5-2a and 5-2c) or less negative (Figures 5-3b and 5-3d). Thus, he will want to put his hedge on in a backwardation market, when the basis is quite positive. This puts him in the best position to benefit from futures changes in the basis. It is important, however, for long hedgers to keep in mind that there is no limit to how positive the basis can become (or to the extent of backwardation). Unpredictable market conditions, such as unanticipated commodity shortages, can cause backwardation to increase sharply.[12]

In addition, when there is a recognizable seasonal pattern in the basis, hedgers may be able to take advantage of it. Figure 6-4, for example, shows a clear seasonality in the heating oil basis: the basis becomes more positive as the heating season (November through March) approaches. At these times, long hedgers are adversely affected while short hedgers benefit. Thus, long hedgers may want to avoid putting on futures positions at such times, or to adjust their hedging strategies to compensate for the adverse basis movement. Short hedgers, in contrast, will want to take advantage of a seasonal move into greater backwardation by putting on positions just prior to the move.

In summary, hedgers can explore historical basis relationships to determine possible seasonalities and to identify basis ranges that have been typical in past years. A basis that is outside the normal bounds may provide an opportunity to improve hedging performance.

The objective of doing *basis hedging*, therefore, is to supplement the basic hedge ratio analysis presented earlier with timing decisions based on predictable basis changes. If these predictions prove to be reasonably accurate, hedging will result in both greater reduction of risk and greater profits. To obtain these benefits, however, hedgers will have to time their hedges, which may require them to remain unhedged for some periods of time. Thus, the added risk of being unhedged must be weighed against the benefits of basis hedging.

Finally, it may be possible to hedge basis variation itself. Often the basis between cash and nearby futures positions is highly correlated with the spread (or price differential) between nearby and distant futures prices. When this is true, a spread position can be used to offset the basis risk in a hedge. Figure 6-5 shows an example of the relationship between the heating oil basis (cash minus near month futures) and a heating oil spread (second month futures minus third month futures). In this case, the more distant spread does not provide a very good hedge of the basis variation.[13]

---

[12]In August 1989, for example, a strike of Peruvian copper miners caused an expectation of an impending copper shortage, sending copper futures prices into deep backwardation (*The New York Times,* August 15, 1989, page D-1, column 1).

[13]For some other commodities there is a closer relationship between the basis and distant spread.

Cents per gallon

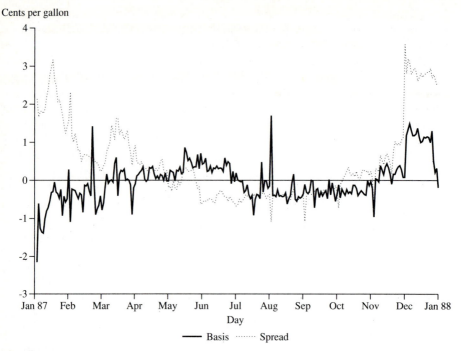

FIGURE 6-5
Heating oil: Basis versus spread (daily from January 1987 to December 1987).

6.6.2 Adjusting for an Unstable Hedge Ratio

In some cases a hedging strategy that uses a constant hedge ratio over the life of the hedge may perform quite poorly. Careful estimation of the minimum-variance hedge ratio may reveal systematic changes in this ratio that can be incorporated into a hedging strategy.

Suppose that it is now January 1989, and that an oil distributor is considering hedging his entire jet fuel inventory with near month heating oil futures. He anticipates having a hedge on for the entire 1989 year, adjusting it periodically to match changes in his inventory. To obtain an estimate of the minimum-variance hedge ratio, he estimates the following regression equation using daily data for 1988:

$$\Delta JET_t = \alpha + \beta \times \Delta HEAT_t + \varepsilon_t$$

where ΔJET_t are daily changes of jet fuel cash prices and $\Delta HEAT_t$ are daily changes of near month heating oil futures prices. The estimate of β is 0.66. Thus, to reduce his risk exposure as much as possible for the entire 1989 year, the distributor devises a hedging strategy for the entire year using a constant hedge ratio of 0.66.

TABLE 6.6
Estimated hedge ratios for individual months (jet fuel cash versus heating oil near month futures using daily data from 1986 to 1988)

Month	Hedge ratio
January	0.69
February	0.74
March	0.51
April	0.48
May	0.43
June	0.60
July	0.79
August	0.63
September	0.82
October	0.60
November	0.53
December	0.85

Suppose, however, that the foregoing regression equation were estimated for each month separately. These results are shown in Table 6.6.[14] The estimated monthly hedge ratios range from a low of 0.43 to a high of 0.85, and are quite variable from month to month. Thus, using a constant-hedge ratio of 0.66 may result in poor hedging performance month-to-month: in some months the distributor may incur substantial net losses.

An alternative hedging strategy is for the distributor to adjust his hedge ratio from time to time—in this case, from month to month. For example, in Janaury he could use the estimated January hedge ratio of 0.69 to determine his futures position; in February a hedge ratio of 0.74; in March a ratio of 0.51; and so forth.

Assume that the oil distributor has to maintain an inventory of 4,200,000 gallons of jet fuel for the first six months of 1989. Using a constant hedge ratio of 0.66, he would sell 66 February futures contracts in January (4,200,000 gallons/42,000 gallons × 0.66). On January 31, 1989 (the last trading day for the February contract), he would *roll* the 66 February contracts into 66 March contracts (i.e., buy February futures and sell March futures), and so forth. An alternative strategy is for the distributor to adjust his hedge ratio each month. He would take a short position in January of 69 contracts in the February futures (4,200,000 gallons/42,000 gallons × 0.69), in February a short position of 74 March contracts, and so forth.

---

[14] The monthly estimates shown in Table 6.6 are estimated using pooled time-series data over the three-year period 1986–1988. In the appendix to this chapter, separate year estimates are also shown. There clearly exists considerable instability in these estimates.

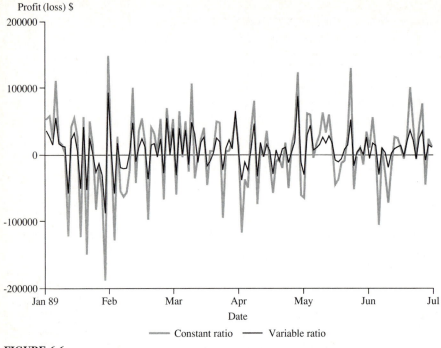

FIGURE 6-6
Daily cash flows: Constant versus variable hedge ratio (hedging jet fuel with near month heating oil futures from January 1989 to June 1989).

Figure 6-6 depicts the daily gains (losses) associated with the two hedging strategies: the constant-hedge-ratio versus the variable-hedge-ratio strategy. Using actual cash and futures prices for the first six months of 1989, Figure 6-6 shows that the variable-hedge-ratio strategy results in less volatile cash flows than does the constant-hedge-ratio strategy. Table 6.7 summarizes the hedging

TABLE 6.7
Constant hedge versus variable hedge ratio: Hedging jet fuel cash using near month heating oil futures (average daily gain (loss) from January 1989 to June 1989)

	Daily gain (loss)	
Position	**Average $**	**Standard deviation $**
Constant hedge ratio = 0.66	(4,576)	58,217
Variable hedge ratio	(2,040)	27,648

performance of these two strategies. Compared to the constant-hedge-ratio, the variable-hedge-ratio strategy reduces the average daily loss and the standard deviation (volatility) by more than 50 percent. Since the objective of the hedge was to reduce risk, the lower standard deviation of daily gains and losses for the variable-hedge-ratio strategy indicates that this strategy is superior to the constant-hedge-ratio strategy.

Gains from adjusting a hedge position in this manner must, of course, be weighed against additional transaction costs that may be incurred. It is also possible that estimated hedge ratios may be so unstable that any hedging strategy is unduely risky. This is a judgement hedgers must make before embarking on a hedging program.

6.7 OUTPUT UNCERTAINTY

In many instances, firms (such as grain and soybean producers) may want to hedge prior to knowing the magnitude of their output (or before knowing the size of their crop). Hedging with a futures position that ex post turns out to be either greater or less than the firm's actual output may result in its net revenue being significantly different from that anticipated, even if all of its expectations about prices are borne out. This is a *quantity* risk that hedgers must face.

The best way to eliminate this risk, of course, is to make accurate forecasts of future production. There is, therefore, a considerable payoff to efforts devoted to making forecasts of future production more accurate. If significant forecast errors are likely, hedgers may do two things: not hedge at all, or adjust their hedge ratios to reflect the output uncertainty. There is, however, no clear procedure for adjusting hedge ratios for output uncertainty.

In some industries rules-of-thumb for making these adjustments have emerged. In agriculture, the rule of *hedging only one-half to two-thirds of expected production* has become commonplace.[15] (Other industries follow different guidelines.) This rule suggests that hedgers should use a hedge ratio lower than the minimum-variance hedge ratio: they should *underhedge*. As we showed earlier in Table 6.5, underhedging results in the hedger remaining on the *hedging efficiency frontier.*

Thus, in the face of significant output uncertainty, a general rule is to use a hedge ratio lower than the minimum-variance hedge ratio (calculated on the basis of the expected output level). However, this is a decision that requires careful consideration in the context of specific hedging circumstances.

---

[15]See, for example, Stephen E. Miller and Kandice H. Kahl, "Performance of Estimated Hedge Ratios Under Yield Uncertainty," *The Journal of Futures Markets*, 9(4): 307–21, 1989.

6.8 MARGINS AND CASH FLOW CONSIDERATIONS

Even a fully hedged position can result in adverse cash flows because of variation margins. As we saw earlier, futures positions are marked-to-market daily. If a price move results in a loss on the futures position, the hedger will have to pay cash (or at least put up Treasury bills) to cover these losses. While the hedger may simultaneously have an offsetting unrealized gain on his cash position, this gain will not result in a compensating cash inflow. For example, a hedger's inventory may appreciate in value because of rising prices, but until it is sold the inventory does not generate an increased cash inflow. Thus, hedgers must be prepared to meet cash demands due to variation margin calls. A gain on the futures position, of course, will result in increased cash *inflows*, which can be invested.

Hedgers, therefore, must be prepared to manage the cash flows associated with hedging. Arranging borrowing facilities to provide funds when needed is an obvious precaution. Having to borrow funds to meet margin calls is another cost of hedging. However, in many cases this cost is offset by the returns on the invested cash inflows generated by favorable price movements.

6.9 MANAGING THE HEDGE

Once a hedge has been established it is important to have in place a system for monitoring it and making adjustments. There also needs to be a systematic evaluation of the effectiveness of the hedge relative to its anticipated (or ex ante measure of) effectiveness. If the hedge has not been successful, the reasons should be identified and steps should be taken to improve hedge effectiveness in the future.

6.9.1 Monitoring the Hedge

In order to monitor the hedge effectively, the following information should be made available on an up-to-date basis:

1. Cash position: The current size of the (cash) position being hedged, how it has changed since the initiation of the hedge, and the dollar gains and losses on this position to date.
2. Futures position: The size of the futures position, and the dollar gains and losses on this position to date.
3. Margins: The total amount of funds dedicated to margin requirements, net financing costs to date, and the adequacy of funding arrangements to meet future margin calls.
4. Basis movements: Changes in the basis should be tracked to see if they are consistent with a priori expectations.
5. New information: As new price data become available, hedge ratios should be recomputed to determine if the hedge ratio being used is consistent with past price relationships.

6.9.2 Adjustments to the Hedge

During the life of a hedge various adjustments may be made, some of which we discussed earlier:

1. **Changes in risk exposure:** If the size of the cash position being hedged changes, the size of the hedging futures position should be changed as well.
2. **Changes in hedge ratio:** During the life of the hedge it may be more effective to change the futures position periodically to reflect known or anticipated changes in the cash-futures price relationship.
3. **New hedging goals:** As new information becomes available, hedgers may change their forecasts and goals; if they prefer more or less risk, hedging strategies should be changed accordingly.
4. **Basis management:** As the basis changes, opportunities may arise for hedgers to take advantage of anticipated basis movements; futures positions may be changed from one contract month to another, and so forth.
5. **Rolling the hedge:** For some hedging strategies it will be necessary to lift periodically futures positions in some months and simultaneously initiate them in other months, or to switch from less liquid to more liquid contract months.

6.9.3 Hedge Evaluation

The final aspect of good hedge management is to evaluate how prior hedging strategies have worked and to determine whether they can be improved. With respect to the goal of reducing risk, an ex post measure of effectiveness is

$$1 - \frac{\text{Variance (gains or losses in hedged position)}}{\text{Variance (gains or losses in unhedged cash position)}}$$

The closer this value is to one, the more successful is the hedge.

This measure should be compared to the earlier a priori measure of hedging effectiveness (see Section 5.5.7), which is estimated prior to putting on the hedge. If there is a significant difference between the ex ante (or anticipated) hedging effectiveness and the ex post hedge effectiveness, we should determine what went wrong. Was our hedge ratio wrong? Did we fail to make obvious hedge adjustments? And so forth.

Finally, the overall cost of the hedging program should be calculated and evaluated to determine the hedger's cost-effectiveness. Brokerage fees, trading costs, and management costs are examples of such expenses. Hedging should then be compared with alternative risk management strategies.

6.10 LEGAL ASPECTS OF HEDGING

Before engaging in a hedging program it is important for firms to be sure that their futures transactions will be recognized as bona fide hedges under the various laws that might apply to them. In particular, such transactions may be exempt from certain laws (or restrictions) or may be eligible for preferred treatment under other laws or regulations.

For example, Section 4a of the Commodity Exchange Act authorizes the Commodity Futures Trading Commission (CFTC) to impose position limits on futures traders, restricting the size of the futures positions that they may hold. These limits are intended to prevent excessive speculation and market congestion (or manipulation). However, bona fide hedging positions are exempt from these limits. Similarly, exchanges commonly impose lower margins on hedgers than on speculators. It is, therefore, advantageous to be a hedger.

The CFTC generally recognizes as bona fide hedging transactions futures positions that have as their purpose the offsetting of price risks incidental to commercial cash market transactions: when fluctuations in the value of the futures position substantially offset changes in the value of the actual or anticipated cash position.[16] This definition is quite general and leaves hedgers with considerable discretion. However, if challenged, hedgers must be prepared to demonstrate the risk-reducing properties of their futures transactions.

Banks, insurance companies, pension funds, money managers, and other regulated entities that commonly use futures to hedge must also be sure that their futures transactions qualify as bona fide hedges under the laws that pertain specifically to them. In particular, hedging transactions are often governed by different accounting principles and by different tax laws than are cash transactions.

6.11   ACCOUNTING FOR FUTURES TRANSACTIONS AND HEDGING POSITIONS

In August 1984, the Financial Accounting Standard Board (FASB) issued Statement No. 80 (FAS 80), "Accounting for Futures Contracts," which provides accounting guidelines for all types of commodity and financial futures contracts (except foreign currency futures).[17]

Statement No. 80 applies both to speculative and hedging futures positions. However, since accounting for speculative positions is relatively simple, most of FAS 80 describes how to account for futures contracts that are being used as hedging instruments. In general, Statement No. 80 requires all futures contracts to be marked to market, consistent with the daily cash settlement requirements imposed by futures exchanges. Increases and decreases in market value must be included in income as they occur *unless* the contract meets certain

---

[16]Regulation 1.3; 17 C.F.R. §1.3.

[17]FAS 80 does not apply to foreign currency futures, forward placements, or option contracts. Accounting for foreign currency futures is covered by FAS 50. The important differences between the two statements are the accounting treatments for the following items: hedges of anticipated transactions, cross-hedging, accounting for gains and losses on hedge transactions, accounting for premium and discounts, and risk assessments.

specified hedge criteria. If these criteria are met, changes in a futures contract's market value can generally be deferred.

6.11.1 Hedge Accounting Principles

Statement No. 80 recognizes two types of hedges: an existing position hedge, and an anticipatory hedge. A futures position that protects against a loss that may result from owning an asset, having a liability, or having a firm forward commitment is a *hedge of an existing position*. A futures position which locks in the price, yield, or interest rate related to a transaction expected to occur in the future is an *anticipatory hedge*.

6.11.2 Hedges of Existing Assets, Liabilities, and Firm Commitments

THE HEDGE CRITERIA. A futures contract that reduces the risk associated with an existing position or a firm future commitment must meet the following criteria to qualify as a valid hedge for accounting purposes:

1. **There must be risk exposure.**
   The position being hedged must expose the company to price risk. Such risk is defined as the sensitivity of a company's income for one or more future periods to changes in the market prices (or yields) of existing assets, liabilities, firm forward commitments, or anticipated transactions. Companies are required to identify and assess such risk using an *enterprise perspective* rather than a *transaction perspective*. This requires the company to evaluate whether its potential risk exposure in one asset (or at one location) is mitigated by an offsetting position in another asset (or by conditions at another location).

2. **There must be risk reduction.**
   The hedging futures position must reduce the economic risk associated with the effect of price changes on the hedged item. Such risk is considered to be reduced if the price of the item being hedged is highly correlated with the price of the commodity underlying the respective futures contract. Thus, gains or losses on the futures contract effectively offset losses or gains on the hedged item.

   A company must, at the inception of the hedge, be prepared to demonstrate that there is likely to be a high correlation between changes in the market value of the futures contract and changes in the fair value of the hedged item, and that this correlation is likely to continue throughout the hedge period. When determining whether such a high correlation is likely, the firm is required to consider such factors as the historical correlation and the changes in this correlation that might be expected at different price levels.[18]

---

[18] While companies may use a variety of approaches to evaluate the expected future correlation, regression analysis is the statistical method commonly used to measure this relationship.

3. There must be designation.

For a futures contract to qualify as a hedge it must be *designated* as such. Accounting for the futures contract as a hedge is prospective: it begins at the time of designation. A company can remove its designation at any time, even if the futures contract continues to reduce a company's risk. However, in this event, the hedge accounting would cease prospectively, beginning at the time the futures contract is no longer designated. There are no specific rules for the designation procedures, but companies should identify through written documentation the individual assets, liabilities, commitments, or anticipated transactions for which a particular futures position is the intended hedge.

ACCOUNTING TREATMENT.   Once a futures contract is classified as a hedge of an *existing asset or liability*, gains and losses on the contract will be deferred and used to offset changes in the carrying value of the hedged item (unless the hedged item is carried at fair market value). Gains and losses on a futures contract that hedges a *firm commitment* are deferred in the balance sheet and become part of the completed transaction when it is recorded. Thus, deferred futures gains and losses are recognized in income at the same time that changes in the value of the other components of the carrying amount of the hedged item are recognized. (For example, an adjustment to the carrying value of inventory held for sale would normally be included in income when the inventory is sold.)

When a futures contract is used to hedge an *asset carried at market value*, Statement No. 80 requires that changes in the market value of the futures contracts be recognized in the same manner as are the unrealized changes in the fair value of the hedged item. For example, if a pension fund sells stock index futures to protect its securities portfolio against a market decline, it must recognize the gains or losses on the futures position as current income, since it also recognizes changes in the fair value of its securities currently.

6.11.3   Anticipatory Hedges

Anticipated transactions are considered to be transactions that a company expects, but is not obligated, to carry out in the future during its normal operation. If a company acquires a futures position as a hedge against such an anticipated transaction, changes in the market value of the futures contracts can be deferred if the hedge criteria discussed in the preceding section *and* the following additional conditions are met:

1. The significant characteristics and expected terms of the anticipated transaction are identified. Such information will normally include the expected date of the transaction, the commodity or financial instrument involved, the expected quantity to be purchased or sold, and the expected hedging period.
2. It is likely that the anticipated transaction will occur. In assessing this likelihood, a company should consider the following:

a. Its financial and operational ability to carry out the transaction
b. The resources committed to the activity surrounding the anticipated transaction
c. The length of time before the transaction is expected to occur
d. The effects of not carrying out the anticipated transaction
e. The probability of achieving the same business objectives using an alternative transaction with substantially different characteristics

   If a company learns that the amount of the anticipated transaction is likely to be less than originally expected, only a pro-rata portion of the futures gain or loss should be recognized currently. If the hedge contract is closed out before the anticipated transaction occurs, any gain or loss on the futures position should continue to be deferred until the anticipated transaction takes place (as long as the required high correlation continues to exist).

6.11.4   Required Disclosure

Companies that account for futures contracts as hedges must disclose the nature of the assets, liabilities, firm commitments, or anticipated transactions that are being hedged. They must also disclose the method of accounting used for the futures contracts and describe the events or transactions that will cause changes in the market value of these contracts to be included in income.

6.12   FEDERAL INCOME TAX CONSIDERATIONS

The 1981 Economic Recovery Tax Act (ERTA) radically changed the tax treatment of futures contracts traded on U.S. markets. ERTA introduced the term *regulated futures contracts* (RFCs) and added Section 1256 to the Internal Revenue Code (IRC). An RFC is defined as any futures contract traded on a domestic commodity exchange or board of trade and subject to a system of daily variation margins. Section 1256, which was subsequently amended by the 1982 Tax Equity and Fiscal Responsibility Act and by the 1984 Deficit Reduction Act, specifies the tax treatment of RFCs, as well as other exchange-traded instruments and certain forward contracts traded in the interbank market.
   For purposes of Federal taxation, there are three general types of RFC transactions, and each of these results in special tax consequences. These are *speculative positions, hedges,* and *mixed straddles.*

6.12.1   Speculative Positions

A speculative RFC position is defined as any RFC that does not qualify as a hedge transaction or that is not part of a mixed straddle. Open positions in RFCs that are speculative in nature are marked-to-market on the last day of the taxable year. Any increases or decreases in the value of the RFCs are recognized as capital gains or losses for tax purposes. *Unrealized* gains or losses are combined with other capital gains or losses that are *realized* during the year as a result of closed RFC transactions. Sixty percent of the net RFC gain or loss is treated as a long-term capital gain or loss, and 40 percent is treated as a short-term gain or loss. This tax treatment is commonly known as the *mark-to-market 60/40 rule*.

6.12.2   Hedges

A futures contract that is accounted for as a hedge under FAS Number 80 may nevertheless not qualify as a hedge for tax purposes. An RFC qualifies as a hedging transaction for tax purposes only if

- The RFC is entered into in the normal course of the entity's trade or business.
- The RFC reduces the risk due to changes in prices, foreign exchange rates, or interest rates (Section 12.5.6 does not define the level of risk reduction necessary to satisfy this requirement).
- The RFC position is identified as a hedge at its inception.
- The hedged item gives rise to ordinary income or loss for tax purposes.

If an RFC meets these criteria and therefore qualifies as a hedge for tax purposes, it is *not* subject to the mark-to-market 60/40 rules. Gains or losses on the futures positions are reported as *ordinary* items in the year the futures positions are closed, in contrast to the *capital* treatment given to speculative RFCs.

6.12.3   Mixed Straddles

The IRC defines a straddle as a position consisting of two or more offsetting positions in actively traded items, in which one position substantially diminishes the risk of loss involved in holding the other position(s). A mixed straddle is a straddle in which at least one—but not all—of the component positions is an RFC (or other Section 1256 contract), and at least one position is a non-Section 1256 contract (e.g., a cash market position) *that is accorded capital gain or loss treatment* under the tax laws. In such a mixed straddle, the RFC does not qualify as a hedge for tax purposes, since the position offsetting the RFC in the straddle is not treated as an ordinary tax item. For example, an RFC that serves as a hedge against marketable equity securities held by a manufacturing company would not qualify as a hedge transaction under Section 1256 because disposition of the securities by the company would result in a capital gain or loss (as opposed to an ordinary income or loss).[19]

---

[19]Tax provisions for mixed straddles are quite complex and beyond the scope of this book. Interested readers should refer to the Internal Revenue Code for further details.

CONCLUSION

Chapters 5 and 6 have discussed the basic concepts and principles applicable to hedging with all types of futures contracts. This discussion, however, is not an exhaustive treatment of hedging. There are many different types of hedges and many possible hedging strategies. Each hedging situation (or problem) is unique, and requires a hedging strategy molded to the specifics of the situation. In each case a careful assessment must be made of the risks to be hedged, and the pros and cons of alternative hedging strategies.

Successful hedging also requires a sound understanding of the particular cash and futures markets involved. All futures contracts are unique: they have different delivery requirements, different pricing conventions, different margin requirements, and so forth. Hedging strategies, therefore, must be suited to the characteristics of particular futures contracts and markets and to the hedger's objectives.

In later chapters we examine several kinds of futures contracts and markets. In each of these chapters hedging examples are provided that are specific to the futures contracts examined. In this way we hope to enrich the reader's understanding of the various hedging strategies and subtleties involved in hedging with futures.

QUESTIONS

1. Define the hedge ratio.
2. Define the minimum-variance hedge ratio.
3. Why is the minimum-variance hedge ratio related to the relative price changes of the hedged commodity and the hedging instrument?
4. Does the example shown in Table 6.4 imply that you should not hedge at all because profits will be lower?
5. In Table 6.5, why is 0.60 the minimum-variance hedge ratio?
6. Given the results in Table 6.5, why would you not use a hedge ratio greater than 0.60?
7. What are some basis relationships that hedgers may be able to take advantage of?
8. When there is output uncertainty, why is underhedging often a rule-of-thumb?
9. What is the difference between the hedge evaluation formula in Section 6.9.3 and the hedge evaluation formula in Section 5.7?
10. What is the distinction between an optimal hedge ratio and a minimum-variance hedge ratio?
11. Describe a hedging example in which there is no basis risk.
12. On June 1, 1990, a textile manufacturer wishes to lock in a price for cotton for the next six months, or until December 1, 1990. He has agreed to supply the U.S. army with one million uniforms on January 1, 1991, at a fixed price that has already been negotiated. He will have to buy 500,000 pounds of U.S.-grown white cotton between June 1 and December 1 in order to make the promised uniforms.

    On June 1 the cash price of cotton is 79.52 cents per pound. This price has risen by more than seven cents in the last month—on May 1, it was 72.20 cents. If the price rises by just three more cents, the textile manufacturer will lose money on the U.S. army contract.

TABLE 6.8
Cotton: Cash and futures prices, and volume and open interest (May 1 to May 31, 1990)

May	Cash price	July 90 futures			Oct 90 futures			Dec 90 futures		
		Price	Volume	Open interest	Price	Volume	Open interest	Price	Volume	Open interest
1	72.20	74.20	3604	16426	69.55	688	3261	67.23	2584	13307
2	72.90	74.90	2358	16436	70.32	371	3424	67.72	1642	13571
3	73.23	74.73	1726	16133	70.10	216	3465	67.38	1269	13843
4	72.26	73.76	3896	15642	69.50	458	3449	66.78	1192	13721
7	72.82	74.32	4645	15086	69.65	212	3458	67.10	2666	14135
8	73.12	74.62	3564	15027	70.15	436	3494	67.49	1172	14152
9	73.97	74.97	3251	15323	70.75	533	3584	67.93	1388	14118
10	74.38	75.38	4518	15676	71.20	768	3760	68.44	1958	14527
11	74.36	75.36	2240	15637	71.35	621	3952	68.37	1785	14603
14	73.92	74.92	2904	15418	70.82	545	4117	67.82	1852	14609
15	74.15	75.15	2624	15675	70.55	371	4071	67.67	1836	14005
16	74.24	75.24	2485	15741	70.33	780	3996	67.91	1765	14054
17	75.15	76.15	3843	16105	71.22	641	4126	68.50	1624	14212
18	75.13	76.13	2147	15906	71.10	331	4118	68.44	1194	14527
21	77.13	78.13	5692	16729	72.23	959	4368	69.10	2564	14812
22	80.02	79.77	7064	17414	72.27	1059	4660	68.86	3004	15119
23	80.10	79.85	7151	17815	71.38	986	4748	68.35	2264	15096
24	79.79	79.54	2701	17412	70.97	555	4791	68.25	1662	15072
25	80.28	80.03	3271	17663	71.95	751	5004	69.08	1953	15252
29	82.28	82.03	4270	18338	72.60	1224	5179	68.81	2341	15366
30	81.38	81.13	4203	16948	72.34	828	5315	68.67	1410	15184
31	78.42	79.92	3275	16600	72.55	537	5301	69.17	1373	15349

He is considering using cotton futures to hedge this price risk. In particular, he needs to decide which among the following cotton futures contracts would be the best to use: the July 90 contract which expires on July 9, the October 90 contract which expires on October 9, or the December 90 contract which expires on December 6.

Table 6.8 provides daily data for May 1990, the immediately preceding month. It provides cash prices, futures prices for the respective futures contracts, and both volume and open interest data for the three contracts.

The textile manufacturer needs to consider the following questions:

a. Based on the above price information for May, which futures contract is likely to provide the most effective hedge? (Show the criterion on which you base your answer.)

b. What are the minimum-variance hedge ratios for each of the three contracts? (Show the work on which you base your conclusion.)

c. Describe the exact futures positions that the manufacturer would assume if he were to use a minimum-variance hedge, using each of the three contracts? (Show your work.)

d. Of what relevance are the volume and open interest figures?

Discuss the pros and cons of hedging with each of the above futures contracts and recommend an overall hedging strategy.

Hint: You may find useful the following regression equations which are estimated with the data provided earlier:

$$\text{General Equation: } \Delta CP_t = \alpha + \beta \times \Delta FP_{t,T} + \epsilon_t$$

where

$T = \text{July}:$	$\Delta CP_t = -0.05 + 1.28\Delta FP_{t,\text{Jul}}$	
	$\quad\quad\quad\;\; (0.11)\quad\; (0.12)$	$(R^2 = 0.86)$
$T = \text{October}:$	$\Delta CP_t = \;\;\, 0.16 + 0.92\Delta FP_{t,\text{Oct}}$	
	$\quad\quad\quad\;\; (0.25)\quad\; (0.44)$	$(R^2 = 0.19)$
$T = \text{December}:$	$\Delta CP_t = \;\;\, 0.27 + 0.27\Delta FP_{t,\text{Dec}}$	
	$\quad\quad\quad\;\; (0.27)\quad\; (0.63)$	$(R^2 = 0.01)$

In addition, the following descriptive statistics were calculated using the May price data:

Price variable	Mean	Standard deviation
ΔCP	0.30	1.19
ΔFP_{Jul}	0.31	0.86
ΔFP_{Oct}	0.18	0.57
ΔFP_{Dec}	0.10	0.43

and the simple correlation coefficients between these variables were

	ΔFP_{Jul}	ΔFP_{Oct}	ΔFP_{Dec}
ΔCP	0.93	0.44	0.10

Students with the relevant statistical background should do the appropriate calculations to reproduce the above regression estimates and descriptive statistics.

SUGGESTED READING

Anderson, R. W. and J. P. Danthine. "Cross-Hedging." *Journal of Political Economy*, Vol. 89 (1981), pp. 1182–1196.

Chang, J. and H. Fang. "An Intertemporal Measure of Hedging Effectiveness." *The Journal of Futures Markets*, Vol. 10, No. 3 (1990), pp. 307–322.

Figlewski, S., Landskroner, Y., and W. Silber. "Tailing the Hedge: Why and How." *The Journal of Futures Markets*, April 1991, pp. 201–212.

Howard, C. and L. D'Antonio. "A Risk-Return Measure of Hedging Effectiveness." *Journal of Financial and Quantitative Analysis*, March 1984, pp. 101–112.

McDonald, R. "Taxes and Hedging of Forward Commitments." *The Journal of Futures Markets*, Summer 1986, pp. 207–222.

Meyers, R. "Estimating Time-Varying Optimal Hedge Ratios on Futures Markets." *The Journal of Futures Markets*, February 1991, pp. 39–54.

Peterson, P. and R. Leuthold. "A Portfolio Approach to Optimal Hedging for a Commercial Cattle Feedlot." *The Journal of Futures Markets*, August 1987, pp. 443–458.

Stulz, R. "Optimal Hedging Policies." *Journal of Financial and Quantitative Analysis*, Vol. 19 (1984), pp. 127–140.

Wilson, W. "Hedging Effectiveness of U.S. Wheat Futures Markets." *Review of Research in Futures Markets*, Vol. 3, No. 1 (1984), pp. 64–79.

APPENDIX: ESTIMATED HEDGE RATIOS FOR INDIVIDUAL MONTHS, JET FUEL CASH VERSUS HEATING OIL NEAR MONTH FUTURES (DAILY PRICES FROM 1986 TO 1988)

		1986	1987	1988	1986–1988
Jan	β	0.72	0.93	0.25	0.69
	s.e.	0.08	0.08	0.66	0.13
	R^2	0.84	0.88	0.01	0.32
Feb	β	0.73	0.89	0.71	0.74
	s.e.	0.07	0.11	0.20	0.05
	R^2	0.87	0.79	0.41	0.81
Mar	β	0.44	1.07	0.46	0.51
	s.e.	0.15	0.07	0.18	0.08
	R^2	0.34	0.93	0.25	0.38
Apr	β	0.39	0.76	0.87	0.48
	s.e.	0.09	0.07	0.10	0.06
	R^2	0.48	0.86	0.81	0.54
May	β	0.43	0.95	0.35	0.43
	s.e.	0.13	0.13	0.11	0.07
	R^2	0.37	0.77	0.38	0.39
Jun	β	0.54	0.86	0.61	0.60
	s.e.	0.09	0.10	0.18	0.07
	R^2	0.66	0.80	0.38	0.58
Jul	β	0.69	0.65	0.98	0.79
	s.e.	0.14	0.10	0.06	0.07
	R^2	0.58	0.70	0.94	0.71
Aug	β	0.46	0.74	1.01	0.63
	s.e.	0.15	0.08	0.10	0.07
	R^2	0.34	0.84	0.83	0.53
Sep	β	0.76	0.59	1.01	0.82
	s.e.	0.09	0.13	0.23	0.08
	R^2	0.81	0.53	0.51	0.62
Oct	β	0.75	0.80	0.15	0.60
	s.e.	0.07	0.09	0.54	0.17
	R^2	0.84	0.80	0.00	0.16
Nov	β	0.53	0.67	0.44	0.53
	s.e.	0.11	0.11	0.17	0.08
	R^2	0.60	0.70	0.29	0.45
Dec	β	0.69	0.99	0.80	0.85
	s.e.	0.12	0.07	0.12	0.06
	R^2	0.65	0.92	0.71	0.75

s.e.: standard error of the estimate

CHAPTER
7

SOCIAL BENEFITS OF FUTURES MARKETS AND THE ROLE OF SPECULATION

7.1 INTRODUCTION

Futures markets are controversial because of the pervasive role of speculation. To critics, futures markets often look like wild speculative orgies. Fortunes are made and lost in the wink of an eye, and the money made by speculators seems too easy and quick: no steel is produced, no buildings are built, and no services are provided.

Futures markets are also controversial simply because they are relatively unknown. Until the last 20 years these markets were largely the province of a small group of hedgers and speculators in agricultural commodities. They were virtually unknown to the legions of Wall Street executives and MBAs—the heart of the financial community.

Finally, people associate futures markets with high leverage and great risk. Traders sell what they do not own and buy what they never intend to possess, simply putting down a small amount of money as margin. Indeed, at times this high leverage has been blamed for certain notorious defaults by traders who were unable to make good on their promises to buy or sell.

Despite these negative images, futures markets provide important social benefits: risk management through hedging, and price-discovery. Neither of these benefits is easy to understand and appreciate. They are conceptually abstract and not readily susceptible to empirical demonstration. They are, nevertheless, quite significant.

This chapter discusses the hedging and price discovery functions of futures markets. It also discusses the contribution that futures markets make to economic welfare, and the critical role that speculators play in bringing about these economic benefits.

7.2   RISK MANAGEMENT

Futures markets do what forward markets do: they provide hedgers with an efficient way of managing price risk. But futures markets often do it better. When futures markets flourish and grow, it is because they provide a cheaper and more efficient way to hedge than do forward markets. This section describes how futures markets achieve this advantage.

Futures markets are the creation of a few key institutional innovations which improve upon forward markets. Two disadvantages of forward markets are: parties to forward contracts are exposed to the risk of default by their counterparties, and forward contracts usually lack liquidity—they cannot be bought and sold (or offset) in a competitive, liquid, secondary market. The institutional structure of futures markets is designed to overcome these disadvantages.

To create liquid markets, futures exchanges introduced standardized futures contracts, centralized trading in a limited number of contracts, and carefully regulated and monitored such trading. To eliminate counter party credit risk, clearing associations were created, guaranteeing contract performance. This guarantee was made credible by the adoption of a system of margin requirements, capital requirements, and mark-to-market accounting procedures, all of which maintain the solvency of clearing members and the integrity of the clearing association. (This is discussed extensively in Chapter 3).

As a consequence of these ingenious innovations, new participants entered futures markets. Traders (speculators and hedgers) who would normally be excluded from participating in forward markets because of this lack of a sufficient credit standing were able to participate freely in futures markets. And, with more traders, together with the centralization of trading on exchange floors in a limited number of standardized contracts, futures markets provided greater liquidity than corresponding forward markets. This enhanced liquidity in turn attracted even more traders, further increasing liquidity in a self-reinforcing process.

Futures markets, therefore, provide more openness, easier entry, greater liquidity, and more competition than most forward markets. As a consequence they provide a lower cost and a more efficient vehicle for hedging price risk.

7.3   PRICE DISCOVERY

The ability of futures markets to provide information about prices—their price discovery role—is an integral component of an efficient economic system. Prices must accurately reflect relative costs of production and relative consumption utilities if an optimum allocation of resources is to be achieved in an economy. Futures markets provide a pricing mechanism through which these relative costs and utilities are brought into alignment, both in the present and over time.

Futures trading takes place on organized futures exchanges, where all trading in a commodity is centralized on the floor of the exchange or through an exchange-supported screen-based computer trading system. Typically, a number of futures contracts on a commodity are traded simultaneously, each calling for delivery of the commodity at a different time in the future. This results in the establishment of many different futures prices for that commodity at any given time. For example, at any point in time there may be as many as 12 futures contracts for crude oil traded, each calling for delivery in one of the next 12 months. Thus, at any moment in time crude oil futures trading results in the establishment of 12 distinct crude oil futures prices, ranging from the price for almost immediate (or near-term) delivery to the price for delivery a year into the future (distant delivery).

All these prices are the result of open and competitive trading on the floors of exchanges and, as such, reflect the underlying supply and demand for a commodity, both in the present and in the future. Or, in the case of prices for future delivery, they reflect current expectations about what supply and demand for a commodity will be at various points in the future. These prices are continuously disseminated throughout the world to the public at large by elaborate exchange-supported price-reporting systems. It is this process of establishing equilibrium futures prices and of making these prices visible to everyone that is commonly known as the *price discovery* function of futures markets.

Futures markets discover equilibrium prices both for current cash prices and for cash prices that will, or may, exist at various times in the future. The latter are often referred to as *expected* cash prices.

7.3.1   Current Cash Prices

Commodities are commonly traded in cash markets by a network of dealers, in which each dealer posts his or her own price. These prices often differ from one another either because dealers operate in geographically segmented markets or because customers are unaware of the price differences that exist. For example, to be sure that he is getting the lowest price available, a gasoline wholesaler must survey the many cash-market dealers. Because conducting such a search is both time-consuming and costly, wholesalers must weigh the potential benefits of finding a lower price against the cost of doing the search.

Futures markets provide highly visible prices against which the current cash prices of dealers can be compared. If the prices of futures contracts for immediate or near-term delivery differ from dealers' cash prices, traders can arbitrage this difference. For example, if cash prices are lower than futures prices, arbitragers will buy the commodity in the cash market and sell futures contracts, locking in a riskless profit. Similarly, if cash prices are higher than futures prices, arbitragers will sell the commodity in the cash market (perhaps by borrowing it and selling it short) and buy futures contracts. Thus, futures and cash prices cannot differ for very long by more than an amount necessary to effect a cash-futures arbitrage.

In addition, since cash-futures arbitrage will occur if *any* dealer's cash price is out of line, such arbitrage will bring all cash prices into alignment with the futures price for a commodity. This means that if a futures market exists for a commodity, the cash prices for that commodity will have to be the same in all regions of the country and for all dealers, or cannot differ by more than the transportation costs involved in moving the commodity around the country or in effecting a cash-futures arbitrage. All cash prices, therefore, will accurately reflect the centralization of the supply and demand for a commodity brought about by trading on a futures exchange. The uniformity and accuracy of current cash prices in reflecting current aggregate supply and demand for a commodity is socially beneficial because it permits consumers to avoid costly searches to assure themselves that they are paying fair prices.

7.3.2 Expected Cash Prices

Futures markets also bring about efficient intertemporal prices, or price discovery. Since futures contracts are traded for delivery of a commodity at various points in the future, they reflect current market expectations about what cash prices will be at those points in the future—or about what the demand and supply for a commodity will be in the future. Futures prices that are considerably higher than current cash prices reflect the market's expectation that there will be a relative shortage of the commodity in the future; lower futures prices reflect an expectation of a relative surplus of the commodity in the future (or, alternatively, of a relative shortage of the commodity in the current period). Through futures trading, therefore, information about the expectations of all market participants—commercial hedgers and speculators—about the supply and demand for a commodity in a future month are assimilated to produce a single futures price for that month.

Information about future cash prices (or expected cash prices) is socially beneficial for two reasons. First, in the case of storable commodities, these prices determine the storage decisions of commercial firms. Higher futures prices signal the need for greater storage, and lower futures prices reduce current inventories. For example, significantly higher futures prices will cause some of a commodity to be withdrawn from current supply and stored for future sale, reducing supply in the current period and increasing supply at a future point in time. Thus, by altering storage decisions in response to intertemporal differences in supply and demand, futures prices adjust the supply of a commodity over time, helping to avoid over- and under-supply conditions.

Second, knowledge of futures prices affects both production and consumption decisions that have the effect of smoothing the supply and demand for a commodity over time. High futures prices signal the need for greater production in the future in order to meet the relative future shortage of the commodity; low futures prices have just the opposite effect. Similarly, low futures prices signal to consumers that it may be beneficial to defer consumption to a later period, thus reducing current demand and alleviating a current shortage.

Thus reflecting expectations about future supply and demand condition, futures prices trigger decisions about storage, production, and consumption that reallocate the supply and demand for a commodity through time in a way that maximizes social welfare. In particular, shortages in the future are alleviated by greater storage and production, and current shortages are alleviated by the deferral of current consumption to a later time period, when cash prices will be lower. Futures markets, therefore, through the discovery of expected cash prices, help to smooth the supply and demand for a commodity over time, and, as a consequence, help to avoid the economic dislocations that flow from sharp discontinuities in the flow of goods and services.

In summary, trading in futures markets establishes and makes visible both current and expected cash prices. The ready availability of this price information reduces search costs and provides signals that guide production, storage, and consumption decisions in ways that contribute to a more efficient allocation of economic resources.

7.4   THE CONCEPT OF A RISK PREMIUM

Understanding the role of speculation in futures markets requires an understanding of the concept of a *risk premium*. This section examines this concept, explains why it exists, and explores its social welfare implications.

7.4.1   What Is an Expected Spot Price?

Central to the concept of a risk premium is the notion of an *expected spot price*. This is the cash price that the market believes will prevail at some point in the future. For example, the expected spot price of heating oil six months from today is the cash price for heating oil that market participants currently believe will prevail six months from today. This price could be higher or lower than the current cash price. If market participants forecast a sharp rise in the demand for oil, or a significant decline in its supply, they will expect higher prices in the future. If the reverse supply and demand forecast is widely-held, they will expect lower prices in the future. The expected spot price, therefore, is a distillation of the individual forecasts of commercial firms, consumers, and speculators about future market conditions.

The expected price can be defined more formally as

$$\hat{P}_{t,t+k} = \exp(P_{t+k}) = \sum_{i=1}^{n} P_{t+k}^{i}(p^{i})$$

where $\exp$ = the expectation of a random variable.

$\hat{P}_{t,t+k}$ = today's expected spot price of a commodity in period $t + k$, or in k days from today, which is day t.

P_{t+k} = the spot price actually occurring in period $t + k$.

P_{t+k}^i = one of many possible spot prices, price i, that may occur in period $t + k$.

p^i = the probability of P_{t+k}^i, or of price i actually occurring in period $t + k$, given the information available at time t. The probabilities over all P_{t+k}^i's must sum to unity.

This definition makes the expected spot price equivalent to the weighted average of all possible spot prices that market participants believe could occur in the future, where the weights reflect the market's assessment of the likelihood (or probability) of a particular price occurring. Table 7.1 contains a simple illustration. The table uses various hypothetical prices that, by assumption, are currently expected to prevail in period $t + k$, together with the associated probabilities, to compute the expected spot price.

7.4.2 Hedging Imbalances and Risk Premiums

To elucidate the role of speculation, let us assume that there are no speculators, only hedgers. What will be the relationship between futures prices and expected spot prices under these conditions?

Figure 7-1 illustrates the determinates of this relationship when only short and long hedgers are present. The vertical (or Y) axis of the graph shows the actual futures prices of a hypothetical commodity. Let us say that these prices in period t are for commodity i for delivery in period $t + k$. These prices are labeled F_1, F_2 and so forth. The horizontal (or X) axis shows the quantity of the commodity that is either demanded (Q_d) or supplied (Q_s) by hedgers.

Figure 7-1 contains one demand schedule (DD') and one supply schedule (SS'). In addition, the horizontal broken line indicates the expected spot price that is *assumed* to prevail at time t ($\exp(P_{t+k})$): the cash price that the market currently expects will prevail in period $t + k$. Actual futures prices in period t may be above, below or equal to the expected spot price. The futures price will be equal to the expected spot price only if the futures price lies on the Y axis at precisely the point where the broken horizontal line intersects the Y axis.

Schedule SS' indicates the quantity of futures contracts that short hedgers wish to sell (or supply) at various futures prices. Hedgers' decisions are determined by the relationship between the current futures price and the expected spot price. When futures prices are well below the expected price, short hedgers will be reluctant to hedge because their expected cost will be high. More specifically, if

TABLE 7.1
Calculating the expected spot price

Prices that may occur in period $t + k$:	$70	$80	$90
Likelihood of occurring:	0.10	0.50	0.40

The expected price, therefore, is

$$\hat{P}_{t,t+k} = \$70 \times (0.10) + \$80 \times (0.50) + \$90 \times (0.40) = \$83$$

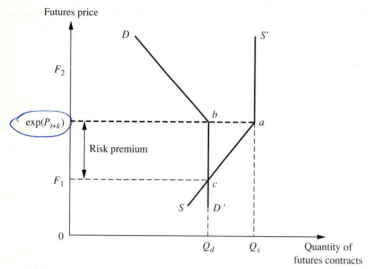

FIGURE 7-1
Net short hedging imbalance *without speculation.*

we assume that a firm hedges by selling futures at price F_1, it will be selling each unit (bushel, gallon, etc.) at a sizeable discount from the price it expects to obtain by waiting until period $t + k$ to sell. This discount is represented by line segment bc, and is called the risk premium. It is the lost income per unit that the short hedger pays to whomever buys the futures contracts that it sells. Thus, in general, the risk premium is the difference between the expected spot price and the prevailing futures price and, as such, is the cost of hedging.

Figure 7-1 shows that the maximum volume of short hedging (Q_s) would occur at point a, where the futures price is equal to the expected spot price. At this futures price the risk premium (and the cost of hedging) is zero. At futures prices above the expected spot price, there are no additional short sales, since hedgers will have already hedged all of their future cash sales. Thus, the line segment aS', which is perpendicular to the X axis, indicates that even higher futures prices will not result in greater short sales by the short hedgers.

Schedule DD' in Figure 7-1 is the same type of schedule for long hedgers. It represents the demands of long hedgers. When futures prices are substantially above expected spot prices, long hedgers will be reluctant to hedge, since they will pay prices that are higher than they expect to pay in period $t + k$. But as futures prices fall, and the differential between the futures price and the expected spot price shrinks, long hedgers will purchase increasing amounts of futures contracts. When the futures price is equal to (or below) the expected spot price, long hedgers will hedge their total future commitments (indicated by the perpendicular line segment bD').

The intersection of the SS' and DD' schedules determines the equilibrium, or market-clearing, futures price. Figure 7-1 depicts a *net short* hedging imbalance. A net short hedging imbalance occurs if the desired quantity of short hedging were to exceed the desired quantity of long hedging at a futures price equal to the expected spot price. This imbalance is shown in Figure 7-1 by line segment ba: the net short imbalance is Q_s minus Q_d.

Figure 7-2 shows the opposite situation: a *net long* hedging imbalance. When the futures price is equal to the expected spot price, desired long hedging exceeds desired short hedging. There is a net long hedging imbalance (which is Q_d minus Q_s). Whether a net short or long hedging imbalance exists depends on fundamental economic factors related to the underlying commodity. Further, a market may have a net short hedging imbalance at one point in time but have a net long hedging imbalance at other times.

In either case, the equilibrium futures price is that which equates the demand and supply of futures contracts. Since by assumption there are no speculators, this is the price that equates the desired short and long hedging. When there is a net short hedging imbalance, as in Figure 7-1, the equilibrium futures price (point c) is below the expected spot price. When there is a net long hedging imbalance, as in Figure 7-2, the equilibrium futures price (point c) is above the expected spot price. In both cases, there is a risk premium (line segment bc) that either short or long hedgers pay.

There is one hypothetical case when the risk premium and the cost of hedging could be zero: when a zero net hedging imbalance exists. When desired short and long hedging are equal at a futures price equal to the expected spot price, there is no risk premium. This case is shown in Figure 7-3. Such a condition is highly unlikely. Experience indicates that there is almost always a hedging imbalance. Thus, the existence of a risk premium is common.

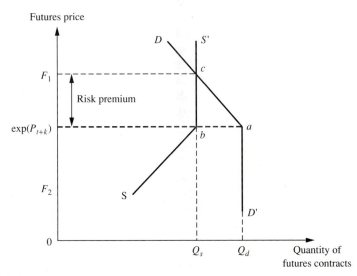

FIGURE 7-2
Net long hedging imbalance *without speculation*.

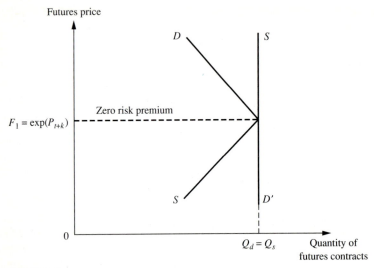

FIGURE 7-3
Zero net hedging imbalance *without speculation*.

To summarize, the existence of a risk premium is the result of a net hedger imbalance. This premium can be either positive or negative, depending on whether there is a long or short hedging imbalance. Further, the larger the risk premium, the greater is the cost of hedging. If the risk premium is large, futures markets may also not perform their price discovery function well, since they may not be good predictors of expected spot prices.

7.5   SPECULATION AND THE MAGNITUDE OF THE RISK PREMIUM

We can now adapt the previous analysis for the presence of speculators. In general, what we will find is that speculation results in smaller risk premiums. Indeed, without any speculation, the net hedger imbalance in many (if not most) futures markets would probably be so great that the size of the risk premium would be prohibitive, eliminating the markets entirely.

The effect of speculation on equilibrium futures prices and risk premiums is displayed in Figures 7-4 and 7-5. Figure 7-1, to reiterate, represents the case of a net short hedging imbalance. *Long* speculation is introduced in this figure by changing schedule DD'. When futures prices fall below the expected spot price, long speculators enter the market and purchase futures contracts. Thus, schedule DD' in Figure 7-1 becomes schedule DD'', in Figure 7-4. Schedule DD'' assumes that the long speculators purchase futures contracts when futures prices fall below the expected spot price. Further, the more that the futures price falls below the expected spot price, the greater is the speculative demand for futures contracts.

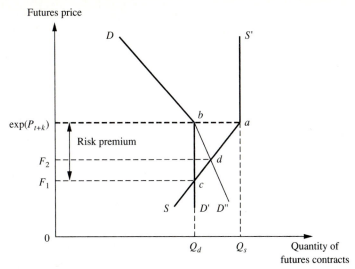

FIGURE 7-4
Net short hedging imbalance *with long speculation.*

The rationale for this assumed speculative behavior is the following. Speculators believe that, over many different time periods, the price that is expected
to prevail at a future point in time (such as $t + k$) will in fact occur. While the
cash price that actually occurs in any particular period, such as $t + k$, may be
higher or lower than the expected price, *on average* speculators will be correct

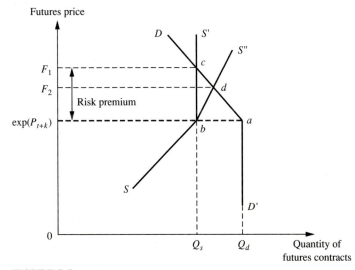

FIGURE 7-5
Net long hedging imbalance *with short speculation.*

in assuming that the expected price will be realized. Thus, by buying repeatedly at futures prices below the expected spot price, long speculators will on average make profits.

Not all speculators, of course, may realize profits. If actual prices turn out to be significantly higher or lower than expected prices, some speculators on those occasions may suffer losses. This is a risk they cannot avoid. The risk of incurring losses, however, diminishes as the difference between the expected price and the futures price increases. If, for example, long speculators buy at futures prices well below the expected spot price, the likelihood of their incurring losses is considerably less. This is the reason that Schedule DD'' in Figure 7-4 shows that as futures prices fall (relative to the expected spot price) speculators purchase greater and greater quantities of futures contracts.

Further, the less risk-adverse are long speculators, the greater (or *flatter*) will be the slope of line segment bD'' of schedule DD'', and the greater quantities of futures contracts they will purchase at a given differential between the futures price and the expected spot price. In the extreme case where long speculators are either *risk-neutral* or *risk-loving*, line segment bD'' would become parallel to the horizontal (or X) axis. (We assume for simplicity that the presence of speculators does not alter line segment Db of schedule DD'': at futures prices above expected spot prices long speculators are unwilling to purchase futures contracts.)

Figure 7-5 shows the effect of speculation when there is a net long hedging imbalance and *short* speculators enter the market. Schedule SS'' reflects the speculative supply of futures contracts at futures prices above the expected price: at these prices the supply of futures contracts (or short selling) is greater than in the absence of short speculators. This occurs because shorts expect to profit as futures prices fall to the expected price level.

The effect of speculation on risk premiums can now be seen in both Figures 7-4 and 7-5. Prior to the introduction of long speculators in Figure 7-1, the intersection of the DD' and SS' schedules occurred at point c: the equilibrium futures price was F_1 and the risk premium was equal to bc. In Figure 7-4, with long speculators in the market, DD' becomes DD'', a new equilibrium occurs at point d, and the equilibrium futures price rises to F_2. As a result, the risk premium paid by short hedgers shrinks by an amount equal to F_2 minus F_1.

Figure 7-5 illustrates that the introduction of short speculation has exactly the same result in a market characterized by a net long hedging imbalance. When short speculation is introduced, schedule SS' changes to SS'', the equilibrium occurs at point d, and the futures price falls from F_1 to F_2. As a result, the risk premium once again shrinks by F_1 minus F_2.

In both Figures 7-4 and 7-5, speculation reduces the risk premium embedded in futures prices and, as a consequence, reduces the cost of hedging. In addition, futures prices become better approximations of expected spot prices. Further, the greater the amount of speculation and the more willing speculators are to take risks, the lower will be the risk premium for a given net hedging imbalance. Thus, more speculation makes futures markets more efficient at performing their hedging and price discovery functions.

TABLE 7.2
Price volatility and speculation (1989)

Commodity	Column 1 Futures price volatility* (mean)	Column 2 Cash price volatility* (mean)	Column 3 Speculation[†] (mean)
(1) Eurodollars (CME)	0.112	0.089	0.328
(2) Crude oil (NYMEX)	2.035	2.119	0.381
(3) S&P 500 (CME)	0.883	1.012	0.345
(4) Soybeans (CBOT)	1.345	1.371	0.541
(5) Corn (CBOT)	1.181	1.395	0.479
(6) German deutschemark (IMM)	0.701	0.675	0.504
(7) Japanese yen (IMM)	0.678	0.667	0.533
(8) Sugar Number 11 (CSCE)	2.488	1.970	0.359
(9) Swiss franc (IMM)	0.794	0.761	0.622
(10) Heat oil Number 2 (NYMEX)	1.950	2.183	0.412
(11) Wheat (CBOT)	0.958	1.154	0.519
(12) British pound (IMM)	0.808	0.738	0.570
(13) Live hogs (CME)	1.552	2.052	0.809
(14) NYSE composite index (NYCE)	0.890	0.692	0.580
(15) T-bill 90-day (CME)	0.120	0.092	0.526
(16) Oats (CBOT)	2.277	1.881	0.535

* mean of monthly standard deviations calculated using daily percentage price changes.

[†] mean of monthly speculation-to-open interest ratios: speculation as a percentage of month-end open interest.

The annual volume of trading in 1989 in the above contracts was
(1)-(3) over 10 million contracts
(4)-(10) between 5 to 10 million contracts
(11)-(15) between 1 to 5 million contracts, and
(16) under 1 million contracts

7.6 CRITICS OF SPECULATION

In contrast to the preceding analysis, critics contend that speculation does more harm than good. Speculators, it is argued, do not trade on the basis of economic fundamentals, but rather respond to a kind of "mob psychology," driving prices irrationally in one direction and then in the other. The result is increased price volatility, which arguably leads to higher risk premiums and less efficient prices, just the opposite result of that shown in Figures 7-4 and 7-5.[1]

The issue, however, is an empirical one: does greater speculation result in increased price volatility? While this is a hotly contested issue, Table 7.2 together with Figures 7-6 and 7-7 provide insightful information on the topic. Table 7.2 shows for 16 different futures markets during 1989 three variables: the volatility of

---

[1]See, for example, G. S. Maddala and Jiscoo Yoo, "Risk Premia and Price Volatility in Futures Markets," *The Journal of Futures Markets*, April 1991, pp. 165-78.

FIGURE 7-6
Price volatility versus speculation (futures prices: 1989).

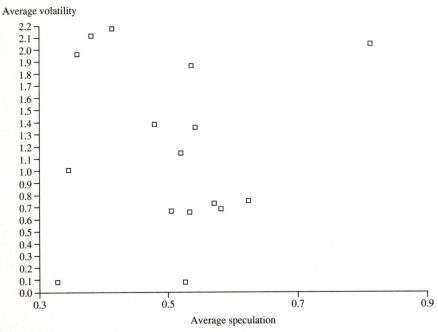

FIGURE 7-7
Price volatility versus speculation (cash prices: 1989).

174

futures prices (column 1), the volatility of cash prices of the underlying commodity (column 2), and the magnitude of speculation in the futures market (column 3). The magnitude of speculation is measured as the percent of total open interest held by speculators, using the CFTC's "Commitments of Traders" data discussed in Section 1.8 of Chapter 1.[2]

Figures 7-6 and 7-7 are scatter plots of the data in Table 7.2. They show the relationship between the magnitude of speculation and the level of price volatility across the 16 commodities. Each small square in these plots represents one of the 16 commodity markets. Clearly, neither Figure 7-6 nor Figure 7-7 reveals a systematic relationship between the volume of speculative trading and price volatility, either with respect to futures or cash prices.

The charge that greater speculation increases risk premiums in futures markets by increasing price volatility does not appear to fit the facts. Thus, the conclusion of Section 7.5—that speculation reduces the size of the risk premium seems valid.

CONCLUSION

Speculators play a vital role in futures markets. Without them futures markets could not exist. Further, the more the speculative activity, the better futures markets perform their critical social functions of providing hedging and price discovery services. It is important, therefore, that speculators be encouraged to participate in futures markets.

Why, then, is speculation such a controversial topic? In the next chapter, which examines the various rationales underlying the regulation of futures markets, some alternative views of speculation are discussed.

QUESTIONS

1. What is meant by the *price discovery* function of futures markets?
2. Which prices do futures markets discover?
3. What price is discovered by a gold futures contract with 6 months left to delivery? What is discovered by a stock index futures contract?
4. What is an expected spot price?
5. What is meant by a *risk premium*?
6. If there were no speculators present in futures markets, under what conditions would there be a zero risk premium?
7. Explain why a net hedger imbalance can result in a risk premium. If there is a net short hedger imbalance, will the risk premium be positive or negative?
8. Explain why the presence of speculators may reduce risk premiums. If speculators are more (rather than less) risk averse, will risk premiums be higher or lower?

---

[2]This is, specifically, the yearly average of each month's ratio of speculative open interest to total open interest. All non-commercial and non-reporting traders are assumed to be speculators. See discussion in Chapter 1, Section 1.8.

9. Which is preferable from an economic welfare perspective: higher or lower risk premiums?
10. What is the argument that supports the view that speculative trading increases risk premiums? What is the evidence?

SUGGESTED READING

Andersen, R. and J. Danthine. "Hedger Diversity in Futures Markets." *Economic Journal*, Vol. 43 (1983), pp. 370–389.

Antonovitz, F. and T. Roe. "Effects of Expected Cash and Futures Prices on Hedging and Production." *The Journal of Futures Markets*, Vol. 6 (Summer 1986), pp. 187–206.

Dusak, C. "Futures Trading and Investor Returns: An Investigation of Commodity Market Risk Premiums." *Journal of Political Economy*, Vol. 81 (1973), pp. 1387–1406.

Junkus, J. "Systematic Skewness in Futures Contracts." *The Journal of Futures Markets*, Vol. 11, No. 1 (February 1991), pp. 9–24.

Kolb, R., J. Jordan, and G. Gay. "Futures Prices and Expected Future Spot Prices." *Review of Research in Futures Markets*, Vol. 2, No. 1 (1983), pp. 110–123.

Ma, C. "Forecasting Efficiency of Energy Futures Prices." *The Journal of Futures Markets*, Vol. 9 (October 1989), pp. 393–420.

Melvin, M. and J. Sultan. "South African Political Unrest, Oil Prices, and the Time Varying Risk Premium in the Gold Futures Market." *The Journal of Futures Markets*, Vol. 10, No. 2 (April 1990), pp. 103–112.

Newberry, D. "When do Futures Destabilize Spot Prices?" *International Economic Review*, February 1987, pp. 291–298.

Stoll, H. and R. Whaley. "Volatility and Futures: Message Versus Messenger." *Journal of Portfolio Management*, Vol. 4 (Winter 1988), pp. 20–22.

Yoo, Jisoo and G. S. Maddala. "Risk Premia and Price Volatility in Futures Markets." *The Journal of Futures Markets*, No. 2 (April 1991), pp. 165–178.

CHAPTER

8

THE ECONOMIC AND HISTORICAL RATIONALES FOR REGULATING FUTURES MARKETS

This chapter provides a conceptual framework for understanding the role of regulation in futures markets. In the next chapter, the current regulatory structure and the specific laws governing futures markets are discussed in detail.

8.1 ALLOCATIVE EFFICIENCY AS A FRAMEWORK FOR UNDERSTANDING REGULATION

Economists view regulation as a mechanism to increase *allocative efficiency*. Since the work of Vilfredo Pareto, an economist who lived nearly a century ago, allocative efficiency has enjoyed a sanctified position in the economist's analytical framework. Maximum allocative efficiency, or, as it is often called, *Pareto optimality,* is attained when it is theoretically impossible to make someone better-off (in economic terms) without making someone else worse-off. When a condition exists where it is possible to improve one person's economic welfare without injuring another's in any way, we are, by definition, not operating at maximum allocative efficiency. Furthermore, even if some people are made worse-off, if the persons made better-off could, in principle, adequately compensate the losers and still be better-off than before, the change is viewed as increasing allocative efficiency (whether or not compensation is actually paid).

The concept of allocative efficiency eschews all individual comparisons of welfare. It does not purport to pass judgement on a change which makes some people better-off but at the cost of making others worse-off. It says nothing about a situation in which Mr. X's wealth is increased by $100 while Mr. Y's is decreased by $100. Many different wealth distributions are consistent with Pareto optimality. From the viewpoint of the theory of allocative efficiency, one wealth distribution is as good as any other. Nevertheless, as value-free as this view is, the concept has been and continues to be a powerful analytical tool. It is still the most persuasive economic rationale for free enterprise and a competitive economy.

The concept also provides an objective guide for determining when and where regulatory interference with free markets is desirable. In particular, when markets fail to attain Pareto optimality, there is said to be *market failure*. Regulation is a potential cure for market failure: regulation could, in principle, be used to make people on net better-off.

8.2 THE CONCEPT OF MARKET FAILURE

Four types of market failure are commonly recognized: natural monopoly, public goods, externalities, and imperfections in the production and dissemination of information. Although the last of these is not entirely distinct from the others, it is a concept of sufficient importance to require separate discussion.

8.2.1 Monopoly

Perhaps the oldest recognized case of market failure is that of *natural monopoly*. This occurs where technology is such that the cheapest way (in the long run) to produce a good or service is for only one firm to produce it. In other words, production is characterized by increasing returns to scale, or by a continuously declining average cost curve.

While production by a single firm under these conditions will result in the lowest unit cost, there will be market failure in the sense that maximum allocative efficiency will not be attained. This occurs because, in order to make a profit, a natural monopolist must set a price above his marginal cost, thereby causing less of the good to be produced and consumed than is consistent with Pareto optimality.[1] Regulation is a common remedy for this situation. Industries such as electric utilities, railroads, telephone, and cable television are examples of regulation based on the existence of natural monopoly.

---

[1]The marginal cost curve of a natural monopolist will lie below his average cost curve, so that setting price equal to marginal cost will result in negative profits. Pareto optimality requires that the ratios of any two prices equal the ratios of their respective marginal costs. This condition is unlikely to be fulfilled if firms do not set prices equal to marginal costs.

Monopoly can also be man-made, as opposed to natural. History is replete with instances of cartels or a few firms dominating a market, either by chance or through calculated effort. Even where natural monopoly does not exist, substantial economies of scale may still exist, resulting in imperfectly competitive markets. To prevent such man-made monopoly power, we have adopted various antitrust laws. These laws, for the most part, are directed at eliminating monopoly power and keeping markets competitive.

Despite important distinctions between natural and man-made monopoly, both are market failures: they distort prices and result in an inefficient allocation of resources.

8.2.2 Public Goods

The second type of market failure is the existence of *public goods*. Pure public goods are those characterized by (1) nonexcludability and (2) a zero marginal social cost of production. Nonexcludability refers to the condition that people cannot be excluded from enjoying (or consuming) the good even though they contribute nothing towards its production. Thus, there is no incentive for the private production of the good. Furthermore, given a marginal social cost of zero, it is suboptimal to exclude anyone from using such a good once it exists, since it costs society nothing for another person to use it. National defense is a classic example. The development of a strategic weapon that assures the security of the United States is characterized by a zero marginal social cost in the sense that another 10 or 10,000 people can enjoy the security it provides without additional cost. Less pure examples of public goods are a lighthouse and a television signal. Once erected, a lighthouse can be used by additional ships at no extra cost. Similarly, a television signal can be enjoyed by one or many persons at the same cost, at least within a given signal area.

A freely competitive market is unlikely to produce pure public goods because of their characteristic of nonexcludability, which prevents the individual (or group) who produces the good from selling it for profit. Each person knows he or she cannot be excluded from enjoying the good once it is produced, even though they contribute nothing to its production. Thus, they have no incentive to rush forward and volunteer to produce it. Instead, they wait for someone else to produce it so they can have a "free ride." As a consequence, public goods may never be produced by private markets.

In practice, many goods are *quasi-public* goods: they have some but not all of the characteristics of pure public goods. We can envision a good that has a zero marginal social cost but which still permits the exclusion of noncontributors, thereby making it profitable to produce. A television signal, for example, can be scrambled so that only paying customers can receive it. Even in this case, however, the result will not be Pareto optimal: if a single price is charged to all subscribers, such a price will exclude customers with a marginal utility lower than the price but still higher than the marginal cost to society of providing the signal to them (which is zero).

Thus, markets fail because public goods either are not produced at all (when it is beneficial in a collective welfare sense to produce them) or, if they are produced, they are produced in less than optimal quantities.

8.2.3   Externalities

Another source of market failure occurs when goods have *external effects*. This happens when the private and social marginal costs (or benefits) of production or consumption diverge. An example is a coal-burning, steel-producing plant, that pollutes the air by emitting sulfur dioxide and other noxious gases. Air pollution imposes costs on nearby residents: wear and tear on property, a dirty environment, and possibly health problems. These costs are properly part of the social costs associated with the production and use of steel, and should be borne by the steel-producing firm and its customers. If these costs are not incorporated into the total cost of producing steel, a divergence will exist between the firm's marginal cost of production (private marginal cost) and society's marginal cost of production (social marginal cost). Private marginal cost will be less than social marginal cost, and the result will be that more steel is produced than is optimal. This is a case of *negative externalities*.

Alternatively, a person who buys garbage collection services in a crowded urban environment benefits others as well as himself. His behavior results in a cleaner, healthier, and more aesthetic environment, which others can also enjoy. Here the social benefits of buying garbage collection services exceed the individual's private benefits, or there are *positive externalities*. If the provision of sanitation service is left entirely to private markets, too little may be purchased, since the price of the service will reflect only private production costs and not the neighborhood benefits associated with the service.

Thus, externalities exist when the private market does not permit the person who benefits others to be remunerated by those so benefited, or when those who are harmed by others cannot demand and obtain compensation from those responsible. Why? Because either no property right is recognizable, or the transaction costs associated with organizing a large group with a small per capita interest are so great as to make impractical concerted private action to recoup damages or capture benefits.

The rationale for government intervention where externalities exist, therefore, is that government can either reduce the transaction costs associated with collective action or effectively coerce certain parties to behave in a different and more socially beneficial way. An example is the imposition of smoke-emission standards on automobile manufacturers. Alternatively, municipal governments frequently provide or arrange for specified (and hopefully optimal) levels of garbage collection service, using their taxing authority and legal powers to coerce collective action.

8.2.4   Information Failures

The final notion of market failure occurs when markets fail to provide the correct amount of information. Achievement of Pareto optimality requires the existence of perfect information or of a perfect market for information. Proponents of informational regulation allege either that there is something special about information as a good that prevents it from being bought and sold as other private goods are, or, that if it is bought and sold, it will not be produced in optimal quantities.

There are two obvious explanations for the occurence of this failure. One is economic in nature; the other is paternalistic. First, information may possess the characteristics of a public good. The first person to obtain information must often incur a substantial cost, in both time and out-of-pocket expenses. Once acquired, however, the information can be passed to others at little or no additional cost. It is, therefore, socially wasteful for people to expend resources to acquire information that others have already obtained. Working together and sharing costs, each person could acquire the information at lower cost.

Could one person incur the cost of acquiring the information and then recoup his expenses by selling it to others, such that the outcome would be the same as had they all joined together at the outset to acquire the information? In most cases the answer will be no. To begin with, the disseminator of the information, in order to recoup expenses incurred in acquiring the information, will have to charge a price greater than the marginal social cost of making the information available to others (which is close to zero). Such a price will therefore exclude users whose marginal utility is less than the price but still greater than the marginal social cost of making the information available. Thus, less information will be made available than is optimal.

This problem is compounded by the incentive that purchasers of information have to resell it. Unlike most commodities, information can be used without being used up. By reselling it a purchaser can recoup some of his purchase price. The possibility of such secondary sales, therefore, complicates the pricing of information. It is difficult to forecast accurately potential sales. This uncertainty destroys the incentive to disseminate information through the usual market mechanism.

There is an alternative, paternalistic, view: consumers may not use information intelligently, even if such information is readily available, and may therefore make incorrect or irrational decisions. Although this view does not enjoy much stature among economists, it is one that has unquestionably received a good deal of attention from public policymakers, especially where the consequences of ignorance and misjudgement can be particularly grave.

Government intervention to correct an informational failure may take several forms. Government itself can assume the responsibility of collecting, evaluating, and disseminating information (either directly or through a franchising relationship); or it can regulate the quality of products and the flow of information between sellers and buyers. Licensing and certification standards, for example, are commonly used to regulate product quality, while labeling requirements, truth-in-advertising standards, and mandatory disclosure requirements are examples of regulations directed at the flow of information.

8.2.5 Regulation Is Not Costless

The market failure framework does not by itself suggest policy prescriptions. At most, it instructs us to consider regulatory intervention when market failure occurs, or it instructs us not to intervene in markets where market failures are not significant. The word *significant* is added, since there is no allowance in the theory for the costs of regulatory intervention. Two such costs have been clearly identified: the cost of a regulatory bureaucracy, and the costs that can result from the perverting effects of regulation on private managers. It is not uncommon for these costs to outweigh the efficiency benefits of regulatory intervention, even when a market failure exists.[2] Thus, the expected benefits of regulatory intervention should exceed the likely direct and indirect costs of regulation.

8.3 EVALUATING THE PERFORMANCE OF FUTURES MARKETS

8.3.1 Allocative Efficiency in Futures Markets

Allocation efficiency in futures markets depends on the ability of these markets to perform their price discovery and risk-shifting functions efficiently. The benefits of price discovery are directly related to the accuracy of futures prices.[3] The more accurate futures prices are in reflecting current and future demand and supply conditions, and therefore in predicting subsequent spot prices, the more efficient they are in conveying information and in allocating resources.

The accuracy of futures prices can be measured in two ways: by whether futures prices are unbiased estimates of subsequent spot prices (or by how large the risk premium is), and by the magnitude of the variance (or spread) of the distribution of futures prices. The less the bias (or risk premium) in futures prices, the more efficient futures markets are as price discovery mechanisms. A high variance of futures prices also makes a high forecast error likely.[4] Unbiasedness and low variance, therefore, suggest an efficient futures market, and vice versa.

With respect to the market's risk management function, a futures contract provides a better hedge the closer is the correlation between changes in futures prices and changes in the price of the asset being hedged.[5] Anything that artificially reduces this correlation makes futures markets less efficient in performing

---

[2]See, for example, H. Averch and L. Johnson, "Behavior of the Firm Under Regulatory Constraint," *American Economic Review,* December 1962, pp. 1051-69; and F. Edwards, "Managerial Objectives in Regulated Industries: Expense-Preference Behavior in Banking," *Journal of Political Economy,* January–February 1977.

[3]For discussion and analysis of this view, see Jerome Stein, "Speculative Price: Economic Welfare and the Idiot of Chance," *Review of Economic and Statistics,* May 1981.

[4]In somewhat different language, this definition of efficiency implies that the social loss associated with an inefficient futures market is directly related to the magnitude of the square of the forecast error between the futures price and the subsequent spot price.

[5]See L.I. Johnson, "The Theory of Hedging and Speculation in Commodity Futures," *Review of Economic Studies,* October 1960; J.L. Stein, "The Simultaneous Determination of Spot and Futures Prices," *American Economic Review,* December 1961; and L.H. Ederington, "The Hedging Performance of the New Futures Markets," *Journal of Finance,* March 1979.

their hedging function. In addition, the more liquid are futures markets, the better they are likely to perform both their hedging and price discovery functions.

8.3.2 Dynamic or Innovational Efficiency

In the long run, the ability of futures markets to allocate resources efficiently will depend on the availability of useful and liquid futures contracts. This, in turn, depends on the willingness and ability of organized exchanges to develop new futures contracts and to improve existing contracts. Unfortunately, we know very little about the factors that drive innovation in futures markets. Are size and diversification of futures exchanges important? What effect does competition among exchanges have? How do various regulations impact innovation? An important dimension of regulation is to formulate a constructive policy related to the approval of new futures contracts and exchanges.[6]

8.3.3 Transactional Efficiency

The transaction costs associated with buying and selling futures contracts are still another aspect of efficiency. Everything else being equal in efficient markets, brokerage and commission costs will be as low as possible. Also, regulatory costs, such as those associated with margin requirements, will be as low as is consistent with well-functioning and safe markets.

The level of transactions costs partially depends on the degree of competition (among commission houses and among brokers) and on the volume of trading. Everything else being equal, greater competition should lower commission rates and narrow bid-asked spreads; and, given the degree of competition, a higher volume of trading should lower commission costs because of economies of scale and narrow bid-asked spreads because of increased liquidity.

8.4 HISTORICAL JUSTIFICATIONS FOR REGULATING FUTURES MARKETS

During the past century critics have pointed to a number of incidents that they contend reveal a failure of futures markets to perform efficiently. This section examines these arguments and relates them to the classic market failures discussed in Section 8.2.

8.4.1 Excessive Speculation

Critics have pointed to excessive speculation as a major reason for regulating futures markets. Speculative overreactions, they contend, result in *runs* in prices,

---

[6]On the subject of innovation in futures markets, see W. Silber, "Innovation, Competition, and New Contact Design in Futures Markets," *The Journal of Futures Markets*, Summer 1981, pp. 123-55.

during which futures prices are determined more by market psychology and game strategy than by underlying economic fundamentals. Such prices, they argue, will not result in an efficient allocation of resources. Thus, fear of destabilizing speculation is one reason for government regulation.

A key question is whether futures markets are especially prone to destabilizing speculation. Are foreign exchange markets, bond markets, stock markets, real estate markets, and so on, any less subject to such speculation? The belief that futures markets are more susceptible to speculative abuses may rest on the unique features of futures markets: specified delivery dates, a narrowly defined deliverable commodity, a large open interest relative to the supply of the deliverable commodity, and high leverage. These characteristics arguably provide a market environment more conducive to speculators having a destabilizing effect in futures markets.

Students of speculation, however, have had great difficulty in establishing, either theoretically or empirically, that speculation has in fact had a destabilizing effect on futures prices (or on prices in any other market, for that matter). Economic theory provides no clear conclusion about the effects of speculation on prices. There is also no conclusive, or even reasonably convincing, empirical evidence to suggest that speculation in futures markets is destabilizing. (See, for example, Section 7.7 in Chapter 7.) Nevertheless, this concern continues to be one of the main underpinnings of regulation in futures markets.

8.4.2 Manipulation

If the history of regulation in futures markets is clear about anything, it is that there is a pervasive belief that futures markets are susceptible to manipulation and monopolistic control.[7] Monopoly power in any market is synonymous with price distortion, which benefits the monopolist (or the manipulator) at the expense of other market participants. Thus, there is market failure in the classic sense. Futures prices are distorted: they do not reflect solely supply and demand conditions (as in competitive markets), and are biased estimates of future cash prices. The result will be a misallocation of resources, with the concomitant welfare loss. In addition, periodic manipulations are likely to increase the variance of the distribution of futures prices, making futures prices on any given day less reliable forecasters of future cash prices.

Monopolistically induced price distortions may also diminish the efficiency of futures markets as hedging vehicles. Such distortions introduce random noise into the variability of futures prices, decreasing the degree of correlation between futures and cash prices.[8]

---

[7] See Section 9.7 in Chapter 9.

[8] The validity of this statement depends on how monopolistic control of futures prices affects cash prices. We assume that there will not usually be a parallel price movement in cash prices.

Finally, monopolistic power in futures markets, as in all other markets, results in unfairness: there is a redistribution of wealth towards those who possess the market power. An unfair market may discourage market participation and reduce trading volume, making markets less liquid and prices more volatile.

Futures markets may be more susceptible to monopolization (or manipulation) than other markets. First, futures contracts have a specific delivery or performance date. Second, they specify a particular commodity for delivery: one's ability to fulfill one's contract obligation by delivering a substitute commodity is highly restricted. Third, futures contracts often trade in a volume many times greater than the supply of the underlying deliverable cash commodity. Thus, traders may be able to acquire market power by acquiring large positions in both futures and the deliverable cash commodity. Inflexible delivery requirements restrict entry in the sense that shorts may not be able to obtain the deliverable commodity in the available time. As a consequence, extensive regulation directed at preventing and discouraging manipulation has been deemed necessary.

8.4.3   Market Liquidity as a Natural Monopoly

A desire to centralize trading also underlies the existing regulatory structure. Centralizing trading at exchanges results in more liquid markets and less variability in futures prices. Less price variability in turn makes futures markets more efficient, as both a price discovery and hedging mechanism. In addition, centralization reduces transaction costs (commission rates, bid-asked spreads, etc.) because of economies of scale and greater liquidity.

Thus, some regulation is directed at restricting entry, with respect to off-exchange competing futures instruments or to competing exchanges. Such regulation limits competition in order to foster greater centralization of trading and greater market liquidity.

8.4.4   Customer Protection

Futures markets are complex and sophisticated markets, and investors may not have the information and expertise to protect themselves. Certain regulations, therefore, such as the licensing requirements for futures commission merchants, representatives, pool operators, and so forth, are directed at protecting users of futures markets and increasing people's confidence in futures markets.

No regulation is without cost, however. Protective regulations, such as reporting requirements, increase the costs of providing futures market services, and these costs must be passed on to users. Higher costs may also discourage the use of futures markets, just the opposite of the intended effect.

Thus, although it is probably impossible to determine whether customer protection regulation increases or decreases the efficiency of futures markets, it nevertheless remains a fundamental underpinning of regulation in futures markets.

8.4.5 Financial Stability

Futures markets have always been characterized by extensive self-regulation directed at assuring that the markets remain financially sound. The soundness of all futures contracts depends on a common supporting institution: the clearing association. If the clearing association becomes bankrupt and fails to make good on its commitments, all futures contracts may become worthless. Clearing associations are like central banks to futures markets. Their failure would undermine the entire industry, sending shock waves throughout the entire financial system. (This concern existed during both the silver crisis of 1980 and the stock market crash of 1987.)

In contrast, the soundness of most financial instruments, like stocks and bonds, depends only on the soundness of the issuer. If the Chrysler Corporation were to fail, Chrysler Corporation's bonds, notes, and stocks might become worthless, but not *all* bonds, notes, or stock would become worthless. While there may be ripple effects of such a failure, there is no direct effect on the soundness of other securities.

The soundness of clearing associations can be viewed as a public good. Their soundness benefits all participants in futures markets. It is impossible to exclude any participant from enjoying the fruits of this financial stability. Thus, everyone should share its costs. But there is a clear incentive to be a "free-rider": to enjoy the benefits without paying a fair share of the costs. Regulation is a way to prevent the incentive to "free-ride" from undermining the soundness of the system.

Exchanges and clearing associations have recognized the critical importance of financial stability and have erected elaborate rules and regulations designed to maintain it. Trading limits, margin requirements, mark-to-market procedures, and capital requirements for members are some of these regulations. In addition, clearing association rules make all members liable for each other's debts up to the "last drop" or to some specified level of capital. Thus, financial stability is a central goal of regulation in futures markets.

CONCLUSION

This chapter has provided a conceptual framework for understanding why the regulation of futures markets is considered necessary. This framework can be used to evaluate the stated purpose of a regulation and to judge its potential effectiveness. The chapter has also described the historical reasons for regulation in futures markets. In the next chapter the current regulatory system which governs futures markets will be described in greater detail. For each type of regulation discussed in Chapter 9, the reader should ask why the regulation is needed, what its objective is, and whether it has succeeded in achieving this objective.

QUESTIONS

1. What does the concept of *allocative efficiency* mean?
2. Give some examples of market failure.

3. Explain how excessive speculation can result in an inefficient allocation of resources.

4. Explain how manipulation can result in an inefficient allocation of resources.

5. Do you believe that regulation should restrict competition in order to foster the centralization of trading?

SUGGESTED READING

Chambers, S. and C. Carter. "U.S. Futures Exchanges as Nonprofit Entities." *The Journal of Futures Markets,* Vol. 10, No. 1 (1990), pp. 79–88.

Easterbrook, F. "Monopoly, Manipulation, and the Regulation of Futures Markets." *Journal of Business,* Vol. 56, Part 2 (April 1986), pp. 103–128.

Edwards, F. "Futures Markets in Transition: The Uneasy Balance between Government and Self-Regulation." *The Journal of Futures Markets,* Vol. 3 (Summer 1983), pp. 191–206.

Edwards, F. "The Regulation of Futures Markets: A Conceptual Framework." *The Journal of Futures Markets,* Vol. 1 (1981 Supplement), pp. 417–440.

Grossman, S. and M. Miller. "Liquidity and Market Structure." *Journal of Finance,* Vol. 43, No. 3 (July 1988), pp. 617–633.

Kyle, A. "A Theory of Futures Market Manipulations." In R. Anderson, *The Industrial Organization of Futures Markets,* D.C. Heath, Lexington, MA, 1984, pp. 141–174.

McDonnell, Jr. W. and S. Freund. "The CFTCs Large Trader Reporting System: History and Development." *Business Lawyer,* May 1983, pp. 917–951.

Pashigan, B. "The Political Economy of Futures Market Regulation." *Journal of Business,* Vol. 59 (April 1986), pp. 55–84.

CHAPTER
9

THE REGULATION
OF FUTURES
MARKETS

Futures markets are regulated both by self-regulatory organizations and the federal government—in specific, by the Commodity Futures Trading Commission (CFTC). Trading on exchanges, known as *contract markets,* is subject to the exclusive jurisdiction of the CFTC.[1] This chapter provides an overview of the regulatory structure applicable to futures markets and describes the major regulatory issues currently being debated.

9.1 THE EVOLUTION OF FEDERAL REGULATION

Federal regulation of futures markets began in 1922, when the Grain Futures Act gave birth to the Grain Futures Administration—a unit of the U.S. Department of Agriculture. In 1922 this was an obvious place for regulatory jurisdiction to originate. Futures trading was at that time almost entirely in agricultural commodities. Amendments to the Grain Futures Act in 1936 renamed it the Commodity Exchange Act, and designated the Commodity Exchange Authority as the federal regulator. The Commodity Exchange Authority was also a unit of the Department of Agriculture, so there was little substantive change in how federal regulation operated. This organizational structure reigned until 1974, when the Commodity

---

[1]The CFTC's exclusive jurisdiction is established in 7 U.S.C. section 2a (1982 and supp. III 1985).

Futures Trading Commission Act of 1974 was passed, creating the CFTC. The CFTC is an independent federal agency and, when created, was envisioned as the futures industry's equivalent of the securities industry's Securities and Exchange Commission (SEC). Today, federal regulation of futures trading is based on four major pieces of legislation: the Commodity Exchange Act, enacted in 1936 and significantly amended in 1968; the Commodity Futures Trading Commission Act of 1974; and the Futures Trading Acts of 1978 and 1982. The combined product of this legislation is known as the Commodity Exchange Act, as amended (CEA). The CEA is administered solely by the CFTC.

Over the 38 years between 1936 and 1975 sweeping changes occurred in futures markets. Most importantly, the types of commodities upon which futures were traded expanded. Metals, such as gold and silver, became significant, and there was growing pressure to trade futures on *financials,* such as foreign currencies and interest rate obligations. The orientation of the Department of Agriculture—to enhance the general welfare of agriculture and American farmers—was ill-suited to oversee this expansion.

Congress responded by creating the CFTC, which consists of five Commissioners appointed by the President and confirmed by the U.S. Senate. The Commissioners serve five-year, staggered terms. The Chairman of the Commission is separately appointed and confirmed, and serves "at the pleasure of the president." The CFTC, like the SEC, places extensive powers in the hands of the Chairman. Unlike the SEC, however, the CFTC is subject to *sunset* provisions, which require that the Congress periodically re-authorize its existence (usually every four years).

The CFTC has regulatory jurisdiction over virtually all persons or entities involved in trading a commodity. This includes contract markets, clearing associations, futures commission merchants (FCMs), floor brokers, trading advisors, commodity pool operators, vendors of commodity options, and those offering instruments known as *leverage contracts*. In addition, the anti-fraud and anti-manipulation provisions of the CEA give the CFTC jurisdiction over all futures traders.

The CFTC has exclusive jurisdiction over all futures contracts initiated by American contract markets. Today the CFTC exercises jurisdiction over futures on interest rate instruments, foreign currencies, stock indexes, and petroleum products—all of which began trading subsequent to 1974.

Federal regulation has three general objectives: (1) to prevent market operations that might interfere with efficient and fair pricing; (2) to prevent conduct harmful to customers, traders, and other market users; and, (3) to maintain the integrity of the markets. These goals might be narrowed and restated as (1) preventing market manipulation; (2) preventing fraud; and, (3) maintaining the financial soundness of clearing associations and FCMs.

The variety, scope, and complexity of the regulations and regulatory procedures directed at achieving these ends are extensive and can be covered only in a general manner in this chapter. Since Chapter 3 discusses clearing associations in some detail, this chapter does not include a discussion of financial soundness regulation since to do so would be repetitive.

9.2 REGULATION OF COMMODITY AND FUTURES OPTIONS

Beginning in 1981 a pilot program for trading options on futures contracts through designated exchanges was initiated by the CFTC. This program was ended in 1988, when the legal status of exchange-traded commodity options was made permanent. Today, the CFTC has exclusive jurisdiction over exchange-traded options on futures contracts.

Both the CEA and the CFTC also permit the trading of off-exchange commodity options under certain limited circumstances. In particular, dealer options on metals are permitted by writers who were in the business of both utilizing and writing options on the underlying commodity prior to May 1, 1978. These writers also must have a net worth of five million dollars; must issue confirmations and other documents to purchasers; and, must comply with a number of segregation, recordkeeping, and disclosure requirements. In addition, CFTC regulations permit off-exchange commodity options if they are sold to a person who is a producer, processor, or commercial user of the underlying commodity and who purchases the option in connection with his business.

Thus, only exchange-traded futures options and a limited category of off-exchange commodity options are permitted in the United States. Participants in these markets are regulated by the CFTC.

9.3 LEGISLATIVE RATIONALE FOR GOVERNMENT REGULATION

Legislative concerns underlying federal regulation parallel the historical reasons for futures market regulation discussed in Chapter 8: excessive speculation, manipulation, and concern about unscrupulous brokers and dealers taking advantage of the unwary public.

The 1936 Commodity Exchange Act states that "transactions in commodities . . . known as 'futures' are affected with a national public interest." They are "carried on in large volume" and "are generally quoted and disseminated." However, the transactions and prices of commodities on "boards of trade are susceptible to speculation, manipulation, and control, and sudden or unreasonable fluctuations in the prices thereof frequently occur as a result of such speculation, manipulation, or control, which are detrimental to the producer or the consumer and persons handling commodities . . . and such fluctuations in prices are an obstruction to and a burden upon interstate commerce . . . and render the relationship imperative for the protection of such commerce and the national public interest therein."[2]

These concerns were echoed 52 years later in connection with the enactment of the Commodity Futures Trading Act of 1974, and again in 1978 when

---

[2]See J. Stassen, "How the Growth of Fundamental Economic Issues Has Been Done Through Legislation Rather Than Research," unpublished manuscript, January 23, 1981, p. 6.

the Futures Trading Act was adopted. The 1978 Act states that a "fundamental purpose of the Commodity Exchange Act is to ensure fair practices and honest dealing on the commodity exchanges and to provide a measure of control over manipulative activity and speculative excesses that demoralize the market to the injury of producers and consumers and the exchanges themselves."[3]

9.4 SELF-REGULATORY ORGANIZATIONS

There are three main self-regulatory organizations: contract markets (or futures exchanges), clearing associations, and the National Futures Association (NFA). Exchanges must be designated (or licensed) by the CFTC, and must meet certain minimal requirements. Exchanges make rules and regulations that are binding on their members, monitor and enforce these rules, impose penalties, hear complaints, and arbitrate internal disputes. The CFTC has oversight responsibility for all exchange rules and for the enforcement of these rules.

Clearing associations were discussed extensively in Chapter 3. Their solvency and sound operation is fundamental to the integrity of futures markets. To this end they impose binding rules on clearing members, carefully monitor members, and enforce their rules to assure the soundness of their members.

The NFA (as well as the CFTC) subjects FCMs to extensive and intensive regulation. FCMs must maintain a specific minimum net capital, segregate customers' funds and securities, and prepare and retain detailed books and records of their operations. Periodically, the NFA audits FCMs.

With respect to exchange and clearing association self-regulation, responsibility for rule-making is vested in governing committees elected by member firms. Members can be viewed as falling basically into three functional classifications: trade houses, commission houses, and the floor group. While some firms may operate in more than one of these groups (as, for example, both a trading house and a commission house), the three groups are distinctive enough to be usefully distinguished.

Each group has different motivations for belonging to an exchange, and may have different perspectives on the objectives and scope of self-regulation. The rules, policies, and procedures adopted by the exchange's governing committees, therefore, can be expected to reflect a complex crystallization of all of the exchange members' motivations as well as some long-run public policy motivations that are likely to become an integral part of the decision-making process of governing committee members.

The motivation of trade houses is to assure that futures exchanges provide for orderly and liquid futures markets, and that they keep the costs of using these markets as low as possible consistent with orderly and liquid markets. Commission

---

[3]Futures Trading Act of 1978, Committee Print, Committee on Agriculture, Nutrition, and Forestry, U.S. Senate, 95th Congress, 2nd Session, 136 (January 1979).

houses are oriented more toward the general public and are interested in generating a high volume of trading among the public. To this end they want the public to view trading futures as both profitable and fair. Trading futures must compare well in terms of the risk-return potential relative to other investments, such as equities and bonds. The floor group, consisting of various kinds of traders and brokers, largely wants to see an active market, with many participants and with substantial movement in prices, either up or down.

In general, all exchange members want to see trading volume increase. Market abuses, disrupting failures, and a public perception of unfairness all work to diminish trading volume. As a group, therefore, exchange members want regulations that prevent these kinds of events from occurring. This is also the goal of government regulation. Thus, the behavior of exchanges and clearing associations as self-regulatory organizations is reasonably consistent with the public interest.

Despite a long history of self-regulation, government regulation of futures markets now plays the major role. There are few actions that an exchange can take without either obtaining prior approval from the CFTC or being subject to the CFTC overturning them at a later time. Self-regulation, therefore, increasingly reflects federal regulatory policy.

9.5   KEY ELEMENTS OF FEDERAL REGULATION

Although the scope of federal regulation is quite broad, there are three critical areas that are basic to understanding the federal regulatory structure. These are the CFTC's *contract designation* authority; its *market surveillance* powers to prevent manipulation; and the regulatory prohibitions of fraudulent trading practices. These are discussed in the three sections that follow.

9.6   CONTRACT DESIGNATION

Sections 4 and 4b of the CEA effectively prohibit all off-exchange futures trading by prohibiting any person from "soliciting, accepting, or making any futures contract unless such orders, contracts, or dealings are executed or consumed by or through a member of a contract market." A contract market is a board of trade or other exchange that has been designated as such by the CFTC. Designation as a contract market is granted on a contract-by-contract basis. Each futures contract proposed by an exchange must be approved by the CFTC before trading can commence. Thus, a contract market is actually an exchange that has received one or more *contract designations* from the CFTC.

Before granting approval to trade a contract the CFTC examines the contract's economic characteristics. Its evaluations are based on what is known as Guideline 1 (which is reproduced in the appendix to this chapter). This guideline specifies four areas of inquiry: (1) a cash market description; (2) an analysis of the terms and conditions of the contract; (3) the *economic purpose* test; and (4) the *public interest* test.

The description of the relevant cash market is simply a background for the other analyses. Analysis of the terms and conditions of the contract is generally the most time-consuming aspect of the CFTC's examination. It analyzes the delivery procedures (such as the delivery dates and locations, the kind and grade of goods to be delivered, the method of calculating invoice prices, and so forth) and the contract's pricing features (such as the price quotations, and the minimum and maximum price fluctuations that are specified). The focus of the CFTC's examination is to assure that an adequate deliverable supply will be available in order to prevent delivery congestion and price manipulation.

The *economic purpose* test requires that exchanges show that the proposed contract will either serve as a basis for pricing (i.e., price discovery) or be used for hedging purposes (i.e., risk-shifting). Analysis of its price discovery benefits normally stresses the difficulty of obtaining price quotes in the cash market and the poor quality and infrequency of cash price quotations. Analysis of the contract's hedging function centers on demonstrating the existence of commercial interest in the contract, and the existence of a price risk that is difficult to hedge with existing alternatives, but which could be successfully hedged with the proposed contract.

Finally, the *public interest* test requires that trading in the contract "not be contrary to the public interest." It is not clear which factors other than those included in the economic purpose test are required to meet this test. Exchanges and the CFTC customarily treat it as a formality.

These requirements make it clear that there are three objectives of contract designation regulation. First, it seeks to protect investors by prohibiting off-exchange trading and by permitting trading only under adequate supervision by exchanges. Bestowing a monopoly position on exchanges also enhances market liquidity. Second, it seeks to curb excessive speculation by requiring that an economic purpose is served by futures trading. Lastly, by scrutinizing a contract's terms and conditions, regulation seeks to prevent manipulation and to assure an orderly futures market.

9.7 MANIPULATION

The CEA makes it a felony to manipulate or attempt to manipulate futures prices. It is important, therefore, that all participants in futures markets understand the implications and potential consequences of their actions. This section describes the applicable regulations and legal standards.

9.7.1 The Statutory Law

The statutory law governing manipulation is contained in the CEA. The CEA provides for the prevention and deterrence of manipulation in three ways.

First, Section 5(d) requires that all Boards of Trade, as a condition for designation as a contract market, prevent the "manipulation of prices and the cornering of any commodity by the dealers or operators upon such Board." Guidelines for contract markets to carry out these responsibilities are provided by the CFTC. Thus, self-regulation has an important place in preventing and policing manipulation.

Second, the CEA bestows substantial powers upon the CFTC to prevent manipulation. Section 6c gives the Commission the power to institute in a Federal District Court an injunctive action against a contract market or other person for violating the Act by "restraining trading in any commodity for future delivery." Section 8a(6) empowers the Commission to communicate to contract markets "the full facts concerning any transaction or market operation." Section 8c(7) grants the Commission the power to alter or supplement contract market rules under various circumstances, including "for the protection of traders or to insure fair dealing." Section 8a(9) gives the Commission emergency powers to intervene directly into contract markets where there is "threatened or actual market manipulation and corners." Finally, Section 9(b) makes manipulation or attempted manipulation a felony punishable by a fine of up to $500,000 ($100,000 for individuals) and by imprisonment up to five years.

Thus, the CEA makes both the industry (via self-regulation) and the CFTC responsible for policing, preventing, and penalizing manipulation and attempted manipulation. Precisely what kinds of trading behavior are viewed as constituting manipulation or attempted manipulation is left to the CFTC and to the courts to determine. Nowhere do the relevant statutes define *manipulation*.

9.7.2   Key Manipulation Cases

The definition of manipulation, or the types of activities that might be considered manipulation, must be inferred from court cases and CFTC decisions. The number of litigated cases dealing with futures market manipulation (or attempted manipulation) has been quite small compared to the immense volume of futures trading over the years. This section reviews the major cases. These cases describe the kinds of trading activities that have been judged to be manipulative, and discuss the legal criteria used to determine whether a pattern of trading activities is illegal or manipulative.

Of the four cases reviewed, three are court decisions and one is an administrative decision by the Commodity Futures Trading Commission. Together, the cases span more than 40 years of futures trading, from 1948 to the present. In three of them the court found manipulation. In the fourth the CFTC found neither manipulation nor attempted manipulation.

GREAT WESTERN FOOD DISTRIBUTORS, INC. v. **BRANNAN (1953).**   Great Western Food Distributors, Inc. was found guilty of manipulating the December 1947 egg futures contract on the Chicago Mercantile Exchange.[4]

---

[4]210 F.2d 474 (7th Circuit 1950).

To make this determination, the court looked at the prices which existed at the close of trading in the contract. It found that at the close of trading the price of the December 47 futures contract was abnormally high compared to the January 48 egg futures contract price. In addition, the court found that both the price of the December 47 futures contract and the cash price of refrigerator eggs were abnormally high relative to the cash price of fresh eggs in December 47. Thus, the finding of *price artificiality* was based largely on historical price spreads at the close of trading.

The court also concluded that Great Western had a dominant market position during the last week of trading, in both the futures and cash markets. It found that Great Western's share of open interest in the December 47 contract was 59.6 percent on December 15, 76.2 percent on December 22, and 73.9 percent at the close of trading. In the cash market for refrigerator eggs in Chicago, Great Western also held 37.6 percent of deliverable supply on December 17, and between 44 and 51 percent during the last three days of trading. These market shares near the close of trading—60 to 75 percent of the open interest and 45 to 50 percent of the cash deliverable supply—were found to constitute *market dominance*.

An important element in the court's decision was its exclusion of fresh eggs and out-of-town refrigerator eggs from deliverable supply, even though these eggs were acceptable for delivery under the terms of the contract. The court excluded them because to deliver them would have imposed on the shorts an unacceptable additional cost: the price of fresh eggs was usually higher and no premium was allowed in the contract for their delivery, and out-of-town refrigerator eggs would have had to be transported to Chicago to satisfy the delivery requirements.

Lastly, the court found that Great Western *intended* to cause price artificiality. The court based this finding on the specific testimony of an employee of Great Western, who stated that his "program was instituted in the hope of a widening spread between December and January prices and that December prices were gradually raised by himself until Great Western was able to liquidate its holdings at an increase in the differential of $4\frac{1}{2}$ to 5 cents."

Thus, a combination of factors led to Great Western's being found to have manipulated the market: the specific intention to raise December egg futures prices, the occurrence of abnormally high December futures prices, and the possession of a dominant market position in both the futures and cash markets. Together, these circumstances are usually characterized as a *corner*—a market condition where the manipulator, through concerted action, acquires monopoly power in both the futures and the underlying cash market and uses it to bring about abnormal futures prices.

CARGILL, INC. v. HARDIN (1971). Cargill was found to have manipulated the May 63 wheat futures contract on the Chicago Board of Trade.[5]

---

[5] 452 F.2d 1154 (8th Circuit 1971). The contract specifies Number 2 soft red winter wheat to be delivered in Chicago.

In deciding this case, the court first found that "the futures price was artificially high and did not reflect basic supply and demand factors for cash wheat." To support this finding it pointed to four types of evidence: the futures price rose an unusual $18\frac{5}{8}$ cents a bushel during the last two trading days (about 13 cents of this increase occurred during the last hour of trading); the May-July futures price spread increased a record amount during the last two trading days; the futures price was out-of-line with the Kansas City wheat futures price; and the futures price was out-of-line with cash wheat prices before and after expiration of the contract.

Second, Cargill was deemed to have a dominant market position because it held 62 percent of the long open interest during the last minutes of trading, and because it held virtually all of the deliverable supply of wheat in Chicago. It should be noted, however, that at 11:02 A.M. on the last day of trading, only some 50 minutes earlier, Cargill held only 24 percent of the open interest.

With respect to its cash market dominance, Cargill's fate was determined when the court excluded from its measure of deliverable supply hard wheat in surrounding areas. While the shorts could have delivered hard wheat in fulfilment of their obligations, it was a more expensive grade of wheat and no premium was allowed to the shorts for delivering it. Thus, this court continued the earlier judicial precedent of excluding from the legal definition of deliverable supply premium qualities of the deliverable commodity.

To reach its determination that Cargill intended to cause artificial prices, the court inferred such intent from the facts together with Cargill's trading behavior. Cargill's trading history in the contract was as follows. In March, 1963, it was short more than 8 million bushels, as a hedger. On April 15, 1963, it liquidated its short position and began to establish a long speculative position, which by May 15 reached the 2 million bushel speculative limit. On May 20, Cargill began to liquidate its long position at high prices. However, at the opening on May 21, the last trading day, it still held 24 percent of the long open interest (1,890,000 bushels). From the opening of trading on the 21st until 11:00 A.M. the futures price declined. During that time Cargill continued to increase its position by purchasing another 100,000 bushels of futures. Trading was to cease at 12:00. At about 11:45 A.M. Cargill submitted a series of limit-sell orders, which allegedly pushed the futures price to almost $2.29, from $2.15 at 11:02 A.M.. Near the close of trading Cargill held 62 percent of the contract's open interest, and at the close had unliquidated holdings of contracts of 365,000 bushels. These it subsequently settled under the auspices of the CBOT by selling warehouse receipts to the shorts at $2.28.

Based on these facts, the court found, first, that Cargill had "inside information" about deliverable supply. On April 12, 1963, just prior to the date that Cargill established its large long position, the USDA published figures showing that there were 2,804,000 bushels of wheat in deliverable grade wheat stored in Chicago. Cargill owned 2,421,000 bushels of this wheat, or about 85 percent of the deliverable supply at the time. Thus, the court reasoned that Cargill knew that by establishing a dominant long futures position it could squeeze the shorts.

Second, the court found that Cargill's submission of a series of limit-sell orders at successively higher prices during the last 15 minutes of trading constituted abnormal trading behavior designed to raise futures prices. Further, it concluded that Cargill's holding of a 2-million bushel long position near the close of trading did not make sound business sense. The cash market was such that had Cargill taken delivery it could not have sold the wheat profitably. Here the court pointed to the fact that, subsequent to the close of futures trading, between the fourth and the thirteenth of June, Cargill sold cash wheat at prices ranging from $2.10 to $2.13 a bushel, well below what it paid for the last futures contracts it bought.

Thus, to determine that manipulation had occurred, the court used information concerning price artificiality, the defendant's dominant futures and cash positions, and an inference of intent to manipulate.

INDIANA FARM BUREAU (1982). In this case, before the CFTC, the complainant alleged that the respondent manipulated the July 73 corn futures contract on the Chicago Board of Trade by attempting to raise the futures price on the last day of trading.[6]

The CFTC dismissed the complaint, arguing that "respondents did not lay the base for a squeeze and it has not been demonstrated that they took any action with the intent to effect an artificial price." While acknowledging that July 73 corn futures prices did increase markedly during the last day of trading, the Commission found this price rise to be the result of a natural squeeze in cash markets due to transportation shortages, heavy export shipments, quality problems, and the failure of shorts to make adequate delivery preparations.

An important aspect of this case is the Commission's attempt to clarify the standard of proof needed to show manipulative intent:

> [We] hold that in order to prove the intent element of a manipulation or attempted manipulation of a futures contract price ... it must be proven that the accused acted [or failed to act] with the purpose or conscious object of causing or effecting a price or price trend in the market that did not reflect the legitimate forces of supply and demand. . . .

An important message contained in *Indiana* is that "where a long has not intentionally created or exploited a congested situation, the long has a contractual right to stand for delivery or exact whatever price for its long position which a short is willing to pay in order to avoid having to make delivery."

Thus, the decision clearly puts traders (the shorts, here) on notice that if another trader (a long, here) does not do something with the specific intent of affecting prices, the losses they may suffer are limited only by market circumstances. The decision appears to say that it is not the exercise of monopoly power that is illegal but a scheme to create monopoly power, whether or not such power is ever exercised.

---

[6]Indiana Farm Bureau, CFTC Dock No. 75-14.

THE HUNTS SILVER CORNER (1989). In a case that has become popularly known as the "Hunts Silver case," the Hunt brothers along with several other defendants were convicted in 1989 of manipulating silver futures prices during the period August 1979 to March 1980. During this period silver futures prices soared from less than $8 an ounce to over $50 an ounce, reaching a peak on January 21, 1980. Figure 9-1 shows the daily closing prices of both near month and distant month (12 months to delivery) silver futures contracts from 1978 through 1981. The defendants were found to have engaged in an elaborate conspiracy to drive up both cash and futures silver prices.

The key facts were that the defendants (the Hunts) (1) acquired large long positions in silver futures, at times reaching nearly 50,000 contracts (250 million ounces of silver); (2) held dominant long positions (as much as 60 percent of all open long positions) in the December 79, February 80, and March 80 futures contracts; (3) engaged in a pattern of requiring delivery as their successive futures positions expired; and, (4) possessed large stocks of physical silver, both bullion and coins.

The plaintiff, who was a short, argued that the defendants, by holding both large futures and cash silver positions and by taking large deliveries, threatened to squeeze the shorts. Unable to acquire silver bullion to make deliveries, the shorts were forced to offset their positions, driving up silver prices to the ben-

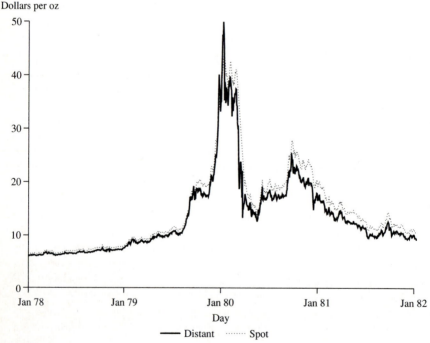

FIGURE 9-1
Silver futures: Spot and distant month prices (January 1978 to December 1981).

efit of the defendants. With the threat of a squeeze pending, the plaintiff contended that traders were generally discouraged from selling futures (since they would be unable to make delivery), further contributing to the upward pressure on futures prices.

Since the case was decided by a jury, it is not clear what factors the jury considered in reaching its decision. However, the decision appears to rest on a finding that the defendants successfully cornered the silver market. An unusual aspect of the case is that the period during which the corner was deemed to have been successful was quite long: at least five months, and possibly as long as seven months. This is an exceptionally long (and unprecedented) period for a delivery squeeze to be effective.

The decision raises two troublesome questions. First, if the theory of the case was that a corner or a squeeze occurred, why is it that the prices of distant month silver futures contracts also rose by nearly the same amount as did the prices of spot or near month contracts? (See Figure 9-1.) A trader short the distant month, with say 12 months or longer to arrange delivery, is unlikely to fear a squeeze. Consequently, a distant month futures contract with an artificially high price should attract a large number of shorts, driving its price down. This did not happen: traders did not sell distant month contracts in large quantity. Could it be that silver prices, rather than being artificially high, were a reflection of fundamental supply and demand factors, such as inflationary expectations?

Second, it is unclear how the defendants were to profit from the squeeze. Even if the squeeze succeeded in artificially raising silver prices for a period of time, prices would inevitably have to fall, as new supplies of silver bullion reached the market (as actually happened in early 1980). Further, the defendants would lose heavily on their physical and futures positions if they attempted to liquidate their holdings. Such sales would almost certainly have caused silver prices to plummet (which in fact did happen when the Hunts were forced to liquidate their positions because of margin problems). Overall, the defendants actually lost $2 billion. The defendants claimed that they did not intend to manipulate silver prices, but only to acquire large stocks of physical silver as an investment against an expected loss in the purchasing power of the dollar (and other paper monies). The jury decided otherwise: that the defendants intended to, and did, cause the prices of futures and cash silver to be artificially high during the 1979–80 period.

SUMMARY. A number of inferences can be drawn from the foregoing decisions. First, an alleged manipulator of a futures market must be found (1) to have caused an *abnormal* or *artificial* futures price, and (2) to have acted with *manipulative intent*. A necessary element is to show that the alleged manipulator held *dominant or controlling positions* in *both* the futures and relevant cash markets.

Second, price artificiality is measured in a variety of ways: absolute levels of futures prices, the relationship between futures and cash prices, various futures spreads, price changes, and so on. The courts have tended to rely heavily on historical price relationships in making a determination of price artificiality.

Third, manipulative intent must almost always be inferred from a trader's actions and conduct. To sustain this burden a plaintiff must show unusual or uneconomic behavior on the part of a defendant, and must show the absence of a plausible nonmanipulative rationale. A complete evaluation of a trader's circumstances and activities is usually required.

Finally, the *Indiana Farm Bureau* case suggests that it is the creation of monopoly power that is illegal, and not the mere exercise of such power by a trader who fortuitously finds himself in possession of monopoly power. The *Indiana* decision protects traders who do not actively seek to manipulate, and permits traders to reap the full benefits of their market positions. Its objective is to discourage manipulation while at the same time encouraging the full use of futures markets for legitimate trading activity.

In circumstances where traders acquire monopoly power because of natural events, rather than as a consequence of intentional monopolistic activity, exchanges may nevertheless intervene under their authority "to preserve orderly markets and prevent manipulation."[7] The narrow legal standards that define manipulation, while perhaps appropriate for the imposition of criminal sanctions, do not restrain exchanges from intervening in a timely and impartial manner to maintain orderly markets. In exercising these rights, exchanges must balance the competing interests of individual traders with the interests of exchanges, exchange members, and the public. In practice, exchanges have considerable discretion to intervene to ensure orderly markets.

9.8 FLOOR TRADING ABUSES

The Commodity Exchange Act prohibits fraudulent and noncompetitive floor trading in order to ensure that customer orders are executed fairly and under competitive market conditions. It also assigns to exchanges a major role in preventing abusive trading practices.

Futures trading takes place in auction markets on the floor of exchanges, where many buyers and sellers compete for orders. In active markets there is considerable noise and confusion, and unscrupulous traders may attempt to take advantage of customers. To prevent this from happening, an *audit trail* of orders and executions is kept for surveillance and investigative purposes. A good audit trail enables both exchanges and the CFTC to determine whether customer orders were executed at prevailing and competitive prices.

The CEA specifically prohibits certain kinds of fraudulent trading practices: *fictitious trades, wash sales, accomodation trades, improper offset* of customer orders, and certain *cross trade*. However, the trading practices that fall under each of these offenses are not always clear. The definitions we have come largely

---

[7]U.S.C. Sec. 7(d)(2sa) of the CEA 1978 requires exchanges to preserve orderly markets and prevent manipulation and other abuses.

from court cases, administrative proceedings before the CFTC, and general market practices.

The following definitions of illegal trading practices can be inferred from prior cases dealing with floor trading abuses.[8] In general, if these trade practices are done knowingly and wilfully, they violate the Commodity Exchange Act.

1. *Wash sales* are buy and sell transactions for the same commodity in the same delivery month that are entered by the same traders, or traders acting in concert, with the intent of having the orders offset each other. Wash sales do not include simultaneous buy and sell transactions entered into for the purpose of changing a trader's position in the exchange's line for delivery notices, and do not include scalping transactions that result in a *scratch* trade that does not have a gain or loss, provided the transaction was entered into for the purpose of making a profit or for other bona fide commercial reasons.

2. *Accomodation trades* are transactions in which a floor broker allows another trader to profit from a customer order held by the floor broker through any arrangement other than by an open and competitive outcry on the floor of the exchange or other transaction permitted by exchange rules. Accomodation trades include but are not limited to

   (a) the undoing or *busting* of a customer's already executed order in order to allow another trader to execute an order at the price of the customer's order or at some other price

   (b) entering into an order with another trader at a pre-determined price in order to allow that trader or any other trader to profit from a customer order

   (c) splitting or adjusting prices during opening or closing rotations except that adjustments for bona fide reporting errors may be corrected in accordance with exchange out-trade procedures

   (d) entering into or executing any futures transactions after the close of trading

   (e) executing a customer limit order through noncompetitive arrangements with any other broker or brokers

   (f) engaging in three-cornered or similar deals where three or some other number of traders engage in noncompetitive trades in order to take advantage of customer orders

   (g) entering into *ginzy* trades or other noncompetitive trading for purposes of split-tick trading or for other purposes

   (h) *cuffing* trades by delaying the filling of customer orders to benefit another trader

   (i) engaging in any activity during trade checking or out-trade procedures in order wrongfully to deprive a customer of profits

---

[8]See Jerry W. Markham, "Prohibition Floor Trading Activities Under the Commodity Exchange Act," *Fordham Law Review*, 58(1): 1–52, 1989.

3. *Cross trades* are prohibited unless conducted in conformance with Regulation 1.39 of the Commodity Exchange Act. Cross trades are any transactions in which a floor broker crosses for execution in the pit a buy and sell order of two different customers. Such orders are to be independently and separately handled by different brokers unless otherwise permitted by exchange rules.

4. A *fictitious sale* is any transaction that is not executed openly and competitively on the floor of the exchange as required by Regulation 1.38.

5. *Pre-arranged trades* are any trades that are arranged prior to their execution in a manner that excludes or impairs the open and competitive execution required by Regulation 1.38.

6. *Frontrunning* is the practice of trading in commodity futures or options contracts with advance knowledge of *material non-public* information about the cash, options, or futures market activities of any dealer, processor, user or consumer of a commodity or customer of the acting party where such activities could reasonably be foreseen to affect market prices and where the information is obtained by the acting party through employment with such persons or through any confidential, fiduciary or any other such special relationship with such persons.

- *Non-public* information is information that has not been disseminated in a manner which makes it generally available to the trading public through recognized channels of distribution.

- *Material* information is information which, if publicly known, would be considered important by a reasonable person in deciding whether to trade a particular commodity interest on a contract market. As used in this section, material information includes, but is not limited to, information relating to present or anticipated cash, futures or option positions or trading strategies.

These definitions are not exhaustive and are constantly evolving as market practices change and new markets develop. In addition, the now infamous FBI "sting operation" in January of 1989 set in motion a number of regulatory reforms, such as the requirement of an improved audit trail and restrictions on dual trading.[9]

9.9   REGULATORY ISSUES

A number of important regulatory issues are currently being debated. These include

- The jurisdictional conflict between the Commodity Futures Trading Commission (CFTC) and the Securities and Exchange Commission (SEC)

---

[9]Undercover FBI agents purchased seats on the Chicago Board of Trade and the Chicago Mercantile Exchange, disguised themselves as floor traders, and secretly recorded hundreds of conversations in trading pits. In July of 1989 federal grand juries returned indictments against 46 floor traders. Subsequently, many of those indicted were acquitted.

- Whether trading in off-exchange instruments that contain significant futures characteristics should be permitted
- Screen-based or electronic trading
- Globalization of futures markets
- Dual trading and the adequacy of the audit trail, and
- The institutionalization of markets and block trading

A full discussion of these issues is not possible. The issues are complex, and there are many different points of view. The discussion in this section is intended only to alert readers to the issues and to stimulate thoughtful analysis of them.

9.9.1 The Jurisdictional Conflict between the CFTC and the SEC

The SEC has regulatory jurisdiction over securities; the CFTC presides over futures. A problem arises because it is not always clear what is a security and what is a futures contract.

A futures contract, roughly speaking, is a fungible promise to buy or sell a particular commodity at a fixed date in the future. Futures contracts are fungible because they have standard terms and each side's obligations are guaranteed by a clearinghouse or a clearing member. Trading is in the futures contract, not the commodity.

A security, roughly speaking, is an undivided interest in a common venture the value of which is subject to uncertainty. Usually this means a claim on the assets and profits of the issuer. Shares of stock, for example, entitle holders to receive dividends and payments on liquidation; bonds promise interest plus a balloon payment of principal at maturity.

Securities are usually associated with capital formation, while futures are associated with price discovery and risk-management (hedging). It might seem, therefore, that a logical division of jurisdiction would be to have the SEC regulate capital formation financial activities and the CFTC regulate hedging instruments.

This is not the way it is. The SEC regulates options on securities, despite the close similarity between options and futures. Options are primarily associated with hedging, and not capital formation. Indeed, synthetic options can be replicated with futures contracts, and vice versa (as we discuss in Chapter 18). However, under section 3(a)(10) of the 1934 Securities and Exchange Act, options written on securities are deemed to be securities, giving the SEC jurisdiction.

The CFTC has a claim to regulate options as well. Options have characteristics similar to futures, and are primarily hedging instruments. This matter came to a head in 1980, when both the SEC and the CFTC asserted jurisdiction over options on securities based on pools of notes. Specifically, in 1980 options were traded on Government National Mortgage Association (GNMA) pass-through certificates. The CFTC argued that these options (as well as other options on financial instruments) were futures under Section 4c(b) of the Commodity Exchange Act (CEA). Further, the CEA gives the CFTC exclusive jurisdiction over futures. Thus, if the CFTC has jurisdiction, the SEC cannot have jurisdiction.

The conflict was resolved by the Johnson-Shad Agreement. (Philip Johnson was the CFTC's Chairman at the time, and John Shad was the SEC's.) This agreement provided that jurisdiction over options follows jurisdiction over the things on which the options are written. Thus, the SEC obtained jurisdiction over options on securities, and the CFTC got jurisdiction over options on futures contracts.

In 1982 this agreement was adopted as legislation by the Congress. A key provision of the legislation is that if an instrument is both a security and a futures contract, the CFTC's jurisdiction is exclusive. However, if the instrument is an option on a security, the SEC's jurisdiction is exclusive.

Do these provisions settle the conflict? Hardly! Each new financial instrument that is invented is apt to renew the conflict. Is it a futures contract, a security or an option? Indeed, this conflict surfaced again recently with respect to *Index Participations* (IPs). Securities exchanges attempted to offer an index security product to compete with stock index futures contracts. They chose IPs, and the SEC approved. The futures exchanges immediately sued to block their introduction, asserting that the new instruments were futures contracts, and not securities. Thus, the CFTC should have jurisdiction, not the SEC, and the instruments should not be traded on a securities exchange but on a futures exchange.

In a 1989 decision, the United States Court of Appeals agreed with the futures exchanges: IPs are futures contracts and the CFTC has jurisdiction.[10] Thus, securities exchanges were not permitted to trade them in the form originally specified. With the continuing development of new financial products this jurisdictional conflict is likely to be repeated over and over again.

9.9.2   Off-Exchange Instruments

This issue involves new instruments that participants do not want to trade on an exchange, preferring to trade them *off-exchange*. Off-exchange instruments are usually not subject to the same degree of regulation as are exchange-traded instruments.

Commodity-backed bonds are an example. In 1980 the Sunshine Mining Company offered to the public silver-index bonds. The bonds were redeemable at an index principal amount, which was the greater of $1000 or the market value of 50 ounces of silver for each $1000 face amount of the bond. If the index

---

[10]Chicago Mercantile Exchange, Board of Trade of the City of Chicago, and Investment Company Institute vs. SEC and Philadelphia Stock Exchange, Inc., Options Clearing Corporation, American Stock Exchange, Inc., and Chicago Board of Options Exchange, Inc., U.S. Court of Appeals, 7th Circuit, Nos. 89-1538, 89-1763, 89-1786, and 89-2012, August 18, 1989.

principal amount was greater than $1000, the company would deliver, in lieu of that amount, 50 ounces of silver for each $1000 face amount of outstanding bonds.[11]

Thus, holders of the bonds benefited from increases in the value of silver but did not suffer if the price of silver declined. Holding the bonds was a way to speculate on rising silver prices, similar to holding either a call option on silver or a long silver futures position. The latter alternatives, however, have to be traded on a futures exchange and are subject to CFTC regulation.

During the 1980s a large number of these hybrid, off-exchange instruments were invented, raising the issue of how (or whether) they should be regulated. In addition, there is concern that off-exchange trading will undermine centralized exchange markets for similar instruments. Off-exchange instruments commonly "free-ride" on the information and regulatory environment created by exchange-traded instruments. If unlimited off-exchange trading were permitted, it might destroy the liquidity of exchange markets, causing injury to the general public. There is also the question of whether users of off-exchange instruments need to be protected against fraudulent and unscrupulous vendors, as are users of exchange-traded instruments.

9.9.3   Screen-Based Trading

The *open-outcry,* auction style market is the traditional way that futures are traded on U.S. exchanges. Advances in computer and communication technologies are threatening this system. New technology may soon make it possible to trade futures (and other financial instruments) by computer. Traders will be able to trade directly with one another via computer screens, bypassing exchange trading floors and possibly even market-makers.

Some form of automated, screen-based trading is already in place in London, Tokyo, Toronto, Amsterdam, Zurich, Frankfurt, Paris, Vancouver, Madrid, Stockholm and Helsinki. The exchanges in these cities are trying hard to attract business from the United States. They are promising lower trading costs, around-the-clock capability, greater liquidity, fairer markets, and better market surveillance based on complete and errorless electronic audit trails.

The success of automated trading systems will depend on their ability to provide uninterrupted service, security, and superior liquidity. Critics contend that such systems will never be able to provide the liquidity that is provided by the current floor-based trading systems. Time will tell.

9.9.4   Globalization of Futures Markets

Trading in futures markets, as well as in other financial markets, has become global for two reasons. There have been enormous advances in the technology of

---

[11]See D. Gilberg, "Regulation of New Financial Instruments Under the Federal Securities and Committee Law," *Vanderbilt Law Review*, 39 (6): 1600–40, 1986.

storing and transmitting information, and there has been progressive elimination of capital controls among developed countries.

Globalization of trading, however, makes international regulatory and jurisdictional conflicts likely, and may require that regulators in different countries agree on who will be responsible for what. In the future, regulatory policies adopted by one country will impact markets in other countries.

Globalization raises the following issues. Is it necessary to harmonize regulations across countries, or should regulators compete with one another? Should countries have to provide reciprocal privileges to competitors from other countries? Will we be able to maintain the integrity of markets when trading and clearing is done on an international, 24 hour basis? Is systemic risk increased by diffusing regulatory responsibility among many countries?

9.9.5 Dual Trading and the Audit Trail

Dual trading is the practice by which floor brokers are permitted to trade for themselves as well as customers. This practice, while creating an inherent conflict of interest for a broker, has nevertheless been permitted because of the belief that it has enhanced the liquidity of futures markets. The regulatory approach has been to regulate brokers' activities to prevent abuse, rather than to prohibit dual trading outright.

In recent years dual trading has come under increased attack. After the 1989 FBI sting operation on the exchange floors it was alleged that floor brokers favored their own accounts over those of their customers, giving themselves the best execution by trading in front of customers. This concern was heightened by the fact that the audit-trail systems employed by exchanges were not precise enough to permit a complete re-creation of trading records.

Under CFTC regulations a brokerage firm that receives a customer order must prepare a written record of the order and must time-stamp that record to the nearest minute. If the order is then transmitted orally to the floor, the order must again be recorded as a floor order and must again be time-stamped when received. After being executed in the pit and returned to the broker's booth, the trade is again time-stamped. The gap in the trading record occurs because there is no requirement that the order be time-stamped when it is executed in the pit. During the time between execution of an order in the pit and the return of the order to the broker's booth prices may change. Floor brokers could take advantage of these price swings by changing the order execution prices.

While exchanges are trying to develop systems that would provide a more complete audit trail, Congress has recently considered legislation that would prohibit dual trading in active contract markets, or for those futures markets with a daily average volume of 7000 contracts or more. This ban would be lifted if an exchange can prove that its audit trail system meets the goal of a fully verifiable audit trail to the extent that it can detect all instances of dual trading violations.

In the future, even greater emphasis will be put on developing better audit trails and on policing floor trader activities. This will undoubtedly be a further catalyst to the development of computer-aided trading technologies.

9.9.6 Institutionalization of Markets and Block Trading

Large institutions, such as pension funds, are playing an increasingly important role in futures markets. This is most evident in the trading of stock index futures and bond futures, which have become major portfolio-management instruments for large financial institutions. These institutions have complained that exchange trading floors do not provide sufficient market liquidity for them to be able to execute large orders at satisfactory prices.

Futures exchanges, in order to cope with large-order trading, are exploring the feasibility of permitting some form of *block* trading, either on or off the exchange floor. In the aftermath of the October 1987 stock market crash, the SEC suggested that it might be appropriate for futures exchanges to consider permitting block trading to better accommodate portfolio trading and its effects.[12]

In futures markets, in contrast to securities markets, there is no specific mechanism for executing a large order in one or more pre-arranged transactions. The entire order must be quoted by open outcry on the floor of the exchange, either as a single bid or offer, or (more realistically) as a series of bids and offers over some period of time. The question, therefore, is whether some form of block trading mechanism similar to that used in securities markets could provide greater market liquidity for institutional traders.

The key to block trading in securities markets is the ability of the upstairs member firm to solicit interest in all or part of a large order from parties on both sides of the trade, to determine a "clean-up" price, and then to arrange for the block to be traded on the exchange floor at that price. This procedure is not permissible on futures exchanges, where there is a requirement of competitive execution on an exchange floor.[13]

A number of block-trading proposals, which would allow some form of pre-arranged trading, are now under discussion at futures exchanges and at the CFTC. One is *sunshine trading*. In this procedure orders would be announced prior to their entry on the floor of an exchange. Traders would be able to contact potential customers before the order is entered for execution in the pit. This procedure, it is hoped, would provide greater market liquidity for large orders, so that a large trade does not have an undue effect on market prices. In the future it is likely that some form of block trading will be instituted in futures markets that is comparable to what is currently done on securities exchanges.

---

[12]SEC Staff Report, "The October 1987 Market Break," 3-18, N.49, February 9, 1988; and the testimony of David S. Ruder, "SEC Recommendations Regarding the October 1987 Market Break," February 13, 1988.

[13]See "Large Order Execution in the Futures Markets," a report by the Committee on Futures Regulation of the Association of the Bar of City of New York, 1989.

CONCLUSION

This chapter has described the major components of the regulatory structure governing futures markets in the United States, and has discussed key regulatory issues that remain unresolved. In other countries, the institutional organization, trading systems, and regulation of futures markets may be quite different. Traders must learn the rules that govern the markets in which they trade. Regulation plays a significant role in the operation of futures markets in all countries.

QUESTIONS

1. Why was the Department of Agriculture the first federal regulator of futures markets?
2. In what year did the CFTC become the federal regulator?
3. Are off-exchange commodity options legal in the United States?
4. What are the general objectives of federal regulation of futures markets?
5. What self-regulatory organizations exist in futures markets? What are the pros and cons of self-regulation versus government regulation?
6. What is the CFTC's contract designation authority?
7. What is the definition of *manipulation*? Describe the main legal elements that must be shown in order to conclude that manipulation has occurred.
8. What argument can you make that the Hunts did not successfully corner the silver futures market in 1979–80?
9. If an FCM is holding an order from a pension fund to sell a large basket of stocks, and prior to selling these stocks the FCM assumes a short S&P 500 stock index futures position, do you believe this FCM's actions constitute frontrunning?
10. Why are there frequent jurisdictional disputes between the CFTC and the SEC? Do you think that competing private interest groups have played a role in fostering this regulatory conflict?
11. Why is the absence of a complete audit trail a problem in futures markets? What are the obstacles to providing a complete audit trail?

SUGGESTED READING

Anderson, R. "The Regulation of Futures Contract Innovations in the United States." *The Journal of Futures Markets*, Vol. 4 (Fall 1984), pp. 297–332.

Domowitz, I. "When Is A Marketplace A Market? Automated Trade Execution in the Futures Market." In *Innovation and Technology in the Markets: A Reordering of the World's Capital Market System*, ed. by D. Siegel, Probus Publishing, Chicago, 1990.

Edwards, L. and F. Edwards. "A Legal and Economic Analysis of Manipulation in Futures Markets." *The Journal of Futures Markets*, Vol. 4 (Fall 1984), pp. 333–366.

Fischel, D. and S. Grossman. "Customer Protection in Futures and Securities Markets." *The Journal of Futures Markets*, Vol. 4 (Fall 1984), pp. 273–296.

Gilberg, D. "Regulation of New Financial Instruments Under the Federal Securities and Commodities Laws." *Vanderbilt Law Review*, Vol. 39, No. 6 (November 1986), pp. 1600–1640.

Johnson, P. M. *Commodities Regulation*, Little, Brown and Company, Boston, 1989.

Kane, E. "Regulatory Structure in Futures Markets: Jurisdictional Competition Between the SEC, the CFTC, and Other Agencies." *The Journal of Futures Markets*, Vol. 4 (Fall 1984), pp. 367–384.

Miller, M. "International Competitiveness of U.S. Futures Exchanges." *Journal of Financial Services Research*, Vol. 4, No. 4 (December 1990), pp. 387–408.

Pietrzak, A. R. "Insider Trading in Futures." *Commodities Law Letter*, Vol. VII, No. 3 (May 1987), pp. 1–7.

Pliska, S. and Catherine Shalen. "The Effects of Regulations on Trading Activity and Return Volatility in Futures Markets." *The Journal of Futures Markets*, Vol. 11, No. 2 (April 1991), pp. 135–152.

APPENDIX: COMMODITY FUTURES TRADING COMMISSION'S GUIDELINE 1, PART 5 (AMENDED)*

Accordingly, the Commission hereby amends Part 5 of Chapter 1 of Title 17 of the Code of Federal Regulations by adding Appendix A which shall read as follows:

Appendix A—Guideline No. 1: Interpretive Statement Regarding Economic and Public Interest Requirements for Contract Market Designation

For purposes of a board of trade seeking designation as a contract market and thereafter for the purpose of demonstrating continued compliance with the requirements of Sections 5 and 5a of the Commodity Exchange Act, the following shall be provided to the Commission.

A. *Description of the Cash Market.* In support of the justification and demonstration to be furnished under Sections B and C of this guideline, a board of trade shall submit with its application a description of the cash market for the commodity on which the contract is based. For purposes of this section, the term cash market includes all aspects of the spot and forward merchandised and for which the contract serves as hedging or price basing function. As applicable to the justification of individual contract terms or the contract's hedging or price basing function, the cash market description shall include:

(1) Production of the underlying commodity, including as appropriate, geographical locations and seasonal patterns in the case of tangible commodities and scheduled issuances in the case of financial instruments.

(2) Consumption of the underlying commodity, including as appropriate, geographical locations and seasonal patterns of intermediate and ultimate consumption in the case of tangible commodities.

(3) The nature and structure of the cash marketing channels including the nature and number of marketing institutions, the nature of the forward contracting market, and the manner in which the price of the commodity is determined at various stages in its marketing.

(4) The prevalent means of market communications, methods of financing commodity ownership, and in the case of tangible commodities the manner in which tangible commodities are transported and stored.

(5) Information provided by the board of trade pursuant to this section shall include statistical data where applicable and where reasonably available. Such data shall cover a period of time sufficient to show accurately the historical patterns of production, consumption and marketing of the commodity which are relevant to the pricing or hedging use of the contract and/or the specification of its terms and conditions. In the absence of a justification for providing data from a shorter period, at least five (5) years of such data should be provided. If the board of trade through reasonable effort cannot obtain sufficient data, interviews with, or statements by, persons having knowledge of the cash market may be used to supplement or, if necessary, substitute for quantitative information.

B. *Justification of Individual Contract Terms and Conditions.* A board of trade shall submit an analysis and justification of significant individual terms and conditions of the contract. Such analysis and justification for each term and condition should be supported in the manner provided by paragraph (5) of Section A of the guideline.

(1) The justification submitted by a board of trade concerning significant contract terms shall include, where applicable, (a) evidence of conformity with the underlying cash market and (b) evidence that the term for condition will provide for a deliverable supply which will not be conducive to price manipulation or distortion and that such a supply reasonably can be expected to be available to the short trader and saleable by the long trader at its market value in normal cash marketing channels. To the extent that a term or condition is not in conformity with prevailing cash market practices, the board of trade shall provide a reason for the variance and demonstrate that the term or condition is necessary or appropriate for the contract and will result in sufficiently available and saleable deliverable supplies.

(2) The justification shall also include, where applicable, the following:

(a) Complete specification of commodity characteristics for par and non-par delivery (such as grade, class, weight, issuer, maturity, rating) including the economic basis for the premiums and discounts, or lack thereof, for differing characteristics. For futures contracts based on debt securities, this shall include an economic justification of the formula to be used for the evaluation of non-par instruments.

(b) All delivery points, including where applicable, for each point:

(i) The nature of the cash market at the delivery point (e.g. auction market, buying station or export terminal);

(ii) A description of the composition of the market;

(iii) The normal commercial practice for establishing cash market values and the availability of published cash prices reflecting the value of the deliverable commodity;

(iv) The level of deliverable supplies normally available, including the seasonal distribution of such supplies; and

(c) A description of the delivery facility (such as warehouse, depository, financial institution) including:

(i) The type(s) of delivery facility at each delivery point;

(ii) The number and total capacity of facilities meeting contract requirements;

(iii) The proportion of such capacity expected to be available for traders who may wish to make delivery and seasonal changes in such proportions; and

(iv) The extent to which ownership and control of such facilities is dispersed or concentrated.

(d) Delivery months. The board of trade shall specify the delivery months and, where applicable, shall describe the relationship of each future delivery month to cyclical variations in deliverable supplies, availability of warehouse space, transportation facilities, cash market activity, and any other factors which may affect the viability of delivery in each such month. The board of trade's justification shall also consider the delivery months for existing contracts which draw on the same deliverable supply.

(e) The permissible delivery pack or composition of delivery units (such as 30 dozen cases of eggs or bonds of the same issue), including a description of any restrictions on the composition of the delivery unit.

(f) The size of the contract unit, and, where relevant,

(i) Information concerning the typical cash market transaction size;

(ii) Information concerning the usual means of transportation for the commodity, including the quantity of the commodity customarily carried by such means; and

(iii) If a storeable commodity is involved, the size of the unit normally handled by commercial storage facilities.

(g) The inspection and certification procedures for the verification of delivery eligibility and, for perishable commodities, the duration of the inspection certificate and any discounts applied to deliveries of a given age.

(h) The delivery instrument (such as a warehouse receipt of demand certificate) and the conditions under which such instrument is negotiable.

(i) The transportation terms at point of delivery (such as F.O.B., C.I.F., proportional rail billing or freight paid to another destination).

(j) The provisions for payment of costs in making and taking delivery, including a description of significant costs (such as inspection, assay, certification, warehouse charges or rail charges).

(k) The minimum price change (minimum price fluctuation), including the manner in which prices for the underlying commodity are normally quoted.

(l) Any restrictions on daily price movements (maximum price fluctuations), including the effect of any such restrictions upon the contract's price and hedging functions; and

(m) A demonstration that the contract terms and conditions, as a whole, will result in a deliverable supply which will not be conducive to price manipulation or distortion.

(3) In the case of the contracts where cash settlements may serve as an alternative to or substitute for physical delivery, information submitted by the board of trade pursuant to this section must include evidence that the cash settlement of the contract is at a price reflecting the underlying cash market, will not be subject to manipulation, and must also include:

(a) an analysis of the price series upon which such settlement will be based, including the series reliability, acceptability, public availability and timeliness.
(b) an analysis of the potential for manipulation of the cash-price series.

C. *Economic Purpose Test.* As a condition of initial and continued designation, a board of trade must demonstrate that the contract meets the economic purpose test. In order to meet the economic purpose test a board of trade shall demonstrate that:

(1) The prices involved in transactions for future delivery in the commodity are, or reasonably can be expected to be, generally quoted and disseminated as a basis for determining prices to producers, processors, merchants or consumers of such commodity or the products or byproducts thereof, or

(2) Such transactions are, or reasonably can be expected to be, utilized by producers, processors, merchants or consumers engaged in handling such commodity (including the products, byproducts or source commodity thereof) in interstate (including foreign) commerce as a means of hedging themselves against possible loss through fluctuations in price.

(3) For purposes of this section, the term hedging means bona fide hedging transactions and positions as defined in 1.3(z)(1) of the Commission's rules.

(4) *Intitial Designation.* To meet the economic purpose test at the time of initial designation, a board of trade must demonstrate that it is reasonable to expect the contract, as specified to be used for hedging and/or price basing by providing an analysis of the potential price basing and hedging uses of the contract which shall include consideration of:

(a) The salient characteristics of the cash market, including the institutions and participants, as described pursuant to Section A of this guideline.

(b) The intended price basing or hedging characteristics of the specific contract terms and conditions, as described pursuant to Section B of this guideline. If a principal commercial use of the contract is expected to be hedging of commodities other than that for which designation is sought ("cross hedging") the board of trade shall supply data which indicates that such use of the contract would constitute appreciable risk reduction.

(c) As requested, statements from or reports of interviews with potential users of the contract which convey specifically the manner and circumstances under which these persons may be expected to utilize the contract for pricing or hedging.

(5) *Continuing Designation.* To justify its continuing designation under the economic purpose requirement, a board of trade designated as a contract market

must demonstrate that trading in the contract for which it is designated has, in fact, served a hedging or price basing function on more than an occasional basis. Such a demonstration shall include:

(a) An evaluation of the actual trading experience in the contract in terms of commercial usage and its use for price basing.

(b) An evaluation of the extent to which commercial participation in the contract constitutes hedging.

D.   *Other Public Interest Requirements*.   As requested, a board of trade shall submit evidence other than that required in sections B and C of this guideline pertaining to the public interest standard contained in Section 5(g) of the Act.

CHAPTER
10

STOCK
INDEX
FUTURES

Introduced in 1982 by the Kansas City Board of Trade, stock index futures contracts are now among the most actively traded futures. Together, these contracts account for about 5 percent of all futures trading in the Unites States. Figure 10-1 shows the growth of trading volume in equity index futures from 1982 to 1990. The most actively traded stock index contract is the Chicago Mercantile Exchange's S&P 500 futures. It alone accounted for 82.2 percent of all trading in stock index futures in 1990.

Since their introduction in the United States, exchanges in foreign countries have also begun trading in equity futures. The most successful are those in London and Japan. Table 10.1 lists the various stock index futures contracts that are presently trading in the United States and abroad.

Stock index futures have been successful because they have proven to be useful in managing large stock portfolios. One of the fastest growing financial sectors during the 1980s has been institutional fund management. Total assets under the management of large institutional investors have grown at the rate of 14 percent a year since 1980: from less than $2 trillion in 1980 to over $6 trillion in 1989. Pension funds are the largest holder of institutional assets, holding some 44 percent. Investment companies (mutual funds) have about 21 percent of these assets. Taken together, institutional investors hold about 45 percent of *all of the stocks* outstanding.

Institutional investors are also active stock traders, accounting for somewhere between 50 and 80 percent of trading volume on the New York Stock Exchange (NYSE), depending on the time period. Further, from 1965 to 1987

214

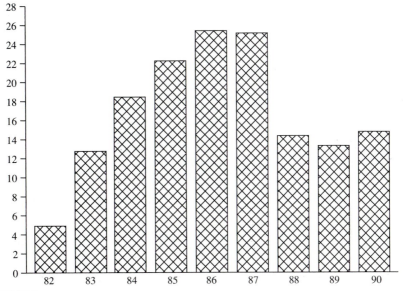

FIGURE 10-1

U.S. stock index futures (annual trading volume: 1982–1990).

the average size of a trade on the NYSE grew from 224 shares to 2112 shares, indicating a growing institutional role.

Another development has been the growth of *index* equity funds. Index funds employ a *passive* portfolio-management strategy. Passive portfolio managers do not attempt to identify under- or over-valued stocks or to predict general movements in the stock market. Instead, they hold a diversified stock portfolio that is designed to mimic a particular stock index (or a particular segment of the equity market). Over $200 billion is now being managed with a passive index strategy.

There are two reasons for this trend toward index fund management. First, there is increasing evidence that an active strategy of picking specific (under-valued) stocks is unlikely to be consistently successful, and that in the long-run an active portfolio strategy is unlikely to out-perform a passive portfolio strategy. Most *efficient market* studies support this conclusion. Second, since the costs associated with an active portfolio strategy (management fees, commissions, and so forth) are significantly greater than those associated with a passive portfolio approach, active portfolio strategies may actually underperform index funds.

These developments have made stock index futures a valuable portfolio management tool and have resulted in the rapid growth of stock index futures markets around the world.

TABLE 10.1
Stock index futures

		1990 Trading volume
I. U.S. futures exchanges		
S&P 500	Chicago Mercantile Exchange	12,139,209
NYSE Composite	New York Futures Exchange	1,574,641
MMI Maxi	Chicago Board of Trade	
(Major Market Index)		951,325
Value Line	Kansas City Board of Trade	52,046
Nikkei 225	Chicago Mercantile Exchange	35,558
Mini Value Line	Kansas City Board of Trade	14,081
TOPIX	Chicago Board of Trade	230
		14,767,090
II. Foreign futures exchanges		
Nikkei 225	Osaka Securities Exchange	13,588,779
Topix	Tokyo Stock Exchange	3,091,041
Bovespa Stock Index	BM&F (Brazil)	2,540,256
CAC 40	MATIF	1,641,398
FTSE 100	London International Financial Futures Exchange	1,443,829
Nikkei 225	Singapore Mercantile Exchange	880,513
EOE Stock Index	Financial Futures Market (Amsterdam)	436,404
All Ordinaries Index	Sydney Futures Exchange	310,004
Hang Seng Index	Hong Kong Futures Exchange	236,003
TSE 35	Toronto Futures Exchange	52,687
DAX	DTB (Germany)	51,363
Swiss Market Index	Swiss Options and Financial Futures Exchange	30,313
Barclay Share Index	New Zealand Futures Exchange	14,475
		24,317,065

10.1   WHAT IS A STOCK INDEX?

Stock index futures contracts are based on complex *cash instruments*. The cash instruments underlying the futures contracts discussed in earlier chapters were conventional commodities: gold, heating oil, corn, and so forth. The cash indexes on which stock index futures are traded are not what would normally be considered a commodity.

There exist many stock indexes, and they are calculated in many different ways. Table 10.2 shows several stock indexes that are widely followed and commonly reported in newspapers. These indexes provide summary measures of changes in the value of particular segments of the equity market—that covered

TABLE 10.2
Stock market indexes, November 22, 1989

STOCK MARKET DATA BANK   11/22/89

MAJOR INDEXES

HIGH	LOW	(12 MOS)	CLOSE	NET CHG	% CHG	12 MO CHG	% CHG	FROM 12/31	% CHG
DOW JONES AVERAGES									
2791.41	2074.68	30 Industrials	2656.78	+ 17.49	+ 0.66	+ 564.50	+ 26.98	+ 488.21	+ 22.51
1532.01	907.72	20 Transportation	1166.43	+ 8.18	+ 0.71	+ 246.95	+ 26.86	+ 196.59	+ 20.27
222.40	181.84	15 Utilities	221.33	+ 1.32	+ 0.60	+ 38.66	+ 21.16	+ 35.05	+ 18.82
1115.15	787.75	65 Composite	1002.45	+ 6.63	+ 0.67	+ 207.80	+ 26.15	+ 176.51	+ 21.37
337.63	251.00	Equity Mkt. Index	320.25	+ 2.01	+ 0.63	+ 67.57	+ 26.74	+ 59.51	+ 22.82
NEW YORK STOCK EXCHANGE									
199.34	150.63	Composite	189.21	+ 1.16	+ 0.62	+ 37.80	+ 24.97	+ 32.95	+ 21.09
237.76	181.16	Industrials	225.58	+ 1.64	+ 0.73	+ 43.48	+ 23.88	+ 36.16	+ 19.09
96.73	73.49	Utilities	95.14	+ 0.50	+ 0.53	+ 21.42	+ 29.06	+ 20.45	+ 27.38
212.37	136.88	Transportation	172.61	+ 0.77	+ 0.45	+ 34.17	+ 24.68	+ 26.01	+ 17.74
173.29	126.98	Finance	160.76	+ 0.21	+ 0.13	+ 32.83	+ 25.66	+ 32.57	+ 25.41
STANDARD & POOR'S INDEXES									
359.80	267.23	500 Index	341.91	+ 2.32	+ 0.68	+ 72.91	+ 27.10	+ 64.19	+ 23.11
410.49	307.64	Industrials	390.58	+ 2.93	+ 0.76	+ 81.13	+ 26.22	+ 69.32	+ 21.58
331.07	213.88	Transportation	269.96	+ 1.93	+ 0.72	+ 53.31	+ 24.61	+ 41.79	+ 18.32
145.28	110.42	Utilities	143.63	+ 0.89	+ 0.62	+ 32.46	+ 29.20	+ 30.99	+ 27.51
35.24	24.28	Financials	32.50	+ 0.05	+ 0.15	+ 7.93	+ 32.28	+ 8.01	+ 32.71
NASDAQ									
485.73	366.09	Composite	455.14	+ 1.00	+ 0.22	+ 87.38	+ 23.76	+ 73.76	+ 19.34
472.42	357.19	Industrials	442.69	+ 0.95	+ 0.22	+ 83.81	+ 23.35	+ 63.74	+ 16.82
550.11	422.20	Insurance	550.11	+ 1.87	+ 0.34	+ 126.60	+ 29.89	+ 120.97	+ 28.19
491.16	422.29	Banks	422.82	+ 0.53	+ 0.13	− 15.12	− 3.45	− 12.49	− 2.87
212.43	158.72	Nat. Mkt. Comp.	199.05	+ 0.43	+ 0.22	+ 39.59	+ 24.83	+ 33.40	+ 20.16
185.12	138.47	Nat. Mkt. Indus.	173.59	+ 0.35	+ 0.20	+ 34.43	+ 24.74	+ 26.17	+ 17.75
OTHERS									
397.03	290.09	Amex	371.72	+ 0.74	+ 0.20	+ 81.63	+ 28.14	+ 65.71	+ 21.47
278.98	223.77	Value-Line (geom.)	256.23	+ 0.87	+ 0.34	+ 32.08	+ 14.31	+ 23.55	+ 10.12
180.78	140.09	Russell 2000	167.18	+ 0.56	+ 0.34	+ 26.77	+ 19.07	+ 19.82	+ 13.45
3523.47	2636.86	Wilshire 5000	3334.98	+ 17.93	+ 0.54	+ 686.78	+ 25.93	+ 596.56	+ 21.78

Source: The Wall Street Journal, November 24, 1989.

by the specific index. A change in a particular index reflects the change in the average value of the stocks included in that index. The number of stocks included in an index could be few, as in the Dow Jones Industrial index, or very many, as in the Wilshire 5000 index, which covers all publically traded U.S. equities.

All stock indexes, however, share common features. First, a certain set (or number) of stocks is specified. Second, a base period is selected, for which the index is defined to be equal to some given value, usually 100.00. Third, a rule is selected for combining the prices of the stocks included in the index to determine the value of the index in periods subsequent to the base period.

Several methods are commonly used to combine the prices (or returns) of individual stocks to determine an index value: (1) weight each stock price (or return) equally; (2) weight by the level of the stock price (a higher price stock receives a heavier weight); or (3) weight each stock price by the market value of the company (a capitalization-weighted index).

In addition, once a weighting scheme is chosen, there are two methods commonly used to compute the average: arithmetic and geometric. An arithmetic mean is a simple average of the component stocks: sum the components and divide by the number of stocks (N). A geometric mean is more complicated: it involves multiplying together each stock's return, taking the Nth root of the product, and multiplying by the value of the index in the previous period.

Table 10.3 provides summary information for each of the major stock indexes. The S&P 500 index is a market value, capitalization-weighted, arithmetic index. It includes the stocks of the 500 largest and most actively traded companies. The average capitalization of companies in the index in December 1989 was about $16 billion, and the total capitalization of all companies in the index was about $8 trillion. The Dow Jones Industrial Average (DJIA) is a price-weighted, arithmetic index, and includes 30 *blue-chip* (large) companies. The Value Line index consists of 1700 selected large and small companies and employs an arithmetic averaging procedure.

Since different stock indexes cover different segments of the stock market, they exhibit different return and volatility patterns. In Table 10.4 the annualized yearly returns as well as the volatility of the major U.S. stock indexes are shown for the 5-year period 1985–1989. The most volatile indexes were the DJIA and the S&P 500, both of which represent large company stocks. Table 10.5 shows the correlations among these indexes for the same time period. While there is a high degree of correlation among all of the indexes, some are more closely related than others. For example, the relationship between the DJIA and the S&P 500 indexes is much closer than that between either of these indexes and the NASDAQ index. This is not surprising since the NASDAQ index includes small stocks while the DJIA and the S&P 500 include only large stocks.

In addition to U.S. stock indexes there are many foreign stock indexes. Most major countries have their own stock markets, and therefore their own stock indexes. Table 10.6 lists the major foreign stock indexes, and Table 10.7 provides annualized yearly returns and volatilities for major foreign stock indexes for the 1985–1989 period.

In order to compare foreign stock indexes with each other and with U.S. stock indexes, Table 10.8 shows the correlations among the various indexes for the 1985–1989 period. It is clear that there is normally very little relationship between stock price movements among various countries: the correlation coefficients are all low. This suggests that there are diversification benefits to be gained by holding a diversified worldwide stock portfolio.

TABLE 10.3
Description of major U.S. stock indexes

	Coverage	Weighting scheme	Method of averaging	Base year
Dow Jones Industrial Average (DJIA)	30 actively traded blue-chip stocks on NYSE	Price	Arithmetic	1885*
Standard & Poor's 500 (S&P 500)	500 companies, 400 industrials, 40 utilities, 20 transportation, 40 financial institutions; NYSE stocks comprise about 93 percent of the Index with AMEX and OTC stocks making up the difference	Market value (capitalization)	Arithmetic	1943
New York Stock Exchange Composite (NYSE)	All NYSE listed companies (approximately 1500 issues)	Market value (capitalization)	Arithmetic	1965
American Stock Exchange Market Value (AMEX)	All AMEX listed companies, common shares, ADRs, warrants	Market value (capitalization)	Arithmetic	1973
Nasdaq Composite (NASDAQ)	All NASDAQ traded stocks (approximately 4000 issues)	Market value (capitalization)	Arithmetic	1971
Value Line (VLA)	1700 selected companies, both blue-chip and smaller, NYSE issues, 14 percent are OTC issues, and 6 percent are AMEX issues	Price	Arithmetic	1961
Wilshire 5000 (W5000)	All companies traded in the United States	Market value (capitalization)	Arithmetic	1980

* The Dow Jones Industrial Average Index was first published on February 16, 1885, and only 14 stocks were included.

TABLE 10.4
U.S. stock indexes: Annualized daily returns and volatilities*
(from January 2, 1985, to September 30, 1989, in percent)

	1985	1986	1987	1988	1989	85–89
DJIA	25.08	20.28	2.23	11.15	28.87	16.89
	(10.28)	(15.36)	(36.46)	(18.23)	(12.11)	(21.09)
S&P 500	24.26	13.59	2.00	11.64	30.52	15.63
	(10.02)	(14.75)	(33.76)	(17.17)	(11.31)	(19.73)
NYSE	24.06	13.04	−0.25	12.21	28.82	14.85
	(9.36)	(13.59)	(31.53)	(15.29)	(10.03)	(18.22)
AMEX	18.73	6.71	−1.11	16.09	31.91	13.52
	(7.78)	(10.47)	(26.96)	(10.05)	(6.49)	(14.73)
NASDAQ	27.19	7.23	−5.38	14.27	28.82	13.60
	(7.97)	(10.18)	(25.41)	(9.95)	(7.25)	(14.17)
VLA	19.30	4.28	−11.20	14.27	22.41	9.15
	(8.20)	(11.53)	(26.52)	(11.44)	(6.95)	(15.03)
W5000	21.37	11.72	−0.73	12.43	29.89	13.76
	(9.30)	(12.78)	(30.05)	(15.16)	(9.40)	(17.78)

* Volatility is measured by the standard deviation of daily returns, and appears in parentheses beneath the annualized mean of the daily returns.

TABLE 10.5
U.S. stock indexes: Correlations of daily rates of return
(from January 2, 1985, to September 30, 1989)

	DJIA	S&P 500	NYSE	AMEX	NASDAQ	VLA	W5000
DJIA	1.0000	0.9817	0.9781	0.7439	0.7429	0.8093	0.9476
S&P 500		1.0000	0.9956	0.7702	0.7744	0.8339	0.9677
NYSE			1.0000	0.8019	0.8035	0.8600	0.9712
AMEX				1.0000	0.9293	0.9365	0.8083
NASDAQ					1.0000	0.9478	0.8171
VLA						1.0000	0.8609
W5000							1.0000

TABLE 10.6
Foreign stock indexes: 1989

| | Nov 23 | Nov 22 | Nov 21 | Nov 20 | 1989 | |
					High	Low
AUSTRALIA						
All ordinaries (1/1/80)	1631.90	1637.70	1629.30	1635.60	1781.80 (29/8)	1412.90 (7/4)
All mining (1/1/80)	834.50	839.10	824.10	828.90	875.10 (29/8)	652.60 (7/4)
AUSTRIA						
Credit Aktien (30/12/84)	407.60	407.48	411.70	416.54	515.09 (11/10)	219.50 (2/1)
BELGIUM						
Brussels SE (1/1/80)	6578.57	6581.19	6548.56	6505.50	6805.28 (26/9)	5519.30 (4/1)
DENMARK						
Copenhagen SE (3/1/83)	358.99	357.22	358.69	358.00	358.99 (23/11)	275.49 (27/2)
FINLAND						
Unitas General (1975)	580.80	591.60	607.50	618.90	815.80 (18/4)	580.80 (23/11)
FRANCE						
CAC General (31/12/82)	517.80	514.10	515.40	516.60	561.60 (11/10)	417.90 (4/1)
Ind. Tendance (30/12/88)	118.40	117.90	117.40	118.60	128.10 (10/10)	97.50 (27/2)
GERMANY						
FAZ Aktien (31/12/58)	648.36	(c)	641.49	648.86	690.91 (10/10)	535.78 (27/2)
Commerzbank (1/12/53)	1911.00	(c)	1888.70	1910.30	2056.80 (10/10)	1595.70 (27/2)
DAX (30/12/87)	1534.68	(c)	1514.09	1532.70	1657.61 (8/9)	1271.70 (13/2)
HONG KONG						
Hang Seng Bank (31/7/64)	2800.79	2812.02	2817.19	2820.28	3309.64 (15/5)	2093.61 (5/6)
IRELAND						
ISEQ Overall (4/1/88)	1677.22	1677.69	1681.78	1683.06	1848.94 (10/8)	1360.64 (10/1)
ITALY						
Banca Com. Ital. (1972)	667.88	665.39	664.98	663.60	734.84 (31/8)	577.49 (28/2)
JAPAN						
Nikkei (16/5/49)	(c)	36286.92	36059.87	35893.58	36286.92 (22/11)	30183.79 (5/1)
Tokyo SE (Topix) (4/1/68)	(c)	2737.20	2717.65	2717.63	2737.20 (22/11)	2366.91 (6/1)
2nd Section (4/1/68)	(c)	3704.55	3692.41	3686.95	3804.11 (9/10)	2774.38 (27/3)

(continued)

TABLE 10.6—cont'd.

	Nov 23	Nov 22	Nov 21	Nov 20	1989	
					High	Low
NETHERLANDS						
CBS Ttl. Rtn. Gen. (End 1983)	252.80	250.80	248.90	251.40	272.70 (21/9)	208.30 (3/1)
CBS All Shr (End 1983)	194.10	192.60	191.10	193.00	210.50 (8/9)	166.70 (1/3)
NORWAY						
Oslo SE (2/1/83)	614.30	609.87	615.08	618.75	695.50 (28/9)	467.17 (2/1)
PHILIPPINES						
Manila Comp (2/1/85)	1375.55	(u)	1386.52	1396.26	1396.26 (20/11)	804.62 (6/2)
SINGAPORE						
Straits Times Ind. (30/12/66)	1378.05	1361.67	1349.42	1345.34	1431.85 (12/10)	1030.69 (4/1)
SOUTH AFRICA						
JSE Gold (28/9/78)	2102.00*	2113.00	2057.00	1977.00	2113.00 (22/11)	1291.00 (15/2)
JSE Industrial (28/9/78)	2575.00*	2572.00	2564.00	2560.00	2838.00 (25/8)	1961.00 (3/1)
SOUTH KOREA**						
Korea Comp Ex. (4/1/80)	890.65	889.15	884.17	889.97	1007.80 (3/4)	846.30 (1/7)
SPAIN						
Madrid SE (30/12/85)	300.14	299.16	297.98	299.35	328.93 (13/9)	268.61 (1/3)
SWEDEN						
Jacobson & P. (31/12/56)	3884.50	3870.60	3928.30	3987.30	4660.30 (16/8)	3333.90 (3/1)
SWITZERLAND						
Swiss Bank Ind. (31/12/58)	750.70	744.40	741.00	743.60	829.10 (6/9)	613.10 (3/1)
TAIWAN**						
Weighted Price (30/6/66)	10094.44	9995.28	10098.60	10269.04	10773.11 (25/9)	4873.01 (5/1)
THAILAND						
Bangkok SET (30/4/75)	762.21	789.27	792.20	777.75	792.20 (21/11)	386.73 (2/1)
WORLD						
M.S. Capital Intl. (1/1/70)	(u)	533.80	530.40	529.20	551.20 (3/8)	487.60 (13/6)

* Subject to official recalculation.

** Saturday Nov. 18: Taiwan Weighted Price: 10309.07. Korea Comp Ex. 900.93.

Base values of all indices are 100 except: Brussels SE, ISEQ Overall and DAX–1,000, JSE Gold–255.7, JSE Industrials–264.3 and Australia All Ordinary and Mining–500; (c) Closed. (u) Unavailable.

Source: Financial Times, November 24, 1989.

TABLE 10.7
Foreign stock indexes: Annualized daily returns and volatilities*
(from January 2, 1985, to September 30, 1989, in percent)

	1985	1986	1987	1988	1989	85–89
Toronto 300 Composite (Canada)	19.24 (8.54)	5.53 (8.73)	3.00 (37.31)	6.99 (9.67)	20.91 (7.68)	10.58 (18.81)
Financial Times 100 FTSE 100, (U.K.)	14.72 (11.91)	16.86 (13.89)	2.33 (28.14)	4.87 (12.56)	34.47 (12.74)	13.49 (17.21)
All ordinaries (Australia)	32.10 (10.46)	38.22 (13.15)	−10.93 (38.43)	11.89 (15.06)	21.47 (15.99)	18.37 (21.43)
Brussell Stock Index (Belgium)	28.93 (10.43)	34.37 (14.52)	−11.38 (28.07)	41.37 (12.09)	27.02 (6.92)	23.89 (16.52)
Copenhagen Stock Index (Denmark)	39.39 (12.35)	−21.24 (14.01)	−1.45 (9.47)	34.37 (8.55)	26.56 (25.48)	14.98 (14.52)
CAC General (France)	38.25 (10.10)	40.16 (18.62)	−34.73 (22.26)	39.09 (15.97)	40.31 (12.16)	23.73 (16.71)
Commerzbank (West Germany)	55.68 (16.79)	4.94 (21.64)	−45.96 (29.24)	25.72 (16.25)	22.47 (12.78)	11.97 (20.57)
Hang Seng Index (Hong Kong)	36.30 (21.94)	38.07 (17.42)	−10.87 (50.32)	15.39 (17.01)	1.77 (40.55)	16.89 (31.63)
Banca Commerce (Italy)	69.57 (17.63)	45.65 (25.59)	−39.13 (20.32)	18.86 (17.44)	25.32 (10.71)	23.91 (18.97)
Nikkei 225 (Japan)	12.58 (9.54)	35.59 (13.91)	14.19 (27.08)	33.06 (13.37)	22.01 (10.48)	23.58 (16.25)
Oslo Stock Index (Norway)	31.18 (16.38)	−9.39 (15.59)	−7.23 (39.21)	33.93 (17.92)	51.76 (15.38)	18.28 (22.93)
Strait Times Index (Singapore)	−25.64 (18.75)	36.15 (18.32)	−7.88 (40.14)	23.39 (16.70)	36.09 (12.10)	11.18 (23.06)
Madrid Stocks Index (Spain)	23.30 (11.29)	45.44 (23.10)	8.64 (28.13)	18.82 (12.87)	22.99 (8.27)	23.89 (18.76)
Jacobsen & P. (Sweden)	24.49 (16.64)	34.59 (17.68)	−12.44 (28.05)	45.98 (13.33)	31.21 (10.62)	24.41 (18.05)

* Volatility is measured as the standard deviation of daily returns, and appears in parentheses beneath the annualized mean returns.

TABLE 10.8
Correlations of percentage daily changes in stock indexes: January 2, 1985, to September 30, 1989

	U.S. (DJIA)	U.S. (S&P 500)	Canada	U.K.	Australia	Belgium	Denmark	France	West Germany	Hong Kong	Italy	Japan	Norway	Singapore	Spain	Sweden
U.S. (DJIA)	1.00	0.98	0.17	0.43	−0.03*	0.15	0.02*	0.17	0.28	0.24	0.07	0.12	0.17	0.14	0.02*	0.18
U.S. (S&P 500)		1.00	0.18	0.43	−0.03*	0.15	0.03*	0.18	0.27	0.24	0.08	0.13	0.17	0.13	0.02*	0.17
Canada			1.00	0.40	0.56	0.13	0.03*	0.15	0.19	0.16	0.15	0.46	0.45	0.50	0.07	0.17
U.K.				1.00	0.27	0.10	0.08	0.20	0.35	0.23	0.16	0.33	0.46	0.30	0.05*	0.34
Australia					1.00	0.20	0.06	0.13	0.20	0.20	0.20	0.43	0.47	0.52	0.23	0.25
Belgium						1.00	0.06	0.13	0.22	0.21	0.12	0.17	0.22	0.29	0.23	0.17
Denmark							1.00	0.08	0.02*	0.08	0.06	0.08	0.05	0.03*	0.08	0.04*
France								1.00	0.34	0.27	0.24	0.18	0.23	0.18	0.22	0.30
West Germany									1.00	0.24	0.24	0.28	0.40	0.21	0.15	0.36
Hong Kong										1.00	0.14	0.19	0.20	0.26	0.19	0.22
Italy											1.00	0.17	0.25	0.14	0.14	0.19
Japan												1.00	0.41	0.40	0.14	0.32
Norway													1.00	0.46	0.16	0.42
Singapore														1.00	0.24	0.28
Spain															1.00	0.17
Sweden																1.00

* Not statistically significant at 5% level. Otherwise, all correlation coefficients are significant at this level.

TABLE 10.9
Contract specifications of stock index futures traded in the United States as of 1990

	Value Line	S&P 500	NYSE Composite	Mini Value Line	MMI Maxi
Inception date	Feb 24, 1982	Apr 21, 1982	May 6, 1982	Jul 29, 1983	Aug 6, 1985
Exchange	KCBT	CME	NYFE	KCBT	CBOT
Ticker symbol	KV	SP	YX	MV	BC
Trading hours (Eastern time)	9:30 A.M. to 4:15 P.M.	9:30 A.M. to 4:15 P.M.	9:30 A.M. to 4:15 P.M.	9:30 A.M. to 4:15 P.M.	9:15 A.M. to 4:15 P.M.
Trading unit	$500 × index	$500 × index	$500 × index	$100 × index	$250 × index
Price quote	Index points	Index points	Index points	Index points	Index points
Contract months	Mar, Jun, Sep, Dec	Mar, Jun, Sep, Dec	Mar, Jun, Sep, Dec	Mar, Jun, Sep, Dec	Monthly
Minimum price fluctuation	0.05 Index point, $25	0.05 Index point, $25	0.05 Index point, $25	0.05 Index point $5	0.05 Index point, $5
Daily price limit	50 points	(2)	28 points	50 points	(2)
Last trading day	Third Friday of contract month	Third Thursday of contract month	Third Thursday of contract month	Third Friday of contract month	Third Friday of contract month
Delivery (1)	Cash-settled	Cash-settled	Cash-settled	Cash-settled	Cash-settled

Note:

1. All futures contracts (except the S&P 500 futures) are cash-settled based on the closing price on the last trading day. S&P 500 futures are cash-settled according to a special opening quotation on the third Friday of the contract month.

2. For the most recent daily price limits and trading halts, contact the respective exchanges.

TABLE 10.10
Contract specifications of major foreign stock index futures as of 1990

	FTSE 100	All ordinaries	Nikkei Dow	Hang Seng Index	Nikkei 225	TOPIX	CAC 40
Inception date	May 3, 1984	Aug 3, 1984	Sep 3, 1986	Dec 31, 1986	Sep 3, 1988	Sep 3, 1988	Mar 1, 1989
Exchange	LIFFE	SYFE	SIMEX	HKFE	OSE	TSE	MATIF
Ticket symbol	ZX	VB	FN	HI			MX
Trading hours (local time)	9:05 A.M. to 4:05 P.M.	9:30 A.M. to 12:30 P.M. 2:00 P.M. to 3:45 P.M.	8:00 A.M. to 2:15 P.M.	10:00 A.M. to 12:30 P.M. 2:30 P.M. to 3:30 P.M.	9:00 to 11:15 A.M. 1:00 to 3:15 P.M.	9:00 to 11:15 A.M. 1:00 to 3:15 P.M.	10:00 A.M. to 5:00 P.M.
Price quote	Index points	Index points	Index points	Index points	Index points	Index points	Index points
Contract months	Mar, Jun, Sep, Dec	Mar, Jun, Sep, Dec	Mar, Jun, Sep, Dec	3 alternate even months	Mar, Jun, Sep, Dec	Mar, Jun, Sep, Dec	(3)
Minimum price fluctuation	0.05 index point, £12.50	0.01 index point, A $10	5 index ¥2500	1 index point, HK $50	¥10,000	¥10,000	0.1 index point, FF20
Daily price limit		None	(1)	300 points	(2)	(2)	50 points
Last trading day	11:20 A.M. of last business day of contract month	Last business day of contract month	Third Wednesday of contract month	Third business day prior to end of contract month	Third business day, prior to tenth of contract month	Third business day, prior to tenth of contract month	4:00 P.M. of last business day of contract month
Delivery	Cash-settled at 11:20 A.M. price on last trading day	Cash-settled at 12:00 P.M. price on last trading day	Cash-settled at closing price on last trading day	Cash-settled at closing price on last trading day	Cash-settled	Cash-settled	Cash-settled at 4:00 P.M. price on last trading day

Note:

1. 10 percent of previous settlement price, expandable to 15 percent.
2. 3 percent of previous settlement price.
3. Three spot months plus one quarterly expiring month.

10.2 STOCK INDEX FUTURES

Futures contracts are traded on various stock indexes. Tables 10.9 and 10.10 provide summary descriptions of the contract specifications of the major stock index futures contracts traded both in the United States and in foreign countries. The most actively traded index is the American S&P 500 index, although within the last few years there has been a remarkable growth in Japanese stock index futures trading (see Table 10.1).

The movement of stock index futures prices is very similar to that of the underlying stock index, as one might expect. Table 10.11 provides annualized average yearly returns for the major U.S. stock index futures and the standard deviations (or volatility) of returns for the 7-year period 1982–1988. Comparing these returns with the relevant underlying cash indexes that were shown earlier in Table 10.4 we can see that there is very little difference in the annual returns between the futures and cash indexes. In general, however, the volatility of the futures indexes is somewhat greater than the cash (spot) stock indexes.

Table 10.12 shows the correlation between daily changes in the various futures indexes and the underlying stock indexes. (The futures indexes used are those for the near month futures contracts.) It is clear that the futures and the spot stock indexes are highly correlated, although the closeness of the relationship varies from year to year and from index to index.

TABLE 10.11
Major stock index futures — Annualized daily returns and volatilities* (near month futures prices, 1982–1988)

	S&P 500	Value Line	NYSE Composite	MMI Maxi
1982	26.58	29.05	26.40	
	(26.62)	(25.66)	(29.01)	
1983	16.54	19.89	17.49	
	(15.98)	(16.09)	(16.17)	
1984	1.39	−7.00	2.16	
	(14.42)	(16.09)	(14.57)	
1985	22.09	17.48	21.69	28.42
	(11.75)	(13.09)	(12.21)	(10.30)
1986	13.48	3.35	13.05	21.09
	(17.01)	(16.43)	(17.35)	(16.28)
1987	1.87	−10.42	−0.43	7.09
	(46.39)	(35.95)	(24.17)	(40.58)
1988	12.73	20.88	13.41	9.45
	(19.29)	(18.47)	(19.32)	(19.99)

* Volatility is measured by the standard deviation of daily percentage changes and is shown in parenthesis beneath the mean percentage daily price changes (or returns).

TABLE 10.12
**Correlations between cash and near month stock index
futures (percentage daily price changes, 1983–1988)**

	1983	1984	1985	1986	1987	1988
S&P 500	0.86	0.88	0.87	0.93	0.96	0.96
NYSE	0.87	0.86	0.87	0.92	0.96	0.95
VLA	0.79	0.78	0.78	0.83	0.87	0.87
MMI			0.95	0.79	0.92	0.94

10.3   SETTLEMENT PROCEDURES OR DELIVERY

In contrast to most futures contracts, which call for physical (or actual) delivery of an underlying cash commodity, stock index futures are nearly always settled by *cash delivery*. No physical commodity (or stock certificate) is delivered by the short. All futures positions that are open at the close of the final trading day in the futures contract are settled by a cash transfer, the amount of which is usually determined by reference to the cash price at the close of trading in the cash market on the last trading day in the futures contract.

The S&P 500 futures contract, however, uses a different settlement procedure. The final trading day for this contract is always a Thursday, and all open contracts at that time are settled according to the *Special Opening Quotation* in the cash market on the following Friday morning. Normally, this quotation is the average of opening (cash) stock prices on Friday morning. If, for example, the futures index is 350 at the close of trading on Thursday, and the *Opening (cash) Quotation* on Friday is 352, the final cash transfer will be $1000 (or $500 × 2 index points), going from the short to the long. This cash transfer will be debited and credited directly to the respective short and long margin accounts.

Stock index futures were the first to employ cash settlement as a substitute for physical delivery. The reason is obvious. A requirement of delivering 500 stocks in the proportions needed to replicate the index underlying the futures contract is more cumbersome and costly than cash settlement.[1] Also, if a long desires to possess actual stocks, he or she can easily purchase such stocks in the cash market.

The effect of cash settlement is to force the futures price to be equal to the cash price at the settlement date. At settlement the futures stock index must be identical to the cash stock index. Thus, although the futures index will (and

---

[1] When introduced in Japan, the Osaka 50 stock index futures required physical delivery. This was one of the factors that led to its swift demise.

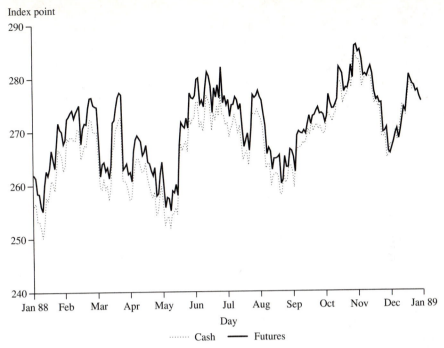

FIGURE 10-2
S&P stock indexes: Cash versus December 1988 futures prices (daily from February 1, 1988, to December 15, 1988).

should) differ from the cash index at most times, the indexes will always be equal at settlement.

Figure 10-2 depicts this convergence property. It graphs both the December 88 S&P futures index and the S&P cash index over the life of the futures contract—February to December 1988.

10.4 STOCK INDEX FUTURES PRICE QUOTATIONS

Table 10.13 shows the price quotations for various stock index futures that appear daily in the Wall Street Journal, as well as the volume and open interest figures for these contracts. The prices in Table 10.13 are as of the close of trading on November 23, 1989. For the S&P 500 index, prices are quoted for three contracts: those with delivery dates in December 89, March 90, and June 90. Almost all of the open positions are in the near month futures: December 89. The lack of trading in distant month contracts suggests that there is little liquidity in these markets. Indeed, it is possible to trade in even more distant contracts, but these are not shown because of low volume and open interest.

The settlement price of the December 89 S&P futures is 342.55. What, then, is the value of a single December S&P 500 futures contract? To calculate

TABLE 10.13

Stock index futures: Price quotations, volume, and open interest for November 23, 1989

FUTURES

S&P 500 INDEX (CME) 500 times index

	Open	High	Low	Settle	Chg	Open High	Low	Open Interest
Dec	341.90	343.35	341.20	342.55	+ 1.00	364.50	298.90	105,909
Mr90	346.10	347.55	345.60	346.80	+ 1.00	369.05	325.80	18,245
June	350.80	351.40	349.75	350.70	+ .90	373.20	332.85	632

Est vol 30,200; vol Tues 41,313; open int 124,801, −423.
Indx prelim High 341.92; Low 339.59; Close 341.91 +2.32

NYSE COMPOSITE INDEX (NYFE) 500 times index

	Open	High	Low	Settle	Chg	Open High	Low	Open Interest
Dec	189.30	190.10	188.95	189.60	+ .55	201.95	161.10	6,049
Mr90	191.55	192.25	191.20	191.80	+ .55	204.20	170.20	408
June	....	....	....	193.95	+ .55	205.45	178.05	73

Est vol 3,605; vol Tues 5,037; open int 6,537, +235.
The index: High 189.22; Low 188.03; Close 189.21 +1.16

MAJOR MKT INDEX (CBT) $250 times index

	Open	High	Low	Settle	Chg	Open High	Low	Open Interest
Dec	528.00	531.80	528.00	531.05	+ 2.60	556.75	487.00	2,998

Est vol 3,000; vol Tues 3,163; open int 3,087, +226.
The index: High 530.85; Low 526.82; Close 530.63 +3.75

—OTHER INDEX FUTURES—

Settlement price of selected contract. Volume and open interest of all contract months.

KC Mini Value Line (KC) 100 times Index
  Dec 286.10 +.30; Est. vol. 50; Open int. 102
KC Value Line Index (KC) 500 times Index
  Dec 285.90 ; Est. vol. 150; Open int. 1,196
  The index: High 285.10; Low 284.06; Close 285.10 +1.05

Source: The Wall Street Journal, November 24, 1989.

this value, the index quotation of 342.55 must be multiplied by $500. Each index point is worth $500. Thus, on November 23, the value of one December 89 contract was $171,275. The 1.00 point change in the December S&P 500 index that appears in Table 10.13 means that the value of each S&P 500 contract increased by $500 from the day before (1.00 × $500 = $500).

Similarly, the value of the Major Market Index futures contract is calculated by multiplying the index by $250. For example, on November 23, the value of the December 89 MMI futures was $132,762.50 ($250 × 531.05); and a 2.60 point change represents a $650 change in the contract value ($250 × 2.60 = $650).

Thus, the value of a particular stock index futures contract is determined by ascribing a specific value to each point in the underlying cash index. To value the contract, you must know the relevant dollar multiple. The higher the dollar value (or multiple) assigned to each index point, the greater is the value of a contract, everything else being equal. Exchanges attempt to select a dollar multiple that will make their futures contracts as attractive as possible to potential users. Too large a contract size may make it too risky for individuals to trade; too small a contract size may make it inefficient for institutions to trade.

10.5 THEORETICAL FUTURES PRICES

The theoretical relationship between the value of stock index futures contracts and cash stock indexes can be described by the cost-of-carry model discussed earlier in Section 4.3.2 of Chapter 4. In equilibrium, the value of the futures contract should be equal to the value of the cash index plus the net cost-of-carry.

Earlier in Chapter 4 the cost-of-carry was defined to be equivalent to the cost of financing: the interest rate that would have to be paid to borrow the necessary funds to buy and carry the asset. *Net* cost-of-carry refers to net financing costs: the cost of financing adjusted for any monetary benefits received as a result of holding (or carrying) the asset.[2] Holders of stock receive dividends; holders of bonds receive interest income.

A model which describes the relationship between stock index futures and cash prices is

$$FP_{t,T} = CP_t + CP_t \times (R_{t,T} - D_{t,T}) \times \frac{T-t}{365}$$

where $FP_{t,T}$ is the stock index futures price (or value) at time t of a contract with settlement date T, CP_t is the price (or value) of the cash index at time t, $R_{t,T}$ is the annualized financing rate for period $T-t$ (in decimal form), and $D_{t,T}$ is the annualized dividend yield on the stocks in the cash index over period $T-t$ (in decimal form). More specifically, $D_{t,T}$ is the *expected* average dividend yield on the stocks that make up the cash stock index over the holding period.[3] Thus, the element in parenthesis is the net financing cost: the borrowing rate minus the dividend yield. When $R_{t,T}$ is greater than $D_{t,T}$ the above formula indicates that the futures price should be above the spot price, or it should trade at a *premium* to the cash. When $R_{t,T}$ is less than $D_{t,T}$ the futures price should be below the spot price, or should trade at a *discount*.

---

[2]There are no significant physical storage costs associated with carrying stock certificates.

[3]This model is technically a *forward* pricing model, since it does not incorporate possible margin flows in determining the theoretical price. Of course, it is well known that forward and futures prices will not be exactly equal if interest rates are stochastic because futures contracts are settled daily and forward contracts are not settled until the contract matures. Several studies have examined the theoretical difference between forward and futures prices in a variety of contexts: J. C. Cox, J. E. Ingersoll, and S. A. Ross, "The Relation between Forward and Futures Prices," *Journal of Financial Economics,* 1981, pp. 321–46; R. A. Jarrow and G. S. Oldfield, "Forward Contracts and Futures Contracts," *Journal of Financial Economics,* 1981, pp. 373–82; and S. F. Richard and M. Sundaresan, "A Continuous Time Equilibrium Model of Forward Prices and Futures Prices in a Multigood Economy," *Journal of Financial Economics,* 1981, pp. 347–72. Nonetheless, various simulations and empirical studies have shown that the difference between forward and futures prices is economically insignificant (see B. Cornell and M. R. Reinganum, "Forward and Futures Prices: Evidence from the Foreign Exchange Markets," *Journal of Finance,* 1981, pp. 1035–45; and, R. J. Rendleman and C. E. Carabini, "The Efficiency of the Treasury Bill Futures Market," *Journal of Finance,* 1979, pp. 895–914). In general, these studies do not find a significant practical difference between futures and forward prices.

TABLE 10.14
Calculation of theoretical stock index futures price

On November 1, 1988, S&P 500 cash index = 279.06.

What is the theoretical price on that date for the December 88 S&P 500 futures contract, which matures on December 15, 1988?

Borrowing cost (r) is assumed to be the 3-month annual T-bill rate: 7.56%

Expected annualized dividend yield (d) = 3.5%, based on historical dividend yields

Carrying period = 44 days

$$F_{t,T} = S_t + S_t(r_t - d_t)\frac{T - t}{365}$$

$$= 279.06 + 279.06 \times (0.0756 - 0.035) \times \frac{44}{365}$$

$$= 279.06 + 279.06 \times (0.0049)$$

$$= \underline{\underline{280.43}}$$

On November 1, 1988, the quoted price for the December 1988 S&P 500 futures contract was 280.15.

Table 10.14 provides an example of how to calculate the theoretical S&P 500 futures index using actual cash index values and the actual borrowing and dividend rates. In this case the theoretical index value is 280.43, is greater than the cash index value of 279.06 because the financing rate is greater than the dividend yield. The theoretical value of the futures contract, therefore, is $140,215 ($500 × 280.43).

10.6 THE EQUIVALENT PORTFOLIO RATIONALE

The foregoing cost-of-carry model for pricing stock index futures is founded on the theoretical equivalency of competing alternative portfolios. Consider the following two investment strategies which should provide investors with the same return:

- Strategy 1:
  Purchase a share of portfolio XYZ stocks and hold it until the end of period T (one year from today). The return on these stocks for this period can be defined as

$$\tilde{R}_1 = \tilde{S}_T - S_0 + D$$

where $\tilde{R}_1$ is the total dollar return at time T, $\tilde{S}_T$ is the stock price at time T, S_0 is the stock price at time of purchase, and D is the dollar dividend paid at time T. A tilde ($\sim$) over a variable indicates a random variable whose value cannot be known in advance. Thus, S_T and R_1 are uncertain. We simplify by assuming that D is known with certainty.

- Strategy 2:
  Instead of buying the stock at the price of S_0, the amount S_0 is invested in a risk-free asset, such as Treasury bills, that pays a yield of r, and simultaneously a futures contract is purchased at price F_0 which calls for delivery of XYZ stocks at T. The dollar return over the holding period (i.e., one year) of this investment will be

$$\tilde{R}_2 = \tilde{F}_T - F_0 + rS_0$$

where $\tilde{F}_T$ is the uncertain futures price at time T, rS_0 is the dollar return on the risk-free asset paid at time T, and F_0 is the futures price at the time the futures contract is purchased.

As discussed earlier, at delivery, or time T, $\tilde{F}_T$ must equal $\tilde{S}_T$ because of the cash settlement procedures used for stock index futures. Thus, the two strategies are equivalent in risk because they both depend only on the uncertain ending values of $\tilde{S}_T$ and $\tilde{F}_T$.

They should, therefore, earn the same return.[4] Hence,

$$\tilde{R}_1 = \tilde{R}_2$$

and

$$\tilde{S}_T - S_0 + D = \tilde{F}_T - F_0 + rS_0$$

and

$$F_0 = S_0 + rS_0 - D$$

This is the identical net cost-of-carry formulation provided in the previous section.

10.7 STOCK INDEX ARBITRAGE

If actual futures and cash prices do not reflect the theoretical relationship described in the previous section, there may be profitable arbitrage opportunities, and stock index arbitrage trading will occur. The following describes, in a simplified setting, why and how such arbitrage occurs.

Suppose that a hypothetical stock portfolio presently has a value of $100, and that it has an annual dividend yield of 3 percent, which is earned evenly throughout the year but paid only at the end of the year. Assume also that the financing rate is 10 percent (accumulating evenly throughout the year). Under these assumptions, the theoretical price of a futures contract on a stock

---

[4]It is assumed that both D and r are known and paid only at the end of period T, there are no taxes, no transaction costs, and all assets can be sold short at any time and the total proceeds from the short sale made available to investors.

index which mirrors this cash stock portfolio, and which has a settlement date of one year from the present, is

$$\$100 + \$100 \times (0.10 - 0.03) = \$107$$

The theoretical futures price is above the current cash price because there is a net carrying cost of $7.

Now suppose that the actual futures price of a one-year contract is $109. An aribtrager can then buy the cash stock at $100, borrowing the funds at 10 percent, and simultaneously sell the futures at $109. At the end of the year, the arbitrager would collect $3 of dividends, deliver the stock portfolio to the long at $109, and repay the loan of $100 plus interest of $10. His net profit would be

$$\$3 - \$10 + (\$109 - \$100) = \$2$$

The arbitrager's profit, therefore, is exactly equal to the difference between the actual and theoretical futures prices:

$$\$109 - \$107 = \$2$$

Since this situation provides a riskless profit opportunity, arbitragers will continue to sell the futures and buy the cash until there is no longer a difference between actual and theoretical futures prices, causing futures prices to fall and cash prices to rise until actual and theoretical futures prices are equal.

Similarly, if the actual futures price were $104, another equilibrating arbitrage would take place. An arbitrager would buy futures at $104, and simultaneously sell the cash portfolio short at $100, investing the proceeds in a risk-free asset at a yield of 10 percent. However, since he borrowed the stock to short it, he will have to pay the lender of the stock a $3 dividend. At the end of the year the arbitrager would collect $110 from the principal and interest on the risk-free asset ($100 + $10), take delivery on the futures contract at $104, and return the stock borrowed plus the $3 in dividends owed. His profit would be

$$\$110 - \$104 - \$3 = \$3$$

Once again, this profit is equal to the difference between the actual and theoretical futures prices:

$$\$107 - \$104 = \$3$$

Such a risk-free profit opportunity cannot exist for long, of course. Arbitragers will continue to arbitrage the difference between actual futures prices and theoretical futures prices until the difference disappears.

Thus, stock index arbitrage is the mechanism that links the cash stock market to the stock index futures market. Arbitragers make sure that futures values do not diverge too much from current cash values plus an adjustment for the net cost-of-carry. This results in a reasonably predictable relationship between cash and futures prices, which is vital to hedgers using stock index futures.

Table 10.15 provides an example of an arbitrage transaction using actual futures and cash index values as well as actual borrowing and dividend rates.

TABLE 10.15
Stock index arbitrage example: S&P 500 Index (futures are underpriced)

Market information on September 15, 1988

Cash index = 270.65

Dec 88 Futures = 271.65 (last trading day was Dec. 15, 1988)

3-month T-bill rate = 7.35%

Dividend yield = 3.5%

Theoretical futures = $270.65 + 270.65 \times (0.0735 - 0.035) \times (91/365)$
= 273.24

Actual futures is undervalued by 1.59 (273.24 – 271.65)

Action: Buy futures, sell cash

Anticipated arbitrage profit (per contract): $1.59 \times \$500 = \$795$

Arbitrage

September 15, 1988

Sell $135,325 stocks when cash index @ 270.65	$135,325
Invest the proceeds in 3-month T-bills @ 7.35%	(135,325)
Buy 1 Dec 88 futures contract @ 271.65	0
Net cash flow	0

Alternative Scenarios on December 15, 1988

Case I: Cash index rises to 300.00

Stand for delivery on 1 Dec 88 futures contract @ 300.00	
Profit: $(300.00 - 271.65) \times \$500$	$ 14,175
Receive invested principal	135,325
Interest earned: $\$135,325 \times 0.0735 \times (91/365)$	2,480
Buy back stocks sold earlier: $\$135,325 \times (300.00/270.65)$	(150,000)
Accrued dividends: $\$135,325 \times 0.035 \times (91/365)$	(1,181)
Net arbitrage profit	799

Case II: Cash index falls to 250.00

Stand for delivery on 1 Dec 88 futures contract @ 250.00	
Loss: $(250.00 - 271.65) \times \$500$	$(10,825)
Receive invested principal	135,325
Interest earned: $\$135,325 \times 0.0735 \times (91/365)$	2,480
Buy back stocks sold earlier: $\$135,325 \times (250.00/270.65)$	(125,000)
Accrued dividends: $\$135,325 \times 0.035 \times (91/365)$	(1,181)
Net arbitrage profit	799

Note: The difference between the anticipated arbitrage profit and the actual arbitrage profit is due to *rounding*.

10.8   THE OBSERVED RELATIONSHIP BETWEEN ACTUAL AND THEORETICAL FUTURES PRICES

In reality, stock index arbitrage may not be as easy and as costless as presumed in the simplified example in Table 10.15. Figure 10-3 plots the actual and theoretical futures prices for the period February 1, 1988, to December 15, 1988, using daily closing (or settlement) price quotations. The actual futures price is for the December 88 S&P 500 futures contract. The theoretical futures price is calculated assuming that the three-month T-bill rate is the relevant borrowing rate and that the annual dividend yield is 3.5 percent. In addition, as required by the pricing formula, an adjustment is made each day for the maturity of the futures contract.

The graph in Figure 10-3 shows that the relationship between the actual and theoretical prices is quite close. On rare occasions, however, there is a difference of as much as two index points. These differences are shown more clearly in Figure 10-4, which plots the difference between actual and theoretical futures prices.

There are several explanations for the observed differences. First, we may have erred in estimating theoretical futures values: the assumed dividend yield may have been wrong, the wrong borrowing rate used, or the cash index value may not have been up-to-date (or simultaneous with futures prices).

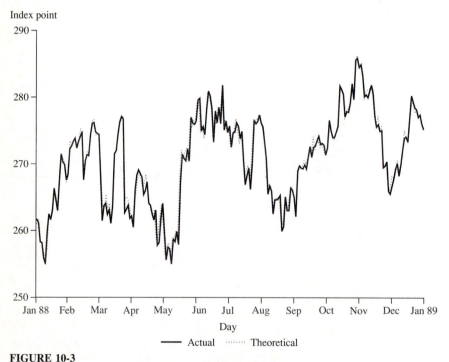

FIGURE 10-3

Actual versus theoretical stock index futures prices (S&P 500 stock index: December 1988 futures, daily from February 1, 1988, to December 15, 1988).

Index point

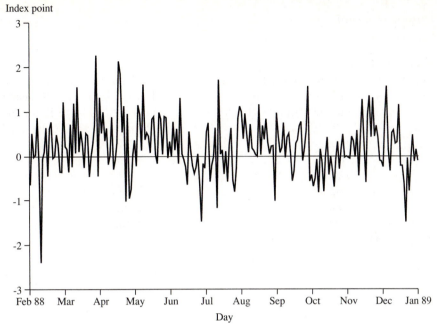

FIGURE 10-4
Differentials between actual and theoretical stock index futures prices (S&P 500 stock index: December 1988 futures, daily from February 1, 1988, to December 15, 1988).

Second, there are transaction costs. Stock index arbitrage requires that large numbers of stocks, as well as futures contracts, must be bought and sold. This involves both commission costs and *execution* costs (such as bid-asked spreads).

Third, the asset underlying a stock index futures contract is in reality more a concept than an asset. It is difficult to buy or short the large number of securities needed, in the proportions required, to duplicate exactly a stock index futures. Fourth, the reported values of the cash stock index may be erroneous because of "stale" price quotations. Index quotations are based on the last sale prices of the component stocks, which may not reflect current bid/asked quotes. Unless an arbitrager has access to current bid/asked quotes, an attractive arbitrage profit opportunity may prove to be a mirage.

Fifth, borrowing the required stocks to short an entire cash portfolio may be difficult. In addition, the requirement that stocks be shorted only in accordance with the *up-tick* rule inhibits arbitrage trading.[5]

---

[5]SEC Rule 10a-1, subject to a number of exceptions of a technical nature, prohibits a short sale: (1) below the last sale price, or (2) at the last sale price unless that price is above the next preceding different price. This requirement is known as the *up-tick test*, since it requires an up-tick in prices. The rule is meant to prevent short sellers from driving down stock prices.

TABLE 10.16
Comparative quarterly annualized dividend yields on various stock indexes (percentages): 1984–1988

		MMI	S&P 500	NYSE Composite
1988	Dec	3.9	3.5	3.6
	Sep	4.0	3.5	3.7
	Jun	3.8	3.4	3.4
	Mar	3.8	3.5	3.9
1987	Dec	3.7	3.6	3.4
	Sep	2.8	2.7	2.9
	Jun	3.0	2.8	2.7
	Mar	3.2	2.9	2.8
1986	Dec	3.7	3.4	3.4
	Sep	3.9	3.5	3.3
	Jun	3.5	3.2	3.2
	Mar	3.6	3.4	3.5
1985	Dec	4.1	3.7	3.6
	Sep	4.7	4.3	4.2
	Jun	4.3	4.0	4.2
	Mar	4.6	4.2	4.4
1984	Dec	5.1	4.5	4.5

Source: Chicago Board of Trade.

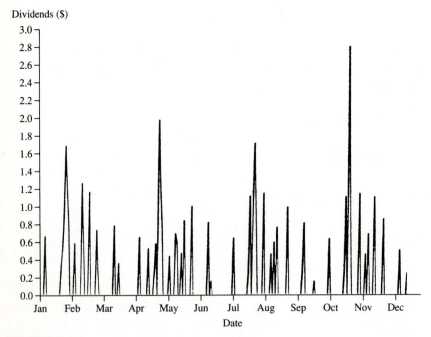

Dividends ($)

FIGURE 10-5
Seasonality of dividend yields for MMI index companies, 1987. (Chicago Board of Trade)

238

Sixth, all proceeds from a short sale are usually not available to potential arbitragers. The extreme case is retail investors. Not only are the short sale proceeds not available to them, but they must post an additional (margin) deposit of 50 percent of the value of the short sale.[6] Brokers-dealers can obtain the use of most but normally not all of the short sale proceeds. Lenders of stocks must be compensated somehow for the credit risk they assume when lending stocks. In most cases this fee is from one to two percent (annual rate) of the value of the shares. Thus, the borrowing rate used in the previous calculations of the theoretical futures price may be too low in that it does not reflect all costs.

Finally, our calculation of the theoretical futures price assumed a constant dividend yield over the holding period. In reality, dividend yields vary (see Table 10.16), and there is a seasonality in dividends. This seasonality is shown in Figure 10-5 for the stocks in the Major Market index, and in Table 10.16 for those in other stock indexes. The dividend yield varies in a nonlinear way: from quarter to quarter, and even from one day to the next (see Table 10.17). Since future dividends are uncertain, arbitragers must use estimates of anticipated dividend yields based on past dividend yields. The estimates of theoretical futures prices shown in Figures 10-3 and 10-4, therefore, are inaccurate because they do not reflect the variation in expected dividend yields.

Given these potential sources of error, it is remarkable how close our simple estimates of theoretical futures prices are to the actual futures prices. It has been estimated that the out-of-pocket transaction costs associated with stock index arbitrage are on the order of one to two index points (see Table 10.18). Thus, the discrepancies between the theoretical and actual futures prices shown in Figure 10-4 are consistently within the transaction cost bounds. The difference exceeds two index points on only three days. The closeness of this relationship suggests that stock index arbitrage has been highly successful in maintaining the theoretical relationship between cash and futures stock index prices.

10.9   STOCK INDEX FUTURES AS A PORTFOLIO MANAGEMENT TOOL

Money managers use stock index futures for basically three purposes: *hedging*, *asset allocation*, and *yield-enhancement*. To protect against a general decline in the stock market, they can hedge by selling stock index futures. One such hedging strategy that has received a great deal of publicity in recent years is *portfolio insurance*. Hedging is covered in the next section.

Asset allocation refers to how institutions distribute their portfolio assets among, for example, equities, bonds, and money market securities. While portfolio managers can restructure their portfolios by buying and selling individual equities, bonds, and money market securities, it is often preferable to use stock index (as well as interest rate) futures to alter the portfolio mix. Using futures is

---

[6]Regulation T, Federal Reserve System.

TABLE 10.17

Expected dividends on MMI stocks during first quarter of 1989, as of January 1989

Date	$	Index points*	Company
January 13	0.80	.280	Procter & Gamble
January 31	0.35	.123	USX
January 31	0.70	.245	Chevron
January 31	0.60	.210	Mobil
February 2	1.10	.385	IBM
February 6	0.55	.192	Exxon
February 9	1.05	.367	DuPont
February 10	1.25	.437	General Motors
February 17	0.37	.129	International Paper
February 14	0.50	.175	Johnson & Johnson
February 17	0.53	.180	MMM
February 17	0.50	.175	Sears
February 27	0.50	.175	Eastman Kodak
February 27	0.30	.105	Coca-Cola
March 1	0.37	.130	Merck
March 2	0.41	.144	General Electric
March 9	1.13	.400	Philip Morris
March 23	0.30	.105	AT&T
March 23	0.70	.245	Dow Chemical
March 30	0.19	.067	American Express

* Quarterly dollar dividend ÷ index divisor ($2.85813).

Source: Chicago Board of Trade.

TABLE 10.18

Transaction costs associated with stock versus stock index futures

	Stocks	Stock index futures
Average price per share/contract	$60	352.00
Number of shares/units	2933*	$500
Market value of portfolio/contract	$176,000	$176,000
Round-trip commission per share/contract**	$0.07	$15
Commission cost	$205.31	$15
Bid/asked spread cost	0.125 index points/share 2933 × 0.125 = $366.63	0.05 index points (or 1 tick per contract) $500 × 0.05 = $25
Total transaction cost:		
Commission plus bid/asked spread	$571.94	$40

* The precise number of shares that would equate a portfolio of stocks with the average stock price to the value of one futures contract is 2933.333 ($176,000/$60).

** Commission that would be paid by large institutional investors.

cheaper: equity and interest rate futures markets are generally more liquid than their cash market counterparts, and trading costs are less (see Table 10.18).

Yield-enhancement refers to a portfolio strategy of holding a "synthetic" stock index fund that is capable of outperforming (or of earning a higher return than) a cash stock index fund. Earlier in this chapter we demonstrated that, if stock index futures are priced according to their theoretical values (the cash index value plus the net carry), a portfolio consisting of a long position in stock index futures and Treasury bills will produce the same return (with the same risk) as a stock portfolio structured to mirror the stock index underlying the futures (see Section 10.6). If, however, stock index futures are incorrectly priced, or their actual value is either greater or less than their theoretical value, a portfolio of stock index futures plus Treasury bills can be constructed that will outperform the corresponding stock portfolio: it will yield a higher return for the identical risk. A yield-enhancement strategy, therefore, takes advantage of such futures mispricing in order to enhance a portfolio's yield or return.

Table 10.19 provides an example of using a synthetic stock index strategy to take advantage of mispricing in the futures market. In this example the near-month futures contract is assumed to be underpriced by 1.40 index points. Thus, the synthetic portfolio strategy is to hold T-bills and simultaneously buy futures contracts. Table 10.19 shows the results of this strategy in comparison to a strategy of simply buying stocks, for three hypothetical market scenarios. In all cases the synthetic portfolio strategy outperforms the cash stock portfolio. The benefits of this strategy, of course, depend both on the degree of futures mispricing and on the size of the portfolio. Table 10.20 provides an example to demonstrate that a yield-enhancement strategy is not useful if there is no futures mispricing.

10.10 HEDGING WITH STOCK INDEX FUTURES

10.10.1 Who Hedges?

Pension funds, mutual funds, life insurance companies, bank trust funds, and university endowment funds hold trillions of dollars of stock. At times portfolio managers wish to reduce their institutions' exposure to a fall in stock values. While still believing that owning stocks is a sound long-term investment strategy, managers may nevertheless want to reduce their equity exposure for short periods of time because of uncertainties about future market developments.

There are several ways this can be done. Simply selling stock and repurchasing it later is one way. But this strategy involves substantial costs. It is relatively expensive to buy and sell stock because of the bid-asked spreads and commission costs. Further, the quantity of stock that institutions trade is often quite large, so that such trades may themselves *move the market*, resulting in poor execution prices.

The liquidity of stock index futures markets have made them the markets of choice for institutional hedging. The S&P 500 futures market can normally absorb

TABLE 10.19
Example of stock index yield enhancement strategy when futures are underpriced

Assumptions

1. Amount to be invested = $10 million
2. Current value of S&P = 340
3. Current value of near-month S&P 500 futures = 342
4. Expected annualized dividend yield = 4%
5. Annualized bond equivalent yield on T-bills = 8%
6. Theoretical futures price = 343.40
7. Margins are posted with T-bills

Alternate investment strategies

1. A portfolio of stocks worth $10,000,000
2. A portfolio of stock index futures and T-bills

$$\text{Long } \$10,000,000 \text{ T-bills}$$

$$\text{Long 58 S\&P futures: } \frac{\$10,000,000}{342 \times 500} = 58.48$$

Hypothetical market scenarios for the value of the S&P index on the settlement date of the futures contract, which is three months from the present:

Case 1: Market increases by 10%: S&P = 374
Case 2: No change: S&P = 340
Case 3: Market decreases by 10%: S&P = 306

Evaluation of the two investment strategies			
	Case I 10% increase	**Case II** No change	**Case III** 10% decrease
a) *Value of portfolio using Strategy 1:*			
Initial investment	10,000,000	10,000,000	10,000,000
Capital appreciation			
10,000,000 × 10% (or −10%)	1,000,000	0	(1,000,000)
Dividend:			
10,000,000 × 4% × $\frac{3}{12}$	100,000	100,000	100,000
Total	11,100,000	10,100,000	9,100,000
b) *Value of portfolio using Strategy 2:*			
Investment in T-bills	10,000,000	10,000,000	10,000,000
Interest on T-bills			
10,000,000 × 8% × $\frac{3}{12}$	200,000	200,000	200,000
Gain (loss) on S&P futures:			
(374 − 342) × 500 × 58	928,000		
(340 − 342) × 500 × 58		(58,000)	
(306 − 342) × 500 × 58			(1,044,000)
Total	11,128,000	10,142,000	9,156,000

TABLE 10.20
Comparison of synthetic stock index portfolio with stock portfolio when there is no futures mispricing and stock market declines by five percent

Assumptions

1. Amount to be invested = $10 million
2. Current value of S&P 500 index = 340
3. Current value of near month S&P futures contract = 343.40
4. Value of the near month S&P 500 at settlement (3 months later) = 323
   (5% decrease)
5. Expected annualized dividend yield = 4%
6. Annualized bond-equivalent yield on T-bills = 8%

Strategy 1: Purchase of stocks

Market value of portfolio that mirrors the index after 5% decrease in market value: $0.95 \times \$10,000,000$	$9,500,000
Dividends	
$0.04 \times \$10,000,000 \times \frac{3}{12}$	100,000
Final value of portfolio	$9,600,000
Net dollar return	$ (400,000)

Strategy 2: Long futures/T-bill portfolio

Number of S&P 500 contracts to be purchased: $\dfrac{\$10,000,000}{343.40 \times \$500} = 58.24$	
Loss on futures:	
$(323 - 343.40) \times 500 \times 58$	$ (591,600)
Value of Treasury bills plus interest:	
$\$10,000,000 \times (1 + 0.08 \times \frac{3}{12})$	10,200,000
Final value of portfolio	$9,608,400
Net dollar return	$ (391,600)*

* The difference in the dollar return for the two strategies is due to rounding of the number of futures contracts purchased.

immense volumes of sell and buy orders without large changes in prices. Bid-asked spreads and commission costs are also lower (see Table 10.18). Many portfolio managers, therefore, hedge with stock index futures rather than by directly altering the composition of their portfolios.

Hedging is also done with stock index options contracts. Institutions obtain *downside* protection by purchasing puts on stock index options. If the stock market falls, the option gives them the right to sell (or put) their stock at the previously higher contracted-for prices. Index option markets, however, have not yet achieved the same degree of liquidity as futures markets, and are more expensive to use. (Hedging with options is covered in Chapter 20.)

10.10.2   Market and Non-Market Risk

There are two types of risk associated with holding equity. The first is *market* or *systematic risk*. The second is *firm specific risk*, often called *unsystematic risk*.

All stocks are exposed to market risk due to changes in the level of interest rates, government trade policies, general economic activity (such as recessions and inflation), changes in tax laws, and possibly war and peace. While some stocks are more affected by these developments than others, all are impacted to some extent.

Firm specific risk, or unsystematic risk, is risk that is specific to a firm or an industry. A particular economic event can cause the price of a specific stock to change sharply, but still have no effect on other stocks. For example, holding stock in IBM subjects the owner to the risk that IBM's earnings may decline. There may be a fall in the demand for mainframe computers, or a competitor may develop a superior computer so that IBM loses market share. The result will be a decline in the value of IBM's stock, and a loss to the holders of IBM stock. Other companies or industries need not be affected by these events.

Modern portfolio theory has shown that unsystematic risk can be eliminated by holding a diversified portfolio of many stocks. Over time some firms (and some industries) will perform better than others, and some worse than others. Which will perform better or worse than expected is difficult to predict. In a properly diversified portfolio these differences will counterbalance: the gain in one stock will offset the loss in another, stabilizing the overall earnings of the portfolio.

Market risk cannot be eliminated by holding a diversified stock portfolio, since every stock will move with the market to some degree. Stock index futures can be used to hedge or manage this risk.

10.11   MEASURING MARKET RISK

A conventional measure of a stock's market risk is the stock's *beta*. Beta (β) is defined as the covariance (cov) between a stock's return and the return on the overall market divided by the variance (var) of return on the market. For stock i, this can be written as

$$\beta_i = \frac{\text{cov}(R_i, R_m)}{\text{var}(R_m)}$$

where R_m is the overall market return on a portfolio consisting of all stocks, and R_i is the return on stock i.

Stock betas can be estimated with regression analysis similar to that discussed earlier in Chapter 6 (Section 6.3.2). Given a series of observed returns over time for stock i ($R_{i,t}$) and for the market portfolio ($R_{m,t}$), the following linear regression can be estimated:

$$R_{i,t} = a + b \times R_{m,t} + e_{i,t}$$

The estimated coefficient b is an estimate of the beta of stock i. The term $e_{i,t}$ is the usual error term.[7]

---

[7]When empirically estimating stock betas it is useful to select a readily available stock index as a proxy for the market portfolio, such as the S&P 500 index.

In this equation the relevant rates of return $(R_{i,t})$ are defined as the change in the stock price in period $t(P_{i,t} - P_{i,t-1})$ plus dividends received in period t $(D_{i,t})$, divided by the price of the stock at the end of period $t - 1$, or as $(P_{i,t} - P_{i,t-1} + D_{i,t})/(P_{i,t-1})$. The major determinate of observed rates of return, therefore, is changes in stock prices. For this reason stock betas are often estimated using only percentage changes in stock prices:

$$\frac{\Delta P_{i,t}}{P_{i,t-1}} = a + b \times \frac{\Delta P_{m,t}}{P_{m,t-1}} + e_{i,t}$$

where $\Delta P_{i,t} = P_{i,t} - P_{i,t-1}$ and $\Delta P_{m,t} = P_{m,t} - P_{m,t-1}$. It has also been shown that similar estimates of stock betas can be obtained by estimating a regression equation using simply absolute price changes rather than percentage changes.[8]

To summarize, the estimate of a stock's beta shows how the value of that stock is likely to change relative to a change in the value of the market portfolio (or a particular stock index). It is often thought of as a stock's *relative* volatility. A beta greater than one indicates that the stock is more volatile than the market. A value of less than one suggests that the stock is less volatile than the market.

To demonstrate the computation and use of stock betas, we have selected a sample of 20 stocks from those listed in the S&P 500 index. These are shown in Table 10.21. The first column in this table is the rank of the company among the 500 companies included in the S&P 500 index, according to a company's total market value in 1988. Some of the companies are among the largest; some are among the smallest. The stocks in Table 10.21 are also diversified among a number of different industries, as shown in the last column of the table. This sample of stocks is used later in the chapter as a representative stock portfolio in order to provide hedging illustrations.

Table 10.22 provides estimates of the betas for the stocks in our 20 company sample, for the 5-year period 1983–1987. Betas are estimated by a regression analysis like that described above, using, alternatively, daily and monthly data. The stock returns used include dividends. The NYSE index is used as a proxy for the market.[9]

Table 10.22 provides beta estimates for individual years as well as for all years taken together so that the stability of the individual stock betas can be seen. For some stocks the betas vary significantly from year to year. The estimates also differ depending upon whether daily or monthly data is used. Thus, when using estimates of stock betas it is important to keep in mind how these estimates are derived and whether they are appropriate for the use intended.

---

[8]William F. Sharpe and Guy M. Cooper, "Risk-Return Classes of New York Exchange Common Stocks," *Financial Analyst Journal*, March-April 1972, pp. 46-54.

[9]Specifically, the capitalization-weighted returns on NYSE stocks were used.

TABLE 10.21
Selected sample of S&P 500 stocks: December 1988*

Rank in S&P 500	Company	Ticket symbol	Market value ($millions)	Asset value ($millions)	Shares outstanding (millions)	Industry type
1	International Business Machine	IBM	66346	73037	590	Computer
4	American Telephone & Telegraph	T	34357	35152	1074	Telecommunication
5	Philip Morris	MO	26992	20295	231	Consumer
11	Mobil	MOB	20434	38820	411	Fuel
17	Dow Chemical	DOW	17232	16239	186	Chemicals
21	Proctor & Gamble	PG	15315	15793	169	Consumer
35	American Express	AXP	12556	142704	417	Nonbank financial
41	Boeing	BA	10382	12608	153	Aerospace
51	Westinghouse Electric	WX	7720	16937	144	Electrical
61	Commonwealth Edison	CWE	6979	20196	212	Utilities
71	Smithkline Beckman	SKB	6427	5017	124	Health care
81	Chrysler	C	5847	48567	233	Automotive
111	Kimberly Clark	KMB	4830	4268	81	Paper
141	Campbell Soup	CIB	4010	4100	129	Food
161	CSX Corp.	CSX	3414	13026	107	Transportation
176	McGraw-Hill	MHP	3203	1758	49	Publishing
181	NCNB Corp.	NCB	3109	29848	86	Banks
211	Newmont Mining	NEM	2710	1715	67	Metals
311	AON	AOC	1815	8266	63	Nonbank financial
341	West Point-Pepperel	WPM	1690	2358	30	Manufacturing

* *Source: Business Week*, 1989 special edition.

TABLE 10.22
Estimates of individual stock betas

Company	Daily data						Monthly data
	83–87	1983	1984	1985	1986	1987	83–87
IBM	1.05	1.26	1.34	1.34	0.91	0.90	0.82
	(0.52)	(0.58)	(0.66)	(0.57)	(0.34)	(0.56)	(0.46)
ATT	1.06	0.65	0.99	1.53	1.16	1.09	0.67
	(0.38)	(0.23)	(0.22)	(0.38)	(0.36)	(0.57)	(0.25)
Phillip Morris	1.09	0.82	1.02	0.98	1.37	1.11	1.07
	(0.39)	(0.21)	(0.38)	(0.20)	(0.39)	(0.58)	(0.53)
Mobil	1.10	1.55	0.96	0.79	0.85	1.15	0.94
	(0.30)	(0.39)	(0.18)	(0.09)	(0.17)	(0.51)	(0.41)
Dow Chemical	1.35	1.51	1.36	1.25	1.21	1.37	1.23
	(0.47)	(0.35)	(0.36)	(0.38)	(0.39)	(0.67)	(0.58)
Proctor & Gamble	0.95	0.68	0.87	0.72	1.13	1.03	0.78
	(0.37)	(0.19)	(0.25)	(0.15)	(0.41)	(0.55)	(0.44)
American Express	1.62	1.57	2.00	1.81	1.41	1.57	1.50
	(0.47)	(0.30)	(0.46)	(0.44)	(0.46)	(0.61)	(0.68)
Boeing	0.95	0.97	1.42	1.73	1.03	0.67	0.99
	(0.24)	(0.16)	(0.35)	(0.37)	(0.27)	(0.24)	(0.40)
Westinghouse Electric	1.45	1.48	1.70	1.74	1.41	1.33	1.43
	(0.48)	(0.41)	(0.48)	(0.30)	(0.46)	(0.65)	(0.66)
Commonwealth Edison	0.66	0.47	0.67	0.49	0.73	0.73	0.50
	(0.23)	(0.15)	(0.09)	(0.08)	(0.28)	(0.45)	(0.23)
Smithkline Beckman	0.89	0.74	0.77	0.93	0.99	0.92	0.92
	(0.30)	(0.14)	(0.22)	(0.22)	(0.39)	(0.41)	(0.45)
Chrysler	1.73	2.66	2.27	1.65	1.35	1.44	1.82
	(0.37)	(0.38)	(0.40)	(0.33)	(0.27)	(0.51)	(0.48)
Kimberly Clark	0.88	0.65	0.56	0.76	1.02	1.01	0.77
	(0.29)	(0.15)	(0.12)	(0.17)	(0.33)	(0.42)	(0.31)
Campbell Soup	0.92	0.54	0.85	0.86	1.21	0.95	0.81
	(0.26)	(0.12)	(0.17)	(0.07)	(0.36)	(0.51)	(0.27)
CSX Corp.	1.23	1.19	1.85	1.48	1.38	0.98	1.44
	(0.36)	(0.27)	(0.43)	(0.29)	(0.42)	(0.42)	(0.69)
McGraw-Hill	1.11	1.09	1.16	1.29	1.16	1.05	1.29
	(0.28)	(0.17)	(0.17)	(0.23)	(0.39)	(0.45)	(0.61)
NCNB Corp.	0.80	0.50	0.69	0.90	1.14	0.79	1.11
	(0.21)	(0.06)	(0.13)	(0.17)	(0.36)	(0.32)	(0.50)
Newmont Mining	0.87	1.09	0.73	0.60	0.59	0.99	1.04
	(0.13)	(0.21)	(0.08)	(0.07)	(0.07)	(0.16)	(0.18)
AON	0.78	0.74	1.26	0.60	0.66	0.73	1.05
	(0.18)	(0.10)	(0.26)	(0.09)	(0.17)	(0.23)	(0.53)
West Point-Pepperel	0.92	0.59	0.79	0.43	0.83	1.17	1.13
	(0.24)	(0.11)	(0.14)	(0.03)	(0.24)	(0.42)	(0.50)

$R_t^j = \alpha + \beta R_t^m + \epsilon_t$

R^j = Individual stock returns with dividends

R^m = Value-weighted return on market including dividends (NYSE stocks)

β = Beta of company j

ϵ_t = Error term for company j

10.12   THE MINIMUM-VARIANCE HEDGE RATIO

As discussed earlier in Chapter 6, a critical decision for hedgers is to determine the appropriate hedge ratio (HR): the ratio of the futures position to the cash position being hedged. A benchmark hedge ratio is the minimum-variance hedge ratio (HR^*), or the value of HR that can be expected to reduce fluctuations in the value of the total portfolio (including the hedge component) to the minimum possible (which may not be zero). This section demonstrates how to construct this hedge ratio for stock index futures. In the next section examples of hedging with stock index futures are provided.

Assume that the minimum-risk hedge ratio succeeds in equating changes in the value of a short stock index futures position with changes in the value of the stock portfolio being hedged. Thus, Δ (value of stock portfolio) $= \Delta$ (value of futures position), which can be restated as

$$\begin{bmatrix} \$ \text{ value of} \\ \text{stock} \\ \text{portfolio} \end{bmatrix} \times \begin{bmatrix} \% \text{ change in} \\ \text{weighted average} \\ \text{portfolio price} \end{bmatrix} = \begin{bmatrix} \$ \text{ value of} \\ \text{futures} \\ \text{portfolio} \end{bmatrix} \times \begin{bmatrix} \% \text{ change in} \\ \text{futures} \\ \text{index} \end{bmatrix}$$

which is identical to

$$\frac{\% \text{ change in weighted average portfolio price}}{\% \text{ change in futures index}} = \frac{\$ \text{ value of futures portfolio}}{\$ \text{ value of stock portfolio}}$$

The right-hand side of this equation is the general definition of a hedge ratio (see Section 6.2 in Chapter 6). In this case, this ratio is, by assumption, the minimum-variance hedge ratio, since it was derived by assuming equal and offsetting changes in the cash and futures portfolios. Thus, the price ratio on the left-hand side of the equation can be used as an estimate of the minimum-variance hedge ratio (HR^*), or

$$HR^* = \frac{\% \text{ change in weighted average portfolio price}}{\% \text{ change in futures index}}$$

We shall call this ratio β_{PF}: the beta of a particular stock portfolio (P) relative to the relevant futures index (F).

How does β_{PF} differ from the beta of portfolio P with respect to a given cash stock index (or β_{PI})? Only in one respect: the futures index (F) may not move on an exact one-to-one basis with the underlying stock index (I).

Table 10.23 demonstrates how a *portfolio beta* can be constructed using in-dividual stock betas. What is the beta of a $2 million stock portfolio consisting of equal dollar investments in the twenty companies shown earlier in Table 10.21? The last column of Table 10.23 provides the individual stock betas, taken from Table 10.22. Since the hypothetical portfolio consists of equal dollar (although not share) holdings of each stock, the portfolio beta is the simple average of the individual stock betas. Thus, for the sample of stocks the portfolio beta (β_{PI}) is

TABLE 10.23
Calculating the portfolio beta using individual stock betas
(hypothetical investment portfolio on May 2, 1988)

	Share price (1)	Number of shares (2)	Dollar investment (3)	Dollar dividend (4)	Stock Beta (5)
IBM	114.125	876	99,974	4.40	1.05
AT&T	26.500	3,774	100,011	1.20	1.06
Phillip Morris	89.752	1,114	99,984	4.48	1.09
Mobil Oil	46.250	2,162	99,993	2.40	1.10
Dow Chemical	82.250	1,216	100,016	2.80	1.35
Proctor & Gamble	76.500	1,307	99,986	2.80	0.95
American Express	23.875	4,188	99,989	0.84	1.62
Boeing	32.156	3,110	100,005	1.60	0.95
Westinghouse	52.750	1,896	100,014	2.00	1.45
Commonwealth Edison	24.000	4,167	100,008	3.00	0.66
Smithkline Beckman	43.297	2,310	100,016	1.76	0.89
Chrysler	23.000	4,348	100,004	1.00	1.73
Kimberly Clark	53.750	1,860	99,975	1.60	0.88
Campbell Soup	26.375	3,791	99,988	0.96	0.92
CSX	27.875	3,587	99,988	1.24	1.23
McGraw-Hill	51.500	1,942	100,013	1.76	1.11
NCNB	21.125	4,735	100,027	1.00	0.80
Newmont Mining	34.750	2,878	100,011	0.60	0.87
AON	23.750	4,211	100,011	1.40	0.78
West Point-Pepperell	30.000	3,333	99,990	0.32	0.92
		Total	2,000,000	Average	1.07

1.07 (see Table 10.23). If unequal dollar investments in the individual stocks were held, the portfolio beta would be the weighted average beta (individual company betas weighted by the size of the respective dollar investments).

As discussed earlier, in most cases a portfolio beta constructed in this manner will not be identical to β_{PF}, since changes in the futures index will not be perfectly correlated with changes in the underlying stock index used to estimate the individual stock betas.[10] Thus, if the portfolio beta is used to estimate the minimum-variance hedge ratio, an adjustment must be made for this factor.

---

[10]It may also be necessary to hedge with a futures index that is different from the market index used to calculate the individual stock betas. This creates a basis risk similar to that which exists in a cross-hedge.

Since it is convenient to use the readily available individual stock betas to construct portfolio betas, we show how to make such an adjustment. A reasonably accurate adjustment is to multiply the portfolio beta by the beta of the stock index relative to the relevant stock index futures contract, which we shall call β_{IF}.[11] The minimum-variance hedge ratio calculation is then

$$HR^* = \beta_{PI} \times \beta_{IF}$$

where β_{IF} is estimated with the following regression equation:

$$\Delta I_t = a + b \times \Delta F_t + e_t$$

where ΔI_t are the percentage changes in the relevant stock market index and ΔF_t are the percentage changes in the futures index. The estimate of b is an estimate of β_{IF}.

10.13   A HEDGING EXAMPLE

Suppose that on May 2, 1988, an investor holds a $2 million stock portfolio consisting of the 20 stocks shown in Table 10.21. The investor is nervous about future market developments and wishes to reduce the risk associated with this portfolio. He does not, however, want to sell the stocks and buy, say, Treasury bills. He believes that the market uncertainties may clarify within the next few months. His objective is to adopt a minimum-risk hedging strategy only for the next few months.

To compute the appropriate hedge ratio the investor decides first to estimate the following regression equation for the period January 2, 1988, to April 30, 1988:

$$\Delta S_t = a + b \times \Delta F_t + e_{i,t}$$

where ΔS_t are the daily percentage changes in the value of the portfolio, and ΔF_t are the daily percentage changes in the S&P 500 futures index. He estimated b to be equal to 0.78.

Alternatively, to check this estimate, the investor uses the formula in the previous section:

$$HR^* = \beta_{PI} \times \beta_{IF}$$

Table 10.24 provides regression estimates of β_{IF} for different cash indexes relative to both the S&P 500 and NYSE futures indexes for the period January

---

[11] Edward Peters, "Hedged Equity Portfolios: Components of Risk and Return," *Advances in Futures and Options Research*, 18: 75–92, 1986.

TABLE 10.24
Estimates of β_{IF} for different cash indexes versus S&P 500 futures and NYSE composite futures using daily data (from January 2, 1985, to March 31, 1989)

	S&P 500 near month futures			NYSE composite near month futures		
Cash Indexes	**β**	**Standard error**	**R^2**	**β**	**Standard error**	**R^2**
DJIA	0.7953	0.0106	0.8447	0.7885	0.0108	0.8382
S&P 500	0.7673	0.0096	0.8615	0.7606	0.0098	0.8544
NYSE	0.7166	0.0090	0.8563	0.7114	0.0091	0.8518
AMEX	0.4903	0.0130	0.5791	0.4884	0.0129	0.5799
NASDAQ	0.4767	0.0124	0.5883	0.4739	0.0124	0.5871
VLA	0.5586	0.0113	0.7027	0.5571	0.0112	0.7053
W5000	0.6647	0.0112	0.7816	0.6599	0.0114	0.7745

2, 1985, to March 31, 1989. The estimates show that β_{IF} is always less than one, indicating that the futures indexes are more volatile than the cash indexes.[12] Thus, the minimum-variance hedge ratio is less than the portfolio beta:

$$HR^* = \beta_{PI} \times \beta_{IF} < \beta_{PI}$$

because $\beta_{IF} < 1$.

The value of β_{PI} is 1.07, which is provided in Table 10.23. To estimate β_{IF} the investor regresses the daily NYSE composite cash index (which was used to estimate the individual stock betas provided in Table 10.22) on the daily S&P 500 near month futures index, for the period immediately preceding May 2, 1988, specifically, January 2, 1988, to April 30, 1988.[13] The estimate of β_{IF} is 0.7166. Thus,

$$HR^* = 1.07 \times 0.7166 = 0.77$$

This is similar but not identical to the first estimate of HR^*, which was 0.78.

Using the preferred estimate of HR^*, 0.78, together with the information in Table 10.21, a minimum-variance hedge can be constructed. On May 2, 1988, the market value of the stock portfolio was $2 million. In addition, on that date the June 88 S&P 500 futures price was 261.70. Hence, the number of June

---

[12]Futures indexes vary more than cash indexes because of changes in the net carry (interest rates and dividend yields), mispricing, and a greater frequency of transactions in futures markets.

[13]We have assumed that the investor has chosen to hedge with S&P 500 futures because it is the most liquid stock index futures market and because it closely tracks his own stock portfolio.

88 futures contracts that should be sold to establish a minimum-risk hedge is $\frac{(\$2,000,000)}{261.70 \times \$500} \times 0.78 = 11.92$, or 12 contracts. The investor chose to hedge with the near-term futures contract because of its superior liquidity. Consequently, if the hedge is maintained beyond June of 1988, the hedge will have to be rolled forward into more distant futures contracts. To implement the hedge, the investor sells 12 June 88 S&P 500 futures contracts at 261.70 on May 2.

Let us see how the hedged portfolio actually performed during the second part of 1988. Assume that, to the surprise of the investor, market conditions remained highly uncertain during the remainder of the year. The investor consequently decided to maintain the hedge through December 1988. To do this he had to roll the short futures position forward as near-term futures contracts expired. More specifically, in June the investor offset his 12 June 88 contracts, and purchased 12 September 88 S&P contracts; on August 31, 1988, he rolled this short position into December 88 futures contracts, and on November 20 he rolled his futures position into March 89 futures contracts. Further, each time when the short futures position was rolled forward the investor recomputed the minimum-variance hedge ratio according to the procedures discussed earlier, making the necessary adjustments to the futures position to maintain a minimum-variance hedge.

Table 10.25 provides an analysis of how the hedged portfolio performed relative to the unhedged portfolio over the nine-month period May 1988 to January 1989. At the beginning of each month both the cash stock portfolio and the short futures position are marked-to-the-market, using prior month-end stock prices and futures prices. The relevant stock prices are reported in Table 10.26. The futures prices can be found in column 7 of Table 10.25. Dividend information can be found in Table 10.23.

Column 10 of Table 10.25 shows the net monthly profit or loss on the hedged portfolio, which can be compared to that of the unhedged stock portfolio in column 4. The cash flows for the hedged portfolio are much smaller than for the unhedged portfolio, as they should be. Thus, the hedging strategy adopted has succeeded in reducing the variance of portfolio returns, and therefore the portfolio risk.

The same conclusion can be reached by examining the comparative monthly rates of return in columns 5 and 12. The volatility of these returns for the hedged portfolio is less than half that of the unhedged portfolio (1.11 percent versus 2.86 percent).

As expected, this reduction in risk does not come free: the average monthly return on the hedged portfolio is significantly less than the return on the unhedged portfolio (1.73 percent compared to 2.13 percent). This is the risk-return tradeoff we discussed in Section 6.5 in Chapter 6.

Investors must decide for themselves whether the reduction in risk from hedging is worth the lost profits. It should be recognized, however, that if stock prices had been more volatile during the hedging period, the reduction in risk could have been much greater than that shown in Table 10.25. In 1988 stock prices were

TABLE 10.25
Analysis of hedged versus unhedged stock portfolio, May 1988 to January 1989

Unhedged stock portfolio

	Beginning of month value $ (1)	Capital gain or (loss) $ (2)	Dividend $ (3)	Cash flow $ (4) = (2) + (3)	Monthly return % (5) = (4)/(1)
May 88	2,000,000.00	42,371.90	9,576.95	51,948.85	2.60
Jun 88	2,051,948.85	129,390.60	10,849.85	140,240.45	6.83
Jul 88	2,192,189.30	17,835.06	1,862.90	19,697.96	0.90
Aug 88	2,211,887.26	(46,431.00)	9,576.95	(36,854.05)	(1.67)
Sep 88	2,175,033.21	94,835.78	10,849.85	105,685.63	4.86
Oct 88	2,280,718.84	77,264.88	1,852.90	79,117.78	3.47
Nov 88	2,359,836.62	(59,682.50)	9,576.95	(50,105.55)	(2.12)
Dec 88	2,309,731.07	40,145.93	10,849.85	50,995.78	2.21
Jan 89	2,360,726.85				
Average				45,090.86	2.13
Standard deviation				61,630.98	2.86

Futures short position

	Number of contracts (6)	Entry (selling) price $ (7)	Exit (buying) price $ (8)	Profit (loss) $ (9)
May 88	12 Jun 88	261.70	262.95	(7,500.00)
Jun 88	12 Sep 88	264.70	275.40	(64,200.00)
Jul 88	12 Sep 88	275.40	273.25	12,900.00
Aug 88	13 Sep 88	273.25	261.10	78,975.00
Sep 88	13 Dec 88	264.10	274.15	(65,325.00)
Oct 88	13 Dec 88	274.15	279.10	(32,175.00)
Nov 88	13 Dec 88	279.10	273.05	39,325.00
Dec 88	13 Mar 89	275.95	280.40	(28,925.00)

Hedged portfolio

	Net profit or (loss) $ (10) = (4) + (9)	Beginning of month value $ (11)	Monthly return % (12) = (10)/(11)
May 88	44,448.85	2,000,000.00	2.22
Jun 88	76,040.45	2,044,448.85	3.72
Jul 88	32,597.96	2,120,489.30	1.54
Aug 88	42,120.95	2,153,087.26	1.96
Sep 88	40,360.63	2,195,208.21	1.84
Oct 88	46,942.78	2,235,568.84	2.10
Nov 88	(10,780.55)	2,282,511.62	(0.47)
Dec 88	22,070.78	2,271,731.07	0.97
Jan 89		2,293,801.85	
Average	36,725.23		1.74
Standard deviation	23,023.51		1.11

TABLE 10.26
Month-end stock prices used in example in Table 10.25
(April 1988 through December 1988, in dollars)

	Apr	May	Jun	Jul	Aug	Sep	Oct	Nov	Dec
IBM	114.125	112.500	127.375	125.750	111.500	115.375	122.625	118.500	121.875
T	26.500	27.125	26.750	26.625	24.875	26.000	28.625	29.875	28.750
MO	89.752	83.876	83.876	91.624	91.876	96.752	95.376	96.624	101.876
MOB	46.250	44.875	43.500	44.750	43.375	42.625	44.375	44.500	45.500
DOW	82.250	82.250	90.875	86.875	83.750	87.000	89.375	85.375	87.750
PG	76.500	76.375	77.500	75.125	74.625	80.000	82.625	81.875	87.000
AXP	23.875	25.250	27.500	28.125	28.625	28.000	27.125	27.000	26.625
BA	32.156	36.656	39.156	40.328	39.328	42.750	43.250	41.328	40.406
WX	52.750	53.250	56.250	54.375	50.125	52.750	52.375	51.500	52.625
CWE	24.000	24.375	28.000	29.875	30.000	30.750	32.000	31.500	33.000
SKB	43.297	41.891	44.625	46.500	45.375	45.125	45.875	45.000	48.125
C	23.000	21.875	24.375	23.375	22.750	24.000	26.625	26.125	25.750
KMB	53.750	52.625	62.000	57.625	57.125	57.375	59.000	58.875	58.250
CIB	26.375	26.500	25.375	26.375	27.000	29.875	32.750	31.625	31.500
CSX	27.875	26.625	26.875	26.750	25.625	30.500	30.750	30.500	31.625
MHP	51.500	54.000	57.750	65.250	66.000	69.500	66.500	61.250	62.250
NCB	21.125	21.750	24.250	23.375	26.750	28.125	28.500	26.875	27.250
NEM	34.750	38.125	41.000	41.500	36.750	35.375	34.875	35.500	33.125
AOC	23.750	24.875	26.375	27.375	27.375	27.250	28.750	27.500	28.000
WPM	30.000	36.250	38.000	36.375	34.125	38.250	44.625	40.000	43.875

Note: Stock symbols in first column corresponds to the companies listed in Table 10.23.

fairly stable. If stock prices had fallen in 1988 like they did on October 19, 1987, the benefits of being hedged would have been considerably greater.

10.14 PORTFOLIO INSURANCE

A stock index futures hedging strategy used extensively in recent years is *portfolio insurance*. Over $60 billion of assets are protected by this technique. This strategy, however, was subject to harsh criticism because of its role in the stock market crash of October 19, 1987.

   Portfolio insurance is essentially a name given to a *dynamic* hedging strategy using stock index futures. By *dynamic* hedging is meant a hedging strategy that continually adjusts the hedge ratio in response to market movements (as opposed to using a constant or *static* hedge ratio). This requires the periodic buying and selling of stock index futures to achieve the desired short futures position. The objective of the short futures position is to protect a stock portfolio from incurring a loss greater than some predetermined amount, or to put a floor underneath the portfolio's value. Pension funds, for example, having a fiduciary obligation to pay future retirement benefits, may not want their portfolios to incur more than a certain loss. The objective of portfolio insurance is similar to that associated with purchasing an index put option. In fact, portfolio insurance seeks to achieve exactly the downside protection that would be obtained by purchasing a stock index put option.

Although the exact nature of the option replicating futures strategy cannot be explained here (options are discussed later in the book), in general it requires the hedger (or portfolio manager) to begin with an initial hedge ratio that is determined by several factors: the risk to be hedged, the level of protection desired, the hedging horizon, and so forth.[14] Later, as the value of the portfolio falls (due to falling stock prices), the hedge ratio is increased. If the value of the portfolio rises instead, the hedge ratio is reduced, possibly to zero. In a falling market, therefore, portfolio insurers sell increasing amounts of stock index futures to generate increasing amounts of profits to make up for previous portfolio losses. In rising markets they are buyers of futures. It is this dynamic buying and selling of futures that has led critics to allege that portfolio insurance has increased stock market volatility. It has proven difficult in practice, however, to identify the effects of portfolio insurance, either theoretically or empirically.

Portfolio insurance programs can also be accomplished by selling and buying stocks directly. Using stock indexes futures, however, is preferred because of the superior liquidity of futures markets (positions of more than $100 million can be executed in a few minutes with a small price impact on the market) and lower trading costs. In addition, using futures does not interfere with individual portfolio managers, who are often part of a larger institutional investment strategy. Individual managers do not have to know that a portfolio insurance strategy is even being implemented.

Portfolio insurance programs can also be done using listed index options, but most institutions have not done so in the past because of significant disadvantages associated with options: option premiums are expensive; options typically do not have expiration dates as distant as futures; and position limits in options, at least in the past, were very restrictive. Further, it has been shown that if the portfolio being insured is a mixture of stocks and bonds, stock index futures can be used more efficiently than options.

---

[14]See Mark Rubinstein and Hayne Leland, "Replicating Options with Positions in Stock and Cash," *Financial Analyst Journal*, July–August 1981, pp. 3–12.

CONCLUSION

This chapter has examined the development, pricing, and uses of stock index futures. It has discussed how stock index futures are used for index arbitrage, asset allocation, and yield-enhancement investment strategies, and how stock index futures can be used to hedge the systematic risk of stock portfolios. The chapter has shown how to compute hedge ratios and how to construct hedge positions when using stock index futures. It has also demonstrated how to implement a stock index hedge, ending with a discussion of portfolio insurance, one of the most popular and controversial stock index hedging strategies. After the stock market crash in October 1987, stock index futures trading was widely criticized as being destabilizing. In the next chapter we examine this controversy in greater depth.

QUESTIONS

1. Explain why the price of a stock index futures contract should be equal to the spot price of the underlying index plus the net cost-of-carry.
2. If futures are expensive relative to the spot index, describe the arbitrage transaction that you would use to profit from this situation. What risks are associated with this type of stock index arbitrage?
3. Can stock index futures contracts be used to hedge both systematic and unsystematic risks? What is systematic risk and how is it measured?
4. How confident are you that the calculated portfolio beta of 1.07 in Table 10.23 is an accurate estimate of the portfolio beta? Explain.
5. Why is the portfolio beta calculated in Table 10.23 not equal to the minimum-variance hedge ratio?
6. In the example in Section 10.13, why is the relationship between the NYSE composite index and the S&P 500 index used to calculate β_{IF}?
7. When rolling the hedge as described in Section 10.13, why would the hedger have to recompute the minimum-variance hedge ratio each time?
8. In the example depicted in Table 10.25, if the investor wished to increase the return on his portfolio and was also willing to take more risk, what would you advise as a hedging strategy? Explain.

SUGGESTED READING

Biermon, H. "Defining and Evaluating Portfolio Insurance Strategies." *Financial Analysts Journal*, Vol. 44 (May/June 1988), pp. 84–87.

Billingley, R. and D. Chance. "The Pricing and Performance of Stock Index Futures Spreads." *The Journal of Futures Markets*, Vol. 8, No. 3 (1988), pp. 303–318.

Bookstaber, R. and J. Langsarn. "Portfolio Insurance Trading Rules." *The Journal of Futures Markets*, Vol. 8, No. 1 (1988), pp. 15–31.

Brennan, M. and E. Schwartz. "Time-Invariant Portfolio Insurance Strategies." *Journal of Finance*, Vol. 43 (June 1988), pp. 283–300.

Figlewski, S. "Hedging Performance and Basis Risk in Stock Index Futures." *Journal of Finance*, Vol. 39 (July 1984), pp. 657–669.

Graham, D. and R. Jennings. "Systematic Risk, Dividend Yield and the Hedging Performance of Stock Index Futures." *The Journal of Futures Markets*, Vol. 7 (February 1987), pp. 1–14.

Kawaller, L., P. Koch, and T. Koch. "The Relationship Between the S&P 500 Index and S&P 500 Index Futures Prices." *Economic Review,* Federal Reserve Bank of Atlanta, May/June 1988, pp.2–9.

MacKinlay, A. and K. Ramaswamy. "Index-Futures Arbitrage and the Behavior of Stock Index Futures Prices." *The Review of Financial Studies*, Vol. 1 (Summer 1988), pp. 137–158.

Modest, D. "On the Pricing of Stock Index Futures." *Journal of Portfolio Management*, Vol. 10 (Summer 1984), pp. 51–57.

Nordhauser, F. "Using Stock Index Futures to Reduce Market Risk." *Journal of Portfolio Management*, Vol. 10 (Spring 1984), pp. 56–62.

CHAPTER

11

THE 1987 STOCK MARKET CRASH AND THE CONTROVERSY OVER STOCK INDEX FUTURES

During the 1980s stock index futures trading soared as more and more institutions holding stock portfolios used stock index futures to manage their risk exposures. In October 1987, in just a few days, the stock market collapsed with unprecedented speed. One consequence of this episode was to turn the searchlight on stock index futures as a possible reason for the near-debacle. Stock index futures were, after all, new instruments, and their effects were still unknown.

This chapter examines the controversy over stock index futures unleashed by the 1987 stock market crash. It discusses the alleged role of stock index futures in precipitating the Crash and the criticisms directed at several popular stock index futures trading strategies. In addition, it reviews and analyzes various regulatory controversies that resulted from government-commissioned studies of the Crash or from proposed legislation aimed at preventing another stock market collapse.

11.1 THE STOCK MARKET CRASH

From the close of trading on Friday, October 16, 1987, to its lowest point on Tuesday, October 20, 1987, a period of just 10 trading hours, the S&P 500 cash index fell by 22 percent. During the same 10 hours the S&P 500 futures index fell by 36 percent.

This precipitous drop in stock prices on October 19 and 20, 1987, and the events that surrounded it, is now known as the "Stock Market Crash of 1987." This crash was the worst ever. Even during the infamous 1929 stock market crash there was no day worse than October 19. (On October 28, 1929, the worst day of the 1929 collapse, the Dow Jones index fell by only 12.82 percent.)

The 1987 Crash was not without warning. In the three prior days, from Wednesday, October 16, through the close on Friday, October 18, the S&P 500 cash index fell by 10 percent. Over the intervening weekend fear overwhelmed investors and produced massive sell orders in the early hours of October 19, before markets in the United States had even opened.

From its high point in August 1987, to its lowest point on Tuesday, October 20, 1987, the stock market fell by 40 percent, a remarkable episode even measured by the cataclysmic events of 1929. Indeed, there are striking similarities between the two crashes. In 1929, the Dow Jones Industrial Average (DJIA) fell by about 34 percent from its peak in September to the end of 1929. In 1987, the DJIA fell by 31 percent from its peak in August to the end of 1987.

The 1987 Crash was not limited to U.S. markets: stock prices plunged throughout the world, in every major stock market. From their respective 1987 highs, the stock market in London dropped 26 percent, and the market in Tokyo fell by 20 percent. In some markets, such as the one in Hong Kong, the collapse was far worse. As a consequence, there have been several extensive government studies of what went wrong.

11.2 THE ALLEGED ROLE OF STOCK INDEX FUTURES TRADING

The most well-known studies of the Crash were those done by the "Brady Commission" and the Securities and Exchange Commission (SEC).[1] The SEC describes the role of futures as follows:

> ...futures trading, and strategies involving the use of futures, were not the 'sole cause' of the so-called market break. Nevertheless, the existence of futures on stock indexes and the use of the various strategies involving 'program trading' (i.e., index arbitrage, index substitution and portfolio insurance) were a significant factor in accelerating and exacerbating the decline.[2]

---

[1] The Brady Commission's report was actually the "Report of the Presidential Task Force on Market Mechanisms," January 1988.

[2] "The October 1987 Market Break," U. S. Securities and Exchange Commission, February 1988, pp. 3–11.

The Brady Commission described what happened as follows:

> Portfolio insurers sold in the futures market, forcing prices down. The downward price pressure in the futures market was then transmitted to the stock market by index arbitrage and diverted portfolio insurance sales. While index arbitrageurs may not have accounted for a substantial part of total daily volume, they were particularly active during the day at times of substantial price movements. They were not, however, the primary cause of the movements; rather, they were the transmission mechanism for the pressures initiated by other institutions.
>
> Finally, there were periods when the linkage between stock and futures markets became completely disconnected, leading to a free-fall in both markets.[3]

Figures 11-1 and 11-2, which are taken from the Brady Commission report, show why the Commission reached its conclusion.[4] The top half of Figure 11-1 depicts the movements of both the S&P 500 cash index and S&P 500 futures index during the day on October 19, 1987. While both indexes fell precipitously during the day, the futures index fell by more than the cash index. The lower half of Figure 11-1 shows the volume of portfolio insurance trading as a percentage of total S&P 500 stock index futures trading volume for half-hour intervals. The Commission concluded that there was a causal relationship between the volume of portfolio insurance trading and both the futures and cash stock price movements.

Figure 11-2 shows, on a different scale, the differences that existed between the cash and futures stock indexes (shown in Figure 11-1) during the day on October 19 at half hour intervals. The futures stock index was well below the cash price index during most of the day. This is in sharp contrast to the pricing theory and price relationships discussed in Chapter 10. We would normally expect stock index futures prices to be higher than cash stock prices, since they are subject to the standard cost-of-carry pricing relationship. However, at one point on October 19 stock index futures prices were at a 45 index point discount to the cash stock index! This led the Brady Commission to conclude that stock index futures prices were causing stock prices to fall.

11.3   MARKET DEVELOPMENTS PRIOR TO THE CRASH

To understand the role played by stock index futures it is necessary to understand developments prior to 1987. The most dramatic development was the key role that stock index futures began to play in securities markets in the years immediately prior to the Crash. In just a few years after their introduction in 1982 stock index futures "became the market of choice for many institutions that trade (stocks)

---

[3] Brady Commission Report, p. 42.
[4] Ibid., pp. 31 and 33.

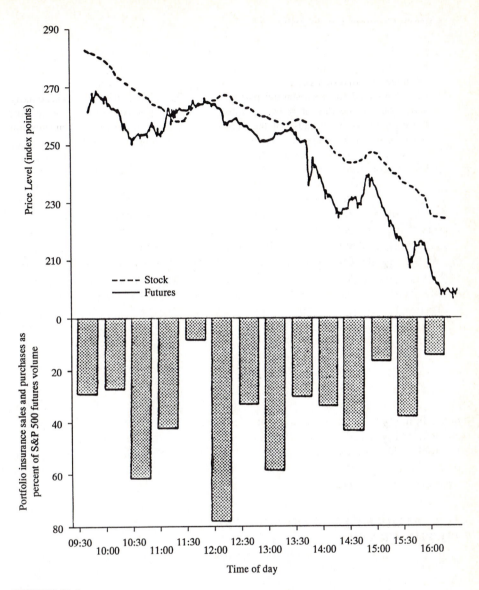

FIGURE 11-1
S&P 500 cash and futures indexes, Monday, October 19, 1987. (Brady Commission Report, p. 31)

Difference in
index points

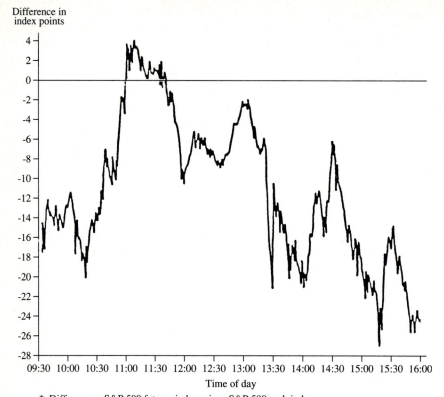

Time of day

* Difference = S&P 500 futures index minus S&P 500 cash index

FIGURE 11-2
S&P 500 price differentials, Monday, October 19, 1987. (Brady Commission Report, p. 33)

actively."[5] Daily trading volume in S&P 500 index futures alone grew to more than two times the average daily dollar volume of trading on the New York Stock Exchange—the equivalent of about $16 billion a day. In addition, options on stock indexes became the fastest growing segment of the options market.

The second development was the sharp increase in the institutionalization of equity markets in the United States. Pension funds and mutual funds grew substantially during the 1980s. Institutional investors now hold equity equal to about 40 percent of the value of all NYSE listed stocks, and in some years account for as much as 80 percent of total trading volume. Block transactions, or large institutional trades, alone account for 50 percent of the volume on the NYSE.

---

[5]See Brady Commission Report, pp. 31-37.

Third, during the 1980s the value of indexed assets under management grew remarkably, to over $200 billion. This in turn resulted in the rapid growth of *program* trading: institutions making large (block) trades simultaneously in many different stocks. (This is sometimes also called *basket* trading.) Currently, as much as 25 percent of all institutional trading is done through program trades.

Fourth, futures markets became *the markets of choice* for this kind of institutional trading because they provided a cheaper and more efficient transaction mechanism. Brokerage fees are much lower in futures markets, and, because of greater market liquidity, execution costs in futures markets are substantially below what they are in the cash (stock) market (see Table 10.18 in Chapter 10). In general, it costs seven to ten times more to execute an equivalent stock trade in the cash market than in the futures market. Put simply, futures exchanges have provided a superior trading vehicle for large institutions.

Fifth, these developments were responsible for the advent and growth of portfolio insurance, a trading strategy discussed in Chapter 10. Used as a substitute for direct selling on the NYSE (through, for example, the placing of limit orders), portfolio insurance trading provided what appeared to be a significantly lower-cost strategy for protecting (or hedging) a stock portfolio. Prior to October 1987, as much as $100 billion of managed portfolio assets were being hedged with this strategy.

Finally, large institutional selling and buying of futures contracts frequently drove futures prices to levels above or below their fair-value levels—the price level consistent with the underlying stock values adjusted for net carrying costs. This in turn resulted in a sharp increase in stock index arbitrage, as well as in yield-enhancing trading activities such as those discussed in Chapter 10.

Thus, the sudden importance of stock index futures trading in equity markets during the 1980s makes it easy to understand why studies of the Crash closely examined the role that futures trading played in the 1987 stock market break.

11.4   THE EVIDENCE

The Brady Commission and the SEC studies point to two pieces of evidence which they believe show the critical role that stock index futures played in the Crash. First, they argue that heavy institutional selling in futures markets, and, in particular, portfolio insurance related selling, precipitated and deepened the fall in stock prices. The Brady Commission claims that on October 19 such sales amounted to 34,500 contracts (equivalent to $4 billion of stocks), which was 40 percent of total S&P futures volume that day, *exclusive* of locals' (or floor traders') transactions.[6] The SEC states that on October 19, stock index arbitrage and substitution programs together with portfolio insurance selling strategies comprised 14.7 percent of total NYSE volume and 21.1 percent of S&P 500 stock volume;

---

[6]Ibid, p. 36. If locals' transactions of $10 billion are included, the percentage falls to 20 percent.

and, that between 1:00 and 2:00 P.M. on that day "the combination of selling from portfolio insurance and index arbitrage totaled more than 40 percent of volume in the stocks comprising the S&P 500 index. Further, such trading totaled more than 60 percent of S&P 500 stock volume during three different 10 minute intervals within that hour."[7] During these periods stock prices fell sharply.

The second piece of evidence relates to the alleged indirect "negative market psychology" effects of futures markets. The Brady Commission states that "the large discount between futures and stocks acted as a 'billboard', worrying many investors that further (stock) declines were imminent."[8] At its low on October 20, for example, the S&P 500 futures price implied a Dow Jones index level of about 1400, which never occurred. The Dow Jones Index never fell below 1700. The SEC argues that

> the knowledge by market participants of the existence of active portfolio insurance strategies created . . . a market 'overhang' effect in both futures and stock markets; this resulted in the maintenance of futures discounts that discouraged institutional traders from participating in the stock market on the buy side, specialists from committing capital to maintain fair and orderly markets, and block positioning firms from maintaining normal levels of activity.[9]

Neither piece of evidence is convincing. First, with respect to the effect of portfolio insurance sales, the fact that such sales were 20 percent of total futures sales on October 19—the largest volume day—suggests that such sales were *not* a dominant feature of the sell-off. Eighty percent of the sales came from other sources! The sell-off was general and not specific to portfolio insurers. Second, looking at particular short time segments, such as 10 minute intervals or even specific hour intervals (as the SEC does), is not a useful mode of analysis. It is always possible to pick an arbitrary small time interval to show that a particular seller's proportion of total sales is whatever percentage we would like to make it—even 100 percent. Evidence drawn from selected short intervals of time is so arbitrary that its meaningfulness is open to serious question. Third, looking at the proportion of total sales accounted for by a particular type of seller does not demonstrate that this selling *caused* the price decline. Prices are determined by both sellers and buyers (and by their expectations). The buyers who were not present on October 19 were just as responsible for the price decline as the sellers who were present. The issue of price determination and causality is considerably more complicated than the studies suggest.

---

[7]SEC report, p. XIII. There is a difference in the numbers reported in the Brady Commission and in both the SEC and CFTC reports. The SEC/CFTC survey numbers are the more accurate. In addition, a distinction should be made between stock index arbitrage trading and portfolio insurance (or hedge) trading. Stock index arbitrage selling constituted only six percent of selling on the NYSE on October 19, and almost nothing on October 20.

[8]Brady Commission Report, p. 40.

[9]SEC Report, p. XIII.

With respect to the alleged "negative psychology" effect of futures, the emphasis is misplaced. The large and unusual discounts that futures prices exhibited on October 19 and on surrounding days were almost certainly due largely to the prevalence of fictitious price quotations on the NYSE. Specialists on the NYSE were unable to cope with the enormous trading volume and order imbalances that occurred and, as a consequence, either failed to conduct continuous trading in stocks or quoted prices at which little trading could be done. Futures prices, on the other hand, continued to reflect market forces. Futures prices fell below quoted stock prices because they reflected market forces, whereas stock prices did not. If this price discount had a negative market impact, it was for good reason: it reflected the current market outlook. Market prices that transmit investors' expectations and psychology do not *cause* prices to fall; they simply represent current supply and demand conditions.

Finally, if the stock market plunge was caused by futures trading activities, how can we explain the fact that the crash was worldwide? Markets in London, Tokyo, Hong Kong, Sydney, Singapore, Paris, Milan, Frankfurt and everywhere else all experienced massive sell-offs on October 19 and 20, despite the absence of significant (or any) stock index futures trading in those markets.[10] These facts suggest that fundamental economic and psychological factors, and not futures-related trading activities, were the primary causes of the 1987 Crash.

11.5   THE AFTERMATH OF THE CRASH: PROPOSED REMEDIES

Subsequent to the Crash a number of regulatory proposals were advanced that supporters believed would stabilize the stock market and prevent another chaotic market decline. These are reviewed in this section.

11.5.1   Curbs on Portfolio Insurance and Program Trading

Although none of the studies of the stock market crash recommended direct curbs on program trading, portfolio insurance, or index arbitrage, there have, nevertheless, been calls to curb or even to ban entirely portfolio insurance and index arbitrage. Under pressure from large clients, a few large brokerage firms "voluntarily" stopped doing index arbitrage for their own accounts subsequent to the Crash.

There are five arguments against restricting these types of trading. First, it is not clear that they in fact increase stock market volatility. They may or may not; we do not know. Second, with the development and increasing dominance of institutional trading, and of index fund management, there are benefits to being able

---

[10]It should be noted that the institutional and market-making systems vary significantly among countries, both in comparison to the United States and to each other. Yet, all markets experienced a sharp and rapid price decline.

to trade the entire market (or to do basket trades). It is cheaper and therefore bene-ficial to the owners or beneficiaries of institutional funds. Third, index arbitrage is necessary in order to link futures and cash prices. Fourth, the volume of portfolio insurance prior to October 19 was "excessive." Users overestimated its benefits. Since the Crash, the volume of portfolio insurance has declined markedly. Finally, there are other ways to curb stock market volatility, without having to sacrifice the benefits of either derivative markets or the new trading strategies. One is to develop market-making systems that provide the necessary market liquidity to support institutional trading. Curbs on particular types of trading, therefore, are unwise.

11.5.2 Higher Futures Margins

Both the SEC and the Brady Commission reports called for higher margins on index futures and options. In its report, the SEC argued that

> . . . low margins contribute to increased speculative trading that, in normal market conditions, contribute to the illusion of almost unlimited liquidity in the futures market. During a market break, however, that liquidity disappears at a rate geo-metrically larger than does liquidity in the lower-leveraged stock market. For these reasons, the Division believes that relatively low margins may contribute to increased concentrated institutional trading and resulting greater price volatility.[11]

The Brady Commission contended that

> All margin requirements have one aspect in common: margins are collateral and control the effective economic leverage achievable in any financial instrument. . . .
> It has long been recognized that margin requirements, through leverage, affect the volume of speculative activity. Controlling speculative behavior is one approach to inhibiting overvaluation in stocks and reducing the potential for a precipitate price decline fueled by the involuntary selling that stems, for example, from margin calls.
> . . . low futures margins allow investors to control large positions with low initial investments. The clear implication is that margin requirements affect intermarket risk and are not the private concern of a single market place. . . .
> To protect the intermarket system, margins on stock index futures need to be consistent with margins for professional market participants in the stock market.[12]

The debate about higher margins is not a debate about whether current mar-gin levels in futures markets are sufficient to maintain market integrity. As we saw in Chapters 2 and 3, futures margins are security deposits, the purpose of which is to insure that futures traders honor their contractual obligations. In the event of a trader default, Futures Commission Merchants (FCMs) and clearing associations are protected by their holding of margin deposits. Futures margins are now established by FCMs and clearing associations, and not by government.

---

[11] SEC Report, p. 65.
[12] Brady Commission Report, p. 65.

Margins are different for different commodities, for different types and sizes of transactions, and can be changed at any time. Their levels are related to the risk associated with specific commodities and transactions. Customers' positions are marked-to-market daily and additional variation margin is called for daily (or even intra-day) if a customer incurs trading losses.

The events of October 1987 showed this system to be remarkably sound. Although substantial margin calls were issued ($3 billion by futures and option exchanges on both October 19 and 20), there were few defaults. Despite an historic market drop, futures markets came through almost unscathed. There were no major FCM defaults, and no clearing association defaults. Whether this system might have cracked had prices continued to fall, and at what point, we do not know. That it did not break in October 1987 is testimony to its strength.

The SEC and Brady Commission recommendations to raise margins on stock index futures to levels similar to those imposed on stocks is based upon a belief that higher margins *reduce speculative activity* and, as a consequence, *increase market stability*. These recommendations do not appear to be based on the events of October 19 and 20, 1987. Higher margins on those days would not have made a difference. Much of the selling in futures markets was by pension funds, trusts, and other large institutions. These institutions do not operate with leverage, and are not constrained by margins. Exchanges also require only hedger margins of these institutions, which are much lower than speculator margins. Thus, at least with respect to the 1987 market plunge, higher futures margins would not have prevented what happened.

Indeed, in 1987 the impact of higher futures margins would have fallen most heavily on speculators. On October 19 and 20 both large and small speculators were net buyers, offsetting rather than reinforcing the sell-order imbalance. If higher margins had been in place during the Crash, the result could very well have been worse: speculators might have been deterred from playing the stabilizing role that they did.

The argument for higher futures margins rests on two propositions: first, that higher margins reduce speculative activity; and, second, that by reducing speculative activity prices will be more stable because excessive price fluctuations will be eliminated. While it is possible that higher margins will reduce speculative activity (as well as other trading), it is not clear that less speculative trading will diminish the magnitude of price movements in either direction. Speculation is as likely to be stabilizing as destabilizing.[13] (See our discussion in Chapter 7, Section 7.7.)

---

[13]There has been a long and inconclusive academic debate about whether speculative activity is on net stabilizing or destabilizing. The results of theoretical models depend critically upon the underlying assumptions that are used. It has also proven difficult to test empirically the effects of speculation. See, for example, M. Friedman, "The Case for Flexible Exchange Rates," *Essays in Positive Economics,* University of Chicago Press, 1953; A. Beja and B. Goldman, "On the Dynamic Behavior of Prices in Disequilibrium," *Journal of Finance*, May 1980, pp. 235-48; and O. Blanchard, "Bubbles, Rationale Expectations, and Financial Markets," *Crises in the Economic and Financial Structure,* Paul Wachtel, ed., Lexington Books, 1982, pp. 295-315.

Stock and other asset prices are determined more by the expectations of asset holders than by trading activity. Asset prices can change sharply with little trading. The value of real estate, for example, can change substantially with few transactions, or even with no transactions. Stock and futures markets are no different. Higher futures margins, which work by increasing trading costs and reducing trading activity, need have no predictable impact on either price levels or price volatility. Lower trading volume does not necessarily mean either lower prices or less volatility.

Higher futures margins are also not without cost. They increase the costs to futures market participants and, in particular, to speculators. This is likely to reduce both the volume of trading and market liquidity, which may result in greater price volatility. In addition, hedgers' costs may rise because less speculation will result in higher risk premiums, as shown in Chapter 7.

In an empirical study of the effects of changes in futures margins, Michael Hartzmark examines trading in wheat, Treasury bonds, pork bellies, and feeder cattle over several years.[14] He finds that higher margin levels reduce open interest and trading volume, but that there is no "statistically significant relationship between margin changes and price volatility." While Hartzmark could only observe small changes in futures margins, his findings suggest that higher margins will result in "certain trader groups being driven from the market, making the market thinner, . . . with the result being less stable futures prices."[15]

The margin issue has been studied extensively in the context of the stock market as well.[16] In general, studies have been unable to conclude that lower stock margins are related to greater price volatility. For example, the Federal Reserve Board investigated the question of whether low margins were the cause of past instability in stock prices or of temporary speculative bubbles.[17] It concluded that

> The evidence and arguments reviewed . . . do not indicate a need for margin regulation to curb short-term speculation . . . ; and
>
> The behavior of stock prices since the enactment of margin regulation also does not support the argument that controlled margin trading will tend to reduce stock

---

[14]Michael L. Hartzmark, "The Effects of Changing Margin Levels on Futures Market Activity, the Composition of Traders in the Market, and Price Performance," *Journal of Business*, 59 (2, part 2): S151-S180, 1986.

[15]Ibid.

[16]See for example, R. Grube, O. Joy, and D. Panton, "Market Responses to Federal Reserve Changes in the Initial Margin Requirements," *Journal of Finance*, June 1979, pp. 659-75; T. Moore, "Stock Market Margin Requirements," *Journal of Political Economy,* April 1966, pp. 158-67; G.W. Douglas, "Risk in the Equity Markets: An Empirical Appraisal of Market Efficiency," *Yale Economic Essays,* Spring 1969, pp. 3-45; W.L. Eckards and D.L. Rogoff, "100 Percent Margins Revisited," *Journal of Finance,* June 1976, pp. 995-1000; J.A. Largay, "100 Percent Margins: Combatting Speculation in Individual Security Issues," *Journal of Finance*, September 1973, pp. 973-86; and J.A. Largay and R. R. West, "Margin Changes and Stock Price Behavior," *Journal of Political Economy*, March/April 1973, pp. 328-39.

[17]The Federal Reserve Board, "A Review and Evaluation of Federal Margin Regulations," 1984.

volatility. Despite the relatively high federal margin levels and the very low levels of margin credit since the early 1930's . . . stock prices have continued to be about as volatile as they were in the 50 years preceding margin regulation.[18]

There is, therefore, no reason to believe that higher margins will reduce price volatility in either the stock or futures markets. The only certainty is that higher margins will impose higher costs on investors and traders, which will reduce trading volume and diminish market liquidity.

11.5.3   Trading Halts

Trading halts, or stopping trading when certain predetermined conditions occur, were first proposed in principle by the Brady Commission. The Brady Commission called such trading halts "circuit breakers," and cited three benefits to adopting them:

> First, they limit credit risks and loss of financial confidence by providing a time-out amid frantic trading to settle up and ensure that everyone is solvent. Second, they facilitate price discovery by providing a "time-out" to pause, evaluate, inhibit panic, and publicize order imbalances to attract value traders to cushion violent movements in the market.
>
> Finally, circuit breaker mechanisms counter the illusion of liquidity by formalizing the economic fact of life, so apparent in October, that markets have a limited capacity to absorb massive one-sided volume. Making circuit breakers part of the contractual landscape makes it far more difficult for some market participants— pension portfolio insurers, aggressive mutual funds—to mislead themselves into believing that it is possible to sell huge amounts in short time periods. This makes it less likely in the future that flawed trading strategies will be pursued to the point of disrupting markets and threatening the financial system.[19]

Trading halts can take many different forms and can be triggered by different pre-determined conditions: price limits, volume limits, order imbalances, prescribed times of the day, and so forth. While the Brady Commission did not recommend a specific type of circuit breaker, it suggested that such mechanisms be coordinated among exchanges and "be formulated and implemented." Subsequent to the 1987 Crash, circuit breakers based on predetermined price limits were adopted by both stock and futures exchanges.

An example of a circuit breaker is the New York Stock Exchange's *50 Point Rule*, which limits stock index arbitrage on days when the Dow Jones Index moves in either direction by more than 50 index points. Once the Dow moves by 50 points during the day, thereafter all index-arbitrage orders must be *stabilizing*. This requires that in a falling (rising) market traders must wait for a price uptick

---

[18]Ibid., pp. 152 and 167.

[19]Brady Commission Report, p.66.

(downtick) to sell (buy). The objective of this rule, obviously, is to prevent index arbitrage from increasing price volatility in the stock market.

There are several arguments against circuit breakers based on price limits. First, if new information requires a price change larger than the allowable price range, trading halts will delay the determination of equilibrium prices. This may result in trading taking place at disequilibrium prices (off the exchange), causing injury to some traders. It also interferes with the price discovery function of markets, since quoted prices will no longer reflect existing economic information.

Second, if markets are closed, traders are deprived of their use at the very time they need them the most: when new information dictates a substantial change in prices. At such times hedgers may want to put on new hedges or to lift prior hedges. Price limits both lock them out and in. The inability to trade at these times could be a serious deterrent to the use of futures markets by hedgers. The prospect of being locked in is an anathema to speculators as well, as it prevents them from getting out when they need to the most.

Further, if market participants know that trading will be halted when prices reach a certain price level, price limits may become self-fulfilling: traders may buy or sell frantically to beat the closing of the market so that they are not locked in. In doing so they will ensure that the limits are hit.

The argument in favor of price limits rests upon the notion that large price movements may be the result of excessive (or irrational) speculation. In this case there may be a reason to slow things down, since market prices are "wrong" to begin with. However, even in this case it is not clear that trading halts will hasten the return to correct prices. Preventing prices from changing may increase the response time of rational traders to disequilibrium prices, slowing the return to more rational prices. Further, at times price limits may have the opposite effect from what we expect: they may increase uncertainty and cause even greater irrational market activity.

Price limits are only one of the many possible types of trading halts. Another that might be employed is to stop trading when large buy or sell order imbalances occur. Market-makers could, for example, delay changing prices for a predetermined amount of time—say 5 or 10 minutes—to see if counterbalancing orders might arise during this time interval. The existence and magnitude of the order imbalance could be disclosed to a broad range of traders, or even to the entire public. In this case the market would remain open for trading at the quoted (or last) price. If the order imbalance were to persist, market-makers might then change prices according to a predetermined schedule, waiting for a short time at each new price for new orders to materialize. At all times, however, the market would remain open for counterbalancing orders.[20]

---

[20]Exchanges might also hold *single-price auctions* one or more times a day, where participants would be advised of order imbalances and where all buy and sell orders would be filled at one time and at one price. If order imbalances were known, new bids might be forthcoming which would balance the market. In this system, markets could clear without specialists or market-makers having to risk their own capital.

In sum, whether or not trading halts are on net beneficial is an open question. Perhaps after we have had the opportunity to observe how they have worked over a number of years we will be able to assess their value.

11.6 EFFECTS ON STOCK MARKET VOLATILITY

The 1987 stock market crash set off a widespread debate about whether stock index futures trading has increased price volatility in the stock market. The evidence, however, suggests that such trading has not in general increased stock market volatility.

Stock market volatility has not been exceptionally high since the introduction of stock index futures in 1982. Table 11.1 shows stock market volatility (measured as the annualized standard deviation of daily percentage price changes) for various time periods before and after the start of stock index trading in 1982. Volatility during 1973–82, the period before the introduction of stock index futures, was similar to the volatility during the four years subsequent to the start of stock index futures trading (1983–1986).[21] Since the October 1987 Crash, however, volatility has been higher.

William Schwert also examined the relationship between stock price volatility measured over 15-minute intervals and the volume of stock index futures trading relative to trading in the stock market. Figure 11-3 depicts this relationship

TABLE 11.1
Annualized volatilities: S&P 500 cash index
(daily: June 1, 1973, to December 31, 1989)

Pre-futures	
June 1, 1973–Apr 20, 1982	14.69%
Post-futures	
1983	13.33%
1984	12.70%
1985	10.12%
1986	14.75%
1987*	18.75%
October 1987	96.99%
1988	17.16%
1989	21.06%

* Excluding October 1987

Volatility is the annualized standard deviation of daily percentage changes in closing index values.

---

[21] See Franklin R. Edwards, "Futures Trading and Cash Market Volatility: Stock Index and Interest Rate Futures," *The Journal of Futures Market*, 8 (4): 421–40, 1988.

Standard deviation
per day (%)

Futures volume/
NYSE volume (%)

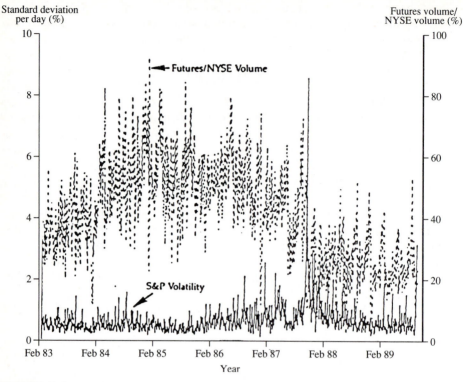

FIGURE 11-3
Volatility of daily returns to S&P 500, based on 15-minute returns within the day, and the ratio
of S&P futures volume to NYSE share trading volume, February 1, 1983–October 19, 1989.
(William Schwert, "Stock Market Volatility," *Financial Analyst Journal*, May/June 1990, pp.
23–34.)

over the six-year period 1983–89. Increased stock index futures trading does not
appear to have resulted in greater stock market volatility.[22]

11.7 EVIDENCE FROM FOREIGN MARKETS

An international comparison of stock market volatility provides evidence about
the effectiveness of regulations aimed at curbing volatility. For example, both the
United States and Japan impose margins of 50 percent or greater on stock transactions, while the United Kingdom has no margin requirements. Price volatility
in London, however, has not been greater than it has been in either New York

---

[22]William Schwert, "Stock Market Volatility," *Financial Analyst Journal,* May/June 1990, pp. 23–34.

or Tokyo. Similarly, of the three countries only Japan has trading halts (based on pre-set price limits), but the Japanese stock market has not been less volatile than the others. Further, the volume of futures trading in equity indexes has been much greater in New York than in either London or Tokyo, but stock market volatility in London and Tokyo has generally not been less than in the United States.

The lack of a relationship between volatility and either margins or circuit-breakers is supported by a study of stock markets in 23 countries by Richard Roll. He examines monthly percentage changes in stock indexes in each of the 23 countries during the period February 1981 to September 1987.[23] Among other tests, Roll estimates the following regression for each market:

$$R_{j,t} = \alpha_j + \beta_j R_{m,t} + \epsilon_{j,t}$$

where $R_{j,t}$ is the monthly percentage change in the stock index of country j for month t, $R_{m,t}$ is the world stock market index monthly percentage change for month t, $\epsilon_{j,t}$ is an unexplained residual, and α_j and β_j are fitted coefficients. The estimated beta, or β_j, therefore, is a measure of the relative volitility of each country's stock market.

To determine the impact of various institutional and regulatory differences across countries, Roll estimates another cross-sectional regression equation using the estimated "βs" from the above equation as the dependent variable. The explanatory variables in this equation are the various institutional and regulatory characteristics (which take the form of zero/one variables) in each of the 23 countries. The estimates show, among other things, no relationship between a market's relative volitility and either margins or price limits. Finally, if just the standard deviation of monthly percentage price changes from February 1981 to September 1987 is compared (a standard measure of stock market volatility), the United States has the lowest level of volatility.

Thus, an international comparison of stock market volatility reveals that the level of volatility is not related either to margin levels or to the use of circuit-breakers.

CONCLUSION

This chapter reviews the controversy over stock index futures trading that was ignited by the collapse of stock prices on October 19, 1987. It examines the role of stock index futures trading during the 1987 stock market crash and discusses the conclusions of several government-sponsored studies of the Crash.

---

[23]Richard Roll, "Price Volatility, International Market Links, and Their Implications for Regulatory Policies," in F. Edwards, *Regulatory Reform of Stock and Futures Markets*, Kluwer Academic Publishers, 1989, pp. 113–48.

The chapter also discusses the pros and cons of proposals to raise margins on futures and to impose circuit-breakers on both the stock index futures market and the underlying cash stock market. Finally, it analyzes the contention that stock index futures trading has increased stock market volatility. Evidence from both foreign and U.S. stock markets suggests that stock index futures trading has not in general increased stock market volatility.[24]

QUESTIONS

1. Describe the kinds of trading in stock index futures that allegedly contributed to the stock market collapse in October 1987. Do you think that this trading caused stock prices on October 19, 1987, to decline by more than they would have otherwise?
2. Do you think that higher margins on stock index futures would reduce stock market volatility? Why?
3. Some exchanges have recently adopted circuit breakers. Explain what they hope to accomplish.
4. Explain the argument that portfolio insurance is a destabilizing influence on stock prices. What is the counter-argument?

SUGGESTED READING

Blume, M., A. Mackinlay, and B. Terker. "Order Imbalances and Stock Price Movements on October 19 and 20, 1987." *Journal of Finance*, Vol. 44 (September 1989), pp. 827–848.

Edwards, F. "Does Futures Trading Increase Stock Market Volatility?" *Financial Analysts Journal*, Vol. 44 (January/February 1988), pp. 63–69.

Edwards, F. "Studies of the 1987 Stock Market Crash: Review and Appraisal." *Journal of Financial Services Research*, Vol. 1, No. 3 (June 1988), pp. 231–252.

Edwards, F. "Taxing Transactions in Futures Markets: Objectives and Effects." Columbia University Center for the Study of Futures Markets, Working Paper #215, 1991.

Gammill, J. and T. Marsh. "Trading Activity and Price Behavior in the Stock and Stock Index Futures Markets in October 1987." *Journal of Economic Perspectives*, Summer 1988, pp. 25–44.

Grossman, S. "Program Trading and Market Volatility: A Report on Interday Relationships." *Financial Analysts Journal*, Vol. 44 (July/August 1988), pp. 18–28.

Kupiec, P. "Initial Margin Requirements and Stock Returns Volatility: Another Look." *Journal of Financial Services Research*, Vol. 3, No. 2/3 (December 1989), pp. 189–203.

Ma, C., R. Rao, and S. Sears. "Volatility, Price Resolution, and The Effectiveness of Price Limits." *Journal of Financial Services Research*, Vol. 3, No. 2/3 (December 1989), pp. 165–200.

Moser, J. "Circuit-Breakers." *Economic Perspectives*, Federal Reserve Bank of Chicago, September/October 1990, pp. 2–13.

Roll, R. "Price Volatility, International Market Links, and Their Implications for Regulatory Policies." *Journal of Financial Services Research*, Vol. 3, No. 2/3 (December 1989), pp. 211–246.

---

[24]It is likely, however, that on certain days, such as the expiration days of stock index futures contracts, volatility has been greater (see Edwards, "Futures Trading and Cash Market Volatility").

SHORT-TERM INTEREST RATE FUTURES

12.1 INTEREST RATE OBLIGATIONS IN GENERAL

Interest rate futures are futures contracts written on *fixed-income* securities or instruments. A fixed-income security or instrument requires the payment of interest in the form of fixed dollar amounts at predetermined points in time, as well as repayment of the principal at maturity of the instrument. These debt obligations are often arbitrarily separated into short-term (*money market*) and long-term (*capital market*) instruments. Money market obligations are defined as having an initial maturity of one year or less and capital market obligations as having initial maturities longer than a year. U.S. Treasury bills are an example of the former; U.S. Treasury bonds are an example of the latter. Futures on short-term debt obligations are covered in this chapter. Futures on long-term debt obligations are examined in Chapter 13.

Treasury bills, along with Treasury notes and bonds, are issued by the U.S. Treasury to finance spending by the U.S. government. Over the years the U.S. government has run budget deficits (expenditures greater than revenues) and has had to borrow huge sums of money from the private sector to finance them. It has done this largely by selling Treasury securities to individuals and financial institutions. As of March 31, 1990, there were $453.1 billion in Treasury bills outstanding, $1,169.4 billion in Treasury notes, and $357.9 billion in Treasury bonds.

In addition to U.S. government obligations, there are many other money and capital market instruments: state and local government bonds (*municipals*), commercial paper, corporate bonds, bank certificates of deposit, mortgage loans and related obligations, and so forth. In short, the cash market for fixed-income debt obligations is enormous.

Dealing in (or holding) interest rate securities entails two types of risk: *interest rate* risk and *default* risk. Default risk is the risk of losing all or some of the principal loaned due to the bankruptcy of the borrower. In general, the greater the possibility (or probability) that a borrower will default (or the lower the borrower's credit-rating), the higher the interest rate that lenders demand. Since U.S. government obligations are generally viewed as being default-free, these obligations carry the lowest interest rate for a given maturity.

A borrower's credit-rating can change during the life of its obligations. If its credit-rating deteriorates, the market will demand a higher yield on its securities, causing the market value of its securities to decline. Even a change in the market's expectations about the possibility of a borrower defaulting can change the value of its debt obligations.

While default risk may at times be quite important, interest rate risk is always a major concern to holders of fixed-income obligations. Interest rate risk is the risk that the price (or market value) of a security will change. The prices of fixed-income securities are directly related to the yields (or interest rates) demanded by investors. These are in turn dependent on macroeconomic factors. At all times investors and traders of fixed-income securities have expectations about the future values of relevant macroeconomic factors: inflation rates, money supply growth rates, economic growth rates, Federal Reserve policy, and so forth. As new economic news becomes available, these expectations change, causing the level of interest rates to change. For example, news which suggests that future inflation rates will be higher than previously anticipated will result in the market demanding a higher yield on all fixed-income securities, causing the prices of outstanding securities to decline.

Yields on outstanding fixed-income securities are adjusted by changes in the prices of these securities. If investors today are willing to buy a fixed-income security only at a price lower than its price yesterday, the result will be a lower market value (price) for the security and a higher yield on the security.

Thus, a change in expectations about future interest rate levels causes changes in the yields demanded by investors, which in turn causes the market value of outstanding fixed-income instruments to change. The more volatile or uncertain are investors' expectations, the more volatile are the prices of fixed-income securities, and the more likely it is that holders of securities will suffer a capital loss.

12.2   INTEREST RATE FUTURES
IN GENERAL

Two factors have contributed to the introduction and growth of interest-rate futures: the enormous growth of the market for fixed-income obligations, both in the United States and in foreign markets, and the increased volatility of interest rates. Both factors have increased the need for an instrument to hedge or manage the interest-rate risk involved in holding and trading fixed-income obligations. Interest-rate futures have been one answer; others have been various forward-contracting instruments, such as interest-rate *swaps*. All of these instruments are designed to enable users to protect themselves against adverse movements in interest rates and in the value of fixed-income securities.

While interest-rate futures have been tried on a number of both short-term and long-term debt instruments, the most successful over the years have been futures on U.S. Treasury bonds, on U.S. 90-day Treasury bills, and on three-month Eurodollar time deposits. This chapter focuses on short-term interest rate futures, and, in particular, on the Treasury bill and Eurodollar futures contracts. The next chapter, Chapter 13, examines long-term interest rate futures, and in particular T-bond futures contracts. Taken together, annual trading in all interest rate futures contracts in the United States surpasses 100 million contracts, and accounts for more than 40 percent of all futures trading in the United States.

Table 12.1 lists the most actively traded short-term interest rate futures contracts both in the United States and abroad. The Eurodollar contract is clearly the dominant contract. Active contracts are also traded in London (3-month Sterling and 3-month Euromark), Paris (3-month PIBOR), Sydney (90-day bank bills), Tokyo (3-month Euroyen), and Singapore (3-month Eurodollar).

TABLE 12.1
Short-term interest rate futures

U.S. exchanges		1990 Volume
3-month Eurodollar	CME	34,695,625
90-day T-bill	CME	1,869,610
1-month LIBOR	CME	84,148
30-day interest rate	CBOT	81,300
3-month T-bill	MidAm	3,884
Total		36,734,567
Foreign exchanges		
3-month Euroyen	TIFFE, Japan	14,413,693
3-month Sterling	LIFFE, U.K.	8,354,922
90-day Bank Bill	Sydney Futures Exchange, Australia	5,015,408
3-month Eurodollar	SIMEX, Singapore	3,469,009
3-month Euromark	LIFFE, U.K.	2,659,641
3-month PIBOR	MATIF, France	1,900,851
3-month Eurodollar	LIFFE, U.K.	1,248,693
3-month Euroyen	SIMEX, Singapore	816,043
3-month Euromark	MATIF, France	393,850
90-day Bank Bill	New Zealand Futures Exchange	281,185
Bankers Acceptance	Montreal Futures, Canada	88,105
3-month ECU	LIFFE, U.K.	64,242
3-month Euromark	SIMEX, Singapore	57,188
3-month HIBOR	Hong Kong Futures Exchange	55,401
3-month Eurodollar	TIFFE, Japan	8,413
Total		38,826,644

12.3   THE TERM STRUCTURE OF INTEREST RATES

Before discussing interest rate futures it is important to understand the yield relationships implicit in the *term structure* of interest rates. The term structure of
interest rates describes the relationship between the *yield-to-maturity* and the maturity of a given fixed-income security. The term structure is typically represented
by a plot of the yields on default-free government securities with different terms-
to-maturity, at a given moment in time. Another name for this yield–maturity
relationship is the *yield curve.*

Figure 12-1 depicts three yield curves for U.S. Treasury securities as they
appeared in the Wall Street Journal on August 1, 1990: one for the day before
(July 31); one for yields a week prior to August 1 (or July 25); one for yields
four weeks prior (or July 3).

Clearly, both the level and the shape of the yield curve for Treasury securities change from day to day, and perhaps even from moment to moment. When
plotting a yield curve, it is important to depict yields only for homogeneous
securities; otherwise the yield–maturity relationship will be confused with other
characteristics of the debt instrument, such as its default risk. The yields shown
in Figure 12-1 are all on U.S. Treasury securities, for which there is no ostensible
default risk.

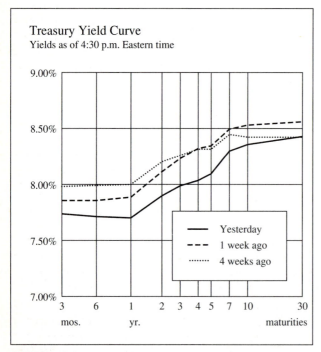

FIGURE 12-1
Treasury yield curve.

The yield relationships depicted in Figure 12-1 show that, over the previous four weeks, long-term securities have had higher yields than short-term securities. For example, on July 31, 1-year rates were about 7.70 percent, 10-year rates about 8.35 percent, and 30-year rates only slightly higher at about 8.42 percent. In general terms, we say that this yield curve is *flat* up to about a 1-year maturity, *upward-sloping* from 1 to 10 years, and only slightly upward-sloping from 10 to 30 years.

In addition, the term structure (or shape of the yield curve) shown in Figure 12-1 remains much the same over the four weeks shown, during which interest rate levels steadily fell. Four weeks earlier, however, the yield curve was slightly *downward-sloping* from 10 to 30 years, rather than slightly upward-sloping over this spectrum of maturities.

While upward-sloping yield curves are the most common, yield curves can also be flat or downward-sloping, depending on economic conditions. Or, they can be upward-sloping over some maturities, downward-sloping over other maturities, and flat over still other maturities.

12.3.1 Spot versus Forward Yields

The *spot* yield on an interest rate instrument is the cash market yield on that instrument at a particular moment in time. Thus, in Figure 12-1 the closing spot yield on a one-year Treasury security on July 31, 1990, is 7.70 percent. A *forward yield* (which is not directly observable) is a term used to describe the market's expectation about what the spot yield will be at some point in the future on a particular maturity instrument (say a 10-year Treasury). One popular theory of the term structure of interest rates, the *expectations* theory, views forward interest rates as unbiased estimators of future spot interest rates. If this theory is correct, forward rates can be inferred from spot rates, as we show below.

12.3.2 Theories of the Term Structure

THE EXPECTATIONS THEORY OF THE TERM STRUCTURE. The prevailing theory of the term structure is the *expectations* theory. At the heart of this theory is a simple proposition: the spot interest rate on a long-term bond will equal an average of the short-term spot interest rates that are expected to occur over the life of the long-term bond. For example, if short-term interest rates during the next 10 years (on say successive 1-year securities) are expected to average 8 percent, the interest rate on a 10-year bond will also be 8 percent. If today's 1-year rate is 8 percent, but interest rates are expected to rise (fall) over the next 10 years, the rate on a 10-year bond will be higher (lower) than 8 percent. Thus, depending on expectations about future spot short-term interest rates, long-term interest rates may be above or below current short-term rates.

Alternatively, the expectations theory states that, on average, today's forward (or expected) rate on a particular instrument is equal to the future spot rate on that instrument. This will be true because arbitrage insures that for different holding periods (or maturities) the expected return must be the same. For example, an investor wishing to make a one-year investment will be indifferent between buying a one-year security today, or a six-month security today and another one six months from now at the then prevailing spot rate. Thus, the current one-year and six-month spot rates (as shown by the yield curve) can be used to infer the future six-month spot rate; or, alternatively, the current six-month and one-year spot interest rates can be used to predict the *forward* six-month interest rate.

Suppose that an investor is deciding between purchasing a six-month instrument or purchasing two consecutive three-month instruments. Both the six-month and three-month spot rates are observable today, and are, respectively, 10 and 9 percent. For the investor to be indifferent between the two investment strategies, what must be the implicit forward rate (or expected spot rate) on the three-month security he will purchase three months from today?

- Choice A: Invest $100 for 6 months at 10%. Total proceeds:
  $100 + ($100 \times 0.10 \times \frac{6}{12}) = 105.00
- Choice B: Invest $100 for 3 months at 9.0%. Total proceeds:
  $100 + ($100 \times 0.09 \times \frac{3}{12}) = 102.25
  Reinvest $102.25 for 3 months at R_3%, where R_3 is the future 3-month spot interest rate. Total proceeds:
  $102.25 + ($102.25 \times R_3 \times \frac{3}{12})$
  Since the return on the two transactions must by assumption be the same:
  $105.00 = $102.25 + ($102.25 \times R_3 \times \frac{3}{12})$
  $R_3 = 0.1076$, or 10.76%

This implied forward rate relationship can be generalized as follows:

$$\left(1 + R_1 \times \frac{t_1}{365 \text{ days}}\right) = \left(1 + R_2 \times \frac{t_2}{365 \text{ days}}\right) \times \left(1 + R_3 \times \frac{t_1 - t_2}{365 \text{ days}}\right)$$

where R_1 is the six-month spot rate, R_2 is the three-month spot rate, R_3 is the implicit three-month forward rate, and t_1 and t_2 are the respective maturities of the spot instruments. Thus, the implicit 3-month forward rate is:

$$R_3 = \left(\frac{1 + R_1 \times \frac{t_1}{365}}{1 + R_2 \times \frac{t_2}{365}} - 1\right) \times \frac{365}{t_1 - t_2}$$

The expectations theory is a powerful theory because it can explain yield curves of different shapes: upward-sloping, downward-sloping, and flat. If short-term yields are expected to rise, it will be upward-sloping; if they are expected to fall, it will be downward-sloping. When long-term rates are above short-term rates (upward-sloping yield curve), the average of future short-term rates is expected to be higher than the current short-term rates, which can obviously only occur if short-term interest rates rise. A downward-sloping yield curve implies the opposite: interest rates are expected to fall. A flat yield curve implies no change in rates.

The expectations theory, however, does not explain an important empirical phenomenon: yield curves are more often upward-sloping than downward-sloping or flat. Since short-term interest rates are just as likely to fall as rise, the expectations theory, therefore, must be supplemented to explain the prevalence of upward-sloping yield curves.

THE LIQUIDITY PREMIUM THEORY. The *liquidity premium* theory, which is often referred to as the *preferred habitat* theory, states that the interest rate on a long-term bond will be equal to the average of the short-term interest rates that are expected to prevail over the life of the bond *plus* a liquidity premium that investors must be paid to get them to hold a long-term bond. The liquidity premium theory, as its name suggests, argues that investors are not indifferent between investments of all maturities, but have a preference for short-term instruments because of their superior liquidity. Short-term instruments have less interest rate risk: prices change less for given changes in interest rate levels. Thus, investors are willing to accept a lower return on short-term securities, everything else being equal. Alternatively, investors must be paid something extra for holding long-term securities. This extra amount is called the liquidity premium.

Thus, there will be a bias toward observing upward-sloping yield curves. Even if future spot rates are expected to be equal to current spot rates, we will observe an upward-sloping yield curve because of the liquidity premium. The liquidity preference theory also implies that the total return on successive short-term investments (say six successive six-month securities) will be less than the return on a three-year security, by the amount of the liquidity premium embedded in the three-year security. Or, alternatively, using today's observable short-term and long-term spot interest rates to predict future short-term spot rates (or to infer forward rates) will result in upward-biased predictions: forward rates will be higher than the pure expectations theory would predict because long-term spot rates contain a liquidity premium.

SUMMARY. The liquidity premium theory is widely accepted as an explanation of the term structure of interest rates. By supplementing the expectations theory with a liquidity premium, this theory is able to explain the prevalence of upward sloping yield curves. In addition, by utilizing the expectations theory, it is able to explain why the yield curve is generally downward-sloping when interest rates are high, and why the opposite is generally true when interest rates are low.

But the liquidity preference theory makes it much more difficult to infer forward rates from the existing term structure, since to do so requires being able to estimate the relevant liquidity premiums. This is not easy. The magnitude of the risk premium is itself variable, and can depend on existing economic conditions and investor psychology.

12.3.3   Forward Rates versus Futures Rates

In our later discussion of interest rate futures contracts it will become clear that the price paid for these futures implies a specific future yield: a spot yield that is expected to prevail at some time in the future. For example, the current yield on a 90-day T-bill futures contract is the spot yield on a (cash) 90-day T-bill that is currently expected to prevail on the expiration date of the futures contract.

The yields on interest rate futures contracts, therefore, are directly comparable to forward yields implied in the term structure of interest rates. As we will see, if futures and forward yields are not identical, there will be an opportunity for profitable arbitrage between futures and cash interest rate instruments.

12.4   TREASURY BILL FUTURES

Prior to the introduction of Eurodollar time deposit futures, the 90-day T-bill contract was the major short-term interest rate futures (see Figure 12-6). The Treasury bill futures contract was introduced in 1976 and is traded on the International Monetary Market (IMM), a division of the Chicago Mercantile Exchange. Contracts are traded on a March, June, September, and December two-year cycle, and call for physical delivery of a 13-week (90-, 91-, or 92-day), $1 million, Treasury bill.

12.4.1   Cash Price Quotations

Treasury bills do not pay explicit interest. Instead, they are sold at a discount relative to their redemption or face value. The difference between the purchase price of a Treasury bill and its face value determines the interest earned by a buyer.

TABLE 12.2
Price quotations
for Treasury bills

Treasury Bills

Rate	Maturity	Bid	Asked	Bid Chg.	Yld.
.00	Jan 25 '90	8.01	7.44	+.27	7.54
.00	Feb 01 '90	7.46	7.28	...	7.40
.00	Feb 08 '90	7.55	7.50	+.05	7.63
.00	Feb 15 '90	7.46	7.41	+.03	7.54
.00	Feb 22 '90	7.51	7.47	+.03	7.62
.00	Mar 01 '90	7.57	7.50	+.05	7.66
.00	Mar 08 '90	7.60	7.56	+.01	7.74
.00	Mar 15 '90	7.64	7.59	+.04	7.78
.00	Mar 22 '90	7.61	7.56	+.02	7.76
.00	Mar 29 '90	7.59	7.56	+.01	7.77
.00	Apr 05 '90	7.67	7.63	+.02	7.85
.00	Apr 12 '90	7.69	7.66	..	7.90
.00	Apr 19 '90	7.75	7.72	...	7.97
.00	Apr 26 '90	7.67	7.63	−.01	7.89
.00	May 03 '90	7.67	7.63	...	7.90
.00	May 10 '90	7.70	7.66	+.02	7.94
.00	May 17 '90	7.66	7.63	−.01	7.92
.00	May 24 '90	7.64	7.59	−.03	7.90
.00	May 31 '90	7.59	7.56	−.02	7.88
.00	Jun 07 '90	7.54	7.50	−.03	7.82
.00	Jun 14 '90	7.60	7.56	...	7.90
.00	Jun 21 '90	7.60	7.56	−.01	7.92
.00	Jun 28 '90	7.56	7.53	−.01	7.89
.00	Jul 05 '90	7.64	7.59	−.02	7.97
.00	Jul 12 '90	7.61	7.56	−.04	7.95
.00	Jul 19 '90	7.58	7.56	−.04	7.96
.00	Aug 02 '90	7.61	7.56	−.03	7.97
.00	Aug 30 '90	7.59	7.56	−.04	7.98
.00	Sep 27 '90	7.56	7.53	+.01	7.97
.00	Oct 25 '90	7.59	7.56	+.03	8.03
.00	Nov 23 '90	7.58	7.53	+.02	8.03
.00	Dec 20 '90	7.50	7.47	−.01	7.99
.00	Jan 17 '91	7.45	7.41	...	7.95

Source: The Wall Street Journal,
January 23, 1990.

Thus, Treasury bill yields are typically quoted on a discount basis: as a percentage of face value rather than of actual funds invested.

Table 12.2 shows price quotations for T-bills as they appeared in the newspaper on January 23, 1990, as of the close of trading on January 22, 1990. The first column is the maturity date of the particular bill. For example, the March 8, 1990, bill has a remaining maturity of 45 days. In the next two columns are the annualized bid and asked discount yields (in percentage), which are the quotes of T-bill dealers.[1] The fourth column shows the daily change (close-to-close) in the bid yield. The final column reports the annualized *bond equivalent yield*,[2] which is calculated by converting the discount yield to a yield based upon the actual price paid for the bill (or the amount invested) using a 365-day year.

The purchase price of a bill is

Face value − Dollar discount = Face value − (Face value)
$$\times (\text{Annualized discount asked yield}) \times (\text{Days to maturity}/360)$$

For example, the purchase price on January 22 of a $1 million T-bill with a maturity date of March 8, 1990 and a discount asked yield of 7.56 percent on January 22, 1990, is

$$\$1,000,000 - \$1,000,000 \times 0.0756 \times \tfrac{45}{360} = \$990,550$$

12.4.2 Futures Quotations and Futures Prices

Table 12.3 contains the contract specifications for T-bill futures and Eurodollar futures (discussed in Section 12.5). Table 12.4 shows the closing quoted T-bill futures prices on January 22, 1990, as they appeared in the newspaper on January 23, 1990. As we have already seen, for each contract (or delivery date) being traded, quotes are reported for the opening, high, low, and settlement prices, and the change in the settlement price from the previous day's close. In addition, the implied annualized discount rate and the day's change in this rate are given. Open

---

[1] Primary issues of Treasury securities are sold at auctions held by the Federal Reserve. There is also a large and liquid secondary market for Treasury securities operated by government securities dealers through a telephone network. In transactions with dealers, customers pay the asked yield when buying and receive the bid yield when selling. The bid-asked spread represents the compensation received by the dealers for making the market. For all interest rate instruments, prices and yields are inversely related. Thus, the bid yield is above the asked yield: the customer's sales price is lower than his purchase price.

[2] Dealers in T-bill markets always quote interest rates on bills on a discount basis. The annualized discount yield is defined as

$$[(\text{Face value} - \text{Price})/\text{Face value}] \times (360/\text{Days to maturity})$$

The discount yield understates the true return on T-bills as measured by the bond-equivalent yield for two reasons. First, the discount yield reflects the percentage gain on the *face value* of the T-bill rather than the percentage gain on the *purchase price* of the T-bill. Second, it takes the year to be 360 days rather than 365 days. The bond-equivalent yield is defined as

$$[(\text{Face value} - \text{Price})/\text{Price}] \times (365/\text{Days to maturity})$$

TABLE 12.3
Summary of contract specifications for 90-day T-bill and three-month Eurodollar futures

Specifications	13-week U.S. Treasury bill	Three-month Eurodollar time deposit
Size	$1,000,000	$1,000,000
Contract grade	New or dated Treasury bills with thirteen weeks to maturity	Cash settlement
Yields	Discount	Add-on
Hours*	7:20 A.M. to 2:00 P.M.	7:20 A.M. to 2:00 P.M.
Months Traded	Mar, Jun, Sep, Dec	Mar, Jun, Sep, Dec
Ticker symbol	TB	ED
Minimum fluctuation in price	.01 (1 basis pt) ($25/pt)	.01 (1 basis pt) ($25/pt)
Last day of trading	The day before the first delivery day	2nd London business day before 3rd Wednesday
Delivery date	1st day of spot month on which 13-week Treasury bill is issued and a one-year T-bill has 13 weeks to maturity	Last day of trading

* Chicago time.

interest and volume figures are also shown in the last column, and at the bottom of the table.

Price quotations for T-bill futures are on an index basis: the index is 100 minus the annualized discount rate (in percent). For example, an annualized discount rate of 9 percent implies an index price of 91. The minimum price fluctuation permitted in trading is one basis point (0.01 percent), which amounts to $25 per contract.

Quoted futures prices are not the dollar prices at which T-bill futures contracts are actually bought and sold. To calculate the dollar futures price it is neces-

TABLE 12.4
Prices of T-bill futures on January 22, 1990

```
TREASURY BILLS (IMM)-$1 mil.; pts. of 100%
                                      Discount    Open
       Open  High  Low  Settle Chg  Settle Chg Interest
Mar    92.65 92.69 92.62 92.65 + .02  7.35 - .02 32,928
June   92.76 92.82 92.76 92.79 + .05  7.21 - .05  5,531
Sept   92.76 92.78 92.76 92.78  ....  7.22  ....    178
   Est vol 4,477; vol Fri 6,082; open int 38,712, -787.
```

Source: The Wall Street Journal, January 23, 1990.

sary to use the T-bill pricing equation discussed in Section 12.4.1. Specifically, if the currently quoted futures price are 92.81 (implying a discount yield of 7.19 percent), the current dollar price of the 13-week T-bill futures contract (FP) will be

$$FP = \$1,000,000 - \$1,000,000 \times \frac{100 - 92.81}{100} \times \frac{91}{360} = \$981,825.28$$

where $\frac{100-92.81}{100}$ is the implied discount yield stated in decimal form.

TABLE 12.5
Short-term interest rates

MONEY RATES

Monday, January 22, 1990

The key U.S. and foreign annual interest rates below are a guide to general levels but don't always represent actual transactions.

PRIME RATE: 10%. The base rate on corporate loans at large U.S. money center commercial banks.

FEDERAL FUNDS: 8¼% high, 8½% low, 8¼% near closing bid, 8 3/16% offered. Reserves traded among commercial banks for overnight use in amounts of $1 million or more. Source: Fulton Prebon (U.S.A.) Inc.

DISCOUNT RATE: 7%. The charge on loans to depository institutions by the New York Federal Reserve Bank.

CALL MONEY: 9¼%. The charge on loans to brokers on stock exchange collateral.

COMMERCIAL PAPER placed directly by General Motors Acceptance Corp.: 8.10% 30 to 44 days; 8.075% 45 to 59 days; 8% 60 to 89 days; 7.90% 90 to 119 days; 7.85% 120 to 149 days; 7.80% 150 to 179 days; 7.50% 180 to 270 days.

COMMERCIAL PAPER: High-grade unsecured notes sold through dealers by major corporations in multiples of $1,000: 8.20% 30 days; 8.15% 60 days; 8.10% 90 days.

CERTIFICATES OF DEPOSIT: 7.70% one month; 7.69% two months; 7.69% three months; 7.68% six months; 7.76% one year. Average of top rates paid by major New York banks on primary new issues of negotiable C.D.s, usually on amounts of $1 million and more. The minimum unit is $100,-000. Typical rates in the secondary market: 8.15% one month; 8.15% three months; 8.20% six months.

BANKERS ACCEPTANCES: 8.05% 30 days; 8% 60 days; 7.95% 90 days; 7.91% 120 days; 7.88% 150 days; 7.85% 180 days. Negotiable, bank-backed business credit instruments typically financing an import order.

LONDON LATE EURODOLLARS: 8 5/16% to 8 3/16% one month; 8 5/16% to 8 3/16% two months; 8⅜% to 8¼% three months; 8⅜% to 8¼% four months; 8 7/16% to 8 5/16% five months; 8 7/16% to 8 5/16% six months.

LONDON INTERBANK OFFERED RATES (LIBOR): 8 5/16% one month; 8⅜% three months; 8 7/16% six months; 8 9/16% one year. The average of interbank offered rates for dollar deposits in the London market based on quotations at five major banks.

FOREIGN PRIME RATES: Canada 13.50%; Germany 10.50%; Japan 4.875%; Switzerland 11%; Britain 15%. These rate indications aren't directly comparable; lending practices vary widely by location.

TREASURY BILLS: Results of the Monday, January 22, 1990, auction of short-term U.S. government bills, sold at a discount from face value in units of $10,000 to $1 million: 7.66%, 13 weeks; 7.58%, 26 weeks.

FEDERAL HOME LOAN MORTGAGE CORP. (Freddie Mac): Posted yields on 30-year mortgage commitments for delivery within 30 days. 10.01%, standard conventional fixed-rate mortgages; 8%, 2% rate capped one-year adjustable rate mortgages. Source: Telerate Systems Inc.

FEDERAL NATIONAL MORTGAGE ASSOCIATION (Fannie Mae): Posted yields on 30 year mortgage commitments for delivery within 30 days (priced at par).9.93%, standard conventional fixed rate-mortgages; 8.75%, 6/2 rate capped one-year adjustable rate mortgages. Source: Telerate Systems Inc.

MERRILL LYNCH READY ASSETS TRUST: 7.67%. Annualized average rate of return after expenses for the past 30 days; not a forecast of future returns.

Source: The Wall Street Journal, January 23, 1990.

Another way of looking at T-bill futures prices is that, if a futures contract expiring at time T is purchased for the above price of $981,825.29, a trader will receive a (discount) yield of 7.19 percent on the 13-week cash T-bill that he takes possession of at time T.

Thus, quoted T-bill futures prices indicate the market's consensus estimate of what spot 13-week T-bill yields *will be* in the future, at the expiration of the futures contract. For example, Table 12.4 shows that, at the close of trading on January 22, 1990, the March 90 T-bill futures price was 92.65. This implies an expected discount yield of 7.35 percent for a 13-week T-bill purchased on March 8, 1990 (the delivery day). On January 22, 1990, the *spot* 13-week T-bill rate was 7.66 percent (see Table 12.5). Thus, the March futures price on January 22, 1990, implies that 13-week T-bill yields will be lower in the future than they are on January 20.

Figure 12-2 plots a series of spot 13-week T-bill rates and the expected 13-week rates implied from the prices of near-month T-bill futures contracts on the same day, for the period January 2, 1986, to September 30, 1989. In general, when futures yields are above spot rates, spot rates are rising; when futures yields are below spot rates, spot rates are declining. The yields on futures contracts, therefore, are forward rates and are predictors of future spot interest rates.

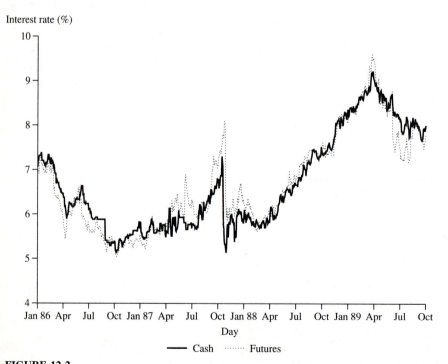

FIGURE 12-2

3-month T-bill rates: Cash versus near-month futures (daily: January 2, 1986, to September 30, 1989).

12.4.3   Delivery Requirements

Depending on the issuing cycle for T-bills and the calendar, a 90-, 91-, or 92-day T-bill may be delivered in fulfillment of a T-bill futures contract. The Treasury issues by auction 13- and 26-week bills each Monday, while 52-week bills are auctioned every month. To insure an adequate supply of deliverable bills, the IMM schedules T-bill futures delivery dates for the three successive business days beginning with the first day of the contract month on which a 13-week bill is issued *and* a one-year bill has a 13-week maturity. Although delivery is always made in the months of March, June, September, and December, the first delivery day in those months will not always be on the same day of the month. For example, the first delivery day for the March 87 contract was March 12, 1987, while the first delivery day for the March 88 contract was March 10, 1988. This schedule ties delivery on a particular futures contract to a specific T-bill maturity date. In general, T-bill futures contracts can be satisfied by delivering either a newly issued 13-week bill or an original-issue 52-week bill with 13 weeks left to maturity. This may mean delivery of a 90-, 91-, or 92-day bill.

12.4.4   Determination of the Delivery Price

If a trader chooses to hold a contract until delivery, the contract is marked-to-market at the close of the last trading day. All longs with open positions at that time must then be prepared to buy the deliverable bill at a purchase price determined by the closing futures price. To calculate the purchase price of the bill the same procedure is used as that described in Section 12.4.2.

If, for example, the final futures price were 92.81 (for an implied yield of 7.19%), the invoice price for a 91-day bill would be

$$\$1,000,000 - \$1,000,000 \times (0.0719) \times \tfrac{91}{360} = \$981,825.28$$

If, alternatively, a 92-day bill were delivered, the invoice price would be $981,625.56.

12.4.5   The Pricing of T-Bill Futures

The concept of a cost-of-carry pricing relationship was discussed in Chapter 4. The cost of financing and storing a commodity or security until delivery is called the cost-of-carry. The convention in financial markets is to apply the term *net carrying cost* to the difference between any interest earned on a security and the cost of borrowing to finance its purchase. In general, the theoretical (cost-of-carry) price of a short-term interest rate futures contract is

$$FP_{t,T} = CP_{t,T} + CP_{t,T} \times (R_{t,T} - D_{t,T}) \times \frac{T - t}{360}$$

where $FP_{t,T}$ is the T-bill futures price at time t of a contract with settlement date T, $CP_{t,T}$ is the price of the cash bill at time t that is deliverable against the futures contract at time T, $R_{t,T}$ is the annualized financing cost for period $T - t$, and

$D_{t,T}$ is the annualized yield on the cash T-bill over period $T - t$. Since T-bills are discount instruments, they do not pay explicit interest (i.e., $D_{t,T} = 0$). (Securities such as T-bonds do pay such interest.) Thus, the cost-of-carry for T-bills is simply the interest expense associated with funding the purchase of the T-bills over the period during which they are held.

To understand the relevance of carrying costs in determining the theoretical price of T-bill futures contracts, consider the March 90 futures contract. The March contract expires on March 8, 1990, and the deliverable cash T-bill on this contract is the 91-day, June 7, 1990, bill. On January 22, 1990, an investor who wishes to possess the June 7 bill has two options. The first is simply to purchase immediately the June 7 cash bill, which has a remaining maturity of 136 days. The second option is to buy the March 90 T-bill futures contract, which expires in 45 days, with delivery on March 8, 1990. At that time, the investor will take possession of the June 7, 91-day T-bill. By using the second option the investor avoids the cost of carrying the June 7 bill for 45 days (from January 23 to March 8). If the market is efficient, however, the March T-bill futures price will reflect this 45-day carrying cost advantage.

Table 12.2 shows that the bid-asked discount yields on the June 7 bill are 7.54 percent and 7.50 percent. The average of these yields is 7.52 percent. Thus, we will state the cash price on January 22, 1990, of the June 7 bill as

$$100 - \left(100 \times 0.0752 \times \tfrac{136}{360}\right) = 97.16$$

Substituting this cash price into the above equation for FP yields the following price for the March 90 futures contract:

$$FP = 97.16 + \left(97.16 \times 0.082 \times \tfrac{45}{360}\right) = 98.16$$

where 8.2 percent is the 45-day term repo rate on January 22, 1990.[3] At the close of trading on January 22, the March 90 futures was quoted at 92.65 (see Table 12.4). Thus, the March 90 futures price was

$$100 - \left(100 \times 0.0735 \times \tfrac{91}{360}\right) = 98.14$$

The actual March 90 T-bill futures price, therefore, is very close to its theoretical (cost-of-carry) price. Indeed, if the actual futures price were to exceed the theoretical price, arbitragers could earn a riskless profit by simultaneously buying the 136-day June 7 bill and selling the March 1990 T-bill futures, and then delivering the bill when the futures contract expired. If the actual price were lower than the theoretical price, reverse cash-and-carry arbitrage would occur.

---

[3]This "term" repo rate was provided by Kidder, Peabody, Inc. The federal funds rate (inter-bank rate) was trading at $8\tfrac{1}{8} - 8\tfrac{2}{8}$ percent on January 22, 1990 (see Table 12.5). A repurchase agreement (more commonly called a repo or RP) is a transaction involving the sale of a security, usually a Treasury security, with a commitment on the part of the seller to repurchase the security after a stated length of time. Repurchase agreements can be viewed as short-term loans collaterized by securities. The interest rate paid by borrowers in the RP market is called the *repo* rate. Because repurchase agreements are a primary funding source for dealers in government securities, the Treasury bill repo rate is typically used to calculate net carrying costs for Treasury bill futures.

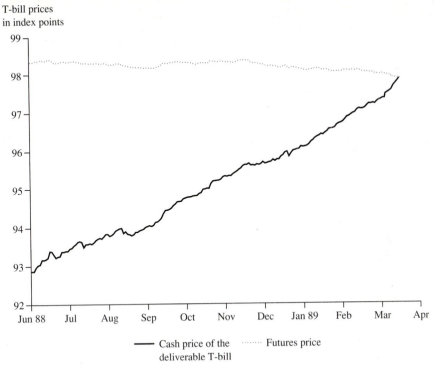

FIGURE 12-3
T-bill prices: Cash versus futures (March 89 contract: June 1, 1988, to March 8, 1989).

Finally, carrying costs fall as the futures settlement date approaches because the time period that a cash position must be held becomes shorter. This causes futures prices to converge to the underlying spot T-bill prices as the delivery date draws near. Figure 12-3 shows the convergence between the prices of the March 89 T-bill futures contract and the deliverable cash T-bill which matures on June 8, 1989. The more deferred is the delivery date of a futures contract, the higher is the carrying cost, and the more the *futures price* exceeds the *cash T-bill price* (alternatively, the lower the *futures yield* is relative to the *cash yield*).

12.4.6   The Implied Repo Rate

The implied repo rate is a measure of the carrying costs that are implicit in the futures-spot price relationship. It is defined as the difference between the actual price of the futures contract and the price of the cash bill, converted to an annualized rate of return, or

$$IRR = \frac{FP_{t,T} - CP_{t,T}}{CP_{t,T}} \times \frac{360}{T - t}$$

where $FP_{t,T}$ and $CP_{t,T}$ are the actual futures and cash prices.

TABLE 12.6
Cash and carry and reverse cash and carry arbitrage examples

As calculated in Section 12.4.6, on January 22, 1990, the implied repo rate on the March 90 T-bill futures contract is 8.07%. Assume, however, that on January 22 the actual 45-day term repo rate is 7.8%.* Since the implied repo rate is above the actual borrowing rate, the March 90 futures contract is overpriced. Thus, it will be profitable for an arbitrager to borrow funds to finance the purchase of a cash T-bill and simultaneously sell the March T-bill futures, locking in a profit of $327 per futures contract:

	Cash flows
On January 22, 1990:	
Purchase $1 million June 7 bill for $971,600	$(971,600)
Borrowing cost @ 7.8%	
Short March futures at 98.14 ($981.400)	0
On March 8, 1990:	
Deliver the June 7 T-bill against the short	
March futures position and receive $981,400	981,400
Less borrowing cost for 45 days:	
$971,600 \times 0.078 \times \frac{45}{360}$	(9,473)
Net arbitrage profit per contract	$ 327

Alternatively, assume that the actual term repo rate is 8.40%, which is substantially higher than the implied repo rate of 8.07%. In this case, the arbitrager will do a *reverse* cash-and-carry arbitrage, buying T-bill futures and shorting the corresponding cash T-bill. When the long T-bill futures expire, the arbitrager will take delivery of the T-bills and use them to eliminate his short cash position. Thus, he will lock in a profit of $402 per futures contract:

	Cash flows
On January 22, 1990:	
Short the June 7 T-bill for $971,600	$971,600
Invest the proceeds at 8.4%	
Go long the March futures at 98.14 ($981,400)	0
On March 8, 1990:	
Interest on investment:[†]	
$971,600 \times 0.084 \times \frac{45}{360}$	10,202
Take delivery of the March futures	
to offset short cash position	(981,400)
Net arbitrage profit per contract	$ 402

---

*The rate differential between the implied repo and the actual term repo is large enough to ensure an arbitrage profit even after transaction costs.

† We assume that the arbitrager is able to invest the entire proceeds of the short sale. This may not always be true.

The implied repo rate reveals the annualized gross rate of return that can be earned by buying a cash T-bill and simultaneously selling a T-bill futures contract with a delivery date $T - t$ days away. Alternatively, it reveals the annualized borrowing rate at which the net return to a cash-and-carry arbitrage transaction will be zero—the no-arbitrage borrowing rate.

Comparing implied repo rates with actual borrowing rates is identical to comparing theoretical and actual futures prices. An implied repo rate above the actual borrowing (repo) rate indicates that futures contracts are overpriced: actual futures prices are higher than theoretical futures prices (the implied borrowing rate is greater than actual borrowing rate). When this is true, it will be profitable for an arbitrager to borrow funds to finance the purchase of a cash T-bill and simultaneously to sell futures.

The implied repo rate on January 22, 1990, for the March 90 contract discussed earlier was

$$IRR = \frac{98.14 - 97.16}{97.16} \times \frac{360}{45} = 8.07\%$$

This rate is lower than the actual 45-day term repo rate of 8.20 percent on January 22, which suggests an arbitrage of buying the futures and shorting a cash

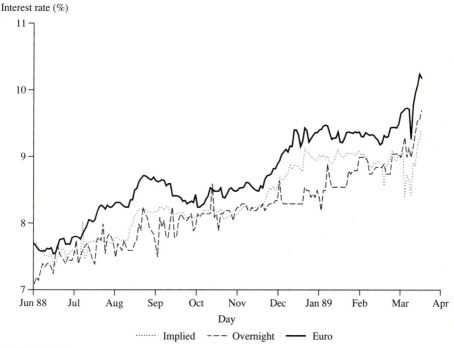

FIGURE 12-4

Implied repo rates versus overnight repo rates and 3-month Eurodollar rates (daily: March 89 futures, from June 88 to March 89).

T-bill. However, there may be transaction costs associated with such arbitrage that eliminate profitable arbitrage. Table 12.6 provides cash-and-carry and reverse cash-and-carry arbitrage examples.

Figure 12-4 plots the daily implied repo rates on the March 90 futures contract for the period from June 1, 1988, to March 13, 1989, as well as alternative borrowing rates, such as the overnight repo rate and the three-month Eurodollar rate. The implied repo rate is highly correlated with these short-term interest rates, as would be expected in an efficient market.

12.5 EURODOLLAR FUTURES

A Eurodollar futures contract calls for the delivery of a $1 million, three-month, Eurodollar time deposit (see Table 12.3). These are non-negotiable, fixed-rate, dollar-denominated time deposits at banks located outside of the United States, primarily in London and European financing centers. Such time deposits are issued by both U.S. and foreign banks. Eurodollar futures contracts call for delivery in March, June, September, and December of each year.

Futures on three-month Eurodollar time deposits were introduced in December 1981, by the IMM in Chicago, and are now the most actively traded short-term interest rate futures contract. Figures 12-5 and 12-6 show the growth of Eurodollar futures trading and the concomitant decline in T-bill futures trading.

Several factors contributed to the explosive growth of Eurodollar futures. First, most major international banks rely heavily on the Eurodollar market for

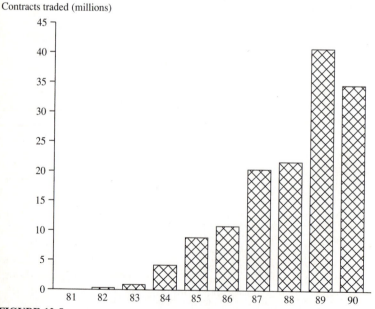

Contracts traded (millions)

FIGURE 12-5
U.S. Eurodollar futures (annual trading volume: 1981–1990).

Contracts traded (millions)

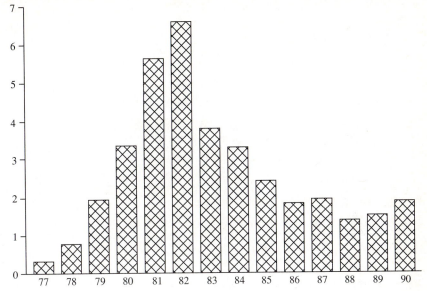

FIGURE 12-6
U.S. Treasury bill futures (annual trading volume: 1977–1990).

short-term funds. To maintain ready access to this market, these banks have become active issuers and purchasers of Eurodollar deposits. Eurodollar futures provide a way that banks can hedge the interest rate risk associated with Eurodollar deposits.

Second, major international corporations have come to rely increasingly on Eurodollar markets for funds. Borrowing rates for these corporations are typically based on the three- or six-month London Interbank Offer Rate (LIBOR), and are often quoted in terms of a certain number of basis points above floating LIBOR. Eurodollar futures, therefore, can be used to hedge (or to lock in) the borrowing costs of these corporations.

Third, Eurodollar futures contracts are traded in Singapore and London as well as in Chicago, and therefore can be traded on a global, 24 hour, basis. Lastly, the cash-delivery mechanism utilized by Eurodollar futures is simpler than the T-bill futures delivery procedures, and has made using Eurodollar futures more attractive.

12.5.1 Eurodollar Time Deposits

Unlike Treasury bills, Eurodollar time deposits pay *add-on* interest. An add-on yield is stated as a percentage of the face amount of the deposit. The rate paid on Eurodollar time deposits is called the London Interbank Offered Rate (LIBOR), and is the interest rate at which major international banks offer to place Eurodollar deposits with one another. Like other money market rates, LIBOR is quoted on an annualized basis and on a 360-day year. Thus, the interest income on a three-month Eurodollar time deposit is simply

Interest return at maturity = Principal × Quoted rate × (90 days / 360 days)

For example, if the principal invested is $1 million and the yield is 10 percent, the three-month return will be $25,000.

12.5.2 Futures Quotations and Futures Prices

Table 12.7 shows price quotations for Eurodollar futures, at the close of trading on January 22, 1990. These prices, similar to T-bill futures prices, are quoted on an index basis: 100 minus the LIBOR on the relevant Eurodollar futures contract. In Table 12-6, the closing price of the March 90 contract is 91.72, and the quoted futures rate is 8.28 percent (100 − 91.72) A change of one basis point in the Eurodollar futures index price is worth $25. Thus, if the price index falls 5 basis points, the value of a futures contract declines by $125.

The yield on a Eurodollar futures contract, like the yield on a T-bill futures contract, reflects the market's assessment about spot interest rate levels in the future. The Eurodollar futures yield represents a prediction about what the three-month spot Eurodollar deposit rate will be in the future. For example, the March 90 Eurodollar futures rate of 8.28 percent indicates that the market expects that in March of 1990 a new three-month Eurodollar deposit will pay 8.28 percent.

Figure 12-7 graphs daily yields on near month Eurodollar futures contracts together with spot three-month Eurodollar deposit rates on the same day, for the period January 1986 through September 1989. When futures rates are above (below) spot rates, the market expects that three-month spot Eurodollar rates will

TABLE 12.7
Prices of Eurodollar futures on January 22, 1990

EURODOLLAR (IMM) − $1 million; pts of 100%

	Open	High	Low	Settle	Chg	Yield Settle	Chg	Open Interest
Mar	91.72	91.74	91.68	91.72	+ .03	8.28	− .03	242,811
June	91.67	91.70	91.64	91.67	+ .03	8.33	− .03	121,659
Sept	91.61	91.64	91.58	91.60	+ .03	8.40	− .03	66,935
Dec	91.40	91.40	91.36	91.37	+ .01	8.63	− .01	44,511
Mr91	91.32	91.33	91.28	91.31	+ .01	8.69	− .01	37,740
June	91.25	91.26	91.22	91.24	....	8.76	....	34,835
Sept	91.23	91.24	91.19	91.21	....	8.79	....	27,624
Dec	91.18	91.18	91.13	91.15	....	8.85	....	19,581
Mr92	91.23	91.23	91.18	91.20	....	8.80	....	17,473
June	91.19	91.19	91.14	91.16	....	8.84	....	11,825
Sept	91.13	91.15	91.09	91.11	....	8.89	....	7,349
Dec	91.03	91.05	90.99	91.01	....	8.99	....	3,713
Mr93	91.05	91.06	91.02	91.02	....	8.98	....	4,676
June	91.00	91.00	90.98	90.98	....	9.02	....	2,885
Sept	90.93	90.95	90.93	90.93	....	9.07	....	2,117
Dec	90.89	90.89	90.87	90.88	+ .01	9.12	− .01	606

Est vol 99,002; vol Fri 143,517; open int 646,340, −6,651.

Source: The Wall Street Journal, January 23, 1990.

Interest rate (%)

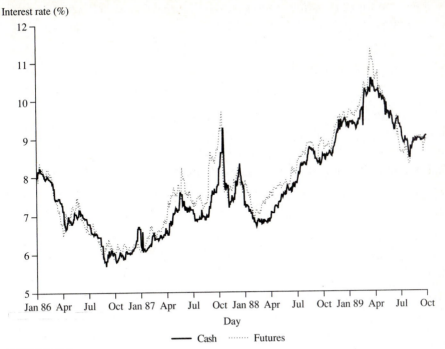

FIGURE 12-7
3-month Eurodollar rates: Cash versus near-month futures (daily: January 2, 1986, to September 30, 1989).

be higher (lower) in the future. In fact, Figure 12-7 shows that when futures rates are above spot rates, spot rates are generally rising, and vice versa.

12.5.3   Delivery and the Determination of Final Settlement Prices

In contrast to T-bill futures, Eurodollar futures employ a cash settlement delivery procedure. The IMM Eurodollar contract was the first futures contract introduced in the United States to utilize cash settlement. Instead of requiring physical delivery, Eurodollar futures are marked to the *cash* price at the close of trading in the contract. Any payments due between longs and shorts at that time are made through the clearinghouse as standard variation margin payments.

To determine the final settlement price for the Eurodollar futures contract, the IMM clearinghouse first determines the spot LIBOR by randomly polling 12 banks actively participating in the London Eurodollar market. It does this at two different times during the last day of trading: once at a randomly selected time during the last 90 minutes of trading, and once at the close of trading. The two highest and two lowest quotes it obtains are deleted from the sample before calculating the average LIBOR rate for that sample. The final settlement price is 100 minus the average of the two sample averages.

When a futures contract requires physical delivery, market forces (i.e., arbitrage) cause the futures price to converge to the spot price of the commodity as the delivery date approaches. Similarly, in the case of a cash-settled contract, marking to the cash price forces the futures price to converge to the cash price at the close of trading on the last day of trading. Figure 12-8 plots the daily yields on the March 89 futures contract together with the daily spot three-month Eurodollar rates for the period from January 1, 1988, to March 19, 1989. It is clear that futures yields converge to spot yields as the delivery date approaches, just as they do when physical delivery is required.

12.5.4 The Pricing of Eurodollar Futures

The concepts discussed earlier in Section 12.3 can be used to price Eurodollar futures. In particular, the futures price should reflect the forward interest rate that is implied by the existing term structure of interest rates.

Suppose that on January 22, 1990, an investor wishes to put his money into Eurodollar deposits until June 17, 1990 (an investment period of 146 days). He has two options. The first is simply to obtain a 146-day Eurodollar time deposit (approximately 5 months). The second is to obtain a 56-day Eurodollar time deposit (approximately 2 months) and simultaneously buy a March 90 Eurodollar futures contract. The March 90 futures expires on March 19, 1990, in 56 days.

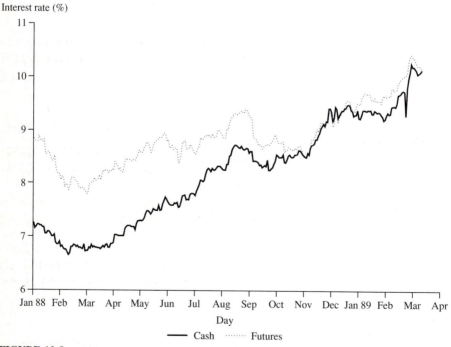

FIGURE 12-8
3-month Eurodollar rates versus March 89 futures rates (daily: January 1988 to March 1989).

In both cases the investor will lock-in a Eurodollar rate for the next 146 days (until June 17, 1990). In an efficiently priced market, the two investment options will yield the same return. If this were not true, there would exist a profitable arbitrage opportunity between the two options. Two securities that are perfect substitutes for one another must have identical yields.

Table 12.5 shows that on January 22, 1990, the two-month London "late" Eurodollar rate was $8\frac{5}{6}$ to $8\frac{3}{16}$ percent, while the five-month rate was $8\frac{7}{16}$ to $8\frac{5}{16}$ percent.[4] The theoretical price for the March 90 Eurodollar futures contract on January 22, 1990, can be calculated as follows:

$$\left(1 + R_1 \times \frac{t_1}{360}\right) = \left(1 + R_2 \times \frac{t_2}{360}\right) \times \left(1 + R_3 \times \frac{t_3}{360}\right)$$

where
t_1 = 146-day investment period, January 23 to June 17, 1990
R_1 = Annualized Eurodollar deposit rate for t_1, 8.3125%
t_2 = 56-day investment period, January 23 to March 19, 1990
R_2 = Annualized Eurodollar deposit rate for t_2, 8.1875%
t_3 = 90-day investment period, March 20 to June 17, 1990
R_3 = Annualized Eurodollar rate on the March 90 futures

Making the substitutions yields

$$\left(1 + 0.083125 \times \frac{146}{360}\right) = \left(1 + 0.081875 \times \frac{56}{360}\right) \times \left(1 + R_3 \times \frac{90}{360}\right)$$

$$R_3 = 0.08285, \text{ or } 8.29\%$$

Thus, the theoretical futures price is 91.71 (100 − 8.29). Table 12.7 shows that on January 22 the March 90 Eurodollar futures settled at 91.72, with a yield of 8.28 percent. This price is almost exactly equal to the theoretical futures price calculated above, which is an indication of the pricing efficiency that prevails in the Eurodollar futures market. The futures yield (R_3), therefore, is equal to the implied forward yield.

If the actual futures price were less than 91.71 (or the futures rate were above 8.29%), arbitragers would borrow for 146 days and invest the proceeds in a 56-day Eurodollar deposit and simultaneously purchase a March 90 Eurodollar futures contract. Alternatively, if the futures were overpriced (or the futures rate were below 8.29%), arbitragers would do the opposite: borrow for 146 days, invest the proceeds in a 146-day Eurodollar deposit, and simultaneously short a Eurodollar futures contract. Thus, to determine if a profitable arbitrage opportunity exists, the implied forward yield can be calculated from the term structure of interest rates and compared to the quoted futures yield. If they are not equal, an arbitrage opportunity may exist.

---

[4]The lower rates of $8\frac{3}{16}$% and $8\frac{5}{16}$% for two months and five months respectively are used in our calculations.

12.6 THE TED SPREAD

Ted Spread = T.Bill FP − Euro Dollar FP
Should always be positive because TB risk < ED risk

The *Ted spread* is the difference between the price of a three-month U.S. Treasury bill futures contract (ticket symbol is TB) and the price of a three-month Eurodollar time deposit futures contract (ticket symbol ED), both with the same expiration month. The spread is quoted as the T-bill futures price minus the Eurodollar futures price. (Alternatively, the Ted spread is the expected yield on a future three-month Eurodollar deposit minus the expected yield on a future three-month T-bill.) Figure 12-9 depicts this spread using the daily settlement prices of near-month T-bill and Eurodollar futures for the period January 1986 through September 1989.

The Ted spread varies significantly over time. Investors view T-bills as less risky than Eurodollars, since T-bills are direct obligations of the U.S. Treasury. While Eurodollar deposits are obligations of major commercial banks, they are not guaranteed by any government (they are not, for example, insured). Though low-risk investments, Eurodollar deposits are not risk-free. A bank may default on its obligations. Thus, T-bills carry a lower rate than Eurodollar deposits. Consequently, the price of a T-bill futures contract is always higher than the price of a Eurodollar futures contract, and the Ted spread is always a positive number.

For example, on January 22, 1990, the March 90 T-bill futures settled at 92.65, for a discount yield of 7.35 percent (see Table 12.4); and the March 90 Eurodollar futures settled at 91.72, for an add-on yield of 8.28 percent (see Table 12.7). The Ted spread, therefore, was 0.93 (92.65 − 91.72), or 93 basis points

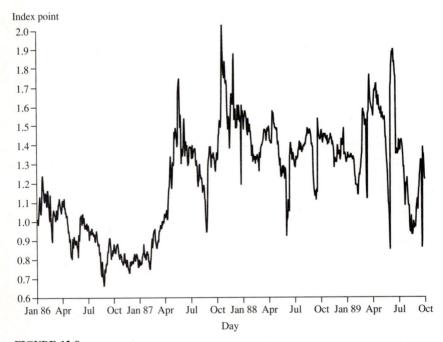

FIGURE 12-9
The Ted Spread: T-bill–Eurodollar (near month futures prices, from January 2, 1986, to September 30, 1989).

(or 93 ticks, each worth $25.00), and was quoted as "93." Figure 12-10 graphs in index points the Ted spread for the March 89 T-bill and Eurodollar futures contracts, for the period May 1, 1987, through March 8, 1989.

The Ted spread is thought of as a *quality* spread. The primary factor causing changes in the magnitude of the spread is a change in perception about the safety of holding a Eurodollar deposit versus a T-bill. If conditions increase the likelihood of bank insolvency, for example, there will be a flight to quality: to T-bills. This will cause the Ted spread to widen, as banks are forced to pay higher Eurodollar rates relative to T-bill yields. Trading the Ted spread, therefore, is a way to speculate on general economic conditions and on the soundness of banks in particular without incurring interest rate risk. In Figure 12-10, the largest spread occurred on October 19, 1987, the day of the 1987 Stock Market Crash, when investors feared that widespread defaults among securities and futures traders might jeopardize the solvency of banks.

12.7 APPLICATIONS USING SHORT-TERM INTEREST RATE FUTURES CONTRACTS

Short-term interest rate futures can be used to hedge interest rate risk and to lock in future investment yields or future borrowing costs. In addition, they can be used to restructure a fixed-income portfolio when economic conditions change.

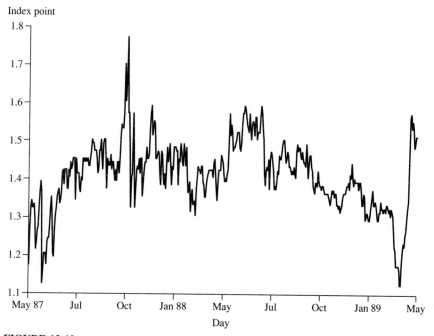

FIGURE 12-10
The Ted Spread: T-bill–Eurodollar (March 89 futures prices, from May 1, 1987, to March 8, 1989).

This section provides examples of using short-term interest rate futures to achieve these objectives.

12.7.1 Short Hedge: Locking in a Borrowing Rate

A short position in interest rate futures can be used to lock in a future borrowing rate. Suppose that on January 22, 1990, a firm knows that it will have to borrow $10 million on March 19, 1990, for three months. A bank agrees to provide these funds at 1 percent above whatever the three-month LIBOR is on March 19, 1990. By coincidence, March 19 is also the last trading day of the March 90 Eurodollar futures contract.

The firm is concerned that in the interim the LIBOR may rise. To protect itself against rising borrowing costs, the firm decides to go short ten March 90 Eurodollar futures as a hedge against an increase in interest rates between January 22 and March 19. Each futures contract is for $1 million, so 10 contracts will balance the $10 million loan. As indicated in Table 12.7, on January 22 the March 90 Eurodollar futures price is 91.72, and the implied three-month Eurodollar rate is 8.28 percent. The three-month LIBOR on January 22, 1990, is 8.375 percent (Table 12.5).

If LIBOR does not change between January 22 and March 19, the firm's borrowing cost for its three-month loan will be

$$\$10,000,000 \times (8.375\% + 1\%) \times \tfrac{3}{12} = \$234,375$$

If LIBOR were to go up, its borrowing cost would increase.

While the firm cannot lock in the January 22 borrowing rate, it can lock in the three-month Eurodollar futures rate of 8.28 percent on January 22, a rate very close to the cash Eurodollar rate on January 22. If it does this, its guaranteed borrowing cost will be

$$\$10,000,000 \times (8.28\% + 1\%) \times \tfrac{3}{12} = \$232,000$$

The following demonstrates how this borrowing cost can be locked in by selling ten March 90 Eurodollar futures contracts on January 22.[5]

Case 1: Three-month LIBOR rises to 9.00% by March 19 (March futures are 91.00).

Interest expense	= (principal) × (annual rate) × $\tfrac{3}{12}$	
	= $10,000,000 × (9%+1%) × $\tfrac{3}{12}$	$250,000
Less: Futures gain	= (price change) × ($25/*bp*) ×10	
	= (91.72 − 91.00) × 100 × 25 × 10	− 18,000
Net borrowing cost		$232,000

---

[5]The final futures price in these examples, as well as those on the following pages, can be determined because at expiration of the futures contract the cash and futures prices are equal.

Case 2: Three-month LIBOR falls to 7.50% by March 19 (March futures are 92.50).

Interest expense	= (principal) × (annual rate) × $\frac{3}{12}$	
	= \$10,000,000 × (7.5% + 1%) × $\frac{3}{12}$	\$212,500
Add: Futures loss	= (price change) × (\$25/bp) ×10	
	= (91.72 − 92.50) × 100 × 25 × 10	+19,500
Net borrowing cost		\$232,000

where bp = a basis point, or 0.01 of a percentage point.

In the first case, a rise in the three-month LIBOR is offset by a gain on the short futures position. In the second case, a fall in the three-month LIBOR, which would lower borrowing costs, is balanced by a loss on the short hedge. In both cases, the firm succeeds in locking in a borrowing cost of \$232,000, or an annual borrowing rate of

$$\frac{\$232,000}{\$10,000,000} \times \frac{12}{3} \times 100\% = 9.28\%$$

which is 1 percent above the three-month implied LIBOR of 8.28 percent on the March 90 Eurodollar futures contract on January 22. Thus, a short hedge using Eurodollar futures allowed the firm to lock in a borrowing rate equal to the implicit forward rate (or the futures rate on the contract).

12.7.2 Long Hedge: Locking in an Investment Yield

A long hedge position in interest rate futures can be used to lock in an investment yield. Suppose that an investor will soon have a large sum of cash to invest for a short period of time. He or she can wait until the funds arrive and invest them at the rate which prevails at that time. Alternatively, the investor can buy T-bill or Eurodollar futures now, locking in a yield.

Assume that on January 22 a corporate treasurer expects to receive \$10 million from an overseas subsidiary in March 1990. He intends to invest the money in three-month T-bills. On January 22, 1990, the three-month T-bill discount yield is 7.66 percent (Table 12.5), and the current implied discount yield on the March 90 T-bill futures is 7.35 percent (Table 12.4). The treasurer infers from the futures yield that the market expects that interest rates will decline in the future. Thus, he decides to go long ten March 90 T-bill futures contracts on January 22 at a price of 92.65, locking in a discount yield of 7.35 percent on the \$10 million he expects to invest in March. On March 7, the last trading day of the March 90 T-bill futures, the treasurer will close out the long futures position and purchase three-month T-bills in the cash market.

The following illustrates how this investment yield can be locked in by initiating a long hedge on January 22, regardless of market conditions on March 7.

Case 1: On March 7, the three-month cash T-bill has a discount yield of 6.70%
(March futures are 93.30)

Price of cash T-bill	$10,000,000 \times [1-6.7\% \times \frac{3}{12}] =$	$9,832,500
Less: Futures gain	$(93.30-92.65) \times 100 \times 25 \times 10 =$	$-16,250$
Effective purchase price		$9,816,250

Annualized discount yield: $\dfrac{\$10,000,000 - \$9,816,250}{\$10,000,000} \times \dfrac{12}{3} \times 100\% = \underline{\underline{7.35\%}}$

Case 2: On March 7, the three-month cash T-bill has a discount yield of 8.00%
(March futures are 92.00)

Price of cash T-bill	$10,000,000 \times [1-8.0\% \times \frac{3}{12}] =$	$9,800,000
Add: Futures loss	$(92.00-92.65) \times 100 \times 25 \times 10 =$	$+16,250$
Effective purchase price		$9,816,250

Annualized discount yield: $\dfrac{\$10,000,000 - \$9,816,250}{\$10,000,000} \times \dfrac{12}{3} \times 100\% = \underline{\underline{7.35\%}}$

In the first case the treasurer purchased futures contracts at a discount rate of 7.35 percent and sold them at 6.70 percent. Since the dollar value of the T-bill futures contract is higher the lower the yield, there is a gain of $16,250 on the long futures position. In the second case there is a loss on the futures position because the three-month discount yield rose to 8.0 percent. In both cases, however, the hedge enabled the treasurer to lock in a discount yield of 7.35 percent on his investment.

12.7.3   Synthetic Interest Rate Securities

A long or short position in interest rate futures can also be used to create *synthetic* securities that have the same cash flows as an alternative cash investment. For example, suppose that a corporate cash manager is instructed to invest $10 million in T-bills for six months, at which time the firm anticipates needing the funds. The manager can fix the rate of return to be earned over this period either by buying six-month T-bills or by simultaneously buying three-month cash T-bills together with three-month T-bill futures. The latter strategy creates a synthetic six-month Treasury bill. A synthetic T-bill can sometimes produce a higher or lower yield than an equivalent cash T-bill, depending on relative yields.

Alternatively, the money manager could create a synthetic six-month T-bill by buying nine-month cash Treasury bills and simultaneously selling three-month T-bill futures. Selling futures contracts shortens the effective maturity of the nine-month T-bill portfolio to six months.

In general, by combining short or long interest rate futures positions with positions in the underlying cash asset it is possible to create a variety of synthetic securities. The following equation is a general statement of the principle underlying the two examples above:

$$\text{Spot} + \text{Futures} = \text{Synthetic security}$$

where a short position is indicated by a minus sign.

Thus, in the first example, a three-month cash T-bill is combined with a *long* three-month T-bill futures position to create a six-month synthetic security. In the second example a nine-month cash bill is combined with a *short* three-month T-bill futures position to create a six-month synthetic security. The cash flows of the synthetic security are the sum of cash flows on the spot and futures positions used to create the security.

12.7.4   Strip versus Stack Hedging Strategies

If an investor or borrower wishes to hedge or to lock in a yield for a long period of time by using interest rate futures, it may be necessary to do a *strip* or a *stack* hedge. A strip hedge utilizes futures positions in a number of different futures contracts, each with a different delivery date that coincides with the hedger's risk exposures. A stack hedge utilizes only futures positions that are concentrated in *nearby* delivery months. While the latter hedging strategy has superior liquidity attributes, it usually entails greater basis risk than a strip hedge. Hedgers must decide whether the greater liquidity is worth the additional basis risk. The following are examples of a strip and stack hedge.

A STRIP HEDGE.   Suppose that on November 1, 1988, a firm estimates that it needs to borrow $10 million for a period of 12 months, beginning December 19, 1988. A bank agrees to provide a variable-rate loan at the quarterly LIBOR plus 100 basis points. Thus, the firm is at risk that interest rates will rise.

The firm can hedge this risk by taking a short interest rate futures position. Futures prices will fall if interest rates rise (100–implied interest rate). Specifically, the firm might hedge for the entire 12-month period by taking a short position on November 1 in each of the following Eurodollar contracts: December 88, March 89, June 89 and September 89 contracts. Each futures contract locks in an interest rate for the three months following its expiration. Thus, the hedge locks in a rate until December, 1990. (The readjustment dates of the loan agreement are assumed to coincide with the expiration dates of the respective Eurodollar futures contracts.)

Table 12.8 provides an example of such a strip hedge, showing the borrowing costs that the firm would have incurred with and without the hedge. It assumes that on November 1, 1988, the firm goes short ten December 88 contracts at a price of 91.41, with a yield of 8.59 percent; ten March 89 contracts at 91.61, with a yield of 8.39 percent; ten June 89 contracts at 91.53, with a yield of 8.47 percent; and ten September 89 contracts at 91.39, with a yield of 8.61 percent. At

TABLE 12.8
Strip hedge example using Eurodollar futures

		Futures positions and transactions			
Date	Spot LIBOR	Dec 88	Mar 89	Jun 89	Sep 89
11/1/88	8.44%	S 10 @ 91.41	S 10 @ 91.61	S 10 @ 91.53	S 10 @ 91.39
12/19/88	9.54%	L 10 @ 90.46			
3/13/89	9.75%		L 10 @ 90.25		
6/19/89	9.44%			L 10 @ 90.56	
9/18/89	8.88%				L 10 @ 91.12
Implied Euro rate		8.59%	8.39%	8.47%	8.61%
Futures gain (loss)		$23,750	$34,000	$24,250	$6,750

S:Short; L:Long

			Hedging results		
Quarter	Firm's loan rate (1)	Quarterly interest expense (2)	Gain (loss) on futures positions (3)	Net interest expense (4) = (2) − (3)	Effective loan rate (5)
Dec 88–Mar 89	10.54%	$ 263,500	$23,750	$239,750	9.59%
Mar 89–Jun 89	10.75%	268,750	34,000	234,750	9.39%
Jun 89–Sep 89	10.44%	261,000	24,250	236,750	9.47%
Sep 89–Dec 89	9.88%	247,000	6,750	240,250	9.61%
Total		$1,040,250	$88,750	$951,500	
Mean	10.40%				9.52%

(1) 1% plus the spot LIBOR for the respective quarter.

(2) Interest expense = principal × annual rate × $\frac{3}{12}$
$$= (\$10,000,000) \times (0.1054) \times \tfrac{3}{12} = \$263,500$$

(3) Futures gain = price change × $25/basis point × 10
  (or loss) $= (91.41 - 90.46) \times 100 \times \$25 \times 10 = \$23,750$

(4) Net interest = interest expense − futures gain (or plus futures loss)
  $= \$263,500 - \$23,750$

(5) Annualized rate $= \dfrac{\text{Net interest}}{\text{Principal}} \times \dfrac{12}{3} \times 100\%$

  $= \dfrac{\$239,750}{\$10,000,000} \times \dfrac{12}{3} \times 100\% = 9.59\%$

expiration of each contract, the futures yield must equal the spot LIBOR because of cash settlement. With the hedge, Table 12.8 shows that the firm's net borrowing cost is $951,500; without the hedge, the cost is $1,040,250. Or, with the hedge the firm's average borrowing rate is 9.52 percent; without the hedge the rate is 10.40 percent. Thus, the hedge succeeded in reducing the borrowing costs significantly.

A STACK HEDGE.   In the previous example, on November 1 the firm assumed an equal number of short positions in the December 88, March 89, June 89 and September 89 Eurodollar futures contracts. However, liquidity in distant contract months is usually much less than in nearby contract months. For example, on November 1, 1988, the following trading volumes and open interest were recorded for the above four Eurodollar futures contracts:

	Trading volume	Open interest
Dec 88	46,903	172,599
Mar 89	29,236	126,082
Jun 89	4,622	49,030
Sep 89	1,670	27,906

To take advantage of the superior liquidity in the nearby contracts, the firm might want to use a stack hedge. One such hedge would be to go short ten December 88 contracts and thirty March 89 contracts, since both contracts appear to have adequate liquidity. The 10 short December contracts will hedge the firm's interest expense for the quarter ending March 89. Ten of the 30 short March contracts will hedge the firm's interest expense for the quarter ending June 89. The additional remaining twenty March contracts are intended as a hedge against subsequent interest rate movements, in the September and December quarters in 1989.

For this hedge to be successful, the firm must hope that if, prior to March 1989, there is an increase in forward interest rates applicable to the September and December quarters, the March 89 futures rates move in a similar way. If this does happen, the gain on the March futures contracts will offset the rise in the subsequent interest expenses. Further, as the June and September contracts become the nearby contracts and gain liquidity, the firm can roll its twenty March short contracts into June and September short positions to protect itself against subsequent rises in interest rates.

Table 12.9 illustrates a stack hedge. We assume that when open interest in the June 89 futures reaches 100,000 contracts (which occurs on January 12, 1989), the firm rolls 20 of its 30 short March futures into June futures, realizing a gain of $57,000. For accounting purposes, 50 percent of this hedge profit ($28,500) is allocated to the June quarter, reducing the interest expense for that quarter. The remaining 50 percent is allocated to the September quarter. Similarly, when open interest in the September contract reaches 100,000 contracts (on February 22, 1989), the firm closes out ten of its remaining twenty June contracts and establishes a short position in the September contract, realizing a gain of $16,000, which is allocated to reducing the interest expense in the September quarter. The firm's total profit from its entire short stack hedge is $94,750, and its total interest expense is $1,040,250 (see Table 12.8). Its *net* interest expense, however, is reduced to $945,500 because of the $94,750 gain on the futures positions.

TABLE 12.9
Stack hedge example using Eurodollar futures

		Futures positions and transactions			
Date	**Spot LIBOR**	**Dec 88**	**Mar 89**	**Jun 89**	**Sep 89**
11/1/88	8.44%	S 10 @ 91.41	S 30 @ 91.61		
12/19/88	9.54%	L 10 @ 90.46			
1/12/89	9.47%		L 20 @ 90.47(a)	S 20 @ 90.42	
2/22/89	9.95%			L 10 @ 89.78(c)	S 10 @ 89.82
3/13/89	9.75%		L 10 @ 90.25(b)		
6/19/89	9.44%			L 10 @ 90.56(d)	
9/18/89	8.88%				L 10 @ 91.12
Implied Euro rate		8.59%	8.39%	9.58%	10.18%
Futures gain (loss)		$23,750	$57,000(a)	$16,000(c)	$(32,500)
			$34,000(b)	$(3,500)(d)	

S:Short; L:Long

			Hedging results		
Quarter	**Firm's loan rate**	**Quarterly interest expense**	**Gain (loss) on futures positions**	**Net interest expense**	**Effective loan rate**
	(1)	(2)	(3)	(4) = (2) − (3)	(5)
Dec 88–Mar 89	10.54%	$263,500	$23,750	$239,750	9.59%
Mar 89–Jun 89	10.75%	268,750	34,000 (b)	234,750	9.39%
Jun 89–Sep 89	10.44%	261,000	28,500 (a)		
			(3,500)(d)	236,000	9.44%
Sep 89–Dec 89	9.88%	247,000	28,500 (a)		
			16,000 (c)		
			(32,500)	235,000	9.40%
Total		$1,040,250	$94,750	$945,500	
Mean	10.40%				9.46%

(1) 1% plus the spot LIBOR for the respective quarter.

(2) Interest expense = principal × annual rate × $\frac{3}{12}$

$\qquad$ = ($10,000,000) × (0.1054) × $\frac{3}{12}$ = $263,500

(3) Futures gain $\quad$ = price changes × $25/basis point × 10
$\quad$ (or loss) $\qquad$ = (91.41 − 90.46) × 100 × $25 × 10 = $23,750

(4) Net interest $\quad$ = interest expense − futures gain (or plus futures loss)
$\qquad\qquad\quad$ = $263,500 − $23,750 = $239,650

(5) Annualized rate = $\frac{\text{Net interest}}{\text{Principal}} \times \frac{12}{3} \times 100\%$

$\qquad\qquad\qquad = \frac{\$239,750}{\$10,000,000} \times \frac{12}{3} \times 100\% = 9.59\%$

Notes: (a) is rolling the 20 March contracts into a June position; (b) is closing out March position; (c) is rolling the June contract into a September position; (d) is closing out June position.

The effectiveness of a stack hedge relative to a strip hedge is determined by movements in the yield curve. A stack and a strip hedge will provide similar hedging effectiveness if the yield curve shifts over time in a parallel fashion. Otherwise they will not. In the example in Table 12.9 the yield curve did not shift in a parallel fashion. For example, on November 1, 1988, the three-month spot LIBOR is 8.44 percent, the March 89 futures contract is at 91.61, and the June 89 futures contract is at 91.53. On January 12, 1989, the spot LIBOR increases to 9.47 percent, the March futures drops 114 basis points to 90.47, and the June futures drops only 111 basis points to 90.42. Thus, each rate changes by a different amount. In the examples in Tables 12.8 and 12.9 these relative yield changes were favorable to the stack hedging strategy, resulting in even lower borrowing costs than the strip hedge achieved. Different relative yield changes, however, could have resulted in the opposite result.

CONCLUSION

After an introductory discussion of interest rate futures in general, this chapter covers short-term interest rate futures. These are futures contracts written on fixed-income securities with less than a one-year original maturity. The most popular of these is the 90-day Eurodollar time deposit futures contract.

Before discussing the specifics of these futures contracts, we examine the cash markets for T-bills and Eurodollar deposits, including the pricing fundamentals implicit in the term structure of interest rates. The chapter then covers the pricing, arbitrage relationships, delivery mechanics, and the various hedging uses of T-bill and Eurodollar futures. In addition, it examines the popular Ted spread.

The chapter concludes with several illustrations of how short-term interest rate futures are used either to hedge interest rate risk or to lock in future investment yields or borrowing costs. We also show how interest rate futures can be used to create synthetic interest rate securities and to restructure a fixed-income portfolio. Finally, our discussion illustrates the difference between a stack and a strip hedging strategy, providing examples of both types of hedges. In the next chapter we continue our discussion of interest rate futures by examining futures contracts written on long-term interest rate obligations.

QUESTIONS

1. What does the *expectation theory* of the term structure say about what determines the five-year bond yield?
2. Why was the *liquidity preference theory* introduced to explain the term structure of interest rates?
3. In Table 12.2 the asked yield on the March 22, 1990, T-bill is 7.56 percent. In Table 12.4 the implied yield on the March 90 T-bill futures contract is 7.35 percent. Why are these yields different? Does this difference imply anything about expectations?
4. Figure 12-3 plots the dollar (invoice) prices of the March 89 T-bill futures contracts as well as the dollar prices of the cash bill that is deliverable on this contract, from June 1, 1988, to March 8, 1989. The T-bill futures contract expires on March 8, 1989,

and the deliverable cash bill matures on June 8, 1989. What is the explanation for the large dollar price discrepancy between the T-bill futures price and the cash price on June 1, 1988. Explain why the two prices converge on March 8, 1989.

In answering this question calculate the dollar prices for both the March 89 T-bill futures and the June 8, 1989, cash T-bill on both June 1, 1988, and March 8, 1989. The relevant prices and yields on these dates were

- On June 1, 1988, the March 89 T-bill futures price was 92.81 and the discount yield for the cash bill was 7.05%.
- On March 8, 1989, the T-bill futures price was 91.40 while the cash bill discount yield was 8.59%.

5. What is the implied repo rate? How is it calculated? If the implied repo rate is lower than the borrowing rate, are futures over- or under-priced? What arbitrage transaction would you engage in?
6. Is it correct to say that, if the market is efficient, the yield on a Eurodollar futures contract for a given three-month time period in the future will be equal to the forward yield for the same time period? What is the difference between the formula in Section 12.3.2 and the pricing formula in Section 12.5.4?
7. Why is the Ted Spread considered to be a quality spread?
8. In the example in Section 12.7.1, why could not the hedger lock in the borrowing rate of 8.375 percent that existed on January 22?
9. What is a synthetic security or investment? Give an example of a synthetic one-year security that involves a short position.
10. What is the distinction between a strip and a stack hedge? What are the pros and cons of each? Is a stack hedge always superior to a strip hedge, as in the examples in Tables 12.8 and 12.9?
11. On April 12, 1991, a treasurer decides to place the company's excess funds in short-term money market instruments until September 15, 1991 (an investment period of 156 days). He is considering two options. The first is a 156-day Eurodollar time deposit and the second is a 66-day Eurodollar time deposit together with a long position in June 91 Eurodollar futures contracts. The June 91 futures expires on June 17, 1991, in exactly 66 days, at which time he can put his funds in a 90-day Eurodollar time deposit. In both cases the treasurer will lock in the Eurodollar rate for the next 156 days.

On April 12, 1991, the treasurer observes the following information:

- The closing price of the June 91 Eurodollar futures contract is 94.00 and it has an implied yield of 6.00 percent.
- The 66-day London "late" Eurodollar rate is 5.875 percent.
- The 156-day London "late" Eurodollar rate is 6.125 percent.

Which investment option provides the treasurer with the best return? Show how you arrive at your answer.

SUGGESTED READING

Allen, L. and T. Thurston. "Cash-Futures Arbitrage and Forward-Futures Spreads in the Treasury Bill Market." *The Journal of Futures Markets,* Vol. 8, (October 1988), pp. 563–573.

Elton, E. J., M. J. Gruber, and J. Rentzler. "Intra-Day Tests of the Efficiency of the Treasury-Bill Futures Market." *Review of Economics and Statistics*, Vol. 66, (February 1984), pp. 129–137.

Hedge, S. and B. Branch. "An Empirical Analysis of Arbitrage Opportunities in the Treasury Bill Futures Market." *The Journal of Futures Markets* Vol. 5, (1985), pp. 407–424.

Hedge, S. and B. McDonald. "On the Informational Role of Treasury Bill Futures." *The Journal of Futures Markets*, Vol. 6, (Winter 1986), pp. 629–644.

Kawaller, I. and T. Koch. "Cash and Carry Trading and the Pricing of Treasury Bill Futures." *The Journal of Futures Markets*, Vol. 4, (1984), pp. 115–123

Lasser, D. "A Measure of Ex-Ante Hedging Effectiveness for the Treasury Bill and Treasury Bond Futures Markets," *Review of Futures Markets*, Vol. 6, No. 2 (1987), pp. 278–295.

MacDonald, J. and S. Hein. "Futures Rates and Forward Rates as Predictors of Near-Term Bill Rates." *The Journal of Futures Markets*, Vol. 9 (1989), pp. 249–262.

MacDonald, S. R. Peterson, and T. Koch. "Using Futures to Improve Treasury Bill Portfolio Performance." *The Journal of Futures Markets*, Vol. 8 (1988), pp 167–184.

McCabe, G. and D. Solberg. "Hedging in the Treasury Bill Futures Market When the Hedged Instrument and the Deliverable Instrument are not Matched." *The Journal of Futures Markets*, Vol. 9, No. 6 (December 1989), pp. 529–538.

Park, H. "Changes in Expectations and the Forecasting Error of Interest Rates: An Error Learning Model of Treasury Bill Futures." *Quarterly Journal of Business and Economics*, Spring 1986, pp. 22–32.

CHAPTER
13

LONG-TERM INTEREST RATE FUTURES

The most actively traded interest rate futures contract in the world is the CBOT's U.S. Treasury bond (T-bond) contract. In 1989 more than 100 million T-bond contracts were traded, nearly twice the volume of Eurodollar futures. Figure 13-1 shows the growth of trading in U.S. T-bond futures from 1977 to 1990. Other successful long-term futures contracts in the United States are the 10-year and 5-year U.S. Treasury note (T-note) contracts. Table 13.1 provides contract specifications for each of these contracts.

On foreign exchanges, the most successful long-term interest rate futures are the 10-year Japanese government bond contract traded on the Tokyo Stock Exchange and the 10-year French government bond contract traded on MATIF in Paris. In addition, the London International Financial Futures Exchange (LIFFE) trades futures on long "gilts" (U.K. government bonds) as well as on U.S., German, and Japanese government bonds; and, the Sydney Futures Exchange trades 10-year Australian government bonds. Table 13.2 shows their respective 1990 trading volumes.

The success of long-term interest rate futures is undoubtedly linked to the growth of the underlying cash markets for government bonds. During the 1980s continuing government budget deficits in all countries, and especially in the United

Contracts traded (millions)

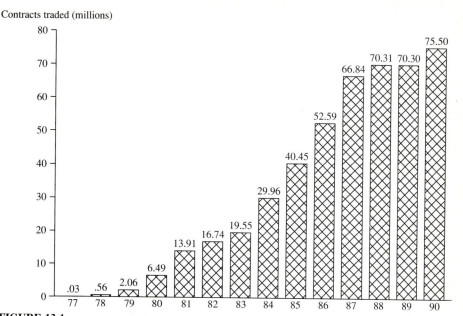

FIGURE 13-1

U.S. T-bond futures annual trading volume, 1977–1990.

States, resulted in an enormous increase in the quantity of bonds issued by governments. As of June 30, 1990, the face value of U.S. government Treasury notes and bonds outstanding was $1527.3 billion. In addition, nongovernmental long-term debt (such as mortgage bonds and corporate bonds) has grown substantially during the last decade. Since a major use of long-term interest rate futures is to hedge the interest rate risk associated with cash positions in government and other long-term debt obligations, it is not surprising that trading in these instruments has risen sharply.

Increased interest rate volatility has also played a role. Since the early 1980s the Federal Reserve has pursued a stable money-growth policy, allowing interest rates to fluctuate more widely. Further, greater uncertainty about inflation rates has resulted in greater interest rate volatility, and long-term debt holders have turned to long-term interest rate futures as a hedge against increased interest rate risk.

As indicated in Table 13.1, the CBOT's T-bond and T-note contracts are identical except for the maturity of the instruments that are acceptable for delivery. The T-bond contract allows delivery of U.S. Treasury bonds with remaining maturities (or earliest call dates) of at least 15 years. The two T-note futures contracts allow delivery of U.S. Treasury notes with remaining maturities of $4\frac{1}{4}$ to $5\frac{1}{4}$ years and $6\frac{1}{2}$ to 10 years. Since the T-bond and T-note futures are very similar, the discussion in this chapter focuses on U.S. T-bond futures, which are the most widely used. The principles and mechanics associated with U.S. T-bond futures are also similar to those applicable to foreign bond futures contracts.

TABLE 13.1
Specifications of leading U.S. long-term interest rate futures contracts

	U.S. T-bond	10-year U.S. T-note	5-year U.S. T-note
Exchange	CBOT	CBOT	CBOT
Date of introduction	August 22, 1977	May 3, 1982	May 6, 1987
Ticket symbol	US	TY	FV
Contract size	$100,000 face value	$100,000 face value	$100,000 face value
Contract months	Mar, Jun, Sep, Dec	Mar, Jun, Sep, Dec	Mar, Jun, Sep, Dec
Price quotation	Points and $\frac{1}{32}$ of a point	Points and $\frac{1}{32}$ of a point	Points and $\frac{1}{32}$ of a point
Tick size	$\frac{1}{32}$ of a point, i.e., $31.25	$\frac{1}{32}$ of a point, i.e., $31.25	$\frac{1}{32}$ of a point, i.e., $31.25
Deliverable grades	U.S. T-bonds that are not callable for at least 15 years and have a maturity of at least 15 years from the first business day of the delivery month	U.S. T-notes with maturity at least $6\frac{1}{2}$ years, but not more than 10 years from the first business day of the delivery month	Any of the four most recently auctioned 5-year U.S. T-notes, with original maturity of not more than 5 years and 3 months, and remaining maturity of not less than 4 years and 3 months, as of the first business day of the delivery month
Last trading day	7th business day preceding the last business day of the delivery month	7th business day preceding the last business day of the delivery month	7th business day preceding the last business day of the delivery month
Last delivery day	Last business day of the delivery month	Last business day of the delivery month	Last business day of the delivery month
Delivery method	Federal Reserve book-entry wire-transfer system	Federal Reserve book-entry wire-transfer system	Federal Reserve book-entry wire-transfer system

TABLE 13.2
Trading volume in long-term interest rate futures: U.S. and foreign exchanges

		1990 Contract volume
U.S. exchanges		
T-bonds (15 years)	CBOT	75,499,257
T-notes ($6\frac{1}{2}$–10 years)	CBOT	6,054,222
T-notes (5 years)	CBOT	2,532,828
T-bonds (15 years)	MidAm	1,461,046
Municipal Bond Index	CBOT	696,861
T-notes (2 years)	CBOT	110,789
Mortgage-backed	CBOT	16,848
Japanese government bonds	CBOT	3,062
Total		86,374,913
Foreign exchanges		
Japanese government bonds (10 years)	Tokyo Stock Exchange, Japan	16,306,571
French government bonds (10 years)	MATIF, France	15,966,096
German government *bunds*	LIFFE, U.K.	9,581,516
Long Gilt (U.K. government bonds)	LIFFE, U.K.	5,643,247
Australian T-bonds (10 years)	Sydney Futures Exchange, Australia	3,173,821
U.S. T-bonds	LIFFE, U.K.	756,201
Government T-bonds	BM&F, Brazil	711,097
Canadian government bonds	Montreal Exchange, Canada	454,058
U.S. T-bonds	Tokyo Stock Exchange, Japan	411,394
Bunds (German government bonds)	DTB, Germany	59,665
ECU bonds	MATIF, France	56,292
Deliverable bonds	Financial Futures Market, Amsterdam	53,798
Japanese bonds	LIFFE, U.K.	46,215
Australian T-bonds (3 years)	Sydney Futures Exchange, Australia	33,753
4-year BTAN T-notes	MATIF, France	27,866
Japanese government bonds (20 years)	Tokyo Stock Exchange, Japan	12,924
Semi-government bonds (10 years)	Sydney Futures Exchange, Australia	4,909
Semi-government bonds (5 years)	Sydney Futures Exchange, Australia	1,788
Total		53,301,211

13.1 THE CASH T-BOND MARKET

The long-term Treasury bond market consists of both Treasury notes and bonds. Treasury notes have original maturities of 10 years or less; Treasury bonds have maturities greater than 10 years and as long as 30 years. These bonds are issued by the U.S. Treasury in refunding cycles that occur quarterly in February, May, August, and November. In most cases the refunding issues include some 3- to 4-year notes, some 7- to 10-year notes, and some 20- to 30-year bonds.

A secondary market for these obligations is made by 46 authorized government bond dealers, who actively buy and sell the securities and are in constant contact with each other. Some of these dealers are large commercial banks; others are associated with large securities firms. Dealers hold an inventory of various government securities (coupon, maturity, etc.) and stand ready to buy and sell them at announced bid and asked prices. The market is an over-the-counter, telephone market.

13.1.1 Quoted Bond Prices

The price and yield quotations for cash bonds that appear in newspapers or on quotation services' screens are typically the quotes of a particular dealer, and are for transactions of $1 million or more. Table 13.3 shows quotations as of

TABLE 13.3
Treasury bond cash quotations, as of December 13, 1989

Rate	Maturity	Bid	Asked	Bid change	Yield
12.00	May 05k	134.17	134.23	+.06	8.03
10.75	Aug 05k	123.25	123.31	+.04	8.03
9.37	Feb 06k	112.15	112.21	+.04	7.97
11.75	Feb 05–10k	131.29	132.03	+.05	8.05
10.00	May 05–10k	116.30	117.04	+.05	8.04
12.75	Nov 05–10k	141.17	141.23	+.06	8.05
13.87	May 06–11k	152.12	152.18	+.06	8.05
14.00	Nov 06–11k	154.08	154.14	+.06	8.05
10.37	Nov 07–12k	121.23	121.29	+.06	8.04
12.00	Aug 08–13k	137.19	137.25	+.05	8.05
13.25	May 09–14k	150.19	150.25	+.07	8.04
12.50	Aug 09–14k	143.12	143.18	+.06	8.05
11.75	Nov 09–14k	136.10	136.16	+.07	8.04
11.25	Feb 15k	135.00	135.06	+.07	7.98
10.62	Aug 15k	128.16	128.22	+.07	7.98
9.87	Nov 15k	120.19	120.25	+.06	7.97
9.25	Feb 16k	113.28	114.02	+.06	7.96
7.25	May 16k	92.12	92.16	+.05	7.93
7.50	Nov 16k	95.02	95.06	+.05	7.93
8.75	May 17k	108.27	108.31	+.06	7.94
8.87	Aug 17k	110.07	110.11	+.05	7.94
9.12	May 18k	113.13	113.17	+.07	7.92
9.00	Nov 18k	112.06	112.10	+.07	7.91
8.87	Feb 19k	110.26	110.30	+.07	7.91
8.12	Aug 19k	102.23	102.27	+.06	7.87

Representative over-the-counter quotations are based on transactions of $1 million or more. Quotes are as of mid-afternoon and are in 32nds: 101-01 means $101\frac{1}{32}$. Net changes are in 32nds. All yields are to maturity and are based on the asked quotes. For bonds callable prior to maturity, yields are computed to the earliest call date for issues quoted above par and to the maturity date for issues below par.

k means that interest is paid semiannually.

Source: The Wall Street Journal, December 14, 1989.

4:00 P.M. Eastern time, for Wednesday, December 13, 1989. Although there are many outstanding government bonds and notes, Table 13.3 shows only bonds with at least 15 years remaining to maturity. (Only these bonds can be delivered in fulfillment of a T-bond futures contract obligation.)

The first column of Table 13.3 shows the coupon rates on the bonds listed in the rows of the table. The second column shows the maturity dates of the bonds. For example, the first bond shown (in the first row) has a coupon of 12 percent and a maturity date of May 2005.[1] The maturity dates of the bonds in Table 13.3 are arranged from the shortest maturity (at the top) to the longest maturity (at the bottom).

The third and fourth columns of Table 13.3 show the dealer's quoted bid and asked prices. If an individual or institution wishes to purchase bonds, they will pay the *asked* price; a seller will receive the *bid* price. The bid-asked spread, or the difference between the bid and asked prices, is the compensation received by dealers for *making the market*. (They do not charge a commission.) For the bonds quoted in Table 13.3, spreads range from 0.12 percent to 0.18 percent of par value. Thus, the dealer cost of buying and selling $100,000 of bonds is between $120 and $180 dollars.[2] There may also be an additional commission if the order is placed with a bank or broker.

Bid and asked prices on bonds are conventionally quoted as a percentage of par value. Fractions of a percentage point are quoted in thirty-seconds. For example, the purchase price of the May 2016 bond, with a coupon of 7.25 percent, is 92.16. This means 92 percent of par value plus $\frac{16}{32}$ of a percentage point of par value. To purchase $100,000 of the May 2016 bonds, therefore, would cost $92,500:

$$(0.92 \times \$100,000) + (0.01 \times \$100,000 \times \tfrac{16}{32})$$

If the same bonds were sold, the seller would receive $92,375:

$$(0.92 \times \$100,000) + (0.01 \times \$100,000 \times \tfrac{12}{32})$$

The fifth column of Table 13.3 is the change in the asked price, from yesterday's quoted price to today's quoted price. For the first bond in Table 13.3 the price increased by $\frac{6}{32}$: a $187.50 increase for each $100,000 of par value.

---

[1] The annual interest payment on a 12 percent coupon bond with a $1000 face value is $120, $12,000 on a bond with a face value of $100,000, and so forth. In Table 13.3, the symbol k signifies that interest is paid semiannually. For the May 2005 bond, the interest payment will be made half in November and half in May. Furthermore, some bonds are callable, meaning that the U.S. government can retire them early by paying their face values to the bondholders. For example, for the February 11.75 percent bond with a maturity date of 2005-10, the first call date is February 15, 2005, and the bond expires on February 15, 2010. The U.S. government has not issued callable bonds in recent years.

[2] The bid and asked price quotations in Table 13.3 are for transactions of $1 million or more. The bid-asked spread may be higher for smaller transactions.

13.1.2   Bond Yields

The last column in Table 13.3 shows the yield on each bond at its current market price. This is the yield-to-maturity on the bond.[3] If, for example, the May 2005 bond is purchased at 134.23 and held to maturity, its effective average annual yield will be 8.03 percent. This yield is much lower than the 12 percent coupon interest rate on the bond. Why? Because the current price of the bond, 134.23, is far above par value. When the bond matures, the holder will receive principal equal only to the bond's par value (or 100 percent of face value). The holder will pay 134.23, but at maturity will receive only 100, resulting in a capital loss. This capital loss must be subtracted from the interest earnings on the bond over its life to determine the net yield-to-maturity on the bond.[4]

To determine the price of a bond we must calculate the present value of its two earnings streams, which occur at different times during the life of the bond: the annual coupon payments, and the repayment of principal at maturity. Or,

Bond price = present value of coupon annuity + present value of face value

In addition, the single interest rate that discounts this series of payments to a sum equal to the bond's current price is referred to as the bond's present yield-to-maturity. This yield is also sometimes called the internal rate of return on an investment in the bond.

The general formula for determining the price of a bond that pays interest semiannually is:

$$P_o = \left[\sum_{t=1}^{2N} \frac{C/2}{(1+R/2)^{(t-1)+(tc/B)}} \right] + \left[\frac{P_T}{(1+R/2)^{(2N-1)+(tc/B)}} \right]$$

where P_o = current quoted price of the bond
$\quad P_T$ = price of the bond at the end of the holding period (which is 100 at maturity)
$\quad R$ = annual yield-to-maturity
$\quad C$ = annual dollar coupon interest
$\quad N$ = number of years to maturity
$\quad tc$ = number of days remaining until the next coupon payment
$\quad B$ = total number of days in a coupon period (if time t is right after a coupon payment, then $tc = B$)

If P_o is known, this formula can be used to calculate the yield-to-maturity (R). Finally, the convention on callable bonds is to assume that they will be called at the earliest possible call date (see footnote to Table 13.3).

---

[3]The yield-to-maturity should not be confused with a bond's *current yield*. The latter is closely approximated by dividing the annual interest payment by the current price of the bond. For the May 2005 bond, for example, the current yield is about 8.91 percent.

[4]Purchasing a bond below par, say at 92.12, will result in a capital gain, which must be added to the interest earned.

13.1.3   Calculating the Bond's Transaction Price

The quoted bond price is not the actual price at which the bonds are bought and sold. If a bond is bought on a date that falls between coupon payments, the buyer of the bond will be the holder of record on the next coupon date, and will receive the full six-month's interest earnings, even though owning the bond for less than six months. To remedy this inequity, the buyer of the bond must pay the seller the *accrued interest* on the bond: the interest earned between the last interest payment and the sale date. The accrued interest on a T-bond is calculated as

$$\left(\frac{B - tc}{B}\right) \times \text{Semiannual coupon payment}$$

where B and tc are as defined above. Thus, the transaction price of a bond at period t is

$$P = (\text{Quoted price}) + (\text{Accrued interest})$$

For example, the 7.25 percent, May 2016 bond pays $3.625 per $100 face value on November 15 and May 15 of each year. At the close of trading on December 13, 1989, the bond had a quoted (asked) price of $92\frac{16}{32}$. If the bond is purchased on December 13, the cash settlement date will be December 14, and the bond will be 29 days into its May 15 coupon period (there will be 152 days remaining until the May coupon payment). The transaction price of a $100,000 May 2016 bond on December 13, 1989, therefore, will be

$$(\$100,000 \times 0.9250) + \left(\$100,000 \times 0.0725 \times \frac{1}{2} \times \frac{29\,\text{days}}{181\,\text{days}}\right)$$

$$= \$92,500 + \$580.80$$

$$= \$93,080.80$$

13.1.4   The Inverse Relationship between Bond Prices and Market Yields

Bond prices are determined in the secondary market by the supply and demand for bonds. If investors believe that the yield-to-maturity on a particular bond is too high, or higher than is being paid on equivalent-risk investments elsewhere, they will purchase the bond, driving its price up until the bond's yield falls to the equilibrium interest rate level. If a bond's yield is deemed to be too low, or below that which can be earned elsewhere, holders will sell the bond until its price falls and its yield rises to the equilibrium level. Arbitrage among the various financial assets will make yields on equivalent-risk assets identical.

Returning to Table 13.3, the yield-to-maturity on bonds with 15- to 20-year maturities was about eight percent on December 13, 1989, with slightly lower yields on the longer-term bonds. All but two of the bonds in Table 13.3, however, have coupons higher than eight percent. Thus, in order to equate the

yields on these bonds to the prevailing 8 percent level of market interest rates, the prices of the bonds will have to be above par, or higher than 100—they will have to sell at a premium. In fact, the price of the 14 percent, November 2006-11 bond is 154.14: it is at a 54.14 point premium. Alternatively, the 7.25 percent, May 2016 bond, which has a coupon below prevailing market yields, has a price of 92.16, or is at a 7.84 point discount.

More formally, this inverse relationship between bond prices and yields can be mathematically derived from the bond pricing formula in Section 13.1.2. This formula makes it clear that a higher R implies a lower bond price, and vice versa.

13.2   DURATION

The bond pricing formula also reveals that the magnitude of the effect of an interest rate change on a bond's price will depend on both the bond's maturity and its coupon level.[5] For a given change in interest rates, the change in bond prices will be greater: i) the longer the maturity of the bond, and ii) the lower the coupon rate on the bond. These relationships exist because more distant cash flows are more affected by the compounding effects implicit in the bond pricing formula.

A bond's *duration* is a useful summary measure of its price sensitivity to interest rate changes. A high-duration bond's price is more sensitive to interest rate changes than is the price of a low-duration bond. Duration incorporates both the maturity effect and the coupon effect into a single numerical measure of a bond's price sensitivity. This measure can be used to compare the price sensitivity of different bonds or even different bond portfolios. As we will see, bonds with low coupons and long maturities have high durations, and bonds with high coupons and short maturities have low durations. [6]

13.2.1   Macaulay's Duration

The duration of a bond is commonly defined as the weighted average of the maturities of the bond's coupon and principal repayment cash flows, where the weights are the fractions of the bond's price that the cash flows in each time period represent. This measure is known as the *Macaulay duration* and is defined as[7]

$$D = \frac{1}{P} \times \sum_{t=1}^{m} \frac{t \times X_t}{(1+r)^t}$$

---

[5]Various tax aspects of bonds that may affect the price-yield relationship are ignored.

[6]The duration of a T-bill depends only on its maturity, since it has no coupon: all cash flows occur at maturity. A longer maturity T-bill, therefore, has a higher duration.

[7]Frederick Macaulay, *Some Theoretical Problems Suggested by the Movements of Interest Rates, Bond Yields, and Stock Prices in the United States Since 1856*, National Bureau of Economic Research, 1938. The Macaulay duration measure assumes a flat term structure.

where D = duration of a bond

X_t = dollar payment on the bond in period t (can be either coupon interest or principal repayment)

r = current annual yield-to-maturity on the bond divided by the number of payment periods in a year (which is two for bonds paying semiannually)

m = number of payment periods

P = transaction price of the bond

Because r is a payment period discount rate and m is the number of periods, this formula measures duration in periods, not in years. To convert to a duration measure in years, the above duration measure must be multiplied by $1/f$, where f is the frequency of coupon payments during a year.

For example, the *period* duration of a two-year note with an 8 percent coupon (paid semiannually), an annual yield-to-maturity of 10 percent, and a market price of 98.0 is 3.7109 (see Table 13.4 for detailed calculations):

$$D = \frac{1}{98}\left[\frac{1 \times 4}{(1 + 0.05)^1} + \frac{2 \times 4}{(1 + 0.05)^2} + \frac{3 \times 4}{(1 + 0.05)^3} + \frac{4 \times 4}{(1 + 0.05)^4} + \frac{4 \times 100}{(1 + 0.05)^4}\right]$$

$$= 3.7109$$

Since the coupon payment period is semiannual, this duration measure is expressed in terms of six-month periods. On an annual basis, the bond's duration is 1.8555 ($3.7109 \times \frac{1}{2}$) years.

TABLE 13.4
Example of duration calculation for two-year note

Market price	=	98.00
Coupon rate	=	8%
Coupon payment	=	Semiannual
Yield-to-maturity	=	10%
Time to maturity	=	2 years

Periods $(t = 1, \ldots, N)$ (1)	Cash flows per $100 face value (X_t) (2)	(1) × (2) (3)	Discount factor $(1 + r)^t$ (4)	Present value of cash flow (3)/(4) (5)	Duration weight (5)/P_0 (6)
1	$4	$4	1.0500	$3.8095	0.0389
2	$4	$8	1.1025	$7.2562	0.0740
3	$4	$12	1.1576	$10.3663	0.1058
4	$4	$16	1.2155	$13.1633	0.1343
4	$100	$400	1.2155	$329.0827	3.3579
				$D =$	3.7109

13.2.2 Modified Duration

Another useful measure of a bond's price sensitivity is *modified duration,* which provides a percentage measure of price volatility. The formula for a bond's modified duration (D_{mod}) is

$$D_{\text{mod}} = \frac{D}{1 + \frac{R}{f}}$$

where D is the Macaulay duration measure (expressed in years), and R and f are as defined earlier. Thus, in our earlier example of the two-year note, the modified duration is

$$D_{\text{mod}} = \frac{1.8555}{1 + \frac{0.10}{2}} = 1.7671$$

A bond's modified duration measures the *percentage change* in a bond's price relative to a given *percentage change* in the bond's yield-to-maturity, or

$$-D_{\text{mod}} = \frac{\%\Delta P}{\%\Delta(1 + R)}$$

Thus, the percentage change in a bond's price can be stated as

$$(\%\Delta P) = -D_{\text{mod}} \times (\%\Delta(1 + R))$$

For example, if the yield-to-maturity on the two-year note in our previous example were to rise by 0.50 percentage points, the percentage change in the price of the note would be

$$(\%\Delta P) = -1.7671 \times (\frac{0.005}{1 + 0.10} \times 100\%)$$

$$= -1.7671 \times 0.4545\%$$

$$= -0.8031\%$$

The price of the two-year note, therefore, will decrease by

$$98.00 \times 0.008031 = 0.79, \text{ or } \tfrac{25}{32}$$

13.2.3 The Duration of a Portfolio

A portfolio's duration can be measured as the weighted average of the durations of each security in the portfolio, where the weights are the market value of each security in the portfolio divided by the total market value of the entire portfolio. The resulting duration is often referred to as the *market-weighted* portfolio duration.

The following example illustrates how to compute the duration of a portfolio consisting of three T-bonds: the 10.37 percent, Nov 2012 T-bond with a face value of $200 million; the 12.00 percent, Aug 2013 T-bond with a face value of $200 million; and, the 11.75 percent, Nov 2014 T-bond with a face value of $100 million. Market prices (averages of the bid-asked prices) for the three bonds are, respectively, 121-26, 137-22, and 136-13. (See Table 13.3.) Expressed in decimal form these prices are, respectively, 121.8125, 137.6875, and 136.4063. The duration of this portfolio is 9.16:

Bond (1)	Bond yield (2)	Bond price (3)	Bond duration (4)	Face value (5)	Market value (6) = (3)×(5) (mil)	Portfolio weight (7) = (6)/655.42	Weighted duration (4)×(7)
10.37 Nov-12	8.04	1.218125	9.288	$200	$243.63	0.37	3.44
12.00 Aug-13	8.05	1.376875	8.926	200	275.38	0.42	3.75
11.75 Nov-14	8.04	1.364063	9.386	100	136.41	0.21	1.97
				$500	$655.42	1.00	9.16

13.2.4 Summary

We have now completed a discussion of the cash T-bond market and the fundamentals of bond prices and yields. Although this discussion may have seemed unrelated to futures markets, a thorough understanding of bond market fundamentals is necessary to understand long-term interest rate futures contracts. The concept of duration will also be important when we turn to using long-term interest rate futures to hedge interest rate risk.

13.3 THE U.S. T-BOND FUTURES CONTRACT

The U.S. T-bond futures contract is more complicated than most futures because of its complex delivery provisions and the wide variety of bonds that can be delivered to satisfy a short's contractual obligation. A T-bond futures contract calls for the delivery of $100,000 face value of U.S. Treasury bonds (or the equivalent) maturing (or not callable) for at least 15 years from the delivery date, with a *notional* (as opposed to an actual) coupon of 8 percent. T-bond futures are, like T-bill and Eurodollar contracts, traded on a March, June, September, and December cycle.

13.3.1 The Delivery Process and Deliverable Bonds

DELIVERY PROCESS. The short initiates the delivery process by choosing which bond to deliver and when to deliver it during the delivery month. The delivery process is a three-day sequence. The day on which the short declares his intention to deliver is called the *position day*. The short can notify the exchange of his intention to deliver until 8 P.M. on the position day, even though the futures market closes at 2 P.M. On the next business day (the *notice day*), the clearinghouse matches the short with the long having the oldest outstanding position, and notifies the respective short and long. By 5:00 P.M. on the notice day the short must state which bond he or she intends to deliver, and must invoice the long for the full amount due, including any accrued interest. The price that the long pays to the short is determined by the settlement price on the position day. Finally, the short must have wired the bonds to the long's bank by 10:00 A.M. of the delivery day (the third day of the delivery sequence). After receipt of the book-entry bonds, the long's bank must make payment by 1:00 P.M. to the short's bank by Fed Funds wire.

DELIVERABLE BONDS.   The T-bond futures contract allows the short to deliver *any* bond with a remaining maturity of at least 15 years to maturity or to the earliest call date. Thus, a short can deliver bonds with a range of coupons and maturity dates, and, consequently, very different market values. To adjust for these differences, the T-bond futures contract specifies *conversion* factors that are used to adjust invoice prices. The conversion factors ensure that the short receives a higher price for delivering a more valuable bond than for delivering a less valuable bond. The conversion factors that were applicable to the outstanding T-bond futures contracts on September 15, 1989, are shown in Table 13.5. All of the bonds in the table have a maturity of at least 15 years and are therefore deliverable on the outstanding futures contracts.

DELIVERY OPTIONS.   An important aspect of the T-bond delivery rules is that they give shorts several *delivery options*. These options are referred to as the

- *Quality Option.* The right to choose which of the many eligible bonds to deliver. The short can maximize his or her return by delivering the *cheapest-to-deliver* bond (discussed in a later section).
- *Timing Option.* The right to choose which day of the month to make delivery.
- *Wild Card Options.* The short has two wild card options. First, he does not have to notify the clearinghouse of his intention to deliver until 8:00 P.M. on the position day, which is six hours after the 2:00 P.M. close of the bond futures market. During this time the short may be able to profit from changes in cash bond prices. Second, the short can wait until 5:00 P.M. on notice day to choose which bond to deliver.

These choices give the short *implied put options.* The market's assessment of the value of these delivery options should be reflected in the futures price. If any of the options have value, T-bond futures prices will be lower than they would otherwise be. Consequently, T-bond futures prices are frequently at a discount to theoretical futures prices, which are calculated without regard to the short's delivery options.

TABLE 13.5
Conversion factors for outstanding T-bond futures contracts, September 15, 1989

	Deliverable T-bonds		T-bond futures contracts							
	Coupon	Maturity	Sep 89	Dec 89	Mar 90	Jun 90	Sep 90	Dec 90	Mar 91	Jun 91
1.	7-1/4	May 15, 2016	0.9180	0.9180	0.9184	0.9185	0.9189	0.9190	0.9194	0.9195
2.	7-1/2	Nov 15, 2016	0.9450	0.9450	0.9453	0.9453	0.9456	0.9456	0.9460	0.9459
3.	8-1/8	Aug 15, 2019	1.0139	1.0141	1.0139	1.0140	1.0138	1.0140	1.0137	1.0139
4.	8-3/4	May 15, 2017	1.0829	1.0825	1.0825	1.0820	1.0820	1.0816	1.0816	1.0811
5.	8-7/8	Aug 15, 2017	1.0968	1.0967	1.0963	1.0962	1.0957	1.0957	1.0952	1.0951
6.	8-7/8	Feb 15, 2019	1.0981	1.0981	1.0977	1.0977	1.0972	1.0972	1.0968	1.0967
7.	9	Nov 15, 2018	1.1121	1.1117	1.1116	1.1111	1.1111	1.1106	1.1105	1.1100
8.	9-1/8	May 15, 2018	1.1256	1.1251	1.1250	1.1245	1.1244	1.1238	1.1237	1.1232
9.	9-1/4	Feb 15, 2016	1.1361	1.1359	1.1353	1.1351	1.1345	1.1343	1.1336	1.1334
10.	9-3/8	Feb 15, 2006	1.1236	1.1229	1.1217	1.1209	1.1297	1.1189	–	–
11.	9-7/8	Nov 15, 2015	1.2039	1.2030	1.2027	1.2018	1.2014	1.2005	1.2001	1.1992
12.	10	May 15, 2005–10	1.1759	1.1742	1.1729	–	–	–	–	–
13.	10-3/8	Nov 15, 2007–12	1.2245	1.2228	1.2216	1.2199	1.2186	1.2168	1.2155	1.2136
14.	10-5/8	Aug 15, 2015	1.2843	1.2837	1.2826	1.2820	1.2808	1.2801	1.2789	1.2782
15.	10-3/4	Aug 15, 2005	1.2436	1.2418	1.2396	1.2378	–	–	–	–
16.	11-1/4	Feb 15, 2015	1.3499	1.3491	1.3477	1.3468	1.3453	1.3444	1.3429	1.3419
17.	11-3/4	Nov 15, 2009–14	1.3711	1.3689	1.3672	1.3649	1.3631	1.3608	1.3589	1.3565
18.	12	May 15, 2005	1.3518	1.3485	1.3458	–	–	–	–	–
19.	12	Aug 15, 2008–13	1.3848	1.3829	1.3802	1.3782	1.3755	1.3733	1.3705	1.3682
20.	12-1/2	Aug 15, 2009–14	1.4427	1.4407	1.4379	1.4358	1.4330	1.4307	1.4278	1.4254
21.	12-3/4	Nov 15, 2005–10	1.4245	1.4208	1.4177	1.4139	1.4107	–	–	–
22.	13-1/4	May 15, 2009–14	1.5141	1.5110	1.5084	1.5052	1.5025	1.4991	1.4963	1.4929
23.	13-7/8	May 15, 2006–11	1.5331	1.5288	1.5250	1.5205	1.5167	1.5120	1.5080	–
24.	14	Nov 15, 2006–11	1.5523	1.5481	1.5444	1.5400	1.5362	1.5316	1.5277	1.5229

Source: Chicago Board of Trade.

TABLE 13.6
Treasury bond futures prices, December 13, 1989

	Open	High	Low	Settle	Change	Yield Settle	Yield Change	Open interest
						Treasury bonds (CBT)—$100,000; pts. 32nds of 100%		
Dec	99-10	99-17	99-06	99-16	+5	8.051	−.016	53,949
Mar 90	99-10	99-18	99-05	99-17	+6	8.048	−.019	218,016
Jun	99-08	99-14	99-02	99-13	+5	8.060	−.016	22,437
Sep	98-29	99-06	98-29	99-06	+5	8.083	−.016	5,294
Dec	98-27	98-29	98-26	98-28	+5	8.115	−.016	3,003
Mar 91	98-10	98-19	98-10	98-19	+5	8.144	−.016	2,425
June	98-09	98-11	98-09	98-11	+5	8.169	−.017	618
Sep	98-02	98-03	98-02	98-03	+4	8.195	−.013	304

Source: The Wall Street Journal, December 14, 1989.

Research suggests that of these options the quality option is the most valuable.[8] However, before discussing how to determine which bond the short should deliver, or which is the cheapest-to-deliver bond, we first need to examine the pricing fundamentals of T-bond futures.

13.3.2   Futures Price Quotations

Table 13.6 shows the closing price quotations for T-bond futures contracts traded on December 13, 1989. The delivery months range from the December 89 (the nearest) to September 91 (the most distant). Columns 2 through 6 contain the open, high, low, and settlement price quotations, and daily price changes for each the contracts.

The pricing convention used for T-bond futures is exactly the same as that used for cash T-bond prices: percentage of par value, with fractions of a percentage point expressed in thirty-seconds. Since each futures contract represents $100,000 of par value bonds, a futures price change of one percentage point (such as from 97-16 to 98-16) means a $1000 change in the contract's value. For example, column 6 in Table 13.6 shows a price increase of $\frac{6}{32}$ for the March 90 contract, which represents an increase of $187.50 in the contract's value. If an investor were long ten March 90 contracts, his gain for the day would be $1875.00.

---

[8]See, for example, G. D. Gay and S. Manaster, "The Quality Option Implicit in Futures Contracts," *Journal of Financial Economics,* 1984, pp. 353-70; G. D. Gay and S. Manaster, "Implicit Delivery Options and Optimal Delivery Strategies for Financial Futures Contracts," *Journal of Financial Economics,* 1986, pp. 41-72; A. Kane and A. Marcus, "The Quality Option in the Treasury Bond Futures Market: An Empirical Assessment," *The Journal of Futures Markets,* 1986, pp. 230-48; S.P. Hedge, "On the Value of the Implicit Delivery Options," in *The Journal of Futures Markets,* October 1989, pp. 421–37.

The seventh column of Table 13.6 shows the respective bond yields implied by the futures settlement prices, and the eighth column shows the daily changes in these yields (in basis points). These are the yields-to-maturity that a purchaser of a T-bond futures contract can expect to earn on the cash T-bond he receives at delivery. For example, a purchaser of a September 91 futures contract at a price of 98.03 would expect to take delivery in September 1991 (nearly two years from December 13, 1989) of a T-bond that would earn a yield-to-maturity of 8.195 percent over the life of the bond.

The last column of Table 13.6 is the open interest for each contract on December 13, 1989. The most liquid are clearly the nearby December 89 and March 90 contracts.

13.3.3 Invoice Prices

The *invoice* price that is paid for T-bonds delivered on a T-bond futures contract is calculated by the following formula:

(Decimal futures settlement price) × (Conversion factor) × ($100,000)
+ Accrued interest on the delivered bond

The *decimal futures settlement price* is the quoted futures price expressed in decimal form (per $1 face value). A quoted futures price of 87-24 becomes a decimal futures settlement price of 0.8775 (24/32nds is expressed as 0.75 of a percentage point). The conversion factor is taken from a table provided by the Chicago Board of Trade, such as Table 13.5. The $100,000 sum in the above formula is the face value of the bonds which underly a T-bond futures contract. Lastly, the accrued interest due on the bond being delivered is calculated as shown in Section 13.1.3.

[handwritten margin note: Converts bond being delivered to]

For example, on December 13, 1989, a trader who is short the December 89 T-bond futures contract decides to deliver the 14 percent, November 2006-11 bond against his short position. This means that he will invoice the long on December 14, based on the settlement price on December 13. From Table 13.6 we know that the quoted settlement price on December 13 was 99.16. In decimal form this price is 0.9950. The applicable conversion factor is 1.5481. Finally, on December 14 there was 29 days of accrued interest on the November 2006 bond, since it last paid interest on November 15, 1989. This amounts to $1121.55 of accrued interest ($100,000 × 0.07 × $\frac{29}{181}$). Thus, the invoice price is

$$(0.9950 \times \$100,000 \times 1.5481) + \$1,121.55 = \$155,157.50$$

For every $100,000 of face value of the November 2006-11 bonds that the short delivers he will receive $155,157.50.

Why should the short receive more than the bond's face value? A short is obligated to deliver $100,000 of principal that will earn 8 percent a year for at least 15 years. In the foregoing illustration, the short has chosen to deliver a bond with an annual coupon of 14 percent (or 7 percent semiannually), a much higher coupon yield. Since the 14-percent bonds will generate greater interest cash flows in the future than would the hypothetical 8 percent bond, they are more valuable.

Alternatively, if the long must pay $155,157.50 for $100,000 face value of the 14 percent, November 2006 bonds, he or she will earn a yield-to-maturity of only 8 percent on the bonds, which is exactly the yield that the short has contracted to provide.

13.3.4   Conversion Factors

The conversion factor for a bond is simply the value of the bond *per $1 face value* computed by discounting the bond's future cash flows by the hypothetical eight percent annual yield. As such, the conversion factor for a bond or note is a function of (i) the bond's time to maturity (or time to first call if callable) from the first day of the delivery month and (ii) the actual coupon rate on the bond or note.[9]

Table 13.7 provides an excerpt from the conversion factor booklet published by the Chicago Board of Trade. The table shows that conversion factors differ by coupon rate and maturity. In particular, in Table 13.5 the conversion factor used for adjusting the price of the $10\frac{3}{4}$ percent, August 15, 2005 bond for delivery against the *September 89 futures contract* is 1.2436, but the conversion factor on this bond for delivery against the *March 90 contract* is only 1.2396. Why? Because in March 1990, the August 2005 bond is closer to maturity than it is in September 1989.

In addition, the closer the coupon of the deliverable bond is to eight percent, the closer the conversion factor is to one. Bonds with coupons higher than eight percent have conversion factors greater than one; bonds with coupons lower than eight percent have conversion factors of less than one. Further, for a given differential between eight percent and the bond's coupon, the longer the bond's maturity, the more its conversion factor will deviate from one.

How well do the conversion factors succeed in bringing invoice prices into line with the prevailing market values of the delivered T-bonds? That depends on how accurately the conversion factors reflect existing relationships among the market values of different bonds with different maturities. If the yield curve is flat at eight percent, the conversion factors will reflect accurately the market value relationships among bonds of all maturities. If the yield curve is not flat at eight percent, the conversion factors will not reflect perfectly the actual market value relationships among bonds. In this case a particular bond will become the best one to deliver. Such a bond is referred to as the *cheapest-to-deliver* bond.

13.4   PRICING T-BOND FUTURES

In theory, T-bond futures prices should be equal to the *adjusted cash prices* of the cheapest-to-deliver bond plus the net cost-of-carry on that bond (which may be positive or negative):

---

[9]For a discussion of how to calculate the conversion factor, see the appendix to this chapter.

TABLE 13.7
U.S. Treasury bond futures conversion factor to yield 8.000%

TERM	10%	10⅛%	10¼%	10⅜%	10½%	10⅝%	10¾%	10⅞%
				COUPON RATE				
15	1.1729	1.1837	1.1945	1.2053	1.2162	1.2270	1.2378	1.2486
15-3	1.1742	1.1851	1.1960	1.2069	1.2178	1.2287	1.2396	1.2505
15-6	1.1759	1.1869	1.1979	1.2089	1.2199	1.2308	1.2418	1.2528
15-9	1.1771	1.1882	1.1992	1.2103	1.2214	1.2325	1.2436	1.2546
16	1.1787	1.1899	1.2011	1.2122	1.2234	1.2346	1.2458	1.2569
16-3	1.1799	1.1911	1.2024	1.2136	1.2249	1.2361	1.2474	1.2587
16-6	1.1815	1.1928	1.2042	1.2155	1.2268	1.2382	1.2495	1.2609
16-9	1.1826	1.1940	1.2054	1.2168	1.2283	1.2397	1.2511	1.2625
17	1.1841	1.1956	1.2071	1.2186	1.2301	1.2416	1.2532	1.2647
17-3	1.1851	1.1967	1.2083	1.2199	1.2315	1.2431	1.2546	1.2662
17-6	1.1866	1.1983	1.2100	1.2216	1.2333	1.2450	1.2566	1.2683
17-9	1.1876	1.1994	1.2111	1.2228	1.2346	1.2463	1.2581	1.2698
18	1.1891	1.2009	1.2127	1.2245	1.2364	1.2482	1.2600	1.2718
18-3	1.1900	1.2019	1.2138	1.2257	1.2376	1.2495	1.2614	1.2732
18-6	1.1914	1.2034	1.2154	1.2273	1.2393	1.2512	1.2632	1.2752
18-9	1.1923	1.2044	1.2164	1.2284	1.2404	1.2525	1.2645	1.2765
19	1.1937	1.2058	1.2179	1.2300	1.2421	1.2542	1.2663	1.2784
19-3	1.1945	1.2067	1.2189	1.2310	1.2432	1.2554	1.2675	1.2797
19-6	1.1958	1.2081	1.2203	1.2326	1.2448	1.2570	1.2693	1.2815
19-9	1.1967	1.2090	1.2213	1.2336	1.2459	1.2582	1.2705	1.2828
20	1.1979	1.2103	1.2227	1.2350	1.2474	1.2598	1.2722	1.2845
20-3	1.1987	1.2111	1.2236	1.2360	1.2484	1.2608	1.2733	1.2857
20-6	1.1999	1.2124	1.2249	1.2374	1.2499	1.2624	1.2749	1.2874
20-9	1.2007	1.2132	1.2258	1.2383	1.2509	1.2634	1.2760	1.2885
21	1.2019	1.2145	1.2271	1.2397	1.2523	1.2649	1.2776	1.2902
21-3	1.2025	1.2152	1.2279	1.2406	1.2532	1.2659	1.2786	1.2912
21-6	1.2037	1.2164	1.2292	1.2419	1.2546	1.2674	1.2801	1.2928
21-9	1.2044	1.2171	1.2299	1.2427	1.2555	1.2683	1.2811	1.2939
22	1.2055	1.2183	1.2312	1.2440	1.2569	1.2697	1.2825	1.2954
22-3	1.2061	1.2190	1.2319	1.2448	1.2577	1.2706	1.2835	1.2964
22-6	1.2072	1.2202	1.2331	1.2461	1.2590	1.2720	1.2849	1.2979
22-9	1.2078	1.2208	1.2338	1.2468	1.2598	1.2728	1.2858	1.2988
23	1.2088	1.2219	1.2350	1.2480	1.2611	1.2741	1.2872	1.3002
23-3	1.2094	1.2225	1.2356	1.2487	1.2618	1.2749	1.2880	1.3011
23-6	1.2104	1.2236	1.2367	1.2499	1.2630	1.2762	1.2893	1.3025
23-9	1.2110	1.2241	1.2373	1.2505	1.2637	1.2769	1.2901	1.3033
24	1.2120	1.2252	1.2384	1.2517	1.2649	1.2782	1.2914	1.3047
24-3	1.2124	1.2257	1.2390	1.2523	1.2656	1.2789	1.2922	1.3055
24-6	1.2134	1.2268	1.2401	1.2534	1.2668	1.2801	1.2934	1.3068
24-9	1.2139	1.2273	1.2406	1.2540	1.2674	1.2808	1.2942	1.3075
25	1.2148	1.2282	1.2417	1.2551	1.2685	1.2820	1.2954	1.3088
25-3	1.2153	1.2287	1.2422	1.2557	1.2691	1.2826	1.2961	1.3095
25-6	1.2162	1.2297	1.2432	1.2567	1.2702	1.2837	1.2972	1.3108
25-9	1.2166	1.2301	1.2437	1.2572	1.2708	1.2843	1.2979	1.3114
26	1.2175	1.2311	1.2447	1.2583	1.2718	1.2854	1.2990	1.3126
26-3	1.2179	1.2315	1.2451	1.2587	1.2724	1.2860	1.2996	1.3133
26-6	1.2187	1.2324	1.2461	1.2597	1.2734	1.2871	1.3007	1.3144
26-9	1.2191	1.2328	1.2465	1.2602	1.2739	1.2876	1.3013	1.3150
27	1.2199	1.2337	1.2474	1.2612	1.2749	1.2887	1.3024	1.3161
27-3	1.2203	1.2340	1.2478	1.2616	1.2754	1.2892	1.3029	1.3167
27-6	1.2211	1.2349	1.2487	1.2625	1.2764	1.2902	1.3040	1.3178
27-9	1.2214	1.2353	1.2491	1.2630	1.2768	1.2907	1.3045	1.3184

(continued)

TABLE 13.7—cont'd.

COUPON RATE

TERM	10%	10⅛%	10¼%	10⅜%	10½%	10⅝%	10¾%	10⅞%
28	1.2222	1.2361	1.2500	1.2639	1.2777	1.2916	1.3055	1.3194
28-3	1.2225	1.2364	1.2503	1.2642	1.2782	1.2921	1.3060	1.3199
28-6	1.2233	1.2372	1.2512	1.2651	1.2791	1.2930	1.3070	1.3209
28-9	1.2235	1.2375	1.2515	1.2655	1.2795	1.2935	1.3074	1.3214
29	1.2243	1.2383	1.2523	1.2664	1.2804	1.2944	1.3084	1.3224
29-3	1.2245	1.2386	1.2526	1.2667	1.2807	1.2948	1.3088	1.3229
29-6	1.2253	1.2394	1.2534	1.2675	1.2816	1.2957	1.3098	1.3238
29-9	1.2255	1.2396	1.2537	1.2678	1.2819	1.2961	1.3102	1.3243
30	1.2262	1.2404	1.2545	1.2687	1.2828	1.2969	1.3111	1.3252
30-3	1.2265	1.2406	1.2548	1.2689	1.2831	1.2973	1.3114	1.3256
30-6	1.2271	1.2413	1.2555	1.2697	1.2839	1.2981	1.3123	1.3265
30-9	1.2273	1.2416	1.2558	1.2700	1.2842	1.2985	1.3127	1.3269
31	1.2280	1.2423	1.2565	1.2708	1.2850	1.2993	1.3135	1.3278
31-3	1.2282	1.2425	1.2568	1.2710	1.2853	1.2996	1.3139	1.3281
31-6	1.2289	1.2432	1.2575	1.2718	1.2861	1.3004	1.3147	1.3290
31-9	1.2290	1.2434	1.2577	1.2720	1.2863	1.3007	1.3150	1.3293
32	1.2297	1.2440	1.2584	1.2728	1.2871	1.3015	1.3158	1.3302
32-3	1.2298	1.2442	1.2586	1.2730	1.2873	1.3017	1.3161	1.3305
32-6	1.2305	1.2449	1.2593	1.2737	1.2881	1.3025	1.3169	1.3313
32-9	1.2306	1.2450	1.2595	1.2739	1.2883	1.3027	1.3171	1.3316
33	1.2312	1.2457	1.2601	1.2746	1.2890	1.3035	1.3179	1.3324
33-3	1.2313	1.2458	1.2603	1.2748	1.2892	1.3037	1.3182	1.3326
33-6	1.2319	1.2464	1.2609	1.2754	1.2899	1.3044	1.3189	1.3334
33-9	1.2320	1.2466	1.2611	1.2756	1.2901	1.3046	1.3191	1.3337
34	1.2326	1.2472	1.2617	1.2763	1.2908	1.3053	1.3199	1.3344
34-3	1.2327	1.2473	1.2618	1.2764	1.2910	1.3055	1.3201	1.3346
34-6	1.2333	1.2479	1.2625	1.2770	1.2916	1.3062	1.3208	1.3354
34-9	1.2334	1.2480	1.2626	1.2772	1.2918	1.3064	1.3210	1.3356
35	1.2339	1.2486	1.2632	1.2778	1.2924	1.3071	1.3217	1.3363
35-3	1.2340	1.2486	1.2633	1.2779	1.2926	1.3072	1.3218	1.3365
35-6	1.2346	1.2492	1.2639	1.2785	1.2932	1.3079	1.3225	1.3372
35-9	1.2346	1.2493	1.2640	1.2786	1.2933	1.3080	1.3227	1.3373
36	1.2352	1.2499	1.2646	1.2792	1.2939	1.3086	1.3233	1.3380
36-3	1.2352	1.2499	1.2646	1.2793	1.2940	1.3088	1.3235	1.3382
36-6	1.2357	1.2505	1.2652	1.2799	1.2947	1.3094	1.3241	1.3389
36-9	1.2358	1.2505	1.2653	1.2800	1.2947	1.3095	1.3242	1.3390
37	1.2363	1.2510	1.2658	1.2806	1.2953	1.3101	1.3249	1.3396
37-3	1.2363	1.2511	1.2659	1.2806	1.2954	1.3102	1.3250	1.3398
37-6	1.2368	1.2516	1.2664	1.2812	1.2960	1.3108	1.3256	1.3404
37-9	1.2368	1.2516	1.2664	1.2813	1.2961	1.3109	1.3257	1.3405
38	1.2373	1.2521	1.2670	1.2818	1.2956	1.3115	1.3263	1.3411
38-3	1.2373	1.2522	1.2670	1.2818	1.2967	1.3115	1.3264	1.3412
38-6	1.2378	1.2527	1.2675	1.2824	1.2972	1.3121	1.3270	1.3418
38-9	1.2378	1.2527	1.2675	1.2824	1.2973	1.3122	1.3270	1.3419
39	1.2383	1.2532	1.2681	1.2829	1.2978	1.3127	1.3276	1.3425
39-3	1.2383	1.2532	1.2681	1.2830	1.2979	1.3128	1.3277	1.3426
39-6	1.2387	1.2536	1.2686	1.2835	1.2984	1.3133	1.3282	1.3432
39-9	1.2387	1.2536	1.2686	1.2835	1.2984	1.3133	1.3283	1.3432
40	1.2392	1.2541	1.2690	1.2840	1.2989	1.3139	1.3288	1.3438

Source: Financial Publishing Co.

Theoretical futures price = (adjusted cash price of cheapest-to-deliver bond)
+ (net cost-of-carry)

where the adjusted cash price is the current cash price of the cheapest-to-deliver bond divided by the conversion factor on the bond that is applicable to the specific futures contract; and the net cost-of-carry is determined by the difference between the prevailing borrowing rate and the coupon yield on the cheapest-to-deliver bond. This relationship, however, will not be entirely accurate if the implicit delivery options discussed in Section 13.3.1 have value. In that event the theoretical futures price will be somewhat lower, since longs will want to be compensated for the implicit put options given to the short. In the discussion which follows, we assume the value of the delivery options to be zero.

The logic of the foregoing theoretical pricing relationship can be readily seen by referring back to the formula for the invoice price discussed in Section 13.3.3. In particular, at expiration of the futures contract, futures prices must converge to the relevant cash price. Otherwise, a profitable arbitrage opportunity would exist. (Remember: the theoretical price is the no-arbitrage price.) Thus, the invoice price on the futures contract should be equal to the purchase price of the cash bond that the short delivers (or the cheapest-to-deliver bond), where the cash price is equal to

$$CP_t \times \$100,000 + \text{Accrued interest}$$

and CP_t is defined as the *quoted* cash price (in decimal form). If this expression for the purchase price of the cash bond is set equal to the invoice price as defined in Section 13.3.3, it is clear that *at delivery* the theoretical futures can be defined as

$$FP^*_{t,T} = \frac{CP^*_t}{CF^*}$$

where $FP^*_{t,T}$ = the theoretical futures price (in decimal form) at time t for a contract deliverable at time T.

CP^*_t = the quoted cash price (in decimal form) of the cheapest-to-deliver bond at time t.

CF^* = the relevant conversion factor on the cheapest-to-deliver bond.

Prior to the contract's expiration, however, this expression will not be accurate because it does not incorporate the net cost-of-carry, which would be necessary to do a cash-and-carry arbitrage. The theoretical (or no-arbitrage) futures price at any time prior to expiration, therefore, will be[10]

$$FP^*_{t,T} = \frac{CP^*_t}{CF^*} + C^*_{t,T}$$

---

[10] This theoretical futures price equation ignores the interest earnings that would be earned by reinvesting the coupon income received during the holding period. This omission makes a trivial difference in the calculation of the theoretical futures price.

where $C^*_{t,T}$ is the net carrying cost (in decimal form) from time t to T (expiration) on the cheapest-to-deliver bond and is defined as

$$C^*_{t,T} = \frac{1}{CF^*}\left[(CP^*_t + AI)(R_t \times \frac{T-t}{360}) - Y \times \frac{T-t}{365}\right]$$

where AI = the accrued interest (in decimal form) on the cash bond from the last coupon payment date to time t.

R_t = the financing rate (generally the repo rate), quoted on a 360-day year basis, in decimal form.

Y = the annual coupon rate on the cash bond.

If the theoretical futures price is not equal to the actual futures price, a profitable arbitrage opportunity will exist. In particular, if the actual futures price were to exceed the theoretical price (or the adjusted cash price of the cheapest-to-deliver bond plus the net carry), arbitragers could profit by shorting futures and purchasing the cheapest-to-deliver bond, and carrying this bond to delivery. Alternatively, if futures prices were cheap, they would do just the reverse: short the cheapest-to-deliver bond and purchase futures. Such cash-and-carry arbitrage would continue until the actual futures price equaled the adjusted price of the cheapest-to-deliver bond plus the net carry (ignoring transaction costs, accrued interest and implicit delivery options).

It is also clear that the theoretical futures price may be higher or lower than the adjusted cash price of the cheapest-to-deliver bond, since the net carry can be either positive or negative. If the borrowing rate were higher than the coupon yield on the bond, the futures price would be higher than the adjusted cash price. If the borrowing rate were lower than the coupon yield, the futures price would be below the adjusted cash price. In addition, as a futures contract approaches its delivery date, the difference between the adjusted cash price of the cheapest-to-deliver bond and the futures price will diminish because the net cost of carry will decline.[11]

Figure 13-2 exhibits these features. It graphs daily futures prices of the September 1989 T-bond contract along with daily adjusted cash prices of the cheapest-to-deliver bond for the period June 1 through September 20, 1989. Table 13.8 lists the bonds which were the cheapest to deliver against the September 89 futures contract during this period. The cheapest-to-deliver bond changed frequently, from one day to the next, ranging from the 9.375 percent, February 15,

---

[11]As discussed in Section 13.3.1, the implied delivery options on a T-bond futures contract may affect the convergence of the futures and cash prices. The two prices will rarely fully converge on the last day of trading, as the short continues to enjoy certain delivery options until the end of the delivery month. Since the long will require some compensation for the short's put options, the actual futures price will typically be at a slight discount to the cash price at expiration. The amount of the discount will vary with the market's evaluation of the remaining implied delivery options.

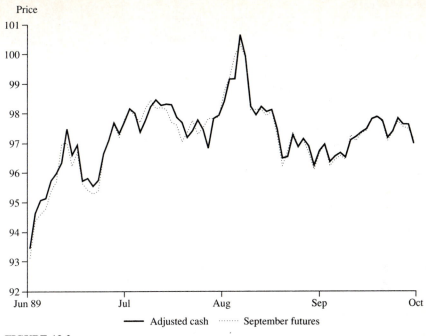

Price

FIGURE 13-2
T-bond futures prices versus T-bond cash prices: Sep 89 futures price versus adjusted cash price of cheapest-to-deliver bond (daily from June 1, 1989, to September 20, 1989).

TABLE 13.8
Cheapest-to-deliver bonds on Sep 1989 futures contract (June 1, 1989 to September 20, 1989)

| Date | September Futures Price | Cheapest-to-Deliver Bonds | | | | |
		Coupon Rate	Maturity Date	Cash Price	Conversion Factor	Adjusted Cash Price
890601	92.938	12.500	Aug 15, 2014	134.563	1.4427	93.27129
890602	94.188	12.000	Aug 15, 2013	130.781	1.3848	94.44056
890605	94.406	13.250	May 15, 2014	143.656	1.5141	94.87900
890606	94.594	12.500	Aug 15, 2014	136.969	1.4427	94.93921
890607	95.188	13.250	May 15, 2014	144.656	1.5141	95.53946
890608	95.500	10.375	Nov 15, 2012	117.281	1.2245	95.77893
890609	96.781	9.375	Feb 15, 2006	108.031	1.1236	96.14747
890612	96.813	12.000	Aug 15, 2013	134.719	1.3848	97.28393
890613	96.031	12.000	Aug 15, 2013	133.500	1.3848	96.40381
890614	96.500	12.000	Aug 15, 2013	133.969	1.3848	96.74234
890615	95.438	10.375	Nov 15, 2012	116.969	1.2245	95.52372
890616	95.219	12.000	Aug 15, 2013	132.406	1.3848	95.61402
890619	95.094	12.500	Aug 15, 2014	137.563	1.4427	95.35073
890621	95.188	12.500	Aug 15, 2014	137.844	1.4427	95.54571
890623	96.406	12.000	Aug 15, 2013	133.563	1.3848	96.44894
890626	96.875	12.000	Aug 15, 2013	134.188	1.3848	96.90027
890627	97.438	12.000	Aug 15, 2013	135.000	1.3848	97.48700
890628	97.000	12.000	Aug 15, 2013	134.500	1.3848	97.12593
890629	97.594	13.250	May 15, 2014	147.656	1.5141	97.52083
890630	97.938	12.000	Aug 15, 2013	135.656	1.3848	97.96093

(continued)

TABLE 13.8—cont'd.

Date	September Futures Price	Cheapest-to-Deliver Bonds				
		Coupon Rate	Maturity Date	Cash Price	Conversion Factor	Adjusted Cash Price
890703	97.719	13.250	May 15, 2014	148.094	1.5141	97.80978
890705	97.500	12.000	Aug 15, 2013	134.563	1.3848	97.17107
890706	97.969	13.250	May 15, 2014	147.719	1.5141	97.56211
890707	98.250	12.000	Aug 15, 2013	135.750	1.3848	98.02859
890710	97.969	13.250	May 15, 2014	148.781	1.5141	98.26385
890711	98.000	13.250	May 15, 2014	148.500	1.5141	98.07806
890712	97.938	12.000	Aug 15, 2013	135.875	1.3848	98.11886
890713	97.500	13.250	May 15, 2014	148.531	1.5141	98.09873
890714	97.406	13.250	May 15, 2014	147.875	1.5141	97.66527
890717	96.844	12.500	Aug 15, 2014	140.656	1.4427	97.49518
890718	97.156	12.000	Aug 15, 2013	134.313	1.3848	96.99054
890719	97.563	12.500	Aug 15, 2014	140.250	1.4427	97.21355
890720	97.094	12.000	Aug 15, 2013	135.125	1.3848	97.57726
890721	97.313	12.000	Aug 15, 2013	134.688	1.3848	97.26133
890724	97.625	7.500	Nov 15, 2016	91.313	0.945	96.62698
890725	97.625	12.500	Aug 15, 2014	140.844	1.4427	97.62514
890726	97.688	12.000	Aug 15, 2013	135.344	1.3848	97.73526
890727	98.531	10.375	Nov 12, 2012	120.250	1.2245	98.20334
890728	99.000	12.000	Aug 15, 2013	137.031	1.3848	98.95385
890731	99.750	14.000	Nov 15, 2011	153.625	1.5523	98.96605
890802	100.125	12.750	Nov 15, 2010	143.094	1.4245	100.4519
890803	99.688	12.000	Aug 15, 2013	138.094	1.3848	99.72111
890804	97.906	10.375	Nov 15, 2012	120.063	1.2245	98.05022
890807	97.938	10.375	Nov 15, 2012	119.688	1.2245	97.74397
890808	97.938	12.500	Aug 15, 2014	141.438	1.4427	98.03666
890809	97.719	12.500	Aug 15, 2014	141.188	1.4427	97.86338
890810	97.875	12.500	Aug 15, 2014	141.281	1.4427	97.92839
890811	97.063	12.500	Aug 14, 2014	140.344	1.4427	97.27857
890814	96.031	12.000	Aug 15, 2013	133.344	1.3848	96.29101
890815	96.531	10.375	Nov 15, 2012	117.969	1.2245	96.34038
890816	97.156	12.000	Aug 15, 2013	134.438	1.3848	97.08080
890817	96.688	10.375	Nov 15, 2012	118.375	1.2245	96.67211
890818	96.906	12.000	Aug 15, 2013	134.250	1.3848	96.94540
890821	96.469	12.500	Aug 15, 2014	139.500	1.4427	96.69369
890822	95.906	12.500	Aug 15, 2014	138.563	1.4427	96.04387
890823	96.469	12.500	Aug 15, 2014	139.281	1.4427	96.54210
890824	96.750	12.500	Aug 15, 2014	139.594	1.4427	96.75871
890828	96.031	12.500	Aug 15, 2014	138.750	1.4427	96.17384
890829	96.250	12.000	Aug 15, 2013	133.438	1.3848	96.35867
890830	96.375	12.000	Aug 15, 2013	133.594	1.3848	96.47154
890831	96.250	11.750	Nov 15, 2014	132.063	1.3711	96.31864
890901	97.063	10.375	Nov 15, 2012	118.656	1.2245	96.90183
890905	96.875	12.000	Aug 15, 2013	134.344	1.3848	97.01314
890906	97.125	11.750	Nov 15, 2014	133.219	1.3711	97.16198
890907	97.219	11.750	Nov 15, 2014	133.375	1.3711	97.27590
890908	97.625	12.000	Aug 15, 2013	135.188	1.3848	97.62240
890911	97.719	12.500	Aug 15, 2014	140.938	1.4427	97.69009
890912	97.500	12.500	Aug 14, 2014	140.750	1.4427	97.56013
890913	96.875	11.750	Nov 15, 2014	132.969	1.3711	96.97965
890914	97.188	12.000	Aug 15, 2013	134.594	1.3848	97.19367
890915	97.531	12.750	Nov 15, 2010	139.094	1.4245	97.64394
890918	97.344	11.750	Nov 15, 2014	133.594	1.3711	97.43548
890919	97.281	11.750	Nov 15, 2014	133.594	1.3711	97.43548
890920	96.938	11.750	Nov 15, 2014	132.719	1.3711	96.79731

2006 bond to the 11.50 percent, August 15, 2014 bond. Figure 13-2 illustrates the convergence property of these two prices as the expiration date of the futures contract approaches. It also shows that the futures price tracks the adjusted cash price reasonably well.[12] Variations in the net cost of carry, therefore, are not large enough to affect this price relationship significantly.

13.5 IDENTIFYING THE CHEAPEST-TO-DELIVER BOND

Identifying the cheapest-to-deliver bond is essential either for pricing T-bond futures or for making optimal delivery decisions. With a *flat* yield curve (which is unlikely), the cheapest-to-deliver bond can be easily determined by using durations:

- If market yields are greater than 8 percent, deliver the bond with the highest duration.
- If market yields are less than 8 percent, deliver the bond with the lowest duration.

As long as the yield curve is flat these rules work well for all levels of interest rates. They work because of the way that conversion factors are calculated. In particular, if market yields are above (below) eight percent, the prices of long-maturity bonds will fall faster (slower) than is implicit in the calculation of the conversion factor. Thus, it becomes optimal to deliver long-maturity (high duration) bonds when yields are above eight percent, and short-maturity (low duration) bonds when yields are below eight percent.

When the yield curve is *not flat,* identifying the cheapest-to-deliver bond on any given day against a particular T-bond contract is a cumbersome computational task. One procedure is to calculate theoretical futures prices using, alternately, each of the eligible cash bonds. The one that yields the *lowest* theoretical futures price will be the cheapest-to-deliver bond. Another method is to derive the implied repo rate for each eligible cash bond. The one with the *highest* implied repo rate will be the cheapest-to-deliver bond.

While both methods are tediously time-consuming, the good news is that almost any broker dealing in futures can readily identify for you the cheapest-to-deliver bond. These firms possess computer programs that continuously calculate the cheapest-to-deliver bond as both futures and cash prices change.

---

[12]The close relationship between movements in futures prices and movements in adjusted cash prices can be seen in the data reported in Table 13.8. A regression of the September futures price on the adjusted cash price yields an intercept term that is not statistically different from zero at the five percent significant level and a slope coefficient that is not statistically different from one at the five percent significant level.

13.5.1   Using Theoretical Futures Prices

The cash bond that yields the *lowest theoretical futures price* is the cheapest-to-deliver bond. In order to identify the cheapest-to-deliver bond, therefore, we can calculate $FP^*_{t,T}$ for all eligible bonds, using quoted cash prices for each bond, the relevant accrued interests, the applicable conversion factors, and the net cost-of-carry on each bond.

Table 13.9 shows the bonds that are deliverable on the March 90 T-bond futures contract and the theoretical futures prices that correspond to each of these cash bonds as of the close of trading on December 13, 1989. Columns 1 and 2 provide the characteristics (coupon and maturity date) of each cash bond. Column 3 is the cash price in decimal form (which is the average of the bid-asked quotes in Table 13.3). Column 4 is the applicable conversion factor, and column 5 is the resulting adjusted cash price. Column 6 is the accrued interest on each bond from the last coupon payment date (either August 15, 1989, or November 15, 1989) to December 14, 1989 (the cash settlement day for purchasing the bond). Column 7 is the net carrying cost computed using the equation in Section 13.4, expressed in decimal form. Column 8 is the theoretical futures price obtained by adding the adjusted cash price (column 5) and the net carrying cost (column 7) together. Column 9 is the implied repo rate (IRR), which is discussed in the section which follows.

Table 13.9 reveals that the 10.375 percent, Nov 2007-12 bond is cheapest to deliver: it has a theoretical futures price of 99.7321 or $99\frac{23}{32}$, which is the lowest. This price is derived as follows:

1. The current cash price of the bond (CP^*_t) is $121\frac{26}{32}$, or, in decimal form, 121.8125.

2. The conversion factor is 1.2216, and the adjusted cash price is 99.7155 (121.8125/1.2216).

3. Since the cash settlement day is December 14, 1989, the bond has 29 days of accrued interest from the last coupon payment day, November 15, 1989. The accrued interest in decimal form, therefore, is 0.8243 ($10.375 \times \frac{29}{365}$).

4. On December 13, 1989, the overnight repo rate is 8.40% and there are 106 days $(T - t)$ remaining from the cash settlement date to the last delivery date of the March 90 T-bond futures contract: March 30, 1990. The net carrying cost is therefore

$$\frac{1}{1.2216}\left[\left((121.8125 + 0.8243) \times 0.084 \times \tfrac{106}{360}\right) - 10.375 \times \tfrac{106}{365}\right] = 0.0165$$

5. Thus, the theoretical futures price $(FP^*_{t,T})$ is simply:

$$99.7155 + 0.0165 = 99.7321$$

The theoretical price of 99.7321 (or $99\frac{23}{32}$) is very close to the actual March 90 futures settlement price of $99\frac{17}{32}$ on December 13, 1989 (see Table 13.6). The

TABLE 13.9
Identifying the cheapest-to-deliver bond: Deliverable bonds on Mar 90 Treasury bond futures, December 13, 1989

Bonds								
Coupon (1)	Maturity (2)	Cash price (decimal) (3)	Conversion factor (4)	Adjusted cash price (3 ÷ 4) (5)	Accrued interest (6)	Net carry (7)	Theoretical futures price (5 + 7) (8)	Implied repo rate (9)
7-1/4	May 2016	92.4375	0.9184	100.6506	0.5760	0.2124	100.8630	3.93
7-1/2	Nov 2016	95.1250	0.9453	100.6294	0.5959	0.2004	100.8298	4.04
8-1/8	Aug 2019	102.7813	1.0139	101.3722	2.6935	0.2457	101.6179	1.58
8-3/4	May 2017	108.9063	1.0825	100.6062	0.6952	0.1568	100.7630	4.26
8-7/8	Aug 2017	110.2813	1.0963	100.5940	2.9421	0.2034	100.7974	4.23
8-7/8	Feb 2019	110.8750	1.0977	101.0067	2.9421	0.2165	101.2232	2.85
9	Nov 2018	112.2500	1.1116	100.9806	0.7151	0.1622	101.1428	3.01
9-1/8	May 2018	113.4688	1.1250	100.8611	0.7250	0.1550	101.0161	3.43
9-1/4	Feb 2016	113.9688	1.1353	100.3865	3.0664	0.1835	100.5700	4.97
9-3/8	Feb 2006	112.5625	1.1217	100.3499	3.1079	0.1233	100.4732	5.29
9-7/8	Nov 2015	120.6875	1.2027	100.3471	0.7846	0.1136	100.4607	5.27
10	May 2005–10	117.0313	1.1729	99.7794	0.7945	0.0086	99.7880	7.53
10-3/8*	Nov 2007–12	121.8125	1.2216	99.7155	0.8243	0.0165	99.7321*	7.72*
10-5/8	Aug 2015	128.5938	1.2826	100.2602	3.5223	0.1419	100.4022	5.52
10-3/4	Aug 2005	123.8750	1.2396	99.9314	3.5637	0.0243	99.9557	6.99
11-1/4	Feb 2015	135.0938	1.3477	100.2402	3.7295	0.1235	100.3637	5.65
11-3/4	Nov 2009–14	136.4062	1.3672	99.7705	0.9336	-0.0113	99.7592	7.63
12	May 2005	134.6250	1.3458	100.0334	0.9534	-0.0978	99.9356	7.03
12	Aug 2008–13	137.6875	1.3802	99.7591	3.9781	0.0137	99.7728	7.60
12-1/2	Aug 2009–14	143.4688	1.4379	99.7766	4.1438	0.0145	99.7911	7.54
12-3/4	Nov 2005–10	141.6250	1.4177	99.8977	1.0130	-0.1233	99.7744	7.57
13-1/4	May 2009–14	150.6875	1.5084	99.8989	1.0527	-0.0629	99.8360	7.37
13-7/8	May 2006–11	152.4688	1.5250	99.9795	1.1024	-0.1516	99.8280	7.40
14	Nov 2006–11	154.3438	1.5444	99.9377	1.1123	-0.1430	99.7947	7.51

*The cheapest-to-deliver bond on December 13, 1989. *Note:* Prices are closing prices on December 13, 1989.

small price discrepancy can be explained by the omitted value of the implied delivery options possessed by the short. As discussed earlier, the actual futures price is normally several thirty-seconds below the theoretical futures price because of the implicit delivery put options, the value of which is not incorporated in the theoretical futures price.

13.5.2   Using Implied Repo Rates

Another way to identify the cheapest-to-deliver bond is to calculate the implied repo rates (IRR) on the alternative eligible cash T-bonds. The bond that yields the *highest implied repo rate* will be the cheapest-to-deliver bond.

Using the cost of carry relationship described in Section 13.4, we can determine the implied repo rate on each bond by finding the implied R that will equate the following equation:

$$C_{t,T} = FP_{t,T} - \frac{CP_t}{CF}$$

where $FP_{t,T}$ is the *actual* futures price, CP_t is the price of the relevant cash bond, CF is the applicable conversion factor, and $C_{t,T}$ is the *implied* net carry. Substituting the definitions stated earlier in Section 13.4, and solving for R yields

$$IRR_t = \left(\frac{360}{T-t}\right)\left(\frac{1}{CP_t + AI}\right)\left(FP_{t,T} \times CF - CP_t + Y \times \frac{T-t}{365}\right)$$

where $FP_{t,T}$, CP_t and the other variables are as defined in Section 13.4 (and are in decimal form). The term in the brackets on the right side of this equation is the dollar difference between the invoice price that will have to be paid at delivery and the cost of the cash T-bond adjusted for the coupon interest earned while holding (or carrying) the bond. Dividing this difference by $(CP_t + AI)$, the *transaction price* of the T-bond (or the funds actually invested), turns this difference into a rate of return, and multiplying by $360/(T - t)$ annualizes this rate of return.

The IRR_t, therefore, represents the riskless rate of return that can be earned on a cash-and-carry arbitrage without borrowing to finance it. Thus, a difference between this rate and the actual borrowing rate (R_t) suggests a profitable arbitrage opportunity. If the IRR_t is greater than R_t, the correct arbitrage is to buy the cash bond and short the futures; if the borrowing rate exceeds the IRR_t, the correct arbitrage is to buy the futures and short the cash bond.[13]

The cash bond with the highest implied repo rate is obviously the one that is most profitable to deliver. It is, therefore, the cheapest-to-deliver bond. Arbitrage will also assure that the futures contract is priced off this bond. If this were not true, there would exist a profitable cash-and-carry arbitrage.

---

[13]The arbitrager must, of course, also take into consideration the implicit delivery options when determining whether a profitable arbitrage exists.

As we saw earlier in Table 13.9, the 10.375 percent, Nov 2007-12 bond was the cheapest to deliver because it had the lowest theoretical futures price. Column 9 of Table 13.9 also shows the implied repo rate for each bond. The 10.375 percent, Nov 2012 has the highest implied repo rate, 7.72 percent. This rate was derived as follows:

IRR_t

$$= \left(\frac{360}{106}\right)\left(\frac{1}{121.8125 + 0.8243}\right)\left(99.53 \times 1.2216 - 121.8125 + 10.375 \times \frac{106}{365}\right)$$

Other bonds with high implied repo rates that are advantageous to deliver are the Nov 2009-14, Aug 2008-13, and Nov 2005-10 bonds.

In summary, the cheapest-to-deliver bond is the one with either the highest implied repo rate or the lowest theoretical futures price.

13.6 HEDGING WITH T-BOND FUTURES

Anyone with a position (short or long) in fixed-rate securities is exposed to potential capital losses due to adverse interest rate changes. Interest rate futures provide a mechanism for managing this risk.

A bank, for example, may make a three-year, fixed-rate loan with funds raised with one-year certificates of deposit. If one-year rates were to rise before the bank could refinance the loan, it could suffer a loss. The bank, therefore, may wish to lock in its future financing costs by going long interest rate futures contracts.

Alternatively, a T-bond dealer holding an inventory of Treasury securities may want to acquire a short position in T-bond futures to hedge against the possibility that interest rates may rise before he can dispose of his inventory, causing him to incur a capital loss. The short hedge insulates the dealer from the adverse effects of a rise in interest rates by protecting his assets against a decline in value. If interest rates rise, the gain in the short futures position will offset losses on the cash assets.

As discussed in earlier chapters, determining the appropriate hedge ratio (HR) is critical to effective hedging. The hedge ratio specifies the magnitude of the futures position that is used in a hedge, and is determined by comparing the relative price sensitivities of the futures and cash instruments. The minimum-variance hedge ratio (HR^*) is the one that minimizes the variance of gains and losses on the hedged portfolio. This variance will be zero on a portfolio consisting of cash bonds and T-bond futures if

$$Q_c \times \Delta CP_t = Q_f \times \$100{,}000 \times \Delta FP_{t,T}$$

where $\quad Q_c$ = the face value of the cash T-bonds.

$\quad\quad \Delta CP_t$ = the change in the price of the cash T-bonds at time t.

$\quad\quad Q_f$ = the number of T-bond futures contracts (each T-bond futures contract has a face value of $100,000).

$\quad\quad \Delta FP_{t,T}$ = the change in the price of the T-bond futures contract being used to hedge during period t.

The minimum-variance hedge ratio, therefore, can be expressed as the ratio of the change in the price of the cash bond to the change in the price of the T-bond futures contract:

$$\frac{Q_f \times \$100,000}{Q_c} = \frac{\Delta CP_t}{\Delta FP_{t,T}}$$

$$HR^* = \frac{\Delta CP_t}{\Delta FP_{t,T}}$$

This hedge ratio is identical to the minimum-variance hedge ratio discussed earlier in Chapter 6. However, since T-bond futures prices track the adjusted spot prices of the cheapest-to-deliver bond, which can change over the life of a futures contract, this ratio must be modified to obtain an accurate measure of the hedge ratio applicable to T-bond futures.

There are two approaches commonly used to determine the minimum-variance hedge ratio for T-bond futures. The first is to use the *duration* measure discussed in Section 13.2.2. The second is to use the *regression methodology* discussed in Chapter 6. Each method has its strengths and weaknesses.

13.6.1   Using Durations to Determine Hedge Ratios

Section 13.4 showed that a close relationship exists between T-bond futures prices and the adjusted cash prices of the cheapest-to-deliver T-bond. Thus, changes in T-bond futures prices can be closely approximated as

$$\Delta FP_t = \frac{\Delta CP_t^*}{CF^*}$$

where ΔCP_t^* are changes in the price of the cheapest-to-deliver bond, and CF^* is the applicable conversion factor. Substituting this expression for ΔFP_t in the hedge ratio equation in the previous section, the minimum-variance hedge ratio becomes

$$HR^* = \frac{\Delta CP_t}{\Delta CP_t^*} \times CF^*$$

To calculate this hedge ratio, we have to identify the cheapest-to-deliver bond and, for a given change in yield, determine by how much both the price of the bond being hedged (CP_t) and the price of the cheapest-to-deliver bond (CP_t^*) will change. For example, if there is a 0.5 percentage point change in the yields on both bonds, by how much will CP_t and CP_t^* change? This will depend on the respective bond durations. As shown in Section 13.2.2, the respective bond durations can be expressed as

$$-D_{CP} = \frac{\%\Delta CP_t}{\%\Delta(1 + R_{CP})_t}$$

and

$$-D_{CP^*} = \frac{\%\Delta CP_t^*}{\%\Delta(1 + R_{CP^*})_t}$$

so that

$$\Delta CP_t = -D_{CP} \times CP_t \times \frac{\Delta R_{CP_t}}{1 + R_{CP_t}}$$

and

$$\Delta CP_t^* = -D_{CP^*} \times CP_t^* \times \frac{\Delta R_{CP_t^*}}{1 + R_{CP_t^*}}$$

where D_{CP} and D_{CP^*} are the respective bond durations, and ΔR_{CP} and ΔR_{CP^*} are the changes in yields on the two bonds. Making the appropriate substitutions into the previously defined hedge ratio equation yields

$$HR^* = \frac{-D_{CP} \times CP_t \times (1 + R_{CP_t^*}) \times \Delta R_{CP_t}}{-D_{CP^*} \times CP_t^* \times (1 + R_{CP_t}) \times \Delta R_{CP_t^*}} \times CF^*$$

With the exception of the yield changes on the respective bonds, all of the variables in this equation can be easily obtained. If, of course, the yield changes on the respective bonds are anticipated to be equal, or

$$\frac{\Delta R_{CP_t}}{\Delta R_{CP_t^*}} = 1$$

then these variables can be deleted entirely from the above equation. If the yield changes are not identical, the relationship between ΔR_{CP_t} and $\Delta R_{CP_t^*}$ must be determined and inserted into the hedge ratio equation.

Assume that on December 13, 1989, an investor purchases $10 million of the 12.00 percent, Aug 2013 bond. To hedge against adverse movements in interest rates, he establishes a short position in the March 90 T-bond futures contract. The Aug 2013 bond has an average cash price of 137.6875 (in decimal form), a yield to maturity of 8.05 percent, and a duration of 8.926. As shown previously, in Table 13.9, on December 13, the cheapest-to-deliver bond on the March 90 T-bond contract is the 10.375 percent, Nov 2012 bond, which has an average cash price of 121.8125 (in decimal form), a yield to maturity of 8.04, and a duration of 9.288. The applicable conversion factor is also 1.2216. Substituting these values into the above formula, and assuming that the changes in the yields on the two bonds are the same, the hedge ratio is

$$HR = \frac{-8.926 \times 137.6875 \times (1 + 0.0804)}{-9.288 \times 121.8125 \times (1 + 0.0805)} \times 1.2216 = 1.33$$

Since the investor wishes to hedge $10 million face value of the 12 percent bonds, to achieve the minimum-variance hedge he will have to short 133 T-bond futures contracts:

$$\left(1.33 \times \frac{\$10,000,000}{\$100,000}\right)$$

13.6.2 Using Regression Analysis to Determine Hedge Ratios

Using duration-based hedge ratios implicitly assumes that the yield curve changes in a parallel fashion over time, or that the yields on both the bond being hedged and the bond which underlies the futures contract always change by the same amount (or that $\Delta R_{CP_t} = \Delta R_{CP_t^*}$). An alternative method for estimating the minimum-variance hedge ratio is regression analysis. This approach takes into account that the two yield changes may not be the same. (The use of regression analysis to estimate hedge ratios was discussed earlier in Chapter 6.)

Specifically, the minimum-variance hedge ratio can be determined by estimating the following equation:

$$\Delta CP_t = \alpha + \beta \times \Delta FP_{t,T} + \epsilon_t$$

where CP_t is the price of the security being hedged. The estimate of β is the minimum-variance hedge ratio:

$$HR^* = \beta = \frac{\Delta CP_t}{\Delta FP_{t,T}}$$

The following two examples illustrate the use of regression analysis to structure a hedge. In these examples, actual market data are used to estimate the hedge ratio and to evaluate the performance of the hedge. The first example involves hedging a portfolio of four Treasury bonds of varying maturities. The second example involves hedging an investment in a corporate bond, the Southern Bell $8\frac{5}{8}$ percent of 2006, which is rated AAA by Standard & Poor's. Although the behavior of corporate bond yields is often different from that of T-bonds, we show that hedging with T-bond futures can still be quite effective in reducing price risk if basis risk is correctly taken into account when computing the hedge ratio.

EXAMPLE 1: HEDGING A PORTFOLIO OF TREASURY BONDS. On July 1, 1989, we wish to hedge a cash portfolio containing $5 million face value of each of the following four Treasury bonds:

- $10\frac{3}{4}$ of Feb 2003
- $9\frac{3}{8}$ of Feb 2006
- $10\frac{3}{8}$ of Nov 2012
- $7\frac{1}{4}$ of May 2016

The average maturity of this portfolio is about 20 years, 5 years longer than the minimum maturity of T-bonds acceptable for delivery against a T-bond futures contract. The portfolio accrues coupon interest of $157,291.67 per month, and has an average annual coupon rate of 9.44 percent. Our objective is to hedge this portfolio against all interest rate (or price) risks. Specifically, we want to minimize the standard deviation of month-to-month changes in the total return on the hedged portfolio, for the period July 1989 through December 1989.

TABLE 13.10
Prices of Treasury bonds used in T-bond portfolio example
(January 87 to June 89)

Month	$10\frac{3}{4}$ of 2003	$9\frac{3}{8}$ of 2006	$10\frac{3}{8}$ of 2012	$7\frac{1}{6}$ of 2016	Value of bond portfolio	Average portfolio price	Change in portfolio price
Jan 87	126.81	116.75	126.00	96.63	$23,311,572.92	116.55	
Feb 87	126.44	116.19	125.25	96.06	23,199,145.83	115.98	−0.57
Mar 87	128.50	117.69	127.31	96.94	23,526,718.75	117.61	1.63
Apr 87	124.56	113.56	123.06	92.56	22,692,291.67	113.43	−4.18
May 87	117.38	106.56	115.50	85.75	21,267,864.58	106.30	−7.13
Jun 87	116.69	106.00	114.56	85.19	21,131,437.50	105.61	−0.69
Jul 87	117.19	106.50	115.19	85.81	21,245,010.42	106.17	0.56
Aug 87	112.91	102.22	110.66	81.28	20,366,583.33	101.77	−4.4
Sep 87	110.94	100.44	108.53	79.94	20,006,156.25	99.96	−1.81
Oct 87	106.50	95.81	103.72	75.50	19,091,729.17	95.38	−4.58
Nov 87	112.50	101.56	109.34	80.81	20,227,302.08	101.05	5.67
Dec 87	111.56	101.28	109.22	80.34	20,138,875.00	100.60	−0.45
Jan 88	113.28	102.94	110.81	82.03	20,472,447.92	102.26	1.66
Feb 88	118.41	108.19	116.56	87.19	21,540,020.83	107.59	5.33
Mar 88	118.75	108.69	117.19	87.72	21,641,593.75	108.09	0.5
Apr 88	114.44	103.91	111.62	82.87	20,667,166.67	103.21	−4.88
May 88	112.62	102.28	109.75	81.22	20,320,739.58	101.47	−1.74
Jun 88	112.06	101.62	109.00	80.44	20,184,312.50	100.78	−0.69
Jul 88	113.78	103.56	110.78	82.28	20,549,885.42	102.60	1.82
Aug 88	111.44	101.47	108.25	79.81	20,079,458.33	100.24	−2.36
Sep 88	110.62	100.81	107.47	79.03	19,929,031.25	99.48	−0.76
Oct 88	113.50	103.72	110.66	81.97	20,526,604.17	102.46	2.98
Nov 88	115.22	105.50	112.66	83.91	20,900,177.08	104.32	1.86
Dec 88	112.91	102.81	110.28	81.56	20,415,750.00	101.89	−2.43
Jan 89	111.56	101.50	109.44	81.25	20,227,322.92	100.94	−0.95
Feb 89	113.84	103.88	112.00	83.62	20,708,895.83	103.34	2.4
Mar 89	110.59	100.62	108.44	80.47	20,048,468.75	100.03	−3.31
Apr 89	111.59	101.78	109.44	81.44	20,256,041.67	101.06	1.03
May 89	112.19	102.47	110.09	82.06	20,385,614.58	101.70	0.64
Jun 89	115.78	106.25	114.25	85.62	21,141,187.50	105.47	3.77

To estimate the minimum-variance hedge ratio, we compare price changes on the individual bonds and changes in the value of the portfolio as a whole during the prior 30 months, from January 1987 through June 1989, to price movements in T-bond futures over the same period. Table 13.10 shows beginning-of-month prices for the four bonds from January 1987 to June 1989. The *value of bond portfolio* column is the sum of the market values of the four bonds. The last two columns give the *average portfolio price* and the *monthly change in the portfolio price*. Table 13.11 provides near month T-bond futures prices as well as monthly changes in these prices for the same period.

TABLE 13.11
Treasury bond near month futures prices
(January 1987 to June 1989)

Month	Futures price	Price changes
Jan 87	99.90	
Feb 87	99.34	−0.56
Mar 87	100.78	1.44
Apr 87	97.71	−3.07
May 87	91.81	−5.90
Jun 87	90.78	−1.03
Jul 87	91.59	0.81
Aug 87	88.18	−3.41
Sep 87	86.03	−2.15
Oct 87	81.75	−4.28
Nov 87	87.12	5.37
Dec 87	86.43	−0.69
Jan 88	88.31	1.88
Feb 88	93.84	5.53
Mar 88	93.68	−0.16
Apr 88	89.28	−4.40
May 88	87.34	−1.94
Jun 88	88.65	1.31
Jul 88	90.62	1.97
Aug 88	88.06	−2.56
Sep 88	86.28	−1.78
Oct 88	90.75	4.47
Nov 88	91.18	0.43
Dec 88	90.53	−0.65
Jan 89	88.28	−2.25
Feb 89	90.90	2.62
Mar 89	87.59	−3.31
Apr 89	88.68	1.09
May 89	89.34	0.66
Jun 89	93.03	3.69

To determine the minimum-variance hedge ratio, we regress the average price changes on the cash portfolio on near month T-bond futures price changes, obtaining the following estimates:

$$\Delta CP_t = -0.14 + 1.006 \times \Delta FP_{t,T}$$
$$R^2 = 0.93$$

The estimate 1.006, therefore, is the minimum-variance hedge ratio. The high R^2 of 0.93 also indicates that T-bond futures prices tracked changes in cash portfolio values extremely well during the estimation period. Thus, to hedge the bond portfolio against interest rate risk a short position of 201 T-bond futures contracts would be appropriate:

$$Q_f = \frac{\$20,000,000}{\$100,000} \times 1.006 = 201$$

Table 13.12 shows the performance of the hedged portfolio and compares it to the performance of the unhedged cash portfolio. It is clear that the hedged portfolio is far less risky: the standard deviation of monthly profits and losses on the hedged portfolio is less than a tenth of what it is on the unhedged portfolio. Also, the average return on the unhedged portfolio is 1.79 percent per month with a standard deviation of 2.76 percent, while the average return on the hedged portfolio is 0.77 percent per month, with a standard deviation of only 0.26 percent. Hedging with T-bond futures, therefore, proved to be quite successful in reducing interest rate risk. However, there was a cost. The average monthly portfolio return fell from 1.79 percent to 0.77 percent.

EXAMPLE 2: HEDGING A CORPORATE BOND.   Assume that at the beginning of July 1989, our objective is to minimize the interest rate risk on a $10 million face value position of Southern Bell $8\frac{5}{8}$ percent of 2006 bonds. Since this is a corporate bond, its yield will behave somewhat differently from a T-bond's. In particular, the price of a corporate bond may change because of changes in the market's perception of its default risk. This risk does not exist for T-bonds. Figure 13-3 shows the general price relationship between corporate bonds and T-bonds over almost a six-year period.

Table 13.13 provides the monthly price data from January 1987 through June 1989 used to estimate the hedge ratio. Regressing the monthly price changes of the corporate bond on the monthly price changes of the near month T-bond futures over the 30-month sample period provided in Table 13.13 yields the following equation:

$$\Delta CP_t = 0.0255 + 0.899 \times \Delta FP_{t,T}$$
$$R^2 = 0.86$$

The R^2 is 0.86, indicating that T-bond futures prices do not track the market value of the corporate bond as well as they did the value of the portfolio of Treasury bonds in the previous example. However, an R^2 of 0.86 is still high,

TABLE 13.12
Performance of hedged Treasury bond portfolio (July 1989–December 1989)

Beginning of month	Unhedged cash position					Futures position		Hedged portfolio (cash + futures)	
	Average portfolio price	Accrued coupon interest (1) $	Change in market value (2) $	Dollar profit (3) = (1) + (2) $	% return	Near month futures price	Profit on futures position (4) $	Net profit (5) = (3) + (4) $	Net % return
June	105.47					93.03			
July	110.44	157,291.67	993,500.00	1,150,791.67	5.46	97.72	(942,690.00)	208,101.67	0.99
August	113.44	157,291.67	599,000.00	756,291.67	3.25	100.38	(534,660.00)	221,631.67	1.00
September	109.68	157,291.67	(751,500.00)	(594,208.33)	(2.53)	97.06	667,320.00	(73,111.67)	0.32
October	108.58	157,291.67	(221,000.00)	(63,708.33)	(0.30)	95.84	245,220.00	181,511.67	0.83
November	112.35	157,291.67	755,500.00	912,791.67	4.22	99.34	(703,500.00)	209,291.67	0.96
December	112.31	157,291.67	(9,500.00)	147,791.67	0.63	99.47	(26,130.00)	(121,661.67)	0.54
Mean				384,958.33	1.79		(215,740.00)	169,218.34	0.77
Standard deviation				608,182.31	2.76		562,184.30	54,028.07	0.26

*Short 201 contracts.

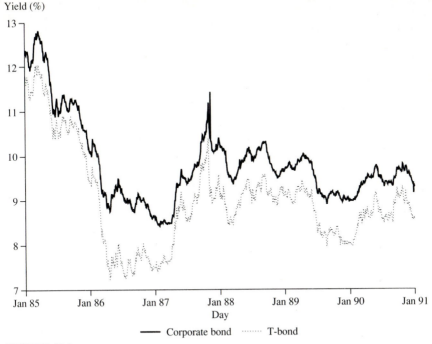

Yield (%)

FIGURE 13-3
T-bond (30-year) versus Moody AAA Corporate bond (20-year) yields: Daily from January 1, 1985, to November 30, 1990.

and suggests a good linear relationship between the two price series. The estimate 0.899 indicates that about 90 T-bond futures contracts are needed to establish a minimum-variance hedge:

$$Q_f = \frac{\$10,000,000}{\$100,000} \times 0.899 = 90$$

Table 13.14 compares the respective performances of the hedged and un-hedged portfolios. The monthly average return on the unhedged portfolio is 1.85 percent, with a standard deviation of 4.57 percent. Hedging reduces the standard deviation of returns by about half (from 4.57% to 2.07%), but also lowers the average monthly return from 1.85 percent to 0.81 percent. Thus, the hedge clearly succeeds in reducing the portfolio's exposure to interest rate risk, but at the cost of lowering profits.

13.6.3 Duration versus Regression

Which technique, duration or regression analysis, is superior for estimating hedge ratios? An advantage of the duration method is that it explicitly utilizes known

TABLE 13.13

Prices of Southern Bell $8\frac{5}{8}$% of 2006 bonds compared to T-bond futures prices

Month	Corporate bond prices	Cash price changes	Near month futures T-bond prices	Futures price changes
Jan 87	98.25		99.90	
Feb 87	99.25	1.00	99.34	−0.56
Mar 87	99.75	0.50	100.78	1.44
Apr 87	96.75	−3.00	97.71	−3.07
May 87	90.78	−5.97	91.81	−5.90
Jun 87	89.13	−1.65	90.78	−1.03
Jul 87	90.00	0.87	91.59	0.81
Aug 87	86.33	−3.67	88.18	−3.41
Sep 87	85.50	−0.83	86.03	−2.15
Oct 87	80.63	−4.87	81.75	−4.28
Nov 87	85.50	4.87	87.12	5.37
Dec 87	86.25	0.75	86.43	−0.69
Jan 88	88.50	2.25	88.31	1.88
Feb 88	92.75	4.25	93.84	5.53
Mar 88	92.87	0.12	93.68	−0.16
Apr 88	88.25	−4.62	89.28	−4.40
May 88	86.50	−1.75	87.34	−1.94
Jun 88	87.00	0.50	88.65	1.31
Jul 88	89.00	2.00	90.62	1.97
Aug 88	86.75	−2.25	88.06	−2.56
Sep 88	86.19	−0.56	86.28	−1.78
Oct 88	89.38	3.19	90.75	4.47
Nov 88	92.50	3.12	91.18	0.43
Dec 88	88.88	−3.62	90.53	−0.65
Jan 89	88.50	−0.38	88.28	−2.25
Feb 89	90.75	2.25	90.90	2.62
Mar 89	87.88	−2.87	87.59	−3.31
Apr 89	87.88	0.00	88.68	1.09
May 89	89.25	1.37	89.34	0.66
Jun 89	92.81	3.56	93.03	3.69

information about the maturity, coupon, and price characteristics of the relevant bonds. This method, however, requires either that we assume what the relationship between ΔR_{CP} and ΔR_{CP*} will be in the future or that we find another way to estimate this relationship.

Regression analysis uses historical data and statistical techniques to estimate hedge ratios. Thus, it depends critically on the implicit assumption that the estimated historical credit market relationships are stable and will continue to hold in the future. If this is not likely, duration may be a preferable procedure.

TABLE 13.14
Performance of hedged corporate bond portfolio (Southern Bell bonds), June 1 to December 31, 1989

Beginning of month	Unhedged cash position					Futures position		Hedged portfolio (cash + futures)	
	Average portfolio price	Accrued coupon interest (1) $	Change in market value (2) $	Dollar profit (3) = (1) + (2) $	% return	Near month futures price	Profit on futures position* (4) $	Net profit (5) = (3) + (4) $	Net % return
June	92.81					93.03			
July	96.75	71,875.00	788,000.00	859,875.00	9.26	97.72	(422,100.00)	437,775.00	4.73
August	97.83	71,875.00	216,000.00	287,875.00	2.98	100.38	(239,400.00)	48,475.00	0.51
September	95.25	71,875.00	(516,000.00)	(444,125.00)	(4.54)	97.06	298,800.00	(145,325.00)	(1.48)
October	94.35	71,875.00	(180,000.00)	(108,125.00)	(1.14)	95.84	109,800.00	1,675.00	0.02
November	96.50	71,875.00	430,000.00	501,875.00	5.32	99.34	(315,000.00)	186,875.00	2.00
December	95.75	71,875.00	(150,000.00)	(78,125.00)	(0.81)	99.47	(11,700.00)	(89,825.00)	(0.94)
Mean				169,875.00	1.85		(96,600.00)	73,275.00	0.81
Standard deviation				431,283.36	4.57		251,724.31	194,033.67	2.07

*Short 90 contracts.

A useful procedure is to estimate hedge ratios using both the duration and regression analysis approaches to see if they yield similar hedge ratios. If they do not, it is important to understand why and to make explicit the underlying assumptions you are using in adopting a particular hedge ratio.

13.7 PORTFOLIO DURATION ADJUSTMENTS

In addition to hedging, long-term interest rate futures can be used to increase or decrease the duration of fixed-income portfolios. For example, adding a short futures position to a bond portfolio will lower the duration of the portfolio, while adding a long futures position to a portfolio will increase its duration.

Suppose that a portfolio manager anticipates a general decline in interest rates and wants to increase the duration of his portfolio to capture the anticipated rally in long-term bonds. He can do this by adding longer-maturity bonds, which will lengthen the average maturity of the cash portfolio and increase its price sensitivity. Alternatively, he may add a long position in T-bond futures to accomplish the same goal. Both strategies will increase the duration of the portfolio, and will result in a larger increase in the value of the portfolio if interest rates fall. However, using T-bond futures to adjust the portfolio duration will usually be the lower cost alternative because of lower transaction costs.

Thus, interest rate futures have numerous money management applications, ranging from hedging interest rate risk to modifying the duration of a portfolio.

CONCLUSION

This chapter completes our discussion of interest rate futures. Chapter 12 examines short-term interest rate futures, and this chapter discusses long-term interest rate futures. Together, the two chapters cover a large body of material dealing with fixed-income securities, both in cash and in futures markets. They include discussions of various fundamental topics such as the term structure of interest rates, the concept of duration, the pricing of fixed-income securities in cash markets, and the relationship between market yields and the prices of fixed income securities. Knowledge of these topics is necessary to understand the pricing of interest rate futures and how interest rate futures are used to hedge interest rate risk.

Today, in every country with futures markets, bond futures are the dominant futures contract. This chapter includes an in-depth analysis of U.S. T-bond futures. It discusses the delivery mechanism used and the pricing of these futures, and it demonstrates how to use these futures to hedge the interest rate risk associated with a fixed-income asset portfolio. The chapter concludes with several examples illustrating the procedures used to construct efficient interest rate hedges.

QUESTIONS

1. If a T-bond is quoted at 91.24, what is the quoted price in dollars of a $100,000 bond?
2. What is the difference between the yield-to-maturity on a bond and the bond's current yield?
3. How does the transaction price of a bond differ from the quoted price of the bond?

4. How is the Macaulay duration of a bond computed?
5. Which bonds are likely to have the highest durations: those with high or low coupons, or those with long or short maturities?
6. Which bonds are deliverable on a T-bond futures contract?
7. What delivery options does a T-bond futures short have?
8. Using the information provided in Tables 13.5 and 13.6, calculate the invoice price that a short would receive by delivering the May 15, 2005-10, 10 percent bond in fulfillment of his or her delivery obligation on the December 89 T-bond futures contract.
9. If the T-bond futures price is higher than the calculated theoretical futures price, what arbitrage transaction would you engage in? Be specific.
10. In general, how can you determine which of the many deliverable T-bonds is the cheapest-to-deliver? Is the May 15, 2005-10, 10 percent bond, for which you calculated the invoice price for question 8, the cheapest-to-deliver bond on the December 89 T-bond futures contract?
11. Assume that on December 13, 1989, you are holding a portfolio of two T-bonds: $500,000 face value of the 14 percent November 2006-11; and $1 million face value of the 9 percent, November 2018. You wish to immunize this portfolio from all interest rate risk by hedging it with March 90 T-bond futures contracts. On December 13, 1989, the following prices, yields, and durations existed:

- the price of the 14 percent, November 2006-11 bond is 154.08, its yield-to-maturity is 8.05 percent, and its duration is 8.00.
- the price of the 9 percent, November 2018 bond is 112.06, its yield-to-maturity is 7.91 percent, and its duration is 9.00.
- the price of the March 90 T-bond futures contract is 99.17, and its yield-to-maturity is 8.048.
- the applicable conversion factors on the 14 percent and 9 percent bonds described above are 1.5444 and 1.1116 respectively.
- the cheapest-to-deliver bond is the August 2019, 8.125 percent bond. The price of this bond is 102.27, and its conversion factor is 1.0139. Its duration is 9.25.

Finally, the following regression equation was estimated:

$$\Delta Y_t = 0.015 + 0.88 \Delta Y_t^*$$

where ΔY_t are the daily changes in the portfolio yield (the weighted average of the yields on the November 2006-11 and August 2018 bonds), and ΔY_t^* are the daily changes in the yield on the August 2019 bond.
Calculate the minimum-variance hedge ratio.

SUGGESTED READING

Arak, M. and L. Goodman. "Treasury Bond Futures: Valuing the Delivery Options." *The Journal of Futures Markets*, Vol. 7 (June 1987), pp. 269–286.

Barnhill, T. and W. Seale. "Optimal Exercise of the Switching Option in Treasury Bond Arbitrages." *The Journal of Futures Markets*, Vol. 8 (October 1988), pp. 517–532.

Batlin, C. "Hedging Mortgaged-Backed Securities with Treasury Bond Futures." *The Journal of Futures Markets*, Vol. 7 (December 1987), pp. 675–695.

Boyle, P. "The Quality Option and Timing Option in Futures Contracts." *Journal of Finance*, Vol. 44 (March 1989), pp. 101–113.

Gay, G. and S. Manaster. "Implicit Delivery Options and Optimal Delivery Strategies for Financial Futures Contracts." *Journal of Financial Economics*, Vol. 13 (May 1986), pp. 41–72.

Hedge, S. "Coupon and Maturity Characteristics of the Cheapest-to-Deliver Bonds on the Treasury Bond Futures Contract." *Financial Analysts Journal*, Vol. 43 (March/April 1987), pp. 70–76.

Kane, A. and A. Marcus. "Conversion Factor Risk and Hedging in the Treasury-Bond Futures Market." *The Journal of Futures Markets*, Vol. 4 (1984), pp. 55–64.

Klendosky, R. and D. Lasser. "An Efficiency Analysis of the T-Bond Futures Market." *The Journal of Futures Markets*, Vol. 5 (1985), pp. 607–620.

Koppenhaver, G. D. "An Empirical Analysis of Bank Hedging in Futures Markets." *The Journal of Futures Markets*, Vol. 10, No. 1 (1990), pp. 1–12.

Maloney, K. and J. Yawitz. "Interest Rate Risk, Immunization and Duration." *Journal of Portfolio Management*, Vol. 13 (Spring 1986), pp. 41–49.

APPENDIX: THE CONVERSION FACTOR AND THE CHEAPEST-TO-DELIVER CONCEPT

The CBOT's T-bond's conversion factor for any particular bond is the bond's price *per $1 face value* (ignoring accrued interest) that the bond would have to have to make its yield to maturity equal to eight percent. This price is computed by using the bond pricing formula (shown below and discussed in Section 13.1.2)

$$P_o = \left[\sum_{t=1}^{2N} \frac{C/2}{(1 + R/2)^{(t-1)+(tc/B)}} \right] + \left[\frac{P_T}{(1 + R/2)^{(2N-1)+(tc/B)}} \right]$$

where R is set equal to eight percent. In other words, the future cash flows on the bond are discounted by an annual yield-to-maturity of eight percent.

The procedure used by the CBOT to calculate conversion factors is slightly different in that the term of maturity, or to the first call, of a bond is determined by rounding down to the nearest quarter of a year. For example, a bond with 22 years, 10 months and 15 days to go until maturity would be considered to have a maturity of 22 years and 9 months. In addition, the first day of the delivery month of the futures contract is used to determine the time to maturity of a bond.

It is important to keep in mind that other exchanges with a T-bond futures contract do not calculate the conversion factor in the same way. For example, the London International Financial Futures Exchange uses a 12 percent discount factor and includes accrued interest in the calculation.

In general, conversion factors are higher the higher the coupon rate (see Table 13.7). A higher coupon rate adds value to the bond by increasing its cash flows.

The relationship between the magnitude of the conversion factor and the *maturity* of a bond depends on whether the bond's coupon is above or below eight percent. If the coupon is above eight percent, bonds with longer maturities will have higher conversion factors. If the coupon is below eight percent, bonds with longer maturities will have lower conversion factors. This relationship can also be seen in Table 13.7.

The concept of the cheapest-to-deliver bond arises because the invoice prices of bonds calculated using the relevant conversion factors may (and usually do) differ from the actual market prices of these bonds. This can occur because the prevailing yield curve is not consistent with that assumed in the conversion factor calculation—flat at eight percent, or because of the existence of liquidity premiums, market segmentation, and tax considerations that affect actual prices.

CHAPTER

14

FOREIGN CURRENCY FUTURES

Foreign currency futures were introduced in 1972 at the Chicago Mercantile Exchange. They were the first financial futures contracts, antedating even interest rate futures by three years. A major impetus to their introduction was the end of *fixed* exchange rates and the widespread adoption of *floating* exchange rates, which resulted in a sharp increase in exchange rate volatility (and therefore in exchange rate risk). A fixed exchange rate is one in which a currency's value is fixed relative to other currencies. Intervention by central banks, buying and selling currencies as needed, is usually required to maintain a fixed rate. In a floating exchange rate regime, currency values are permitted to change freely to reflect the underlying private sector demand and supply for currencies.

The fixed exchange rate system that existed prior to 1973 was formalized in 1944 when the International Monetary Fund was created. At that time major western countries established par values for the major currencies vis-a-vis the U.S. dollar, which was then pegged to gold (specifically, $35 per troy ounce of gold). Currencies were permitted to fluctuate one percent above or below their par values. At these limiting values, central banks intervened to prevent greater departures from the par values.[1]

---

[1] If the price of a country's currency were to rise to its upper intervention limit, central banks would supply that currency and drive its price down. They could do this either by selling the currency or taking foreign currency in payment (reducing the demand for the currency). Alternatively, if the exchange rate were at its lower limit, central banks would buy the currency and drive its price up.

This system worked reasonably well until the dollar became significantly overvalued. Large U.S. balance of payments deficits resulted in a greater supply of dollars being available than foreigners wished to hold at the established exchange rates. As a consequence, in 1971 the dollar exchange rate was changed to permit a devaluation of the dollar, and exchange rate limits were expanded to $2\frac{1}{4}$ percent on either side of par value. (This was the Smithsonian Agreement.) These adjustments, however, were not sufficient to restore currency stability, and in February of 1973 the dollar was permitted to float freely.

Today we have a mixture of floating and fixed exchange rates. The dollar is relatively free to float vis-a-vis other major currencies, tempered by central banks intervening to prevent extreme exchange rate changes or excessive volatility. In contrast, the European Monetary System (EMS), consisting of most western European countries, maintains fixed exchange rates (within specific limits) among the currencies of the countries belonging to the EMS. The end of the fixed exchange rate system understandably resulted in dollar exchange rates becoming more volatile than in preceding years. As a consequence, international transactions involving foreign currencies are subject to significant currency risk.

An example of this risk is the following. Suppose that a U.S. automobile importer contracts on October 1, 1989, to take delivery of German automobiles one year later at a price in Deutschemarks (DM) that is agreed upon on October 1. At the October 1 mark-to-dollar exchange rate of 2, the U.S. importer can calculate his or her future dollar cost for the automobiles. In a year, however, when the importer will have to pay for the automobiles, the exchange rate may be different. If the mark were to appreciate against the dollar, or the mark-to-dollar exchange rate were to fall below 2, the importer's dollar cost for the automobiles would rise, perhaps substantially. Figure 14-1 shows that the mark did in fact appreciate from October 1989 to October 1990: the exchange rate went from 2 to about 1.54. This appreciation of the mark would have imposed a cost increase on the importer of nearly $(2.00 - 1.54)/2.00 = 23$ percent!

Figure 14-1 shows the movement of the U.S. dollar–Deutschemark spot exchange rates from 1987 to 1990. It is obvious that exchange rates can be quite volatile. Table 14.1 provides the annualized daily volatility of the U.S. dollar exchange rates vis-a-vis the major foreign currencies, from 1985 to 1990.[2]

Foreign currency futures provide a mechanism for managing currency risk. In addition, they can be used to speculate on changes in exchange rates. This chapter covers the fundamentals of foreign currency futures and provides examples of how they can be used to hedge currency risk.

---

[2]Compare these volatilities with those for stock indexes in Table 10.4 of Chapter 10.

DM/$

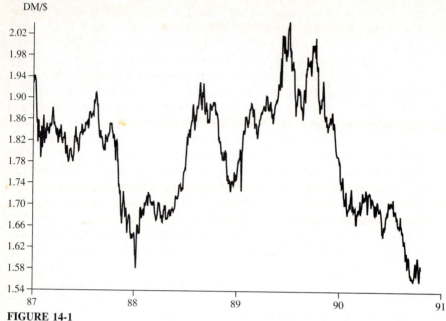

FIGURE 14-1
Deutschemark spot exchange rates (DM/$) (daily, from January 1987 to September 1990).

TABLE 14.1
Annualized daily volatility of major foreign currencies:*
Daily spot exchange rates from January 1985
to September 1990 (in percent)

	1985–1990	1985	1986	1987	1988	1989	1990
DM	11.99	15.15	12.28	11.33	9.65	12.56	9.31
¥	11.50	11.89	11.97	11.17	10.39	11.85	11.55
SF	14.08	16.28	13.22	13.47	10.50	15.78	14.53
£	12.16	17.37	11.05	10.33	10.31	12.05	9.38
CD	4.92	5.13	4.91	4.52	5.64	4.15	5.09
AD	12.94	17.53	12.83	10.46	10.56	12.77	12.00
FF	11.92	15.14	12.52	10.78	9.46	12.54	9.48

*Annualized standard deviation of daily percentage changes.

DM: Deutschemark
¥: Japanese yen
SF: Swiss franc
£: British pound
CD: Canadian dollar
AD: Australian dollar
FF: French franc

14.1 THE FOREIGN CURRENCY MARKET

14.1.1 Why Does It Exist?

The currency (or money) of any country, whether it is U.S. dollars or French francs (FF), is simply another financial asset. Someone who holds a checking account denominated in French francs, for example, is holding French currency. This French franc balance may be used to purchase French goods (such as wine) or French assets (such as a house in France or a bond issued by the French government), just as we would use a dollar checking account balance to purchase goods or assets in the United States denominated in dollars.

If people in every country purchased only the goods and services produced in that country, or the assets located in that country, there would be no need to have a foreign currency market. No one would need to hold a foreign currency, even for a short period of time.

In today's economy, however, there is a huge volume of international transactions, and a market for foreign exchange is a necessary concomitant to these transactions. In all developed countries a plethora of foreign goods are imported, requiring importers to obtain the foreign exchange (or foreign currency) needed to purchase these goods. Not surprisingly, therefore, the trading activity in any particular currency is directly related to the volume of international trade conducted in that currency.

In addition, financial assets, such as stocks and bonds, are traded actively across borders. Banks raise funds by accepting deposits in one currency and making loans in another currency. Japanese pension funds use Japanese yen to buy stocks and bonds in the United States, and American pension funds use dollars to buy Japanese and European financial assets. All of these transactions require the purchase or sale of a foreign currency. As cross-border trading in financial assets has grown, so, therefore, has trading in foreign exchange.

14.1.2 The Cash Market

In 1989, the average daily trading in foreign currencies in the United States alone was about $500 billion. Most of this trading was in six currencies: Deutschemarks, Japanese yen, British pounds, Swiss francs, Canadian dollars, and French francs. The spot foreign exchange market is similar to the over-the-counter market for securities. There is no centralized meeting place (or exchange), and no fixed opening and closing time. Some foreign exchange dealers are open 24 hours a day. There are also no requirements for participation, other than the informal acceptance of other participants.

Banks do most of the foreign exchange business. Through correspondent relationships with banks in other countries, banks have ready access to foreign currencies. Foreign currency transactions usually do not involve a physical transfer of currency, but simply a bookkeeping entry among banks. (Banks customarily maintain balances with foreign banks in the currency of the foreign bank's country.)

In addition to spot transactions, banks and other foreign exchange dealers regularly buy and sell currencies for forward delivery—delivery at some time in the future. This forward currency market provides many of the same economic functions as currency futures. After discussing currency futures, we will return (in Section 14.6) to a comparison of currency futures and foreign exchange forward contracts.

14.2 FOREIGN EXCHANGE QUOTATIONS

Foreign exchange quotations can be confusing to the uninitiated because currencies are quoted in terms of (or relative to) other currencies. They may also be quoted in different ways. A common convention is to quote exchange rates in terms of U.S. dollars($). For example, the French franc exchange rate is quoted as so many FF per $ (FF/$). If a dollar buys six French francs, the FF/$ exchange rate is 6 (6/1). Alternatively, the same exchange rate can be quoted in terms of how many dollars a French franc can buy, or as a $/FF exchange rate. In this case the dollar exchange rate is quoted as 0.1667 (1/6), which is simply the reciprocal of the former dollar exchange rate:

$$\$/FF = \frac{1}{FF/\$}$$

or, alternatively,

$$FF/\$ = \frac{1}{\$/FF}$$

Table 14.2 shows exchange rate quotations as they appeared in the Wall Street Journal on August 10, 1990. The quotations are for 3 P.M. on August 9, the previous day, and are for amounts of $1 million or more. Transactions of less than $1 million take place at less favorable exchange rates. The quotations are those of only one dealer, Bankers Trust Company, and are the selling (or the ask) rates: the exchange rate someone pays to buy foreign currency from Bankers Trust. If someone wants to sell foreign currency to Bankers Trust, they will receive the bid price, which will always be lower than the ask price. The bid prices are not quoted in Table 14.2. As in other over-the-counter markets, the dealer receives the difference between the bid and ask rates as payment for making-the-market.

The quotations in the first two columns of Table 14.2 are in terms of dollars (or cents) per unit of a foreign currency: 18.692 cents per FF, $1.868 per British pound (£), and so forth. The quotations appearing in the last two columns are expressed as units of a foreign currency per dollar: 5.35 FF per dollar, 0.5353 £ per dollar, and so forth.

In the spot market, exchange rates are normally quoted on a per-dollar basis (or as so many units of a foreign currency (FC) per dollar (FC/$)), except for the British pound which is almost always quoted on a dollar-per-pound basis ($/£). The foreign exchange cash market observes a two-day settlement

TABLE 14.2
Exchange rate quotations: August 9, 1990

EXCHANGE RATES

Thursday, August 9, 1990
The New York foreign exchange selling rates below apply to trading among banks in amounts of $1 million and more, as quoted at 3 p.m. Eastern time by Bankers Trust Co. Retail transactions provide fewer units of foreign currency per dollar.

Country	U.S. $ equiv. Thurs.	Wed.	Currency per U.S. $ Thurs.	Wed.
Argentina (Austral) ...	.0001784	.0001784	5605.07	5605.07
Australia (Dollar)	.8005	.7945	1.2492	1.2587
Austria (Schilling)	.08901	.08933	11.23	11.20
Bahrain (Dinar)	2.6522	2.6522	.3771	.3771
Belgium (Franc)				
Commercial rate	.03046	.03060	32.83	32.69
Brazil (Cruzeiro)	.01408	c.01405	71.02	c71.15
Britain (Pound)	1.8680	1.8700	.5353	.5348
30-Day Forward	1.8572	1.8592	.5384	.5379
90-Day Forward	1.8369	1.8378	.5444	.5441
180-Day Forward	1.8080	1.8094	.5531	.5527
Canada (Dollar)	.8711	.8711	1.1480	1.1480
30-Day Forward	.8669	.8668	1.1535	1.1537
90-Day Forward	.8595	.8598	1.1634	1.1630
180-Day Forward	.8511	.8513	1.1750	1.1747
Chile (Official rate)	.003463	.003463	288.80	288.80
China (Renminbi)	.211752	.211752	4.7225	4.7225
Colombia (Peso)	.001980	.001980	505.09	505.09
Denmark (Krone)	.1644	.1649	6.0840	6.0625
Ecuador (Sucre)				
Floating rate	.001099	.001099	910.00	910.00
Finland (Markka)	.26667	.26767	3.7500	3.7360
France (Franc)	.18692	.18751	5.3500	5.3330
30-Day Forward	.18662	.18722	5.3584	5.3414
90-Day Forward	.18590	.18649	5.3792	5.3622
180-Day Forward	.18486	.18544	5.4095	5.3925
Greece (Drachma)	.006369	.006390	157.00	156.50
Hong Kong (Dollar) ...	.12867	.12862	7.7720	7.7750
India (Rupee)	.05767	.05767	17.34	17.34
Indonesia (Rupiah) ...	.0005400	.0005400	1852.02	1852.02
Ireland (Punt)	1.6843	1.6797	.5937	.5953
Israel (Shekel)	.4865	.4865	2.0556	2.0556
Italy (Lira)	.0008556	.0008589	1168.76	1164.25
Japan (Yen)	.006676	.006673	149.80	149.85
30-Day Forward	.006679	.006676	149.73	149.78
90-Day Forward	.006679	.006676	149.73	149.78
180-Day Forward	.006680	.006678	149.70	149.75
Jordan (Dinar)	1.5221	1.5221	.6570	.6570
Kuwait (Dinar)	z	z	z	z
Lebanon (Pound)	.001488	.001488	672.00	672.00
Malaysia (Ringgit)	.3702	.3702	2.7015	2.7010
Malta (Lira)	3.2680	3.2680	.3060	.3060
Mexico (Peso)				
Floating rate	.0003481	.0003481	2873.00	2873.00
Netherland (Guilder) .	.5559	.5579	1.7990	1.7925
New Zealand (Dollar) .	.6015	.6020	1.6625	1.6611
Norway (Krone)	.1619	.1630	6.1750	6.1350
Pakistan (Rupee)	.0463	.0463	21.60	21.60
Peru (Inti)	.00000677	.00000677	147754.14	147754.14
Philippines (Peso)	.04292	.04292	23.30	23.30
Portugal (Escudo)	.007163	.007163	139.60	139.60
Saudi Arabia (Riyal) ..	.26596	.26596	3.7600	3.7600
Singapore (Dollar)	.5540	.5536	1.8050	1.8065
South Africa (Rand)				
Commercial rate	.3857	.3857	2.5927	2.5927
Financial rate	.2597	.2591	3.8506	3.8595
South Korea (Won)	.0013976	.0013976	715.50	715.50
Spain (Peseta)	.010215	.010246	97.90	97.60
Sweden (Krona)	.1712	.1715	5.8400	5.8300
Switzerland (Franc) ...	.7440	.7477	1.3440	1.3375
30-Day Forward	.7435	.7470	1.3450	1.3387
90-Day Forward	.7421	.7455	1.3475	1.3414
180-Day Forward	.7401	.7437	1.3512	1.3447
Taiwan (Dollar)	.037050	.036765	26.99	27.20
Thailand (Baht)	.03903	.03903	25.62	25.62
Turkey (Lira)	.0003770	.0003773	2652.52	2650.41
United Arab (Dirham) .	.2723	.2723	3.6725	3.6725
Uruguay (New Peso)				
Financial	.000810	.000810	1234.00	1234.00
Venezuela (Bolivar)				
Floating rate	.02123	.02123	47.10	47.10
W. Germany (Mark) ..	.6262	.6285	1.5970	1.5910
30-Day Forward	.6260	.6283	1.5974	1.5915
90-Day Forward	.6254	.6277	1.5990	1.5932
180-Day Forward	.6239	.6261	1.6027	1.5973
SDR	1.36422	1.36315	.73302	.73359
ECU	1.29884	1.29669	....	....

Special Drawing Rights (SDR) are based on exchange rates for the U.S., West German, British, French and Japanese currencies. Source: International Monetary Fund.

European Currency Unit (ECU) is based on a basket of community currencies. Source: European Community Commission.

z-Not quoted. c-corrected.

Source: The Wall Street Journal, August 10, 1990.

period. For example, an importer buying spot French francs on Wednesday, August 8, at the Wednesday quotation, will actually pay for and receive the francs on Friday, August 10.

Table 14.2 also provides forward exchange rate quotations for currencies for which active forward markets exist. Specifically, it shows 30-day, 90-day, and 180-day forward rates for British pounds (£), Canadian dollars (CD), French francs (FF), Japanese yen (¥), Swiss francs (SF), and Deutschemarks (DM). These are the most actively traded currencies in the spot market.

Discussions of foreign currencies frequently utilize the terms *depreciated* and *appreciated* to describe changes or movements in exchange rates. A currency is said to depreciate against another currency when it becomes *less valuable* vis-à-vis that currency: when a unit of that currency buys fewer units of the other currency than before. A currency is said to appreciate against another currency when it becomes *more valuable* vis-à-vis that currency: when one of its units buys more units of the other currency than before. For example, in Table 14.2, the Deutschemark is shown depreciating against the dollar from August 8 to August 9 (from .6285 to .6262), while the Japanese yen appreciated against the dollar (from .006673 to .006676). Alternatively, the same currency movements can be viewed as the dollar appreciating against the mark and depreciating against the yen.

14.3   CROSS EXCHANGE RATES

In Table 14.2 all foreign currencies are quoted in terms of dollars. This became the standard practice because in the past most international currency transactions were done in dollars. Increasingly, however, international transactions are now being done in currencies other than the dollar. For example, a French importer buying German automobiles may use FF to buy DM directly, rather than first buying dollars and then using the dollars to buy DM. In this case the relevant cross exchange rate is the number of DM that each FF can buy. As a consequence, major currencies are now also quoted as cross exchange rates. Table 14.3 shows the cross currency rate quotations for the key currencies.

Each of the exchange rates in Table 14.3 are quoted directly in terms of the other seven major currencies. Because of the existence of an active trading market in currencies, the cross rates for two currencies must be consistent with the currencies' respective exchange rates in terms of dollars. If this were not true, riskless and profitable arbitrage opportunities would exist.

In particular, the equilibrium (or no-arbitrage) relationship between the cross rate for two currencies (say FF and DM) and their respective dollar exchange rates is:

$$\frac{FF}{DM} = \frac{FF/\$}{DM/\$}$$

TABLE 14.3
Key currency cross rates: August 9, 1990

Key Currency Cross Rates Late New York Trading August 9, 1990								
	Dollar	Pound	SFranc	Guilder	Yen	Lira	D-Mark	FFranc	CdnDlr
Canada	1.1470	2.1426	.85387	.63761	.00766	.00098	.71845	.21435	......
France	5.3510	9.996	3.9835	2.9746	.03572	.00458	3.3517	....	4.6652
Germany	1.5965	2.9823	1.1885	.88749	.01066	.00137	....	.29836	1.3919
Italy	1168.5	2182.8	869.87	649.56	7.800	....	731.91	218.37	1018.7
Japan	149.80	279.83	111.516	83.273	....	.12820	93.830	27.995	130.60
Netherlands ..	1.7989	3.3603	1.3392	....	.01201	.00154	1.1268	.33618	1.5684
Switzerland ...	1.3433	2.5093	....	.74673	.00897	.00115	.84140	.25104	1.1711
U.K.	.53533	....	.39852	.29759	.00357	.00046	.33532	.10004	.46672
U.S.	....	1.8680	.74444	.55590	.00668	.00086	.62637	.18688	.87184

Source: Telerate

Source: The Wall Street Journal, August 10, 1990.

For example, in Table 14.3 the FF/DM cross rate is 3.3517, which is almost identical to the relevant dollar exchange rates in Table 14.2:

$$\frac{FF/\$}{DM/\$} = \frac{5.350}{1.597} = 3.35$$

The small discrepancy between these rates is undoubtedly due to the fact that the cross rates are quotes from Telerate while the dollar exchange rates are quotes of Bankers Trust Co. In addition, all of the rates may not be quoted at exactly the same time of the day.

An important reason for the increase in the cross-trading of currencies is that the Deutschemark and the Japanese yen are beginning to rival the dollar as the world's pre-eminent currency. Germany and Japan both have strong currencies, large and robust economies, a reputation for sound economic policies with a strong anti-inflation tilt, and a stable political environment. A 1990 survey by the Federal Reserve Bank of New York revealed that the mark dominates currency trades in which the dollar is not involved. According to the survey report, the mark was involved in 95 percent of all reported cross-currency trades.[3] Table 14.4 shows the correlations among the major foreign currencies, using daily spot exchange rates from January 1985 to September 1990. The Deutschemark displays a high correlation with the Swiss franc, British pound, Japanese yen, and French franc.

TABLE 14.4
Correlations among major foreign currencies: Daily spot exchange rates from January 1985 to September 1990

	DM	¥	SF	£	CD	AD	FF
DM	1.00	0.74	0.88	0.79	0.28	0.23	0.95
¥		1.00	0.69	0.65	0.14	0.24	0.73
SF			1.00	0.71	0.26	0.22	0.84
£				1.00	0.28	0.28	0.78
CD					1.00	0.18	0.26
AD						1.00	0.25
FF							1.00

All correlations are statistically significant at conventional levels of significance.

---

[3]"Strong Mark Forcing Dollar to Move Over," *New York Times*, August 28, 1990, B1, Col. 4.

14.4 DETERMINANTS OF EXCHANGE RATE LEVELS

Like any other commodity, the demand and supply for a currency determines its equilibrium exchange rate. A currency in great demand relative to its supply will have a high exchange rate: a unit of the currency will have a high value in terms of other currencies.

The fundamental factors that determine the demand and supply of a currency are

1. Balance of payments
2. Government policies
3. Expectations

BALANCE OF PAYMENTS. A country's balance of payment is the net inflow or outflow of that country's currency after summing up all of its transactions with other countries. These transactions include the exports and imports of its goods and services, foreign investment in the country, foreign investments by the country's citizens abroad, foreign aid, and governmentally directed central bank transactions. The major economic factors that determine a country's balance of payments are its national income and price levels, and interest rate levels relative to those in other countries.

A country's currency is in demand when the country has a balance of payments surplus, in which case its currency value is usually strong. A balance of payments deficit usually results in a declining currency value. In the later half of the 1980s both Germany and Japan enjoyed balance of payments surpluses, and both countries had strong currencies. Conversely, the United States experienced substantial balance of payments deficits and a declining currency value.

GOVERNMENT POLICIES. Governments, through their central banks, often intervene in foreign exchange markets to influence currency values. If central banks decide to buy a currency, they support its value; if they sell a currency, they depress its value.

In the European Monetary System (EMS) members have agreed to intervene in spot currency markets to maintain currency values among members, but *not* to intervene with respect to outside currencies (such as the dollar).[4] Currency exchange rates among members are maintained within $2\frac{1}{4}$ percent above and below the agreed par values (except for the Italian lira, which is permitted to vary by 6 percent).

In addition, government policies with respect to inflation, tariffs, import quotas, and exchange controls can all have an impact on currency values. Polit-

---

[4]The EMS consists of Britain, Belgium, Denmark, France, West Germany, Ireland, Italy, Luxembourg, and the Netherlands.

ical instability can also cause economic policy uncertainty and result in a weak currency value.

EXPECTATIONS. Expectations may at times be the predominant factor influencing foreign exchange rates. An expectation that a currency's value will soon change often results in a massive flow of short-term capital, either into or out of that currency, resulting in an actual change in the currency's value. A belief that a particular currency is undervalued (overvalued) relative to fundamentals will result in an inflow (outflow) of short-term capital to (from) that country. A reason often given by central banks for intervening in foreign exchange markets is that such intervention is necessary to curb excessive exchange rate volatility caused by erroneous (and volatile) expectations.

TABLE 14.5
Currency futures and trading volume

		1990 Trading volume
U.S. exchanges		
Deutschemark	CME	9,169,230
Japanese yen	CME	7,437,235
Swiss franc	CME	6,524,893
British pound	CME	3,410,333
Canadian dollar	CME	1,408,799
U.S. dollar index	NYCE	565,164
Australian dollar	CME	105,241
Deutschemark	MidAm	82,534
Swiss franc	MidAm	75,819
Japanese yen	MidAm	54,283
British Pound	MidAm	25,846
ECU	NYCE	12,150
Canadian dollar	MidAm	9,287
Dollar/yen diff	CME	3,727
Dollar/mark diff	CME	1,478
Dollar/pound diff	CME	1,064
French franc	CME	50
Total		28,887,133
Foreign exchanges		
U.S. dollar	BM&F, Brazil	608,203
Japanese yen	SIMEX, Singapore	116,421
Deutschemark	SIMEX, Singapore	64,269
Japanese yen	TIFFE, Japan	28,883
U.S. dollar	New Zealand Futures Exchange	3,848
British pound	SIMEX, Singapore	2,623
New Zealand dollar	New Zealand Futures Exchange	597
Sterling	LIFFE, U.K.	143
Australian dollar	Sydney Futures Exchange, Australia	38
Total		825,025

14.5 CURRENCY FUTURES

Futures are traded on seven currencies: Australian dollars, British pounds, Canadian dollars, Deutschemarks, French francs, Japanese yen and Swiss francs. Table 14.5 lists the trading volumes in these futures in 1990. The bulk of the futures trading is in Deutschemarks, Japanese yen and Swiss francs. The Deutschemark and the Japanese yen contracts are, respectively, the eighth and ninth most active futures contracts traded in the United States.

About 29 million currency futures contracts were traded on U.S. exchanges in 1990, accounting for about 10 percent of all futures trading in the U.S. In contrast, the volume of currency futures trading on foreign exchanges is quite low. This is undoubtedly due to the Chicago Mercantile Exchange (CME) introducing currency futures much earlier than foreign exchanges. The CME has also succeeded in holding this market, despite intense competition from foreign exchanges.[5] Figure 14-2 shows the growth of currency futures trading from 1973 to 1990.

Table 14.6 lists the specifications of the most active currency futures contracts. The contracts are quite similar to one another, the major difference being the

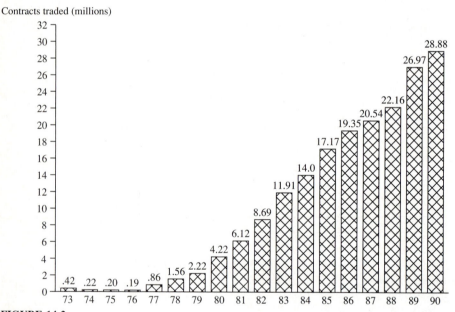

Contracts traded (millions)

FIGURE 14-2
U.S. foreign currency futures: Annual trading volume, 1973-1990.

---

[5]The only foreign exchange successful in trading currency futures is the Singapore Mercantile Exchange, which is a partner of the CME, jointly clearing futures contracts with the CME. Trading in Singapore primarily occurs when the CME is closed, during the night, and is in the same contracts traded on the CME.

TABLE 14.6
Foreign currency futures contract specifications

	British pound (£)	Canadian dollar (CD)	Deutschemark (DM)	French franc (FF)	Japanese yen (¥)	Swiss franc (SF)	Australian dollar (AD)
Trading unit	BP62,500	CD100,000	DM125,000	FF250,000	JY12,500,000	SF125,000	AD100,000
Quotations	US $ per pound	US $ per Canadian $	US $ per mark	US $ per franc	US $ per yen	US $ per franc	US $ per Australian $
Minimum price change	.0002 = $12.50	.0001 = $10.00	.0001 = $12.50	.00005 = $12.50	.000001 = $12.50	.0001 = $12.50	.0001 = $10.00
Price limit*	None	None	None	None	None	None	None
Contract months actively traded			March, June, September, December				
Trading hours			7:20 A.M. to 2:00 P.M. (Chicago time)				
Last trading day			Futures trading terminates at 9:16 A.M. on the second business day immediately preceding the third Wednesday of the contract month.				
US dollar value as of August 9, 1990	$116,750	$87,110	$78,275	$46,730	$83,450	$93,000	$80,500
Delivery day			Delivery by wire transfer on the third Wednesday of the contract month.				

*There is an opening price limit between 7:20 A.M.–7:35 P.M. Otherwise there are no price limits.

quantity of the currency represented by one futures contract. These range from 62,500 British pounds to 12,500,000 Japanese yen. In dollar terms, however, all but one of the contracts have a value between \$78,000 to \$120,000 (see Table 14.6).[6]

14.5.1 Futures Price Quotations

Table 14.7 provides price quotations for currency futures contracts as they appeared in the Wall Street Journal on August 10, 1990. The quotations are as of the close of trading on August 9, 1990, and display, for each contract, the usual open, high, low, and settlement prices for that day, as well as the open interest. Currency quotations also include the high and low *lifetime* prices for each contract, or the highest and lowest prices recorded thus far during the life of the particular contract. In addition, following the quotations for each contract (on the last line), both the estimated total trading volume for the current day and the actual trading volume and total open interest for the previous day are given.

TABLE 14.7
Currency futures price quotations:
August 9, 1990

```
                                         Lifetime      Open
              Open  High  Low Settle Change High Low Interest
JAPANESE YEN (IMM) 12.5 million yen; $ per yen (.00)
Sept   .6682 .6692 .6673 .6677 + .0002  .7410 .6268 54,991
Dec    .6684 .6690 .6676 .6677 + .0002  .7165 .6290  3,182
Mr91   .6685 .6685 .6685 .6676   ....   .6850 .6315  1,313
   Est vol 16,065; vol Wed 22,580; open int 59,486, +9.
   W. GERMAN MARK (IMM) – 125,000 marks; $ per mark
Sept   .6272 .6285 .6256 .6260 – .0023  .6343 .5410 70,405
Dec    .6264 .6270 .6242 .6249 – .0023  .6331 .5764  3,318
Mr91   .6255 .6258 .6240 .6235 – .0024  .6303 .5820    379
   Est vol 20,690; vol Wed 32,278; open int 74,114, –2,287.
   CANADIAN DOLLAR (IMM) – 100,000 dlrs.; $ per Can $
Sept   .8667 .8672 .8661 .8669 + .0011  .8672 .8093 31,601
Dec    .8568 .8574 .8568 .8573 + .0011  .8574 .8050  3,530
Mr91   .8493 .8494 .8491 .8495 + .0011  .8494 .7990  4,358
June   .8419 .8419 .8419 .8422 + .0011  .8419 .7995  1,828
Sept    ....  ....       .8359 + .0011  .8335 .7985  1,032
   Est vol 2,905; vol Wed 4,580; open int 42,349, –143.
   BRITISH POUND (IMM) – 62,500 pds.; $ per pound
Sept  1.8560 1.8600 1.8536 1.8550 –.0014 1.8644 1.5290 37,716
Dec   1.8262 1.8296 1.8238 1.8248 –.0014 1.8360 1.5640  1,721
Mr91  1.8012 1.8012 1.7970 1.7976 –.0014 1.8012 1.6580    516
   Est vol 5,855; vol Wed 10,160; open int 39,953, +307.
   SWISS FRANC (IMM) – 125,000 francs-$ per franc
Sept   .7443 .7470 .7426 .7432 – .0041  .7525 .6020 42,733
Dec    .7418 .7450 .7401 .7412 – .0042  .7499 .6300  1,430
Mr91    ....  ....  .7398 – .0042       .7470 .6500    467
   Est vol 16,590; vol Wed 21,762; open int 44,682, +693.
   AUSTRALIAN DOLLAR (IMM) – 100,000 dlrs.; $ per A.$
Sept   .7955 .7972 .7941 .7961 + .0054  .8001 .7240  2,560
   Est vol 551; vol Wed 417; open int 2,567, –157.
   U.S. DOLLAR INDEX (FINEX) 500 times USDX
Sept   87.98 88.08 87.79 88.07 + .20 100.43 87.21  3,032
Dec    88.52 88.60 88.50 88.73 + .19  96.46 87.94  1,680
   Est vol 713; vol Wed 1,549; open int 4,744, –205.
   The Index: High 87.76; Low 87.55; Close 87.75 +.17
```

Source: The Wall Street Journal, August 10, 1990.

[6]The quotations in Table 14.2 are used to calculate these values.

Quotations for currency futures on U.S. exchanges are in terms of dollars per unit of a foreign currency. This is the opposite of the spot market quotation convention. It is important, therefore, to identify the quotation convention being used. In the remainder of this chapter, to prevent confusion, we specify the exchange rate quotation convention that is being used in parentheses immediately following the stated spot or futures exchange rate (such as $S_t(DM/\$)$ for the spot DM-dollar exchange rate at time t, and $F_{t,T}(\$/DM)$ for the futures dollar-DM exchange rate at time t for delivery in period T).

14.5.2 Pricing of Currency Futures

Similar to many other futures that we have studied, currency futures prices have a cash-and-carry relationship with spot exchange rates. In particular, futures prices converge to underlying spot prices on the last futures trading day, as net carrying costs go to zero. Figure 14-3 shows this convergence occurring between the December 89 DM futures price (exchange rate) and the spot DM exchange rate on December 18, 1989 (the last trading day of the December contract).

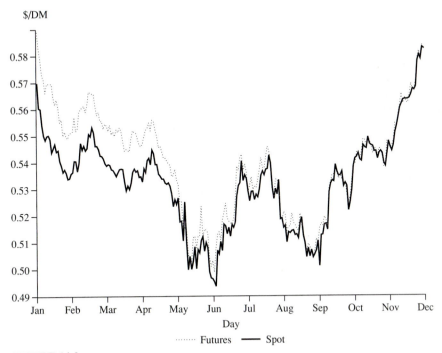

FIGURE 14-3
DM exchange rates ($/DM): Spot versus December 89 futures (daily: from January 1989 to December 1989).

The theoretical currency futures price is the price at which a profitable cash-and-carry (or reverse cash-and-carry) currency arbitrage does not exist. In a currency cash-and-carry arbitrage, one purchases the foreign currency at time t, carries it from t to T, and then sells it at time T at a price locked in by a short futures position acquired at time t. This is the same arbitrage transaction as buying gold at t, holding it from time t to T, and selling it at time T at a price locked in with a short gold futures position at time t. Consider the following arbitrage transaction:

1. At time t convert Q amount of U.S. dollars (Q_t^{US}) into a foreign currency (FC) at the current spot dollar-foreign currency exchange rate ($S_t(\$/FC)$), obtaining Q_t^{FC} amount of foreign currency:

$$Q_t^{FC} = Q_t^{US} \times \frac{1}{S_t(\$/FC)}$$

2. Invest Q_t^{FC} in a riskless security denominated in FC for the period t to T, at an annual interest rate of R^{FC}. At time T this investment will yield Q_T^{FC}:[7]

$$Q_T^{FC} = Q_t^{FC} \times \left(1 + R^{FC} \times \frac{T-t}{360}\right)$$

3. At time t short futures contracts on currency FC that expire at time T in an amount equal to Q_T^{FC}. This will lock in a future exchange rate of $F_{t,T}(\$/FC)$, which will yield the following quantity of U.S. dollars at time T (Q_T^{US}):

$$Q_T^{US} = Q_T^{FC} \times F_{t,T}(\$/FC)$$

Making the appropriate substitutions, and rearranging, yields

$$Q_T^{US} = Q_t^{FC} \times \left(1 + R^{FC} \times \frac{T-t}{360}\right) \times F_{t,T}(\$/FC)$$

$$= Q_t^{US} \times \frac{1}{S_t(\$/FC)} \times \left(1 + R^{FC} \times \frac{T-t}{360}\right) \times F_{t,T}(\$/FC)$$

$$= Q_t^{US} \times \frac{F_{t,T}(\$/FC)}{S_t(\$/FC)} \times \left(1 + R^{FC} \times \frac{T-t}{360}\right)$$

Thus, the dollar return on the *foreign* investment can be stated as

$$\frac{Q_T^{US}}{Q_t^{US}} = \frac{F_{t,T}(\$/FC)}{S_t(\$/FC)} \times \left(1 + R^{FC} \times \frac{T-t}{360}\right)$$

---

[7]By convention, in the interbank market a 365-day year is used for Australian dollars, British pounds and Canadian dollars, but a 360-day year is used for all other foreign currencies.

4. In equilibrium, at which no profitable arbitrage opportunity exists, the return on a riskless *dollar* investment for the same period, or

$$1 + R^{US} \times \frac{T - t}{360}$$

must be the same as the dollar return on the riskless *foreign* currency investment, or

$$1 + R^{US} \times \frac{T - t}{360} = \frac{F_{t,T}(\$/FC)}{S_t(\$/FC)} \times \left(1 + R^{FC} \times \frac{T - t}{360}\right)$$

This in turn implies a no-arbitrage equilibrium condition of

$$F_{t,T}(\$/FC) = S_t(\$/FC) \times \left(\frac{1 + R^{US} \times \frac{T-t}{360}}{1 + R^{FC} \times \frac{T-t}{360}}\right)$$

This equation, therefore, defines the theoretical currency futures price, since the theoretical futures price is nothing more than the no-arbitrage futures price. It shows that the theoretical price is a function of the prevailing spot exchange rate and relative U.S. and foreign interest rates.[8]

For example, on August 9, 1990, the U.S. three-month annual interest rate was 8.00 percent, the West German three-month rate was 8.51 percent, and the spot \$/DM exchange rate was 0.6262 (Table 14.2). Using the above formula, the theoretical futures price on August 9 of the December 90 contract (expiring on December 17, 1990) is:

$$F_{t,T}(\$/DM) = 0.6262 \times \frac{1 + 0.08 \times \frac{130}{360}}{1 + 0.0851 \times \frac{130}{360}} = 0.6251$$

In fact, at the close of trading on August 9, the December 90 DM futures price was quoted at 0.6249, very close to the calculated theoretical price.

14.5.3 Covered Interest Rate Parity

The equation derived in the previous section,

$$F_{t,T}(\$/FC) = S_t(\$/FC) \times \left(\frac{1 + R^{US} \times \frac{T-t}{360}}{1 + R^{FC} \times \frac{T-t}{360}}\right)$$

---

[8]The following, simpler, expression is a good approximation to this equation:

$$F_{t,T}(\$/FC) = S_t(\$/FC) \times \{1 + (R^{US} - R^{FC}) \times \frac{T - t}{360}\}$$

where R^{US} and R^{FC} are the annualized interest rates in the respective currencies.

is often called the *Interest Rate Parity* formula, or, alternatively, the *Covered Interest Arbitrage* formula. This term derives from the fact that the equation describes the equilibrium relationship between four interrelated markets — the domestic and foreign deposit markets, and the spot and futures currency markets.[9] The word *covered* signifies that arbitrage strategies can be used to lock in a riskless return on an investment in a foreign currency asset. When the equilibrium condition depicted by the interest rate parity formula holds for all currencies, only the same riskless rate of return can be earned on all foreign currency investments.

If this condition does not hold, arbitrage will occur that will re-establish the equilibrium relationships. For example, if U.S. interest rates are too *low* relative to German interest rates, investors will want to hold German deposits. They will buy spot marks and sell forward marks, raising the spot exchange rate for marks and depressing the forward rate for marks. This will continue until marks sell at a forward discount to dollars that reflects exactly the German-U.S. interest rate differential. Alternatively, if U.S. interest rates are too *high* relative to German interest rates, the opposite will occur: marks will be sold in the spot market and bought in the forward market until there exists a forward mark premium sufficient to offset the interest-rate differential.

Thus, if actual exchange rates and interest rates do not correspond to the no-arbitrage equilibrium conditions described by the interest rate parity formula, cross-border arbitrage will occur: currencies will be bought and sold until spot and futures exchange rates change to reflect current international interest rate differentials. In addition, the cash flows associated with such arbitrage may alter relative interest rates in some countries, which will in turn change the equilibrium exchange rate relationship.

As a general rule, a country's currency will sell at a forward discount vis-à-vis a country with lower interest rates, and will sell at a forward premium vis-à-vis of a country with higher interest rates. As discussed earlier, on August 9, 1990, the U.S. three-month interest rate was 8.00 percent, and the West German three-month interest rate was 8.51 percent. Since U.S. interest rates are lower than German interest rates, the forward *dollar* (DM/$) exchange rate should be at a premium to the spot dollar exchange rate (DM/$). In fact, on August 9, 1990, the exchange rate on the December 90 futures contract was 0.6249 ($/DM), or 1.6003 (DM/$), while the spot $/DM exchange rate was 0.6262, or 1.5969 (DM/$).[10]

For the interest rate parity relationship shown above to hold, arbitragers must be able to buy and sell currencies freely, and to have unimpeded access to investments in foreign countries. The imposition of cross-border capital controls, foreign exchange controls, discriminatory taxes, and other impediments to foreign

---

[9] *Deposit* markets are bank markets in which short-term lending and borrowing occur.

[10] The convention is to quote forward premiums and discounts in terms of units of foreign currency per U.S. dollars.

investment and international capital flows, therefore, may interfere with the establishment of the interest rate parity equilibrium relationships.

14.5.4 Identifying a Foreign Currency Arbitrage

A simple way to determine if a profitable riskless currency arbitrage opportunity exists is to calculate the implied repo rate on a foreign currency investment and compare this rate to the *actual* U.S. borrowing (or lending) rate. Using the equation derived in steps 3 and 4 of Section 14.5.2, which defines the return on a foreign currency investment, we can state the annualized implied repo rate (IRR) on that investment as

$$IRR = \left\{ \frac{F_{t,T}(\$/FC)}{S_t(\$/FC)} \times \left(1 + R^{FC} \times \frac{T-t}{360}\right) - 1 \right\} \times \frac{360}{T-t}$$

With actual values for $F_{t,T}$, S_t, and R^{FC}, this equation can be solved to obtain the annualized implied repo rate.

For example, on August 9, 1990, the following yields and prices existed:

- Spot exchange rate $(S_t(\$/DM)) = 0.6262$
- December 90 futures price $(F_{t,T}(\$/DM)) = 0.6249$
- Four-month German interest rate $(R^{FC}) = 8.51\%$
- Time-to-maturity $(T - t) = 130$ days (August 10 to December 17, 1990)

Thus, the IRR on a 4-month mark investment was 7.92 percent:[11]

$$\left\{ \frac{0.6249}{0.6262} \times \left(1 + 0.0851 \times \frac{130}{360}\right) - 1 \right\} \times \frac{360}{130} = 0.0792$$

Table 14.8 provides an example of an arbitrage transaction that a U.S. investor would do if the U.S. borrowing rate were *lower* than the IRR on a foreign investment; and Table 14.9 illustrates the arbitrage transaction that this investor would do if the U.S. investment return were *higher* than the IRR on a foreign investment.[12]

14.6 FORWARD VERSUS FUTURES CURRENCY CONTRACTS

Active forward markets exist in several currencies. While precise volume figures do not exist, the forward currency market is probably many times larger

---

[11] We assume for the purpose of the illustration that the four-month interest rate is identical to the 130-day interest rate.

[12] If in these examples the investor were German, the transaction would be a little different bcause we would want the net arbitrage profit to be stated in DM rather than dollars.

TABLE 14.8
Case 1: Cash-and-carry foreign currency arbitrage: IRR > U.S. interest rate (U.S. interest rate is 7.00%)

	Cash flows
August 9, 1990	
1. Borrow US$1,000,000 at 7.00% for 130 days	US$ 1,000,000
2. Convert the dollar proceeds at the prevailing spot exchange rate of 0.6262 (US$/DM) and obtain DM of [$1,000,000/0.6262]	(US$ 1,000,000) DM 1,596,934
3. Invest the DM proceeds in DM-denominated securities at an interest rate of 8.51% for 130 days	(DM 1,596,934)
4. Sell DM forward contract (matures on Dec 17, 1990) for an amount of DM1,646,009 at a future exchange rate of 0.6249(US$/DM) (Note: DM1,646,009 includes both the principal and future interest income. See point 5 below.)	0
	0
December 17, 1990	
5. Receive matured DM-investment	
principal DM 1,596,934	
plus: interest income 49,075	
[DM1,596,934 × 0.0851 × (130/360)]	DM 1,646,009
6. Deliver the DM proceeds against the short DM forward position and obtain dollar proceeds of [DM1,646,009 × 0.6249]	(DM 1,646,009) US$ 1,028,591
7. Return the borrowed dollars	
principal US$ 1,000,000	
plus: interest expense 25,278	(US$ 1,025,278)
[$1,000,000 × 0.07 × (130/360)]	
Net arbitrage profit	US$ 3,313

Note: If futures contracts were used in this example, the arbitrager would have to go short 13 Dec 90 DM futures (DM1,646,009/DM125,000 = 13.17) and would incur the residual risk associated with the extra 0.17 futures contract (or DM21,009). Thus, to avoid any unanticipated exchange gain (loss) due to rounding the number of futures contracts, forward contracts are used in the example.

than the currency futures markets. The main participants in forward markets are large commercial firms and institutional traders, who use these markets to acquire currencies and to hedge forward commitments. Participants in currency futures markets are generally smaller commercial firms and speculators, although large firms also use futures in conjunction with forward markets. Futures and forward currency markets reinforce each other, increasing the overall liquidity of foreign exchange markets.

Forward and futures currency contracts differ in the following ways: the terms of forward contracts are not standardized as are futures contracts; in forward

TABLE 14.9
Case 2: Reverse cash-and-carry foreign currency arbitrage: IRR < U.S. interest rate (U.S. interest rate is 9.00%)

		Cash flows
August 9, 1990		
1. Borrow DM 1,500,000 at 8.51% for 130 days		DM 1,500,000
2. Convert the DM proceeds at the prevailing spot exchange rate of 0.6262 (US$/DM) and obtain US$ of [DM1,500,000 × 0.6262]		(DM 1,500,000) US$ 939,300
3. Invest the dollar proceeds in U.S. securities at an interest rate of 9.00% for 130 days		(US$ 939,300)
4. Buy DM forward contract (matures on Dec 17, 1990) for an amount of DM1,546,096 at a future exchange rate of 0.6249(US$/DM) (Note: DM1,546,096 includes both the principal and future interest expense. See point 7 below.)		0
		0
December 17, 1990		
5. Receive matured U.S.-investment		
principal	US$ 939,300	
plus: interest income	30,527	US$ 969,827
[$939,300 × 0.09 × (130/360)]		
6. Deliver the U.S. dollars against long forward position and receive DM [DM1,546,096 × 0.6249(US$/DM)]		US$ 966,155 DM 1,546,096
7. Return the borrowed DM		
principal	DM 1,500,000	
plus: interest expense	46,096	(DM 1,546,096)
[DM1,500,000 × 0.0851 × (130/360)]		
Net arbitrage profit		US$ 3,672

Note: If futures contracts were used in this example, the arbitrager would have to go long 12 Dec 90 DM futures (DM1,546,096/DM125,000 = 12.37) and would incur the residual risk associated with the extra 0.37 futures contract (or DM46,096). To avoid any unanticipated exchange gain (loss) due to rounding the number of futures contracts, forward contracts are used in the example.

markets there is neither a clearinghouse guarantee nor the associated regulatory oversight; there are no initial or variation margin requirements (or marking-to-market); and settlement normally occurs by delivery of the currency (rather than by offset). Table 14.10 summarizes the main differences between forward and futures currency contracts.

The characteristics of forward contracts make it easy to understand why participation in forward markets is limited to large firms and institutions. With no margin requirements and no clearinghouse oversight, each participant in the forward market directly bears the credit risk of the other contracting party. Thus, only participants with credit-standings beyond reproach are acceptable to other participants.

TABLE 14.10
Futures and forward currency contracts compared

	Forward	Futures
Size of contracts	Tailored to individual needs	Standardized
Delivery date	Tailored to individual needs	Standardized
Contract prices	Established by the bank or broker via telephone contact with limited number of buyers and sellers	Determined by open auction among buyers and sellers on exchange floor
Participants	Banks, brokers, multinational companies, commodity pools, and institutional funds	Banks, brokers and multinational companies, commodity pools, institutional funds and small traders.
Commissions	Set by spread between dealer's buy and sell price	Published brokerage fee
Margins	None but compensating bank balances may be required	Margin deposit required
Clearing operation (financial integrity)	Handling contingent on individual banks and brokers. No separate clearinghouse.	Handled by exchange clearinghouse. Daily settlements to the market and variation margin requirements.
Marketplace	Over the telephone worldwide and computer networks	Central exchange floor with worldwide communications
Accessibility	Limited to large customers	Open to anyone who needs hedge facilities or has risk capital with which to speculate
Regulation	Self-regulating	Self-regulating and regulated by the Commodity Futures Trading Commission
Frequency of delivery	More than 90% settled by actual delivery	Actual delivery less than 1% of volume
Price fluctuations	No daily limit	No daily limit

14.7 APPLICATIONS OF FOREIGN CURRENCY FUTURES

14.7.1 Hedging with Currency Futures

Hedging foreign currency transactions is often necessary to protect the profit expected on ordinary international business transactions. Exchange rates can be quite volatile and unpredictable, and can eliminate anticipated profits in a short period of time. Fortunately, this currency risk can be hedged with currency futures.

A long hedge (i.e., buying currency futures contracts) protects against a rise in a foreign currency's value. A short hedge (i.e., selling currency futures contracts) protects against a decline in a foreign currency's value. A long hedge, for example, might be used by a U.S. importer who must pay in a foreign currency or by a borrower of a foreign currency who now holds a U.S. dollar investment but will in the future have to repay the foreign currency loan. In both instances there is an exposure to the risk that the foreign currency will become more expensive. In contrast, a short hedge might be used by a U.S. exporter who expects to be paid in a foreign currency, or even by a non-U.S. importer who buys goods with U.S. dollars.

THE LONG HEDGE. On August 9, 1990, a U.S. importer signs a contract to buy German machinery for a total cost of DM 1,250,000. The payment date is December 17, 1990. The importer is facing the risk that the mark may appreciate between August and December. On August 9, the spot DM exchange rate ($/DM) is 0.6262, while the December 90 DM futures price is 0.6249. In order to protect against an adverse movement in exchange rates, the importer decides to go long 10 December 90 DM futures contracts (each futures contract calls for delivery of DM 125,000) at the price of 0.6249. On December 17 (the last trading day of the December 90 DM futures contract), he plans to offset the futures position and purchase DM 1,250,000 in the spot market. This allows him to fix the purchase cost of the machinery at US$781,125 [DM1,250,000×0.6249($/DM)] on August 9, regardless of the market conditions that prevail on December 17. The following demonstrates the outcome of this hedging strategy under alternative scenarios.

Case 1:	DM appreciate to 0.6400 on December 17, 1990:	
	Purchase cost: DM 1,250,000 × 0.6400 ($/DM)	= US $800,000
	Less: Futures gain of (0.6400 − 0.6249) × 125,000 × 10	= − 18,875
	Net purchase cost:	= US $781,125

Case 2:	DM depreciates to 0.6100 on December 17, 1990:	
	Purchase cost: DM 1,250,000 × 0.6100 ($/DM)	= US $762,500
	Plus: Futures loss of (0.6100 − 0.6249) × 125,000 × 10	= + 18,625
	Net purchase cost:	= US $781,125

THE SHORT HEDGE. On August 9, 1990, a U.S. exporting firm signs a contract to sell U.S. goods to a British firm. It will receive £1,000,000 for payment on September 17, 1990, which coincides with the last trading day of the September 90 £ futures contract. Fearing that the pound will depreciate against the dollar between now and September 17, the U.S. firm decides to protect itself by going short 16 September 90 £ futures contracts (each contract calls for delivery of £62,500). The September 90 £ futures price on August 9 is 1.8550 ($/£). The spot £ exchange rate on August 9 is 1.8680. The U.S. firm will offset its futures position on September 17 and sell the £1,000,000 it receives from the

British firm in the spot market. By hedging this way, the U.S. firm will be guaranteed a sales revenue of US$1,855,000 [£1,000,000 × 1.8550($/£)], independent of the market conditions that exist on September 17. This is illustrated by the following:

Case 1:	BP appreciates to 1.8893 on September 17, 1990:	
	Sales revenue: £1,000,000 × 1.8893 ($/£)	= US $1,889,300
	Less: Futures loss of (1.8550 − 1.8893) × 62,500 × 16	= − 34,300
	Net sales revenue:	= US $1,855,000

Case 2:	BP depreciates to 1.8000 on September 17, 1990:	
	Sales revenue: £1,000,000 × 1.8000 ($/£)	= US $1,800,000
	Plus: Futures gain of (1.8550 − 1.8000) × 62,500 × 16	= + 55,000
	Net sales revenue:	= US $1,855,000

In both of the above hedging examples, an adverse exchange rate move was counterbalanced by profits on the futures position. However, in both cases the hedger did not profit from a *favorable* movement in exchange rates. Since the hedger's objective, nevertheless, was to eliminate foreign currency risk, the hedge must be judged a success.

14.7.2   Synthetic Foreign Currency Futures Contracts

U.S. dollar-denominated futures contracts can be used to create *synthetic* foreign currency futures contracts. By buying one currency futures and simultaneously selling another currency futures it is possible to create the equivalent of a currency futures contract denominated in a currency other than U.S. dollars, or to establish a cross-currency futures spread.

Suppose that a money manager expects the mark to appreciate relative to the yen. He can buy mark futures and sell yen futures, locking in a future exchange rate between the yen and the mark:

$$F_{t,T}(\yen/\mathrm{DM}) = \frac{F_{t,T}(\$/\mathrm{DM})}{F_{t,T}(\$/\yen)}$$

This position will be profitable under the following conditions:

1. Both the mark and the yen appreciate with respect to the dollar, but the mark appreciates more.

2. Both the mark and the yen depreciate with respect to the dollar, but the mark depreciates less.
3. The mark appreciates relative to the dollar, and the yen depreciates relative to the dollar.

In the first two cases, only one leg of the spread is profitable, but the profits on this leg exceed the losses on the other leg. In the last case both legs of the spread generate gains. It should be clear that the reverse spread (i.e., long yen and short marks) will be profitable under the opposite conditions. These results, however, will occur only if the futures positions are established in the correct proportions: equal *dollar-value* futures positions on both legs of the spread.

14.7.3 Hedging with Synthetic Cross Rate Futures Contracts

Suppose that on August 9, 1990, a Japanese manufacturer agrees to purchase equipment from a German company for DM 10,000,000. The payment date is December 17, 1990 (the last trading day of *all* December 90 foreign currency futures contracts on the CME). The manufacturer fears that the mark will appreciate relative to the yen prior to December. If that happens, the cost (in yen) of the equipment will increase.

The Japanese manufacturer decides to hedge against a possible mark appreciation by using a synthetic yen-denominated mark futures contract to lock in the exchange rate between the yen and the mark on August 9. He goes long the December mark futures contract and goes short the December yen futures contract, both of which are denominated in dollars. On August 9, the price of the December 90 yen futures contract ($/¥) is 0.006677, and the price of the December 90 mark futures contract ($/DM) is 0.6249.

To obtain the required quantity of marks for the equipment purchase, the manufacturer takes a long position of 80 DM December futures contracts:

$$\frac{\text{DM}\,10,000,000}{\text{DM}\,125,000} = 80$$

These contracts lock in a dollar cost of $6,249,000 on December 17:

$$\text{DM}\,10,000,000 \times 0.6249(\$/\text{DM}) = \$6,249,000$$

But the Japanese manufacturer must also be sure that he will be able to obtain $6,249,000 in December with the yen he has available. To guarantee this, he goes short the December 90 yen futures contracts, locking in the future dollar-yen exchange rate for December 17. Based on the December 90 yen futures contract price on August 9, he needs to sell 935,899,356 yen in order to receive $6,249,000 (i.e., $\frac{\$6,249,000}{0.006677}$). He therefore has to go short approximately 75 yen futures contracts on August 9:

$$\frac{¥935,899,356}{¥12,500,000} = 74.87$$

Thus, by taking a long position of 80 DM futures contracts and a short position of 75 ¥ futures contracts, the Japanese manufacturer creates a synthetic yen-dominated mark futures contract which locks in the rate at which he will exchange yen for marks on December 17, the date of his purchase of the German equipment. By doing so he avoids the risk associated with fluctuations in the yen/mark exchange rate. Specifically, the manufacturer locks in a yen/mark cross exchange rate of 93.59:

$$F_{t,T}(¥/DM) = \frac{F_{t,T}(\$/DM)}{F_{t,T}(\$/¥)} = \frac{0.6249}{0.006677} = 93.59$$

14.8 EURO RATE DIFFERENTIAL FUTURES CONTRACTS

Trading in *Euro rate differential* futures contracts (commonly known as *DIFFs*) began on July 6, 1990, on the Chicago Mercantile Exchange. These contracts are based upon interest rate differentials between three-month Eurodollar deposit offered rates (LIBOR) and the offered rates on three-month Europounds, Euromarks, and Euroyen deposits. Contracts are traded on a quarterly cycle and are cash-settled at expiration. Similar to other Eurodollar contracts, the price of a DIFF contract is quoted as an index, calculated by subtracting the nondollar Eurocurrency rate from the Eurodollar rate, and then deducting the difference from 100.

DIFF contracts, while ostensibly short-term interest rate futures contracts, are relevant to foreign currency futures. They allow traders to take positions on interest-rate differentials between dollar and nondollar deposits without incurring a currency exposure risk. In the absence of these contracts, interest rate arbitrage between countries involves several corresponding foreign currency transactions in order to lock in the interest rate differential (see Section 14.5.4). In addition, since exchange rates are partly determined by relative movements in interest rates in different countries, DIFF contracts can be useful in hedging foreign currency risk.

Whether DIFF contracts will prove to be a useful addition to the futures contracts already available, only time will tell us.

CONCLUSION

Volatile exchange rates have made foreign currency risk management an increasingly important part of financial management in international corporations and banks. We review both the interbank currency market and the organized futures markets for foreign currencies. The pricing fundamentals of currency futures are examined as well as the relationships between spot and futures exchange rates.

In addition, cross border interest rate arbitrage is discussed, and it is shown that currency futures are an integral part of such arbitrage. Finally, various examples are given of how currency futures can be used to hedge foreign exchange risk, including the use of synthetic currency futures contracts to lock in cross exchange rates.

QUESTIONS

1. What is the distinction between a fixed and floating exchange rate system?
2. What are the two quotation conventions employed in spot currency markets, and how are they related?
3. What is a cross exchange rate? In an efficient market, what is the relationship between cross exchange rates and dollar exchange rates?
4. Determine whether the exchange rates for Canadian dollars and Dutch guilders in Table 14.2 are consistent with the relevant cross exchange rate in Table 14.3.
5. Are currency futures cash settled contracts?
6. Are currency futures quoted as units of a foreign currency per dollar, or dollars per unit of a foreign currency?
7. The theoretical price of a foreign currency futures contract is determined by a cost-of-carry relationship. What are the elements of this relationship?
8. Why should a U.S. investor be able to earn the *U.S.* riskless rate of return on investments in foreign currencies?
9. Show how to calculate the annualized implied repo rate (IRR) on a foreign currency investment. If the IRR is higher than the dollar borrowing rate, describe the appropriate arbitrage transaction.
10. Assuming that on August 9, 1990, the seven-month interest rate in the United Kingdom were 10 percent, and the seven-month interest rate in the United States were 8 percent, does a profitable arbitrage opportunity exist? Explain how you arrived at your answer. Describe and reproduce the transactions involved in doing the arbitrage. Calculate the expected arbitrage profit (use Tables 14.2 and 14.7).
11. Why are the participants in the forward currency markets generally much larger than in the futures market?
12. If a U.S. exporter agrees to accept payment in the future in a foreign currency, what is his currency risk exposure? How would he hedge this risk with futures contracts? Assuming that he will be paid 1 million Swiss francs, what should his futures position be?
13. What is a synthetic currency futures contract? How do you create one?
14. On October 8, 1990, the following interest rate and exchange rate relationships existed:
    (a) Yield:
        - 10-year U.S. government bonds: 8.67%
        - 10-year Japanese government bonds: 7.42%
        - 10-year British gilts: 11.71%
    (b) Exchange rates:
        i. Spot:
            - $¥/\$ = 130.75$
            - $\$/£ = 1.9740$

    ii. Six-month forward:
   - ¥/$ = 130.88
   - $/£ = 1.9260

(Note: The U.S. dollar is at a forward premium to both the Japanese yen and the British pound.)

    An investment advisor recommends that you, as a Japanese, buy U.S. 10-year bonds, and hedge your exchange rate risk by selling dollars forward six months, where you will obtain an additional premium because dollars are at a forward premium to yen. Evaluate this strategy.

    The same investment advisor recommends that an American buy 10-year British gilts, and hedge by selling British pounds forward six months, even though the pound is at a forward discount to the dollar.

    Evaluate this strategy. In making your evaluations, consider the following:

- What is the annual rate of return on the recommended investments? (Show the appropriate calculations.)
- Do these investments entail any risk? Explain your answer.

    Assuming that interest rate parity theory holds, what does the implied term structure look like in the respective countries?

    Finally, if you have identified a risk exposure in these investments, do you have any suggestions about how this risk could be hedged with futures?

SUGGESTED READING

Benet, B. "Commodity Futures Cross Hedging of Foreign Exchange Exposure." *The Journal of Futures Markets*, Vol. 10, No. 3 (1990), pp. 287–306.

Cavanaugh, K. "Price Dynamics in Foreign Currency Futures Markets." *Journal of International Money and Finance*, Vol. 6, No. 3 (1987), pp. 295–314.

Chang, J. and L. Shanker. "Hedging Effectiveness of Currency Options and Currency Futures." *The Journal of Futures Markets*, Vol. 6, No. 2 (1986), pp. 289–305.

Grammatikos, T. and A. Saunders. "Stability and the Hedging Performance of Foreign Currency Futures." *The Journal of Futures Markets*, Vol. 3, No. 3 (1983), pp. 295–305.

Hammer, J. "Hedging and Risk Aversion in the Foreign Currency Market." *The Journal of Futures Markets*, Vol. 8 (December 1988), pp. 657–686.

Hodrick, R. and S. Srivastava. "Foreign Currency Futures." *Journal of International Economics*, Vol. 22 (1987), pp. 1–24.

Kodres, L. "Tests of Unbiasedness in Foreign Exchange Futures Markets: The Effects of Price Limits." *The Review of Futures Markets*, Vol. 7, No. 1 (1988), pp. 138–166.

Korajczyk, R. "The Pricing of Forward Contracts for Foreign Exchange." *Journal of Political Economy*, Vol. 93 (April 1985), pp. 346–368.

Levine, R. "The Pricing of Forward Exchange Rates." *Journal of International Money and Finance*, Vol. 8, No. 2 (1989), pp. 163–179.

CHAPTER 15

COMMODITY FUTURES

This chapter covers those futures markets that were not explicitly covered in previous chapters. The remaining futures contracts fall into three commodity groupings: agricultural (including livestocks and the so-called *soft* commodities), energy, and metals (both precious and industrial). Trading in these commodity futures, taken together, constitutes about 40 percent of total trading on U.S. futures exchanges (see Table 1.1 in Chapter 1).

This chapter is not the first encounter readers of this book have had with commodity futures. The discussion and examples in Chapter 4, which covered the pricing fundamentals of futures, focused on silver, copper, and heating oil futures. Similarly, in Chapters 5 and 6, which dealt with hedging, much of the discussion utilized commodity futures. We have, therefore, already covered the pricing and hedging fundamentals of commodity futures. It remains only to describe more comprehensively the particular futures contracts that are traded in these markets.

The organization of the chapter is as follows. Section 15.1 briefly reviews the pricing fundamentals of commodity futures. This review is a summary of material already covered in Chapter 4. Section 15.2 examines agricultural commodity futures; Section 15.3 covers energy futures; Section 15.4 discusses precious-metal futures; Section 15.5 covers industrial-metal futures; and Section 15.6 contains a brief discussion of hedging with commodity futures.

15.1 PRICING FUNDAMENTALS

A key difference between commodity futures and financial futures is that commodity futures are often subject to the existence of a convenience yield. The concept of a *convenience yield* was discussed extensively in Chapter 4 (in Sections 4.3.5 and

4.3.6). Commodity futures prices may also exhibit seasonal patterns uncommon for financial futures.

The basic pricing formula for commodity futures is

$$FP_{t,T} = CP_t + CC_{t,T} - Y_{t,T}$$

where $FP_{t,T}$ = futures price in period t for delivery at time T.

CP_t = price of the underlying cash commodity at time t.

$CC_{t,T}$ = total per unit net cost of carrying the commodity from time t to T.

$Y_{t,T}$ = convenience yield (measured in dollars per unit of the underlying commodity) for period t to T.

Thus, the convenience yield implicit in a commodity futures price is

$$Y_{t,T} = (CP_t + CC_{t,T}) - FP_{t,T}$$

where $CP_t + CC_{t,T}$ represents the full-carry futures price.[1] If the actual futures price is less than the full-carry futures price, or

$$FP_{t,T} < (CP_t + CC_{t,T})$$

the underlying commodity is said to have a convenience yield.

Predicting commodity futures prices is difficult because of unanticipated variations in convenience yields. Understanding these variations requires a thorough knowledge of the economic fundamentals of the underlying cash commodity market. Since commodity markets differ significantly from one another, there are no easy and reliable generalizations. Heating oil is quite different from soybeans, and both are very different from copper.

In the next four sections of the chapter the leading futures contracts in each of the commodity futures groups are described. This discussion makes clear the extensive scope and variety of the cash markets that are involved.

15.2 AGRICULTURAL FUTURES

15.2.1 Trading and Growth

Table 15.1 lists the leading agricultural commodity futures contracts both in the U.S. and on foreign exchanges together with their respective trading volumes in 1990. Cocoa, coffee, sugar, and cotton are often referred to as *soft* commodity futures. In the United States, the three most active agricultural contracts—corn, soybean, and sugar #11—account for almost half of the total trading volume in this group.

Figure 15-1 shows annual trading volume in agricultural futures from 1981 to 1990. Although there is considerable variation from year to year, there is no

---

[1]This formula, as we noted earlier, ignores the possibility that various delivery options may exist which have value. To the extent that a particular commodity has a delivery option with a recognizable value, this formula would have to be modified.

TABLE 15.1
Agricultural and soft futures (major contracts: 1990 trading volume)

| | U.S. | | | Foreign | |
Contract	Exchange	Trading volume	Contract	Exchange	Trading volume
Corn	CBOT	11,423,027	Raw sugar	Tokyo Sugar Exchange*	6,375,354
Soybeans	CBOT	10,301,905	American soybeans	Tokyo Grain Exchange*	4,401,165
Sugar #11	CSCE	5,424,801	Raw sugar	Osaka Sugar Exchange*	2,837,839
Soybean meal	CBOT	4,904,471	Red beans	Tokyo Grain Exchange*	2,739,687
Soybean oil	CBOT	4,658,302	Rubber	Tokyo Commodity Exchange*	2,308,449
Live cattle	CME	3,797,376	Cotton yarn	Tokyo Commodity Exchange*	1,865,880
Wheat	CBOT	2,876,270	Imported soybeans	Osaka Grain Exchange*	1,824,590
Live hogs	CME	2,241,272	Cocoa	London Fox, U.K.	1,701,586
Coffee "C"	CSCE	1,774,050	Red beans	Osaka Grain Exchange*	1,526,872
Cocoa	CSCE	1,635,917	Rubber	Kobe Rubber Exchange*	1,383,394
Soybeans	MIDAM	1,565,641	Dried cocoon	Toyahashi Dried Cocoon Exchange*	1,328,122
Cotton #2	NYCE	1,534,611	Cotton yarn	Nagoya Textile Exchange*	1,209,007
Pork bellies	CME	1,303,129	Coffee	London Fox, U.K.	1,170,176
Wheat	KCBT	1,136,234	Dried cocoon	Maebashi Dried Cocoon Exchange*	1,159,978
Others		2,511,342	Sugar	London Fox, U.K.	896,400
	U.S. Total	57,088,348			

* Exchange located in Japan.

Contracts traded (millions)

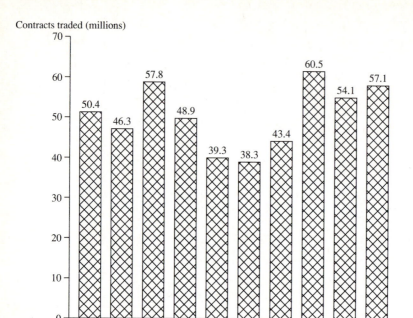

FIGURE 15-1
U.S. agricultural and soft futures (Annual trading volume: 1981–1990).

overall growth trend. Trading volume in 1990 is similar to what it was in 1983. In contrast, from 1960 to 1980 there was a 19-fold increase in the trading of agricultural and soft commodity futures (see Table 1.1 in Chapter 1). Most of this growth, therefore, occurred during the 1960–1980 period, rather than during the 1980s.

15.2.2 Contract Specifications and Delivery

Tables 15.2, 15.3, and 15.4 provide the contract specifications for the main agricultural commodities, broken up by grains, soft commodities, and meat futures. In general, futures on these commodities are traded for delivery in many different months. For example, there are seven contract months for soybeans and eight contract months for soybean oil. Also, futures trading usually continues into the delivery month, although for sugar #11 and coffee "C" it ceases prior to the delivery month.[2] All of the contracts permit the short to designate when she intends to make delivery during the delivery month. Finally, in some contracts, like wheat, the short is given an option to choose which among several approved deliverable grades of the commodity she wishes to deliver. In addition, she may be able to choose among several different permissible delivery locations.

---

[2]In this chapter, the terms *contract months* and *delivery months* are used interchangeably.

TABLE 15.2
Specifications of major U.S. grain futures contracts

	Soybeans	Corn	Soybean meal	Soybean oil	Wheat
Exchange	CBOT	CBOT	CBOT	CBOT	CBOT
Symbol	S	C	SM	BO	W
Trading unit	5000 bushels	5000 bushels	100 tons	60,000 pounds	5000 bushels
Deliverable grade	No. 2 Yellow at par and substitutions at differentials set by the exchange	No. 2 Yellow at par and substitutions at differentials set by the exchange	One grade of meal only with minimum protein of 44%	One grade of crude soybean oil only	No. 2 Soft Red, No. 2 Hard Red Winter, No. 2 Dark Northern Spring, No. 1 Northern Spring at par, and other permissible substitutions
Price quotation	Cents and quarter cents per bushel	Cents and quarter cents per bushel	Dollars and cents per ton	Dollars and cents per pound	Cents and quarter cents per bushel
Tick size	1/4 cent per bushel, $12.50 per contract	1/4 cent per bushel, $12.50 per contract	10 cents per ton, $10 per contract	1/100 of a cent per pound, $6 per contract	1/4 cent per bushel, $12.50 per contract
Contract months	Jan, Mar, May, Jul, Aug, Sep, Dec	Mar, May, Jun, Sep, Dec	Jan, Mar, May, Jul, Aug, Sep, Oct, Dec	Jan, Mar, May, Jul, Aug, Sep, Oct, Dec	Mar, May, Jul, Sep, Dec
Last trading day	Seven business days before the last business day of the contract month	Seven business days before the last business day of the contract month	Seven business days before the last business day of the contract month	Seven business days before the last business day of the contract month	Seven business days before the last business day of the contract month

TABLE 15.3
Specifications of major U.S. soft commodities futures contracts

	Sugar #11	Cotton #2	Cocoa	Coffee "C"
Exchange	CSCE	NYCE	CSCE	CSCE
Symbol	SB	CT	CC	KC
Trading unit	112,000 pounds	50,000 pounds	10 metric tons	37,500 pounds
Deliverable grade	Raw centrifugal cane sugar	Strict low middling $1\frac{1}{16}$ inch U.S. grown white cotton	Exchange–set tolerances for defects, bean count, bean size, and other standards	Arabica coffee
Price quotation	Cents per pound	Cents per pound	Dollars per ton	Cents per pound
Tick size	1/100 cent per pound, $11.20 per contract	1/100 cent per pound, $5 per contract	$1 per metric ton, $10 per contract	1/100 cent per pound, $3.75 per contract
Contract months	Jan, Mar, May, Jul, Oct	Mar, May, Jul, Oct, Dec	Mar, May, Jul, Sep, Dec	Mar, May, Jul, Sep, Dec
Last trading day	Last business day of the month preceding the contract month	17th business day of the contract month	11th business day before the first business day of the contract month	One business day prior to the first business day of the contract month

TABLE 15.4
Specifications of major U.S. meat futures contracts

	Live cattle	Live hogs	Pork bellies
Exchange	CME	CME	CME
Symbol	LC	LH	PB
Trading unit	40,000 pounds	30,000 pounds	40,000 pounds
Deliverable grade	USDA Choice Grade or better fat cattle (steers)	USDA Grade No. 1, No. 2 and No. 3 barrows and gilts	USDA approved, frozen pork bellies, cut and trimmed
Price quotation	Cents per pound	Cents per pound	Cents per pound
Tick size	$0.00025 per pound, $10 per contract	$0.00025 per pound, $7.50 per contract	$0.00025 per pound, $10 per contract
Contract months	Feb, Apr, Jun, Aug, Sep, Oct, Dec	Feb, Apr, Jun, Jul, Aug, Oct, Dec	Feb, Mar, May, Jul, Aug
Last trading day	20th calendar day of the contract month	20th calendar day of the contract month	6th business day prior to the end of the contract month

15.2.3   Invoice Prices and Delivery Differentials

When alternative delivery grades are permitted, there is an adjustment in the contract invoice price when a short delivers something other than the *par grade*. The par grade is defined as the deliverable grade for which there is no price adjustment. If the short delivers something other than the par grade, there is an exchange-specified adjustment in the invoice price. (This is similar to the conversion factors for T-bond futures contracts discussed in Chapter 13.)

For grain futures, *additive grade adjustment* factors are specified by the exchange prior to the beginning of trading in the contract. For example, the CBOT wheat futures contract specifies four par delivery grades and seven other deliverable grades, with associated adjustment factors (usually plus or minus one cent per bushel from the price of the par grade). The invoice price for wheat futures is calculated according to the following formula:

$$\text{Invoice price} = \text{Quoted futures price} + \text{Adjustment factor}$$

Suppose that the settlement price of wheat futures on the last day of trading is $2.53 per bushel, and that the short decides to deliver 5000 bushels of Number One soft red wheat. Number One soft red is not a par grade wheat. It is a more valuable grade of wheat, and therefore has an adjustment factor of plus one cent per bushel. The invoice price, consequently, will be:

$$\text{Invoice price} = \$2.53 \text{ per bushel} + \$.01 \text{ per bushel} = \$2.54 \text{ per bushel}$$

As we have seen in Chapter 13 for T-bond futures, whenever there are multiple delivery grades together with exchange-determined invoice price adjustments,

TABLE 15.5
**Cash price quotations: Agricultural
and soft commodities
(December 10, 1990)**

CASH PRICES

Monday December 10, 1990.
(Closing Market Quotations)

GRAINS AND FEEDS

	Mon	Fri	Yr.Ago
Barley, top-quality Mpls., bu	n2.25-.35	2.25-.35	3.20
Bran, wheat middlings, KC ton	70.00	69.00	95.00
Corn, No. 2 yel. Cent-Ill. bu	bp2.28	2.27	2.29½
Corn Gluten Feed, Midwest, ton ..	85.-110.	85.-100.	96.50
Cottonseed Meal,			
Clksdle,Miss. ton...........................	145.00	145.00	175.75
Hominy Feed,Cent-Ill. ton	80.00	80.00	83.00
Meat-Bonemeal, 50% pro. Ill. ton.	205.-210.	205.-210.	215.00
Oats, No. 2 milling, Mpls., bu	n1.28-.30	1.28-.30	1.74½
Sorghum, (Milo) No. 2 Gulf cwt ...	4.64	4.60	4.60
Soybean Meal,			
Decatur, Illinois ton..........	163½-167½	163½-167½	179.50
Soybeans, No. 1 yel Cent.-Ill. bu ...	bp5.88	5.87	5.69
Wheat,			
Spring 14%-pro Mpls. bu....	2.81½-.85½	2.81½-85½	4.22½
Wheat, No. 2 sft red, St.Lou. bu	bp2.75	2.72½	4.22½
Wheat, No. 2 hard KC, bu	2.79¼	2.79	4.38½
Wheat, sft wht; del Portland Ore. .	2.86	2.84	4.64

FOODS

Beef, Carcass, Equiv.Index Value,			
choice 1-3,550-700lbs.	123.50	122.75	n.a.
Beef, Carcass, Equiv.Index Value,			
select 1-3,550-700lbs.	112.10	111.35	n.a.
Broilers, Dressed "A" NY lb	x.5315	.5113	.5006
Butter, AA, Chgo., lb.	1.03¼	1.03¼	1.25
Cocoa, Ivory Coast, $metric ton ...	g1,436	1,395	1,148
Coffee, Brazilian, NY lb.	n.82	.82	.70
Coffee, Colombian, NY lb.	n.93½	.94	n.a.
Eggs, Lge white, Chgo doz.	.77-.83	.77-.83	.91½
Flour, hard winter KC cwt	7.45	7.35	10.40
Hams, 17-20 lbs, Mid-US lb fob	.76-.87	z	1.00
Hogs, Iowa-S.Minn. avg. cwt	48.00	48.50	49.00
Hogs, Omaha avg cwt	47.00	48.00	49.00
Pork Bellies, 12-14 lbs Mid-US lb ..	.55-.57	.52-.55	.40
Pork Loins, 14-18 lbs. Mid-US lb ...	1.03-.06	1.02-.03	.95
Steers, Tex.-Okla. ch avg cwt	81.25	81.00	77.00
Steers, Feeder, Okl Cty, av cwt	100.75	10.00	90.25
Sugar, cane, raw, world, lb. fob ...	.0971	.0967	.1368

FATS AND OILS

Coconut Oil, crd, N. Orleans lb.	xxn.17	.17	.21¾
Corn Oil, crd wet mill, Chgo. lb. ...	n.26	.26	.23
Corn Oil, crd dry mill, Chgo. lb. ...	n.27¼	.27¼	.23¼
Cottonseed Oil, crd Miss Vly lb. ...	n.24½	.24½	.20½
Grease, choice white, Chgo lb.	n.12½	.12½	.12
Lard, Chgo lb.	n.14½	.14½	.13
Palm Oil, ref. bl. deod. N.Orl. lb ...	n.17½	.17½	.15¼
Soybean Oil, crd, Decatur, lb.	.2185	.2188	.1917
Tallow, bleachable, Chgo lb.	b.13¾	.13¾	.14
Tallow, edible, Chgo lb.	n.15	.15	.16½

FIBERS AND TEXTILES

Burlap, 10 oz 40-in NY yd	n.2885	.2885	.2815
Cotton 1 1/16 str lw-md Mphs lb ...	.6900	.6768	.6041
Wool, 64s, Staple, Terr. del. lb.	2.20	2.20	3.50

b: bid
bp: country elevator bids
g: main crop, ex-dock, warehouses, Eastern Seaboard,
north of Hatteras
n: nominal
x: less than truckloads
xx: f.o.b. tankcars
z: not quoted
n.a.: not available

Source: The Wall Street Journal, December 11, 1990.

the short will deliver the *cheapest-deliverable grade*. To determine this grade, the short adjusts the spot (or market) price of each deliverable grade by the relevant exchange adjustment factor. The cheapest-deliverable grade will be the one with the lowest delivery-adjusted spot price.[3]

15.2.4 Cash and Futures Price Quotations

Table 15.5 provides cash price quotations typically shown for agricultural commodities. Table 15.6 shows price quotations for the futures contracts traded on these commodities. In contrast to financial futures, there is generally a direct correspondence between cash and futures price quotations for commodities. For example, corn is quoted as so many cents per bushel in both cash and futures markets, live cattle is quoted as cents per pound in both cash and futures markets, and so forth.

As explained in Chapter 4, a carry pricing relationship commonly applies to commodities that are easily storable and in abundant supply. Agricultural commodities that are easily storable and deliverable include cocoa, coffee, corn, cotton, oats, orange juice, soybeans, soybean oil, and wheat. Commodities that are not storable, and hence frequently not subject to a carry pricing relationship, are live cattle, live hogs, and feeder cattle.

15.2.5 The Determination of Agricultural Futures Prices: The Case of Soybean Futures Prices

To illustrate the kinds of factors that affect agricultural futures prices, this section examines soybean futures prices. In Table 15.6 soybean futures display a complex forward price structure. A carry relationship generally exists for the January 91 through August 91 contracts, and from the November 91 contract forward. The August 91 to November 91 contracts, however, display backwardation. This overall price structure mirrors the agricultural cycle: the crop year for soybeans begins on September 1 and ends on August 31. Soybean prices are usually lowest at harvest time (i.e., November) and move higher during the marketing year (or crop year), as storage, interest and insurance costs accumulate over time. Toward the end of the crop year, soybean stocks dwindle, so that an increase in demand can have a sizeable effect on prices. Consequently, the prices of July and August soybeans in one crop year are sometimes higher than November soybeans of the next crop year. Further, since next year's soybeans are not available until November, if there is a shortage in July there is no limit to how far July futures prices can trade above November futures prices. Thus, it is common for soybean futures contracts to be in a carry relationship from November through July or August, but

---

[3]The delivery of something other than the *par grade* can be treated as a delivery option that has potential value, similar to a *timing* or *location* delivery option.

TABLE 15.6
Price quotations for agricultural and soft futures (December 10, 1990)

	Open	High	Low	Settle	Change	Lifetime High	Lifetime Low	Open Interest
–GRAINS AND OILSEEDS–								
CORN (CBT) 5,000 bu.; cents per bu.								
Dec	226¾	227¼	225¾	226¾	+ ¾	296½	215½	8,217
Mr91	237¼	238	236¾	238	+ 1	302½	227¼	90,300
May	244¾	245¾	244½	245½	+ 1	306½	235	34,581
July	250¾	252¼	250½	252	+ 1½	308¼	241½	45,286
Sept	250¼	252¼	250¼	252	+ 1¾	287½	240¼	5,776
Dec	249¾	252	249½	252	+ 2½	275	242½	16,739
Mr92	257	258¼	257	258¼	+ 2	262	249	638
Est vol 28,000; vol Fri 23,590; open int 201,537, −2,421.								
OATS (CBT) 5,000 bu.; cents per bu.								
Dec	111¼	111¼	110½	110¼	....	194¼	103½	76
Mr91	121½	121½	120¼	120½	− ¼	201	115½	7,664
May	126¼	127	126¼	126	− ¼	183¾	122	2,453
July	132½	132½	132	132	+ ¼	164¾	127½	1,334
Est vol 1,000; vol Fri 419; open int 11,623, −11.								
SOYBEANS (CBT) 5,000 bu.; cents per bu.								
Jan	596	598¼	591½	595¾	+ ¾	692	564¼	43,398
Mar	611	613½	607	610½	+ ½	703	578½	30,820
May	626	627	620¾	624¾	+ 1	711	592	17,812
July	637	638¾	632¾	636¾	+ 1¼	718	603½	17,726
Aug	639	640	636	639½	+ 2¼	695	607½	2,768
Sept	627½	628½	625½	628	+ 1¼	670	601	2,781
Nov	625½	627	622½	625¾	+ 1½	674	601½	9,106
Ja92	637½	638	636	637	+ 1¾	642½	615½	270
Est vol 35,000; vol Fri 30,784; open int 124,713, +195.								
SOYBEAN MEAL (CBT) 100 tons; $ per ton.								
Dec	174.50	175.70	173.80	175.00	+ .40	205.50	169.20	3,435
Ja91	176.50	177.90	175.60	176.70	+ .10	204.00	171.50	24,927
Mar	181.80	183.00	180.50	181.90	+ .30	212.00	174.50	22,221
May	185.20	186.20	184.20	185.80	+ 1.10	208.00	175.80	10,031
July	188.50	189.30	187.70	188.70	+ .60	209.00	177.50	6,114
Aug	189.00	190.00	189.00	189.60	+ 1.50	199.00	176.50	1,558
Sept	188.00	189.00	188.00	188.60	+ 1.60	193.50	175.50	2,166
Oct	187.40	187.50	187.40	187.00	+ 1.20	190.00	181.20	907
Dec	188.00	189.20	188.00	189.10	+ 1.00	190.00	181.50	2,184
Ja92	....	....	....	187.50	+ .50	186.00	183.50	123
Est vol 20,000; vol Fri 28,172; open int 73,665, −1,482.								
SOYBEAN OIL (CBT) 60,000 lbs.; cents per lb.								
Dec	21.55	21.55	21.36	21.50	− .03	25.55	19.75	1,662
Ja91	21.72	21.76	21.54	21.66	− .07	25.55	19.81	26,223
Mar	22.10	22.10	21.90	21.98	− .12	25.61	19.85	22,826
May	22.38	22.38	22.20	22.28	− .04	25.65	20.25	13,480
July	22.45	22.54	22.40	22.46	− .09	25.70	20.90	6,846
Aug	22.45	22.45	22.43	22.35	− .07	25.50	21.25	1,922
Sept	22.35	22.35	22.32	22.32	− .07	25.10	21.25	1,652
Oct	....	....	....	22.35	....	24.90	21.30	1,149
Dec	22.30	22.30	22.20	22.22	+ .02	24.75	21.30	1,622
Ja92	....	....	....	22.12	− .03	22.95	21.31	228
Est vol 17,000; vol Fri 15,900; open int 77,610, −1,300.								
WHEAT (CBT) 5,000 bu.; cents per bu.								
Dec	252	254¾	252	253¼	+ ¼	380	238	1,029
Mr91	266½	268¼	265½	267¼	+ 1	382½	256	24,604
May	274½	276	273½	274¾	+ 1	373	264½	9,189
July	279	280	277	278¾	+ ¼	355	271¾	9,364
Sept	284½	284½	284½	284½	+ ¾	326	278½	744
Dec	295	295½	295	296	+ 1¼	318	289	587
Est vol 12,000; vol Fri 9,762; open int 45,517, −574.								

	Open	High	Low	Settle	Change	Lifetime High	Lifetime Low	Open Interest
–LIVESTOCK & MEAT–								
COCOA (CSCE)–10 metric tons; $ per ton.								
Dec	1,190	1,212	1,190	1,212	+ 24	1,558	965	269
Mr91	1,223	1,245	1,216	1,241	+ 14	1,581	985	16,028
May	1,265	1,285	1,259	1,281	+ 11	1,572	1,000	6,693
July	1,301	1,319	1,297	1,319	+ 12	1,590	1,060	7,701
Sept	1,356	1,356	1,356	1,356	+ 16	1,515	1,264	3,979
Dec	....	....	....	1,388	+ 16	1,535	1,325	5,895
Mr92	....	....	....	1,422	+ 16	1,538	1,396	573
Est vol 2,962; vol Fri 4,109; open int 41,238, −1,386.								
COFFEE (CSCE)–37,500 lbs.; cents per lb.								
Dec	88.00	88.90	88.00	88.40	− .10	109.50	80.50	753
Mr91	91.80	92.20	91.30	91.60	− .60	112.00	84.35	28,708
May	94.10	94.20	93.25	93.85	− .70	113.00	87.00	6,674
July	96.35	96.60	95.90	96.20	− .75	111.50	89.25	2,360
Sept	98.45	98.50	98.00	98.40	− .75	113.50	91.80	1,580
Dec	101.50	101.50	101.25	101.30	− .50	116.00	95.35	408
Est vol 3,491; vol Fri 7,338; open int 40,509, +214.								
SUGAR–WORLD (CSCE)–112,000 lbs.; cents per lb.								
Mar	9.54	9.74	9.54	9.73	+ .13	15.22	9.08	55,716
May	9.64	9.80	9.64	9.79	+ .11	15.05	9.10	25,272
July	9.69	9.84	9.68	9.84	+ .10	14.90	9.17	14,767
Oct	9.69	9.82	9.69	9.83	+ .09	14.40	9.19	15,806
Mr92	....	....	....	9.90	+ .06	10.14	9.36	241
Est vol 6,981; vol Fri 12,500; open int 111,802, −269.								
COTTON (CTN)–50,000 lbs.; cents per lb.								
Mar	74.85	76.87	74.85	76.25	+ 1.32	77.70	63.82	613
May	74.37	76.00	74.37	75.57	+ 1.20	77.40	64.40	18,895
July	74.03	75.15	74.00	74.75	+ .79	78.38	65.67	10,364
Oct	68.20	68.65	68.20	68.60	+ .40	72.85	66.77	5,331
Dec	65.70	66.10	65.63	65.95	+ .32	69.10	64.95	806
Mr92	....	....	....	66.65	+ .35	68.50	65.85	3,316
Est vol 15,000; vol Fri 7,139; open int 39,620, −298.								

–FOOD & FIBER–

	Open	High	Low	Settle	Change	Lifetime High	Lifetime Low	Open Interest.
PORK BELLIES (CME) 40,000 lbs.; cents per lb.								
Feb	65.10	66.70	64.20	66.70	+ 2.00	73.80	49.40	8,278
Mar	64.20	65.67	63.40	65.67	+ 2.00	73.45	49.20	1,845
May	64.30	65.87	63.40	65.87	+ 2.00	73.12	49.50	2,014
July	63.50	64.97	62.90	64.97	+ 2.00	72.80	50.15	579
Aug	62.00	62.52	62.00	62.52	+ 2.00	70.05	51.60	173
Est vol 4,229; vol Fri 4,724; open int 12,889, −52.								
CATTLE–LIVE (CME) 40,000 lbs.; cents per lb.								
Dec	79.97	80.75	79.97	80.70	+ .77	80.75	71.00	12,065
Fb91	76.35	77.00	76.25	76.87	+ .70	77.80	72.50	23,825
Apr	76.20	76.95	76.20	76.87	+ .65	78.05	74.00	14,820
June	74.10	74.65	74.10	74.55	+ .50	75.45	72.15	10,112
Aug	72.70	73.12	72.70	72.92	+ .35	73.85	70.35	3,915
Oct	72.70	73.05	72.70	72.90	+ .47	73.05	70.70	2,566
Dec	73.75	74.00	73.70	73.80	+ .40	74.00	71.75	502
Est vol 18,739; vol Fri 15,042; open int 67,805, −1,219.								
HOGS (CME) 30,000 lbs.; cents per lb.								
Dec	49.25	50.30	49.20	49.95	+ .67	56.10	44.25	4,744
Fb91	48.30	49.00	48.07	48.87	+ .70	53.15	46.20	15,618
Apr	45.80	46.65	45.75	46.50	+ .65	49.90	43.60	4,909
June	49.55	50.70	49.45	50.00	+ .45	53.75	47.70	2,723

Source: The Wall Street Journal, December 11, 1990.

to display backwardation from July or August to November (as shown in Table 15.6).

Figure 15-2 plots the daily settlement prices of the July 90 and November 90 soybean futures contracts, from June 1, 1989, to July 20, 1990. July and November contracts are selected because July is the last major *old crop* month, while November is the first major *new crop* month. The July–November spread, therefore, represents an *intercrop* spread, with delivery dates in two different crop years.

Dollars per bushel

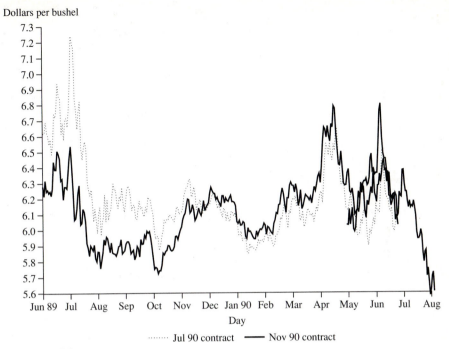

FIGURE 15-2
Soybean futures prices (daily from June 1989 to July 1990).

The link between crop years is the *carry-over*: soybeans not consumed during one crop year are carried over into the next year. It is this carry-over that links futures prices in different crop years. In particular, when there is a decrease in demand in one crop year, carryover to the next crop year will increase and prices in that year will generally fall. In years of *very weak* demand, old-crop prices may even fall below new-crop prices, resulting in a negative spread (i.e., July futures trading at a discount to November futures). However, since soybeans will be carried over to the new crop year, November futures prices will not exceed July futures prices by more than the cost of storage, interest, and insurance associated with carrying the soybeans from July to November. Thus, while there is no limit to how much July futures prices can exceed November futures prices (when a shortage of soybeans exists in July), November futures prices cannot exceed July futures prices by more than the cost of carrying soybeans from July to November. Figure 15-2 demonstrates these pricing relationships. In July 1989, the July price is above the November price, while in July 1990, the reverse is true.

Other supply factors also can affect soybean prices. For example, if during the growing season higher production is anticipated due to an increase in planted acreage, or perhaps because of favorable weather conditions, November prices may fall. However, the prospect of lower prices in the future will reduce current demand, driving down July futures prices. As a result, July prices may fall faster than November prices, causing the typical backwardation spread to narrow. Alternatively, a reduction in planted acreage or unfavorable weather conditions may drive July prices up more than November prices because soybean users, faced with uncertainty about the size of the future crop, try to buy the remaining soybean supplies.

Thus, understanding agricultural futures prices requires a thorough understanding of the economics of the particular agricultural commodity markets.

15.2.6   The Crush Spread

A popular agricultural futures spread is the *crush spread*. The processing of soybeans into soybean oil and soybean meal is called *crushing*. The crush spread is the simultaneous purchase (sale) of *soybean* futures and the sale (purchase) of soybean *oil* and soybean *meal* futures. The crush spread is the expected gross processing margins (GPM) of soybean processors. The GPM reflects the current cost of the raw material, soybeans, relative to the current prices of the processed meal and oil.

Crush spreads are generally quoted as the difference between the combined sales value of the meal and oil produced by a bushel of soybeans and the price of a bushel of soybeans. Because soybeans are traded in cents per bushel, soymeal in dollars per metric ton, and soyoil in cents per pound, soymeal and soyoil prices are converted to cents per bushel to provide a simple spread quotation.[4] In addition, it is commonly assumed that a 60-pound bushel of soybeans yields about 48 pounds of meal and 11 pounds of oil (there is a processing loss of approximately 1 pound). These yields imply that to replicate the crush spread requires buying and selling futures contracts in a yield equivalent ratio: 10 soybean contracts, 12 meal contracts, and 9 oil contracts.[5] The following formula can be used to calculate the crush spread (in dollars per bushel):

$$\text{Crush} = \left(\frac{P_{SM}}{2,000} \times 48\right) + (P_{SO} \times 11) - P_{SB}$$

where P_{SM}, P_{SO} and P_{SB} are the prices for soybean meal, soybean oil, and soybeans respectively.

The following illustrates the computation of the November–December 91 crush spread (or the GPM) using the futures settlement prices from Table 15.6 for soybean, soybean meal, and soybean oil:

soybeans: $6.2534 per bushel (November 91 contract)

soybean meal: $189.10 per ton (December 91 contract)

soybean oil: $0.2222 per lb (December 91 contract)

---

[4]There are 60 pounds in a bushel, and 2000 pounds in a metric ton.

[5]The customary crush package is in multiples of 50,000 bushels. For example, 50,000 bushels of soybeans (or 10 soybean contracts) × 48 lb/bushel = 2,400,000 lb of meal; 2,400,000 lb of meal ÷ 2,000 lb/ton = 1,200 tons of meal (or 12 meal contracts); and 50,000 bushels of soybeans × 11 lb of oil/bushel = 550,000 lb of oil (or 9 oil contracts). For simplicity, however, some traders use a one-to-one contract ratio: one soybean contract, one meal contract, and one oil contract.

$$\text{Crush Spread} = \left(\frac{\$189.10}{2,000} \times 48\right) + (\$0.2222 \times 11) - \$6.2534 = \$0.7292/\text{bushel}$$

The one-month time span between the soybean and the two soybean product futures contracts (i.e., November vs. December) in the above example reflects the time involved in the crushing process.

A soybean processor is subject to both input and output price risks. An increase in the price of soybeans (an input) increases costs. Decreases in oil and meal prices (outputs) reduce the processor's revenue. Futures in all three commodities allow a processor either to hedge each of these price risks separately or to use the crush spread to hedge against an unfavorable change in his GPM—a hedging technique called *putting on the crush spread*. The latter entails buying soybean futures contracts to fix the input cost and simultaneously selling soybean oil and soybean meal futures to lock in the output prices.

If the crush spread becomes less than the actual processing margin, it may be advantageous to put on a *reverse crush spread*. This involves selling soybean futures and simultaneously buying meal and oil futures, in order to profit from a widening of the spread. If soybean processors are losing money, they will cut back production, reducing the amount of soybean products in the marketplace and causing higher product prices. In addition, processors will buy fewer soybeans, resulting in lower soybean prices. Thus, the crush spread will widen, and the reverse spread position can be closed at a profit.

In the past the crush spread has varied widely. Figure 15-3 plots the crush spread from January 1985 to December 1990, calculated with daily near month futures prices for the soybean complex.[6] Crush spreads are commonly put on when the spread is wide and reverse crush spreads are put on when the spread is narrow.[7]

15.3 ENERGY FUTURES

15.3.1 Recent Developments in Energy Markets

Oil is the largest cash commodity in the world. During the past 10 years increased reliance on spot oil markets and increased price volatility of energy products fostered the development of energy futures markets. To understand why energy futures markets developed in the 1980s some knowledge of recent developments in cash oil markets is necessary.

---

[6] The crush spread has a seasonal pattern. The spread tends to be widest (meaning the products are worth more relative to the soybeans) at harvest time. At that time there is an abundant supply of soybeans and soybean prices are at the lowest levels of the year, and the demand for meal and oil is usually strong.

[7] The sharp drop in the crush spread in July 1989 was related to the alleged manipulation of the July 89 soybean futures contract in July 1989 by Ferruzzi which resulted in a sharp increase in soybean prices, and in negative processing margins. Immediately after the emergency action taken by the Chicago Board of Trade to force liquidation of positions, soybean futures prices collapsed and gross processing margins returned to being positive.

Dollar per bushel

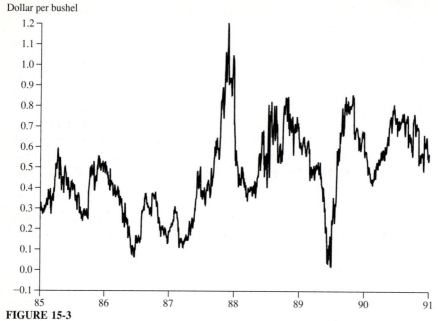

FIGURE 15-3
Soybean crush spread (daily: near month futures prices from 1985 to 1990).

A refiner buys crude oil, refines it and subsequently sells the refined products (primarily heating oil and gasoline). The cost of crude oil constitutes more than 85 percent of total refining costs. The supply and cost of crude oil has undergone major changes over the past two decades. In the 1970s, about 70 percent of all internationally traded crude oil was sold by the OPEC (The Organization of Petroleum Exporting Countries) to major oil companies at official prices, generally under three-year contracts. The dramatic oil price increase triggered by the Arab Embargo in 1973–74 and the Iranian revolution in 1978–79 encouraged both energy conservation and the development of non-OPEC oil reserves. As demand contracted and supply expanded, a crude oil surplus developed, and spot prices fell well below official prices. Oil companies, as a result, turned increasingly to the spot market for supplies, enticed by low prices and a reduced need to secure dependable supplies. By the mid-1980s as much as 65 percent of all crude oil transactions were on a spot basis, and the duration of the remaining term contracts was considerably shorter than in earlier years.

Although OPEC continued to maintain official prices, discounting became commonplace, as suppliers struggled to maintain market share. In OPEC the roles of swing producer and price stabilizer were increasingly assumed by Saudi Arabia. In late 1985 the Saudis decided to have OPEC institute a system of *netback pricing,* whereby the price of crude oil is determined by the value of refined products. Under this system there was no longer a structural stabilization mechanism for oil prices. When product prices fell, refiners cut runs, reduced their demand for crude, and put downward pressure on crude prices, and vice versa.

In December 1986 OPEC abandoned netback pricing, and returned to a fixed price system. But the price and production goals of OPEC members proved incompatible. Finding that they could set either prices or the volume of production, but not both, they adopted a flexible pricing formula. Under this system, crude prices for term contracts are set at the spot price of one or more key *indicator* crudes, averaged over several days, plus or minus quality and transportation differentials. Typical contracts also provide for some volume flexibility, resulting in term contracts designed to mimic the flexibility of spot market prices. To further ensure market sensitivity, OPEC reviews the price and volume formulas monthly or quarterly. By 1989 more than 50 percent of internationally traded crudes were being sold under these term contracts. Thus, the growth of spot oil markets and the increased price volatility of energy products set the stage for the development and growth of energy futures markets.

15.3.2 Trading and Growth

The trading of energy futures in the United States is conducted on the New York Mercantile Exchange (NYMEX), the world's leading energy futures exchange. Table 15.7 shows the 1990 trading volume of the major energy futures contracts, both in the United States and overseas. Heating oil futures were introduced in 1978, followed by crude oil and unleaded gasoline futures in 1983 and 1985 respectively. Today, the NYMEX energy futures complex includes crude oil, heating oil, gasoline, residual fuel oil, propane and natural gas, as well as crude oil, heating oil, and gasoline options.

Energy futures were not traded prior to 1978 because there was little day-to-day price volatility in energy products. During the 1960s and 1970s crude oil prices were tightly controlled by OPEC together with large globally integrated oil companies. In addition, in the United States energy prices were regulated by the federal government. By the early 1980s, however, OPEC had lost its monopolistic grip on oil markets, and deregulation was in the process of freeing energy prices to respond to market conditions.

TABLE 15.7
Major energy futures contracts: 1990 trading volume

Contract	Exchange	Trading volume
U.S.		
Crude oil	NYMEX	23,686,897
Heating oil	NYMEX	6,376,871
Unleaded gasoline	NYMEX	5,205,995
Others		171,532
	U.S. total	35,441,295
Foreign		
Crude oil	IPE, U.K.	4,083,092
Gas oil	IPE, U.K.	2,603,095
High sulphur fuel oil	SIMEX, Singapore	213,918

Figure 15-4 shows that annual trading in energy futures had grown to over 30 million contracts in just 10 years. This constitutes more than 10 percent of total futures trading in the United States. Crude oil is now the third most actively traded U.S. futures contract: its volume is more than double that of corn, soybeans, or gold (introduced in 1921, 1937, and 1975, respectively). The NYMEX's crude oil futures price has also become a benchmark price on which all crude oil spot transactions are based.

15.3.3   Contract Specifications and Delivery

Table 15.8 provides the specifications for the leading energy futures contracts. Contracts are traded for delivery in all months, for at least 15 months into the future. A unique feature of energy futures contracts (i.e., heating oil and gasoline) is that the *long* is given the option of when to take delivery during the delivery month. (All non-energy futures contracts give the *short* the right to determine when to deliver.) The long can call for delivery any time after the fifth business day of the delivery month, but all deliveries must be completed before the last business day of the month. More specifically, the long specifies a consecutive five-day period (the so called *five-day window*) during which the short is required to complete delivery. In practice, longs and shorts frequently agree to change the mode, location, or timing of deliveries subsequent to formal delivery nominations, which are made at the beginning of the delivery month (see Chapter 2, Section

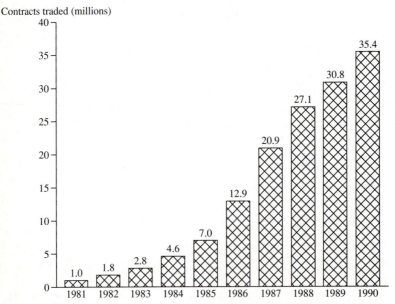

Contracts traded (millions)

FIGURE 15-4
U.S. energy futures (annual trading volume: 1981–1990).

TABLE 15.8
Specifications of major U.S. energy futures contracts

	Crude oil	Heating oil	Unleaded gasoline
Exchange	NYMEX	NYMEX	NYMEX
Symbol	CU	HO	HU
Trading unit	1000 barrels	42,000 gallons	42,000 gallons
Deliverable grade	Par crude: West Texas Intermediate 0.4% sulfur, 40 API gravity; other deliverable crude oil grades with 0.05% sulfur by weight or less, not less than 34 API gravity and not more than 45 API gravity	Industry standards for fungible No. 2 heating oil specifications	Industry standards for fungible northern grade, unleaded regular gasoline
Price quotation	Dollars per barrel	Cents per gallon	Cents per gallon
Tick size	$0.01 per barrel, $10 per contract	$0.01 per gallon, $4.20 per contract	$0.01 per gallon, $4.20 per contract
Contract months	All months	All months	All months
Last trading day	3rd business day prior to the 25th calendar day of the month preceding the delivery month	Last business day of the month preceding the delivery month	Last business day of the month preceding the delivery month

2.6.3 for a discussion of EFPs and ADPs). The futures settlement price on the last trading day is the invoice price used for delivery.

CASH AND FUTURES PRICES. Table 15.9 shows cash price quotations on December 10, 1990 for energy products that are commonly traded in cash markets. Table 15.10 provides the quotations for crude oil, heating oil, and gasoline futures prices on the same date. The deliverable grade of oil on the crude oil futures contract is West Texas Intermediate, which is quoted in the cash market at $26.90 a barrel (Table 15.9). The settlement price for January 91 crude oil futures is also $26.90 a barrel (Table 15.10). The closeness of the cash and futures prices exists because the January 91 contract expires on December 20, 1990—only 10 days later. Cash and futures prices for both heating oil and gasoline are also shown in Tables 15.9 and 15.10.

Backwardation is a common characteristic of energy futures prices. In Table 15.10, for example, all three contracts display backwardation in their pricing structures. This implies that there are significant convenience yields on energy products for immediate or near-term delivery. In heating oil, for example, producers' inventories usually peak in the fall, while heating oil consumption does not peak until sometime later in the heating season—January or February. An unexpected surge in oil consumption, therefore, can result in a shortage of heating oil and backwardation in the pricing structure.

TABLE 15.9
Cash price quotations for energy products
(December 10, 1990)

OIL PRICES

Monday December 10, 1990.

CRUDE GRADES OFFSHORE-d	Mon	Fri	Yr. Ago
European "spot" or free market prices			
Arab lt.	hn26.10	cn25.45	17.60
Arab hvy.	hn21.10	cn20.45	16.35
Iran. lt.	hn25.60	cn24.95	17.55
Forties	hn28.95	cn28.30	19.40
Brent (Dec)	h28.85	c28.55	19.55
Bonny lt.	hn29.60	cn28.95	19.65
Urals-Medit.	hn27.85	cn27.20	18.75
DOMESTIC-f			
Spot market			
W. Tex. Int Cush			
(2525-2600) (Jan)	h26.90	26.60	20.70
W.Tx.sour, Midl (2325-2465)	hn25.42	25.00	19.34
La. sw. St.Ja (2575-2650)	h28.18	c27.78	21.31
No. Slope del USGULF	hn24.85	24.35	19.09

Open-market crude oil values in Northwest Europe around 17:50 GMT in dlrs per barrel, for main loading ports in country of origin for prompt loading, except as indicated.

REFINED PRODUCTS			
Fuel Oil, No. 2 NY gal.	g.8250	.8110	.6825
Gasoline, unlded, premium			
NY gal.	g.7100	.7025	n.a.
Gasoline, unlded, reg.			
NY gal.	g.6850	.6700	.5110
Propane, Mont Belvieu,			
Texas, gal.	g.3850	.3875	.2900
Butane, normal, Mont Belvieu,			
Texas, gal.	g.5425	.5475	n.a.

a-Asked. b-Bid. c-Corrected. d-as of 11 a.m. EST in Northwest Europe. f-As of 4 p.m. EST. Refiners' posted buying prices are in parentheses. g-Provided by Oil Buyers Guide. h-Dow Jones International Petroleum Report. n.a.-Not available. z-Not quoted. n-Nominal. r-Revised.

Source: The Wall Street Journal, December 11, 1990.

TABLE 15.10
Futures price quotations for crude oil, heating oil, and gasoline
(December 10, 1990)

	Open	High	Low	Settle	Change	Lifetime High	Lifetime Low	Open Interest
CRUDE OIL, Light Sweet (NYM) 1,000 bbls.; $ per bbl.								
Jan	27.40	27.65	26.80	26.90 +	.32	38.20	17.86	51,163
Feb	26.65	26.95	26.30	26.52 +	.36	36.80	~18.15	37,018
Mar	26.05	26.12	25.65	25.74 +	.35	35.40	18.40	24,146
Apr	25.25	25.35	24.85	24.95 +	.28	33.90	18.03	16,158
May	24.80	24.80	24.25	24.31 +	.26	32.70	18.03	13,410
June	24.15	24.20	23.60	23.81 +	.26	31.50	18.30	12,395
July	23.80	23.95	23.30	23.45 +	.26	30.40	18.31	9,818
Aug	23.60	23.60	23.05	23.20 +	.26	29.50	19.05	8,979
Sept	23.40	23.40	22.85	23.02 +	.26	28.72	19.10	5,402
Oct	23.15	23.15	22.75	22.89 +	.28	28.40	19.63	6,717
Nov	23.00	23.00	22.65	22.79 +	.30	28.10	19.10	6,796
Dec	23.05	22.05	22.60	22.72 +	.32	27.70	19.45	16,056
Ja92	22.75	22.75	22.50	22.67 +	.34	27.60	20.90	5,988
Feb	22.85	22.85	22.45	22.62 +	.35	27.00	21.20	3,292
Mar	22.30	22.30	22.30	22.57 +	.35	26.75	21.20	4,011
Apr	22.30	22.30	22.30	22.52 +	.34	26.50	20.75	10,593
May	22.25	22.25	22.25	22.47 +	.32	24.58	21.25	1,440
June	22.20	22.40	22.20	22.42 +	.30	23.70	22.23	4,249
Sept	....	....	....	22.27 +	.25	24.00	23.00	675
Dec	....	....	....	22.22 +	.20	24.00	21.85	447
Est vol 48,039; vol Fri 68,556; open int 238,853, −2,090.								
HEATING OIL NO. 2 (NYM) 42,000 gal.; $ per gal.								
Jan	.8160	.8250	.8080	.8097 +	.0180	1.0725	.5295	29,525
Feb	.7850	.7920	.7760	.7776 +	.0152	1.0200	.5260	17,696
Mar	.7400	.7400	.7270	.7282 +	.0081	.9650	.5070	10,354
Apr	.6950	.6950	.6810	.6810 +	.0046	.9200	.4930	5,253
May	.6620	.6625	.6590	.6512 +	.0011	.8850	.4840	2,357
June	.6475	.6475	.6400	.6322 −	.0014	.8575	.4840	4,591
July	.6425	.6425	.6230	.6252 −	.0019	.8500	.4855	4,572
Aug	.6430	.6450	.6250	.6287 −	.0024	.8507	.5350	3,561
Sept	.6450	.6450	.6450	.6402 −	.0019	.8428	.6550	1,829
Oct	....	....	....	.6472 −	.0019	.8500	.6579	301
Nov	.6685	.6685	.6685	.6542 −	.0019	.7800	.7182	362
Dec	.6770	.6770	.6770	.6617 −	.0014	.8262	.6350	6,338
Ja92	....	....	....	.6657 −	.0009	.8200	.8200	30
Est vol 17,798; vol Fri 17,889; open int 86,769, +279.								
GASOLINE, Unleaded (NYM) 42,000 gal.; $ per gal.								
Jan	.6875	.6950	.6760	.6773 +	.0126	.9625	.4910	13,750
Feb	.6950	.7050	.6840	.6867 +	.0125	.9500	.4985	13,823
Mar	.7025	.7140	.6975	.6975 +	.0099	.9500	.5065	11,518
Apr	.7475	.7475	.7350	.7350 +	.0114	.9825	.5490	7,033
May	.7360	.7360	.7300	.7290 +	.0130	.9700	.5545	3,044
June	.7210	.7210	.7170	.7120 +	.0140	.9550	.5490	2,516
July	.6995	.6995	.6995	.6950 +	.0150	.8270	.7325	930
Aug	.6775	.6835	.6775	.6780 +	.0160	.9050	.5350	1,122
Sept	.6670	.6670	.6670	.6630 +	.0170	.9025	.6975	1,307
Oct	....	....	....	.6390 +	.0180	.8675	.6850	1,177
Dec	....	....	....	.6160 +	.0195	.7525	.6300	153
Est vol 9,986; vol Fri 12,413; open int 56,392, +452.								

Source: The Wall Street Journal, December 11, 1990.

Figures 15-5 and 15-6 show the highly cyclical nature of both heating oil inventories and the consumption of heating oil during the 1980s. Depending on the congruence of these cycles, heating oil futures prices can display either a full-carry or a backwardation pricing structure. Figure 15-7 plots the daily settlement prices of the August 90, December 90, and February 91 heating oil futures contracts during 1990. The August to December contracts show a carry relationship, while the December to February contracts display backwardation, the extent of which varies over time.

In Chapter 4, Figure 4-6 displays the monthly convenience yields implicit in heating oil futures prices over the 1987–88 season. It reveals that convenience yields are highest during the late winter and early spring months, when heating

Number of barrels (thousands)

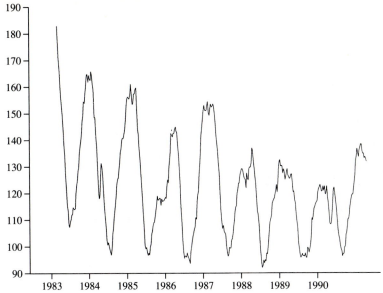

FIGURE 15-5
Weekly U.S. heating oil inventory (January 1983 to December 1990).

Number of barrels (in millions)

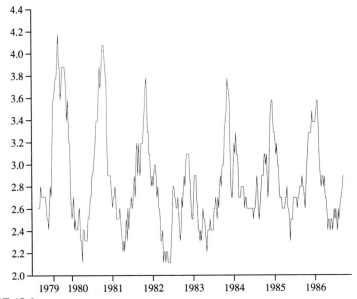

FIGURE 15-6
Weekly U.S. heating oil consumption (July 1979 to August 1986).

Cents per gallon

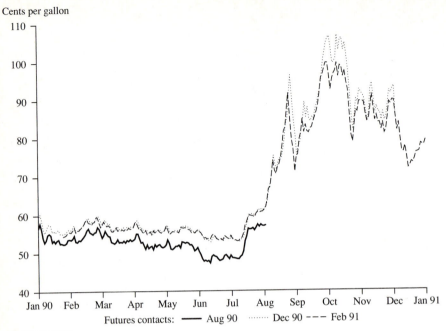

FIGURE 15-7
Heating oil futures prices (daily: from January 1990 to December 1990).

oil consumption often exceeds anticipated levels and inventories are low. During the summer months the reverse is true. Figures 15-8 and 15-9 reinforce this conclusion. Figure 15-8 shows the constant one-month and three-month spreads for heating oil futures from 1981 to 1986, while Figure 15-9 shows the one-month convenience yields over the same period of time, both in the United States and in Europe (on the IPE). The convenience yield (and therefore backwardation) peaks during late winter months and is lowest during summer months. These graphs clearly demonstrate that heating oil prices vary from nearly a full-carry relationship during the summer to sharp backwardation during late winter and early spring. This pattern appears to be quite seasonal. Thus, similar to agricultural futures, users of energy futures must understand the economics of energy markets in order to understand the price relationships that exist in energy futures markets.

15.3.4   The Crack Spread

A well-known energy futures spread is the *crack spread*. A crack spread is the simultaneous purchase (sale) of crude oil futures and sale (purchase) of petroleum product futures contracts (i.e., heating oil and gasoline). The magnitude of this spread reflects the cost of refining crude oil into petroleum products.

Refining crude oil takes time: time to refine, to ship, and to sell the derivative products. During this time a refiner is at risk that product prices may fall, reducing

Price spread (Cents per gallon)

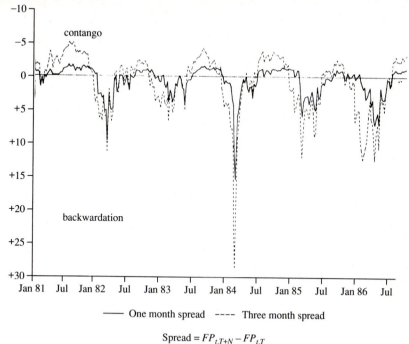

Spread = $FP_{t,T+N} - FP_{t,T}$

FIGURE 15-8
Heating oil spreads (weekly futures prices 1-1-81 to 8-29-86).

his *gross refining margin*. The crack spread can be used to hedge this risk: hedgers can lock in the differential between their input costs and output prices, protecting their profit margins.

Crack spread ratios reflect the amounts of heating oil and gasoline that are produced from each barrel of crude oil (which can change over the year). On average, a barrel of crude oil yields 49 to 55 percent gasoline, 20 to 24 percent heating oil, 6 percent jet fuel, 6 to 11 percent residual fuel and 3 to 6 percent naptha. The remainder is asphalt and butane.

As a consequence, the traditional refining spread is 3-2-1: three barrels of crude are assumed to yield two barrels of gasoline and one barrel of heating oil.[8] However, the most quoted crack spread on the New York Mercantile Exchange is 2-1-1, largely because it is easy to compute.

---

[8] The traditional 3-2-1 refining spread reflects the notion that a barrel of crude oil yields about twice as much gasoline as heating oil. Recently, the increasing dependence on heavier imported crudes, the demand for high-octane unleaded gasoline, and changes in refining technology have combined to alter barrel yields. Many refiners now think that a 5-3-2 spread more nearly reflects reality. That spread implies that it takes five barrels of crude to produce three barrels of gasoline and two barrels of heating oil.

Cents per gallon

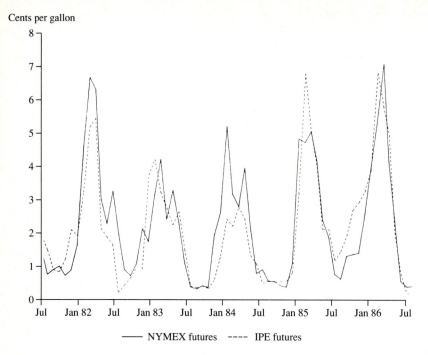

——— NYMEX futures   - - - - IPE futures

NYMEX is the New York Mercantile Exchange heating oil contract;
IPE is London's International Petroleum Exchange gas-oil contract.

FIGURE 15-9
One-month heating oil convenience yields (monthly July 81 to June 86).

Crack spreads are quoted in terms of dollars per barrel. Since product prices are quoted in cents per gallon but crude prices are quoted in dollars per barrel, the following formula is used to calculate crack spread quotations:[9]

$$\text{Crack spread} = \frac{(N_{HU} \times P_{HU} \times 42) + (N_{HO} \times P_{HO} \times 42) - (N_{CL} \times P_{CL})}{N_{CL}}$$

where N_{HU}, N_{HO}, and N_{CL} represent the number of unleaded gasoline, heating oil, and crude oil futures contracts respectively. (The number of product contracts bought (sold) must be equal to the number of crude oil contracts sold (bought), or $N_{HU} + N_{HO} = N_{CL}$). P_{HU} and P_{HO} are, respectively, the prices of unleaded gasoline and heating oil futures, expressed in dollars per gallon, and P_{CL} is the price of crude oil futures, expressed in dollars per barrel.

Thus, the 3-2-1 January–February 91 crack spread on December 10, 1990, would be calculated as follows (see Table 15.10):

---

[9]There are 42 gallons in one barrel.

February 91 gasoline: $0.6867 a gallon

February 91 heating oil: $0.7776 a gallon

January 91 crude oil: $26.90 a barrel

$$\text{Crack spread} = \frac{(2 \times \$0.6867 \times 42) + (1 \times \$0.7776 \times 42) - (3 \times \$26.90)}{3}$$

$$= \$3.214/\text{barrel}$$

The one-month time span between the crude oil and product futures contracts (i.e., January vs. February) in the foregoing spread reflects the time involved in the refining process.

Figure 15-10 plots the 3-2-1 crack spread from 1985 through 1990, calculated with daily settlement prices for the near month futures contracts. There is considerable variation in the spread: in 1990 alone it ranged from a low of about $1 to a high of almost $12. Such changes in the magnitude of the spread obviously reflect the relative volatility of the prices of crude oil and its derivative products. If derivative product prices fall (rise) relative to crude prices, the spread narrows (widens).

If the spread is expected to narrow, it is appropriate to *put on the spread*: to be short the derivative products and long crude oil. Refiners commonly take this position to protect their refining margins. If the spread is expected to widen, a speculator might short crude oil and go long gasoline and heating oil (sometimes

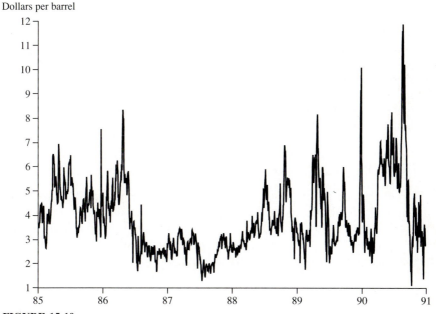

FIGURE 15-10

Energy crack spread (3-2-1): Daily near month futures prices, 1985 to 1990.

called a *reverse crack spread*). More generally, crack spread positions permit a trader to speculate on the relative price relationships between crude oil and its derivative products, without having to speculate on the absolute price levels of either crude oil or the derivative oil products. Trading the crack spread is less risky than outright positions in the component oil products because crude oil, gasoline, and heating oil prices tend to move together, although obviously not by the same amounts. Indeed, trading the crack spread simulates the risk and return associated with actually operating a refinery.

15.4 PRECIOUS METALS FUTURES

Metals fall into one of two commodity classifications: precious or industrial. For some metals the distinction is less clear than for others. At one end of the spectrum is gold, which is traded primarily because of its ability to act as a store of value. Historically, when investors have become anxious about paper currencies, perhaps because of rampant inflation, they have turned to holding gold and other precious metals as a way to preserve the purchasing power of their wealth. In general, therefore, precious metals are those which are in relatively short supply, so that they retain their values despite vicissitudes in aggregate economic activity.

At the other end of the spectrum are industrial metals, like copper, aluminum, zinc, lead, nickel, and tin.[10] These are purchased almost exclusively for industrial uses. Thus, an industrial metal's value is tied closely to the demand for and supply of that metal, which depends importantly on the health of particular sectors of the economy.

Some metals, like silver, are hybrid: they lie in the metals spectrum somewhere between the precious and industrial classification extremes. At times silver trades primarily as an industrial metal; at other times it may trade as a precious metal, depending on economic conditions. When trading metals, therefore, it is important not to lose sight of the multiple factors that may affect metal prices. This section discusses futures contracts on precious metals. Futures trading on industrial metals is covered in the next section.

15.4.1 Trading and Growth

Futures contracts are traded on the following precious metals: gold, silver, platinum, and palladium. During the 1970s trading in all metal futures grew significantly (see Table 1.1 in Chapter 1), but this growth slowed appreciably during the 1980s. Figure 15-11 shows that the annual trading volume in precious metal futures in the Unites States has not grown during the 1980s.

---

[10]Industrial metals are also known as *base* metals.

Contracts traded (millions)

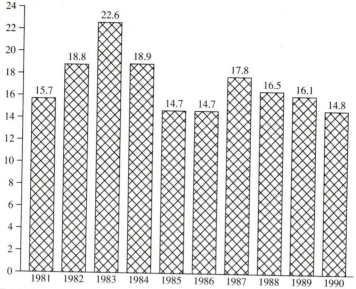

FIGURE 15-11
U.S. precious metals futures (annual trading volume: 1989–1990).

15.4.2 Contract Specifications and Delivery

Table 15.11 provides the trading volume in the leading precious metal futures contracts on U.S. and foreign exchanges. Table 15.12 provides the contract specifications for the three most active U.S. precious metals futures. The terms of these contracts are quite similar to one another. Each contract specifies a delivery period of about a month, during which futures trading continues. The short, as usual, has the option of specifying when during the delivery month he wishes to make delivery, and is permitted to deliver metal that lies within a specified acceptable range of quantities and quality grades. Delivery must also take place at one of the exchange-approved warehouses.

The three-day delivery procedures for the COMEX gold futures contract is typical. The short initiates delivery by stating his intention to make delivery two days later. This is the first day of the three-day delivery period, and is called the *presentation date*. The futures price used for calculating the invoice price is the settlement price on that day. On the second day (the *notice date*), the clearinghouse notifies the long with the oldest outstanding position that delivery will occur on the next day. On the third day (the *delivery date*), the short delivers the gold to the long and the long pays the short. The earliest presentation date for a contract is the second-to-last business day of the month preceding the delivery month for the contract, and the latest presentation date is the third-to-last day of the delivery month.

The COMEX gold futures contract permits delivery of gold bullion bars with a weight of between 95 and 105 ounces and with a fineness of 99.5 percent or

TABLE 15.11
Major precious metals futures contracts: 1990 trading volume

Contract	Exchange	Trading volume
U.S.		
Gold	COMEX	9,730,041
Silver	COMEX	3,913,609
Platinum	NYMEX	820,934
Palladium	NYMEX	95,642
Others		252,621
	U.S. total	14,812,847
Foreign		
Gold	Tokyo Commodity Exchange, Japan	6,873,304
Platinum	Tokyo Commodity Exchange, Japan	3,269,193
Silver	Tokyo Commodity Exchange, Japan	504,332

TABLE 15.12
Specifications of major U.S. precious metal futures contracts

	Gold	Silver	Platinum
Exchange	COMEX	COMEX	NYMEX
Symbol	GC	SI	PL
Trading unit	100 troy ounces	5000 troy ounces	50 troy ounces
Deliverable grade	Not less than 0.995 fineness, approved by a refiner listed by COMEX	Not less than 0.999 fineness, approved by a refiner listed by COMEX	99.9% platinum
Price quotation	Dollars per ounce	Cents per ounce	Dollars per ounce
Tick size	$0.10 per troy ounce, $10 per contract	$0.001 per troy ounce, $5 per contract	$0.10 per troy ounce, $10 per contract
Contract months	The first three consecutive months; any Jan, Mar, Jul, Sep, and Dec falling within a 23-month period beginning with the current month	The first three consecutive months; any Jan, Mar, Jul, Sep, and Dec falling within a 23-month period beginning with the current month	Jan, Apr, Jul, Oct
Last trading day	3rd last business day of the contract month	3rd last business day of the contract month	4th last business day of the contract month

greater. In practice, bullion bars that carry the stamp of an exchange-approved refiner will meet these specifications. The invoice price that a short receives depends on the exact weight and fineness of the gold bar that is delivered. Specifically, the invoice price is

$$\text{Invoice price} = \text{Settlement futures price} \times \text{Weight} \times \text{Fineness}$$

For example, the settlement price of the December 90 gold futures contract on December 10, 1990, was $374.20 per ounce (see Table 15.13). If on that date the short were to state his intention to deliver 100 ounces of bullion bars with a 99.5 percent fineness, he would receive $37,232.90 for each futures contract:

$$\$37,232.90 = (\$374.20)(100)(0.995)$$

On the other hand, if the short were to deliver 95-ounce gold bars with a 99.7 fineness, the invoice price for each futures contract would be $35,442.35:

$$\$35,442.35 = (\$374.20)(95)(0.997)$$

TABLE 15.13
Futures price quotations for precious metals (December 10, 1990)

	Open	High	Low	Settle	Change	Lifetime High	Lifetime Low	Open Interest
—METALS								
COPPER-HIGH (CMX)—25,000 lbs.; cents per lb.								
Dec	110.40	111.20	110.00	109.90	− .25	131.20	91.50	4,402
Ja91	110.00	110.85	109.60	110.80	+ 1.30	126.40	94.00	1,368
Feb	109.00	109.80	108.90	109.80	+ 1.60	115.80	99.50	817
Mar	106.40	108.40	106.30	108.00	+ 2.00	122.60	92.30	20,671
Apr	106.00	106.00	106.00	107.20	+ 2.00	115.50	99.85	241
May	105.15	106.70	105.00	106.40	+ 2.05	117.80	97.00	3,091
June	104.25	104.25	104.25	105.60	+ 2.00	109.00	102.30	179
July	102.00	105.30	103.80	104.80	+ 2.10	113.50	96.50	2,812
Aug	....	....	....	104.30	+ 2.10	107.00	103.30	131
Sept	103.00	104.00	102.80	103.90	+ 2.20	110.50	95.50	2,311
Oct	....	....	....	103.45	+ 2.25	106.00	102.50	141
Dec	101.50	102.10	101.50	102.45	+ 2.45	108.50	94.50	3,058
Est vol 4,700; vol Fri 7,844; open int 39,527, +1,169.								
GOLD (CMX)—100 troy oz.; $ per troy oz.								
Dec	372.00	375.70	372.00	374.20	+ 3.90	455.50	357.00	3,326
Fb91	374.50	377.80	374.40	375.90	+ 3.80	457.50	362.00	55,543
Apr	377.00	380.60	377.00	378.70	+ 3.80	526.00	366.20	18,147
June	380.50	383.10	380.20	381.70	+ 3.70	466.20	372.00	12,770
Aug	387.00	387.00	384.20	384.50	+ 3.60	468.00	375.00	5,515
Oct	....	....	....	387.50	+ 3.50	476.00	385.00	1,705
Dec	389.50	389.50	389.50	390.60	+ 3.50	483.00	384.00	7,442
Fb92	....	....	....	393.80	+ 3.50	456.50	391.90	3,098
Apr	....	....	....	396.90	+ 3.50	446.00	394.00	2,063
June	....	....	....	400.20	+ 3.50	467.00	398.50	3,752
Aug	....	....	....	403.60	+ 3.50	423.50	412.50	192
Est vol 29,000; vol Fri 27,079; open int 113,554, +1,018.								
PLATINUM (NYM)—50 troy oz.; $ per troy oz.								
Ja91	415.00	418.00	413.50	417.20	+ 3.80	551.00	388.10	8,739
Apr	420.00	423.00	419.00	422.40	+ 4.00	554.50	394.50	6,077
July	424.50	424.50	423.50	426.40	+ 4.10	528.50	400.00	1,834
Oct	427.00	431.00	426.00	430.40	+ 4.10	513.00	415.00	553
Est vol 3,183; vol Fri 5,211; open int 17,233, +979.								
SILVER (CMX)—5,000 troy oz.; cents per troy oz.								
Dec	407.0	408.5	403.0	405.0	− 0.5	742.0	403.0	881
Mr91	415.5	417.0	411.5	412.8	− 0.7	665.0	411.0	54,338
May	422.0	422.0	418.5	418.4	− 0.8	647.0	417.0	7,191
July	427.0	427.0	423.0	424.0	− 0.8	667.5	423.0	4,046
Sept	430.0	430.0	430.0	429.5	− 0.9	654.0	430.0	2,009
Dec	438.3	438.3	337.5	437.4	− 0.9	623.5	437.5	3,582
Mr92	....	....	....	445.8	− 1.0	613.0	447.0	1,067
May	....	....	....	451.7	− 1.0	589.0	462.0	835
July	....	....	....	457.6	− 1.0	557.0	467.0	388
Est vol 11,000; vol Fri 12,010; open int 74,432, +104.								

Source: The Wall Street Journal, December 11, 1990.

Thus, the fineness of the metal acts as a *multiplicative* grade-adjustment delivery factor for adjusting invoice prices, similar to the additive grade-adjustment delivery factors we encountered earlier in this chapter for agricultural futures. This multiplicative delivery factor is also similar to the conversion factors encountered in our discussion of T-bond futures in Chapter 13 (Section 13.3.4).

15.4.3   Cash and Futures Prices

Metals are traded for both spot and forward delivery in international cash markets. Metal dealers stand ready to buy or sell metals at quoted prices. Table 15.14 shows the cash prices quoted on December 10, 1990, for the most actively traded metals in the cash market.

There are often many different cash prices quoted for a particular metal. For example, there are seven gold prices quoted in Table 15.14. The Krugerrand, Maple Leaf, and American Eagle quotes are for particular kinds of gold coins. The quotes for gold bullion are by different gold dealers (Engelhard or Handy &

TABLE 15.14
Cash price quotations for metals (December 10, 1990)

METALS			
Aluminum			
ingot lb. del. Midwest	q.69¼-.71¼	.69¼-.71¼	.74¾
Copper			
cathodes lb.	p1.13-.17	1.13-.17	1.09½
Copper Scrap, No 2 wire N Y lb	k.88	.86	.82½
Lead, lb.	p.37-.40	.37-.40	.39
Mercury 76 lb. flask NY	q185-195	185.-195.	294.00
Steel Scrap 1 hvy mlt Chgo ton	104.-108.	104.-108.	.96½
Tin composite lb.	q3.7621	3.7481	4.0449
Zinc Special High grade lb	q.61898	.61898	.73⅛
MISCELLANEOUS			
Rubber, smoked sheets, NY lb.	n.47	.47	n.a.
Hides, hvy native steers lb., fob ...	.84	.84	.90
PRECIOUS METALS			
Gold, troy oz			
Engelhard indust bullion	375.34	372.08	416.86
Engelhard fabric prods	394.11	390.68	437.70
Handy & Harman base price	374.05	370.80	415.50
London fixing AM 372.25 PM ...	374.05	370.80	415.50
Krugerrand, whol	a376.05	372.50	418.50
Maple Leaf, troy oz.	a386.75	383.00	431.50
American Eagle, troy oz.	a386.75	383.00	431.50
Platinum, (Free Mkt.)	423.00	418.50	510.50
Platinum, indust (Engelhard)	418.00	423.00	507.50
Platinum, fabric prd (Engelhard)	518.00	523.00	607.50
Palladium, indust (Engelhard) ...	93.50	93.50	141.75
Palladium, fabrc prd (Englhard)	108.50	108.50	156.75
Silver, troy ounce			
Engelhard indust bullion	4.050	4.090	5.750
Engelhard fabric prods	4.334	4.376	6.153
Handy & Harman base price	4.050	4.100	5.735
London Fixing (in pounds)			
Spot (U.S. equiv. $4.0975)	2.0980	2.1335	3.5725
3 months	2.1675	2.2025	3.7030
6 months	2.2320	2.2660	3.8360
1 year	2.3550	2.3905	4.0880
Coins, whol $1,000 face val	a3,105	3,100	4,195

a-Asked. b-Bid. bp-Country elevator bids to producers. c-Corrected. d-Dealer market. e-Estimated. f-Dow Jones International Petroleum Report. g-Main crop, ex-dock, warehouses, Eastern Seaboard, north of Hatteras. j.-f.o.b. warehouse. k-Dealer selling prices in lots of 40,000 pounds or more, f.o.b. buyer's works. n-Nominal. p-Producer price. q-Metals Week. r-Rail bids. s-Thread count 78x54. x-Less than truckloads. z-Not quoted. xx-f.o.b. tankcars.

q: Metals Week, p: Producer Price, a: Asked price

Source: The Wall Street Journal, December 11, 1990.

Harmon), or are quotes at different times during the day (such as the London A.M. fix, which is the gold price at 10:30 A.M., or the London P.M. fix, which is the price of gold at 4:30 P.M., London time).

Precious metal futures prices usually display a carry pricing relationship. Earlier, in Chapter 4, we used precious metal futures prices to illustrate a full-carry pricing relationship. The prices in Table 15.13 show a carry relationship for gold, silver, and platinum. In Figure 15-12 daily settlement prices are plotted for the June 90, October 90, and December 90 gold futures contracts. These also clearly exhibit a consistent cost-of-carry relationship.

15.4.4 The Gold and Silver Ratio

A commonly traded precious metals spread is the gold/silver ratio. This ratio is the price of gold divided by the price of silver, and is the number of ounces of silver required to equal the value of one ounce of gold. For example, on December 10, 1990, December 90 gold futures were $374.20 an ounce, while December 90 silver futures were $4.05 an ounce (see Table 15.13). Thus, the gold/silver ratio was 92.40: one ounce of gold had the same market value as 92.40 ounces of silver.

Trading gold/silver spreads requires predicting the relative price movements of gold and silver. If the ratio is expected to decline (rise), traders will sell (buy) gold futures and simultaneously buy (sell) silver futures.

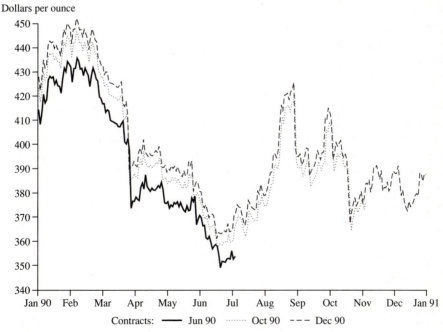

FIGURE 15-12
Gold futures prices (daily prices: January 1990 to December 1990).

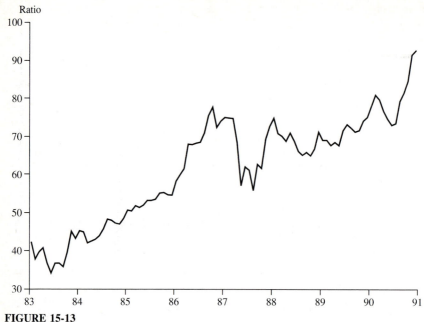

FIGURE 15-13
Gold/silver ratio (monthly: near month futures prices, 1983 to 1990).

The gold/silver ratio has varied widely over time. Figure 15-13 plots this ratio from 1983 to 1990. Many traders, however, believe that a normal value for the ratio is about 40. Thus, when the ratio exceeds 40, they often sell gold futures and buy silver futures, anticipating that the ratio will decline. Conversely, when the ratio is below 40, traders often buy gold futures and sell silver futures, anticipating and increase in the ratio.

This long-term price relationship between gold and silver has varied significantly. It is difficult, therefore, to conclude that a normal ratio value exists. Figure 15-13 shows that the ratio has continued to rise throughout the 1980s. The relative value of gold has been increasing, mainly because the price of silver has declined significantly. A possible reason for this price decline is that silver has been losing its status as a precious metal, and has become more like an industrial metal. Further, the supply of silver currently exceeds industrial demand, and this over-supply situation is expected to continue into the future (see Chapter 16, Section 16.1.3).

15.5   INDUSTRIAL METAL FUTURES

15.5.1   Trading and Growth

The volume of futures trading in industrial metals on U.S. exchanges, which is shown in Figure 15-14, is relatively small. The London Metal Exchange (LME) dominates world trade in industrial metals. As shown in Table 15.15, the only active industrial metal futures traded in the United States is Commodity Exchange's

Contracts traded (millions)

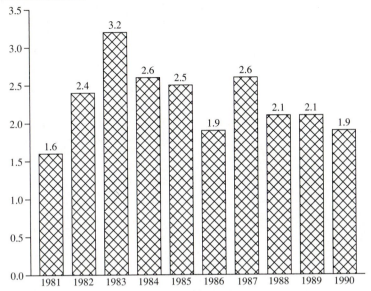

FIGURE 15-14
U.S. industrial metal futures (annual trading volume: 1981–1990).

copper contract. However, even the trading volume in copper is much higher on the LME.[11] Total trading volume on the LME increased by 32 percent in 1990, from 10.08 million in 1989 to 13.35 million contracts.

Trading on the LME is closely tied to cash (or physical) metal markets. Since its establishment in 1876, the LME has set global benchmark prices for aluminum, copper, zinc, lead, nickel, and tin.[12] The LME differs from other futures exchanges in several aspects. This section provides a brief overview of how the LME operates and of the pricing of industrial metal futures.[13]

15.5.2 The London Metal Exchange

In the nineteenth century England imported large quantities of metals from South America, Africa, and Asia. Because of the time that elapsed between a cargo

---

[11]The contract size of the LME copper is 25 long tons while the COMEX contract calls for delivery of 25,000 pounds of copper. Since each long ton equals 2,204.62 pounds, the LME contract size is more than 2.2 times greater than that of the COMEX contract. When comparing the actual tonnages of copper (not just number of contracts) traded on the two exchanges, trading volume on the LME is at least seven times greater than it is on COMEX.

[12]Only copper and tin were traded on the LME in the early years.

[13]For a detailed description of the organizational structure of the LME, see the Rules and Regulations of the London Metal Exchange and the International Commodities Clearing House.

TABLE 15.15
Major Industrial metal futures contracts: Annual trading volume

Contract	Exchange	Trading volume		
		1990	1989	1988
U.S.				
High grade copper	COMEX	1,853,185	1,929,095	2,112,549
Foreign				
Copper—grade A	LME	5,993,965	4,520,793	3,336,700
Aluminum—high grade	LME	4,355,720	3,036,892	2,098,047
Zinc*	LME	1,448,107	1,330,386	713,866
Lead	LME	611,756	576,671	485,173
Nickel	LME	582,210	482,995	343,734
Tin	LME	361,196	129,180	—

*Includes both special high grade and high grade zinc.

ship leaving port and the eventual delivery of the metal to warehouses in other parts of the world, metal dealers and producers faced substantial price risk while awaiting the arrival of their cargoes. The LME emerged as a marketplace where metal cargoes could be hedged by trading them on an *arrival of ship* basis. Because of this origin, the LME actively trades both cash and forward contracts, on which delivery is common. However, LME *forward* contracts are similar (but not identical) to the futures contracts traded on U.S. exchanges.

LME CONTRACT SPECIFICATIONS.   LME contracts are traded both on specific contract months as well as on specific contract dates. A unique feature of all LME contracts is that they call for delivery on specific *prompt* dates (i.e., settlement dates), rather than in particular delivery months.[14] Valid contract dates are every LME business day between (and including) the *cash date* and the *three-month date*, and every third Wednesday during the fourth to the twenty-seventh month.[15] In other words, there is a contract maturing every LME business day during the *intermediate* period (i.e., between the cash and three-month dates), whereas forward contracts exceeding three months are available only on a monthly basis. These monthly forward contracts are settled on the third Wednesday of the contract month. The three-month contract is the most actively traded of the prompt dates.

A *cash date* contract requires delivery two business days from the current calendar day; a *three-month date* contract requires delivery three months from the current date. For example, a cash contract traded on December 12, 1990 (Wednes-

---

[14]In this section, prompt dates, contract dates, and settlement dates are used interchangeably.

[15]Contracts for copper, aluminum, and zinc, the three most heavily-traded metals, are traded up to 27 months forward. Contracts for other metals, lead, nickel, and tin, are traded only up to 15 months forward.

day), will become prompt on December 14, 1990 (Friday), and the three-month contract will become prompt on March 12, 1991.[16] Similarly, a cash contract traded on December 13, 1990 (Thursday), will become prompt on December 17, 1990 (Monday), whereas the three-month contract prompt date will be March 13, 1991.

The peculiar design of LME contract dates reflects trading practices in the physical market. When the LME was first established no contracts were traded beyond a three-month period. Legend has it that three months was the average voyage time to ship copper from either Chile or Peru to England. Whatever the reason, the three-month period appeared to reflect the time it took for cargoes to be shipped, unloaded, and transferred to warehouses where delivery could be made. Contracts with daily prompt dates between cash and three-month contracts enabled hedgers to adjust positions daily in the event of late or early arrival of a shipment. The particular specifications and delivery requirements for LME metal contracts are provided in Table 15.16.

LME TRADING HOURS AND PROCEDURES. The LME houses both an open outcry market and a 24-hour, inter-office, telephone market. The open outcry market occurs when the Ring dealing members of the LME meet twice a day on the floor of the Exchange to conduct *Ring* trading: a morning session from 11:50 A.M. to 1:25 P.M. (London time), and an afternoon session from 3:20 P.M. to 5:00 P.M..[17] As shown in Table 15.17, each Ring session actually consists of a series of five-minute trading sessions for each of the metals. Aluminum trades for five minutes, copper for five minutes, and so forth, twice around.[18] Trading in the Ring is conducted by dealers calling out their bids and offers to others in the Ring.[19]

Since trading in the Ring is confined to very brief time periods, traders with large positions may not be able to execute all of their orders within the

---

[16]The last trading day for any contract date is two business days before the settlement date. Thus, a cash contract traded on December 12 is settled on December 14. Similarly, the last trading day for the three-month contract is March 8, 1991.

[17]Ring trading is equivalent to pit trading. However, rather than standing in the pit, ring dealing members sit at their designated seats to conduct trading. The tradition of the Ring was born in 1876, when a member would chalk a large circle on the floor of the room and, at the cry of "Ring, Ring," those wishing to trade would take their accustomed places around it. One minor difference between ring trading and pit trading is that all six metals are traded in the same ring in a designated order, while only one commodity is traded in each pit.

There are different types of memberships at the LME, but only Ring dealing members are authorized to trade in the Ring. Ring members bear a heavy financial burden in maintaining a Ring dealing status.

[18]The order in which the metals are traded in the Ring changes from time to time, at the discretion of the LME.

[19]Typically, Ring trading starts with dealers offering to buy or sell metal for various dates. However, with so many different prompt dates and limited Ring dealing time, dealers usually trade only the cash and three-montn dates, which then determine the prices for the intermediate contract dates.

TABLE 15.16
Contract specifications of LME industrial metal futures

	Aluminum	Copper	Zinc	Lead	Nickel	Tin
Price quotation	US$/ton	Sterling/ton	US$/ton	Sterling/ton	US$/ton	US$/ton
Contract size	25 ton	25 ton	25 ton	25 ton	6 ton	5 ton
Minimum price fluctuation	$1 per ton	50 pence per ton	$1 per ton	25 pence per ton	$1 per ton	$1 per ton
Contract months	Daily to 3 months then monthly to 27 months	Daily to 3 months then monthly to 27 months	Daily to 3 months then monthly to 27 months	Daily to 3 months then monthly to 15 months	Daily to 3 months then monthly to 15 months	Daily to 3 months then monthly to 15 months
Quality*	Primary aluminum of minimum 99.70% purity with maximum permissible iron content 0.2% and maximum permissible silicon content 0.10%	Electrolytic copper in the form of either cathode (Grade A) or wirebars (Grade A of standard dimensions in the weight range 110 kgs to 125 kgs)	Special high-grade zinc of minimum 99.995% purity, and weighing not more than 55 kgs each	Refined pig lead of minimum 99.97% purity and not more than 55 kgs each	Primary nickel of minimum 99.8% purity	Refined tin of minimum 99.85% purity and the weighing range between 12 kgs and 50 kgs
Quantity tolerance	2%	2%	2%	2%	2%	2%

*Deliveries of all metals must be of brands listed on the LME-approved list for that metal.

412

TABLE 15.17
LME Ring trading hours (London time)*

First session		Second session	
Tin	11:50–11:55	Lead	3:20–3:25
Aluminum	11:55–12:00	Zinc	3:25–3:30
Copper	12:00–12:05	Copper	3:30–3:35
Lead	12:05–12:10	Aluminum	3:35–3:40
Zinc	12:10–12:15	Tin	3:40–3:45
Nickel	12:15–12:20	Nickel	3:45–3:50
Copper	12:30–12:35	Lead	4:00–4:05
Tin	12:40–12:45	Zinc	4:05–4:10
Lead	12:45–12:50	Copper	4:10–4:15
Zinc	12:50–12:55	Aluminum	4:15–4:20
Aluminum	12:55–1:00	Tin	4:20–4:25
Nickel	1:00–1:05	Nickel	4:25–4:30
Kerb trading	1:05–1:25	Kerb trading	4:30–5:00

*As of February, 1991.

alloted times. In earlier days, participants then retreated to the "kerb" outside the LME building to continue trading. Recognizing the inevitability of *kerb trading*, the LME set aside a limited period *after* each official trading session for such activity, inside the trading room. In specific, after the morning and afternoon trading sessions, a 20–25 minute kerb trading period occurs, during which traders can deal in any metal in an open outcry market.

Another unique feature of the LME trading system is that it allows extensive inter-office, telephone trading to take place before and after Ring trading. In fact, a majority of transactions is done via this telephone network, which links traders throughout the world. A trade made on the telephone is as binding between LME members as if it were done in the Ring. Further, contracts traded in the Ring or over the telephone are both cleared through the International Commodities Clearing House.

There is also no set time during the day for either the commencement or cessation of such trading. Traders decide their own trading hours. For many international metal companies, when the trading day ends in London, the LME book is passed to the New York office, then later to the Tokyo desk, and after the close of trading in Tokyo, back to London. Thus, trading takes place 24 hours a day.

Inter-office trades customarily outnumber Ring and kerb trades by a considerable margin. Table 15.18 provides the percentage of total LME trades done during Ring and kerb hours on January 9, 1991, as an example. On average, less than five percent of total trading volume occurs during Ring hours.

OFFICIAL LME PRICES.   Official LME prices are closing settlement prices distributed by the LME, and are set by an exchange committee. During the morning ring-trading session, at least three members of the exchange's quotation committee (selected from the ring dealing members) are present. After the morning ring-

TABLE 15.18
London Metal Exchange trading statistics:
January 9, 1991

Commodity	Total trading volume (a)	Trading volume during ring and kerb (b)	(a)/(b) (in percent)
Aluminum	12455	440	3.53
Copper	25062	1198	4.78
Nickel	5115	113	2.21
Lead	1749	162	9.26
Tin	2131	262	12.29
Zinc	3694	206	5.57

Source: International Commodities Clearing House.

trading session in each metal is completed, these members determine the best bid and offer prices for each metal at the close of trading. Official daily settlement prices are then announced for cash, 3-month, and 15-month contracts. Prices for other contract dates are not officially announced, but it is always possible to obtain a price quote for immediate dates from a broker.

LME official bid and ask prices are widely reported by the news media. Table 15.19 provides an example of these quotations for three-month forward contracts. The official quotation currency for copper and lead is pounds sterling, while aluminum, zinc, nickel, and tin are quoted in U.S. dollars.[20]

TABLE 15.19
London Metal Exchange: Price
quotations (December 10, 1990)

London Metal Exchange Prices

Quotations in pounds sterling per metric ton at the close of second ring trading in the afternoon.
Monday December 10, 1990.

	Bid	Chg.	Asked	Chg.
Aluminum—Hi—Spot (z)	1526.00	− 37.00	1528.00	− 37.00
3 months	1562.00	− 34.00	1563.00	− 34.00
Copper—Cath—Hi—Spot	1279.00	− 20.00	1280.00	− 21.00
3 months	1285.00	− 14.00	1286.00	− 13.00
Lead—Spot	327.00	− 2.00	328.00	− 3.00
3 months	336.00	− 2.00	337.00	− 1.50
Nickel—Spot (z)	8225.00	− 25.00	8275.00	− 25.00
3 months	8055.00	− 45.00	8100.00	− 25.00
Zinc—Sp Hi—Spot (z)	1300.00	+ 13.00	1305.00	+ 15.00
3 months	1271.00	+ 16.00	1275.00	+ 17.00

z - Prices quoted in U.S. dollars.

Source: The Wall Street Journal, December 11, 1990.

---

[20]The LME also provides official exchange rates to convert official sterling prices into U.S. dollar prices. Although copper and lead are traded in sterling during Ring hours, they are normally quoted in U.S. dollars in the telephone network market.

INTERPRETING CASH AND FORWARD LME PRICE QUOTATIONS. The three-month forward contract is the only LME contract quoted in absolute price levels. Other LME contracts are normally quoted in terms of a spread relative to the three-month price. This is obviously quite different from the typical pricing convention used in futures markets, where all contracts are quoted in terms of price levels.

Table 15.20 shows typical LME bid-ask quotes for various contract dates (obtained from an LME member) for aluminum, copper, and zinc on February 27, 1991. An absolute price is quoted only for the three-month contract date. All other contract dates are quoted as a spread relative to the three-month price.

Using copper as an example, on February 27, 1991, the bid-ask quotes for the three-month contract were $2414-$2416 per metric ton, meaning $2414 bid and $2416 ask. The first spread quote, "Cash/3M: 57-67B," indicates that the price differential between the cash contract and the three-month contract is $57 bid and $67 ask. The "B" signifies that the market is in backwardation: the cash price is above the three-month price. Thus, absolute bid and ask price levels for the cash date are computed as

TABLE 15.20
LME forward price quotations on February 27, 1991
(Broker—Dealer quotations)

Aluminum		Copper		Zinc	
3 months	$1575–1576	3 months	$2414–2416	3 months	$1197–1200
Cash/3M	29–30 C	Cash/3M	57–67 B	Cash/3M	11–13 B
Cash/Mar	8–9 C	Cash/Mar	17–20 B	Cash/Mar	5–6 B
Mar/Apr	9–10 C	Mar/Apr	22–25 B	Mar/Apr	1–3 B
Apr/May	8–9 C	Apr/May	13–16 B	Apr/May	12–14 B
May/3M	2–3 C	May/3M	5–8 B	May/3M	3–5 B
3M/Jun 91	6–8 C	3M/Jun 91	5–15 B	3M/Jun 91	2–4 B
3M/Jul 91	14–17 C	3M/Jul 91	20–30 B	3M/Jul 91	4–7 B
3M/Aug 91	22–26 C	3M/Aug 91	35–45 B	3M/Aug 91	6–10 B
3M/Sep 91	29–34 C	3M/Sep 91	45–55 B	3M/Sep 91	8–13 B
3M/Oct 91	35–40 C	3M/Oct 91	60–70 B	3M/Oct 91	10–15 B
3M/Nov 91	40–45 C	3M/Nov 91	70–90 B	3M/Nov 91	11–16 B
3M/Dec 91	45–50 C	3M/Dec 91	80–100 B	3M/Dec 91	13–18 B
3M/Jan 92	50–55 C	3M/Jan 92	90–110 B	3M/Jan 92	15–20 B
3M/Feb 92	55–60 C	3M/Feb 92	100–120 B	3M/Feb	17–24 B
3M/Mar 92	60–65 C	3M/Mar 92	110–130 B	3M/Mar 92	19–26 B
3M/Apr 92	64–69 C	3M/Apr 92	120–140 B	3M/Apr 92	22–29 B
3M/May 92	68–79 C	3M/May 92	130–150 B	3M/May 92	25–35 B
Ave 1991	$1570–1590	Ave 1991	$2370–2400	Ave 1991	$1165–1185
Ave 1992	$1645–1665	Ave 1992	$2240–2280	Ave 1992	$1160–1180
Ave 1993	$1685–1715	Ave 1993	$2130–2180		

C: Contango
B: Backwardation
3M: 3 months contract
Ave: Average price for longer-term forward contracts
Source: Metallgesellschaft.

	Bid	**Ask**
Three-month price	$2,414	$2,416
Cash/3M (B) spread	+ 57	+ 67
Cash price:	$2,471	$2,483

Alternatively, the February 27 quotation "3M/Jul 91: 20-30 B " indicates that the spread between the three-month contract and the July 91 contract (prompt on July 17, 1991, the third Wednesday of the month) is $20 bid and $30 ask, and that the market is in backwardation: the three-month price is above the July price. The absolute July 91 bid and ask prices are therefore:[21]

	Bid	**Ask**
Three-month price	$2,414	$2,416
3M/Jul 91 (B) spread	− 30	− 20
July 91 price:	$2,384	$2,396

A "C" in a price quotation signifies a contango price relationship: the nearby price is below the distant price. In Table 15.20, the three-month aluminum bid-ask quotes are $1575–1576 per metric ton, and the cash to three-month spread is quoted as "Cash/3M: 29-30 C." Thus, the respective cash price levels are

	Bid	**Ask**
Three-month price	$1,575	$1,576
Cash/3M (C) spread	− 30	− 29
Cash price:	$1,545	$1,547

LME DELIVERY PROCEDURES.   The standard LME contract calls for the delivery of registered LME grade metals on the due date, from and to an LME approved warehouse.

Warehouse warrants are the LME's unit of currency, and are used to make delivery. Such warrants are issued by approved warehouses for specific tonnages of metals. A weight tolerance is provided for in the contract, as well as a specified

---

[21] Since the market is in backwardation, the absolute price level of the July contract is derived by subtracting the spread quote from the three-month price quote. Simply subtracting the $20 bid quote from the three-month bid price of $2414, and the $30 ask quote from the three-month ask price of $2416, will result in a July bid price of $2394 and an ask price of $2386. This would make the bid price greater than the ask price, which is not possible. Therefore, to obtain the absolute price levels for the July date, *cross subtraction* is required: the ask spread quote is subtracted from the three-month bid price, and the bid spread quote is subtracted from the three-month ask price.

latitude with respect to the shape and weight of individual pieces making up a warrant lot (see Table 15.16). Trades are settled at the price agreed to and on the exact tonnage specified in the contract–the *round tonnage*. Any weight discrepancy between this round tonnage and that shown on the actual warrant is accounted for separately. The usual permitted tolerance is plus or minus 2 percent, providing an overall tolerance of 4 percent.

The LME maintains a list of approved warehouses located at listed delivery points. Originally confined to ports in the United Kingdom, the list has been considerably extended: first to Rotterdam, later to ports in northwestern Europe and the Mediterranean, and most recently to Singapore, Japan, and the United States.[22] The short has the option to deliver warrants from *any* warehouse against his open contract positions. The long, therefore, may have to swap warrants with other buyers to obtain the metal at a warehouse of his choice.[23]

A significant proportion of contracts traded on the LME results in delivery. Table 15.21 compares the NYMEX's crude oil futures contract with the LME's contracts in terms of their frequency of delivery. Less than one-tenth of one percent of the total crude oil contracts traded result in physical delivery, whereas more than 3 percent of traded LME contracts result in physical delivery.

THE TIN CRISIS AND THE "NEW" LME.   The "tin crisis" in October 1985 significantly changed the clearing system used by the LME from a *principals* market to a *cleared* market. Prior to this episode, LME ring members traded with each other on a *principal-to-principal* basis. No deposits (or margins) were required between ring members. Each ring member was granted a credit line, officially called his *Permitted Open Indebtedness*. This was the maximum net amount that a ring member could owe to all other ring members collectively without having to post additional collateral. Similarly, margin deposits were normally not required of customers, although LME members had the right to call their customers for margin money if they wished. Finally, LME contracts were not processed through a clearinghouse and were not guaranteed by a clearing association.

The tin market collapsed in 1985 when the International Tin Council failed to support tin prices. Beginning in 1956, the International Tin Council had supported tin prices through the use of both export controls and a buffer stock operation conducted primarily on the LME. On October 24, 1985, this support operation collapsed, leaving outstanding commitments of over £300 million with banks and brokers. When the Tin Council's member governments declined either to inject additional capital or to acknowledge responsibility for the Tin Council's debts, tin prices fell by 40 percent, putting LME dealers on the brink of bankruptcy and

---

[22]Warehouses in Singapore, Japan, and the United States are available for certain metals. For example, the newly opened LME warehouse (in February 1991) in Baltimore is for aluminum only.

[23]For market participants who do not want to take delivery on the settlement day, the LME and ICCH have special provisions which allow the open positions to be cash settled.

TABLE 15.21
Comparison of physical deliveries: NYMEX's crude oil versus LME base metals contracts, July 1988 to December 1990

Month	NYMEX crude oil			All LME metals		
	Total deliveries	Total trading volume	Deliveries as a percentage of trading volume	Total deliveries	Total trading volume	Deliveries as a percentage of trading volume
Jul 1988	1,145	1,245,338	0.09	26,236	619,724	4.23
Aug 1988	663	1,386,447	0.05	28,080	646,763	4.34
Sep 1988	370	1,749,649	0.02	29,063	767,132	3.79
Oct 1988	501	1,392,173	0.03	21,687	755,461	2.87
Nov 1988	747	1,515,671	0.05	22,389	791,379	2.83
Dec 1988	360	2,084,784	0.02	23,316	717,505	3.25
	3,786	9,374,062	0.04	150,771	4,297,964	3.51
Jan 1989	633	1,835,871	0.03	21,909	729,532	3.00
Feb 1989	2,092	1,546,401	0.14	20,757	735,683	2.82
Mar 1989	1,995	1,721,178	0.12	25,965	839,022	3.09
Apr 1989	990	1,660,365	0.06	20,445	834,827	2.45
May 1989	1,306	1,785,917	0.07	23,917	821,661	2.91
Jun 1989	785	2,080,341	0.04	24,384	825,383	2.95
Jul 1989	2,761	1,939,674	0.14	27,439	764,912	3.59
Aug 1989	2,035	1,795,504	0.11	31,001	859,818	3.61
Sep 1989	807	1,701,036	0.05	32,375	922,536	3.51
Oct 1989	412	1,498,690	0.03	30,083	957,857	3.14
Nov 1989	720	1,403,674	0.05	29,674	825,105	3.60
Dec 1989	747	1,695,989	0.04	31,037	707,713	4.39
	15,283	20,664,640	0.07	318,986	9,824,049	3.25
Jan 1990	2,336	1,440,891	0.16	29,447	907,892	3.24
Feb 1990	200	1,596,653	0.01	32,967	904,007	3.65
Mar 1990	1,270	1,787,762	0.07	35,462	1,080,795	3.28
Apr 1990	1,267	1,553,551	0.08	33,559	911,469	3.68
May 1990	2,028	1,734,940	0.12	30,515	941,085	3.24
Jun 1990	940	2,045,612	0.05	36,588	891,759	4.10
Jul 1990	1,494	1,886,448	0.08	31,233	1,115,376	2.80
Aug 1990	1,805	1,966,514	0.09	47,563	1,232,516	3.86
Sep 1990	3,164	2,198,274	0.14	44,573	1,264,766	3.52
Oct 1990	1,168	2,201,622	0.05	50,231	1,221,184	4.11
Nov 1990	2,344	2,303,477	0.10	45,520	1,182,510	3.85
Dec 1990	816	2,304,318	0.04	46,959	964,953	4.87
	18,832	23,020,062	0.08	464,617	12,618,312	3.68

Source: New York Mercantile Exchange for crude oil data, and International Commodity Clearing House for LME data.

threatening the very existence of the LME. Subsequently, the LME's tin market was closed, and a thorough re-examination of its trading practices and general operations was conducted.[24] The result was that the International Commodities Clearing House (ICCH) became the clearinghouse and guarantor for all LME contracts. The LME is also now a "Recognized Investment Exchange" under the U.K. Financial Services Act of 1986, and operates in a fashion similar to other futures exchanges.[25]

15.5.3 Determinants of Industrial Metal Prices

Industrial metal prices fluctuate in an unpredictable manner. There are no apparent seasonal cycles. As primary inputs to industrial production, industrial metal prices are related to the strength of the general economy and to the pace of inflation. Figure 15-15 compares the MG Base Metal Index (a consumption-weighted price index based on the six LME metals—aluminum, copper, zinc, lead, nickel, and tin) with percentage changes in U.S. industrial production.[26] The two data series suggest a close relationship between base metal prices and the pace of general economic activity.

Industrial metal futures prices sometimes display a carry relationship, and at other times a backwardation relationship. Figures 15-16 and 15-17 show cash and three-month LME forward prices for aluminum and copper from 1981 to 1990. It is common for industrial metal futures prices to be in backwardation during peaks in business cycles (such as in late 1989), when industrial demand is high relative to supply, but to be in a carry relationship during periods of slack demand (such as in the early 1980s). However, individual metal prices respond differently to the business cycle because of fundamental supply and demand differences. Thus, the

---

[24]Tin trading was suspended on the LME from November 1985 to May 1989. Trading in tin was resumed on June 1, 1989.

[25]Traditionally, the LME was known for its predilection for discretionary rather than mandatory margin calls on members and their clients. However, all LME members who are also members of the clearinghouse (in the LME this includes all ring members) have now accepted the ICCH as their counterparty to exchange contracts, and therefore stand ready to meet margin calls on them. In addition, under the Financial Services Act, money from customers must be kept in a segregated account, separate from the clearing member's own funds. Clearing members are required to issue margin calls on these segregated accounts as soon as a deficiency of funds occurs. However, should a customer (usually a large commercial company) choose not to have its account segregated, the clearing member may issue a credit line to this unsegregated client. Once a credit line is granted, margin calls are not issued to this client until losses exceed the credit limit. The clearing member assumes a financing role by charging customers interest for drawing on credit lines, and paying interest on unrealized gains on open positions. Credit lines are generally granted only to creditworthy customers with active trading relationships with clearing members.

[26]The MG Base Metal Index is the world's first base metal price index, and was developed by Metallgesellschaft in Germany. The weight assigned to each metal in the Index is based on relative western-world consumption in 1985, the base year. In this index, aluminum accounts for 42.6%, copper 25.4%, zinc 16.0%, lead 13.6%, nickel 1.9%, and tin 0.5%.

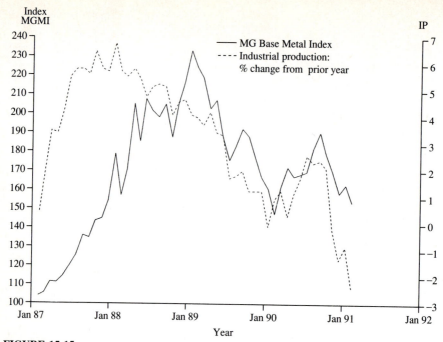

FIGURE 15-15
MG Base Metal Index (MGMI) versus U.S. industrial production (monthly: January 1987 to February 1991).

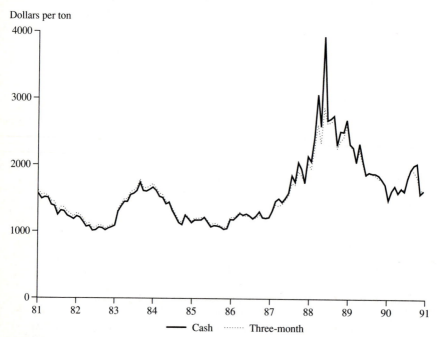

FIGURE 15-16
Cash versus three-month forward aluminum prices (monthly: January 1981 to December 1990).

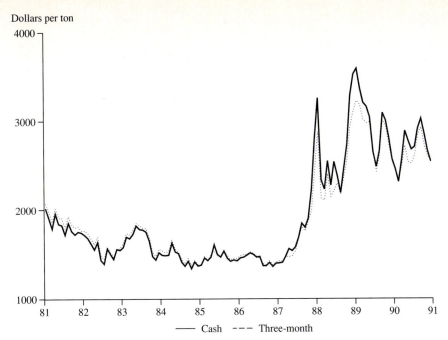

Dollars per ton

—— Cash --- Three-month

FIGURE 15-17
Cash versus three-month forward copper prices (monthly: January 1981 to December 1990).

TABLE 15.22
Maximum backwardation: LME cash and three-month forward prices (U.S. dollars per ton)

	1987	1988	1989	1990	87-90
Aluminum	$200.00	$1340.00	$249.00	$20.00	$1340.00
	(11.00%)	(31.24%)	(10.08%)	(1.21%)	(31.24%)
					(Jun 13, 88)
Copper	$589.16	$600.67	$372.07	$371.84	$589.16
	(21.57%)	(21.49%)	(10.64%)	(12.91%)	(21.57%)
					(Nov 11, 87)
Zinc	$69.69	$165.00	$240.00	$156.00	$240.00
	(7.48%)	(9.71%)	(14.63%)	(8.76%)	(14.63%)
					(Dec 15, 89)
Lead	$110.57	$90.60	$81.28	$417.03	$417.03
	(15.89%)	(12.40%)	(11.81%)	(34.32%)	(34.32%)
					(Mar 14, 90)
Nickel	$534.61	$5850.00	$1650.00	$610.00	$5850.00
	(7.71%)	(28.91%)	(11.05%)	(6.00%)	(28.19%)
					(Apr 26, 88)

Notes: Backwardation: in $ = Cash price − 3 month forward price

$$\text{in \%} = \frac{(\text{Cash price} - 3 \text{ month forward price})}{\text{Cash price}} \times 100\%$$

Since tin trading was suspended on the LME from November 1985 to May 1989, tin is not included in the table.

degree of price backwardation varies among metals, and over time. Table 15.22 shows the yearly *maximum* backwardation in individual metals during each year from 1987 to 1990. It is clear that all of the metals have experienced significant backwardation at some time, and that backwardation is a common occurrence.

15.6 HEDGING

Chapter 6 discussed the concepts and methodologies which underlie the use of commodity futures to hedge price risks associated with related commodities. Examples using commodity futures were provided that demonstrated how to estimate hedge ratios and how to construct and manage an efficient hedging strategy (see Section 6.3.2). Since the concepts and techniques discussed in Chapter 6 are directly applicable to hedging with the futures contracts discussed in this chapter, to repeat that discussion here would be unnecessarily redundant.

CONCLUSION

This chapter describes the major commodity futures contracts currently traded in the United States and on foreign exchanges. It covers agricultural and soft commodities, energy futures, and both precious and industrial metals futures. The fastest growing segment of these markets is energy futures.

For each of these commodity groupings, the chapter describes the volume and growth of trading, the characteristics of the major futures contracts traded, the delivery specifications and procedures used, the relevant cash and futures price quotations, and the pricing relationships that exist. In addition, it discusses commonly traded futures spreads, such as the crush and crack spreads.

Since all of the fundamental pricing and hedging concepts discussed earlier in Chapters 4, 5, and 6 are applicable to commodity futures, this chapter does not repeat that discussion. Readers wishing to acquire a full understanding of commodity futures should read this chapter along with Chapters 4, 5, and 6.

QUESTIONS

1. Which of the various commodity futures markets have grown dramatically during the 1980s?
2. What is the crush spread? What is the crack spread?
3. On January 10, 1990, the February crude oil price was $22.90 a barrel, the March unleaded gasoline futures price was 63.56 cents a gallon, and the March heating oil futures price was 61.87 cents per gallon. Calculate the following crack spreads: 2-1-1; 3-2-1; and 5-3-2.
4. Explain the difference between an additive and a multiplicative delivery adjustment factor. Give an example of each.
5. Explain how a producer of soybean oil and meal can use futures to hedge an anticipated reduction in his gross processing margin. Assume that, on December 10, 1990, the producer is planning to crush 500,000 bushels of soybeans. What crush spread position should he take?

6. Explain why many commodity futures prices periodically experience backwardation, while such backwardation is uncommon for financial futures.
7. In mid-August 1990, the Iraqi invasion of Kuwait caused the November–December 90 crack spread (2-1-1) to widen to $7.56 a barrel. How can you explain this spread? As a speculator, what position would you take? Why? What happened to the spread subsequently?
8. If you are a producer of oats and wish to hedge against a fall in oat prices, how would you go about determining whether an existing grain futures contract could be used to hedge this price risk effectively?
9. How do London Metal Exchange price quotations differ from typical U.S. futures exchange price quotations?

SUGGESTED READING

Emmet, E. and D. Vaught. "Risk and Return in Cattle and Hog Futures." *The Journal of Futures Markets,* Vol. 8 (1988), pp. 79–87.

Fama, E. and K. French. "Commodity Futures Prices: Some Evidence on Forecast Power, Premiums, and the Theory of Storage." *Journal of Business,* Vol. 60 (January 1987), pp. 55–73.

Fama, E. and K. French. "Business Cycles and the Behavior of Metals Prices." *Journal of Finance,* Vol. 43 (1988), pp. 1075–1093.

Gross, M. "A Semi-Strong Test of the Efficiency of the Aluminum and Copper Markets at the LME." *The Journal of Futures Markets,* Vol. 8 (1988), 67–77.

Hayenga, M. and D. DiPietre. "Hedging Wholesale Meat Prices: Analysis of Basis Risk." *The Journal of Futures Markets,* Vol. 2 (1982), pp. 131–140.

Johnson, R., C. Zulauf, S. Irwin, and M. Gerlow. "The Soybean Complex Spread: An Examination of Market Efficiency From the Viewpoint of a Production Process." *The Journal of Futures Markets,* Vol. 11, No. 1 (February 1991), pp. 25–38.

Kuhn, B. "A Note: Do Futures Prices Always Reflect the Cheapest Deliverable Grade of the Commodity?" *The Journal of Futures Markets,* Vol. 8 (February 1988), pp. 99–102.

Marcus, A. and D. Modest. "Futures Markets and Production Decisions." *Journal of Political Economy,* Vol. 92 (June 1984), pp. 409–426.

Milonas, N. "Measuring Seasonalities in Commodity Markets and the Half-Month Effect." *The Journal of Futures Markets,* Vol. 11, No. 3 (June 1991), pp. 331–346.

Stevens, S. "Evidence for a Weather Persistence Effect on the Corn, Wheat, and Soybean Growing Season Price Dynamics." *The Journal of Futures Markets,* Vol. 11, No. 1 (February 1991), pp. 81–88.

Witt, H., T. Schroeder, and M. Hayenga. "Comparison of Analytical Approaches for Estimating Hedge Ratios for Agricultural Commodities." *The Journal of Futures Markets,* Vol. 7 (1987), pp. 135-146.

CHAPTER

16

TRADING METHODS AND STRATEGIES

Trading futures as a speculator is no different from trading any other commodity or asset. Success depends on the ability to predict future price levels and to manage risk successfully.

If a speculator can accurately predict prices, he can be short or long at the appropriate time to profit from the impending price movements. In this case, there will be no risk, since the speculator knows with certainty what is going to happen to prices.

In reality, even successful traders frequently forecast price movements incorrectly and take losses. The risk of such losses must, therefore, be carefully managed. The trader's objective, obviously, is to make profits when his forecasts are correct that are greater than the losses he incurs when his forecasts are wrong. It is possible for a trader to be successful even when his price forecasts are incorrect more often than not, so long as his losses when he is wrong are smaller than are his profits when he is right. This is the result that a trader hopes to achieve by adopting a particular trading strategy.

This chapter discusses alternative approaches used by traders to forecast prices and to manage risk. Two techniques are commonly used to forecast prices: *fundamental* and *technical* analysis. Both are examined in this chapter and examples of each are provided. In addition, various strategies for managing trading risk are discussed.

16.1 FUNDAMENTAL ANALYSIS

Fundamental analysis seeks to identify the fundamental economic and political factors that determine a commodity's price. It is basically an analysis of the (current and future) supply and demand for a commodity in order to determine if a price change is imminent, and in which direction and by how much prices are expected to change.

The fundamentalist approach requires gathering substantial amounts of economic data and political intelligence, assessing the expectations of market participants, and analyzing this information to predict future price movements. It is a time-consuming and tedious process. Sometimes large econometric models are used, but more often simpler analytical forecasting frameworks are employed. In either case, fundamental analysis requires that traders have a thorough knowledge of the workings of underlying commodity markets, be able to evaluate and interpret basic economic and market conditions, and understand how futures prices relate to underlying cash prices.

16.1.1 Analyzing a Commodity

Various factors affect the supply and demand for a commodity. Supply factors include production factors, such as input costs and raw material shortages, weather patterns, available inventories, and foreign imports. For example, abnormally low heating oil inventories in January may result in higher oil prices, bad weather can mean lower agricultural crop yields and higher future prices, and a labor strike at copper mines can interrupt production and raise copper prices.

The demand for a commodity is affected by such factors as general economic conditions, general price levels, the prices of substitute commodities, seasonal consumption patterns, government policies, international commodity agreements, and exports. In addition, the exports and imports of a commodity will be affected by changes in currency exchange rates and by specific government policies motivated by political objectives.

With respect to financial assets, like stocks and bonds, government and central bank policies both in the United States and in foreign countries can be of critical importance. Also, expectations about future policy changes and about general inflation rates are of key importance. For foreign currency rates, international trade and capital flows are central.

Fundamental analysis, therefore, requires that the major determinates of a commodity's demand and supply be identified and evaluated. This information must be updated constantly, on a daily, weekly, or monthly basis, or whenever possible, to identify shifts in demand or supply that may indicate coming price changes.

16.1.2 Sources of Information

Much of the important fundamental information is publicly available through government and privately published reports. The following sources are frequently used:

TABLE 16.1
Economic statistics release schedule

January 1991

Monday	Tuesday	Wednesday	Thursday	Friday
	1 New Year's Day Markets closed (in Tokyo, markets are closed through 1/3) Banks closed	**2** NAPM index (10:00 A.M. EST) Nov.: 41.3% Dec.: —— Construction (10:00 A.M. EST) Nov.: +1.3% Dec.: —— 10-day auto sales (12/11–12/20)	**3** In Washington, D.C.: Congress convenes Jobless claims (for week ended 12/22) (8:30 A.M. EST) New home sales (10:00 A.M. EST) Oct.: −3.5% Nov.: —— M1, M2, M3 (for week ended 12/24) (4:30 P.M. EST)	**4** Unemployment (8:30 A.M. EST) Nov.: 5.9% Dec.: —— Factory orders (10:00 A.M. EST) Oct.: +2.8% Nov.: —— Non-farm payrolls (8:30 A.M. EST) Nov.: −178K Dec.: —— 10-day auto sales (12/21–12/31) LTD: Currency opt. (CME)
7 Treasury auction 3 & 6 month bills	**8** Consumer credit (target date) Oct.: +2.4% Nov.: —— Treasury auction: 30-year REFCORP bonds	**9** Treasury auction: 7-year notes	**10** Jobless claims (for week ended 12/29) (8:30 A.M. EST) Wholesale trade (10:00 A.M. EST) Oct.: + 0.1% Nov.: —— M1, M2, M3 (for week ended 12/31) (4:30 P.M. EST) Treasury auction: 52-week bills	**11** PPI (8:30 A.M. EST) Nov.: +0.5% Dec.: —— LTD: Crude oil opt. (NYMEX) Mortgage backed Fut & opt (CBOT)

14	15	16	17	18
Treasury auction: 3 & 6 month bills LTD: Currency fut. (CME) Eurodollar fut. (CME)	U.N. deadline for Iraq expires In Japan: Adults day. Markets closed. Retail sales (8:30 A.M. EST) Nov.: −0.1% Dec.: ___ 10-day auto sales (1/1–1/10)	CPI (8:30 A.M. EST) Nov.: +0.3% Dec.: ___ Industrial production (9:15 A.M. EST) Nov.: −0.8% Dec.: ___ Capacity utilization (9:15 A.M. EST) Nov.: 82.6% Dec.: ___ Inventory sales ratio (9:00 A.M. EST) Oct.: 1.48 Nov.: ___	Jobless claims (for week ended 1/4) (8:30 A.M. EST) Housing starts (8:30 A.M. EST) Nov.: −0.3% Dec.: ___ Building permits (8:30 A.M. EST) Nov.: −1.4% Dec.: ___ M1, M2, M3 (for week ended 1/17) (4:30 P.M. EST)	Trade balance (7:30 A.M. EST) Oct.: −11.60Bn. Nov.: ___ LTD: S&P500opt. (CBOT) U.S. Bond opt. (CBOT) 10-year note opt. (CBOT) 5-year note opt. (CBOT) Silver opt. (CBOT) MMI (CBOT)
21	22	23	24	25
Martin Luther King Day Banks closed At the CME, Ags, currencies, & interest rates closed at 12:00 noon At the CBOT, financials close at 12:00 noon	Treasury auction: 3 & 6 month bills LTD: Crude oil fut. (NYMEX)	Beige Book released for February 5–6 FOMC Meeting Treasury auction: 2-year notes	Jobless claims (for week ended 1/12) (8:30 A.M. EST) M1, M2, M3 (for week ended 1/14) (4:30 P.M. EST) 10-day auto sales (1/11–1/20) Treasury auction: 5-year notes	GNP (8:30 A.M. EST) Q3 '90: + 1.4% Q4'90: ___ Corporate profits (8:30 A.M. EST) Q3'90: + 8.0% Q4'90: ___ U.S. Export Price Index (10:00 A.M. EST) Nov.: ___ Dec.: ___ U.S. Import Price Index (10:00 A.M. EST) Nov.: ___ Dec.: ___
28	29	30	31	
Personal income & outlays (10:00 A.M. EST) Nov.: +0.2% Dec.: ___ Treasury auction: 3& 6 month bills LTD: 1000 oz. silver (CBOT) 5000 oz silver (CBOT) Kilo gold (CBOT) 100 oz gold (CBOT)	In Washington, D.C. President Bush delivers the State of the Union Address Durable goods (8:30 A.M. EST) Nov.: − 10.5% Dec.: ___ Employment Cost Index (target date)	Leading indicators (8:30 A.M. EST) Nov.: ___ Dec.: ___	Jobless claims (for week ended 1/19) (8:30 A.M. EST) Agricultural prices (3:00 P.M. EST) Nov.: ___ Dec.: ___ M1, M2, M3 (for week ended 1/21) (4:30 P.M. EST) LTD: 30-day interest (CBOT)	

Source: Indosuez Carr Futures Inc.

1. **Government Agencies.** The United States Department of Agriculture (USDA) is the predominant source of statistical and fundamental supply and demand information on grains, livestocks, meats, and soft commodities traded in the United States. The USDA publishes a variety of reports covering different aspects of a commodity: detailed summaries of weekly activity in a particular commodity market, extensive reviews of factors influencing prices and supply and demand conditions, information on foreign crop production and demand, and analyses of developments in import and export markets. The Department of Energy provides information on the supply and demand in various petroleum markets. Government agencies, such as the Department of Commerce and the Labor Department, release important macroeconomic statistics, such as the Consumer Price Index, the Producer Price Index, leading indicators, industrial production, gross national product, capacity utilization, and unemployment figures, on a monthly or quarterly basis.

2. **Futures Exchanges.** Futures exchanges issue daily, weekly, monthly, and annual reports on commodities traded on that exchange. They are often the major source of information on those commodities. They also publish statistical data on prices, volume, open interest, warehouse stocks, and market activities.

3. **Newspapers and Magazines.** Most metropolitan daily newspapers provide at least some commodity prices and brief analyses of current market activity. Some newspapers, like the *Journal of Commerce* and *The Wall Street Journal*, have a large section devoted to commodity and futures trading. They include daily futures and cash price tables, stories on actively traded commodities, comprehensive volume and open interest data, and provide coverage of major business and financial news that affect commodity prices. *Futures* magazine also provides fundamental reports on commodities, discusses trading strategies, and lists dates of forthcoming governmental reports relevant to futures markets. Trade papers are also a good source of information. For example, the *American Metal Market* provides good coverage of prices and developments regarding both precious and industrial metals. Similarly, *Platts Daily Oilgram* and *Petroleum Intelligence Weekly* provide extensive coverage of energy markets and energy product prices.

4. **Brokerage Houses.** Most large brokerage houses have an economic and commodity research department which compiles statistical information and provides information to clients, along with an interpretation of its potential impact on prices. Many of these firms publish weekly market newsletters and offer daily telexes containing pertinent current data and the firm's evaluation of various commodities. Some firms also publish periodic special in-depth studies of a single commodity or related group of commodities. Table 16.1 provides a typical financial market calendar put out monthly by most brokerage houses to alert clients to the release dates for important economic information.

5. **Electronic Data Bases.** There are a growing number of electronic data bases and news services that traders can access, such as the Dow Jones and the Knight-Ridder news services. A listing of many available electronic data services can be found in *Futures* magazine's annual "Reference" issue.

16.1.3   Case Study: Silver

The purpose of analyzing the supply and demand of a commodity is to predict future prices. By updating this analysis as monthly, weekly, and even daily information becomes available, analysts hope to recognize shifts in supply and demand that signal significant price changes. Table 16.2 provides an excerpt from an article on silver which appeared in *The Wall Street Journal* on January 14, 1991,[1] illustrating the use of fundamental analysis to forecast long-term silver prices. In addition, the appendix to this chapter provides an example (for soybeans) of the kind of fundamental analysis that a trader might want to do before beginning to trade a particular futures market.

16.2   TECHNICAL ANALYSIS

Technical analysis is the study of historical prices for the purpose of predicting prices in the future. Technical analysts frequently utilize charts of past prices to identify historical price patterns. These price patterns are then used to forecast prices. This is why technical traders are often referred to as *chartists.*

Technical analysis has grown in popularity since the development of powerful microcomputers. Computers permit the storage and rapid retrieval of large data bases, and enable complex and sophisticated analyses of historical prices. Many different microcomputer software programs are readily available for analyzing and identifying price patterns.

Technical analysts believe that fundamental analysis does not provide sufficient information for successful trading. Supply and demand analysis, they argue, is not timely enough to be useful. Fundamental analysis relies on data and variables that are available only at weekly, monthly, or even quarterly intervals (for example, the CPI figures for March 1991 are not released by the Department of Commerce until April 12, 1991). In the interim, new information creates expectations about what the values of these variables will be, and this information is quickly impounded in market prices.

Futures traders, they argue, must be sensitive to short-run price movements. Losses in the short-run require margin payments and entail the loss of equity. To be right about prices two years from now but wrong until then may be just as costly as not being right at all. A trader's losses in the short-run may prevent his or her ever getting to the long-run.

A basic belief of technical analysts is that market prices themselves contain useful and timely information. Prices quickly reflect all available fundamental information, as well as other information, such as participants' expectations and the "psychology of the market."

---

[1] Stanley W. Angrist, "Silver Prices Continue to Languish as Supply Outstrips Demand and Production is Maintained," *The Wall Street Journal,* January 14, 1991, p. 14, Col. 3.

TABLE 16.2
Case study: A fundamental analysis of silver

Silver Prices Continue to Languish as Supply Outstrips Demand and Production Is Maintained

By Stanley W. Angrist

Staff Reporter of The Wall Street Journal

To be bullish on silver, one must be long on patience.

Any investor who bought silver on the last day of 1979 and sold it on the last day of any subsequent year would have had a big loss on the investment, ranging from 44% if the silver was sold at the end of 1980 to 85% if sold on the last day of 1990. Put another way, the price of silver has risen on a year-end to year-end basis only twice in the past 11 years; the larger gain was 34% in 1982 from the end of 1981.

In that context, it isn't surprising that silver languishes under $4.50 an ounce, its lowest level since 1976, despite the threat of imminent war, possibly sky-high oil prices and eroding confidence in the U.S. banking system.

Two problems dog the silver market: There is too much of the metal compared with demand for it, and more keeps being produced no matter how low the price falls. Rhona O'Connell, senior precious metals analyst in the London office of Shearson Lehman Brothers International,

says that since 1982 enough silver has been added to world stocks to satisfy 17 months of Western demand at projected 1991 rates of use.

While the stockpile buildup is slowing, she says, supplies remain more than ample. "At the close of 1990, the silver price in real terms [adjusted for inflation] was near to a 19-year low, and Lehman expects it to go lower," Ms. O'Connell says.

The only scenario that Ms. O'Connell envisions producing a "knee-jerk rally" in silver would be an extremely short war in the Middle East, which could lead traders to speculate that an economic recovery was on the way and that oil prices would fall significantly. But if a Mideast conflict is prolonged, "hedging would be done in gold, and silver would continue to drift lower as the recession was extended."

Philip Gotthelf, publisher of the Commodity Futures Forecast, a market letter for traders, also sees little hope for higher prices. "Many silver bulls saw the opening [of Eastern] Europe as a great stimulus for silver," he says, but industrialization of

those countries will take far longer than optimists had hoped.

"East Europeans won't be rushing to buy cameras and take extensive trips for which they would need lots of film. They are going to be far more concerned about buying bread," Mr. Gotthelf says. Photographic uses account for about half of silver consumption world-wide.

Moreover, silver has lost all pretense of being a monetary metal, says Ted Arnold, metals specialist for Merrill Lynch in London. "I don't know of any major central banks that hold silver today to back currency," he says. The only chance for silver to soar again is "if the great American public rediscovered the metal as an investment." But, he says, "I believe that love affair is well and truly dead."

One reason so much silver keeps being produced, Mr. Arnold points out, is that about 63% of world output costs nothing because it is a byproduct of copper, lead, zinc and gold mining. "Silver would still be mined by these producers, no matter what its selling price," Mr. Arnold asserts.

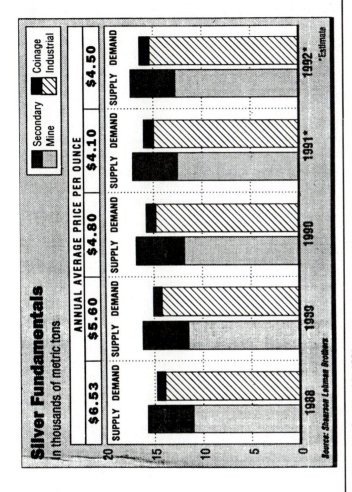

Source: The Wall Street Journal, January 14, 1991.

Critics of technical analysis, on the other hand, see no reason to believe that there exist historical price patterns that will be repeated in the future. New information, they argue, arrives in the market in a random fashion, so that repetitive price patterns are unlikely. It is also not clear what other information is contained in prices, and why this information should result in nonrandom price patterns.

Despite these criticisms, technical analysis remains alive and well, and is the favored methodology among futures traders. It has been estimated that more than 80 percent of professional trading advisors associated with commodity funds rely solely on technical trading systems.[2]

16.3 CHART ANALYSIS

Chart analysis plots or graphs historical prices in order to identify price patterns which can then be used to predict the future direction of prices. Charting is the basic tool of technical analysis. Chartists rely primarily on three bodies of data: prices (monthly, weekly, daily, and intra-day), trading volumes, and open interest levels. They also often use charts to capture shifts in market sentiment and market psychology. This section describes the most common types of charts used by traders.

16.3.1 Price-Pattern Recognition Charts

The goal of any chart analyst is to find consistent, reliable, and logical price patterns with which to predict future price movements. The most commonly used price-pattern recognition charts are: *bar* charts, *line* charts, and *point-and-figure* charts.

BAR CHARTS. Figure 16-1 shows a daily bar chart (sometimes called a *vertical line chart*) of the December 90 S&P futures contract. Each day's (or week's, or month's) trading activity is marked by a single vertical line on the graph. This line connects the high and low prices for the trading period (such as a day), indicating the price range. The horizontal "tick" on the right side of the vertical line shows the closing price for the period. These charts are used, for example, to identify one-day (or one-week, etc.) price reversals, such as those indicated in Figure 16-1. A one-day price reversal occurs in a rising (falling) market when prices make a new high (low) for the current advance (decline) but then close lower (higher) than the previous day's close.

LINE CHARTS. In a line chart only the closing prices are plotted for each time period, usually a day. Figure 16-2 portrays a line chart for the same December 90 S&P futures contract.

---

[2]See Scott H. Irwin and B. Wade Brorsen, "Public Funds," *The Journal of Futures Markets,* 5:463–485, 1985; and, Louis P. Lukac, B. Wade Brorsen, and Scott H. Irwin, "Similarity of Computer Guided Technical Trading System," *The Journal of Futures Markets,* 8(1): 1–14, 1988.

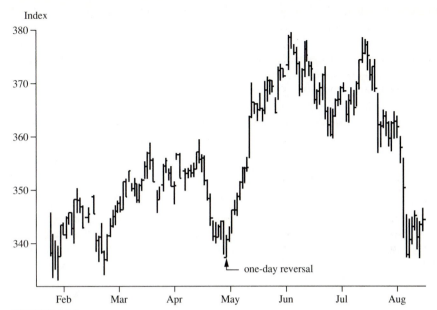

FIGURE 16-1
Bar chart: Dec 90 S&P 500 futures contract (daily prices, January 1990 to August 1990).

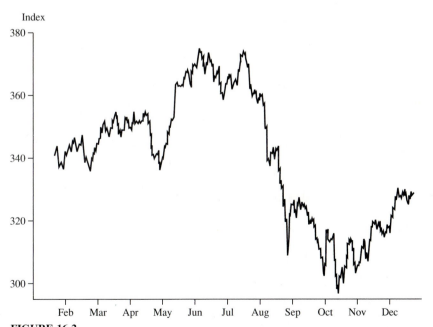

FIGURE 16-2
Line chart: Dec 90 S&P 500 futures contract (daily prices, January 1990 to December 1990).

POINT-AND-FIGURE CHARTS.   Point-and-figure charts (sometimes called *reversal* charts) are constructed by filling in boxes with either an X (indicating a price increase) or an O (indicating a price decrease).[3] A price increase or decrease is defined as a price change that exceeds a specified magnitude. A price change less than that magnitude does not receive an X or O in the chart. If prices are rising, the appropriate Xs are entered in a particular column. When prices begin to decline, a new column is started, and Os are entered in that column.[4] Each price reversal results in the start of a new column.

To plot prices on a point-and-figure chart, the chartist starts with a sheet of graph paper, making a scale along the vertical axis of the paper. Each box on the graph represents a given change in price: $1, 50 cents, 1 cent, or whatever. The flexibility in this system lies in the choice of scale (or the size of box). The smaller the size, the more sensitive the chart is to price moves and to price reversals.

The objective of a point-and-figure chart is to provide a smoothing effect on the price changes that appear in a bar chart in order to detect significant price trends and reversals. Point-and-figure charts can also be used to generate buy and sell signals. For example, a buy signal occurs when an X in a new column surpasses the highest X in the immediately preceding X column; a sell signal is given when an O in a new column is below the lowest O in the previous O column. These are simple buy and sell signals. Point-and-figure chart devotees recognize other more complex signals and formations, such as the penetration of *resistance* and *support* levels. These are used both to generate buy and sell signals and to determine where stop-loss orders should be placed.

Figure 16-3 shows a point-and-figure chart for November 89 crude oil futures prices. Each box represents a 12-cent change in price. Each column reversal, therefore, requires a price move of twenty-four cents in the opposite direction.

Bar charts and line charts have the advantage of being the simplest to construct. They take only seconds a day to keep current, and give a clear and up-to-date picture of price movements. However, some technical analysts feel that merely knowing the high–low price range and the closing price is insufficient. They believe it is important to follow prices within the day's trading range, where most of the activity occurs. Thus, a point-and-figure chart, which is similar to a frequency distribution of prices during the day, is a useful supplement.

16.3.2   Common Technical Price Patterns

Chart analysis uses both trendlines and geometric formations to predict market *tops* and *bottoms,* as well as future price movements. The most popular technical price patterns are: support and resistance, trendlines, double tops and bottoms, and head-and-shoulders.

---

[3]A reversal chart, more generally, is the one in which a price trend is reversed by a predetermined minimum price change in the opposite direction.

[4]Any price increase or decrease of the specified magnitude is recorded. Thus, there may be many such price changes *within* a day. Bar charts and line charts do not use these *intra-day* prices.

$/barrel

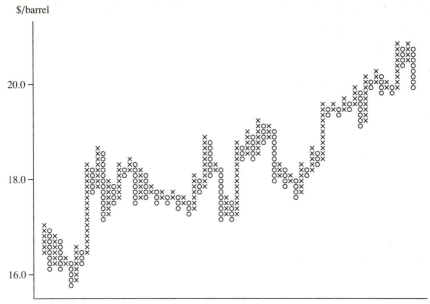

FIGURE 16-3
Point-and-figure chart: Nov 89 crude oil futures contract (daily prices, January 16 to October 20, 1989).

SUPPORT AND RESISTANCE LEVELS. A *support level* is a price level at which there appears to be substantial buying power to keep prices from falling further. Such a support level is shown in Figure 16-4 for March 91 corn futures during the period January 1990 to February 1991.

A *resistance level* is a price level at which there appears to be substantial selling pressure which keeps prices from rising further. Figure 16-5 illustrates a resistance level for March 91 Swiss franc futures during the February 1990 to February 1991 period.

A *congestion area* occurs when prices move sideways, fluctuating up and down within a well-defined range, with no clear-cut movement in either direction for a considerable time period. Both Figures 16-4 and 16-5 show examples of congestion areas. When prices break out of such a congestion area, either by penetrating support or resistance levels, it is a signal to sell or buy, respectively.

TRENDLINES. A common trading strategy is to identify a trend and then go with the trend. A *trendline* on a chart is frequently identified by a straight line connecting periodic highs and lows on a price chart. An *uptrend* can consist of a sequence of either rising price highs or rising price lows. Figure 16-6 shows an uptrend line inferred from December 90 daily Deutschemark futures prices. This is a support trendline because it is drawn along rising price *lows*. A *downtrend* is a sequence of either falling lows or falling highs. Figure 16-7 illustrates a downtrend inferred from daily MG base metal futures prices. This is a resistance trendline because it is drawn along falling price *highs*.

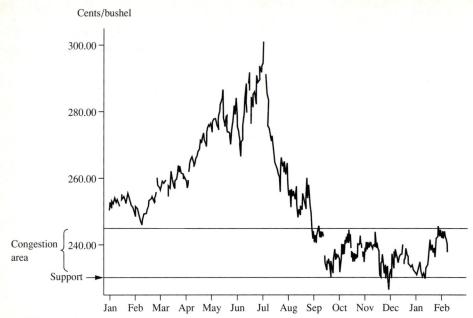

FIGURE 16-4
Support level and congestion area: Mar 91 corn futures contract (daily prices, January 1990 to February 1991).

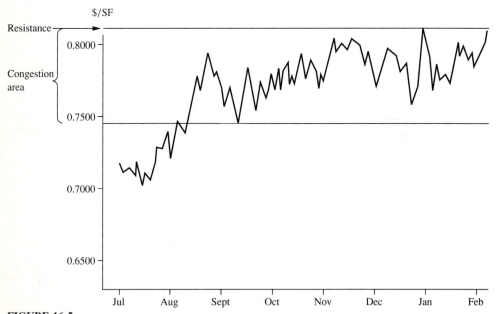

FIGURE 16-5
Resistance level and congestion area: Mar 91 Swiss franc futures contract (daily prices, February 1990 to February 1991).

FIGURE 16-6
Support uptrend line: Dec 90 Deutschemark futures contract (daily prices, June 1990
to December 1990).

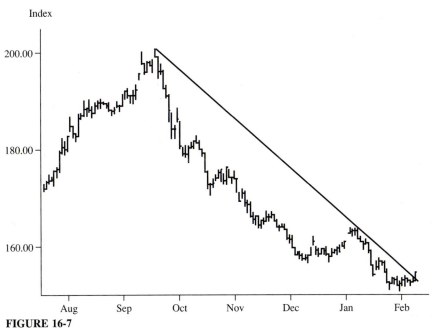

FIGURE 16-7
Resistance downtrend line: MG base metal index 3-month futures (daily prices, July 1990
to February 1991).

Generally, when prices penetrate (or go above) a resistance uptrend line, this is a signal to buy. When prices go below a support downtrend line, this is a signal to sell or go short.

DOUBLE TOPS AND BOTTOMS. *Double tops* or *bottoms* are frequently used to identify a price reversal. In an uptrend, the failure of prices to exceed a previous price peak on two occasions is considered a double top. This is a warning signal that the uptrend may be about to end and a downtrend to commence. However, the formation of a double top is not considered confirmed until falling prices penetrate the previous low from above. Figure 16-8 shows the formation of a double top in March 91 S&P futures in June and July of 1990, and its confirmation in August.

A double bottom is just the mirror image of this price pattern. This occurs when falling prices fail to penetrate previous support levels on two occasions, followed by the upside penetration of the previous price high.

HEAD-AND-SHOULDERS TOPS AND BOTTOMS. *Head-and-shoulders* formations are among the most frequently used technical patterns for identifying a price reversal. This formation consists of four phases: the left shoulder, the head, the right shoulder, and the penetration of the neckline. A head-and-shoulders reversal pattern is complete only when the neckline is penetrated, either in an upward or downward direction.

Figure 16-9 shows a nearly complete *head-and-shoulders top* for March 91 pork bellies futures. The broken line indicates the price movements that are still

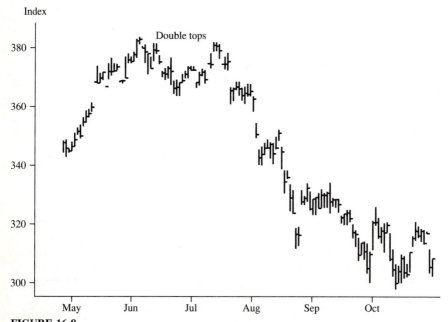

FIGURE 16-8
Double top: Mar 91 S&P 500 futures contract (daily prices, May 1990 to October 1990).

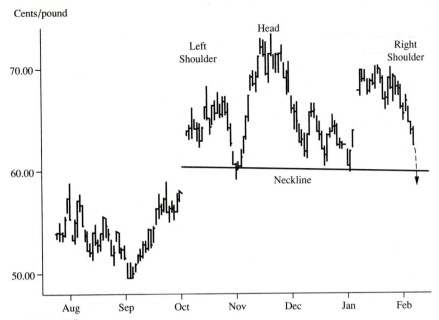

FIGURE 16-9
Head-and-shoulders top in progress: Mar 91 pork bellies futures contract (daily prices, August 1990 to February 1991).

required to complete the formation: prices must penetrate the neckline from above to indicate the beginning of a downtrend.

A *head-and-shoulders bottom* is the inverse of a head-and-shoulders top: it is the same formation turned upside down. Figure 16-10 illustrates this price pattern for New York Composite Index futures. The formation was complete when the neckline was penetrated from below in November, indicating a reversal from a downtrend to an uptrend.

16.3.3 Market Trend Analysis

Market trend analyses use more complex price charts as well as volume and open interest figures to determine both the existence of price trends and the strength of these trends.

MOVING AVERAGES. *Moving averages* are used to determine price trends and trend changes. A moving average is a statistical technique for smoothing price movements in order to identify trends more easily. A simple *n-day* moving average is the average of the most recent *n* daily closing (or other) prices. For example, a five-day moving average is the average of the last five daily closing prices, a 25-day moving average is the average of the last twenty-five days, and so forth. The number of days used to compute the average determines the sensitivity of the average to new price movements. The more days that are used, the less sensitive

Index

FIGURE 16-10

Head-and-shoulders bottom: New York composite index (daily prices, August 1990 to February 1991).

is the average. Weighted moving averages can also be constructed. If greater weights are given to more recent prices, the average becomes more sensitive to price changes.

Sometimes traders use two moving averages to determine buy and sell decisions. For example, using a slow moving average (more days) together with a fast moving average (fewer days) generates the following trading strategies:

1. Buy when the faster moving average goes above the slower one. Sell when the faster moving average goes below the slower one. Figure 16-11 illustrates these trading strategies by superimposing a 5-day moving average and a 20-day moving average on a bar chart for 3-month aluminum forward prices, from July 1990 to February 1991. A buy signal on the chart is indicated by a B, while a sell signal is indicated by an S.

2. Buy when prices are above *both* the fast and slow moving averages. Sell when prices are below *both* moving averages. Figure 16-12 shows both buy (B) and sell (S) signals generated by these trading rules when applied to MG Base Metal Index 3-month forward prices during the period July 1990 to February 1991. (5-day and 18-day moving averages are used in this example.)

MOMENTUM AND OSCILLATOR. Rate of change indicators, such as *momentum* and *oscillator* indexes, are used as leading indicators of price changes. They are based upon price *changes* rather than price levels, and are used to determine

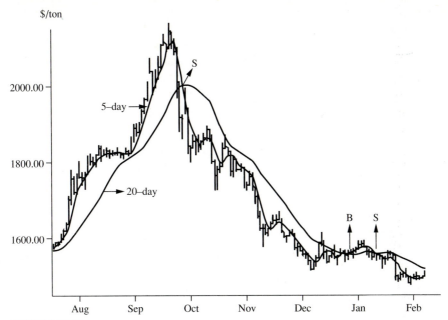

FIGURE 16-11
Moving averages: 5-day versus 20-day aluminum three-month forward prices (London Metal Exchange), July 1990 to February 1991.

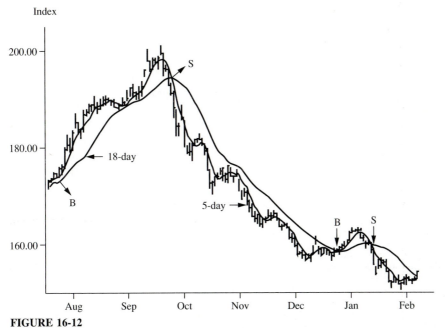

FIGURE 16-12
Moving averages: 5-day versus 18-day MG base metal index three-month forward prices (July 1990 to February 1991).

when a price trend (either up or down) is weakening or strengthening, or losing or gaining momentum.

A *momentum index* measures the acceleration or deceleration of a price advance or decline by using absolute price movements over a fixed time interval. To calculate a five-day momentum index, for example, net price changes occurring over five-day periods are calculated. These (positive and negative) price changes are then plotted around a zero line. Positive price changes are plotted above the zero line, and negative price changes below the line.

Figure 16-13 plots a five-day momentum index at the bottom along with the corresponding daily price chart at the top, using December 90 coffee futures prices. A rising index above the zero line signifies an increase in upward momentum, and a falling index below the zero line means an increase in downward momentum. Alternatively, a rising index below the zero line reflects a decrease in downward price momentum, and a declining index above the zero line signifies a decrease in upward momentum.

The use of momentum values as trend indicators is straightforward. A buy signal occurs whenever the value of the momentum index turns from negative to positive, and a sell signal occurs when it turns from positive to negative. Once a position is entered, a high momentum index also serves as a confirmation of the correctness of the trade.

Momentum indexes are used to identify *overbought* and *oversold* markets as

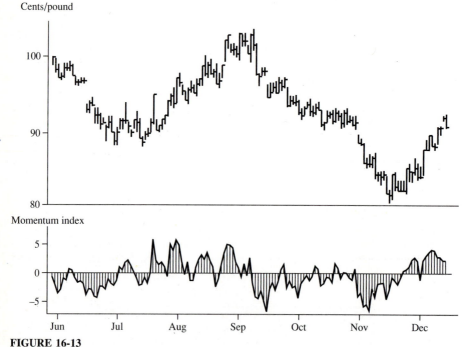

FIGURE 16-13

Five-day momentum index: Dec 90 coffee futures prices (June 1990 to December 1990).

well. A market is considered overbought (oversold) when it can no longer sustain the strength of the current uptrend and a downward (upward) price movement is imminent. Momentum values are bounded in both directions by the maximum move possible during the time interval represented by the span of the momentum. The attainment of a maximum positive or negative momentum value is considered to indicate the end of a trend, and signals to traders either to begin liquidating their positions before prices actually reverse direction or to initiate positions in advance of a market turnaround.

An *oscillator index* is a normalized form of a momentum index. One problem with the momentum index is that it lacks a predetermined upper and lower boundary. Thus, by dividing the momentum value (the price change over n days) by a specified divisor normalizes the index so that movements fall within a range of -1 and $+1$.[5] Using a normalized momentum, or the oscillator, the upper and lower boundaries become volatility-adjusted at any level. When a value is reached near the upper or lower bounds of $+1$ and -1, the market is considered to be overbought (near $+1$) or oversold (near -1). As a general rule, traders buy when the oscillator index is in the lower end of the range, and sell when it is in the upper end of the range. If the index crosses the zero line, it suggests a reversal of a price trend. Figure 16-14 provides an example of an oscillator index obtained by normalizing the five-day momentum index shown in Figure 16-13.

VOLUME AND OPEN INTEREST. Figure 16-15, at the top, shows a bar chart for December 90 S&P futures prices during 1990. At the bottom of the chart, total trading volume and open interest for *all* S&P futures contracts are shown. Daily volume is represented by a vertical bar at the bottom of the chart under each day's price. Open interest is plotted as a solid line above the daily volume bar. Official volume and open interest figures are reported a day later than futures prices.

Technical analysts believe that volume and open interest provide information about whether a price move is strong or weak. A few common beliefs about open interest are the following:

1. If prices are rising and open interest and volume are increasing, new money is thought to be flowing into the market, reflecting aggressive new buying. This is considered bullish.
2. If prices are rising but open interest and volume are declining, the rally is thought to be caused primarily by short covering (holders of losing short positions covering those positions by buying). Money is leaving rather than entering the market. This combination is considered to be bearish because the uptrend will probably end once the short covering is completed.

---

[5]There are several ways to normalize an index. The simplest way to do this is to divide the latest momentum value by the maximum possible price move for the time period being covered. Thus, if prices were rising substantially, the divisor would change as well, giving the technique a means of adjusting for varying volatility.

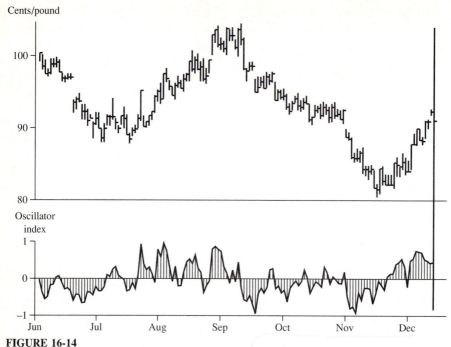

FIGURE 16-14
5-day Oscillator: Dec 90 coffee futures prices (June to December 1990).

3. If prices are falling and open interest and volume are rising, new money is thought to be flowing into the market, reflecting aggressive new short selling. This action increases the likelihood that the downtrend will continue, and is considered bearish.

4. If prices are falling and open interest and volume are declining, the price decline is considered to be the result of discouraged or losing longs liquidating their positions. This is interpreted as indicating a weak downtrend, and is bullish.

These views, however, are highly controversial. Changes in open interest and volume are subject to alternative interpretations, and there has been little research that confirms the importance of open interest and volume as price indicators.

16.3.4 Structural Analysis

Structural analysis seeks to identify repeatable price patterns, utilizing both charting and quantitative analysis. Two common types of repeatable price patterns are *seasonal* and *cyclical*. Seasonal patterns refer to recognizable price movements over a crop or a calendar year. Cyclical patterns refer to price patterns that occur consistently independent of seasons, and may occur over either long or short periods of time.

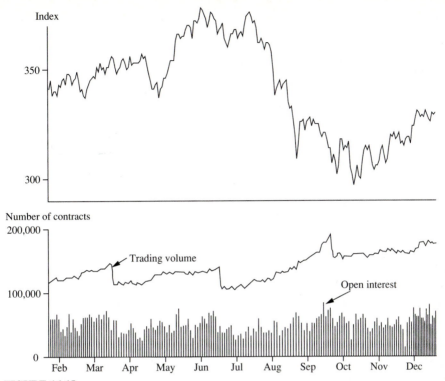

FIGURE 16-15
Total volume and open interest in all S&P 500 futures contracts and Dec 90 S&P 500 futures prices (January to December 1990).

As discussed in Chapter 15, many commodities exhibit seasonal price patterns. For example, agricultural commodities show a tendency for prices to register lows at a certain time of the year and highs at another time of year. For example, since at harvest supply is usually greater than demand, prices are often low.

Cyclical price patterns are much harder to identify and to validate, and are therefore seldom relied on by traders. A well-known cyclical theory, however, is the *Elliot Wave Theory*.[6] Elliot contends that there is a cyclical rhythm in nature that pertains to all aspects of life. According to the theory, a major bull market consists of five waves, followed by a bear market consisting of three waves. Further, the five-wave bull market is made up of three *up legs* and two *down legs*, and the three-wave bear market consists of a downswing, a rally, and a final downswing. In addition, Elliot argues that within major cyclical trends there are intermediate and minor trends.

To pique the reader's curiosity, Figure 16-16 depicts what appears to be a currently evolving price pattern in the stock market. It shows annual

[6]Ralph Elliot, *Nature's Law: The Secret of the Universe,* 1942.

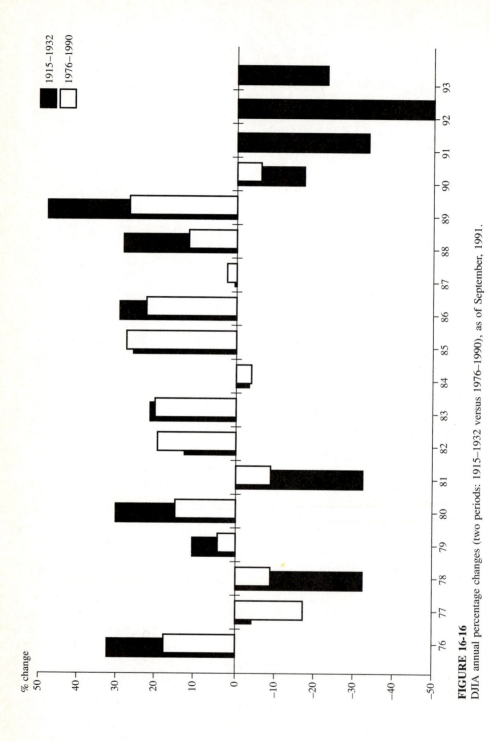

FIGURE 16-16

DJIA annual percentage changes (two periods: 1915–1932 versus 1976–1990), as of September, 1991.

percentage changes in the Dow Jones Industrial Average (DJIA) during two long periods associated with our two most severe stock market crashes: 1915–1932 and 1976–1990. The DJIA's annual percentage change is shown on the vertical axis of the figure, and the relevant years on the horizontal axis. The black bars represent the percentage changes in the earlier years (1915–1932), while the white bars show the percentage changes in the recent years (1976–1990).[7]

It is startling that the direction of the change in stock prices has been the same for the first fifteen years of each period, up to 1990. The pattern suggests that stock prices will decline in the 1991–93 period.

16.4 TRADING SYSTEMS

Whether fundamental or technical analysis is used to forecast price movements, traders need to develop a trading system or strategy. Traders have to know when to enter and exit the market, and how to manage risk.

A trading system often employs more than one technical indicator. This section provides an example of one such system developed by two academics: the CRISMA trading system for stock.[8]

Their system makes use of three technical indicators: a particular stock's price performance relative to the performance of a general stock market index, the stock's recent price performance relative to its performance during some period in the past, and the volume of trading in the stock. The specific criteria that must be met before buying a stock are

1. The stock's 50-day moving average must intersect the stock's 200-day moving average from below at a time when the slope of the latter's plotted course is greater than or equal to zero. In other words, current stock prices must be rising relative to levels in previous periods.
2. The stock's *relative strength indicator* over the past four weeks must have a slope greater than or equal to zero. Relative strength is the percent change in a stock's (or commodity's) price relative to the percent change in some general stock market index (such as the S&P 500 index). This criterion ensures that the stock's performance over the most recent period is better or at least equal to the performance of the market as a whole.
3. The cumulative volume graph for the stock, from beginning to ending point over the previous four weeks, must have a slope greater than zero. This is considered to indicate that rising prices in the stock are associated with increased trading activity.

---

[7]The authors would like to thank Michael Belkin at Salomon Brothers for this example.

[8]Stephen W. Pruitt and Richard E. White, "The CRISMA Trading System: Who Says Technical Analysis Can't Beat the Market?" *The Journal of Portfolio Management,* Spring 1988, pp. 55–88; and Stephen W. Pruitt and Richard E. White, "Exchange-Traded Options and CRISMA Trading," *The Journal of Portfolio Management,* Summer 1989, pp. 55–56.

Finally, to guard against *whipsaws*, or false signals, a last filter is used. Even if all of the above criteria are satisfied, a stock is nevertheless purchased only after its price advance reaches 110 percent of the price level established by the intersection of the 50-day and 200-day moving averages. This provides a 10 percent cushion for error.

Once purchased, a stock is subsequently sold when either its price falls below the 200-day moving average price or rises above 120 percent of the price level established by the intersection of the 50-day and 200-day moving averages. This rule, therefore, has the trader either taking profits after a 9 percent increase

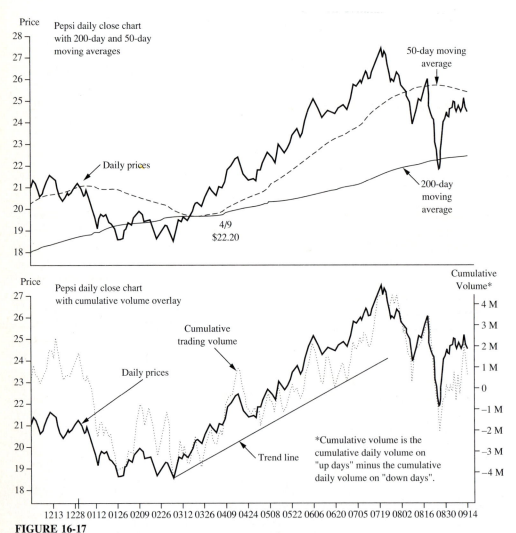

FIGURE 16-17
The CRISMA trading system for Pepsi stock, December 1989 to September 1990. (Knight-Ridder Trade Center)

in prices or taking losses after less than a 10 percent decline in prices (since the 200-day moving average price will still be rising even if current prices are declining).

Thus, this trading system, like others, generates both buy and sell signals. In addition, a trading system can be used to provide guidelines for selling short and subsequently repurchasing.

An example of the CRISMA system applied to Pepsi's stock for the period December 1, 1989, to September 14, 1990, is provided in Figure 16-17.[9] On the top half of the figure, a daily bar chart of Pepsi's stock price over 200 days is shown along with the stock's 50-day and 200-day moving average prices. The bottom half of the figure shows daily closing prices of the stock as a solid line, and the stock's cumulative trading volume as a dotted line.

The system generated a buy signal on April 9, 1990. On that date the price of the stock hit $22.20, which was 110 percent of the price established by the intersection of the 50-day and 200-day moving averages ($20.20). Also, the 50-day average had crossed the 200-day average from below when the 200-day average was rising, and the stock's cumulative trading volume had been rising over the past four weeks. A sell signal occurred in June, when the stock's price hit $24.75, which was 120 percent of the $20.20 price.

Pruitt and White tested this model for 204 stocks over the period 1976 to 1985. The stocks that were selected by the CRISMA system, they claim, generated a mean annualized excess return of between 26.65 and 35.65 percent over alternative *buy-and-hold* strategies, assuming zero transaction costs; or, alternatively, these stocks generated an excess return of from 6.13 to 15.13 percent assuming a 2 percent transaction cost. [10]

The CRISMA system is just one of an infinite variety of trading systems that could be devised. There is, as might be expected, intense debate about whether such trading systems can be profitable in the long run. Academics, especially, doubt their usefulness. Since trading systems are developed using historical data, it is easy to fall prey to the trap of making the system fit the data. It is relatively simple to find a system that explains historical price movements, but much more difficult to find one that succeeds in accurately predicting future price movements, at least for very long.[11]

---

[9] The authors would like to thank Stephen Goldstein of Knight-Ridder Trade Center for suggesting this example.

[10] S. Pruitt and R. White, "The CRISMA Trading System," pp. 57–58.

[11] For a sampling of the academic literature, see Louis P. Lukac and B. Wade Brorsen, "The Usefulness of Historical Data in Selecting Parameters for Technical Trading Systems," *The Journal of Futures Markets,* 9: 55–66, 1989; Scott H. Irwin and J.W. Uhring, "Do Technical Analysts Have Holes in Their Shoes?" *The Review of Futures Markets,* 3: 264-77, 1984; Christopher K. Ma and Luc A. Soenen, "Arbitrage Opportunities in Metal Futures Markets," *The Journal of Futures Markets,* 8: 199–209, 1988; W. Tomek and S. Querin, "Random Processes in Prices and Technical Analysis," *The Journal of Futures Markets,* 4: 15–23, 1988; and Salih N. Neftci and Andrew J. Policano, "Can Chartists Outperform the Market? Market Efficiency Tests for Technical Analysis," *The Journal of Futures Markets,* 4: 465–78, 1984.

Despite pervasive academic criticism, however, the majority of professional traders continue to rely, fully or partially, on some type of trading system to make decisions. Sometimes these systems are supplemented with fundamental analysis, but most often they are technical-analysis-based systems, some more formally developed than others. Trading systems enjoy a particularly strong following among professional commodity traders.

16.5   RISK MANAGEMENT AND THE ALLOCATION OF PORTFOLIO EQUITY

An important element of any trading system is risk management. Traders must determine how to allocate their equity to achieve their trading objectives. They must, specifically, decide what the overall leverage in their portfolio should be, and how much of their equity to commit to each futures position in their portfolio.

There are no simple rules for making these decisions. A speculator's preference for risk will partially determine these decisions. A preference for greater risk, for example, usually results in the adoption of greater overall leverage.

Given a speculator's risk preference and objectives with respect to return and risk, there still remains the question of allocating portfolio equity across commodities in the portfolio: determining the number of futures contracts to hold of each commodity in the portfolio. A common strategy is to allocate portfolio equity according to volatility, or to hold positions in each commodity such that the likely daily dollar loss is the same for all positions.

Assume, for example, that a trader does not wish to risk losing more than five percent of the portfolio's trading equity on any single position, and that he does not want to commit more than 60 percent of the total portfolio equity to margin deposits supporting his futures positions (keeping 40 percent in reserve to meet variation margin calls). In this case, the maximum daily loss the trader is willing to take on any *single* position is

$$\text{Maximum potential daily loss} = 0.05 \times (0.60 \times \text{total equity})$$

His allocation decision rule, therefore, is

$$\begin{bmatrix} \text{Maximum} \\ \text{potential} \\ \text{daily loss} \end{bmatrix} = \begin{bmatrix} \text{Worst-case daily change} \\ \text{in price of a particular} \\ \text{futures contract} \end{bmatrix} \times \begin{bmatrix} \text{Size} \\ \text{of} \\ \text{contract} \end{bmatrix} \times \begin{bmatrix} \text{Number} \\ \text{of} \\ \text{contracts} \end{bmatrix}$$

Thus, his position sizes are determined by

$$\begin{bmatrix} \text{Number of} \\ \text{contracts} \end{bmatrix} = \frac{0.05 \times (0.60 \times \text{total equity})}{\begin{bmatrix} \text{Worst-case daily change} \\ \text{in price of a particular} \\ \text{futures contract} \end{bmatrix} \times \begin{bmatrix} \text{Size} \\ \text{of} \\ \text{contract} \end{bmatrix}}$$

Suppose that a speculator's total equity is $500,000, and that he is planning to hold a portfolio consisting of gold, crude oil, and S&P 500 futures. Further, suppose that the likely worst-case daily price move for gold is estimated to be

$12.70 an ounce (or $1270 per contract), to be $3.21 per barrel for crude oil (or $3210 per contract), and to be 9.89 index points for the S&P 500 futures (or $4945 per contract). These estimates are based on the distribution of daily absolute price changes during 1990 for the respective commodities, and are equal to the mean plus three standard deviations of the daily price changes (see Table 16-3). Inserting these values in the above equation along with the size of the respective contracts yields the following position sizes (or number of contracts, N), rounded to the nearest integer:

- Gold:

$$N = \frac{0.05 \times (0.60 \times \$500,000)}{\$1270} = 12$$

- Crude oil:

$$N = \frac{0.05 \times (0.60 \times \$500,000)}{\$3210} = 5$$

- S&P 500 index:

$$N = \frac{0.05 \times (0.60 \times \$500,000)}{\$4945} = 3$$

Thus, the speculator would initially hold a total of 20 contracts, allocated according to the above formulas. Over time, this portfolio allocation would have to be adjusted to reflect changes in total portfolio equity as well as changes in estimates of the likely worst-case price volatility for each of the commodities in the portfolio. As shown in Table 16-3, volatility can change significantly. In addition, to the extent that the price movements of different commodities are correlated, these relationships must be incorporated into the above risk analysis.

Other frameworks for making portfolio allocation decisions exist. Traders must adopt a procedure they are comfortable with and that is consistent with their objectives and risk preferences. The important point is that they must make decisions in a systematic way. Trading in a disorganized and undisciplined manner is almost always a recipe for disaster.

16.6   MEASURING VOLATILITY

In the previous section the allocation of equity among the different portfolio positions was partially determined by a commodity's expected price volatility. How should this price volatility be estimated?

A common method is to use historical data on daily price changes to predict future price volatility. While there are a number of sophisticated statistical techniques available that do this, a simple one is to use an estimate of the standard deviation of past daily absolute price changes.

$$\sigma = \frac{\sqrt{\sum_{i=1}^{n}(x_i - \overline{x})^2}}{n}$$

TABLE 16.3
Mean and standard deviations of absolute daily price and contract value changes for the top ten futures contracts: 1989–1990

| | 1990 | | | | | 1989 | | | | |
| | | | Dollar value per contract | | | | | Dollar value per contract | | |
	Mean (μ) (1)	Standard deviation (σ) (2)	μ + 1σ (3)	μ + 2σ (4)	μ + 3σ (5)	Mean (6)	Standard deviation (7)	μ + 1σ (8)	μ + 2σ (9)	μ + 3σ (10)
T-bond price	14/32	12/32				12/32	10/32			
Contract value	($437.50)	($375.00)	$812.50	$1187.50	$1562.50	($375.00)	($312.50)	$687.50	$1000.00	$1312.50
Eurodollar price	0.04	0.05				0.07	0.08			
Contract value	($100.00)	($125.00)	$225.00	$350.00	$475.00	($175.00)	($200.00)	$375.00	$575.00	$775.00
Crude oil price	0.72	0.83				0.29	0.36			
Contract value	($720.00)	($830.00)	$1550.00	$2380.00	$3210.00	($290.00)	($360.00)	$650.00	$1010.00	$1370.00
S&P 500	2.87	2.34				2.00	2.58			
Contract value	($1435.00)	($1170.00)	$2605.00	$3775.00	$4945.00	($1000.00)	($1295.00)	$2290.00	$3580.00	$4870.00
Corn price	2.03	1.80				2.28	2.23			
Contract value	($100.00)	($90.00)	$190.00	$280.00	$370.00	($114.00)	($115.00)	$229.00	$344.00	$459.00
Soybeans price	5.24	4.62				7.18	6.74			
Contract value	($262.00)	($231.00)	$493.00	$724.00	$955.00	($359.00)	($337.00)	$696.00	$1033.00	$1370.00
Gold price	2.89	3.27				2.39	2.30			
Contract value	($289.00)	($327.00)	$616.00	$943.00	$1270.00	($239.00)	($230.00)	$469.00	$699.00	$929.00
Deutsche price	0.0032	0.0027				0.0029	0.0024			
Contract value	($400.00)	($337.50)	$737.50	$1075.00	$1412.50	($362.50)	($300.00)	$662.50	$962.50	$1262.50
Yen price	0.000040	0.000035				0.000037	0.000035			
Contract value	($500.00)	($437.50)	$937.50	$1375.00	$1812.50	($462.50)	($437.50)	$900.00	$1337.50	$1775.00
Swiss franc price	0.0045	0.0038				0.0037	0.0032			
Contract value	($562.50)	($475.00)	$1037.50	$1512.50	$1987.50	($462.50)	($462.50)	$862.50	$1262.50	$1662.50

where σ is the standard deviation, n is the number of daily price changes observed, x_is are the daily absolute price changes, and $\overline{x}$ is the mean of the daily absolute price changes during the period.

If the distribution of daily absolute price changes is approximated by a normal distribution, it is reasonable to expect that about 99 percent of the time the daily price change will not exceed the mean of the distribution plus three standard deviations. (Or, alternatively, on about 95 percent of the days the price change will not exceed the mean plus two standard deviations, $\mu + 2\sigma$.)

Table 16.3 provides the means and the standard deviations of the daily absolute price changes for the 10 most active futures contracts, calculated by using all trading days during 1989 and 1990 respectively. For each commodity near-month futures prices are used to estimate these means and standard deviations. Taking 1990 as an example, column 1 is the average value of the absolute price changes (μ), and column 2 is the value of the standard deviation (σ) of these price changes. The corresponding dollar values per contract are in brackets underneath the means and standard deviations of the price changes. Columns 3, 4, and 5 are, respectively, the mean plus one, two, and three standard deviations, expressed in dollar values per contract. For example, in 1990 the average daily absolute price change for crude oil is $0.72 a barrel, and the standard deviation is $0.83. Thus, we would expect that on about 99 percent of days crude oil prices would not change by more than $3.21 a barrel ($0.72 + $0.83 × 3), or by more than $3210 per contract. This could be considered a worst-case price change.

Using this procedure to estimate expected (or future) price volatility requires that the estimates of the mean and standard deviation be updated continuously. They can, for example, be recalculated every day, using the past 50 (or 100, etc.) trading days; or, greater importance might be attached to current volatility by weighting current price changes more heavily.

No matter how price volatility is estimated, traders need to keep in mind that historical volatility is not always a reliable predictor of future volatility. Judgments about future volatility should take into account current market conditions as well as historical price changes. (A further discussion of price volatility is contained in Section 19.5.)

16.7 KEEPING A TRADING DIARY

Another key to successful trading is maintaining a daily trading diary of the positions held, changes in the market value of these positions, actions taken, and the reasons for these actions. Tables 16.4 and 16.5 provide examples of the kinds of daily records that traders should keep.

Table 16.4 is a summary statement of a trader's daily equity position for his entire portfolio. This information is essential for assessing the success or failure of a trading strategy. It also alerts traders to their risk exposure—large daily changes in portfolio equity indicate significant risk exposure. Table 16.4, for example, shows that on some days the trader's equity experienced sizeable changes, such as on November 7 and 12. Equity changes of this magnitude clearly indicate that the trader is vulnerable to significant losses.

TABLE 16.4
Trading journal: Summary of equity position

1990 Date	Beginning equity	Closing equity	Dollar change from previous day	Percent change from previous day	Cumulative percent change from inception
10/11	$1,000,000	$1,000,500	$500	0.05%	0.05%
10/12	1,000,500	1,001,175	675	0.07%	0.12%
10/15	1,001,175	1,003,425	2,250	0.22%	0.34%
10/16	1,003,425	1,001,188	(2,238)	−0.22%	0.12%
10/17	1,001,188	974,875	(26,313)	−2.63%	−2.51%
10/18	974,875	979,000	4,125	0.42%	−2.10%
10/19	979,000	969,000	(10,000)	−1.02%	−3.10%
10/22	969,000	995,250	26,250	2.71%	−0.48%
10/23	995,250	989,625	(5,625)	−0.57%	−1.04%
10/24	989,625	1,039,313	49,688	5.02%	3.93%
10/25	1,039,313	974,000	(65,313)	−6.28%	−2.60%
10/26	974,000	988,750	14,750	1.51%	−1.13%
10/29	988,750	949,350	(39,400)	−3.98%	−5.07%
10/30	949,350	928,688	(20,663)	−2.18%	−7.13%
10/31	928,688	957,563	28,875	3.11%	−4.24%
11/1	957,563	1,063,888	106,325	11.10%	6.39%
11/2	1,063,888	1,072,490	8,602	0.81%	7.25%
11/5	1,072,490	1,164,115	91,625	8.54%	16.41%
11/6	1,164,115	1,077,415	(86,700)	−7.45%	7.74%
11/7	1,077,415	950,877	(126,538)	−11.74%	−4.91%
11/8	950,877	967,040	16,163	1.70%	−3.30%
11/9	967,040	1,154,853	187,813	19.42%	15.49%
11/12	1,154,853	1,405,252	250,400	21.68%	40.53%
11/13	1,405,252	1,511,052	105,800	7.53%	51.11%
11/14	1,511,052	1,540,853	29,800	1.97%	54.09%
11/15	1,540,853	1,540,853	0	0.00%	54.09%
11/16	1,540,853	1,536,865	(3,988)	−0.26%	53.69%

Note: Equity value includes both realized and unrealized gains and losses.

TABLE 16.5
Trading journal: Position summary (S&P 500 stock index)

Date	Positions	Number of contracts	Purchase price	Unrealized gain/loss	Selling price	Realized gain/loss	Cumulative realized gain/loss	Stop price	Dollar gain/loss if exit at stop	Percent gain/loss if exit at stop	Comment
11/8	Long	20	304.20	$56,000			0	302.50	(17,000)	−1.79%	
	Long	1	306.30	1,750			0	305.50	(400)	−0.04%	
	Long	1	310.12	(160)			0	305.50	(2,310)	−0.24%	
	Long	2	313.60	(3,800)			0	308.00	(5,600)	−0.59%	
11/9	Long	20	304.20	113,500			0	305.00	8,000	0.83%	
	Long	1	306.30	4,625			0	305.00	(650)	−0.07%	
	Long	1	310.12	2,715			0	306.00	(2,060)	−0.21%	
	Long	2	313.60	1,950			0	307.00	(6,600)	−0.68%	
	Long	10	313.15	12,000			0	310.00	(15,750)	−1.63%	
11/12	Long	20	304.20	163,000			0	305.00	8,000	0.69%	
	Long	1	306.30	7,100			0	305.00	(650)	−0.06%	
	Long	1	310.12	5,190			0	306.00	(2,060)	−0.18%	
	Long	2	313.60	6,900			0	307.00	(6,600)	−0.57%	
	Long	10	313.15	36,750			0	309.00	(20,750)	−1.80%	
11/13	Long	20	304.20	149,500			0	308.00	38,000	2.70%	
	Long	1	306.30	6,425			0	309.00	1,350	0.10%	
	Long	1	310.12	4,515			0	309.00	(560)	−0.04%	
	Long	2	313.60	5,550			0	309.00	(4,600)	−0.33%	
	Long	10	313.15	30,000			0	310.00	(15,750)	−1.12%	
	Long	10	320.20	(5,250)			0	314.00	(31,000)	−2.21%	
11/14	Liquidate all open positions:										
	Long	20	304.20		321.80	$176,000	$176,000				
	Long	1	306.30		321.80	7,750	183,750				
	Long	1	310.12		321.80	5,840	189,590				
	Long	2	313.60		321.80	8,200	197,790				
	Long	10	313.15		321.80	43,250	241,040				
	Long	10	320.20		321.80	8,000	249,040				
11/15							249,040				
11/16							249,040				

Table 16.5 provides a daily record of trading activity in one portfolio position: the S&P 500 index. Here the trader is using *stop prices* to control risk exposure. His potential losses are shown in the right-hand columns of the table, and are calculated on the basis of the positions being stopped out at the stop prices. These are conservative estimates, of course, since traders will not always get their stop prices. On the far right of the table there is also space provided for a brief explanation of the decisions made during the day.

Keeping the kind of information shown in Tables 16.4 and 16.5 current, along with maintaining a more extensive analytical diary explaining the trading decisions made, are essential to a systematic and disciplined approach to trading. Such information indicates when changes in a trading strategy are called for and provides for systematic management of risk. Probably the most serious error made by nonprofessional traders is not keeping this information current, and therefore delaying decisions that would have been made earlier had this information been available in a timely fashion and been fully evaluated.

CONCLUSION

This chapter briefly describes fundamental and technical analysis, the two approaches used by traders to forecast price changes and to make buy and sell decisions. Of the two approaches, technical, or chart, analysis is the more popular among commodity traders. The chapter discusses the logic underlying charting and provides illustrations of the most commonly used chart analyses. There are, however, many books which examine the subtleties of technical analysis in greater detail. This chapter is intended as an introduction to trading, providing only enough detail for readers to grasp the basic concepts and methodologies underlying technical analysis. Those wishing to pursue the subject in greater depth should consult additional sources.

Fundamental analysis attempts to utilize basic economic and political information to predict the future demand and supply for a commodity. Technical analysis essentially ignores fundamental factors in favor of elaborate and often complex analyses of historical price patterns. However, neither fundamental nor technical analysis provides a complete trading system, especially during periods of erratic or indecisive market conditions. Fundamental traders who have studied and understand basic market conditions are less likely to lose perspective and abandon a position that is fundamentally sound, or to assume a position that is fundamentally unsound. On the other hand, technical analysis can aid in anticipating the short-term direction and duration of price movements, and may help to detect shifts in market psychology that underlie the ebb and flow of price movements. A sound trading strategy can be developed by combining aspects of both approaches, coupled with sensible risk-management policies. The chapter suggests procedures that traders can adopt to ensure a disciplined approach to trading.

In summary, traders must determine what and when to buy and sell, and how much to buy and sell of each commodity, know how to manage risk, and maintain disciplined trading records.

QUESTIONS

1. Describe how fundamental analysis is used to predict prices.
2. Technical analysis utilizes a variety of charting techniques. What is the purpose of charting? Give an illustration using a particular chart.
3. Why do you think technical analysis is more popular with traders than fundamental analysis?
4. Do you agree with the view that if open interest rises when prices are rising (falling), this is a bullish (bearish) signal.
5. Describe the elements of a successful trading system or strategy other than forecasting prices. What are the key decisions that traders must make?
6. How would you define and measure portfolio risk? Describe procedures for managing this risk.
7. What trading records should traders maintain?

SUGGESTED READING

Goldenberg, D. "Trading Functions and Futures Price Movements." *Journal of Financial and Quantitative Analysis*, Vol. 23 (December 1988), pp. 465-481.

Irwin, S. and W. Uhrig. "Do Technical Analysts Have Holes in Their Shoes?" *Review of Research in Futures Markets,* Vol. 3, No. 3, (1984), pp. 264-277.

Lukac, L. P., B. W. Brorsen, and S. H. Irwin. "The Usefulness of Historical Data in Selecting Parameters for Technical Trading Systems." *The Journal of Futures Markets,* Vol. 8 (February 1989), pp. 55-65.

Lukac, L. P., B. W. Brorsen, and S. H. Irwin. "A Test of Futures Market Disequilibrium Using Twelve Different Technical Trading Systems." *Applied Economics,* May 1988, pp. 623-639.

Murphy, J. A. "Futures Fund Performance: A Test of the Effectiveness of Technical Analysis." *The Journal of Futures Markets,* Vol. 6 (Summer 1986), pp. 175-186.

Neftci, S. N. and A. J. Policano. "Can Chartists Outperform the Market?: Market Efficiency Tests for Technical Analysis." *The Journal of Futures Markets,* Vol. 4 (Winter 1984) pp. 465-478.

Peterson, P. and R. Leuthold. "Using Mechanical Trading Systems to Evaluate the Weak Form Efficiency of Futures Markets," *Southern Journal of Agricultural Economics,* July 1982, pp. 147-151.

Silber, W. "Market Behavior in an Auction Market: An Analysis of Scalpers in Futures Markets." *Journal of Finance,* Vol. 38 (September 1983), pp. 937-954.

APPENDIX: EXAMPLE OF FUNDAMENTAL ANALYSIS: THE SOYBEAN COMPLEX, FEBRUARY 5, 1991

Background Analysis

The soybean complex consists of the actual bean and two byproducts: soybean meal and soybean oil. The uses of the soybean itself are quite limited, but the products are found in many feed, food, and industrial products. The United States is the largest bean grower, accounting for approximately 60 percent of world output, while South America provides a dependable harvest in the off-season.

Livestock feed is the largest source of demand for soybean meal, which provides large amounts of protein. Consequently, the size of the livestock population affects the demand for meal. There is a direct correlation between U.S. prosperity and increased consumer demand for beef and poultry. USDA projections for live-stock and the economy are therefore important factors determining meal demand. Oil is used mainly in edible consumer products, such as margarine, shortening, and table oils. It has limited industrial uses.

Availability and the prices of substitute products are also important factors in affecting demand. For example, a variety of animal and vegetable oils compete aggressively with soybean oil. Palm oil, in particular, is a competitor. Palm oil generally comes from Malaysia and Indonesia. Currently, a large storm is forecast for this region, and crop availability has come into question.

Foreign demand for the U.S. crop (i.e. exports) is also important. The U.S. government has recently suspended a sizeable export agreement with Pakistan. This has forced Pakistan, traditionally a major importer of oil, to tap the South American market, which has been an increasing supplier in world markets. Other international factors, such as exchange rates, the state of foreign economies, and political events also influence foreign demand for the U.S. crop. Recently, the United States has refused to expand export credits to the Soviet Union, the largest importer of grains, which should have a depressing effect on prices.

Supply is chiefly affected by plantings, weather, and crop yields. Prices, the availability of substitutes, subsidies, and crop rotations all influence planting inten-tions. Typically, the government releases its first planting estimates in mid-March. However, a special early estimate was released yesterday to gauge farmers' reac-tions to revisions in the acreage program. These estimates are not reliable because there is still ample time for farmers to change their planting intentions. Once the crop is in the ground, weather and disease are the major factors. Finally, the crop must be successfully harvested before a final crop is obtained. Throughout the season, the USDA and numerous private firms issue survey estimates of the soy-bean crop as well as other agricultural crops. During the season price movements are generally based on these supply estimates, although occasional surprises in demand can affect prices.

The pricing of soybean futures is highly dependent on the gross processing margin, or the *crush spread*. This is a measure of the difference between the cost of the soybean and the value of the derivative oil and meal. A certain dollar spread must be maintained to cover processing and related costs. The current March crush spread is trading at 60.71 cents, with the range for the past year between 45 and 75 cents.

Soybean futures trade in months that match the growing season. March coin-cides with planting intentions; July with planting germination; August and Septem-ber with growing; and November with harvesting. January is the off-season. Meal and oil follow the same seasonal pattern, except that the November contract is replaced by contracts in both October and December. Spread relationships often exist that differ from a full carry relationship. As would be expected, near the end of a crop year (July) and at the beginning of a new crop year (November), the relationship is quite variable. Supply is uncertain and backwardation is prevalent. Figures 16A-1a, b, and c show the relationship between the July and November futures prices during the last three years.

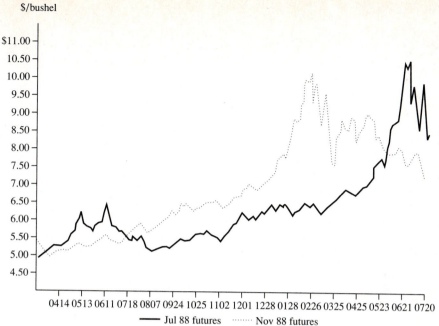

FIGURE 16A-1a

Soybean July and November futures prices, March 15, 1988 to July 20, 1989.

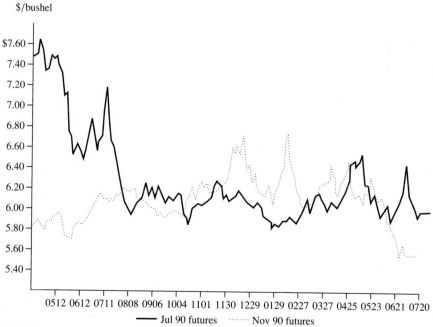

FIGURE 16A-1b

Soybean July and November futures prices, April 13, 1989 to July 20, 1990.

$/bushel

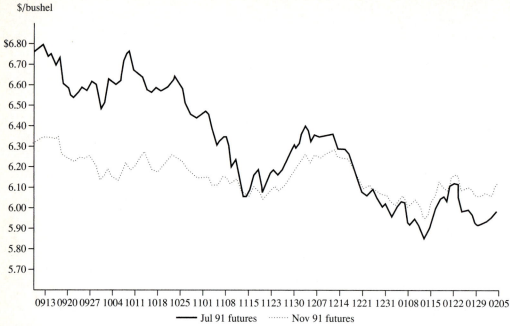

FIGURE 16A-1c
Soybean July and November futures prices, September 1, 1990 to February 5, 1991.

Current and Future Prices

Figures 16A–2a, b, and c provide price charts for the March 91 contracts in the soybean complex. Currently we are experiencing the highest level of soybean inventories since the 87–88 season. Also, South America has had a record high of soybean exports during the October to December period. These factors, together with the economic recession and the recent change in acreage requirements by the government, create a bearish long-term outlook for soybeans. In the near term, however, prices should be relatively stable, except for the usual crop-scare rallies due to weather conditions in South America. Brazil has been experiencing dry weather, which is something to be watched. March 91 soybean prices have steadily declined over the life of the contract, from a high of $7.03 per bushel to a low of $5.595 per bushel. Currently they are trading at $5.7025 per bushel. Thus, current soybean prices have already incorporated the bearish factors discussed above.

Since the Soviet Union is the largest source of foreign demand for soybean meal, recent developments in the Soviet Union cast a bearish outlook for this commodity. Nevertheless, soybean meal prices should remain relatively stable. Closing prices for the nearby March meal contract have ranged from about $205 per ton to $160.60 per ton, and the contract is currently trading near its low at $166.10 per ton.

Soybean oil faces stiff competition in the future. The latest USDA report indicates that, in reaction to the new acreage programs, more oilseed crops, such as sunflower, are expected to be planted. Additionally, there appears to be an increased focus on low-fat substitutes, such as canola oil made from rapeseed.

FIGURE 16A-2a

Soybeans: March 91 futures (daily settlement prices from January 19, 1990, to February 4, 1991).

FIGURE 16A-2b

Soybean meal: March 1991 futures (daily settlement prices from February 23, 1990, to February 4, 1991).

Cents/pound

FIGURE 16A-2c

Soybean oil: March 1991 futures (daily settlement prices from January 19,1990, to February 4,1991).

The near March oil contract has ranged from a 25.61 cent per pound high to a 19.85 cent low, with yesterday's close at 21.12 cents per pound.

Recommended Trading Strategy

Although the present outlook for grain prices is bearish, it is our opinion that there exists an upside potential. Current prices already reflect the existing bearish factors, so that there does not appear to be much downside risk. An examination of prices over the last ten years shows that soybeans are at their lowest levels. Also, given the current South American weather problems, and Soviet exports at historic lows, any bullish news could turn the market around. Therefore, we should be buyers on price dips in beans and meal, but take no position in oil due to the substitutability condition. Further, if distant spreads come into a full-carry pricing relationship, we should sell the distant contract and buy the near contract in order to catch a move toward backwardation as the growing season commences. Finally, once having taken a long position, we have to be attentive to further developments with respect to the demand factors discussed above. If demand conditions deteriorate further, we should be prepared to reconsider our long strategy.[1]

---

[1]The authors wish to thank Robert Silvay, a former Columbia University student, for assistance in preparing this appendix.

CHAPTER

17

SPECULATORS: WHO ARE THEY AND WHO WINS AND LOSES?

This chapter describes what is known about speculative trading in futures markets. It discusses who the speculators are, how they trade, what kind of trading strategies they use, and who makes and loses money. Although there is not an abundance of information available about speculators (most prefer to keep their activities confidential), this chapter pulls together and summarizes the various studies that have been done. Our discussion distinguishes between two types of speculators: those who trade (or manage) their own funds, and those who participate in futures markets indirectly through *commodity funds* — pooled investment funds that employ professional money managers.

17.1 THE ROLE AND VOLUME OF SPECULATION

Chapter 7 identified three contributions that speculators make to futures markets. First, they absorb the risks that hedgers wish to shed. To encourage speculators to perform this function, hedgers pay a *risk premium* to speculators. In general, the greater the volume of speculation, the lower will be the risk premium, and the less costly it will be to hedge.

Second, speculative trading enhances the efficiency of the price discovery process. By buying and selling, speculators cause prices to reflect underlying economic conditions. When current futures prices are good predictors of future cash prices, markets are more efficient at allocating resources. Third, speculative trading enhances market liquidity and lowers the transaction costs associated with using both futures and the underlying cash markets.

The volume of speculative trading in futures markets is substantial. The only available statistics, those produced by the Commodity Futures Trading Commission (CFTC) in its monthly report "Commitments of Traders in Futures," suggest that speculation constitutes more than half of the total trading volume.

The CFTC monthly reports provide summaries of month-end open interest positions held by commercial and non-commercial traders in specific commodities. The CFTC compiles these data from daily reports that *large traders* are required to file. Large traders are those holding positions at the end of the day in excess of a position level specified by the CFTC, where all contract months are aggregated. For example, in November 1990, the specified reportable positions were 400 contracts for Eurodollars, 250 contracts for crude oil, 100 contracts for copper, 25 contracts for coffee, and so forth.

Table 17.1 reproduces the CFTC's November 1990, month-end summary report for Eurodollar futures. In the column "Open interest," total open interest is reported for the current month (November 1990) under three headings: "All," "Old," and "Other." These differ only in the way that spread positions are counted. In "All" futures, "Spreading" includes each trader's reported long and short positions in the *same market* without regard to which crop or calendar year the legs of the spread are held. In "Old" futures, "Spreading" includes only each trader's balanced long and short positions *within* a crop or calendar year. If the legs of the spread are held in *different* crop or calendar years, the spread is not included. "Other" futures is simply the difference between the "All" and "Old" figures.[1]

Of the reportable positions, commercial traders are usually hedgers — they are self-declared hedgers, and their main line of business is usually directly related to the commodity that underlies their futures positions. Non-commercial traders are largely speculators. It is not clear which traders the non-reportable positions represent. Since this category encompasses only small traders, it seems reasonable to assume that it consists mostly of speculators. It is also important to keep in mind that day traders, who do not hold positions overnight and are therefore probably speculators, are not included in any of these open interest categories.

To determine the proportion of total open interest accounted for by hedgers versus speculators in Eurodollar futures in November, 1990, we add the *commercial* long and short positions and divide the resulting sum by the sum of *total* long and short positions for both reportable and non-reportable positions (see Table 17.1). This yields 59.25 percent. Thus, hedgers account for 59.25 percent of total Eurodollar open interest. Speculators, therefore, must account for the remaining

---

[1] Because of intra-market spreading between crop or calendar years, the sum of spreading positions on the long and short sides, or non-commercial long or short positions in "Old" and "Other" futures, will not necessarily equal the figure shown for "All" futures.

TABLE 17.1
Eurodollars (3-month) — International Monetary Market commitments of traders in all futures combined and indicated futures, November 30, 1990

FUTURES	OPEN INTEREST	NON-COMMERCIAL LONG ONLY	NON-COMMERCIAL SHORT ONLY	NON-COMMERCIAL LONG AND SHORT (SPREADING)	COMMERCIAL LONG	COMMERCIAL SHORT	TOTAL LONG	TOTAL SHORT	NONREPORTABLE LONG	NONREPORTABLE SHORT

(CONTRACTS OF $1,000,000 FACE VALUE)

	OPEN INTEREST	NC LONG ONLY	NC SHORT ONLY	NC SPREADING	COMMERCIAL LONG	COMMERCIAL SHORT	TOTAL LONG	TOTAL SHORT	NONREP. LONG	NONREP. SHORT
ALL	724,558	60,997	10,061	13,699	397,836	460,821	472,532	484,581	252,026	239,977
OLD	168,756	20,669	8,634	0	103,757	101,215	124,426	109,849	44,330	58,907
OTHER	555,802	46,032	7,131	7,995	294,079	359,606	348,106	374,732	207,696	181,070

CHANGES IN COMMITMENTS FROM OCTOBER 31, 1990

	OPEN INTEREST	NC LONG ONLY	NC SHORT ONLY	NC SPREADING	COMMERCIAL LONG	COMMERCIAL SHORT	TOTAL LONG	TOTAL SHORT	NONREP. LONG	NONREP. SHORT
ALL	20,451	7,326	2,247	1,164	-2,261	43	6,229	3,454	14,222	16,997

PERCENT OF OPEN INTEREST REPRESENTED BY EACH CATEGORY OF TRADERS:

	OPEN INTEREST	NC LONG ONLY	NC SHORT ONLY	NC SPREADING	COMMERCIAL LONG	COMMERCIAL SHORT	TOTAL LONG	TOTAL SHORT	NONREP. LONG	NONREP. SHORT
ALL	100.0%	8.4	1.4	1.9	54.9	63.6	65.2	66.9	34.8	33.1
OLD	100.0%	12.2	5.1	0.0	61.5	60.0	73.7	65.1	26.3	34.9
OTHER	100.0%	8.3	1.3	1.4	52.9	64.7	62.6	67.4	37.4	32.6

NUMBER OF TRADERS IN EACH CATEGORY:

NUMBER OF TRADERS		NC LONG ONLY	NC SHORT ONLY	NC SPREADING	COMMERCIAL LONG	COMMERCIAL SHORT	TOTAL LONG	TOTAL SHORT
ALL	201	25	17	8	108	118	139	138
OLD	110	11	7	0	50	70	61	77
OTHER	167	20	11	5	97	93	120	107

CONCENTRATION RATIOS

PERCENT OF OPEN INTEREST HELD BY THE INDICATED NUMBER OF LARGEST TRADERS

	BY GROSS POSITION				BY NET POSITION			
	4 OR LESS TRADERS		8 OR LESS TRADERS		4 OR LESS TRADERS		8 OR LESS TRADERS	
	LONG	SHORT	LONG	SHORT	LONG	SHORT	LONG	SHORT
ALL	21.8	17.2	28.2	27.0	13.3	11.0	17.9	17.0
OLD	24.9	16.1	36.2	26.5	19.0	12.2	28.1	17.2
OTHER	23.1	20.2	29.6	29.6	14.5	13.7	18.6	20.2

Source: Commodity Futures Trading Commission.

40.75 percent. Since these figures do not include day-traders, they may understate the importance of speculative trading.

The magnitude of speculation varies with the market. Table 17.2 provides the percentage of total open interest accounted for by speculators in each of the 16 active futures markets over the entire 1989 year (calculated by averaging the monthly percentages as calculated in the preceding paragraph). The magnitude of speculation varies from a low of 32.8 percent (Eurodollars) to a high of 80.9 percent (live hogs). The average over all markets is 50.27 percent. Speculative trading appears to constitute a larger proportion of total trading in markets with lower trading volume.

TABLE 17.2
Volume of speculation in selected futures markets during 1989

Commodity (exchange)	Speculation as percentage of open interest: Monthly mean*
(1) Eurodollars (CME)	32.8
(2) Crude oil, light, sweet (NYMEX)	38.1
(3) S&P 500 (CME)	34.5
(4) Soybeans (CBOT)	54.1
(5) Corn (CBOT)	47.9
(6) German Deutschemark (CME)	50.4
(7) Japanese yen (CME)	53.3
(8) Sugar #11 (CSCE)	35.9
(9) Swiss franc (CME)	62.2
(10) Heating oil No. 2 (NYMEX)	41.2
(11) Wheat (CBOT)	51.9
(12) British pound (CME)	57.0
(13) Live hogs (CME)	80.9
(14) NYSE Composite Index (NYCE)	58.0
(15) T-bill 90-day (CME)	52.6
(16) Oats (CBOT)	53.5
Overall average	50.3

*Speculative open interest as a percentage of total month-end open interest: mean of monthly percentages over the year.

The annual volume of trading in 1989 in the above contracts was:
(1)–(3) over 10 million contracts;
(4)–(10) between 5 and 10 million contracts;
(11)–(15) between 1 and 5 million contracts; and
(16) under 1 million contracts.

Data Source: "Commitment of Traders in Futures," Commodity Futures Trading Commission, 1989.

17.2   A PROFILE OF THE SMALL SPECULATOR

Information about small speculators in futures markets comes primarily from two surveys conducted in 1983: one by the Chicago Board of Trade (CBOT) and one by *Barron's*.[2] These surveys report that small speculators tend to have higher income levels and more education than the general population. The medium 1983 annual income of futures speculators reported in the *Barron's* survey was $85,200, and between 67 and 80 percent of the traders attended or completed college.

The main reason given by respondents for trading futures, not surprisingly, was a desire to make money. Table 17.3 reports answers to a survey question asking individuals why they trade futures. Other than the perceived profit potential, the main reasons given are "low margins" and "the excitement of trading." "Low margins," however, are not independent of the "profit motivation," since high leverage increases the opportunity to make large profits.[3]

The objectives of small futures traders also appear to be different from those of investors in other assets. Table 17.4 summarizes answers to a question about the objectives of futures traders compared to other investors. Futures traders are relatively less concerned both about the safety of their capital and about earning a steady income than are investors in general, and are relatively more attracted by the prospect of earning large short-term trading profits. There is, clearly, a noticeable difference in how futures traders value the possibility of making substantial short-term trading profits.

Questions about the opinions and attitudes of traders also revealed the following: futures markets are too sophisticated for the average investor, requiring a great deal of time to master; futures trading is psychologically rewarding; and, futures are a good way to beat inflation. Table 17.5 provides the responses to the *Barron's* survey questions on these issues.

Both the CBOT and the *Barron's* survey indicate that futures traders are quite active. Table 17.6 shows that almost 38 percent of futures traders executed 48 or more trades during the year prior to the survey; and more than 20 percent of traders had more than 96 trades during the year. Small futures traders appear to be much more active than small stock market participants. Turnover statistics on the New York Stock Exchange, for example, suggest that small investors hold a stock on average for more than two years.

---

[2]Chicago Board of Trade, "Profile of U.S. Futures Markets," Part 1, *Retail Traders 1983–84,* Chicago, 1983; and, Barron's National Business and Financial Weeks, *Markets for Futures and Options,* 1983. See also Dennis Draper, "The Small Public Trader in Futures Markets," *Futures Markets: Regulatory Issues,* edited by A. Peck, American Enterprise Institute, Washington, D.C., 1985, pp. 211–69.

[3]In Tables 17.3 through 17.5, the column "Total respondents" includes all survey respondents, both those who traded futures and those who did not. The Barron's study sampled 2000 of its subscribers. Of the 1178 respondents, only 24.2 percent said that they either had traded futures in the past or were currently trading futures. The column labeled "Respondents currently trading futures" shows the responses of only those trading futures.

TABLE 17.3
**Reasons for initial decision to invest in futures: *Barron's*
and CBT surveys, 1983 (percent)**

Reason	Total respondents	Respondents currently trading futures
Profit potential	61.8	78.5 (53.5)
Low margins	28.4	41.5 (12.9)
Excitement	20.0	41.5 (7.2)
Diversification	16.4	27.7
Broker's recommendation	15.3	15.4 (6.6)
Portfolio protection	14.2	12.3
Recommendation of a friend or associate	9.5	6.2
Lack of activity in other investments	8.4	9.2 (1.7)
Response to an advertisement	4.7	1.5

Note: Numbers in parentheses are percentages from Chicago Board of Trade data.
Barron's study permitted multiple answers; the CBT study permitted only one answer
(the most important factor).

Sources: *Barron's* National Business and Financial Weeks; Chicago Board of Trade
survey; and D. Draper, "The Small Public Trader in Futures Markets."

TABLE 17.4
Primary investment objectives: *Barron's* survey, 1983

Reason	(Percent)	
	Total respondents	Respondents currently trading futures
Long-term growth/capital appreciation	76.4	60.6
Safety of capital	39.8	19.7
Inflation hedge	32.3	33.3
Additional current income	32.3	15.2
Short-term gains/trading profits	29.0	69.7

Sources: *Barron's* National Business and Financial Weeks; and D. Draper,
"The Small Public Trader in Futures Markets."

TABLE 17.5
Opinions about futures trading: *Barron's* survey, 1983

	(Percent)	
Reason	Total respondents*	Respondents currently trading futures*
Too sophisticated for average investor	82.4	84.6
Requires too much time to stay on top of market	82.1	70.8
Too risky	79.4	56.9
Too many futures products offered	34.7	44.6
Requires too much money	28.8	20.0
Is psychologically rewarding	25.6	72.3
Great opportunity to beat inflation	40.3	78.5

*Percentage that strongly agree or tend to agree with statement.
Sources: *Barron's* National Business and Financial Weeks; and D. Draper, "The Small Public Trader in Futures Markets."

Finally, when asked about their sources of information about commodity markets, small traders said they relied primarily on their own analyses of trading systems, supported by information taken from articles, newsletters, and other publications. Although traders noted the need for brokers, they did not appear to place a great deal of weight on brokers' recommendations.

TABLE 17.6
Number of investment transactions in past 12 months: *Barron's* survey, 1983

	(Percent)
Number of transactions	Respondents currently trading futures*
1–5	3.1
6–11	10.6
12–23	27.3
24–47	19.7
48–71	12.1
72–95	4.5
96 or more	21.2
Median (number)	34.0
Average (number)	45.0

*Percentage of respondents. Percentages do not add to 100.0 because of nonresponses.
Sources: *Barron's* National Business and Financial Weeks; and D. Draper, "The Small Public Trader in Futures Markets."

In summary, the typical small speculator in futures markets appears to be well-educated, to have a relatively high income, and to be motivated primarily by a desire to make money. In addition, speculators trade quite actively, focus on short-term results, and rely on their own analyses and trading systems to determine what to trade and how to trade it.

17.3 LARGE SPECULATORS: COMMODITY FUNDS

There are two types of institutions in futures markets that are active speculative traders: public and private *commodity funds*. A commodity fund is an investment trust, syndicate, or similar form of enterprise that is engaged in the business of investing its pooled funds in futures, options, and leverage contracts. As an institution, commodity funds are similar to mutual funds or investment companies in securities markets, which also pool individual investors' funds.

Commodity funds usually hold a diversified portfolio of futures contracts. They can also be either long or short futures. There are two types of commodity funds: *public* and *private*. A public fund is one whose shares can be purchased by the general public. A private fund is usually called a *pool* and is limited to fewer than 35 investors.[4]

Commodity funds offer small speculators two benefits. First, by pooling the funds of many investors, they provide a vehicle for trading a large and diversified portfolio of futures contracts. Second, they provide professional money management and trading expertise. This often includes a proprietary trading system or strategy developed by the fund's trading advisors.

There has been significant growth in the volume of assets managed by commodity funds during the 1980s. Figure 17-1 shows the number of public funds in existence during the 1980s, and Figure 17-2 shows the volume of assets under management by *public* commodity funds for each year during the 1980s. These assets have increased six-fold since 1986. The growth of private pools has probably been even greater. The attractiveness of commodity funds as an investment has increased because of the expansion of financial futures markets, the increased volatility of markets, and perhaps because of disenchantment with the stock market after the 1987 Stock Market Crash (note the large increase in 1987 in Figure 17-2).

Commodity funds are active and large speculative traders. It has been estimated that in 1984, when commodity funds were much smaller than they are today, they held more than 20 percent of the open interest in the nearby contracts in the 10 most active futures contracts.[5] Thus, commodity funds represent a grow-

---

[4]Private pools are sometimes called *managed futures accounts*. Private pools may have an unlimited number of *accredited* investors — people having a net worth of $1 million each or an annual income in excess of $200,000 — but can have no more than 35 *unaccredited* investors.

[5]Wade D. Brorsen and Scott H. Irwin, "Futures Funds and Price Volatility," *The Review of Futures Markets,* 6:118–35, 1987.

Total number of
public futures funds

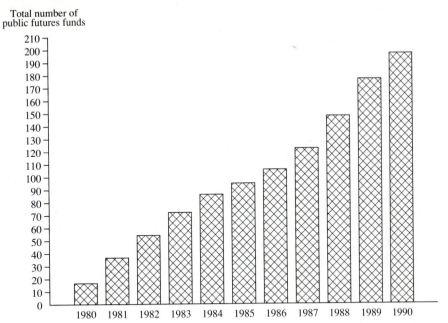

FIGURE 17-1
Total number of public futures funds. (Managed Accounts Reports)

Billions of dollars

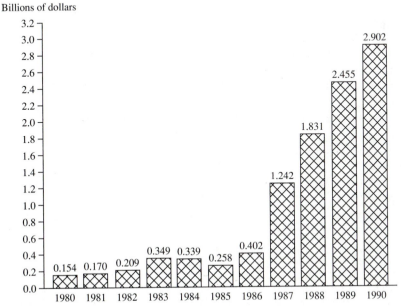

FIGURE 17-2
Equity growth of public futures funds. (Managed Accounts Reports)

ing institutional speculative presence in futures markets, the full implications of which are not yet clear.

17.4 THE PERFORMANCE OF TRADERS IN GENERAL

17.4.1 Early Studies

There is considerable controversy about who makes money in futures markets. Do speculators prosper at the expense of hedgers? Do large speculators earn more than small speculators? Although there have been at least a half dozen studies of this issue over the past 35 years, conclusions differ significantly.

One reason for these differences is the poor quality of the data that researchers have had to use. While a few studies have utilized actual trading histories of individuals, such data are hard to come by.[6] Traders consider this information proprietary and are usually unwilling to disclose it, even well after the fact.

Other studies have utilized the CFTC's aggregate month-end large-trader reports discussed earlier in Section 17.1.[7] These studies, however, have had to use hypothetical trading rules and hypothetical transaction prices to evaluate returns. Their findings, therefore, are disputable.

Taken together, however, the studies generally support the following conclusions: (1) small speculators usually lose money (Stewart, Houthakker, Rockwell, Hieronymus, and Ross); and, (2) large speculators profit at the expense of large hedgers (Rockwell, Chang, and Houthakker).

17.4.2 Recent Studies

A recent study by Michael Hartzmark utilizes the normally confidential data which underlie the CFTC's Commitment-of-Traders reports.[8] Large traders are required to submit daily reports to the CFTC describing their end-of-day positions. Using these positions, together with daily settlement prices, Hartzmark estimated daily

---

[6]See W. B. Stewart, "An Analysis of Speculative Trading in Grain Futures," Technical Bulletin No. 1001, Washington: U.S. Department of Agriculture, 1949; Thomas A. Hieronymus, *Economics of Futures Trading for Commercial and Personal Profit,* 2nd edition, New York: Commodity Research Bureau, 1977; Richard Teweles, Charles V. Harlow, and Herbert L. Stone, *The Commodity Futures Game: Who Wins? Who Loses? Why?* New York: McGraw Hill, 1977; and Ray L. Ross, "Financial Consequences of Trading Commodity Futures Contracts," *Illinois Agricultural Economics,* 1975, pp. 27–31.

[7]See Hendrik S. Houthakker, "Can Speculators Forecast Prices?" *Review of Economics and Statistics,* 38:143–51, May 1957; Charles S. Rockwell, "Normal Backwardation, Forecasting, and Returns to Commodity Futures Traders," in *Selected Writings on Futures Markets,* Vol. 2, edited by A. Peck, Chicago Board of Trade, 1977; and Eric C. Chang, "Returns to Speculators and the Theory of Normal Backwardation," *Journal of Finance,* 40: 193-208, March 1985.

[8]Michael Hartzmark, "Returns to Individual Traders of Futures: Aggregate Results," *Journal of Political Economy,* 85: 1292–1306, 1987.

gains and losses for each reporting trader.[9] In total, his data include more than a million daily observations on positions held by individual traders in all contract maturities, and over a half million observations for individual traders where all contract maturity positions are aggregated.

Hartzmark's findings differ sharply from those of earlier studies. After examining nine separate commodity markets over the period July 1, 1977, to December 31, 1981, he concluded that large commercial traders (hedgers) do *not* incur losses but instead earn substantial profits, while large non-commercial traders (speculators) do *not* earn significant profits.[10] As a group, however, large traders earn significant profits. Thus, it must be true that small traders as a group lose money (since futures markets are a "zero-sum game"). Since small (non-reporting) traders are very likely to be speculators, it also seems reasonable to conclude that small speculators are net losers.

Contrary to previous studies, therefore, Hartzmark finds that only large hedgers consistently earn profits. Large speculators sometimes make money and sometimes lose money, but on average just about break even. Small speculators consistently incur losses.

Table 17.7 reports Hartzmark's results for the specific commodity markets he examined, broken up by long and short positions. These data suggest several additional conclusions. First, taken as a group, hedgers earn greater profits when they are short than when they are long (see columns 2 and 3). Second, for large non-commercial traders the gross gains and losses on short and long positions are almost equal (see columns 4 and 5).[11] Success for large speculators, therefore, appears to be independent of whether they are long or short. Thus, a speculator's ability to forecast prices appears to determine his success, rather than his being opposite a hedger.

Finally, column 7 in Table 17.7 indicates that over all markets fewer than half of the traders have positive returns (46 percent). This statistic, however, does not tell the whole story. Hartzmark reports a large degree of skewness in the distribution of trader returns: of all large commercial traders, the five most successful hedgers (0.1 percent of all commercial traders in the sample) account for

---

[9] Hartzmark did not have actual trading histories and transaction prices, and was required to make several critical operational assumptions, such as what the transaction prices were. His data also do not capture day trading, since only positions at the end of the day need be reported.

[10] The distinction between commercial and non-commercial traders is not always clear. Sometimes a commercial trader also speculates. However, to be designated as a commercial trader or hedger, Hartzmark requires that the trader's business be directly related to the commodity that underlies the futures position, and if a trader holds both speculative and hedging positions, his position must be dominated by hedging commitments. Nevertheless, Hartzmark's findings are vulnerable to this data problem. In an even more recent study, Hartzmark attempts to correct this data problem. See his "Luck versus Forecast Ability: Determinants of Trader Performance in Futures Markets," *Journal of Business,* 64: 49–74, 1991.

[11] Column 4 in Table 17-7 shows the losses of all unsuccessful traders summed, and column 5 shows the profits of all successful traders summed.

TABLE 17.7
Performance measures by market and trader type (returns in millions of dollars)

Market and trader type	Net dollar returns			Gross dollar return		Number of traders*		Number of observations	
	Total (1)	Net long (2)	Net short (3)	Total losses (4)	Total gains (5)	Total	Positive return (%) (7)	On single positions (8)	Aggregated daily (9)
Oats:									
All traders	10.28†‡	-0.85	11.14	-4.61	14.88	179	46.9	42,925	18,860
Commercial	9.63	-0.26	9.90	-1.78	11.41	50	56.0	24,669	11,321
Noncommercial	0.64	-0.59	1.24	-2.83	3.47	129	43.4	18,256	7,539
CBT wheat:									
All traders	59.14	-117.72	176.85	-213.00	272.14	703	48.9	156,628	79,982
Commercial	42.94	-78.54	121.48	-137.41	180.35	236	47.9	81,253	44,518
Noncommercial	16.19	-39.18	55.37	-75.59	91.79	467	49.3	75,375	35,464
MGE wheat:									
All traders	19.01	15.43	3.58	-25.06	44.06	164	54.9	43,180	24,088
Commercial	21.17	19.03	2.14	-20.00	41.17	101	53.5	38,668	21,307
Noncommercial	-2.17	-3.60	1.44	-5.06	2.89	63	57.1	4,512	2,781
KBT wheat:									
All traders	2.15	-36.45	38.72	-117.92	120.07	269	46.8	80,398	45,117
Commercial	2.62	-30.96	33.69	-105.66	108.28	172	48.3	67,155	39,053
Noncommercial	-0.47	-5.49	5.03	-12.26	11.80	97	44.3	13,243	6,064
Combined wheat:									
All traders	80.30	-138.74	219.15	-355.98	436.27	757	49.1	280,206	149,187
Commercial	66.73	-90.47	157.31	-263.07	329.80	270	48.1	187,076	104,878
Noncommercial	13.53	-48.27	61.84	-92.91	106.48	487	49.7	93,130	44,309
Pork bellies:									
All traders	80.56‡	-51.65	132.20	-115.48	196.00	1,106	49.7	262,614	122,599
Commercial	79.05†‡	3.96	75.10	-4.19	83.24	41	58.5	36,968	14,829
Noncommercial	1.48	-55.61	57.10	-111.29	112.76	1,065	49.4	225,646	107,770

Live cattle:								
All traders	66.85	250.25	−183.30	−346.11	412.96	1,058	51.3	216,053	99,326
Commercial	−130.27	24.47	−154.74	−232.90	102.63	238	34.9	63,827	30,989
Noncommercial	197.12†‡	225.78	−28.56	−113.21	310.33	820	56.1	152,226	68,337
Feeder cattle:								
All traders	104.55†‡	109.58	−5.04	−87.96	192.50	711	46.7	70,064	32,340
Commercial	559.09	−276.46	835.60	−157.41	716.50	227	54.2	45,586	23,800
Noncommercial	75.42†‡	74.12	1.27	−36.10	111.52	467	49.7	47,297	20,346
T-bonds:								
All traders	390.02†	−1012.68	1403.85	−609.95	999.97	1,713	44.8	225,954	90,541
Commercial	559.09	−276.46	835.60	−157.41	716.50	227	54.2	45,586	23,800
Noncommercial	−169.07†‡	−736.22	568.25	−452.54	283.47	1,486	43.3	180,368	66,741
T-bills:								
All traders	120.44	−147.49	267.97	−268.12	388.56	1,491	44.0	184,302	72,727
Commercial	114.96†	−35.77	150.73	−46.85	161.81	211	53.6	47,439	21,042
Noncommercial	5.48	−111.72	117.24	−221.27	226.75	1,280	42.2	136,863	51,685
All markets:								
All traders	853.00†	−991.58	1845.97	−1788.21	2641.14	4,567	46.0	1,282,118	585,580
Commercial	728.32†	−339.07	1067.59	−758.06	1486.38	971	45.3	428,332	197,433
Noncommercial	124.60	−652.51	778.38	−1030.15	1154.78	3,728	46.3	853,786	388,147
Small traders	−853.00	991.58	−1845.97	⋯	⋯	⋯	⋯	⋯	⋯

* The total number of traders in all markets does not equal the sum of all traders in each market since certain traders participate in more than one market. In addition, 132 traders were designated as being one type of trader (i.e. commerical or noncommercial) in one market and the other type in another market.

†Denotes mean of distribution of individual returns that is different form zero at a 5 percent probability level.

‡Denotes mean of distribution of monthly returns that is different from zero at a 10 percent probability level.

Source: Hartzmark, "Returns to Individual Traders of Futures."

58 percent of the group's total net profits. A few hedgers, therefore, do remarkably well.

An even more recent study, by Maddala and Yoo, uses the CFTC's *Commitment of Traders* data and examines 11 futures markets during the years 1977 to 1988, and arrives at just the opposite conclusion: they find that large speculators consistently make money, while large hedgers consistently lose money.[12] However, they too find that small speculators do *not* make money.

More specifically, Maddala and Yoo find that in agricultural commodities markets large speculators make average profits that are generally higher than the average losses incurred by large hedgers. This implies that, on average, small speculators lose money in these markets. In foreign currency futures markets, they find that large speculators' profits are about equal to large hedgers' losses, implying that small speculators neither make nor lose money. Maddala and Yoo argue that large speculators are able to earn profits consistently for two reasons: they receive a risk premium from hedgers for bearing risk, and they are better informed than small speculators.

17.4.3   Implications

Academic studies, clearly, have not resolved the issue of who makes and loses money in futures markets. If there is a majority conclusion, it appears to be that large speculators generally make profits, at the expense of both small speculators and large hedgers. This finding, if correct, would support the traditional view of futures markets as insurance markets in which speculators earn a risk premium for willingly taking on the risks that hedgers transfer to them (as discussed in Chapter 7).

17.5   THE PERFORMANCE OF COMMODITY FUNDS

Commodity funds are large, professionally managed, speculators. Their performance, therefore, may provide further evidence of how large and diversified speculators fare in futures markets.

17.5.1   Aggregate Net Returns

The performance of public funds can be gauged from data on net profits (or net returns). Specifically, the equity invested in a commodity fund is represented by shares in the fund held by investors (similar to a mutual fund). Increases or decreases in the value of a fund's total equity, due to its trading activities,

---

[12]G. S. Maddala and Jisoo Yoo, "Risk Premia and Price Volatility in Futures Markets," *The Journal of Futures Markets,* April 1991, pp. 165–78.

are reflected in changes in the value of the shares issued by the fund. A fund's aggregate net return is

Net return $= Gross\ realized\ trading\ profits\ (losses)$

$+$ Unrealized trading profits (losses)

$-$ Management and incentive fees

$-$ Administrative costs

The relationship between a fund's costs and its *gross* returns is discussed later in the chapter.

Table 17.8 provides the average annual (aggregate) *net rates of return* for all public funds in existence during the years 1984 to 1989.[13] End-of-the-month values are used to compute these average rates of return (shown in column 1), assuming continuous compounding. Column 2 provides the standard deviation of these aggregate rates of return over the 12 months of the year. Column 3 shows the average Sharpe Ratio for each year, column 4 provides the number of funds in existence each year, and column 5 shows the average annual T-bill rate.

TABLE 17.8
Annual rates of return of public commodity funds, 1984–1989

Year	Annual rate of return (percent)	Annualized standard deviation (percent)	Sharpe ratio	Number of funds	Annual treasury bill rate (percent)
	(1)	(2)	(3)	(4)	(5)
1984	7.51	24.27	−0.10	65	9.84
1985	6.63	21.94	−0.05	76	7.72
1986	−14.21	21.37	−0.95	83	6.16
1987	32.47	20.62	1.31	90	5.46
1988	5.97	25.45	−0.01	101	6.34
1989	−8.80	18.49	−0.93	101	8.37

1. The annual rate of return for commodity funds is based upon the average monthly rates of return for all funds compounded to yield an annual rate of return.

2. The Sharpe ratio is: (the mean annual return minus the mean annual T-bill rate) divided by the annualized standard deviation. Since commodity funds returns have little or no correlation with other assets, such as stocks and bonds, the Sharpe Ratio is a reasonable performance measure. The relevant T-bill returns are shown in column 5 of the above table.

3. The number of funds that existed at both the beginning and the end of the year. Thus, if a fund dissolved during the year it was not included in our sample. This may impart a positive bias to the above results.

Data Source: Monthly Reports issued by Managed Accounts Reports, Inc., 220 Fifth Avenue, N.Y., NY 10001.

---

[13] For information on earlier years, see Scott H. Irwin and B. Wade Brorsen, "Public Futures Funds," *The Journal of Futures Markets, 5*: 463–85, 1985.

Figure 17-3 plots the annual rates of return and standard deviations shown in Table 17.8. In two of the six years shown the average net rate of return was negative. The most profitable year was 1987, a year in which stock prices plummeted. In 1987 the average net rate of return for all commodity funds was almost 33 percent.

Despite occasional high returns, investing in commodity funds does not appear to be particularly attractive. Table 17.9 provides comparable annual rates of return for other commonly held assets: common stocks of large companies (the S&P 500 index), small stocks, long-term corporate bonds, long-term government bonds, and Treasury bills. In general, the mean annual return for commodity funds is low compared with the other investments, while the risk (the standard deviation) is relatively high. In addition, the Sharpe Ratios for commodity funds shown in column 3 of Table 17.8 are low by most standards and vary significantly.

17.5.2 The Distribution of Fund Returns

The riskiness of commodity funds can be seen in the distributions of the net annual rates of return for public funds. Figures 17-4 through 17-9 provide annual frequency distributions of the net annual rates of return for individual public

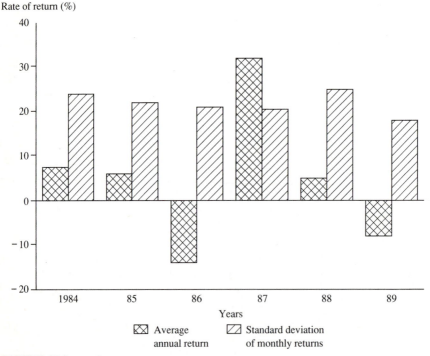

FIGURE 17.3
Average yearly return: 1984–1989.

TABLE 17.9
Returns on comparable investments, 1984–1989

	(Percent)	
	Average of annual rates of return	Average of annualized standard deviations
Commodity funds	4.93	22.03
Common stock (S&P 500 Index)	18.40	15.99
Small stocks	8.10	16.36
Long-term corporate bonds	15.63	8.93
Long-term government bonds	15.99	11.10
U.S. Treasury bills	7.32	0.23

Data Source: Managed Account Reports, and "Stocks, Bonds, Bills, and Inflation: 1989 Yearbook" published by R.C. Ibbotson Associate, Inc.

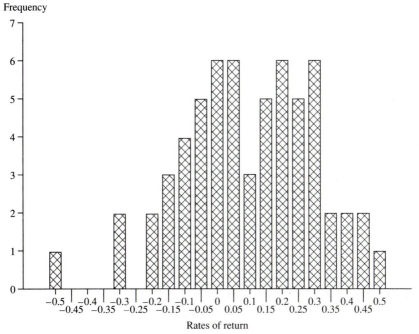

FIGURE 17-4
Frequency distribution of the rates of return on commodity funds in 1984.

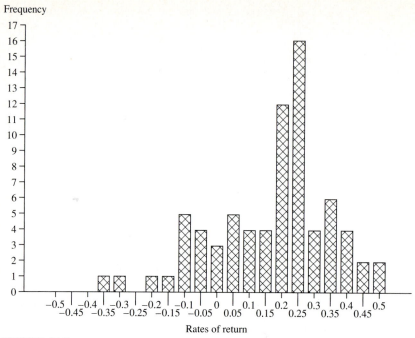

FIGURE 17-5
Frequency distribution of the rates of return on commodity funds in 1985.

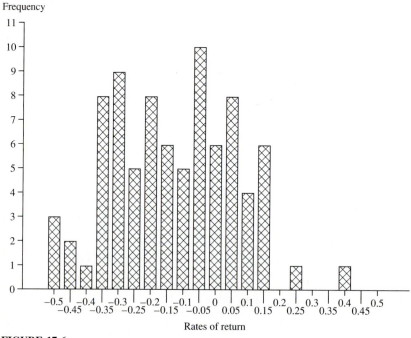

FIGURE 17-6
Frequency distribution of the rates of return on commodity funds in 1986.

480

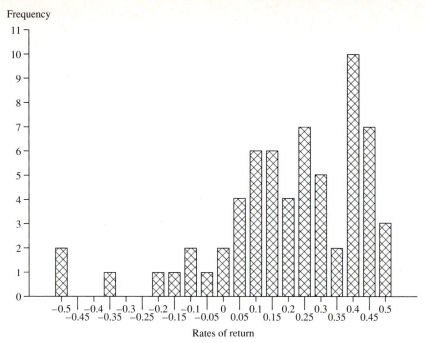

FIGURE 17-7
Frequency distribution of the rates of return on commodity funds in 1987.

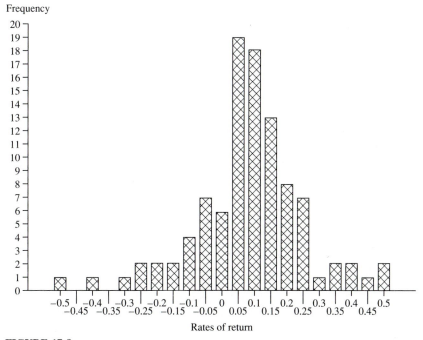

FIGURE 17-8
Frequency distribution of the rates of return on commodity funds in 1988.

Frequency

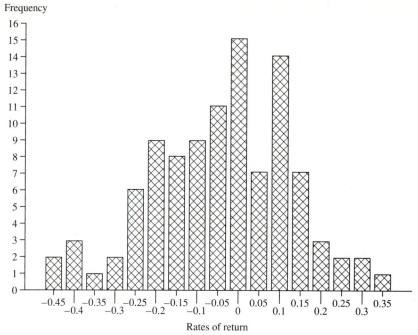

FIGURE 17-9
Frequency distribution of the rates of return on commodity funds in 1989.

funds in existence each year from 1984 to 1989.[14] In general, fund returns had a negative *skewness* in every year but 1987.[15] Table 17.10 provides a measure of the skewness of the return distributions for each year from 1984 to 1989. The exception was 1987, when many funds did extraordinarily well.

In contrast to these results, research on other investment assets suggests that return distributions are generally positively skewed. For example, Lorie and Fisher report positive skewness for common stock returns.[16] Thus, commodity fund returns exhibit a relatively high standard deviation and a negative skewness in their return distributions.

---

[14]These distributions may have a positive bias because funds that ceased to operate during the year are not included.

[15]Skewness is a measure of the symmetry of a return distribution. Positive skewness indicates a greater probability of large high returns relative to low returns. Skewness in commodity fund returns is discussed in Edwin J. Elton, Martin J. Gruber and Joel Rentzler, "The Performance of Publicly Offered Commodity Funds," *Financial Analysts Journal*, July–August 1990, pp. 23–30.

[16]L. Lorie and L. Fisher, "Some Studies of the Variability of Returns on Investments in Common Stocks," *Journal of Business*, April 1970.

TABLE 17.10
Cross-sectional skewness
of commodity fund returns

Year	Skewness
1984	−0.008
1985	−0.003
1986	−0.006
1987	0.0019
1988	−0.004
1989	−0.001

17.5.3 Implications: Commodity Funds as an Investment

These findings raise the question of why investors place their money with public commodity funds. Net returns are low, and the risk is high. One possibility is that investors view funds as a hedge against price inflation. Researchers, however, have not found a significant positive correlation between fund returns and the Consumer Price Index, so that commodity funds do not appear to be a hedge against price inflation.[17]

Another possibility is that commodity funds provide a significant diversification benefit when included in a portfolio of stocks and bonds. Irwin and Brorsen, for example, find that if public commodity funds are included in portfolios of stocks and U.S. Treasury securities, the "efficient investment frontier" shifts upward: portfolio risk is reduced by 0.6 to 3.7 percentage points without a reduction in portfolio return.[18] Further research on this issue is necessary, however, before definitive conclusions can be reached.

17.5.4 Aggregate Gross Returns Are Positive

The findings discussed above, however, still do not answer the question of how large professional speculators fare in commodity markets. Aggregate *net* returns do not provide this answer. Net returns are *after costs,* and the costs associated with commodity funds are high. To determine how well fund managers fare, we need to examine *gross* returns. This requires creating pro forma aggregate gross returns for funds by adjusting the available data on net returns. Scott Irwin did

---

[17] See Elton, Gruber and Rentzler, p.27.

[18] Irwin and Brorsen, "Public Futures Funds," pp. 475–79. See also Anthony F. Herbst and Joseph P. McCormack, "An Examination of the Risk-Return Characteristics of Portfolios Combining Commodity Futures Contracts with Common Stocks," Columbia Futures Center Working Paper No.124, 1986; Elton, Gruber and Rentzler argue that there are no diversification benefits.

this for public funds for the 1978 to 1988 period. He took the average net monthly return for a public fund, added back an estimate of the fund's likely total costs, and subtracted the interest earnings that were part of its reported net return. This procedure yielded an estimate of a fund's gross returns derived solely from its trading activities.[19]

Using these estimates for an individual fund's gross returns, Irwin generated an aggregate annual gross rate of return of 22.4 percent for all public funds for the entire 1979–88 period, and a standard deviation for these returns of 22.6 percent. These estimates suggest that professional fund managers are in fact successful speculators, which is consistent with the studies that find that large speculators on average make net profits (see Section 17.4). Thus, if a large investor in a commodity fund, such as a pension fund, is able to negotiate lower management fees, the returns may be attractive.[20]

CONCLUSION

This chapter has examined speculative activity in futures markets to determine who the speculators are, what their motivations and objectives are, and how well they do. Particular attention was paid to commodity funds, since these are large institutional speculators which have experienced rapid growth in recent years.

There is considerable controversy about how well speculators do. Small speculators do not appear to fare well, while the evidence on large speculators is mixed. Most studies find that large speculators make money, but some conclude that on average they just about break even. There are also big differences in how individual speculators fare: some do very well while others do quite poorly. In general, however, the evidence appears to support the view that speculators earn a risk premium by bearing the risks that hedgers give up. One conclusion is clear: speculating in commodity markets is risky business.

QUESTIONS

1. The volume of speculation is much greater in some futures markets than in others (see Table 17-2). How can you explain these differences?
2. Do you think that the proportion of open interest accounted for by speculators (or non-commercial traders) is a good indication of the volume of speculative trading?
3. Why do speculators say that they trade futures? Is the evidence on how speculators fare consistent with the reasons they give?
4. Do large speculators make more money than small speculators? Do you think that large speculators have an advantage over small speculators?

---

[19]To make the pro forma adjustments, Irwin used estimates of the costs incurred by investors in *private* funds. Estimates of gross returns would be higher if the higher public fund costs were used. See the appendix to this chapter.

[20]The authors understand that institutional investors in funds do in fact pay lower management fees.

5. The findings of some studies suggest that on average large hedgers make money. If this is correct, who loses money? What data problems exist that make these results questionable?

6. Why have commodity funds grown in recent years?

7. Does the evidence on commodity fund returns suggest that funds are good investments?

8. Would you consider a commodity fund to be a risky investment? Why?

9. How can you justify investing money in a public commodity fund?

10. The incentive fees charged by commodity funds are quite high (See the appendix to this chapter). Do you think this fee structure is reasonable? Give arguments on both sides of the question.

11. On average, the aggregate net annual returns of commodity funds are low. Does this indicate that large professional speculators do poorly in commodity markets?

SUGGESTED READING

Bernard, V. and T. Frecka. "Commodity Contracts and Common Stock as Hedges Against Relative Consumer Price Risk," *Journal of Financial and Quantitative Analysis,* Vol. 22 (June 1987), pp. 169-188.

Bodie, Z. and V. Rosansky, "Risk and Return in Commodity Futures." *Financial Analysts Journal,* Vol. 36 (May/June 1980), pp. 27-39.

Brorsen, B. W. and S. H. Irwin. "Examination of Commodity Fund Performance." *Review of Research in Futures Markets,* Vol. 4, No.1 (1985), pp. 84-105.

Chang, E. "Returns to Speculators and the Theory of Normal Backwardation." *Journal of Finance,* Vol. 40, No. 1 (March 1985), pp. 193-208.

Edwards, F. and C. Ma. "Commodity Pool Performance: Is the Information Contained in Pool Prospectuses Useful?" *The Journal of Futures Markets,* Vol. 8 (October 1988), pp. 589-616.

Elton, E., M. Gruber, and J. Rentzler, "Professionally Managed, Publicly Traded Commodity Funds," *Journal of Business,* Vol. 60 (April 1987), pp. 175-199.

Hartzmark, M. "Returns to Individual Traders of Futures: Aggregate Results." *Journal of Political Economy,* December 1987, pp. 1292-1306.

Hartzmark, M. "Luck Versus Forecast Ability: Determinants of Trader Performance in Futures Markets." *Journal of Business,* Vol. 64, No. 1 (1991), pp. 49-74.

Herbst, A. and J. McCormack. "An Examination of the Risk/Return Characteristics of Portfolios Combining Commodity Futures Contracts with Common Stocks." *The Review of Futures Markets,* Vol. 6, No. 3 (1987), pp. 416-425.

APPENDIX: ESTIMATING AVERAGE OPERATIONAL AND MANAGEMENT FEES

Irwin estimates that the various average operational and management fees for both public and private commodity funds are

	Public commodity funds	Private commodity pools
Management fees as % of equity	5.0	2.0
Commissions as % of equity	9.3	2.5
Incentive fees as % of gross trading profits	20.0	25.0
Total fees as % of equity	18–20	10–12

Source: Scott H. Irwin, Terry R. Krukemyer, and Carl R. Zulauf, "Investment Performance of Public Commodity Pools: 1979–1989," unpublished paper, January 1991.

CHAPTER 18

THE
FUNDAMENTALS
OF OPTIONS

Options are deferred delivery contracts that give buyers the right, but not the obligation, to buy or sell a specified commodity or security at a set price on or before a specified date. Today options are traded on commodities and financial assets as diverse as foreign exchange, bank time deposits, U.S. Treasury securities, petroleum products, stocks, stock indexes, and metals. This chapter, and Chapters 19 and 20, cover the fundamentals of option contracts: how they work, how they are priced, how they are traded by speculators, and how they are used by commercial firms to hedge risks associated with underlying assets.

Options on commodities have existed in different forms since 1860 for products as diverse as gold, wheat, and tulip bulbs. An active over-the-counter market in stock options has also existed in the United States for nearly a century. The following section reviews the history of option trading in the United States on both securities and commodities.

18.1 THE EVOLUTION OF OPTION TRADING IN THE UNITED STATES

18.1.1 Options on Securities

Options exercisable in stock have been traded actively for nearly a century in the over-the-counter market under the auspices of the Put and Call Dealer Association. Options were first traded on an organized exchange in 1973, when the Chicago Board Options Exchange (CBOE) came into existence. The CBOE listed standardized call options on 18 common stocks. In 1975 and 1976 the American, Philadelphia and Pacific Stock Exchanges also began trading call options on common stocks, and, in 1977 put options were listed on all of these exchanges. The volume of option trading on exchanges has grown rapidly: options are now traded on over 400 stocks.

In the 1980s securities exchanges expanded the scope of option trading to include options on other financial assets. In 1982 the American Stock Exchange began trading options on T-bills, T-notes, T-bonds, and gold, and the Philadelphia Stock Exchange introduced options on foreign currencies. In 1983 the CBOE began trading options on the Standard and Poor's 100 stock index. Exchange options now exist on a wide variety of securities.

18.1.2   Options on Commodities and Futures

Commodity options, or options on commodities rather than securities, have had a stormy existence in the United States since 1860. First traded on major grain exchanges, such options were met with immediate opposition from farm groups who petitioned state governments to prohibit them. Farmers believed that speculation in futures and options caused volatile grain prices. As a result of this opposition, grain exchanges such as the Chicago Board of Trade denied option traders the protection of the exchange. However, this did not deter trading in options, and the rule was subsequently eliminated in 1869.

The opposition of farm groups continued, and in the early 1890s, when grain price suffered a sharp decline, Congress came very close to adopting a general ban on options. In 1921, Congress finally acted, passing the Futures Trading Act, which imposed a prohibitive tax on earnings from option trading. This was quickly followed by the Grain Futures Act in 1922, which required exchanges and their members to maintain extensive records of option trading and authorized the Secretary of Agriculture to conduct investigations of exchange operations.

The opposition to option trading climaxed in the 1930s. On July 19 and 20, 1933, wheat prices collapsed dramatically, and option trading quickly became the scapegoat. In 1936 Congress passed the Commodity Exchange Act, which banned commodity option trading in the following commodities: wheat, cotton, rice, corn, oats, barley, rye, flaxseed, grain sorghums, mill feeds, butter, eggs, and potatoes. In 1938 this list was expanded to include wool, in 1940 to include fats, oils, cottonseed meal, cottonseed, peanuts, soybeans, and soybean meal, and in 1968 to include livestock, livestock products, and frozen orange juice. As a result, commodity options disappeared from the listings of U.S. exchanges.

Meanwhile, commodity options continued to prosper in London, and American brokerage firms became intermediaries through which their American customers traded London options. Options were available in London on cocoa, coffee, copper, silver, sugar, lead, tin, and zinc. By the early 1970s the popularity of London options had become widespread.

A final scandal in the early 1970s rocked the option market. Some U.S. option dealers sold over-the-counter options to the public at excessively high premiums and without covering their short option positions through ownership of the underlying commodity. When these dealers later failed, imposing substantial losses on customers, Congress began an extensive review of federal regulation of commodity futures and option trading.

The result was the Commodity Futures Trading Commission Act (CEA) of 1974, and the creation of the Commodity Futures Trading Commission (CFTC). The CEA continued the prohibition of exchange-traded options on commodities banned prior to 1974, but empowered the CFTC either to extend this prohibition to other commodities covered under the new act or to permit options on previously banned commodities under conditions the Commission deemed appropriate.

The CFTC responded by proposing regulations governing options traded *off-exchange* by firms already engaged in the offer and sale of the physical commodity on which the options were written. In 1977 the CFTC licensed 60 firms to transact business in London and *dealer* options.[1]

Sales abuses continued, however, and in June 1978, the CFTC temporarily suspended all sales of commodity options in the United States. The only exceptions were commercial and dealer options where the firms writing the options were able to demonstrate financial capability. This exception permitted certain existing commercial option dealers to remain in business.

In 1978 the Futures Trading Act reinforced the ban on option trading but also directed the CFTC to develop a regulatory structure that would permit the lifting of this ban. In September 1981, the CFTC initiated an option pilot program for exchange-traded commodity options. Eight futures exchanges subsequently submitted applications to trade options on futures contracts, including options on precious metals, agricultural products, and financial instruments. Trading in options on T-bonds, sugar, and gold futures began in late 1982. These were quickly followed by options on S&P 500 and NYSE stock index futures in January of 1983, and by options on foreign currency, live cattle, soybeans, wheat, cotton, and silver futures in 1984. Today, on most futures exchanges options are traded on some futures contracts.

18.1.3   Current Regulatory Structure

Option markets are regulated by both the Securities Exchange Commission (SEC) and the CFTC. In December 1981, the Chairman of the SEC, which regulates all security exchanges, and the Chairman of the CFTC agreed that the SEC would have exclusive jurisdiction over options on cash *security instruments,* such as stocks and T-bonds, while the CFTC would have exclusive jurisdiction over options on all futures contracts and on all physical commodities other than securities. This agreement became known as the Johnson–Shad Accord, and was ratified by

---

[1]*Dealer* options are sold by dealers in the underlying physical commodity and must be covered by the dealer's inventory of the commodity.

the Congress in late 1982. Thus, the SEC now regulates foreign currency options traded on the Philadelphia Stock Exchange while the CFTC regulates options on foreign currency futures traded on the Chicago Mercantile Exchange. This division of authority has understandably resulted in some regulatory conflicts, which are discussed more extensively in Section 9.9.1 of Chapter 9.

18.2   TERMINOLOGY AND DEFINITIONS

18.2.1   What Is an Option Contract?

The buyer (or owner) of an option contract has a *right*, but not an obligation, to buy or sell a specific quantity of a given asset at a specified price at or before a specific date in the future. To acquire this right, the buyer pays a premium to the seller (also called the *option writer*). If the buyer chooses to exercise his right to buy or sell the asset, the seller of the option has an *obligation* to deliver or take delivery of the underlying asset. The potential loss to an option seller is unlimited. In contrast, if the buyer chooses not to exercise his right, but to allow the option to expire, his loss is limited to the premium paid.

A *call option* gives the buyer, who pays the premium, the right to *purchase* the underlying asset. The contract specifies an *exercise* or *strike* price at which the asset can be purchased at or prior to the option's maturity date. Buyers may choose not to exercise this right if market conditions are not favorable. A *put option* gives the buyer the right to *sell* an underlying asset at a specific exercise price at or prior to the option's maturity date.

The option holder's right to exercise the option expires on the expiration date of the contract. The option's expiration date is different from the exercise date. The *exercise date* is the date upon which the option is actually exercised. The *expiration date* is the last day upon which the option may be exercised.

Two common types of options are *European* and *American*.[2] A European option contract may be exercised only on the contract's expiration date. The expiration date and the exercise date (if the option is exercised by the holder) must, therefore, be the same. An American option contract can be exercised at any time prior to the contract's expiration date, at the holder's discretion. Thus, the exercise date of an American option can be different from its expiration date. American options are understandably more valuable than otherwise identical European options because of the exercise flexibility they give buyers.[3]

---

[2] In the United States American options are normally traded.

[3] The latest development in the option market is the *Asian* option. Currently, Asian options are not traded on organized exchanges, but are over-the-counter instruments. These contracts are valued on the basis of the average value of the underlying asset during the life of the option. This is in contrast to the payoff of a standard European or American option, which is dependent on the value of the underlying asset on the exercise date. This is discussed more fully later in the chapter.

18.2.2 Exchange-Traded versus Over-the-Counter Options

EXCHANGE-TRADED OPTIONS. *Exchange-traded* option contracts, like futures contracts, are standardized and are traded on organized (and government designated) exchanges. An exchange-traded option specifies a uniform underlying instrument, one of a limited number of strike prices, and one of a limited number of expiration dates. Strike-price intervals and expiration dates are determined by the exchange where the option is traded. Tables 18.1 and 18.2 show, as examples, specifications for the kinds of exchange-traded option contracts available in the United States. Performance on option contracts is guaranteed by a clearing corporation that interposes itself as a third party to all option contracts. This eliminates default risk for option buyers, or the risk that the seller of an option will fail to meet his or her obligations. Thus, just as for futures, contract standardization together with a clearing corporation guarantee provide the fundamental structure for exchange-traded options.

Once an exchange-traded option contract has been purchased, contract obligations may be fulfilled in one of these three ways:

1. The buyer allows the option to expire unexercised. All of the premium is retained by the seller, and the seller's obligation is discharged.
2. The buyer exercises his right on or before the expiration date. The seller must then adhere to the terms of the option contract, and accept the other side of the position. The seller keeps all of the premium.
3. Either or both the buyer and/or the seller executes an offsetting transaction in the option market, eliminating all future obligations—the buyer sells or the seller buys another option with *identical terms*. In this case, the rights or obligations under the original option are, in effect, transferred to a new option holder or grantor. Thus, neither the buyer nor the seller of an option needs to hold an option until expiration, provided he is willing to accept or pay the current market premium required to close out (or offset) his position.

Buyers of exchange-traded put and call options are not required to deposit margin funds, since their loss exposure is limited to the premium paid for the option. Sellers of put and call options, in contrast, are required to maintain margin accounts, since they are exposed to considerable risk (see Section 18.4.1).

OVER-THE-COUNTER OPTIONS. *Over-the-counter* (OTC) options are custom-tailored agreements sold directly by dealers rather than through an exchange. Major commercial and investment banks, for example, write custom-tailored interest rate and currency options for commercial customers. The terms of these contracts—the amount of the underlying asset, the strike price, the expiration date, and so forth—are negotiated by the parties to the contract.

TABLE 18.1
Contract specifications: Options on physicals (selected examples)

	Individual stocks	S&P 100 index	Deutschemark	Gold
Exchange	CBOE	CBOE	PHLX	AMEX
Trading hours*	9:30 A.M. to 4:10 P.M.	9:30 A.M. to 4:10 P.M.	4:30 A.M. to 2:30 P.M. (Mon–Fri) 6:00 P.M. to 10:00 P.M. (Sun–Thu)	9:00 A.M. to 2:30 P.M.
Underlying asset	Common stocks listed on the NY Stock Exchange and the American Stock Exchange, and qualified securities traded over the counter	S&P 100 stock index (cash settled)	DM 62,500 (delivery of currency to approved depository in country of origin)	100 fine troy ounces of gold bullion (cash settled)
Contract months	Two nearby months, plus quarterly months of Mar, Jun, Sep, and Dec; cycles are extended eight months out	Four nearby months	Two nearby months plus quarterly months of Mar, Jun, Sep, and Dec	Feb, Apr, Jun, Aug, Oct, and Dec, four months traded at any one time
Minimum price fluctuation	$\frac{1}{16}$ or $6.25 per contract	$\frac{1}{16}$ or $6.25 per contract	$0.0001 per DM or $6.25 per contract	$0.10 per troy ounce, or $10 per contract
Strike prices	Vary among stocks (usually $5.00 or $2.50 interval)	5 index point interval	$0.01 interval	$10 interval below $500 and $20 interval at/above $500
Daily price limit	None	None	None	None
Speculative position limit	Depends on a given stock's outstanding shares and volume	25,000 contracts, but no more than 15,000 contracts in the front month	6000 contracts	2000 contract maximum per position
Last trading day	Third Friday of an expiring contract month	Third Friday of an expiring contract month	Friday before third Wednesday of the month	Third Friday of the expiration month
Exercise	American	American	Both American and European styles are available	American

* Eastern time.

TABLE 18.2
Contract specifications: Options on futures contracts (selected examples)

	T-bond futures	Eurodollar futures	Crude oil futures	Deutschemark futures
Exchange	CBOT	CME	NYMEX	CME
Trading hours*	9:00 A.M. to 3:00 P.M.(Mon–Fri) 6:00 P.M. to 9:30 P.M. (Sun–Thu)	8:20 A.M. to 3:00 P.M.	9:45 A.M. to 3:10 P.M.	8:20 A.M. to 3:00 P.M.
Underlying asset	One CBOT U.S. T-bond futures contract	One CME Eurodollar futures contract	One NYMEX crude oil futures contract	One CME Deutschemark futures contract
Contract months	Mar, June, Sept, Dec	All twelve calendar months†	Six consecutive months	All twelve calendar months†
Minimum price fluctuation	$\frac{1}{64}$ or $15.63 per contract	0.01 index point or $25 per contract	$0.01 per barrel or $10 per contract	$0.0001 per DM or $12.50 per contract
Strike prices	2 points ($2000) interval	0.25 index point interval	$1 interval	$0.01 interval
Daily price limit	3 points above or below the prior day's settlement price	None	None	Trading ceases when the corresponding futures contract locks limit at the opening price limit
Last trading day	Noon on the last Friday preceded by at least five business days	Second London bank business day immediately preceding the third Wednesday of the contract month	First Friday of the month prior to the contract month	Second Friday immediately preceding the third Wednesday of the contract month
Exercise	American	American	American	American

* Eastern time.

†The underlying instrument for the three monthly option expirations that fall within a single quarter is the quarter-end futures contract. For example, the exercise of a January, February, or March option will all result in a position at the strike price in the March futures contract.

TABLE 18.3
Top 10 option contracts: U.S. and foreign

Contract	Exchange	1990 Trading volume*
U.S. exchanges		
S&P 100	CBOE	68,846,535
T-bond futures	CBOT	27,315,411
S&P 500 futures	CME	11,212,505
Eurodollar futures	CME	6,859,625
XMI	AMEX	5,579,911
Crude oil futures	NYMEX	5,254,612
Deutschemark	PHLX	4,891,902
Deutschemark futures	CME	3,430,374
Yen futures	CME	3,116,130
Yen	PHLX	2,990,431
Foreign exchanges		
Nikkei 225 futures	Osaka, Japan	9,187,741
10-year French government bond futures	MATIF, France	7,410,305
Swedish OMX Index	SOM, Sweden	5,168,766
Swiss Market Index	SOFFEX, Switzerland	4,655,114
FTSE 100	LTOM, U.K.	2,412,083
CAC 40	MONEF, France	2,389,816
Dutch Stock Index	EOE, Netherlands	1,975,365
German Bund futures	LIFFE, U.K.	1,804,178
Short sterling futures	LIFFE, U.K.	1,376,543
3-month PIBOR futures	MATIF, France	709,736

* Number of option contracts.

Source: Futures Industry Association, Inc. and *Futures and Options World*.

18.2.3   Options on Physicals versus Options on Futures

Options on physicals are options that can be exercised to obtain a position in a physical or actual asset. *Options on futures* are those that result in the acquisition of a futures position upon exercise. Table 18.3 shows the most active exchange-traded option contracts in the United States and abroad, together with their respective trading volumes in 1990. Option contracts on the CBOE's S&P 100 cash index and on the CBOT's T-bond futures are the most actively traded. Tables 18.1 and 18.2 provide the specifications of the leading option contracts.

18.3   OPTIONS ON PHYSICALS

This section examines options on physicals. Section 18.4 discusses options on futures. Not surprisingly, many of the option mechanics covered in this section apply equally to options on futures.

18.3.1 Individual Stock Options and the Basics of Option Pricing

Options on individual stocks are undoubtedly the most widely known option contracts and are traded on many stock and option exchanges. The largest option exchanges in the United States are the Chicago Board Options Exchange, the American Stock Exchange, the Philadelphia Stock Exchange and the Pacific Stock Exchange.

Table 18.4 provides price quotations for stock options traded on the CBOE, for November 1, 1990. For example, on November 1 the closing price for Alcoa stock was 53\frac{1}{4}$ (column 1), and options were listed for five different strike prices: $50, $55, $60, $65, $70 (column 2). Prices (or premiums) for both call and put options are shown in columns 3 through 8, for expiration dates in November 90, December 90, and January 91.[4] Each option contract represents 100 shares of stock. If an option is not traded or offered for a particular expiration date, an r or s appears in the quotation table for calls and puts respectively.

For example, the January 91 call option on Alcoa stock with a strike price of $55 had a premium of 2\frac{1}{2}$ on November 1. A buyer of this option, therefore, would have to make an immediate payment of $2.50 per share (or $250 per contract) to the writer of the option.

A few simple properties of option pricing are readily apparent from Table 18.4:

1. **The Level of the Strike Price.** Call options with lower strike prices are more valuable: they give the buyer the right to purchase the underlying asset at a lower price. For example, the Alcoa Jan 50 call has a premium of 5\frac{1}{2}$, while the Jan 55 call premium is only 2\frac{1}{2}$. Similarly, put options with higher strike prices are more valuable: they give buyers the right to sell at a higher price. Thus, the Nov 50 put costs only $$\frac{5}{8}$, while the Nov 55 put has a premium of 2\frac{5}{8}$.

2. **Intrinsic Value versus Time Value.** Option premiums have two components: *intrinsic value* and *time value*. If the current stock price is above the strike price of a call (or below the strike price of a put), the option has intrinsic value. An option with intrinsic value is said to be *in-the-money*. An option with no intrinsic value is said to be either *at-the-money* or *out-of-the-money* (i.e., the current stock price is equal to or below the strike price for a call or is equal to or above the strike price for a put). If the strike price is equal to the current stock price, an option is said to be *at-the-money*. The following summarizes the relationship between an option's strike price and the market price of the underlying asset:

---

[4]Expiration dates for options traded on the CBOE are the third Friday of the expiration month.

TABLE 18.4
Price quotations for stock options: November 1, 1990

CHICAGO BOARD

Option & NY Close	Strike Price	Calls—Last Nov	Calls—Last Dec	Calls—Last Jan	Puts—Last Nov	Puts—Last Dec	Puts—Last Jan
Alcoa	50	3½	r	5½	⅝	r	r
53¼	55	r	1⅝	2½	2⅝	3½	r
53¼	60	r	7/16	r	r	r	r
53¼	65	r	s	½	r	s	12
53¼	70	r	s	⅛	r	s	17
AmGenl	22½	r	4⅝	r	r	r	r
27	25	2⅜	3⅝	r	5/16	1¼	2⅛
27	30	5/16	1	1⅝	3	r	r
27	35	1/16	s	⅝	r	s	r
27	40	s	s	5/16	s	s	r
AmStr	40	4⅞	5⅞	r	⅝	r	1 11/16
AT&T	25	r	s	r	r	s	⅛
34¾	30	4½	4⅞	5	1/16	5/16	7/16
34¾	35	⅝	1¼	1⅝	1	1⅜	1½
34¾	40	s	s	5/16	s	s	r
Amrtch	60	r	7⅜	r	r	½	1⅛
66⅞	65	r	3¾	4¾	⅝	1⅝	2½
66⅞	70	r	1⅛	1¾	r	r	r
Atl R	110	s	s	r	s	s	⅞
130⅜	115	s	s	r	s	s	1¼
130⅜	120	r	r	r	r	r	1 15/16
130⅜	125	6⅛	7⅝	r	1	2⅜	3⅜
130⅜	130	r	r	5¾	2½	3⅞	4¾
130⅜	135	⅝	1⅞	3⅛	r	r	7⅜
130⅜	140	1/16	s	1¾	r	s	r
130⅜	145	r	s	1	r	s	r
Avon	22½	r	r	r	r	¾	r
25	25	⅝	1½	2⅜	1	r	r
25	30	3/16	r	¾	r	r	r
BankAm	15	r	s	r	r	s	7/16
19⅜	17½	2	r	2¾	¼	⅞	1
19⅜	20	⅝	1 1/16	1⅛	r	1⅝	1⅞
19⅜	22½	1/16	¼	⅝	r	r	r
BankNY	12½	r	r	r	r	½	r
14¾	15	11/16	13/16	1¼	1⅛	1¼	r
14¾	17½	r	r	⅝	r	r	r
14¾	20	r	r	⅜	r	r	r
BattlM	5	r	r	2	r	r	r
6¾	7½	1/16	⅜	¾	⅞	r	1¼
6¾	10	r	s	¼	r	s	r
6¾	12½	r	s	⅛	r	s	r
BellAtl	45	7¾	r	r	r	r	⅝
52⅞	50	3¼	4⅜	4⅜	r	1¼	r
52⅞	55	r	1⅜	1¾	r	r	r
Beth S	10	1 9/16	r	r	r	¼	r
11⅜	12½	⅛	7/16	¾	r	r	r
24⅛	25	½	1¼	2⅛	r	2¼	2¾
24⅛	30	r	⅜	¾	r	r	r
Upjohn	30	7	r	7¼	r	r	½
36¾	35	2⅜	3⅛	3⅞	⅜	1 3/16	1 11/16
36¾	40	9/16	1 5/16	1⅞	3⅜	4⅛	r
36¾	45	3/16	9/16	15/16	s	s	r
36¾	50	⅛	5/16	⅜	r	r	r
Weyerh	17½	1	r	r	r	r	⅝
18⅛	20	r	r	½	r	r	r
18⅛	25	s	s	r	s	s	7½
Xerox	25	4½	r	r	⅛	9/16	¾
30¼	30	1¼	1¾	2½	¾	1⅞	2¼
30¼	35	r	5/16	¾	r	r	6⅛
		Nov	**Dec**	**Feb**	**Nov**	**Dec**	**Feb**
AlexAl	17½	r	r	r	⅜	r	r
19⅛	20	r	r	1 3/16	1½	r	r
Amdahl	10	1¾	2	r	r	r	r
11⅝	12½	⅜	½	r	r	r	1¾
11⅝	15	r	⅛	r	r	r	r
A E P	30	r	r	⅜	2⅛	r	r
AlnGrp	55	r	s	r	⅜	s	r
63⅞	60	3¼	r	r	1	2¼	3⅝
63⅞	65	1½	r	r	2⅝	4¾	r
63⅞	70	r	r	r	r	8¾	r
63⅞	80	r	s	r	17⅝	s	r
Amoco	45	10⅛	s	s	r	s	s
55⅛	50	r	r	r	⅛	r	1¼
55⅛	55	1¼	2⅛	3¼	r	1⅞	3
55⅛	60	⅛	⅝	1¼	r	r	r
A M P	35	7⅝	r	r	r	r	⅝
42⅝	40	2¾	3½	3	⅜	1⅜	r
42⅝	45	¼	1	r	r	4⅜	r
Baxter	22½	3¼	r	r	r	r	9/16
25½	25	1	1½	2⅛	7/16	1	r
25½	30	r	r	⅜	r	r	r
Blk Dk	10	r	r	⅞	⅞	r	r
9½	15	r	s	¼	r	s	r
Bng o	43⅜	2	s	s	⅞	s	s
44	50	r	s	s	6⅜	s	s
44	60	1/16	s	s	r	s	s
Boeing	35	r	s	10½	r	s	r
44	40	4½	r	6¾	¼	¾	1½
44	45	1⅛	2⅜	3½	1⅞	2¾	3¾
44	50	3/16	¾	1¾	6⅜	6¼	6½
44	55	1/16	r	⅞	11	r	11¼
Bois C	20	2¼	3	r	r	1⅛	1⅝
22⅛	22½	1	1	1 11/16	1¼	r	r
22⅛	25	⅜	½	1½	3⅝	r	r
C B S	150	r	r	r	2⅛	r	6½
155⅝	155	r	r	r	3½	6½	r
155⅝	160	3⅜	r	9⅜	6¼	r	r
155⅝	195	1/16	s	r	r	s	r
Heinz	30	3	r	r	r	½	s
33	30	s	s	s	s	s	1
33	35	r	⅝	1½	r	r	r
I T T	40	4¼	5	5¾	¼	r	r
44⅜	45	½	1½	2 9/16	1 9/16	2	r
44⅜	50	1/16	r	1 1/16	r	6	r
44⅜	55	r	⅛	r	r	r	r
K mart	25	¼	½	1⅜	1⅝	2	r
23⅝	30	r	r	¼	r	r	r
LandsE	10	r	r	r	r	1 3/16	r
Litton	75	1¼	3⅝	6½	2¼	2½	4⅝
75¼	80	⅜	1	r	r	r	r
Loews	70	r	r	r	r	1⅞	r
75⅝	75	r	5½	r	r	r	r
75⅝	80	15/16	r	5¼	5⅛	r	r
75⅝	85	r	r	3¼	r	r	r
75⅝	90	r	11/16	r	r	14	r
LongvF	10	r	r	r	r	¾	r
9¾	12½	r	r	r	r	r	2⅞
MayD o	40	1½	r	r	r	r	r
MayDS	35	4½	r	r	r	r	r
39½	40	1¼	r	r	1½	r	4
McCawC	12½	r	r	1 9/16	r	r	r
Mc Don	22½	3⅜	r	r	¼	r	r
25½	25	1¼	1⅞	2⅞	½	1 3/16	1⅝
25½	30	r	3/16	¾	r	4½	r
25½	35	s	r	r	s	9⅝	r
N C R	40	r	r	r	r	½	r
48¼	45	r	r	r	r	r	2⅜
48¼	50	⅝	1⅞	3½	2½	r	4¾
48¼	55	r	½	r	7	6¾	r
48¼	60	r	r	r	r	r	11¾
NorSo	35	r	r	r	r	⅝	r
36¾	40	r	⅝	r	3⅜	3¾	r
NorTel	22½	r	r	r	r	r	7/16
26⅛	25	r	r	2 13/16	3/16	11/16	1¼
Oracle	5	11/16	1	r	r	7/16	r
5½	7½	r	¼	9/16	1¾	r	r
5½	10	r	r	r	r	r	4½
5½	20	s	1/16	r	s	r	r
OutbdM	7½	r	2	r	r	r	r
9¼	10	r	9/16	r	1¼	r	r
9¼	12½	r	r	r	r	3⅝	r
Pall	35	s	r	⅛	s	r	r
ParaCm	30	5¼	r	6½	⅛	⅜	r
35⅝	35	1½	2⅝	3½	15/16	1¾	2⅝
35⅝	40	¼	⅞	1 13/16	r	r	r
35⅝	45	r	7/16	15/16	r	r	r
35⅝	50	s	3/16	s	s	r	s
R P M	20	r	5/16	⅝	r	r	r
RalPur	80	s	r	s	s	1	s
94⅛	85	s	r	r	s	1½	2 15/16

(*continued*)

Market scenarios	Call options	Put options
Market price > strike price	In-the-money	Out-of-the-money
Market price = strike price	At-the-money	At-the-money
Market price < strike price	Out-of-the-money	In-the-money

For example, at the current Alcoa stock price of $\$53\frac{1}{4}$, the Nov 50 Alcoa call is in-the-money (its intrinsic value is positive), while the Nov 50 put is out-of-the-money (it has no intrinsic value). Why, then, does the latter option have a premium of $\$\frac{3}{8}$? Because it still has *time value*.

Table 18.5 provides a breakdown of the two components of an option premium using Alcoa stock options with a strike price of $55 as an example. At the current stock price of $53.25, both the Dec 55 and the Jan 55 calls are out-of-the-money and, therefore, have no intrinsic value. The premiums for those options

TABLE 18.4—cont'd.

Biogen	17½	r	r	r	¼	r	r
19¼	20	r	r	r	1⅜	r	r
19¼	22½	r	9/16	r	r	r	r
19¼	25	r	r	r	5¾	r	r
19¼	30	s	s	3/16	s	s	r
Biomet	30	r	13/16	r	r	r	r
27	35	r	s	7/16	r	s	r
Bolar	5	1/16	s	r	1⅞	s	2
3	10	s	s	r	s	s	6¾
Borind	15	r	s	9⅛	r	s	r
23	17½	r	s	7	r	s	r
23	20	4⅛	4⅜	5¾	r	r	r
23	22½	r	r	r	1⅛	2 1/16	r
23	25	⅝	1 11/16	3	1 15/16	3⅜	r
BurlN	25	7/16	⅝	r	r	r	r
CarnCr	10	r	r	r	1/16	r	¾
13	12½	r	r	1¾	r	r	1⅜
13	15	⅛	r	¾	r	r	r
Cntocr	30	r	r	8⅛	r	r	r
37	35	r	r	r	1	r	r
37	40	r	r	r	r	r	5⅛
ChamDv	17½	r	r	1	r	r	r
CmpAsc	5	2⅛	r	2	r	r	r
7¼	7½	3/16	⅜	⅝	r	⅞	r
7¼	10	r	1/16	s	s	s	s
Chryslr	10	1¼	r	1¾	r	9/16	¾
11⅛	12½	1/16	5/16	⅝	r	r	2 5/16
11⅛	15	s	s	3/16	s	s	r
CIGNA	30	5⅜	r	5⅝	7/16	1¼	r
34⅞	35	1⅜	2⅛	2½	1⅝	3½	r
34⅞	40	r	r	r	5½	r	r
34⅞	55	s	s	⅛	s	s	r
CinBel	20	r	r	1 3/16	r	r	r
20⅝	22½	r	r	⅜	r	r	r
Citicp	10	2	2⅛	2½	3/16	½	11/16
11⅞	12½	5/16	¾	1	1¼	1½	1½
11⅞	15	1/16	⅛	5/16	r	r	3¼
11⅞	17½	r	s	⅛	5⅝	s	6¼
11⅞	20	r	s	1/16	8⅛	s	8⅞
11⅞	22½	s	s	1/16	s	s	10⅞
Delta	50	8½	s	r	5/16	s	1½
58⅝	55	3¾	r	r	⅝	1¾	2⅞
58⅝	60	1	r	4	2⅛	4⅜	r
58⅝	65	r	⅝	1 9/16	r	r	r
DiaSrk	20	⅜	r	r	r	r	r
18¾	22½	r	r	5/16	r	r	r
EKodak	35	5⅜	5½	5¾	⅛	½	15/16
40	40	1⅜	2	2⅝	1⅛	2	2⅜
40	45	⅛	5/16	⅝	r	r	r
Elan	15	r	r	2¼	¼	r	r
17	17½	⅜	r	r	1¼	r	r

Cadenc	15	r	2 1/16	r	r	r	r
16⅝	20	r	5/16	r	r	r	r
CapCit	370	r	r	r	3¾	9½	r
390⅞	380	19¼	r	r	8	15	r
390⅞	390	r	r	r	11⅝	r	r
390⅞	400	8	14¼	r	19¼	r	r
390⅞	410	3¾	r	r	19⅞	r	37
390⅞	420	2	s	18¾	r	s	r
390⅞	430	¾	r	r	r	r	48
390⅞	440	r	4½	r	r	r	r
390⅞	450	¼	r	r	r	r	r
390⅞	470	r	s	r	r	s	80½
Coke	35	10⅜	s	r	1/16	s	½
45⅛	37½	7⅜	s	s	r	s	s
45⅛	40	5½	r	7	¼	¾	1 5/16
45⅛	42½	2⅞	s	s	½	s	s
45⅛	45	1⅛	2	3¼	1⅛	2	2½
45⅛	50	⅛	½	1⅜	5¼	r	r
CocaCE	12½	r	r	r	r	r	⅝
13⅝	15	⅛	¼	11/16	r	r	r
Colgat	60	r	8⅛	r	r	r	r
66¾	65	2¼	r	5	⅞	r	r
66¾	70	¼	r	2⅝	4⅛	r	r
66¾	75	r	s	1 13/16	r	s	r
Cmw Ed	30	3⅞	r	4	r	r	⅜
33⅞	35	3/16	⅜	¾	r	r	2½
C Data	7½	r	r	r	¼	⅝	r
8¼	10	r	r	11/16	r	r	r
8¼	22½	r	s	s	14½	s	s
Corng	35	r	r	r	r	r	1
40	40	r	2	r	1	r	r
Diebld	30	r	r	3¼	r	⅞	1¼
32¾	35	⅜	⅞	1⅝	2⅝	r	4⅛
32¾	40	1/16	s	⅝	8⅜	s	r
32¾	45	1/16	s	r	r	s	r
Edwrds	17½	r	⅞	r	r	r	r
ForstL	40	r	r	r	½	1⅜	r
42	45	r	1⅛	r	r	r	r
FptMc	35	1	r	r	r	r	1⅝
36	40	r	r	r	4⅛	r	r
GnCine	20	r	r	⅞	1½	r	r
Gn Dyn	22½	1 11/16	r	3⅛	r	r	r
23⅜	25	⅝	1 1/16	1⅞	r	r	r
23⅜	30	1/16	s	r	r	s	r
Harris	17½	r	r	⅞	r	r	r
Hewlet	25	2¾	r	r	5/16	¾	1⅜
27⅛	30	5/16	⅞	1 11/16	3	r	4⅛
27⅛	35	1/16	r	¾	r	r	8½
27⅛	40	r	s	5/16	r	s	r
27⅛	50	1/16	s	r	r	s	r
Honw n	75	r	r	r	⅛	r	1¾

94⅛	90	6	10½	10⅛	1⅛	2¾	4⅜
94⅛	95	2½	4	r	3¼	5⅞	5⅞
94⅛	100	⅞	2¾	6½	6	7½	10
94⅛	105	⅛	1½	4¾	13	12½	r
94⅛	110	⅛	1 3/16	3	16½	r	r
Safewy	12½	r	r	11/16	r	r	2
SherW	30	r	r	r	r	r	1⅛
33½	35	r	r	2	2½	r	r
SwAir	20	r	r	11/16	r	r	r
StoTch	10	r	r	r	¼	5/16	r
14¾	12½	1⅝	r	3¼	r	¾	r
14¾	15	¼	1⅜	r	r	r	r
14¾	17½	1/16	r	1⅛	r	r	r
14¾	22½	s	r	¼	s	r	r
Syntex	50	3⅞	5	6	¼	1 1/16	r
53⅞	55	¾	2 1/16	4⅛	2	2⅞	4⅝
53⅞	60	r	9/16	1¾	6⅛	r	r
53⅞	65	s	¼	r	s	r	r
53⅞	70	s	1/16	r	s	r	r
Tektrn	15	r	1 3/16	2	r	9/16	r
Telcrd	30	5⅝	7	r	13/16	r	r
35	35	3¼	4⅛	5⅝	2 11/16	r	r
35	40	1⅛	r	r	5½	r	r
35	45	¼	¾	r	9⅞	r	r
Toys o	23⅜	s	⅝	s	s	2½	s
Toys	17½	3⅝	r	r	r	r	r
21⅞	20	1¾	2½	3½	⅜	1	r
21⅞	22½	⅜	1 1/16	2	1⅜	2⅛	2⅝
21⅞	25	⅛	5/16	1⅜	4⅛	3½	4⅜
21⅞	30	r	⅛	⅜	8¾	r	r
UCamp	30	3	r	r	r	r	r
33⅛	35	r	⅞	r	r	3¼	3⅞
33⅛	40	r	r	r	7⅛	r	r
Waban	5	r	1⅜	2 3/16	r	r	r
6½	7½	r	5/16	11/16	r	r	r
Walmrt	22½	r	r	r	⅛	7/16	r
27	25	2⅜	3⅛	4⅛	7/16	⅞	1¾
27	27½	s	1½	s	s	1¾	s
27	30	⅛	½	1⅝	3	3¼	4
27	35	r	1/16	⅜	r	r	r
27	32½	s	⅛	s	s	6⅜	s
Whirlp	15	r	r	r	r	r	⅝
18	17½	r	r	r	r	r	1½
18	20	r	r	r	1 11/16	r	r
Whitmn	17½	r	1¼	1¾	r	r	r
18¼	20	r	r	r	1⅞	r	r

Total call vol 216,004 **Call open int** 2,675,311
Total put vol 173,401 **Put open int** 1,700,972

r-Not Traded. s-No Option.

Source: The Wall Street Journal, November 2, 1990.

TABLE 18.5
Intrinsic value versus time value Alcoa stock options: November 1, 1990

Market price: \$53.25

Strike price: \$55.00

	Calls		Puts	
	Dec 90	Jan 91	Nov 90	Dec 90
Expiration date	Dec 21, 90	Jan 18, 91	Nov 16, 90	Dec 21, 90
Option premium	$\$1\frac{5}{8}$	$\$2\frac{1}{2}$	$\$2\frac{5}{8}$	$\$3\frac{1}{2}$
Intrinsic value	0	0	$\$1\frac{3}{4}$	$\$1\frac{3}{4}$
Time value	$\$1\frac{5}{8}$	$\$2\frac{1}{2}$	$\$\ \frac{7}{8}$	$\$1\frac{3}{4}$

TABLE 18.6
Price quotations for index options: November 1, 1990

Thursday, November 1, 1990

OPTIONS

Chicago Board

S&P 100 INDEX

Strike	Calls—Last			Puts—Last		
Price	Nov	Dec	Jan	Nov	Dec	Jan
265	....	....	35⅜	1⅛	4½	7
270	20⅝	25	29⅝	1 9/16	5½	8
275	19	22½	26½	2 3/16	6⅝	9¼
280	15	19¼	....	2⅞	7¾	11
285	11¼	17	19½	4⅛	9¼	13
290	7⅝	14	17¾	5¾	10¾	14
295	4⅞	11¼	14¾	7⅞	13	....
300	2 13/16	8¼	11¼	11	15⅜	19
305	1 9/16	5⅞	9	15	18¾	21¼
310	13/16	4⅛	7⅛	19	22	....
315	½	2¾	5¼	22⅞	25	....
320	¼	1¾	3⅝	29⅝	28⅞	30⅞
325	⅛	1 1/16	....	....	....	....
330	1/16	½	....	39	41½	....
335	1/16	....	....	....	....	....
340	....	¼	....	....	....	....
345	....	⅛	....	....	....	....
350	....	⅛	....	....	....	....

Total call volume 110,884 Total call open int. 422,166
Total put volume 103,084 Total put open int. 396,575
The index: High 293.15; Low 287.24; Close 292.76, +2.93

S&P 500 INDEX

Strike	Calls—Last			Puts—Last		
Price	Nov	Dec	Mar	Nov	Dec	Mar
250	....	....	....	3/16	1⅜	5
275	....	....	40¾	13/16	3⅞	10
280	....	....	....	....	1 9/16	4¾
285	....	....	....	1 9/16	....	....
290	18¾	....	....	2 1/16	6⅞	14
295	14¾	....	....	3⅛	8	14¾
300	11	17¼	....	4	9¾	16½
305	7⅜	14⅜	21¼	5⅝	11⅜	19¼

Strike	Calls—Last			Puts—Last		
Price	Nov	Dec	Jan	Nov	Dec.	Jan
550	1 1/16	6⅛	....	....	....	....
555	11/16	4¼	....	....	....	....
560	7/16	3⅝	....	....	....	48⅜
565	5/16	2 3/16	6⅞	....	....	....
570	¼	....	....	....	....	....
580	1/16	1	....	....	....	....
585	1/16	1	....	....	....	....
590	....	½	....	....	....	....
595	....	⅜	....	....	....	....

Total call volume 9,257 Total call open int. 66,608
Total put volume 5,660 Total put open int. 63,047
The index: High 519.32; Low 508.74; Close 517.77, +4.98

INSTITUTIONAL INDEX

Strike	Calls—Last			Puts—Last		
Price	Nov	Dec	Jan	Nov	Dec	Jan
290	....	....	....	⅞	....	....
295	....	....	....	⅞	....	....
300	....	....	....	1 1/16	....	....
305	....	....	....	1½	....	....
310	....	....	....	2⅛	....	....
315	17½	....	....	2⅞	8¼	....
320	14⅜	....	....	4⅛	....	....
325	10⅛	....	....	6¾	....	....
330	7⅜	....	16¾	8⅜	14¾	15½
335	4¾	11⅛	15⅜	....	....	....
340	2 15/16	8¾	....	....	....	....
345	1¾	....	....	....	....	....
355	⅜	....	....	....	....	....
360	¼	....	....	....	....	....
370	....	11/16	....	....	....	....

Total call volume 1,181 Totai call open int. 33,976
Total put volume 1,065 Total put open int. 49,551
The index: High 331.39; Low 324.89; Close 331.07, +3.33

INTERNATIONAL MARKET INDEX

Strike	Calls—Last			Puts—Last		
Price	Nov	Dec	Jan	Nov	Dec	Jan
275	....	....	....	1⅞	....	....

Philadelphia Exchange

GOLD/SILVER INDEX

Strike	Calls—Last			Puts—Last		
Price	Nov	Dec	Jan	Nov	Dec	Jan
80	....	....	....	....	1¾	....
85	7⅝	....	....	....	....	4¾
95	1¾	....	....	....	....	....
100	⅞	....	....	....	....	....
105	....	1⅞	....	....	....	....

Total call volume 96 Total call open int. 634
Total put volume 43 Total put open int. 702
The index: High 91.10; Low 89.58; Close 90.92, +1.14

VALUE LINE INDEX OPTIONS

Strike	Calls—Last			Puts—Last		
Price	Nov	Dec	Jan	Nov	Dec	Jan
230	....	2⅜	....	....	....	....
240	....	....	....	....	23	....

Total call volume 5 Total call open int. 1,402
Total put volume 1 Total put open int. 4,861
The index: High 217.85; Low 216.23; Close 217.84, +0.95

NATIONAL O-T-C INDEX

Strike	Calls—Last			Puts—Last		
Price	Nov	Dec	Jan	Nov	Dec	Jan
250	5¼	....	....	....	....	....
265	⅞	....	....	....	....	....
270	9/16	....	....	....	....	....
275	⅜	....	....	....	....	....

Total call volume 31 Total call open int. 240
Total put volume 0 Total put open int. 22
The index: High 251.12; Low 247.45; Close 251.12, +1.31

UTILITIES INDEX

Strike	Calls—Last			Puts—Last		
Price	Nov	Dec	Jan	Nov	Dec	Jan
205	....	....	....	....	....	1¼
210	....	9⅛	....	....	1⅞	....

310	4¾	11½	....	7⅝	13⅜	21½
315	2⅞	8½	....	10⅝	15¾	....
320	1⅝	6¼	13	16⅝	21	....
325	⅞	3¾	12⅞	19⅜	21¾	....
330	½	2¾	10½	23½	27½	30½
335	¼	2	8½	28¼	....	35
340	1/16	1 3/16	....	....	35	....
345	1/16	....	5¾	....	36⅞	....
350	....	5/16	....	....	....	....
360	....	....	2	....	....	....
375	....	1/16	....	....	....	....
380	....	1/16	....	....	....	....
385	....	....	½	....	....	....

Total call volume 19,854 Total call open int. 350,233
Total put volume 18,872 Total put open int. 506,737
The index: High 307.27; Low 301.61; Close 307.02, +3.02

American Exchange

MAJOR MARKET INDEX

Strike	Calls—Last			Puts—Last		
Price	Nov	Dec	Jan	Nov	Dec	Jan
440	....	....	....	5/16	3¼	....
450	....	....	....	13/16	....	7¾
460	....	....	....	1 1/16	6	....
470	....	....	....	1¾	9	....
475	....	....	....	2 1/16	8⅝	....
480	....	....	....	2 9/16	....	....
485	....	....	....	3⅜	....	....
490	....	....	....	3¾	11⅜	....
495	....	....	....	4½	13½	....
500	21¾	....	....	5½	14¾	....
505	19¾	27¼	....	6⅝	17¾	19⅝
510	15⅛	....	....	8	20½	....
515	12¼	....	....	10¼	....	....
520	9⅜	18⅛	....	12¼	....	....
525	7¼	14	....	19	....	....
530	5⅛	15	....	17¾	....	....
535	3¾	11¾	....	22	27⅜	....
540	2 9/16	9	16⅛	34⅛	....	....
545	1¾	....	....	....	....	....

300	....	....	....	....	15	....
310	1⅜	....	....	....	....	....

Total call volume 10 Total call open int. 303
Total put volume 23 Total put open int. 367
The index: High 296.33; Low 292.09; Close 292.37, −4.61

JAPAN INDEX

Strike	Calls—Last			Puts—Last		
Price	Nov	Dec	Jan	Nov	Dec	Jan
190	....	....	....	....	1⅛	....
200	....	....	....	⅝	2¼	....
210	....	....	....	⅞	....	....
215	....	....	....	1⅛	4¼	....
220	....	....	....	1¾	5¼	....
225	....	....	....	2¾	6½	8½
230	....	....	....	3⅝	8½	10⅝
235	....	17	....	5⅛	9½	11¾
240	8¼	....	....	7	....	....
245	5⅝	....	....	9	13¼	15¼
250	3¼	8⅜	....	11¾	15⅞	....
255	1¾	....	....	....	18¾	....
260	1⅛	4⅜	....	19¼	....	....
265	¾	....	....	....	....	....

Total call volume 263 Total call open int. 5,179
Total put volume 1,328 Total put open int. 10,184
The index: High ....; Low ....; Close 243.30, −7.78

OIL INDEX

Strike	Calls—Last			Puts—Last		
Price	Nov	Dec	Jan	Nov	Dec	Jan
230	....	....	....	1	4¼	....
235	11¼	....	....	....	....	....
245	....	....	....	4¾	....	....
250	....	....	....	8¼	....	....
255	....	....	....	11½	....	....
265	....	1 9/16	....	....	....	....
275	....	⅝	....	....	....	....
280	....	⅜	....	....	....	....

Total call volume 44 Total call open int. 328
Total put volume 81 Total put open int. 264
The index: High 246.25; Low 243.41; Close 245.85, +1.87

215	5⅜	....	....	1 3/16	....	....
220	1½	3⅝	....	....	....	....

Total call volume 208 Total call open int. 2,125
Total put volume 50 Total put open int. 1,774
The index: High 220.86; Low 218.16; Close 220.86, +3.14

Pacific Exchange

FINANCIAL NEWS COMPOSITE INDEX

Strike	Calls—Last			Puts—Last		
Price	Nov	Dec	Mar	Nov	Dec	Mar
175	28¾	....	....	....	....	....
190	....	....	....	1½	....	....
195	11⅝	....	....	....	....	....
200	7⅝	....	....	2 15/16	....	....
205	4½	....	....	4⅜	8¾	....
210	2⅜	....	....	8½	....	....
215	⅞	....	....	....	....	....
235	....	....	....	....	28⅞	....

Total call volume 371 Total call open int. 5,716
Total put volume 196 Total put open int. 1,675
The index: High 205.72; Low 201.82; Close 205.22, +1.87

N.Y. Stock Exchange

NYSE INDEX OPTIONS

Strike	Calls—Last			Puts—Last		
Price	Nov	Dec	Jan	Nov	Dec	Jan
155	....	....	....	11/16	3¼	....
160	....	....	....	1⅞	4½	....
162½	....	....	....	....	4¾	....
165	3⅞	9⅛	....	2 5/16	5⅝	....
170	2¼	....	....	5½	7¼	....
175	½	2¼	....	....	11⅝	....
177½	¼	....	....	....	....	....
180	⅛	....	....	....	....	....

Total call volume 177. Total call open int. 5,342.
Total put volume 124. Total put open int. 2,245.
The index: High 167.69; Low 165.07; Close 167.59, +1.42

Source: The Wall Street Journal, November 2, 1990.

reflect only the time value component. Alternatively, both the Nov 55 and the Dec 55 puts are in-the-money and have positive intrinsic values. The latter option premiums reflect both intrinsic and time value components.

3. **The Relationship of Time Value to Time to Expiration.** The longer the time remaining until an option's expiration, the higher its premium tends to be, everything else being equal. This is because a longer time period provides more opportunity for the price of the underlying asset to move to a level where the option is in-the-money, and where the purchase or sale of the asset at the specified strike price will be profitable.[5] Thus, an option with six months remaining until expiration will have a higher premium than will an option with the same strike price but with only three months until expiration. In Table 18.5, for example, the Alcoa Jan 55 call has a higher premium than the Dec 55 call, and the Dec 55 put has a higher premium than the Nov 55 put. The difference is the option's time value, which is the difference between the actual option premium and the intrinsic value of the option. Since the time value of an option declines to zero as the time to the option's expiration date diminishes, an option is known as a *wasting asset.* The sensitivity of option premiums to time to expiration is analyzed in greater detail in Chapter 19.

The magnitude of an option's time value reflects the potential of the option to gain intrinsic value during its life. A deep out-of-the-money option has little potential to gain intrinsic value because to do so asset prices will have to change substantially. Therefore, it will have little time value. Similarly, a deep in-the-money option is as likely to lose intrinsic value as to gain it, and as a consequence also has little time value. Generally, time value is at a maximum when an option is at-the-money. At this point there is no intrinsic value to lose, but there is a roughly 50–50 chance of gaining intrinsic value.

18.3.2 Stock Index Options

In recent years exchange-traded options have been introduced on a variety of cash commodities. The most popular of these are options on stock indexes (see Table 18.3). A stock index option gives the buyer the right to buy or sell a specific basket of stocks (or stock index) at a specified price. Normally, at exercise of the option any profits or losses incurred are determined by cash settlement, rather than by physical delivery of the underlying basket of stocks.

Options are available on many different stock indexes.[6] Table 18.6 shows typical premiums for index options as of the close of trading on November 1,

---

[5]Whether an option will be exercised depends on the relationship between the strike price and the underlying stock price. An option holder will exercise only when he can make a gross profit. An in-the-money option is likely to be exercised; an out-of-the-money option is unlikely to be exercised. At-the-money options may or may not be exercised.

[6]Readers should refer to Chapter 10 for a detailed discussion of stock indexes.

1990. For example, the closing price of the CBOE S&P 100 index call option with a strike price of 295 for December 90 expiration is $11\frac{1}{4}$. A buyer, therefore, would pay a premium of $1125 ($11\frac{1}{4}$ × $100) for the right to buy the S&P 100 index at 295 at any time between November 2, 1990, and December 21, 1990 (the expiration day of the S&P 100 index options).[7]

Suppose that the S&P 100 index rises to 320.50. If the buyer exercises the option, he will make a net profit of $1425, computed as follows:

Value of stock index: 320.50 × $100 = $32,050
Exercise price: 295 × $100 = $29,500
Exercise value: $32,050 − $29,500 = $2550
Premium: 11.25 × $100 = $1125
Net profit: $2550 − $1125 = $1425

The option seller, therefore, will lose $1425. Alternatively, if the S&P 100 index were to remain below 295.00 until the expiration of the option, the buyer would lose his entire premium of $1125, and the option seller will have a profit of $1125.

18.3.3 Currency Options and Interest Rate Options

Table 18.7 provides price quotations for currency and interest rate options as of November 1, 1990. A currency option gives the buyer the right to buy or sell a fixed quantity of a specified currency in exchange for a specific quantity of another currency, in a ratio determined by the strike price of the option. For example, a buyer of a Philadelphia Stock Exchange Deutschemark December 90 call option with a strike price of $0.6650 acquires the right to purchase DM 62,500 at an exchange rate of 0.6650($/DM), or for $41,562.50. For this right, on November 1, a buyer would pay a premium of 1.13 cents per DM, or $706.25 [DM62, 500 × 0.0113($/DM)] per option contract. (See Table 18.1 for specific contract details.)

Options on interest rate (or fixed income) instruments exist for both long-term and short-term instruments. Options on long-term interest rate instruments, such as U.S. Treasury notes and bonds or British gilts, are among the most popular option contracts (see Table 18.3). Using U.S. T-bond options as an example, assume that a buyer of a CBOE U.S. T-bond December 90 call option with a strike price of 100 acquires the right to purchase $100,000 of 30-year T-bonds at face value on or before December 21, 1990. For this right, on November 1, 1990, he would have

---

[7]The S&P 100 index option contract expires on the third Friday of the contract month. The dollar value of the S&P 100 index is defined as $100 per index point (see Table 18.1).

TABLE 18.7
Price quotations for interest rate and currency options: November 1, 1990

CURRENCY

OPTIONS

PHILADELPHIA EXCHANGE

Option & Underlying	Strike Price	Calls—Last Nov	Calls—Last Dec	Calls—Last Mar	Puts—Last Nov	Puts—Last Dec	Puts—Last Mar
50,000 Australian Dollars-cents per unit.							
ADollr	...75	r	r	r	r	0.37	r
78.47	...77	1.68	r	r	0.37	r	r
78.47	...79	0.47	r	r	r	r	r
78.47	...80	0.25	r	r	r	2.66	r
78.47	...81	r	r	r	2.89	r	r
31,250 British Pounds-cents per unit.							
BPound	185	r	r	r	r	0.72	r
194.78	187½	r	r	r	0.40	1.15	4.05
194.78	.190	r	4.40	r	0.55	r	r
194.78	192½	1.85	r	r	1.70	r	r
194.78	.195	1.84	2.80	r	2.34	4.00	r
194.78	197½	r	1.28	r	4.00	r	r
194.78	.200	r	r	2.66	6.00	r	r
50,000 Canadian Dollars-cents per unit.							
CDollr	...81	r	r	r	r	r	0.25
85.87	...85	r	r	r	r	0.57	1.67
85.87	...86	r	r	r	0.68	1.15	2.17
85.87	.87½	r	0.08	r	r	r	r
50,000 Canadian Dollars-European Style.							
CDollar	86½	0.09	r	r	r	r	r
62,500 German Marks-cents per unit.							
DMark	.. 61	r	r	r	r	r	0.35
66.52	...62	r	r	r	r	0.14	r
66.52	...63	r	r	r	r	0.27	r
66.52	.63½	r	r	s	r	0.30	s
66.52	...64	r	r	r	0.13	0.34	r
66.52	.64½	1.95	r	s	0.18	0.42	s
66.52	...65	1.54	r	r	0.20	0.60	r
66.52	.65½	r	r	s	0.36	r	s
66.52	...66	0.90	1.37	2.13	0.51	0.99	r
66.52	.66½	0.71	1.13	s	0.81	1.35	s
66.52	...67	0.50	0.92	1.50	1.04	r	r
66.52	.67½	r	0.42	s	r	r	s
66.52	...68	0.18	0.49	r	r	r	r
62,500 German Marks-European Style.							
66.52	...62	r	r	r	r	r	0.55
66.52	.64½	r	r	s	0.19	r	s
66.52	...65	r	r	2.40	r	r	r
66.52	...69	r	r	0.83	r	r	r
6,250,000 Japanese Yen-100ths of a cent per unit.							
JYen	... 66	s	s	s	r	r	0.07
76.66	...67	r	r	r	r	r	0.09
76.66	...68	r	r	r	r	r	0.16
76.66	...70	r	r	r	r	r	0.32
76.66	...71	r	r	r	r	r	0.44
76.66	...72	r	4.47	r	r	0.22	r
76.66	.72½	r	r	s	r	0.30	s
76.66	...73	r	3.63	r	r	0.33	r
76.66	...74	r	r	r	0.18	0.50	r
76.66	.74½	r	r	s	0.34	0.65	s
76.66	...75	1.98	r	r	0.43	0.89	r
76.66	.75½	r	r	s	0.55	1.03	s
76.66	...76	1.34	r	2.35	0.83	1.28	1.86
76.66	.76½	0.98	1.46	s	1.07	1.46	s
76.66	...77	0.68	1.20	1.97	1.16	1.65	r
76.66	.77½	r	1.07	s	r	r	s
76.66	...78	0.42	0.91	1.51	r	2.37	3.10
76.66	.78½	r	0.66	s	r	r	s
76.66	...79	0.24	0.65	1.26	r	r	3.63
76.66	.79½	0.20	r	s	r	r	s
76.66	...80	0.16	0.43	0.90	r	r	r
76.66	.80½	0.10	r	s	r	r	s
76.66	...81	0.08	0.25	r	r	r	r
76.66	.81½	0.08	r	s	r	r	s
76.66	...82	0.03	r	0.50	r	r	r
76.66	...83	r	0.10	0.39	r	r	r
6,250,000 Japanese Yen-European Style.							
76.66	...72	4.32	r	r	r	r	r
76.66	...73	r	3.78	r	r	r	r
76.66	...75	r	r	r	0.44	r	r
76.66	...78	0.34	r	r	r	r	r
62,500 Swiss Francs-cents per unit.							
SFranc	..70	r	r	r	r	s	0.27
78.57	...73	r	r	r	r	0.20	r
78.57	...74	r	r	r	r	0.28	r
78.57	...75	r	r	r	0.17	r	r
78.57	...76	r	r	r	0.40	r	r
78.57	.76½	r	r	s	r	0.82	s
78.57	...77	r	r	2.80	r	r	r
78.57	...78	r	r	r	0.78	1.25	r
78.57	...80	0.38	0.70	r	r	r	r
78.57	...81	s	0.33	r	s	r	r
78.57	.81½	r	0.26	s	r	r	s
78.57	...82	r	0.30	r	r	r	r
62,500 European Currency Units-cents per unit.							
ECU	134	3.95	r	r	r	r	r

Total call vol. 19,709 Call open int. 342,671
Total put vol. 13,657 Put open int. 344,149
r—Not traded. s—No option offered.
Last is premium (purchase price).

INTEREST RATE

OPTIONS

Thursday, November 1, 1990

For Notes and Bonds, decimals in closing prices represent 32nds; 1.01 means 1 1/32. For Bills, decimals in closing prices represent basis points; $25 per .01.

Chicago Board Options Exchange

U.S. TREASURY BOND—$100,000 principal value

Underlying Issue	Strike Price	Calls—Last Nov	Calls—Last Dec	Calls—Last Jan	Puts—Last Nov	Puts—Last Dec	Puts—Last Jan
8¾% (ybe)	100	....	1.28	....	....	....	....
due 8/2020		....	....	....	....	....	....

Total call vol. 1 Call open int. 6
Total put vol. 0 Put open int. 20

3 p.m. prices of underlying issues supplied by The Chicago Corp.: T-Bonds 8¾% 100.18. T-Notes 8½% 101.13.

OPTIONS ON SHORT-TERM INTEREST RATES

Strike Price	Calls—Last Nov	Calls—Last Dec	Calls—Last Jan	Puts—Last Nov	Puts—Last Dec	Puts—Last Jan
75	....	⅛	....	....	....	....
77½	....	1/16	....	....	....	....
80	....	1/16	....	....	....	....

Total call volume 90 Total call open int. 1,583
Total put volume 100 Total put open int. 1,855
IRX levels: High 71.00; Low 70.40; Close 70.50, −0.50

OPTIONS ON LONG-TERM INTEREST RATES

Strike Price	Calls—Last Nov	Calls—Last Dec	Calls—Last Jan	Puts—Last Nov	Puts—Last Dec	Puts—Last Jan
80	....	....	5⅞	....	¼	....
82½	....	....	....	¼	....	....
85	1 5/16	2	....	⅝	1 5/16	....
87½	¼	15/16	1 5/16	2 5/16	2¾	....
90	1/16	....	....	4⅝	4½	....

Total call volume 145 Total call open int. 1,052
Total put volume 224 Total put open int. 1,630
LTX levels: High 86.32; Low 85.47; Close 85.62, −0.69

Source: The Wall Street Journal, November 2, 1990.

to pay a premium of $1\frac{28}{32}$, or \$1875 (\$100,000 × 0.01 + \$31.25 × 28). (See Table 18.1 for the T-bond option contract specifications.)

18.4 OPTIONS ON FUTURES

Table 18.8 provides the trading volume for U.S. futures options by commodity grouping from 1985 to 1990. Table 18.9 lists all of the futures option contracts traded on futures exchanges in the United States, as well as their respective trading volumes in 1990. Tables 18.10a, 18.10b, and 18.10c (pp. 508–511) contain typical price quotations for futures options as of the close of business on November 1, 1990.

An *option on a futures contract* is like other exchange-traded options, except that holders acquire the right to buy or sell a futures contract on an underlying asset, rather than the asset itself. For example, a buyer of an S&P 500 futures *call* option has the right to take a *long* position in the S&P 500 futures contract at the specified strike price, whereas a buyer of an S&P 500 *put* futures option has the right to take a *short* position in the S&P 500 futures at the specified strike price.

The seller of a futures option assumes the obligation of taking a futures position opposite that of the option buyer. For example, the seller of an S&P 500 *call* futures option must be ready to take a *short* position in the S&P 500 futures; and, the seller of an S&P 500 *put* futures option must be ready to accept a *long* S&P 500 futures position.[8]

All futures options in the United States are *American*: they can be exercised on any trading day. Option buyers and sellers can also liquidate their obligations at any time before exercise by selling or buying an identical option contract, thereby offsetting their positions (just as in futures markets).

Unlike a stock option, or other physical options, a cash exchange in the amount of the exercise price does not occur when a futures option is exercised. Rather, a futures option holder acquires a long or short futures position, where the acquisition futures price is equal to the strike price of the option. Subsequently, as the acquired futures position is marked-to-market at the close of the trading day, holders of long futures positions can withdraw cash in an amount equal to the current futures price less the option strike price (if positive), and holders of short futures positions can withdraw an amount equal to the strike price less the current futures price (if positive). Thus, when a futures option is exercised the holder receives a futures contract with an unrealized gain equal to the exercisable value of the option.

Suppose that on November 1, 1990, an investor buys a CME S&P 500 index futures call option for December expiration with a strike price of 310.00, at

---

[8]When an option is exercised, an option writer is randomly chosen by the clearing association and assigned to take the related futures position.

TABLE 18.8
U.S. trading in futures options: 1985–90*

			Numbers of option contracts			
	1985	1986	1987	1988	1989	1990
Total	20,044,744	31,770,613	46,185,985	49,137,490	55,446,130	64,103,094
Interest rates	12,821,488 (63.96%)	20,136,225 (63.38%)	25,842,477 (55.95%)	23,312,073 (47.44%)	28,073,883 (50.63%)	35,336,832 (55.12%)
Foreign currencies	2,216,315 (11.06%)	4,411,316 (13.89%)	7,062,113 (15.29%)	7,623,383 (15.51%)	9,119,520 (16.45%)	8,588,796 (13.40%)
Agriculturals	1,746,290 (8.71%)	2,546,041 (8.01%)	4,309,280 (9.33%)	8,832,658 (17.98%)	8,113,952 (14.63%)	9,610,229 (14.99%)
Precious metals	1,974,949 (9.85%)	2,231,516 (7.02%)	3,008,214 (6.51%)	2,579,182 (5.25%)	2,366,450 (4.27%)	2,686,774 (4.19%)
Equity indexes	1,285,702 (6.42%)	2,182,748 (6.87%)	2,083,926 (4.51%)	758,131 (1.54%)	1,201,111 (2.17%)	1,672,425 (2.61%)
Energy	–	135,266 (0.43%)	3,260,642 (7.06%)	5,606,093 (11.41%)	6,316,183 (11.39%)	6,097,107 (9.51%)
Nonprecious metals	–	127,501 (0.40%)	612,850 (1.33%)	402,792 (0.82%)	234,035 (0.42%)	107,387 (0.17%)
Others	–	–	6,483 (0.02%)	23,178 (0.05%)	20,996 (0.04%)	3,544 (0.01%)

*The percentage of total futures option volume is shown in parentheses beneath the volume figures.
Source: Futures Industry Association, Inc.

TABLE 18.9
Exchange-traded options on futures contracts

	1990 Trading volume
Chicago Board of Trade	
T-bonds	27,315,411
Soybeans	2,089,382
Corn	2,116,302
T-notes (10 year)	936,754
Wheat	482,941
Soybean meal	181,429
Soybean oil	138,089
T-notes (5 year)	87,440
Muni bonds	85,613
Mortgage backed	19,231
Silver	1,398
	33,453,990
Chicago Mercantile Exchange	
Eurodollar	6,859,625
Deuschemark	3,430,374
Japanese yen	3,116,130
Swiss franc	1,130,447
S&P 500	1,638,131
Live cattle	713,276
British pound	501,187
Canadian dollar	283,609
Feeder cattle	168,310
Live hogs	171,306
Pork bellies	46,286
Australian dollar	27,381
Lumber	29,717
T-bill	32,283
	18,148,062
New York Mercantile Exchange	
Crude oil	5,254,612
Unleaded gasoline	435,685
Heating oil	406,810
	6,097,107
Commodity Exchange	
Gold	1,931,804
Silver	747,499
High grade copper	107,387
	2,786,690
Coffee Sugar & Cocoa Exchange	
Sugar	2,393,016
Cocoa	344,944
Coffee	282,566
	3,020,526

(continued)

TABLE 18.9—cont'd.

	1990 Trading volume
New York Cotton Exchange	
Cotton	284,991
Frozen concentrated orange juice	63,029
U.S. dollar index	99,668
5-year U.S. T-note	0
	447,688
New York Futures Exchange	
NYSE Composite Index	25,501
CRB Index	3,544
	29,045
Kansas City Board of Trade	
Wheat	65,794
Mid-Atlantic Commodity Exchange	
Soybeans	23,578
Soft-red winter wheat	3,408
Gold	2,324
	29,310
Minneapolis Grain Exchange	
American spring wheat	4,509
European spring wheat	22
	4,531

Source: Futures Industry Association, Inc.

a premium of 11.40, or $5700 (see Table 18.10b). Assume that after five weeks the Dec 90 S&P futures contract is at 330.00, and that the investor exercises the option and acquires a long S&P futures position of 310.00. The investor will have an *unrealized* profit on the futures position of $10,000 [(330.00 − 310.00) × $500]. To realize this profit immediately the investor can offset: sell a December 90 S&P 500 futures at 330.00. If he does not do this, there is no guarantee that he will realize the $10,000 profit, since S&P 500 futures prices fluctuate continuously. If he does offset, the net profit on the option will be $4300, which is $10,000 minus the $5700 premium paid on November 1.

18.4.1   Margins

Exchange-traded options are subject to a margin system similar to that applied to futures contracts and discussed earlier in Chapters 2 and 3. In the case of options, however, margins are normally imposed only on the sellers (or writers) of options. Buyers of options customarily pay the entire premium due at the purchase date, and, since they are not exposed to losses due to changes in the price of the underlying asset, no margin is required. Option sellers, in contrast, are exposed to unlimited potential losses due to changes in the underlying asset price. Consequently, they are required to post margin deposits to guarantee that they will ultimately fulfill their contractual obligations (if and when the buyer of the option exercises against them).[9]

Just as for futures transactions, option sellers deposit cash or acceptable securities as initial margin with their brokers, and individual brokerage firms set margin levels, subject to the minimum margin requirements established by exchanges.[10]

The systems used by exchanges to set minimum margins are complex and vary substantially among exchanges. Different exchanges utilize different methodologies for determining initial margin requirements, treat outright and spread positions differently, assess variation margins in different ways, and have different rules for what offsets can be applied. There are, however, some common features among these systems that are similar to those used in futures markets:

- Initial margin levels are based on a calculation of the largest likely daily loss.
- Variation margins are determined by marking-to-the-market the option's value, or by the daily changes in the option's value.

Differences among exchanges exist mainly in the details and procedures used to determine the size of these margins.[11]

A good example of an option margining system is the Chicago Mercantile Exchange's (CME) Standard Portfolio Analysis of Risk (SPAN) system. SPAN utilizes a *portfolio approach* to determine the risk on futures option positions. More

---

[9]Until recently, futures exchanges in London used a margin system in which both buyers and sellers of futures options were margined. For both futures and options positions, for example, a delta-based margining system was used to determine the initial and variation margins. Delta can be veiwed as a risk component of an option position (the concept of delta is discussed in detail in Chapter 19). There are four important features of a delta-based margining system:

1. The initial margin for a futures option position is determined by multiplying the initial margin for a futures contract position by the option's risk factor (i.e., the delta). An additional prudential risk margin is also required for a short option position.
2. Both short and long option positions are marked to market, and subject to variation margins.
3. There is a full automatic offset of initial margins for options and futures/options combinations that involve risk offsets.
4. In contrast to the initial margin on a futures position, which remains constant until delivery, the initial margin on an option position can vary as the risk factor of the position varies but will never exceed the full margin on a futures contract.

In 1991, LIFFE, the IPE, and FOX changed their margin systems to a SPAN system, which is discussed later in this section.

[10]For options on securities, the Federal Reserve Board has authority to establish minimum margins.

[11]See, for example, footnote 9.

TABLE 18.10a
Price quotations for futures options: November 1, 1990

INTEREST RATE
FUTURES OPTIONS

T-BONDS (CBT) $100,000; points and 64ths of 100%

Strike	Calls—Last			Puts—Last		
Price	Dec-c	Mar-c	Jun-c	Dec-p	Mar-p	Jun-p
88	4-04	4-23	4-37	0-12	0-61	1-40
90	2-20	3-00	3-20	0-27	1-35	....
92	0-61	1-57	2-20	1-04	2-26	3-15
94	0-19	1-08	1-38	2-26	3-41	4-28
96	0-05	0-40	1-03	4-12	5-05	....
98	0-01	0-23	0-42	6-08	6-50	....

Est. vol. 200,000, Wed vol. 27,985 calls, 40,707 puts
Open interest Wed 393,965 calls, 476,244 puts

T-NOTES (CBT) $100,000; points and 64ths of 100%

Strike	Calls—Last			Puts—Last		
Price	Dec-c	Mar-c	Jun-c	Dec-p	Mar-p	Jun-p
94	2-24	2-46	....	0-10	0-49	....
95	1-33	2-03	....	0-17	1-04	....
96	0-53	1-31	1-51	0-37	1-31	....
97	0-22	1-02	....	1-07	2-00	....
98	0-10	0-45	....	1-57	....	....
99	0-04	0-30	....	2-51	....	....

Est. vol. 4,700, Wed vol. 488 calls, 628 puts
Open interest Wed 16,728 calls, 20,872 puts

MUNICIPAL BOND INDEX (CBT) $100,000; pts. & 64ths of 100%

Strike	Calls—Settle			Puts—Settle		
Price	Dec-c	Mar-c	Jun-c	Dec-p	Mar-p	Jun-p
87	2-28	2-36	....	0-22	1-14	....
88	1-47	....	....	0-41	....	....
89	1-10	1-34	....	1-04	2-09	....
90	0-46	1-10	....	1-39	2-47	....
91	0-27	....	....	2-20	....	....
92	0-14	....	....	....	....	....

Est. vol. 76, Wed vol. 1 calls, 0 puts
Open interest Wed 11,226 calls, 11,272 puts

5 YR TREAS NOTES (CBT) $100,000; points and 64ths of 100%

Strike	Calls—Last			Puts—Last		
Price	Dec-c	Mar-c	Jun-c	Dec-p	Mar-p	Jun-p
97	2-20	....	....	0-02	....	....
98	1-24	1-36	....	0-05	....	....
99	0-38	0-61	....	0-19	....	....
100	0-11	0-35	....	....	....	....
101	0-03	....	....	....	....	....
102	....	....	....	....	....	....

Est. vol. 770, Wed vol. 150 calls, 240 puts
Open interest Wed 8,736 calls, 5,041 puts

MORTGAGE-BACKED (CBT) $100,000; pts. and 64ths of 100%

Strike	Calls—Settle			Puts—Settle		
Price	Nov-c	Dec-c	Jan-c	Nov-p	Dec-p	Jan-p
Cpn	9.5	9.5	9.5	9.5	9.5	9.5
97	2-12	2-13	....	0-03	0-16	0-25
98	1-16	1-24	1-29	0-10	0-31	....
99	0-33	0-53	....	....	....	....

Strike	Dec-c	Mar-c	Jun-c	Dec-p	Mar-p	Jun-p
100	0-11	....	....	1-05	1-26	....
101	0-02	0-12	....	1-60	2-13	....
102	....	....	....	2-58	....	....

Est. vol. 30, Wed vol. 0 calls, 10 puts
Open interest Wed 812 calls, 1,126 puts

EURODOLLAR (IMM) $ million; pts. of 100%

Strike	Calls—Settle			Puts—Settle		
Price	Dec-c	Mar-c	Jun-c	Dec-p	Mar-p	Jun-p
9175	0.41	0.66	0.69	0.02	0.06	0.13
9200	0.20	0.46	0.50	0.06	0.10	0.19
9225	0.08	0.30	0.35	0.19	0.18	0.27
9250	0.03	0.17	0.23	0.39	0.30	0.39
9275	0.01	0.10	0.14	0.61	....	....
9300	.0004	0.06	0.09	....	....	....

Est. vol. 23,189, Wed vol. 11,272 calls, 8,579 puts
Open interest Wed 240,052 calls, 181,667 puts

EURODOLLAR (LIFFE) $1 million; pts. of 100%

Strike	Calls—Settle			Puts—Settle		
Price	Dec-c	Mar-c	Jun-c	Dec-p	Mar-p	Jun-p
9175	0.40	0.68	0.70	0.02	0.06	0.12
9200	0.19	0.48	0.52	0.06	0.11	0.19
9225	0.07	0.31	0.37	0.19	0.19	0.29
9250	0.02	0.19	0.24	0.39	0.32	0.41
9275	0.00	0.10	0.15	0.62	0.48	0.75
9300	0.00	0.06	0.08	0.87	0.69	0.75

Est. Vol. Thur, 0 Calls, 10 Puts.
Open Interest Wed 3,933, Calls, 2,427 Puts.

LONG GILT (LIFFE) £50,000; 64ths of 100%

Strike	Calls—Settle			Puts—Settle		
Price	Dec-c	Mar-c	Jun-c	Dec-p	Mar-p	
82	2-32	3-35	....	0-12	0-53	....
83	1-45	2-56	....	0-25	1-10	....
84	1-01	2-18	....	0-45	1-36	....
85	0-36	1-50	....	1-16	2-04	....
86	0-18	1-23	....	1-62	2-41	....
87	0-09	1-00	....	2-53	3-18	....

Est. Vol. Thur, 1,575 Calls, 2,825 Puts.
Open Interest Wed 18,440, Calls, 25,782 Puts.

—OTHER INTEREST RATE OPTION—

Final or settlement prices of selected contract. Volume and open interest are totals in all contract months.

Treasury Bills (IMM) $1 million; pts. of 100%

Strike	Dec-c	Mar-c	Jun-c	Dec-p	Mar-p	Jun-p
9325	0.14	0.55	....	0.10	0.09	0.13

Est. vol. 164. Wed vol. 566. Op. Int. 6,875.

CBT—Chicago Board of Trade. CME—Chicago Mercantile Exchange. FINEX—Financial Instrument Exchange, a division of the New York Cotton Exchange. IMM—International Monetary Market at Chicago Mercantile Exchange. LIFFE—London International Financial Futures Exchange.

Source: The Wall Street Journal, November 2, 1990.

TABLE 18.10b
Price quotations for futures options: November 1, 1990

CURRENCY TRADING

FUTURES OPTIONS

JAPANESE YEN (IMM) 12,500,000 yen; cents per 100 yen

Strike	Calls—Settle			Puts—Settle		
Price	Nov-c	Dec-c	Mar-c	Nov-p	Dec-p	Mar-p
7550	1.39	1.94	....	0.31	0.85	....
7600	1.05	1.64	2.35	0.47	1.06	1.85
7650	0.76	1.37	....	0.68	1.29	....
7700	0.54	1.14	1.88	1.96	1.56	2.36
7750	0.37	0.94	....	1.29	1.84	....
7800	0.25	0.77	1.48	1.67	2.18	2.93

Est. vol. 17,665, Wed vol. 7,550 calls, 5,819 puts
Open interest Wed 104,606 calls, 119,647 puts

DEUTSCHEMARK (IMM) 125,000 marks; cents per mark

Strike	Calls—Settle			Puts—Settle		
Price	Nov-c	Dec-c	Mar-c	Nov-p	Dec-p	Mar-p
6550	1.18	1.61	....	0.18	0.61	....
6600	0.81	1.30	2.01	0.31	0.80	1.67
6650	0.51	1.03	....	0.51	1.03	....
6700	0.32	0.81	1.57	0.82	1.31	2.23
6750	0.19	0.64	....	1.19	....	....
6800	0.11	0.49	1.20	1.61	1.99	2.82

Est. vol. 18,857, Wed vol. 3,091 calls, 3,998 puts
Open interest Wed 66,199 calls, 91,183 puts

CANADIAN DOLLAR (IMM) 100,000 Can.$, cents per Can.$

Strike	Calls—Settle			Puts—Settle		
Price	Nov-c	Dec-c	Mar-c	Nov-p	Dec-p	Mar-p
845	0.96	1.18	1.18	0.06	0.27	....
850	0.57	0.84	0.95	0.16	0.44	1.42
855	0.28	0.57	0.76	0.37	0.67	....
860	0.10	0.37	0.59	0.70	0.96	2.05
865	0.03	0.22	0.46	1.13	1.30	....
870	0.01	0.13	0.35	....	1.70	2.80

Est. vol. 615, Wed vol. 320 calls, 332 puts
Open interest Wed 7,482 calls, 8,467 puts

BRITISH POUND (IMM) 62,500 pounds; cents per pound

Strike	Calls—Settle			Puts—Settle		
Price	Nov-c	Dec-c	Mar-c	Nov-p	Dec-p	Mar-p
1875	5.94	6.68	7.06	0.18	0.96	3.76
1900	3.68	4.86	5.76	0.46	1.62	4.90
1925	1.94	3.38	4.58	1.18	2.62	6.02
1950	0.82	2.20	3.64	2.56	3.92	7.46
1975	0.30	1.40	2.84	4.54	5.58	....
2000	0.12	0.86	2.16	....	7.50	10.90

Est. vol. 1,574, Wed vol. 749 calls, 489 puts
Open interest Wed 13,469 calls, 14,068 puts

SWISS FRANC (IMM) 125,000 francs; cents per franc

Strike	Calls—Settle			Puts—Settle		
Price	Nov-c	Dec-c	Mar-c	Nov-p	Dec-p	Mar-p
7750	1.66	1.95	....	0.34	0.94	....
7800	1.02	1.66	2.57	0.50	1.14	2.13
7850	0.75	1.40	....	0.73	1.38	....
7900	0.53	1.18	2.12	1.01	1.65	2.65
7950	0.37	0.97	....	....	....	....
8000	0.25	0.80	1.71	1.73	2.28	3.23

Est. vol. 3,638, Wed vol. 1,318 calls, 1,256 puts
Open interest Wed 29,923 calls, 41,520 puts

—OTHER CURRENCY FUTURES OPTIONS—

Final or settlement prices of selected contracts. Volume and open interest are totals in all contract months.

Australian Dollar (IMM) $100,000; $ per $

Strike	Nov-c	Dec-c	Mar-c	Nov-p	Dec-p	Mar-p
7800	0.69	1.28	....	0.64	....	....

Est. vol. 23. Wed vol. 40. Op. Int. 3,990.

FINEX—Financial Instrument Exchange, a division of the New York Cotton Exchange. IMM-International Monetary Market at Chicago Mercantile Exchange. LIFFE-London International Financing Futures Exchange.

INDEX TRADING

FUTURES OPTIONS

S&P 500 STOCK INDEX (CME) $500 times premium

Strike	Calls—Settle			Puts—Settle		
Price	Nov-c	Dec-c	Mr-c	Nov-p	Dec-p	Mar-p
300	12.20	17.55	....	3.80	9.25	16.00
305	8.70	14.35	23.70	5.25	10.95	17.80
310	5.80	11.40	20.95	7.35	12.95	19.90
315	3.55	8.80	18.20	10.10	15.25	22.10
320	2.10	6.55	15.20	13.60	17.95	24.50
325	1.15	4.70	13.35	17.65	21.05	27.00

Est. vol. 4,084; Wed vol. 2,663 calls; 1,589 puts
Open interest Wed ; 35,885 calls; 38,478 puts

—OTHER INDEX FUTURES OPTIONS—

NYSE COMPOSITE INDEX (NYFE) $500 times premium

Strike	Calls—Settle			Puts—Settle		
Price	Nov-c	Dec-c	Jan-c	Nov-c	Dec-c	Jan-c
1.68	3.60	6.50	8.85	3.25	6.25	7.60

Est. vol. 89, Wed vol. 34 calls, 14 puts
Open interest Wed 887 calls, 926 puts
CBT—Chicago Board of Trade. CME—Chicago Mercantile Exchange. NYFE—New York Futures Exchange, a unit of the New York Stock Exchange.

Source: The Wall Street Journal, November 2, 1990.

TABLE 18.10c
Price quotations for futures options: November 1, 1990

COMMODITY FUTURES OPTIONS

Thursday, November 1, 1990.

AGRICULTURAL

CORN (CBT) 5,000 bu.; cents per bu.

Strike	Calls–Settle			Puts–Settle		
Price	Dec-c	Mar-c	May-c	Dec-p	Mar-p	May-p
210	19¾	29½	....	⅛	¼	½
220	11	19½	26	⅝	1⅛	1½
230	3⅝	13	19½	3¾	4	3¼
240	¾	7¾	13½	10¾	7¾	6⅝
250	¼	4¼	8⅞	20⅛	15	12
260	⅛	2½	6	30⅝	22¼	19

Est. vol. 8,000, Wed vol. 5,460 calls, 7,403 puts
Open interest Wed 120,753 calls, 65,923 puts

SOYBEANS (CBT) 5,000 bu.; cents per bu.

Strike	Calls–Settle			Puts–Settle		
Price	Jan-c	Mar-c	May-c	Jan-p	Mar-p	May-p
575	38½	....	....	1¼	....	....
600	19½	35	47	6¾	7¼	7¾
625	8	21	32	20½	18¾	17¼
650	3⅝	12½	21½	41	35	31¼
675	1¾	7½	14½	63¾	54½	48½
700	¾	4¼	9½	....	76½	68

Est. vol. 7,000, Wed vol. 3,801 calls, 1,729 puts
Open interest Wed 44,866 calls, 24,763 puts

SOYBEAN MEAL (CBT) 100 tons; $ per ton

Strike	Calls–Settle			Puts–Settle		
Price	Dec-c	Jan-c	Mar-c	Dec-p	Jan-p	Mar-p
170	10.70	....	....	.40	....	.75
175	6.20	....	....	1.10	.95	1.30
180	3.25	5.50	9.50	2.75	3.00	3.00
185	1.50	3.50	7.00	6.20	5.75	5.35
190	1.00	2.40	5.25	10.70	9.40	8.25
195	.40	1.30	3.25	15.00	....	11.70

Est. vol. 400, Wed vol. 539 calls, 518 puts
Open interest Wed 11,192 calls, 5,503 puts

SOYBEAN OIL (CBT) 60,000 lbs.; cents per lb.

Strike	Calls–Settle			Puts–Settle		
Price	Dec-c	Jan-c	Mar-c	Dec-p	Jan-p	Mar-p
20	1.660	....	....	.010	....	....
21	.700	....	....	.030	.030	.120
22	.220	.450	....	.550	.400	.400
23	.050	.200	.550	1.400	1.100	1.030

COFFEE (CSCE) 37,500 lbs.; cents per lb.

Strike	Calls–Settle			Puts–Settle		
Price	Dec-c	Mar-c	My-c	Dec-p	Mar-p	May-p
80	8.86	12.70	....	.01	.35	....
85	3.88	8.58	10.88	.03	1.08	1.38
90	.28	4.93	7.20	1.20	2.43	2.70
95	.02	2.65	5.13	6.17	5.04	5.50
100	.01	1.55	3.38	11.16	9.05	8.88
105	.01	.80	2.13	16.16	13.30	12.63

Est. vol. 2,059; Wed vol. 576 calls; 735 puts
Open interest Wed; 14,757 calls; 15,399 puts

SUGAR–WORLD (CSCE) 112,000 lbs.; cents per lb.

Strike	Calls–Settle			Puts–Settle		
Price	Dec-c	Mar-c	My-c	Dec-p	Mar-p	May-p
9.00	.89	1.05	1.16	.15	.33	.39
9.50	.55	.78	....	.32	.56	....
10.00	.35	.57	.66	.58	.82	.88
11.00	.12	.28	.40	1.37	1.53	1.59
12.00	.05	.17	.24	2.28	2.36	2.47
13.00	.03	.09	.16	3.26	3.30	3.39

Est. vol. 8,949; Wed vol. 5,586 calls; 1,819 puts
Open interest Wed; 155,539 calls, [illegible] 880 puts

COCOA (CSCE) 10 metric tons; $ per ton

Strike	Calls–Settle			Puts–Settle		
Price	Dec-c	Mar-c	My-c	Dec-p	Mar-p	May-p
1000	162	233	284	1	11	21
1100	64	154	198	3	32	35
1200	3	87	133	42	66	70
1300	1	47	84	140	123	121
1400	1	25	50	240	198	187
1500	1	15	32	340	293	269

Est. vol. 1,056; Wed vol. 480 calls; 267 puts
Open interest Wed; 15,234 calls, 16,304 puts

OIL

CRUDE OIL (NYM) 1,000 bbls.; $ per bbl.

Strike	Calls–Settle			Puts–Settle		
Price	Dec-c	Jan-c	Fb-c	Dec-p	Jan-p	Feb-p
33	2.92	....	....	0.75	3.40	4.95
34	2.27	3.95	4.05	1.10	3.95	5.65

80	0.05	0.15	0.37	3.05	....	....
82	0.00	0.05	0.17	5.00	....	....
84	0.00	....	....	....	....	....

Est. vol. 4,657, Wed vol. 657 calls, 983 puts
Open interest Wed 18,440 calls, 28,999 puts

HOGS–LIVE (CME) 30,000 lbs.; cents per lb.

Strike	Calls–Settle			Puts–Settle		
Price	Dec-c	Feb-c	Apr-c	Dec-p	Feb-p	Apr-p
52	1.15	1.20	0.75	0.92	3.30	....
54	0.37	0.70	0.50	2.15	....	....
56	0.12	0.35	....	3.90	....	....
58	0.02	0.20	....	5.80	....	....

Est. vol. 210, Wed vol. 295 calls, 205 puts
Open interest Wed 5,248 calls, 5,770 puts

PORK BELLIES (CME) 40,000 lbs.; cents per lb.

Strike	Calls–Settle			Puts–Settle		
Price	Feb-c	Mar-c	May-c	Feb-p	Mar-p	May-p
58	7.35	....	....	3.00	....	4.65
60	6.20	....	....	3.85	....	5.60
62	5.20	....	....	4.85	....	6.60
64	4.25	4.25	....	5.85	6.70	7.70
66	3.52	3.55	....	6.97	....	8.85
68	2.90	....	....	....	....	....

Est. vol. 28, Wed vol. 20 calls, 100 puts
Open interest Wed 938 calls, 1,407 puts

–METALS–

COPPER (CMX) 25,000 lbs.; cents per lb.

Strike	Calls–Last			Puts–Last		
Price	Dec-c	Mar-c	May-c	Dec-p	Mar-p	May-p
105	8.65	8.90	8.40	0.15	4.30	5.50
110	4.50	6.10	6.10	1.00	6.40	8.10
115	1.45	4.10	4.20	2.95	9.30	11.10
120	0.35	2.70	2.90	6.850	12.80	14.80
125	0.10	1.70	2.00	11.50	16.70	18.60
130	0.05	1.10	1.35	16.50	21.10	23.00

Est. vol. 425, Wed vol. 121 calls, 135 puts
Open interest Wed 4,357 calls, 4,490 puts

GOLD (CMX) 100 troy ounces; dollars per troy ounce

Strike						
24	.020	.050	.250	2.350	2.080	1.750
25	.020	.040	.160	3.330	3.060	....

Est. vol. 500, Wed vol. 423 calls, 325 puts
Open interest Wed 8,925 calls, 10,375 puts

WHEAT (CBT) 5,000 bu.; cents per bu.

Strike	Calls–Settle			Puts–Settle		
Price	Dec-c	Mar-c	May-c	Dec-p	Mar-p	May-p
240	22¼	....	....	....	....	....
250	12½	....	....	½	1	1¾
260	5	18¾	....	2½	2¼	3¾
270	1⅞	12½	21¼	10	5½	6½
280	⅝	7¼	15¼	18¼	10¼	10¼
290	¼	4	10¾	28	16¾	15¼

Est. vol. 1,700, Wed vol. 1,395 calls, 1,329 puts
Open interest Wed 44,683 calls, 12,211 puts

WHEAT (KC) 5,000 bu.; cents per bu.

Strike	Calls–Settle			Puts–Settle		
Price	Dec-c	Mar-c	May-c	Dec-p	Mar-p	May-p
250	....	....	....	....	½	....
260	....	....	....	2	1½	....
270	3	10¾	20	6	4¼	7¾
280	1½	6½	14	14	9	12
290	½	3¾	10	23½	16½	17½
300	½	2¼	7	33½	24½	24

Est. vol. 105, Wed vol. 78 calls, 5 puts
Open interest Wed 11,014 calls, 3,591 puts

COTTON (CTN) 50,000 lbs.; cents per lb.

Strike	Calls–Settle			Puts–Settle		
Price	Dec-c	Mar-c	My-c	Dec-p	Mar-p	May-p
73	1.85	3.45	....	0.06	1.65	2.05
74	0.95	2.80	3.45	0.16	2.00	2.45
75	0.30	2.30	2.95	0.51	2.70	2.95
76	0.10	1.90	2.55	1.31	3.10	....
77	0.01	1.65	....	2.22	....	....
78	0.01	1.35	1.80	3.22	4.40	....

Est. vol. 850; Wed vol. 1,207 calls; 291 puts
Open interest Wed; 17,302 calls; 13,505 puts

ORANGE JUICE (CTN) 15,000 lbs.; cents per lb.

Strike	Calls–Settle			Puts–Settle		
Price	Jan-c	Mar-c	My-c	Jan-p	Mar-p	May-p
100	....	....	....	0.70	....	....
105	8.90	....	....	1.50	7.15	....
110	5.65	11.70	....	3.15	....	....
115	3.25	9.55	....	5.75	....	....
120	1.70	7.75	....	9.15	14.90	....
125	0.80	6.00	....	13.20	....	....

Est. vol. 90; Wed vol. 49 calls; 127 puts
Open interest Wed; 2,058 calls; 535 puts

Strike						
35	1.75	3.50	3.75	1.45	4.50	6.29
36	1.40	3.20	3.45	2.23	5.18	7.00
37	1.00	2.85	3.20	2.83	5.85	7.72
38	.70	2.55	2.95	3.53	6.51	....

Est. vol. 16,844; Wed vol. 11,502 calls; 10,859 puts
Open interest Wed; 124,383 calls; 125,143 puts

HEATING OIL No.2 (NYM) 42,000 gal.; $ per gal.

Strike	Calls–Settle			Puts–Settle		
Price	Dec-c	Jan-c	Fb-c	Dec-p	Jan-p	Feb-p
86	.0642	.1331	.1391	.0205	.0880	....
88	.0527	.1236	.1316	.0209	.0985	.1195
90	.0427	.1146	.1220	.0390	.1095	.1299
92	.0325	.1060	.1150	.0488	.1209	....
94	.0255	.0980	.1070	.0618	.1329	.1549
96	.0190	.0910	.1020	.0753	.1460	.1699

Est. vol. 2,769; Wed vol. 898 calls; 263 puts
Open interest Wed; 15,535 calls; 13,175 puts

GASOLINE–Unleaded (NYM) 42,000 gal.; $ per gal.

Strike	Calls–Settle			Puts–Settle		
Price	Dec-c	Jan-c	Fb-c	Dec-p	Jan-p	Feb-p
88	.0640	.0975	.1000	.0210	.1013	....
90	.0520	.0900	....	.0290	....	.1425
92	.0390	.0825	....	.0360	.1263	.1565
94	.0310	.0755	....	.0480	.1350	....
96	.0240	.0690	.0750	.0610	....	....
98	.0190	.0630	....	.0760	....	....

Est. vol. 964; Wed vol. 98 calls; 419 puts
Open interest Wed; 4,008 calls; 7,718 puts

–LIVESTOCK–

CATTLE-FEEDER (CME) 44,000 lbs.; cents per lb.

Strike	Calls–Settle			Puts–Settle		
Price	Nov-c	Jan-c	Mar-c	Nov-p	Jan-p	Mar-p
84	3.35	2.85	2.55	0.02	1.40	3.05
86	1.47	1.75	1.50	0.12	2.30	4.00
88	0.27	0.92	0.90	0.92	3.47	....
90	0.00	0.40	0.50	2.65	....	....
92	0.00	....	....	....	....	....
94	....	....	....	....	....	....

Est. vol. 325, Wed vol. 240 calls, 370 puts
Open interest Wed 3,287 calls, 7,491 puts

CATTLE-LIVE (CME) 40,000 lbs.; cents per lb.

Strike	Calls–Settle			Puts–Settle		
Price	Dec-c	Feb-c	Apr-c	Dec-p	Feb-p	Apr-p
74	3.12	1.85	2.50	0.12	1.22	1.65
76	1.42	0.87	1.45	0.42	2.22	2.55
78	0.37	0.37	0.75	1.37	3.67	3.82

Strike	Calls–Last			Puts–Last		
Price	Dec-c	Jan-c	Feb-c	Dec-p	Jan-p	Feb-p
360	23.20	30.00	31.50	0.70	3.30	5.30
370	14.50	22.40	24.60	1.60	5.50	8.20
380	7.70	15.90	18.90	4.60	9.10	12.00
390	3.40	10.90	13.90	10.30	14.00	16.90
400	1.50	7.30	10.30	17.90	20.30	23.00
410	0.80	4.90	7.40	27.20	27.70	29.80

Est. vol. 5,500, Wed vol. 5,470 calls, 2,253 puts
Open interest Wed 111,738 calls, 37,123 puts

SILVER (CMX) 5,000 troy ounces; cents per troy ounce

Strike	Calls–Last			Puts–Last		
Price	Dec-c	Mar-c	May-c	Dec-p	Mar-p	May-p
375	50.9	63.4	69.5	0.3	3.8	5.4
400	26.8	44.8	50.5	1.2	9.0	11.5
425	7.0	26.6	35.5	6.4	17.0	20.5
450	2.5	16.5	24.5	26.9	31.7	33.0
475	1.0	11.0	17.0	50.4	51.2	50.0
500	0.6	6.5	12.0	75.0	71.7	69.5

Est. vol. 3,700, Wed vol. 1,649 calls, 805 puts
Open interest Wed 61,487 calls, 22,375 puts

–OTHER FUTURES OPTIONS–

Final or settlement prices of selected contracts. Volume and open interest are totals in all contract months.

Lumber (CME) 150,000 bd.ft., $ per 1,000 bd.ft.

Strike	Jan-c	Mar-c	May-c	Jan-p	Mar-p	May-p
190	3.40	6.00	....	5.80	4.50	....

Est. vol. 212. Wed vol. 13. Op. Int. 2,036.

Oats (CBT) 1,000 bu.; cents per bu.

Strike	Dec-c	Mar-c	May-c	Dec-p	Mar-p	May-p
120	4	14	....	3	3	....

Est. vol. 75. Wed vol. 99. Op. Int. 1,700.

Silver (CBT) 1,000 troy oz.; cents per troy oz.

Strike	Dec-c	Feb-c	Apr-c	Dec-p	Feb-p	Apr-p
425	3.0	30.0	....	....	....	....

Est. vol. 10. Wed vol. 0. Op. Int. 681.

Soybeans (MCE) 1,000 bu.; cents per bu.

Strike	Jan-c	Mar-c	May-c	Jan-p	Mar-p	May-p
625	8	21	32	20½	18¾	17¼

Est. vol. 200. Wed vol. 202. Op. Int. 4,090.

Wheat (MPLS) 5,000 bu.; cents per bu.

Strike	Dec-c	Mar-c	May-c	Dec-p	Mar-p	May-p
260	3½	16	....	4½	4	....

Est. vol. 1. Wed vol. 29. Op. Int. 1,603.

Source: The Wall Street Journal, November 2, 1990.

specifically, it simulates how the value of an option seller's entire option/futures position would change under a number of different but possible market scenarios, involving changes in both the level and the volatility of the underlying futures prices.[12] It then sets a required minimum margin large enough to cover the largest one-day loss generated by the alternative simulations. As the value of the option position changes from day to day due to changes in prices, daily margin calls (or payments) are made.

This system, like futures margining systems, is designed to protect option buyers from defaults by option writers, and, ultimately, to maintain the solvency of the option clearinghouse and the integrity of option markets.

18.5   FUTURES VERSUS OPTIONS ON FUTURES

While exchange-traded futures and option contracts are similar in many respects, there are important distinctions between them. This section examines the similarities and differences between futures and options on futures. Table 18.11 provides a summary of the key differences between the two contracts. Most of these differences have already been discussed in earlier sections of this chapter. The different risk exposure and profit potentials indicated in Table 18.11 will also be illustrated by the various risk-return payoff diagrams provided later in this section.

While the number and variety of futures and option trading strategies are virtually unlimited, as we will see in Chapter 20, there are a few futures and option positions that are basic to all trading strategies. These positions, once mastered, can be modified and combined to create a variety of complex futures and option strategies. In this section the profit and loss potential of the basic futures and option positions are illustrated graphically in a format known as *payoff analysis*. Our illustrations utilize the actual prices of options on the December 90 S&P 500 futures contract, as of the close of trading on November 1, 1990 (provided in Table 18.10). The specifications for these futures and option contracts are provided in Table 18.12.

18.5.1   Long and Short Futures Positions

Before examining options it is useful to look at the payoff diagram for a futures contract. Unlike options, the risk-return structure for long and short futures positions is symmetric. The holder of a long (short) futures position gains (loses) if the futures price increases (decreases), and vice versa.

---

[12]In determining possible scenarios, historical price experience of the relevant futures contracts is the primary input.

TABLE 18.11
Key differences between futures and options on futures

Alternative positions	Trader's rights	Trader's obligations	Premium paid or received	Margins required	Risk exposure	Profit potential
Futures contract buyer	—	Accept commodity at contract price	—	Yes	Unlimited	Unlimited
Futures contract seller	—	Deliver commodity at contract price	—	Yes	Unlimited	Unlimited
Call option buyer	Buy futures contract at strike price	None	Paid	No	Limited	Unlimited
Call option seller	—	Sell futures contract at strike price	Received	Yes	Unlimited	Limited
Put option buyer	Sell futures contract at strike price	None	Paid	No	Limited	Unlimited
Put option seller	—	Buy futures contract at strike price	Received	Yes	Unlimited*	Limited

* The seller's risk is, however, limited in that the price of an asset cannot fall below zero.

TABLE 18.12
Contract specifications: S&P 500 futures and futures options

	S&P 500 futures	Futures options on S&P 500
Description of index	The S&P 500 Stock Price Index is a capitalization-weighted index comprising 500 of the largest and most actively traded domestic industrial stocks.	The S&P 500 Stock Price Index is a capitalization-weighted index comprising 500 of the largest and most actively traded domestic industrial stocks.
Ticker symbol	Futures: SP Cash: INX	Calls: CS Puts: PS
Contract size	$500 × the S&P 500 Stock Price Index	One S&P 500 futures contract
Strike price intervals	N/A	5.00 point intervals
Minimum price change	.05 index points = $25.00 per contract	.05 index points = $25.00 per contract*
Trading hours	8:30 A.M. to 3:15 P.M. Chicago time	8:30 A.M. to 3:15 P.M. Chicago time
Contract months	March, June, September, December	All twelve calendar months†
Last day of trading	The Thursday prior to the third Friday of the contract month.	March, June, September, December: the Thursday prior to the third Friday. Other eight months: the third Friday.
Settlement procedure	Cash settlement. All open positions at the close of the final trading day are settled in cash in accordance with the Special Opening Quotation on the following Friday morning. There is no delivery of securities. Final gains and losses are charged to the margin accounts, based on the opening values of the S&P 500 stocks. If a stock does not open on Friday, its last sale price is used.	Except on the final trading day of March, June, September, and December options, exercise of a call results in a long futures position at the strike price in the underlying contract month; and exercise of a put results in a short position at the strike price in the underlying contract month. Any short position open at the end of a trading day is liable to the assignment of a futures position via exercise.
		Exercise of a March, June, September, or December option on the settlement day results, in effect, in cash settlement for the in-the-money amount. Expiring in-the-money options for these expirations only will be automatically exercised.

* A trade may occur at a nominal price (.002 = $1) if it results in liquidation for both parties of deep out-of-the-money option positions.

† The underlying instrument for the three monthly option expirations that fall within a quarter is the quarter-end futures contract. For example, the exercise of a January, February, or March option will all result in a position at the strike price in the March futures contract.

Profit/loss per contract
(Thousands of dollars)

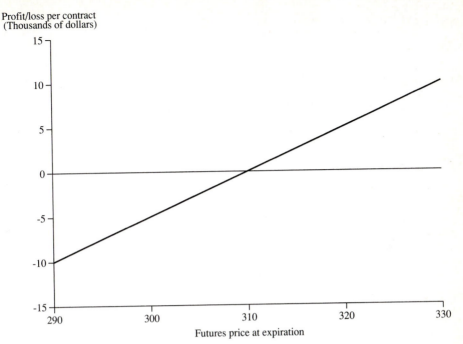

FIGURE 18-1
Long futures: Dec 90 S&P 500 futures (purchased at 310).

Figure 18-1 is the payoff diagram for a simple long position of one December 90 S&P 500 futures, purchased at 310.00 on November 1.[13] The ultimate profit or loss associated with this long futures position will depend on the value of the Dec S&P 500 futures contract on December 20 (the last trading day for the futures contract). If the S&P 500 index closes at 310.00 on December 20, the long futures position has a zero payoff: there will be neither a gain nor a loss. If the S&P index closes at 320.00, the futures position will yield a profit of $5000 (10.00 × $500). If the index finishes at 300.00, the position will result in a loss of $5000. Thus, the potential payoff on the futures position can be depicted by an upward-sloping, 45-degree line, which intersects the zero-profit axis at the purchase price of 310.00.

Figure 18-2 shows a similar payoff diagram for a short position of one December 90 S&P futures, sold at 310.00. A short futures position has a payoff diagram that is the mirror image of the long futures payoff diagram: a 45-degree, downward-sloping line, intersecting the zero-profit axis at 310.

[13]On November 1, 1990, the December 90 S&P futures contract settled at 308.45. (See Table 18.13). Strike prices of the S&P futures contract are set at 5.00 index point intervals, such as 305.00, 310.00 and 315.00. To simplify our analysis, a 310.00 settlement price for the December S&P 500 futures on November 1 is assumed. Thus, in our subsequent analyses of the Dec 310 calls and puts, these are treated as at-the-money options.

TABLE 18.13
S&P 500 futures prices: November 1, 1990

FUTURES

S&P 500 INDEX (CME) 500 times index

	Open	High	Low	Settle	Chg	High	Low	Open Interest
Dec	305.80	309.40	302.40	308.45	+ 1.65	379.50	295.60	145,177
Mr91	308.45	311.90	305.10	311.00	+ 1.65	384.00	298.00	7,858
June	313.80	314.50	308.00	314.00	+ 1.80	386.00	300.00	1,127

Est vol 52,486; vol Wed 44,988; open int 154,189, +663.
Indx prelim High 307.27; Low 301.61; Close 307.02 +3.02

NYSE COMPOSITE INDEX (NYFE) 500 times index

	Open	High	Low	Settle	Chg	High	Low	Open Interest
Dec	166.80	168.70	165.00	168.20	+ .90	206.50	161.25	4,651
Mr91	168.00	169.50	166.25	169.40	+ .90	183.00	163.85	288

Est vol 7,800; vol Wed 6,305; open int 4,969, −32.
The index: High 167.69; Low 165.07; Close 167.59 +1.42

MAJOR MKT INDEX (CBT) $250 times index

	Open	High	Low	Settle	Chg	High	Low	Open Interest
Nov	515.50	518.50	507.25	517.35	+ 2.50	544.25	491.25	5,903
Dec	517.15	520.25	510.00	519.50	+ 2.50	540.80	493.25	1,261

Est vol 3,000; vol Wed 3,034; open int 7,237, −120.
The index: High 519.26; Low 508.74; Close 517.77 +4.98

Source: The Wall Street Journal, November 2, 1990.

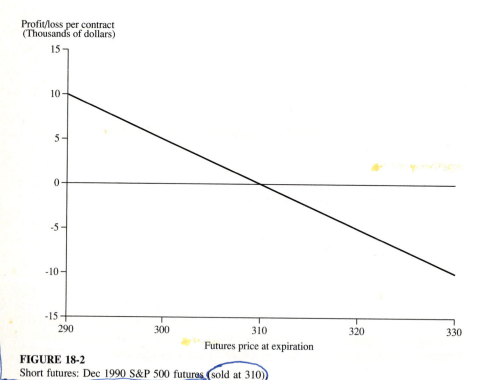

FIGURE 18-2

Short futures: Dec 1990 S&P 500 futures (sold at 310)

Profit/loss per option
(Thousands of dollars)

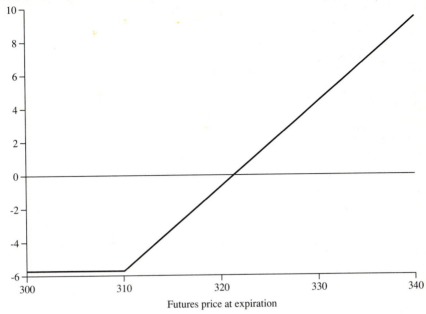

Futures price at expiration

FIGURE 18-3
Long call: Dec 310 S&P 500 call.

18.5.2 Basic Option Positions: Calls and Puts

LONG A CALL. Figure 18-3 shows the profit and loss payoff diagram for an investor who is long a call option. Specifically, he purchases an S&P 500 Dec 310 call option at a premium of 11.40, or $5700 (see Table 18.10). This gives him the right to buy the underlying futures contract at a price of 310 at any time during the life of the option (i.e., prior to December 20, 1990). He will realize a profit at expiration only if the intrinsic value of the option at that time is greater than the premium paid.[14] This will occur only if the S&P 500 futures price increases by enough to cover the premium on the option.

The profit or loss on the call option contract at expiration is calculated by subtracting the premium paid from the value of the option at expiration, which is the amount by which the futures price exceeds the strike price of the option. The break-even price level is 321.40, which is derived by adding the strike price

---

[14]Payoff analysis shows the value of a futures or option position only at the time of expiration of the contract. As such, it shows only the intrinsic value of an option, since at expiration there can be no time value. By offsetting the contract prior to its expiration, investors may make greater or lesser profits than those shown in a payoff diagram.

(310.00) and the premium paid (11.40) together. Thus, if S&P 500 futures prices ultimately exceed 321.40, the investor will make a profit. If Dec S&P 500 futures prices decline, and the option moves out-of-the-money, the buyer will not exercise the option and his loss will equal the $5700 premium paid.

An important decision for an investor is to determine which call option to purchase. Option premiums are higher for options with a longer time remaining until expiration, because such options provide more time for the market to move in a favorable direction. It is also generally possible to purchase this additional time at a proportionately lower cost: a six-month option does not usually cost twice as much as a three-month option.

Equally important is the decision about the strike price of the option: should an at-the-money, out-of-the-money, or in-the-money option be purchased? Premiums are higher for at-the-money and in-the-money options, since these options have a greater chance of eventually being profitable. An out-of-the-money option costs less and has a smaller chance of being profitable. Figure 18-4 compares the profit and loss profiles of three kinds of call options on the December 1990 S&P 500 futures, using option prices on November 1, 1990 (see Table 18.10): the Dec 300 call (in-the-money), the Dec 310 call (at-the-money), and the Dec 320 call (out-of-the-money).

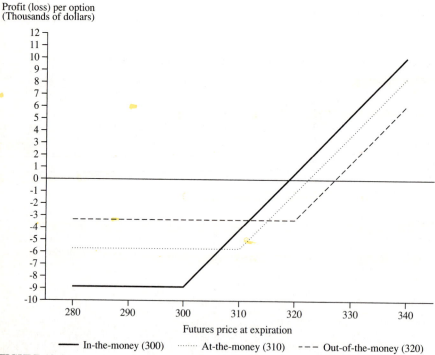

FIGURE 18-4

Long calls: In–, at–, and out-of-the-money (Dec 1990 S&P 500 futures option calls).

Profit/loss per option
(Thousands of dollars)

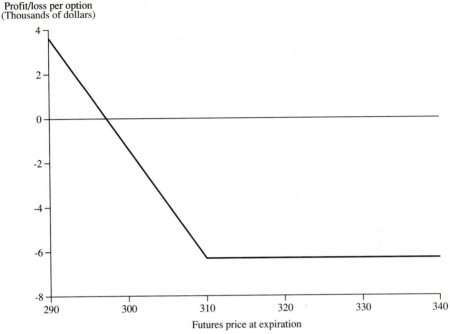

Futures price at expiration

FIGURE 18-5
Long put: Dec 310 S&P 500 put.

LONG A PUT. An investor anticipating a decline in the stock market may purchase an S&P 500 futures put option, which gives him the right to assume a short S&P 500 futures position at the option's strike price. In this case he will profit if S&P futures prices decline during the life of the option.

Figure 18-5 shows the payoff diagram for a long put position on an at-the-money Dec 1990 S&P 500 futures option. On November 1, the premium for this option is 12.95 (or $6475). Thus, the break-even futures price is 297.05 (310 minus 12.95). The investor will have a net profit only if the futures price declines to a level below 297.05.

SHORT A CALL. Writing a simple *uncovered* (or *naked*) call option exposes writers to unlimited potential losses.[15] The principal motivation for writing options is to earn the premium. In periods of stable or declining prices, call option writing can result in attractive profits by capturing the declining time value of an option.

---

[15] *Covered* options are those for which the writer has a corresponding offsetting position in the asset underlying the option. (See Section 20.2.1 in Chapter 20 for further discussion of covered option strategies.) Naked options do not have corresponding offsetting positions, and are therefore more risky.

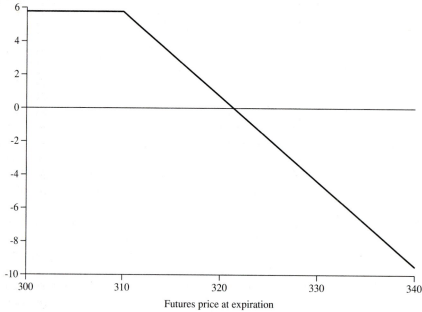

Profit/loss per option
(Thousands of dollars)

Futures price at expiration

FIGURE 18-6
Short call: Dec 310 S&P 500 call.

Figure 18-6 provides the payoff diagram for a call option writer (or seller) of the S&P 500 Dec 310 call. In contrast to a long option position (see Figure 18-3), a call option seller has an unlimited loss potential if prices rise, and a profit potential that is limited to the premium received. The call buyer has an unlimited profit potential and a limited loss potential, just the opposite.

The seller of an S&P call option receives the premium from the option buyer in return for assuming the obligation to take a short position in the futures contract at the strike price if the buyer exercises the option. Since S&P futures options are American style, writers may have to assume this short position at any time during the life of the option. Sellers can eliminate this obligation by buying back (or offsetting) the call prior to its exercise.

The strategy of writing uncovered calls reflects an investor's expectations and tolerance for risk. Writing an at-the-money S&P 500 call is appropriate when investors believe that underlying stock prices are likely to remain either unchanged during the life of the option or, if they do change, move lower. Further, while the premium earned by writing an out-of-the-money call option is less, such an option provides a greater margin for error with respect to future stock prices. An investor willing to write an in-the-money call option, for a corresponding higher premium, implicitly believes there is a small likelihood of higher stock prices in the future.

Profit/loss per option
(Thousands of dollars)

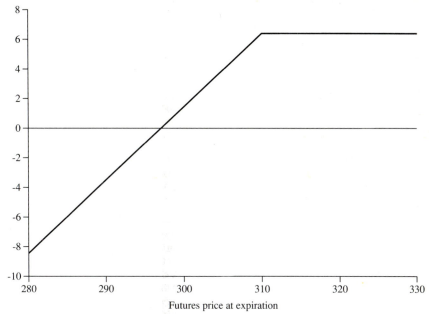

Futures price at expiration

FIGURE 18-7
Short put: Dec 310 S&P 500 put.

SHORT A PUT.   The payoff diagram for a short position in the Dec 310 S&P
500 put option is shown in Figure 18-7 (Compare this diagram with Figure 18-5.)
The seller (writer) of an S&P 500 put option is obligated to take a long S&P 500
futures position if the option is exercised. If the futures price is at or above the
put's strike price at expiration, of course, the put option will expire worthless,
and the seller will keep the entire premium. If, however, S&P 500 futures prices
fall below the strike price of the put option by an amount exceeding the premium
received, the seller will suffer a loss. This loss is unlimited, and depends on the
magnitude of the decline in S&P 500 futures prices. Writers of put options are
obviously betting on either stable or rising stock prices in the future. In periods of
stable or rising prices put option writing can result in attractive profits by capturing
the declining time value of an option.

18.5.3   Covered Option Positions

A *covered* option position involves the purchase or sale of an option in combination with an offsetting (or opposite) position in the asset which underlies
the option. As indicated earlier, call writers incur losses when prices rise, and
put writers suffer losses when prices fall. Thus, short puts can be covered with a

short position in the underlying asset, and short calls can be covered with a long position in the underlying asset:

$$\text{Covered call sale } = \text{ short call } + \text{ long futures}$$

$$\text{Covered put sale } = \text{ short put } + \text{ short futures}$$

18.5.4 Synthetic Futures and Options

Synthetic futures positions are created by combining two option positions such that the resulting payoff diagram is the same (or nearly the same) as that of an outright futures position.

Synthetic long futures positions are created by combining *long call options* with *short put options* having the same strike price. For example, on November 1 an investor can establish a synthetic long futures position by purchasing the Dec 310 call for 11.40 ($5700) and writing the Dec 310 put for 12.95 ($6475). If S&P 500 futures prices rise prior to expiration, the gain on the call option will be similar to the gain that would occur on a long futures position; if futures prices fall, the loss on the short option position will match the loss that would occur on the long futures position. This synthetic long futures position is depicted in Figure 18-8, which shows a profit profile similar to that of the long S&P futures position shown in Figure 18-1.[16]

Synthetic short futures are created by combining *long puts* with *short call options* having the same strike price. Like a short futures position, a synthetic short futures position increases in value when prices decline and decreases in value when prices increase. Figure 18-9 shows the profit profile of a synthetic short futures position, which is similar to that shown in Figure 18-2. In general, the cost of establishing either synthetic futures position is the difference between the respective call and put premiums. In summary:

$$\text{Synthetic long futures } = \text{ long call } + \text{ short put}$$

$$\text{Synthetic short futures } = \text{ long put } + \text{ short call}$$

Synthetic option positions are created by combining options and futures positions. In particular, a synthetic long call option is created by combining a long put option with a long futures position; and, a synthetic long put option is created by combining a long call option with a short futures position. Synthetic call and put options are discussed more fully in Section 20.2.2 of Chapter 20.

---

[16]The synthetic long futures line is not identical to the line in Figure 18-1: it intersects the zero profit line at a price below 310. This difference occurs because both the call and put options are *not* exactly at-the-money options. Consequently, the call and put premiums are not identical. However, if both at-the-money call and put options were available for the 308.45 strike price, the lines in Figures 18-1 and 18-8 would be identical. The relationship of call and put premiums for options on futures contracts, as opposed to stocks, is discussed in Section 19.4.2 of Chapter 19.

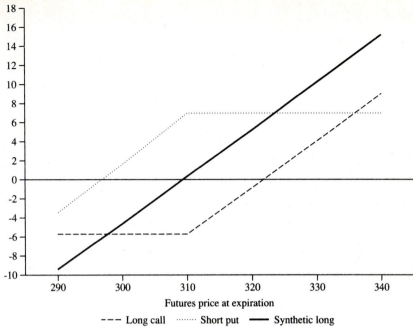

FIGURE 18-8
Synthetic long futures: Dec 1990 S&P 500 futures (long Dec 310 call & short Dec 310 put).

Profit (loss) per contract
(Thousands of dollars)

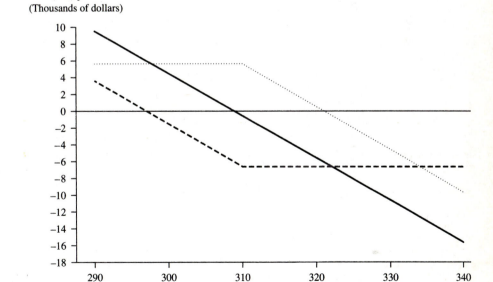

FIGURE 18-9
Synthetic short futures: Dec 1990 S&P 500 futures (short Dec 310 call & long Dec 310 put).

CONCLUSION

This chapter provides an overview of the fundamentals of options. It describes the evolution of option trading in the United States, the various types of option markets that exist, the difference between exchange-traded and OTC options, the various kinds of exchange-traded options that can be bought and sold, and the fundamentals of option prices. In addition, the differences between options on physicals and options on futures are examined. Finally, the chapter provides a payoff-diagram analysis of the basic option positions, showing a profit and loss profile for each type of position. Among other examples, it shows how different combinations of options can be used to create synthetic futures positions.

In the next chapter the pricing of options is discussed in greater detail, and in Chapter 20 the various option trading and hedging strategies are examined.

QUESTIONS

1. It is said that an option writer has a contingent liability. Upon what is this liability contingent?
2. Why is the option writer potentially subject to unlimited losses?
3. What is the difference between an American and a European option?
4. How does an option on a futures contract differ from an option on physicals? What does the seller of an S&P 500 futures option get when the option is exercised?
5. Why might an out-of-the-money option have a positive premium?
6. How does the length of the time to expiration of an option contract affect its premium?
7. The premium on an S&P 500 futures put option with a strike price of 325 for December 90 is 17.95. How much does the buyer pay? What is the premium in dollars of a copper call futures option with a strike price of 110 for May delivery? See Table 18.10b.
8. Why is an option writer required to post margin while an option buyer normally is not?
9. If an investor expects stock prices to fall in the future, what kind of option should she buy? What kind of option should she write?
10. What is a synthetic futures position? Why would an investor assume a synthetic futures position rather than a simple futures position?

SUGGESTED READING

Ross, S. A. "Options and Efficiency." *Quarterly Journal of Economics,* February 1976, pp. 75–89.

Rubinstein, M. "An Economic Evaluation of Organized Options Markets." *Journal of Comparative Corporate Law and Securities Regulation,* June 1979, pp. 49–64.

Stoll, H. and R. Whaley. "The New Option Markets." In *Futures Markets: Their Economic Role,* ed. by Anne Peck, American Enterprise Institute for Public Policy Research, Washington, D.C., 1986, pp. 205–282.

CHAPTER
19

OPTION
PRICING

The price that an option buyer pays and that an option seller receives is the premium on the option. Like every other price, the premium on a particular option is determined by the demand for and supply of that option. This chapter discusses the factors which underlie the demand for and supply of an option, and how these factors interrelate to determine equilibrium (or fair value) premiums.

Knowledge of how options are priced is important for two reasons: to determine whether the existing option premiums are correct, and to identify profitable trading and arbitrage opportunities. In addition, option pricing models can often be used to value non-exchange-traded assets that contain option-like features.

This chapter begins with an explanation of the *put-call parity* relationship that exists between put and call option premiums. This price relationship is driven by arbitrage among the various related instruments (or assets). As such, it can be thought of as an arbitrage pricing model of option premiums.

The second section of the chapter discusses two well-known theoretical option pricing models: the Black-Scholes model, and the Black futures option model. These models are widely used by both practitioners and academics.

The final part of the chapter contains a sensitivity analysis of premiums, showing how premiums change when the underlying pricing factors change. Understanding these pricing relationships is necessary to assess the potential profitability and risk associated with the various option positions.

Readers should be forewarned that option pricing models rely on a fairly sophisticated level of mathematics which, unfortunately, is unavoidable. We have, however, tried to include in the chapter enough nonmathematical materials and exposition to permit readers to grasp the fundamental intuitions behind the various option pricing models even without fully understanding the mathematics underlying them.[1]

19.1   THE PUT-CALL PARITY PRICING RELATIONSHIP: COMMON STOCK

As discussed in Chapter 18, buying a call option together with a short position in the underlying asset creates a synthetic long put, while buying a put option in conjunction with a long asset position creates a synthetic long call option. In a market where arbitrage among all assets (or instruments) is possible, there should, therefore, exist a systematic price relationship among the various assets that can be combined to create equivalent synthetic assets.

This pricing relationship is known as the *put-call parity*, and requires that the price of a European put option on one share of stock that does not pay dividends should be equal to the combined value of a call option on one share of the same stock, with the same strike price and time to expiration as the put option, a short position of one share in the underlying stock, and a riskless investment of an amount equal to the present value of the strike price. In other words, the equilibrium put option price is

$$P = C + K \exp^{-rt} - S$$

where
P = current market price of a European put option to sell one share.
C = current market value of a European call option to buy one share.
r = riskless interest rate covering the life of the option.
t = time to expiration of the put (and call) option.
K = strike price for the put (and call) option.
S = current market price of the underlying stock.
$\exp^{-rt}$ = the exponential present value factor.

Alternatively, the price of a call option should be equal to the price of a put option with the same strike price and expiration date plus a sum equal to the current price of the underlying asset minus the price of a risk-free investment in an amount equal to the present value of the option's strike price, or

$$C = P + S - K \exp^{-rt}$$

---

[1]For a more complete discussion of option pricing models, see J. C. Cox and M. Rubinstein, *Options Markets*, Prentice-Hall, 1988.

If either of these relationships is violated, and there are no transaction costs, margins, and taxes, arbitragers can make a certain profit on a zero investment by selling the relatively overpriced option and using the proceeds to buy the relatively underpriced option together with the appropriate related positions in the underlying asset and debt instruments. Taken together, the latter positions create a synthetic option which completely hedges the risk associated with the short position in the overpriced option.

For example, if call prices are too high relative to put prices, an arbitrager can lock in a riskless profit by selling a call and simultaneously buying a put, borrowing the amount $K \exp^{-rt}$ at the risk-free rate, and buying the underlying asset. The latter creates a synthetic long call position which balances the short call position.

Alternatively, if put prices are too high relative to call prices, an arbitrager can lock in a riskless profit by selling the overpriced put and simultaneously buying a call, selling the underlying asset, and lending the amount $K \exp^{-rt}$ at the risk-free rate (which creates a synthetic long put).

To see the logic behind the put-call parity pricing relationship, consider an investment in the following positions, along with their associated payoffs at expiration: write a call option and buy a put option on one share of the same underlying stock, both with the same strike price (K) and the same expiration date (t); borrow $K \exp^{-rt}$ by selling zero-coupon bonds in that amount with maturity t; and buy one share of the underlying stock at price K.

These positions generate a current cashflow of $C - P - S + K \exp^{-rt}$, and have the following payoffs at expiration, depending on what happens to stock prices:

	Current cashflow	Expiration date	
		$S^* \leq K$	$S^* > K$
Write call	C	0	$K - S^*$
Buy put	$-P$	$K - S^*$	0
Buy stock	$-S$	S^*	S^*
Borrow	$K\exp^{-rt}$	$-K$	$-K$
Net		0	0

where S^* is the market price of the underlying stock at the expiration date.

If, at the expiration date, the stock price (S^*) is less than the strike price ($S^* \leq K$), the put will be worth $K - S^*$ and the call will expire worthless. If, on the other hand, at expiration the stock price is greater than the strike price ($S^* > K$), the call writer will lose $S^* - K$, and the put will expire worthless. In both cases, however, the investor will own the stock at expiration, worth S^*, and will have to pay K. In addition, in both cases the cashflow at expiration will be zero. Thus, a no-arbitrage equilibrium pricing relationship requires that the initial investment necessary to set up these riskless positions must be zero, or that

$$C - P - S + K \exp^{-rt} = 0$$

which in turn implies that

$$P = C + K \exp^{-rt} - S$$

and

$$C = P + S - K \exp^{-rt}$$

This shows that if S is equal to K, or both the call and put options are at-the-money, the call option premium must nevertheless be greater than the put option premium, since the strike price K is being discounted. Further, this difference increases the longer the time to expiration and the higher the interest rate (or discount factor).[2]

19.2 OPTION PRICING IN GENERAL: FUNDAMENTAL DETERMINANTS

In Chapter 18, the profit and loss profiles for various basic option positions were constructed based on the value of the underlying asset at the option's expiration date. In that analysis, an option's value depends on only two variables—the asset price at expiration, and the option's strike price. However, prior to expiration the value of an option will depend upon all of the following variables:

• the current value of the underlying stock or asset (S)
• the option's strike price (K)
• the anticipated volatility of the price of the underlying asset (σ)
• the time remaining until the option expires (t)
• the current level of the risk-free interest rate (r)

This set of variables affects both put and call values, but not always in the same way. Table 19.1 provides a summary of the impact of each of the five variables on the value of calls and puts, holding the other variables constant. In addition, the relationship of the option premium to each of these factors taken alone is depicted graphically in Figures 19-1 to 19-10 for S&P 100 stock index options on November 1, 1990 (see Table 18-6).[3]

---

[2]Later in the chapter we show that for options on some instruments, such as futures contracts, at-the-money call and put option premiums are equal.

[3]In particular, the Black-Scholes option pricing model is used. This model is discussed in the next section. In formulating these graphs we have ignored the dividend yield aspect of the S&P 100 Index. See footnote 12 for a detailed discussion of the impact of dividends on the valuation of stock options.

TABLE 19.1
Determinants of option values

Pricing factors	Effect of an increase in each pricing factor on the option value, holding other factors constant	
	Call premium	Put premium
1. Current asset price	Increase	Decrease
2. Strike price (K)	Decrease	Increase
3. Volatility (σ)	Increase	Increase
4. Time to expiration (t)	Increase	Increase
5. Interest rate (r)	Increase	Decrease

Figures 19-1 to 19-10 are generated using a standard option pricing model for which the basic data inputs are

- current S&P 100 cash index = 292.76
- strike price = 290.00
- expected annualized volatility of the S&P 100 index = 28%
- time to expiration = 50 days (December 90 options expire on December 21, 1990)
- interest rate = 7.12%

For example, to generate the relationship between the premium and the value of the S&P 100 index (Figure 19-1), we allow the S&P 100 index to vary while holding all of the other above variables constant.

19.2.1 Call Options

The importance of the *underlying asset price* and the *strike price* in determining option values before expiration is obvious. As shown in Figure 19-1, call option values increase as underlying asset prices (i.e., the S&P 100 index) rise, holding everything else constant. Similarly, the lower the strike price, the higher the call value (see Figure 19-2).

The impact of an asset's price *volatility* is less apparent. Volatility can be viewed as a measure of the dispersion of possible future asset prices. The higher the volatility, the greater the likelihood that the asset will do either very well or very poorly. A call option holder, however, while being able to capture the full dollar benefit from favorable price outcomes, will not suffer a loss from unfavorable price outcomes, since in these cases he will not exercise the call. Consequently, the higher the price volatility over the lifetime of a call, the higher is its value, everything else being equal. This positive relationship is clearly shown in Figure 19-3.

Time to expiration (t) measures the remaining life of an option. One way a longer time to expiration works is through its relationship to volatility. Over a long period of time, much can happen. Even an asset with a low volatility may

Premium in index points

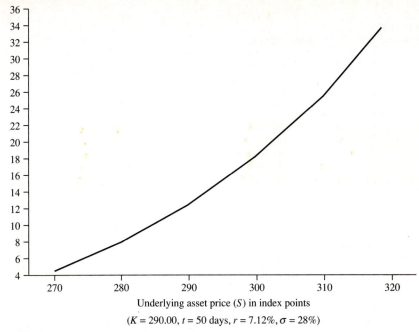

Underlying asset price (S) in index points

$(K = 290.00, t = 50 \text{ days}, r = 7.12\%, \sigma = 28\%)$

FIGURE 19-1
The relationship of a call option premium to the underlying asset price (S): S&P 100 stock index.

Premium in index points

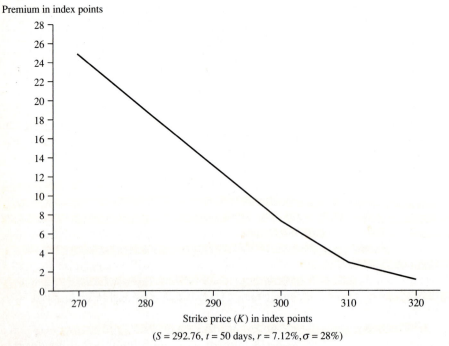

Strike price (K) in index points

$(S = 292.76, t = 50 \text{ days}, r = 7.12\%, \sigma = 28\%)$

FIGURE 19-2
The relationship of a call option premium to the strike price (K): S&P 100 stock index.

Premium in index points

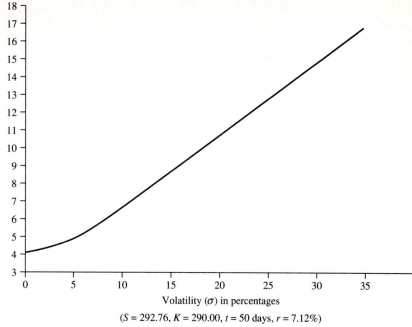

Volatility (σ) in percentages

($S = 292.76$, $K = 290.00$, $t = 50$ days, $r = 7.12\%$)

FIGURE 19-3
The relationship of a call option premium to the volatility (σ): S&P 100 stock index.

Premium in index points

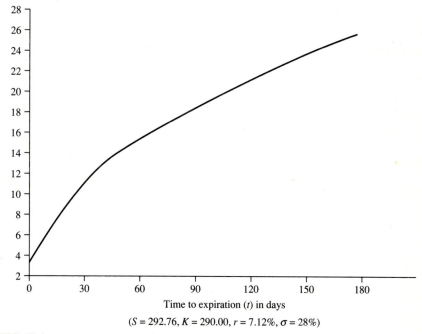

Time to expiration (t) in days

($S = 292.76$, $K = 290.00$, $r = 7.12\%$, $\sigma = 28\%$)

FIGURE 19-4
The relationship of a call option premium to the time to expiration (t): S&P 100 stock index.

Premium in index points

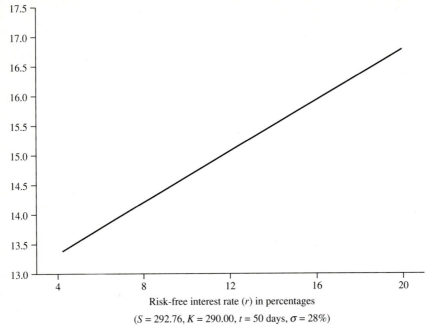

(S = 292.76, K = 290.00, t = 50 days, σ = 28%)

FIGURE 19-5
The relationship of a call option premium to the interest rate (r): S& P 100 stock index.

eventually experience a favorable price move. Call premiums, therefore, tend to be higher the more time remaining before expiration (see Figure 19-4). This time-value premium, however, shrinks to zero as the expiration date approaches. Options, consequently, are often referred to as *wasting assets.*[4]

The effect of *interest rates* is less obvious. The higher the interest rate, the lower the present value of the (strike) price that the call buyer has contracted to pay in the event of exercise. Thus, a higher interest rate has the same effect as does lowering the strike price: higher interest rates result in higher call values (see Figure 19-5). The effect of the interest rate is also related to an option's time to expiration. Since, for a given interest rate, the present value of the option's strike price decreases as t increases, everything else equal, variations in time to expiration will affect the call value through their effect on present values.[5]

---

[4] In practice, it appears that time value declines by very small increments per unit of time in the early stage of an option's life, but then declines at an increasing rate as the expiration date approaches.

[5] The role of interest rates in the determination of option premiums is complex and varies from one type of option to another. The positive relationship between a stock option's call value and the interest rate does not hold for options on futures, for example. This topic is discussed later in the chapter.

Premium in index points

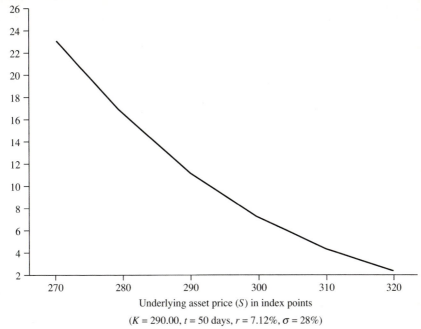

Underlying asset price (S) in index points

$(K = 290.00, t = 50 \text{ days}, r = 7.12\%, \sigma = 28\%)$

FIGURE 19-6

The relationship of a put option premium to the underlying asset price (S): S&P 100 stock index.

19.2.2 Put Options

The effects of stock prices, strike prices, and interest rates on put option values are just the reverse of those for a call. However, stock volatility and time to expiration, by raising the probability of favorable price movements, increase both put and call values. These relationships are depicted for put options in Figures 19-6 to 19-10, respectively.

In the next section the relationship between these factors and the price of an option is examined in the context of a formal mathematical model: the *Black-Scholes model*. This model yields an exact formula for pricing European call options on non-dividend-paying stocks.

19.3 THE BLACK-SCHOLES MODEL

The Black-Scholes (B-S) option pricing model is probably the most well-known and widely used pricing model in finance. Initially developed in 1973 by two academics, Fischer Black and Myron Scholes, the model was designed to price European options on non-dividend-paying stocks.[6] Subsequent work by other aca-

---

[6]Fischer Black and Myron Scholes, "The Pricing of Options and Corporate Liabilities," *The Journal of Political Economy,* June 1973, pp. 637–59.

Premium in index points

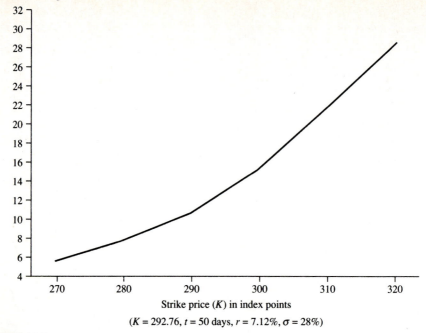

$(K = 292.76, t = 50 \text{ days}, r = 7.12\%, \sigma = 28\%)$

FIGURE 19-7

The relationship of a put option premium to the strike price (K): S&P 100 stock index.

Premium in index points

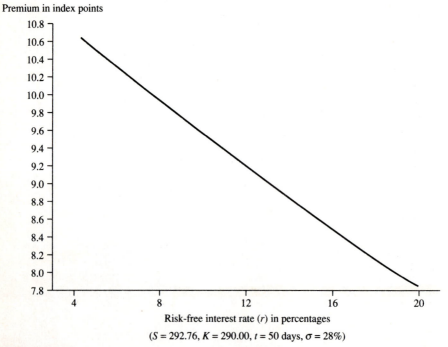

$(S = 292.76, K = 290.00, t = 50 \text{ days}, \sigma = 28\%)$

FIGURE 19-8

The relationship of a put option premium to the interest rate (r): S&P 100 stock index.

Premium in index points

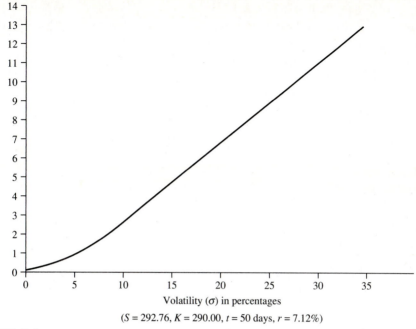

Volatility (σ) in percentages

($S = 292.76$, $K = 290.00$, $t = 50$ days, $r = 7.12\%$)

FIGURE 19-9

The relationship of a put option premium to the volatility (σ): S&P 100 stock index.

Premium in index points

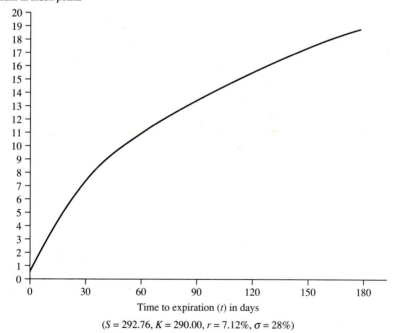

Time to expiration (t) in days

($S = 292.76$, $K = 290.00$, $r = 7.12\%$, $\sigma = 28\%$)

FIGURE 19-10

The relationship of a put option premium to the time to expiration (t): S&P 100 stock index.

demics has modified the model to make it applicable to American options, options on dividend-paying stock, and options on other instruments, such as futures contracts. An understanding of the basic Black-Scholes model, however, is fundamental to option pricing theory. While the mathematical concepts that underlie the model are complex, the pricing relationships upon which it rests are intuitively logical and are similar to those discussed earlier in the chapter. Thus, rather than explaining the derivation of the B-S model, we simply state the B-S pricing formula and show how to use it to price options.

The foundation of the model is the construction of a hypothetical risk-free portfolio, consisting of long call options and short positions in the underlying stock, on which an investor earns the riskless rate of interest. Utilizing this portfolio together with information about current stock prices and interest rates, and by hypothesizing likely values of the stock at expiration of the option, Black and Scholes derive the following equations for pricing European call options on non-dividend-paying stocks:[7]

$$C = SN(d_1) - K \exp^{-rt} N(d_2)$$

$$d_1 = \frac{ln(S/K \exp^{-rt})}{\sigma \sqrt{t}} + 0.5\sigma \sqrt{t}$$

$$d_2 = d_1 - \sigma \sqrt{t}$$

where C, S, K, r, and t are as previously defined.

σ is the annualized volatility of stock returns (specifically, the standard deviation of stock returns).

$ln(.)$ is the natural logarithm.

$N(.)$ is the cumulative probability distribution function for a standardized normal variable.[8]

These equations look complicated, but are easy to use. The appeal of the model is its simple closed-form solution, which lends itself to fast computations. The B-S model requires only five inputs, four of which are easily obtainable: the current stock price, the option's strike price, the riskless rate of interest, and the option's time to expiration. The only variable that is not directly observable

---

[7]The put option value can be easily derived from the call option value using the put-call parity relationship discussed earlier.

[8]Understanding normal and log-normal distributions is essential for option pricing. Appendix 1 provides a discussion of the normal probability distribution and compares the normal and log-normal distributions graphically. A random variable has a log-normal distribution if the natural logarithm of the variable is normally distributed. The B-S option pricing model assumes that stock prices are *log-normally* distributed. If stock prices were *normally* distributed, this would imply that it is equally likely for a stock price to move up or down. But there are natural factors that impede price movements in the downward direction. For example, a stock's price cannot drop below zero. These considerations make a log-normal distribution assumption more reasonable.

is the expected volatility of the stock's return, which is customarily estimated using historical data. The various techniques employed to estimate this volatility parameter are discussed in Section 19.5.

19.3.1 An Example: Computing the Value of a Call Option Using Black-Scholes

While the Black-Scholes pricing formulas are readily available on computers and calculators, it is useful to work through an application. Assume that on November 1, 1990, we want to price a Dec 90 European call option on Disney stock,

where S = \$92.00

K = \$95.00

t = 50 days, or $\frac{50}{365}$ (which equals 0.137) of a year (the option expires on December 21, 1990)

r = 7.12%

σ = 35%

Also assume that Disney stock does not pay dividends.

The call option value is derived as follows:

1. Compute the present value of the strike price:

$$Ke^{-rt} = \$95 \exp^{(-0.0712)(0.1370)} = \$94.08$$

2. Compute d_1 and d_2:

$$d_1 = \frac{ln(S/K \exp^{-rt})}{\sigma \sqrt{t}} + 0.5\sigma \sqrt{t}$$

$$d_1 = \frac{ln(\$92.00/\$94.08)}{0.35 \sqrt{0.1370}} + (0.5)(0.35) \sqrt{0.1370} = -0.1082$$

$$d_2 = d_1 - \sigma \sqrt{t}$$

$$d_2 = -0.1082 - 0.35 \sqrt{0.1370} = -0.2377$$

3. Compute $N(d_1)$ and $N(d_2)$:[9]

$N(d_1)$ and $N(d_2)$ are the values in the cumulative standard normal distribution that correspond to d_1 = −0.1082 and d_2 = −0.2377. In other words, they are the probabilities that the price at expiration will be 0.1082 and 0.2377 standard deviations below the mean, (i.e., 0). These probabilities can be found by using the procedure described in Appendix 1 and Table 19A.1, and are

---

[9]See Appendix 1 for a discussion of how to utilize the standard normal distribution table to derive $N(d_1)$ and $N(d_2)$.

$$N(d_1) = 0.4570$$

$$N(d_2) = 0.4061$$

4. Compute the fair value of the call option:

$$C = (\$92.00)(0.4570) - (\$95.00)(0.4061) = \$3.46$$

On November 1, 1990, the actual market price for Disney's Dec 95 call option was $4.00. In computing the option value in this example, we have ignored the fact that Disney stock pays dividends and that the option is American, not European. Thus, our computed value should be lower than the option's market value because it does not reflect either the dividend income or the potential benefits of the right of early exercise.[10]

19.3.2   Modifications of the Black-Scholes Model

The Black-Scholes option pricing model is based on a number of restrictive assumptions:

1. The underlying asset cannot pay discrete dividends or accrue interest payments.
2. The option being valued is European (it cannot be exercised before the expiration date).
3. The risk-free interest rate is constant over the life of the option.
4. The underlying asset returns are normally distributed, with constant mean and standard deviation.
5. All asset markets are perfectly efficient, with continuous trading and zero transaction costs, and no taxes.
6. The short selling of securities with full use of proceeds is permitted.

As mentioned earlier, the Black-Scholes model was originally developed for pricing European call options on non-dividend-paying stocks. In practice, stocks pay dividends, some types of options allow early exercise, interest rates

---

[10]A number of empirical studies have attempted to test the accuracy of option pricing models by seeing whether profitable arbitrage opportunities exist. Some find that such opportunities do exist if transaction costs are not considered, but that even small transaction costs eliminate these opportunities. Other studies find that profitable arbitrage opportunities still exist when transaction costs are considered. One problem with all of these studies is their use of closing price quotations to determine the price of the options. If trading is thin, options may not be purchasable at quoted prices. See D. Chiras and S. Manaster, "The Information Content of Option Prices and a Test of Market Efficiency," *Journal of Financial Economics,* 6: 213–34, 1978; D. Galai, "A Test of Market Efficiency of the Chicago Board Options Exchange," *Journal of Business,* 50: 167–97, 1977; and R. Trippi, "A Test of Option Market Efficiency Using a Random-Walk Valuation Model," *Journal of Economics and Business,* 29: 93–98, 1977.

are not constant, and trading may not be continuous. Thus, the simple assumptions underlying the Black-Scholes model are often violated in practice.[11]

To value options when one or more of the above assumptions is violated, a number of alternative option pricing models have been developed that are basically modifications of the Black-Scholes model.[12] These include models to value American options and models that price options on different assets, that permit non-constant risk-free interest rates, that allow changing stock volatility, and that incorporate discontinuous stock price movements.[13]

---

[11]Many researchers have found that the original Black-Scholes model is quite robust even when some of these basic assumptions are violated.

[12]The Black-Scholes model, for example, can be used to price European options on dividend-paying stocks. In this case, the stock price is reduced by the present value of all the expected dividends paid during the life of the option, where the discounting is done from the ex-dividend dates and at the risk-free rate. A dividend is included in the calculations only if its ex-dividend date occurs during the life of the option. Further, the Black-Scholes formula is applicable to pricing American call options on non-dividend-paying stocks, since early exercise of an option is never optimal. See Robert Merton, "Theory of Rational Option Pricing," *Bell Journal of Economics and Management Science,* Spring 1973, pp. 141–83; and Clifford Smith, "Option Pricing: A Review," *Journal of Financial Economics,* January–March 1976, pp. 3–51.

With respect to American call options on dividend-paying stocks, there is some probability that, just before the stock goes ex-dividend, the call will be exercised. This implies that there is a finite ex-dividend stock price above which the call will be exercised (and below which the call will be held). On the boundary, the call option holder will be indifferent. In order to capture the possibility of early exercise, an approximate pricing procedure is used. See Richard Roll, "An Analytic Valuation Formula for Unprotected American Call Options on Stocks with Known Dividends," *Journal of Financial Economics,* November 1977, pp. 251–58; Richard Geske and Richard Roll, "On Valuing American Call Options with the Black-Scholes European Formula," *Journal of Finance,* 39: 443–55, 1984; and Robert Whaley, "On the Valuation of American Call Options on Stocks with Known Dividends," *Journal of Financial Economics,"* June 1981, pp. 207–11.

The pricing of American put options is less clear. It can be optimal to exercise American put options on non-dividend-paying stocks prior to expiration. An American put option should be exercised early if it is sufficiently deep in-the-money (i.e., the stock price is sufficiently low). However, dividends make it less likely that an American put option will be exercised early. It can, for example, be shown that it is never worth exercising an American put on a dividend-paying stock immediately prior to an ex-dividend date. Thus, to price an American put option, numerical analysis is often used. See Michael Parkinson, "Option Pricing: The American Put," *Journal of Finance,* January 1977, pp. 21–36; Michael Brennan and Eduardo Schwartz, "The Valuation of American Put Options," *Journal of Finance,* May 1977, pp. 449–62; and H.E. Johnson, "An Analytic Approximation to the American Put Price," *Journal of Financial and Quantitative Analysis,* March 1983, pp. 141–48.

In sum, analytic formulas for valuing European puts and calls are available for options on both dividend-paying and non-dividend-paying stocks. In the absence of dividends, American calls have the same values as European calls. When there are dividends, American calls can still sometimes be valued analytically using approximate procedures. There is, however, no analytic formula for the valuation of an American put option on either a dividend or a non-dividend-paying stock.

[13]See G. Barone-Adesi and R. Whaley, "Efficient Analytic Approximation of American Option Values," *Journal of Finance,* 42:301–20, 1987; J. C. Cox and S. A. Ross, "The Valuation of Options for Alternative Stochastic Processes," *Journal of Financial Economics,* 3:145–66, 1976; J. C. Cox, M. Rubinstein, and S. A. Ross, "Option Pricing: A Simplied Approach," *Journal of Financial Economics,* 7:229–63, 1979; and R. Merton, "Option Pricing When Underlying Stock Returns are Discontinuous," *Journal of Financial Economics,* 4:125–44, 1976.

Among these alternative models, the *binomial* option pricing model has proven to be one of the most popular. This model can be used to value American put options as well as options on a stock that pays dividends. In addition, it has proven useful in valuing a variety of tailor-made options that are sold over-the-counter. Appendix 2 provides a description of the binomial option pricing model.

Modifications of the Black-Scholes model have also been made in order to price options on different (non-stock) assets, such as options on physical commodities, foreign currencies, debt instruments, and futures contracts. A brief discussion of models that are particularly relevant to the focus of this book is provided below.

1. **Foreign Currencies.** The deliverable instrument on a foreign exchange option is a fixed amount of the underlying foreign currency. In Chapter 14 we show that the forward premium or discount on foreign currencies is determined by the difference between the riskless interest rates in the relevant countries, or by the interest rate parity relationship. Thus, *both foreign and domestic* interest rates play a role in the valuation of foreign currency options, in contrast to the B-S model in which only the domestic interest rate is involved. Garman and Kohlhagen have modified the B-S model to price foreign currency options by incorporating both foreign and domestic riskless interest rates.[14]

2. **Debt Instruments.** Most approaches to option valuation assume that the riskless interest rate is constant over the life of the option, and that there is little correlation between movements in short-term interest rates and underlying asset prices. While this may be a reasonable assumption for stocks and many physical commodities, it is not for options on debt instruments (e.g., T-bonds and T-notes). In general, there is a positive correlation between long-term and short-term interest rate movements, and, therefore, a negative relationship between the underlying bond prices and short-term interest rates. Thus, a rise in short-term rates will cause T-bond prices to decline and, consequently, call option prices to decline. Further, rising short-term rates will increase the discount factor and cause option prices to decline even further. Several modified option pricing models have been developed to account for these added complexities.[15]

---

[14]M. B. Garman and S. W. Kohlhagen, "Foreign Currency Option Values," *Journal of International Money and Finance,* 2:231–37, 1983; I. Giddy, "Foreign Exchange Options," *The Journal of Futures Markets,* Summer 1983, pp. 143–66.

[15]G. Courtadon, "The Pricing of Options on Default-free Bonds," *Journal of Financial and Quantitative Analysis,* 1982, pp. 71–100; and M. Brennan and E. Schwartz, "Alternative Methods for Valuing Debt Options," Working Paper 888, University of British Columbia, Vancouver, B.C., 1982; R. Rendelman and B. Barter, "The Pricing of Options on Debt Securities," *Journal of Financial and Quantitative Analysis,* 15: 11–24, 1980.

3. Futures Contracts. A model to value options on futures contracts (or futures options) has been developed by Fischer Black and is discussed in the next section.[16]

Finally, the Black-Scholes model can be generalized to price options on a variety of assets, including securities, commodities, currencies, futures, and forward contracts.[17] This generalized option pricing model is discussed in Appendix 3.

19.4 THE BLACK MODEL FOR FUTURES OPTIONS

The original Black-Scholes option pricing model is based on the intuition that a riskless hedge portfolio which consists of stock options together with related positions in the underlying stock must yield the riskless interest rate on any funds invested. In the case of futures options, such a riskless portfolio, consisting of a position in futures options and an offsetting position in the underlying futures contract, requires no initial investment, and therefore should not earn any return. Based on this insight, Fischer Black developed the following futures option pricing equation:

$$C_f = \exp^{-rt}[FN(d_1^*) - KN(d_2^*)]$$

$$d_1^* = \frac{ln(F/K)}{\sigma_f \sqrt{t}} + 0.5\sigma_f \sqrt{t}$$

$$d_2^* = d_1^* - \sigma_f \sqrt{t}$$

where the variable definitions are the same as those in the Black-Scholes model, except that

- C_f is the premium on a call option on a futures contract.
- F is the current futures price.
- σ_f is the expected annualized volatility of the futures returns (where returns are defined as percentage changes in futures prices).

Since no initial investment is required in establishing a position in a futures contract, there is no interest rate term (r) in the d_1^* and d_2^* equations. The Black model was originally devised for valuing European options on forward contracts. However, if the riskless rate of interest is assumed to be constant during the life of the futures option, this model is equally applicable to valuing European futures options.

---

[16]Fischer Black, "The Pricing of Commodity Contracts," *Journal of Financial Economics,* 1976, 167-79.

[17]James F. Meisner and John A. Richards, "Option Premium Dynamics: With Applications to Fixed Income Portfolio Analysis," in *Advances in Bond Analysis and Portfolio Strategies,* edited by F. Fabozzi and D. Garlicki, Chicago: Probus Publishing, 1987, pp. 395–415.

19.4.1   An Example: Using the Black Model to Value Futures Options

On November 1, 1990, the following data for the 305-strike call option on the December 90 S&P 500 futures existed:

- $F = 308.45$
- $K = 305.00$
- $r = 7.12\%$
- $t = 49$ days, or $\frac{49}{365}$ (which equals 0.1342) of a year (the option expires on December 20, 1990)
- $\sigma_f = 28\%$

1. Compute $N(d_1^*)$ and $N(d_2^*)$:

$$d_1^* = \frac{ln(F/K)}{\sigma_f \sqrt{t}} + 0.5\sigma_f \sqrt{t}$$

$$d_1^* = \frac{ln(308.45/305.00)}{0.28 \sqrt{0.1342}} + (0.5)(0.28) \sqrt{0.1342} = 0.1605$$

$$N(d_1^*) = 0.5636$$

$$d_2^* = d_1^* - \sigma_f \sqrt{t}$$

$$d_2^* = 0.1605 - 0.28 \sqrt{0.1342} = 0.0579$$

$$N(d_2^*) = 0.5231$$

2. Compute the Dec 305 call option value:

$$C_f = \exp^{-rt}[FN(d_1^*) - KN(d_2^*)]$$

$$= \exp^{(-0.0712)(0.1342)}[(308.45)(0.5636) - (305.00)(0.5231)]$$

$$= 14.16$$

In fact, Table 18.10 shows that the market value on November 1 of the Dec 305 call option on the Dec 90 S&P 500 futures was 14.35, which is very close to the computed theoretical value.[18]

---

[18]The S&P 500 futures options are American style while the Black futures option pricing model is for European exercise. Thus, it is not surprising that the theoretical value computed above is less than the actual option price, since it does not incorporate the right of early exercise.

19.4.2 The Put-Call Parity Relationship for Futures Options

As discussed in Section 19.1, the price of a European put option on one share of stock that does not pay dividends should be equal to the combined value of a call option on one share of the same stock with the same strike price and time to expiration, a riskless investment of an amount equal to the present value of the put's strike price, and a short position of one share in the underlying stock. Thus, the equilibrium put option price is

$$P = C + K \exp^{-rt} - S$$

In the case of futures options, however, no initial investment is required to buy or sell a futures contract (in contrast to buying or selling stock). Thus, there is no need to borrow money, and the above put-call parity relationship for futures options simplifies to

$$P_f = C_f + K - F$$

where the subscript (f) indicates a futures option contract. This equation states that the put premium will equal the call premium plus the difference between the strike price and the underlying futures price (i.e., $K - F$). Since at-the-money calls and puts have no intrinsic value (i.e., $K = F$, or $K - F = 0$), their premiums are identical.

On November 1, 1990, the Dec 310 call premium (C_f) on the December 90 S&P 500 futures option was 11.40 index points (see Table 18.10b), and the December 90 S&P futures price was 308.45 (see Table 18.13). Based on the put-call parity relationship, the no-arbitrage Dec 310 put option premium should have been

$$P_f = C_f + K - F$$
$$= 11.40 + 310.00 - 308.45$$
$$= 12.95$$

As shown in Table 18.10b, the market price for the Dec 310 put option on November 1, 1990, was exactly 12.95 index points.

If the Dec 310 put were not priced at 12.95, either the call or the put, or both, would be mispriced. If the option were overpriced, an arbitrager would sell the option. If underpriced, he would buy the option. In each case he could lock in the disparity between the fair market value and the prevailing market price by establishing the corresponding offsetting position. In particular, arbitragers would engage in either conversion or reverse conversion arbitrage, which are discussed and illustrated in the following sections.

Put Undervalued, Call Overvalued

CONVERSION ARBITRAGE. Table 19.2 provides a conversion arbitrage example assuming that the Dec 310 S&P futures put option is *undervalued* by 0.95 index points. A conversion transaction entails the sale of a call, and the purchase of a put together with the purchase of the underlying futures (a synthetic call), where the put and call share a common strike price and expiration date.

Arbitrage

TABLE 19.2
Options on futures: Conversion arbitrage

Prices on November 1, 1990:

December 90 S&P futures	=	308.45 index points
Dec 310 call option	=	11.40 index points
Dec 310 put option	=	12.95 index points

In Section 19.4.2, we showed that the no-arbitrage Dec 310 put premium is also 12.95 index points. Suppose, however, that the Dec 310 put were at 12.00 index points, or that the put option were underpriced. In this case, the correct arbitrage transaction is to do a conversion: buy puts, buy futures, and sell calls.
The expected arbitrage profit would be $(12.95 - 12.00) \times \$500 = \$475$.

November 1, 1990:

	Cash flows
i) Buy one Dec 310 put at 12.00 ($12.00 \times \$500$)	$(6,000)
ii) Go long one Dec 90 S&P futures at 308.45	0
iii) Sell one Dec 310 call at 11.40 ($11.40 \times \$500$)	5,700
Net option premium paid	$ (300)

December 20, 1990:

	Gain (loss)
If Dec 90 S&P futures price is at 320.00, or $F > K$:	
i) Loss on the put (the premium)	$(6,000)
ii) Long futures position is offset by being assigned a short futures position at the 310 strike price, for a gain of $[(310 - 308.45) \times \$500]$	775
iii) Retain the call premium	5,700
Net arbitrage profit	$ 475
If Dec 90 S&P futures price is at 290, or $F < K$:	
i) Cost of the put (the premium)	$(6,000)
ii) Long futures position is offset by exercising the put to acquire a short position at the 310 strike price, for a gain of $[(310 - 308.45) \times \$500]$	775
iii) Retain the call premium	5,700
Net arbitrage profit	$ 475

In the example in Table 19.2, the arbitrager buys the undervalued Dec 310 put at 12.00, goes long the December 90 futures at 308.45, and sells the Dec 310 call at 11.40, locking in an arbitrage profit of $475. If, by December 20, the option's expiration day, the December 90 futures price rises above the 310 strike price to 320, the Dec 310 put will be worthless and the arbitrager will lose the entire $6000 option premium paid on November 1. However, the arbitrager will retain the $5700 call option income. In addition, when the Dec 310 call is exercised, the arbitrager will be assigned a short futures position at 310, for a net gain of $775. In sum, the arbitrager realizes a net profit of $475.

If, on the other hand, by December 20, the December 90 futures price declines to 290, the arbitrager will exercise the in-the-money put, acquiring a short futures position at 310, and will close out his existing long futures position for a gain of $775. Also, since the call will be out-of-the-money, the arbitrager will have a profit on the call equal to the entire call premium. After subtracting the put option premium paid earlier, the arbitrager again realizes a net gain of $475.

Thus, the conversion transaction permits the arbitrager to lock in a profit of $475, no matter which way futures prices move. The profit from a conversion can be determined by comparing the difference between the call and put premiums with the difference between the underlying market price and the strike price, or by the formula

(Call premium − put premium) − (underlying price − strike price)

$$[(11.40 - 12.00) - (308.45 - 310.00)] \times \$500 = \$475$$

Put Overvalued, Call Undervalued

REVERSE CONVERSION ARBITRAGE. Reverse conversion arbitrage transactions (or simply *reversals*) are similar to conversion transactions except that all of the legs of the transactions are reversed. Instead of selling calls, buying puts, and buying the underlying instruments, the arbitrager buys calls, sells puts, and sells the underlying instrument, where once again the put and call share a common strike price and expiration date. A reverse conversion is done when the put is *overvalued* or the call is *undervalued*. Table 19.3 provides an example of reverse conversion arbitrage assuming that the Dec 310 put is overvalued.

The profit from a reverse conversion can also be determined by comparing the difference between the put and call premiums with the difference between the strike price and the underlying market price, or by the formula

(Put premium − call premium) − (strike price − underlying price)

$$[(14.00 - 11.40) - (310 - 308.45)] \times \$500 = \$525$$

19.5 ESTIMATION OF PRICE VOLATILITY

In all of the option pricing models the expected volatility of the underlying asset returns (or of the percentage changes in prices) is an important determinant in the price of an option. Such volatility reflects the potential of a particular call or put to move into-the-money, permitting profitable exercise. Accordingly, option sellers demand a higher premium and option buyers are more willing to pay a higher premium if expected volatility is higher.

Expected volatility is not directly observable. Different methods have been developed to estimate or to predict this volatility over the life of an option. The two most common approaches are to use historical and implied volatility estimates.

TABLE 19.3
Options on futures: Reverse conversion arbitrage

Prices on November 1, 1990:

December 90 S&P futures   =   308.45 index points
Dec 310 call option   =   11.40 index points
Dec 310 put option   =   12.95 index points

In Section 19.4.2, we showed that the no-arbitrage Dec 310 put premium is also 12.95 index points. Suppose, however, that the Dec 310 put were at 14.00 index points, or that the put option were overpriced. In this case, the correct arbitrage transaction is to do a reverse conversion: sell puts, sell futures, and buy calls. The expected arbitrage profit would be $(14 - 12.95) \times \$500 = \$525$.

November 1, 1990:

	Cash flows
i) Sell one Dec 310 put at 14.00 (14.00×$500)	$7,000
ii) Go short one Dec 90 S&P futures at 308.45	0
iii) Buy one Dec 310 call at 11.40 (11.40×$500)	(5,700)
Net option premium received	$1,300

December 20, 1990:

	Gain (loss)
If Dec 90 S&P futures price is at 320.00, or $F > K$:	
i) Gain on the put (the premium)	$7,000
ii) Short futures position is offset by exercising the call option to obtain a long futures position at the 310 strike price, for a gain of $[(308.45 - 310) \times \$500]$	(775)
iii) Cost of the call	(5,700)
Net arbitrage profit	$ 525
If Dec 90 S&P futures price is at 290, or $F < K$:	
i) Retain the entire put premium	$7,000
ii) Short futures position is offset by being assigned a long futures position at the 310 strike price, for a loss of $[(308.45 - 310) \times \$500]$	(775)
iii) Cost of the call	(5,700)
Net arbitrage profit	$ 525

19.5.1   Historical Price Volatility

Price volatility refers to the degree of variability of price changes. A commonly used measure of this volatility is the standard deviation of previous (or historical) daily, weekly, or even monthly percentage changes in prices.[19]

Depending on which data interval is used to calculate the standard deviation of prices, annualized price volatility (σ) is obtained by multiplying the calculated standard deviation by the square root of the number of periods, or

For monthly data: $\sigma = \sqrt{12} \times$ monthly standard deviation

For weekly data: $\sigma = \sqrt{52} \times$ weekly standard deviation

For daily data: $\sigma = \sqrt{252} \times$ daily standard deviation[20]

Using previous data to estimate price volatility implicitly assumes that past price volatility is a good predictor of price volatility in the future. This assumption may not always be appropriate.

For example, suppose that on November 1, 1990, an investor wishes to compute the no-arbitrage premiums for options on the December 90 S&P 500 futures contract. To use the Black model he must first obtain an estimate of the expected price volatility of the December 90 futures contract for the period November 2 to December 20. He decides to look first at historical price volatility.

Table 19.4 provides historical prices for the December 90 S&P futures contract from September 3 to October 31, 1990, or for the two months prior to November 1. The third column in the table provides the daily percentage changes of futures prices. In addition, the table gives the standard deviations of the percentage price changes for both September and October: 1.02 percent and 1.66 percent. Thus, the annualized price volatilities for September and October are 16.19 percent and 26.35 percent respectively.

These estimates make it clear that different time periods can give totally different estimates of volatility. Investors using historical price volatility, therefore, must select a previous time period which they believe reflects conditions similar to those that they expect will exist during the period covered by their option

---

[19]The percentage price change is often calculated as the difference between the natural logarithms of the current and previous prices. Thus, the standard deviation (sd) of percentage price changes is computed as

$$sd = \frac{\sum_{t=1}^{N}(X_t - \overline{X})^2}{N}$$

where N = number of observations

$X_t = \ln(Y_t / Y_{t-1})$, i.e., the percentage price change

Y_t = asset price in period t

$\overline{X}$ = arithmetic mean of the X_t

[20]There are 252 trading days in a year.

TABLE 19.4
Historical price volatility: S&P 500 Dec 90 futures contracts,
September 3 to October 31, 1990

Date	Futures price	Percentage change (in %)	Date	Futures price	Percentage change (in %)
Sep 03	326.35		Oct 01	318.25	3.76
Sep 04	327.80	0.44	Oct 02	318.35	0.03
Sep 05	328.50	0.21	Oct 03	313.70	−1.47
Sep 06	324.10	−1.35	Oct 04	315.30	0.51
Sep 07	327.75	1.12	Oct 05	314.85	−0.14
Sep 10	325.10	−0.81	Oct 08	317.40	0.81
Sep 11	325.30	0.06	Oct 09	305.75	−3.74
Sep 12	325.70	0.12	Oct 10	302.20	−1.17
Sep 13	321.75	−1.22	Oct 11	297.35	−1.62
Sep 14	319.30	−0.76	Oct 12	301.70	1.45
Sep 17	321.20	0.59	Oct 15	306.00	1.42
Sep 18	321.60	0.12	Oct 16	301.25	−1.56
Sep 19	318.40	−1.00	Oct 17	300.60	−0.22
Sep 20	314.35	−1.28	Oct 18	308.15	2.48
Sep 21	314.75	0.13	Oct 19	313.05	1.58
Sep 24	307.50	−2.33	Oct 22	315.50	0.78
Sep 25	311.40	1.26	Oct 23	313.80	−0.54
Sep 26	308.30	−1.00	Oct 24	315.45	0.52
Sep 27	302.80	−1.80	Oct 25	311.40	−1.29
Sep 28	306.50	1.21	Oct 29	303.30	−2.64
			Oct 30	305.75	0.80
			Oct 31	305.40	−0.11

Daily standard deviations: Annualized standard deviations:
September: 1.02% $1.02\% \times \sqrt{252} = 16.19\%$
October: 1.66% $1.66\% \times \sqrt{252} = 26.35\%$

contracts. Further, they must determine the length of the time period to use to estimate volatility, how to weight the observations, and whether to use weekly, daily, or, if available, transaction data. In practice, most investors simply rely on *daily* price data.

19.5.2 Implied Price Volatility

Implied price volatility is an estimate of expected volatility that can be derived from actual option premiums. It is the volatility that the marketplace currently expects. *priced into the option already.*

More specifically, if observed option premiums are taken as a given, the only variable in the Black-Scholes (or in the Black) option pricing model that is not directly observable is price volatility. Thus, instead of using the model to solve for the option premium, the model can be solved for the price volatility that is consistent with the market-determined option premium. The resulting estimate is commonly known as the implied price volatility.

The following example illustrates how to calculate the implied price volatility embedded in the 310 call premium on the December 90 S&P 500 futures on November 1, 1990, using the Black model. As shown in Table 18.10, the price of this option is 11.40, and the December 90 S&P futures price is 308.45. In addition, the risk-free interest rate is 7.12 percent and there are 49 days remaining until expiration of the option. Thus

$$C_f = \exp^{-rt}[FN(d_1^*) - KN(d_2^*)]$$

and

$$11.40 = \exp^{(-0.0712)(0.1342)}[(308.45)N(d_1^*) - (310.00)N(d_2^*)]$$

$$d_1^* = \frac{\ln(308.45/310.00)}{\sigma_f^* \sqrt{0.1342}} + 0.5\sigma_f^* \sqrt{0.1342}$$

$$d_2^* = d_1^* - \sigma_f^* \sqrt{0.1342}$$

Solving these equations for the implied volatility (σ_f^*) yields

$$\sigma_f^* = 27.16\%$$

Solving for σ_f^* requires tedious iterative calculations. Fortunately, there are many software programs and option calculators available that can quickly make these computations. Option traders, therefore, can compare their own expectations of future price volatility with the implied price volatility. If these are not consistent with one another, either the option premium is wrong or the trader's expected volatility estimate is wrong.

Table 19.5 provides the volatilities that are implied by the different option premiums (for different strike prices) on the December 90 and March 91 S&P 500 futures options, on November 1, 1990. Different premiums for these options, for

TABLE 19.5
Implied volatilities: S&P 500 futures options, November 1, 1990

Strike price	December 90 call		March 91 call	
	Market price (points)	Implied volatility (%)	Market price (points)	Implied volatility (%)
300	17.55	29.39		
305	14.35	28.31	23.70	27.92
310	11.40	27.16	20.95	27.45
315	8.80	26.06	18.20	26.73
320	6.55	25.00	15.20	25.42
325	4.70	24.02	13.35	25.41
Current futures price:		308.45		311.00
Time to expiration:		49 days		140 days

TABLE 19.6
Volatility of Dec 90 S&P 500 futures prices:
November 1 to December 20,1990

Date	Futures price	Rate of change (in %)
Nov 01	308.50	1.01
Nov 02	313.25	1.53
Nov 05	315.65	0.76
Nov 06	311.80	−1.23
Nov 07	307.15	−1.50
Nov 08	308.30	0.37
Nov 09	315.60	2.34
Nov 12	320.95	1.68
Nov 13	319.30	−0.52
Nov 14	321.70	0.75
Nov 15	318.30	−1.06
Nov 16	317.90	−0.13
Nov 19	320.45	0.80
Nov 20	317.00	−1.08
Nov 21	317.25	0.08
Nov 22	317.85	0.19
Nov 23	315.60	−0.71
Nov 26	317.60	0.63
Nov 27	319.25	0.52
Nov 28	319.05	−0.06
Nov 29	317.15	−0.60
Nov 30	323.90	2.11
Dec 03	324.30	0.12
Dec 04	327.00	0.83
Dec 05	330.40	1.03
Dec 07	328.40	−0.61
Dec 10	329.10	0.21
Dec 11	328.20	−0.27
Dec 12	331.40	0.97
Dec 13	329.75	−0.50
Dec 14	326.95	−0.85
Dec 17	326.60	−0.11
Dec 18	330.60	1.22
Dec 19	330.10	−0.15
Dec 20	329.80	−0.09

Daily standard deviation: 0.93%
Annualized standard deviation: $0.93\% \times \sqrt{252} = 14.76\%$

the *same delivery date*, imply different implied volatilities. These differences may be due to imperfections in the data, or to traders assigning different probabilities to premature exercise, according to whether the option is in- or out-of-the-money.

The existence of different implied volatility estimates for options with the same expiration dates raises the question of which of the implied volatilities is the most accurate prediction of future price volatility. A common approach is to form a weighted average of the implied volatilities, where the weights reflect a trader's view of the potential accuracy of the volatility estimates. This is often called the *composite implied price volatility.*[21]

19.5.3 Summary

Which volatility estimate—historical or implied—provides the best prediction of future volatility? Table 19.6 shows the December 90 S&P 500 futures prices that actually occurred during the period from November 1 through December 20, 1990. The actual volatility during this period was 14.76 percent, much lower than either the historical or implied price volatility estimates. Neither the historical volatilities in Table 19.4 nor the implied volatilities in Table 19.5 were, therefore, very accurate predictors of actual volatility. Thus, expected price volatility is continually changing and is difficult to predict.[22]

19.6 SENSITIVITY OF OPTION PREMIUMS

Equally important with understanding how options are priced is to understand how option premiums change when the basic pricing factors change. In Section 19.2 the relationships of option premiums to the underlying asset price, price volatility, time to expiration, and interest rates were discussed briefly. This section further examines the *sensitivity* of option premiums to these factors.

Table 19.7 provides a sensitivity analysis of the premiums for various December 90 S&P 500 futures options on November 1, 1990. The first row of Table 19.7 shows the actual (market) option premiums on November 1. In the second and third rows these premiums are disaggregated into their intrinsic and time-value components. As discussed earlier in Chapter 18, intrinsic value is the amount by

---

[21]The composite implied volatility is an important tool in option trading. The common procedure is to assign a heavier weight to options that are close to the money, have longer maturities, and are actively traded. Generally, the more active a market is, the more efficient is the market. Most weighting systems used in commercial computer packages also weight option implied volatilities according to the sensitivity of a particular option premium to changes in volatility.

[22]Several studies have shown that the accuracy of estimates of historical volatilities can be increased by using daily open, high, and low prices in addition to closing prices. See M. Garman and M. Klass, "On the Estimation of Security Price Volatilities from Historical Data," *Journal of Business,* 53: 67–78; and M. Parkinson, "The Extreme Value Method for Estimating the Variance of the Rate of Return," *Journal of Business,* 53: 61–65, 1980.

TABLE 19.7
Sensitivity analysis: Dec 90 S&P 500 futures options, November 1, 1990

			Strike price			
	300	**305**	**310**	**315**	**320**	**325**
			Call options			
Market value	17.5500	14.3500	11.4000	8.8000	6.5500	4.7000
Intrinsic value	8.4500	3.4500	0.0000	0.0000	0.0000	0.0000
Time value	9.1000	10.9000	11.4000	8.8000	6.5500	4.7000
Delta	0.6204	0.5586	0.4962	0.4348	0.3758	0.3203
Gamma	0.0119	0.0123	0.0125	0.0123	0.0119	0.0112
Theta (per day)	0.1179	0.1232	0.1253	0.1242	0.1202	0.1137
Lambda (per 1%)	0.4239	0.4408	0.4465	0.4413	0.4259	0.4020
Rho (per 1%)	−2.3560	−1.9260	−1.5300	−1.1810	−0.8790	−0.6310
			Put options			
Market value	9.2500	10.9500	12.9500	15.2500	17.9500	21.0500
Intrinsic value	0.0000	0.0000	1.5500	6.5500	11.5500	16.5500
Time value	9.2500	10.9500	11.4000	8.7000	6.4000	4.5000
Delta	−0.3701	−0.4319	−0.4943	−0.5557	−0.6147	−0.6702
Gamma	0.0119	0.0123	0.0125	0.0123	0.0119	0.0112
Theta (per day)	0.1195	0.1239	0.1250	0.1229	0.1179	0.1105
Lambda (per 1%)	0.4239	0.4408	0.4465	0.4413	0.4259	0.4020
Rho (per 1%)	−1.2420	−1.4700	−1.7390	−2.0470	−2.4100	−2.8260

Actual December 90 S&P 500 futures price on November 1, 1990 is 308.45 (see Table 18.13).

which an option (call or put) is in-the-money. An option's time value is the amount by which the actual option premium differs from the intrinsic value, or

$$Premium = intrinsic\ value + time\ value$$

For example, on November 1 the December 90 S&P 500 futures price was 308.45, and the premium on the Dec 315 put was 15.25. Thus, the intrinsic value portion of the premium was 6.55 index points, and the time value component was 8.70 index points.

Table 19.7 also displays two obvious characteristics of option premiums. First, for a *given price* of the underlying asset (or futures), the intrinsic value of a call (put) increases as the strike price of the option decreases (increases); and second, the time value is highest for options at-the-money or close to being at-the-money. The latter occurs because an at-the-money option has the highest likelihood of gaining intrinsic value relative to the likelihood of its losing intrinsic value. More specifically, a deep out-of-the-money option has little potential to gain intrinsic value, and a deep in-the-money option has about as much potential to lose intrinsic value as to gain it. In contrast, an at-the-money option has no intrinsic value to lose, but still has about a 50–50 chance of gaining intrinsic value.

Finally, rows 4 through 8 in Table 19.7 provide various measures of the sensitivity of option premiums to each of the underlying pricing factors. These are discussed below.[23]

19.6.1 Delta: Changes in Option Prices Relative to the Underlying Futures Price

For a given option, an increase in the underlying asset price causes call premiums to increase and put premiums to decrease (everything else being constant). The change in the price of a call option (C_f) with respect to a given change in the underlying futures (F) or asset price is called the option's *delta* (δ).

More specifically, delta is defined as:

$$\delta = \frac{\partial C_f}{\partial F} > 0$$

For example, a delta of 0.4962 on the December 310 S&P 500 futures call option means that a unit change in the underlying futures price (such as from 308.45 to 309.45) will cause a 0.4962 unit (or index point) change in the call option premium—from 11.40 to 11.8962. The relationship between option prices and underlying asset prices, however, is nonlinear. This nonlinear relationship is readily apparent in row 4 of Table 19.7, and is shown graphically in Figure 19-11 for the Dec 310 call premium and in Figure 19-12 for the Dec 310 put premium.[24]

More specifically, the value of a call option's delta always varies between 0 and 1. Deep out-of-the-money options are little affected by changes in the underlying price, and have deltas close to 0. Deep in-the-money option premiums consist almost entirely of intrinsic value. Consequently, such premiums are closely related to the underlying asset prices, and have deltas close to 1. At-the-money options have deltas around 0.5. For example, in Table 19.7, the Dec 310 call option has a delta close to 0.5; the Dec 325 call, which is out-of-the-money, has the lowest delta; and the Dec 300 call, which is in-the-money, has the highest delta. Thus, the delta of a call option increases as the option goes more in-the-money and decreases as the option goes further out-of-the-money.[25] For a put option, the negative value of the delta will increase as the option goes more in-the-money (see Table 19.7).

Knowledge of an option's delta can be used to determine hedge ratios when hedging with options. For example, a delta of 0.4962 indicates that a riskless portfolio can be constructed by combining 202 long Dec 310 call options with a short

---

[23]Discussion in these sections focuses on call options. However, the analysis is equally applicable to put options, unless otherwise indicated.

[24]The put option's delta is negative.

[25]Readers can also refer to Table 20.21 in Chapter 20, which shows May 89 crude oil futures options ($15 strike price) for the period December 1, 1988, to March 31, 1989. This table shows how the value of delta changes as the option moves from at-the-money to deep in-the-money.

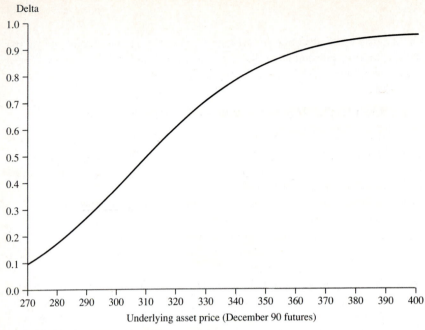

FIGURE 19-11
The Delta of a call option as a function of the underlying asset price. (December 90 S&P 500 futures options, strike price = 310).

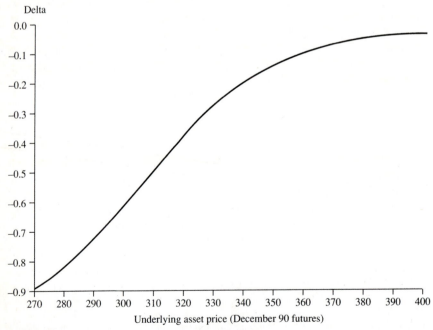

FIGURE 19-12
The Delta of a put option as a function of the underlying asset price (December 90 S&P 500 futures options, strike price = 310).

554

position of 100 Dec 90 futures contracts, or by using options and futures in a proportion indicated by the option's delta.[26] In Section 20.6 of Chapter 20 we discuss how to utilize an option's delta to construct hedged and balanced option positions.

19.6.2 Gamma: The Rate of Change of Delta

The *gamma* of an option is a measure of the *change* of an option's delta with respect to the underlying asset price. Technically, it is the second derivative of the option premium with respect to the asset (or futures) price (i.e., $\frac{\partial^2 C_f}{\partial F^2}$), and it is sometimes referred to as the option's curvature.

For example, Table 19.7 shows a gamma of 0.0125 for the Dec 310 call option. This indicates that a unit change in the underlying futures price (from, say, 308.45 to 309.45) will result in the option's delta changing by 0.0125 (from 0.4962 to 0.5087). A high gamma indicates that the slope of the delta curve is changing quickly as the underlying price changes, or that there is a high degree of nonlinearity or convexity (or curvature) in the option's delta. Figure 19-13 shows

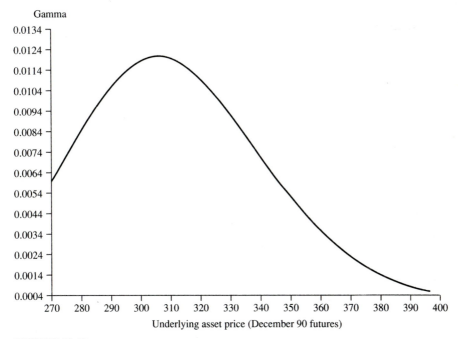

FIGURE 19-13
The Gamma of a call option as a function of the underlying asset price (December 90 S&P 500 futures options, strike price = 310).

---

[26]The option hedge ratio is obtained by taking the reciprocal of the delta. In this example, a delta of 0.4962 results in a hedge ratio of 2.02 ($\frac{1}{0.4962}$). The delta is also the prime determinant of the risk factor used by exchanges to determine margins on options.

this nonlinearity by graphing the gamma of the Dec 310 call option in relation to the underlying futures price.

Options that are both exactly at-the-money *and* close to expiration have the highest gammas. If, however, an option is close to expiration, but is either in- or out-of-the-money, its gamma will go to 0. At expiration the premium will equal the intrinsic value of the option, so its delta will either be 0 when the option is out-of-the-money or 1 when it is in-the-money. In both cases, therefore, the gamma will be 0.

An option with a high gamma is less attractive to an option writer. A high gamma means that as the option moves into-the-money, the delta increases at a faster pace, accelerating the short's losses; or, alternatively, as the option moves out-of-the-money, the delta decreases faster, attenuating the short's gain.[27] Since changes in delta always work against the option seller, an option with a delta that is highly sensitive to changes in the underlying price (or with a gamma that is large) is more risky to the seller. Alternatively, high gamma options are more attractive to option buyers.

19.6.3   Lambda: Changes in Option Prices Relative to Changes in Volatility

Lambda is the change in the option's price with respect to a unit change in the volatility of the option's underlying asset price (or $\frac{\partial C_f}{\partial \sigma_f} > 0$).[28] More specifically, the lambdas shown in Table 19.7 measure the changes in option premiums for a percentage point change in the option's (implied) volatility. For example, a lambda of 0.4465 on the Dec 310 call indicates that a 1 percentage point increase in volatility (i.e., from, say, 27.16 percent to 28.16 percent) results in a 0.4465-unit change in the option premium (i.e., from 11.40 to 11.8465).

Lambda lies between zero and infinity, and declines as the option approaches expiration. If lambda is high, an option's value is very sensitive to small changes in volatility. A low lambda, on the other hand, indicates that volatility changes have little impact on the value of an option. Lambda is at its maximum value for at-the-money options with long terms to expiration. Figure 19-14 shows the lambda of the Dec 310 call option in relation to the underlying futures price. The option's lambda is highest when the December 90 futures price is at 310, or when the option is at-the-money.

---

[27]If gamma is small, delta changes only slowly, and adjustments to keep a portfolio delta-neutral need only be made infrequently. However, if gamma is large, delta is highly sensitive to the price of the underlying asset and it will be risky to leave a delta-neutral portfolio unchanged for any length of time. Section 20.6 in Chapter 20 provides a detailed discussion of the delta hedging technique.

[28]Lambda is also referred to as *kappa*.

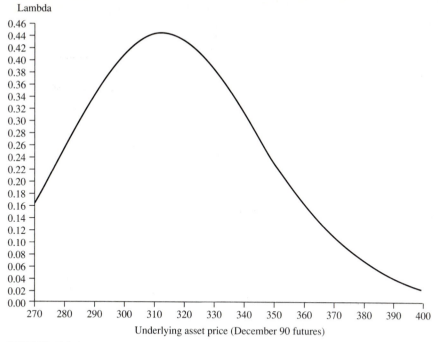

Lambda

Underlying asset price (December 90 futures)

FIGURE 19-14

The Lambda of a call option as a function of the underlying asset price (December 90 S&P 500 futures options, strike price = 310).

19.6.4 Theta: Changes in Option Prices Relative to Time to Expiration

Theta measures the change in the option premium with respect to time to maturity, or $\frac{\partial C}{\partial t} > 0$. The longer an option's time to expiration, the more valuable it is. However, as the time to expiration decreases, the option becomes less valuable. More specifically, the theta in Table 19.7 measures the change in the option premium for a one-day change in the option's time to maturity. For example, a theta of 0.1253 on the Dec 310 call indicates that the option premium will decline by 0.1253 between today and tomorrow (a reduction in the life of the option), assuming that all other factors remain the same. High theta options are attractive to option sellers because options have a high rate of time decay.

The value of theta lies between zero and the total value of the option. As the option approaches expiration, the theta increases in value; in other words, the time value of an option erodes more quickly in the last few days of an option's life.

Figure 19-15 graphs the theta of a call option with respect to whether the option is in-, at-, or out-of-the-money. The value of theta is highest when the

Theta

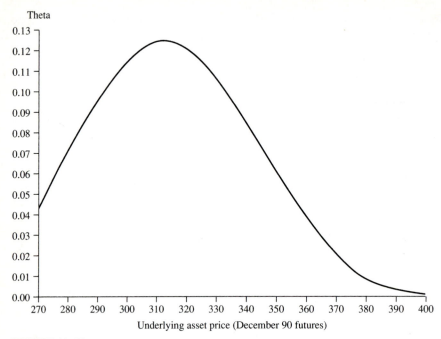

FIGURE 19-15
The Theta of a call option as a function of the underlying asset price (December 90 S&P 500 futures options, strike price = 310).

option is at-the-money. Thus, for a given time to expiration, most option writers prefer to sell options that are close to the money.

19.6.5 Rho: Changes in Option Prices Relative to Interest Rates

Rho is the change in an option's price with respect to a percentage point change in the interest rate ($\frac{\partial C_f}{\partial r}$). It measures the sensitivity of the value of an option to interest rates. As already discussed in Section 19.2, the role of the interest rate in the determination of option premiums is complex and varies from one type of option to another. The relationship is positive between stock option premiums and the interest rate, while for options on futures the relationship is negative. Table 19.7 shows how the value of rho changes among in-the-money and out-of-the-money options.

? see
Table 19.1
pg 529

19.7 APPLICATIONS OF OPTION PRICING

In the last decade, option pricing models have been applied with increasing success to all kinds of securities with option-like characteristics. This section describes some of the more common instruments that contain option features, and are therefore subject to option pricing methodology.

19.7.1 Interest Rate Options

Interest rate option features are embedded in many products and services now offered by financial institutions. These include callable and putable bonds, mortgage-backed securities with implicit prepayment options, installment loans, certificates with early redemption rights, and redeemable insurance contracts.

- **Callable and Putable Bonds.** Bonds are often issued with a call feature (callable bonds) which allows the issuing firm to buy back the bonds at a predetermined price in the future. Putable bonds are bonds with an embedded put option which allows investors to force a company to redeem the bonds at a predetermined price at a future date. The value of these call and put provisions, like any other option contract, depends on the strike prices, time to expiration, and the volatility of interest rates.

- **Deposit Accounts with Early Withdrawal Features.** Banks provide customers with fixed-interest-rate certificate of deposit accounts for given time periods. Customers are allowed to withdraw their money early if they are prepared to pay a prestipulated penalty. In the presence of interest-rate uncertainty, this early withdrawal feature may be valuable to customers, despite the early withdrawal penalty. The early withdrawal feature can be viewed as an option. If interest rates rise above the fixed deposit rate, customers may choose to exercise their option and withdraw their funds. If one views the certificate of deposit as a security that pays a coupon interest, the holder can be viewed as owning a putable bond. When interest rates rise, the holder can put this bond to the bank at a strike price equal to the value of the account less the predetermined penalty. In providing this early withdrawal feature, the bank is essentially writing put options on interest rates. Thus, the bank can use an option pricing framework to establish its cost of providing this feature. Moreover, the bank can offset its risk by purchasing corresponding put options.

- **Mortgages.** Virtually all mortgages contain provisions that allow homeowners to repay prior to maturity. This provides homeowners with an option to refinance at better terms if interest rates decline. This amounts to mortgagees holding call options and mortgagors writing call options.

- **Interest Rate Caps.** When the yield curve is upward sloping, borrowers often prefer to use cheaper short-term funds to finance long-term projects. In doing so, they risk rising future interest rates. To limit (or cap) this risk, many borrowers pay financial institutions an up-front fee to guarantee a ceiling on future interest rates. If interest rates stay below the ceiling rate, their cost of funds will fluctuate with the prevailing market rate. However, if interest rates are above the ceiling rate, the rate paid by the borrowers will be the agreed-upon ceiling rate.

This agreement divides the interest rate risk between the two parties: the borrower retains the interest rate exposure up to the ceiling rate, and the lender accepts the risk above that level. In providing an interest rate cap, the bank is writing an interest rate put option on the loan, and the borrower is purchasing this put. The borrower will exercise the option to put the loan to the lender if interest rates exceed the ceiling rate (or the cap).

- **Collars.** Purchasing an interest rate cap and selling an interest rate floor on the same interest rate instrument is called *purchasing a collar*. A collar defines the maximum and minimum range (or the cap-and-floor) within which borrowing costs can move. If interest rates rise above the ceiling, the borrower obtains financing at the ceiling rate. If interest rates fall below the floor, the borrower must pay the floor rate. Borrowers participate in falling rates only down to the floor, while lenders bear the risk that rates will increase above the ceiling. Collars, therefore, are extensions of interest rate cap agreements, and allow borrowers and lenders to share the interest-rate risk in an agreed-upon way.

- **Captions, Floortions, and Swaptions.** Recent innovations are *captions, floortions,* and *swaptions,* which are options on caps, floors, and swaps, respectively. Options on caps, floors and swaps give the purchaser the right to buy (or sell) these instruments. The customer specifies the maturity, the strike price, and the form of exercise (European or American). Captions and floortions, therefore, are basically options on options, or *compound* options.

All of the above instruments contain implicit interest rate options that can be valued with option pricing methodologies.[29]

19.7.2 Corporate Securities

The application of option pricing to the valuation of corporate securities is referred to as *contingent claim analysis.* The original Black and Scholes paper emphasized the fact that corporate liabilities could be viewed as a combination of simple option contracts. Since then, contingent claim analysis has been used to value all types of corporate securities, including equity, discount bonds, subordinated debt, compound options, lease agreements, optional bonds, incentive contracts, warrants, and convertibles. Numerical methods are usually required to obtain

---

[29]See B. Brennan and E. Schwartz, "Saving Bonds, Retractable Bonds and Callable Bonds," *Journal of Financial Economics,* August 1977, pp. 67–88; C. Cox, J. Ingersoll and S. Ross, "An Analysis of Variable Rate Loan Contracts," *Journal of Finance,* 35: 389–404, 1980; P. Jones and S. Mason, "Valuation of Loan Guarantees," *Journal of Banking and Finance,* 4: 89–107, 1980; C. Smith, "Applications of Option Pricing Analysis," in *Handbook of Financial Economics,* edited by J. Bicksler, New York, North-Holland Publishing Company, 1979, pp. 79–121; and K. Dunn and J. McConnell, "Valuation of GNMA Mortgage-Backed Securities," *Journal of Finance,* 35: 599–616, 1981.

pricing solutions for these securities. This section briefly reviews the basis for the use of these valuation techniques with respect to corporate securities.[30]

- **Corporate Bonds.** In lending money to companies bondholders can be viewed as having purchased the firm and as having sold a call option to the shareholders. Similarly, in issuing debt, shareholders can be viewed as having surrendered the firm to bondholders and, in exchange, received a call option which allows them to buy back the firm for the face value of the debt (FV) at the maturity of the debt. Within this framework, shareholders can also be viewed as owners of the assets of the firm who have borrowed the present value of FV and have purchased a put. If, at maturity, the value of the firm is less than FV, shareholders can default on the loan, and exercise their in-the-money put option to deliver the firm to the bondholders. Thus, the valuation of corporate bonds should reflect the values of these option contracts.

- **Stock Warrants.** A *warrant* is an instrument that gives the owner of the warrant an option to purchase a fixed number of shares of stock at a designated price over a specific time period. When issued, most warrants have a maturity of between three and five years. Since holders of warrants do not receive dividends or interest, the value of the warrants derives solely from their option feature. As such, warrants can be viewed as call options issued by firms. When warrants are exercised, however, the firm's equity is diluted, which must be taken into consideration when valuing warrants.

- **Minimum or Maximum of Two Risky Assets.** A wide variety of financial instruments have a put or call payoff function that depends on the minimum or maximum prices of two risky assets. Examples include secured debt, foreign currency bonds, optional bonds, and certain compensation contracts.

---

[30]See F. Black and J. Cox, "Valuing Corporate Securities: Some Effects of Bond Indenture Provisions," *Journal of Finance,* 31: 351–68, 1976; M. Brennan and E. Schwartz, "Convertible Bonds: Valuation and Optimal Strategies for Call and Conversion," *Journal of Finance,* 32: 1699–1716, 1977; G. Constantinides and R. Rosenthal, "Strategic Analysis of the Competitive Exercise of Certain Financial Options," *Journal of Economic Theory,* 32: 128–38, 1984; D. Emanuel, "Warrant Valuation and Exercise Strategy," *Journal of Financial Economics,* 12: 211–36, 1983; R. Geske and H. Johnson, "The Valuation of Corporate Liabilities, as Compound Options: A Correction," *Journal of Financial and Quantitative Analysis,* 19: 231–32, 1984; S. Mason and R. Merton, "The Role of Contingent Claims Analysis in Corporate Finance," in *Recent Advances in Corporate Finance,* edited by E. Altman and M. Subrahmanyam, Howewood, Illinois: Dow Jones-Irwin, 1985; J. McConnell and J. Schallheim, "Valuation of Asset Leasing Contracts," *Journal of Financial Economics,* 12: 237–61, 1983; R. Merton, "On the Pricing of Corporate Debt: The Risk Structure of Interest Rates," *Journal of Finance,* 29: 449–70, 1974; C. Smith and J. Zimmerman, "Valuing Employee Stock Option Plans Using Option Pricing Models," *Journal of Accounting Research,* 14: 357–64, 1976; and R. Stulz, "Options on the Minimum or the Maximum of Two Risky Assets: Analysis and Applications," *Journal of Financial Economics,* 10: 161–85, 1982.

CONCLUSION

This chapter examines the fundamentals of option pricing. The factors that determine the premiums for call and put options—the price of the underlying asset, the option's strike price, the option's time to expiration, the expected volatility of the underlying asset price, and the level of the risk-free interest rate—are discussed and illustrated with examples using actual option prices. In addition, the relationship between put and call premiums, or the put-call parity pricing relationship, is explained.

The basic theoretical models used to price options are also discussed. Specifically, both the Black-Scholes option pricing model and the Black model for pricing futures options are examined, and examples are provided of how to use these models to generate fair-value (or no-arbitrage) option prices. The discussion shows how the put-call parity pricing relationship can be applied to futures options, and provides examples of the kind of price arbitrage that would occur if actual option prices were to diverge from theoretical or no-arbitrage values. Finally, since the expected price volatility of the underlying asset is a component of all option pricing models, and since this variable cannot be directly observed, a discussion of how to estimate price volatility is included.

The chapter also provides an analysis of the sensitivity of option premiums with respect to the various pricing factors discussed earlier. A particularly important aspect of this discussion is the analysis of an option's delta—the change in the option's premium for a given change in the price of the underlying asset. Delta is used for a variety of purposes, from establishing hedge ratios to setting margin requirements on option writers.

Option pricing models have been applied with increasing success to all kinds of securities with option-like characteristics. The chapter concludes with a brief discussion of some financial instruments that have embedded option features.

QUESTIONS

1. Based on the data used in the example in Section 19.4.1, calculate the theoretical premium for the Dec 300 call on the December 90 S&P 500 futures, as of the close of trading on November 1, 1990, using the Black pricing model. How does this value compare to the actual premium on November 1 (see Table 18.10)?

2. Calculate the theoretical premium for the Dec 300 put option on the December 90 S&P 500 futures as of the close of trading on November 1, 1990. How does this value compare to the actual put premium on that day? (Hint: use the put-call parity relationship and the call value obtained in question 1.)

3. If the call premium calculated in question 1 were two index points higher than the actual market premium for that call on November 1, what arbitrage transaction would you perform to profit from this price discrepancy? What would be your arbitrage profit? Show how you calculated this.

4. What is implied price volatility? If the Dec 310 call premium on the December 90 S&P 500 futures, on November 1, 1990, were 15 rather than 11.40 index points (as shown in Section 19.2), what would be the implied price volatility? What do you think

happened to stock option prices immediately after the stock market crash in October 1987 (see Chapter 11)?

5. If you were a futures commission merchant, what factors would you consider in determining the level of initial margin to require of your option-writing customers? How would you determine the appropriate variation margins to require or to pay out? Explain your answer.

SUGGESTED READING

Barone-Adesi, G. and R. Whaley. "Efficient Analytic Approximation of American Option Values." *Journal of Finance,* Vol. 44 (June 1987), pp. 301–320.

Becker, S. "Standard Deviations Implied in Option Prices as Predictors of Future Stock Price Variability." *Journal of Banking and Finance,* Vol. 5 (1981), pp. 363–381.

Black, F. "The Pricing of Commodity Contracts." *Journal of Financial Economics,* Vol. 3 (September 1976), pp. 167–179.

Black, F. and M. Scholes. "The Pricing of Options and Corporate Liabilities." *Journal of Political Economy,* Vol. 81 (1973), pp. 637–654.

Bodurtha Jr., J. and G. Courtadon. "Tests of an American Option Pricing Model on the Foreign Currency Options Market." *Journal of Financial and Quantitative Analysis,* Vol. 22 (June 1987), pp. 153–168.

Bookstaber, R. and J. McDonald. "A Generalized Option Valuation Model for the Pricing of Bond Options." *Review of Research in Futures Markets,* Vol. 4, No. 1 (1985), pp. 60–73.

Camerer, C. "The Pricing and Social Value of Commodity Options." *Financial Analysts Journal,* Vol. 38 (Jan/Feb 1982), pp. 62–67.

Cotner, J. "Index Option Pricing: Do Investors Pay for Skewness?" *The Journal of Futures Markets,* Vol. 11, No. 1 (February 1991) pp. 1–8.

Cox, J., S. Ross, and M. Rubenstein. "Option Pricing: A Simplified Approach." *Journal of Financial Economics,* Vol. 7 (1979), pp. 229–263.

Geske, R. and K. Shastri. "Valuation by Approximation: A Comparison of Alternative Option Valuation Techniques." *Journal of Financial and Quantitative Analysis,* Vol. 20 (March 1985), pp. 45–72.

Hoag, J. "The Valuation of Commodity Options." In *Option Pricing,* ed. by Menachem Brenner, D.C. Heath, Lexington, MA, 1983, pp. 183–221.

Johnson, H. and D. Shanno. "Option Pricing When the Variance is Changing." *Journal of Financial and Quantitative Analysis,* Vol. 22 (June 1987), pp. 143–151.

Merton, R. C. "Theory of Rational Option Pricing." *Bell Journal of Economics and Management Science,* Vol. 4 (1973), pp. 141–183.

Ritchken, P. and L. Sankarasubramanian. "On Valuing Complex Interest Rate Claims." *The Journal of Futures Markets,* Vol. 10, No. 5 (Oct. 1990), pp. 443–456.

Whaley, R. "Valuation of American Futures Options: Theory and Empirical Tests." *Journal of Finance,* Vol. 41 (March 1986), pp. 127–150.

Wilson, W. "Option Price Behavior in Grain Futures Markets." *The Journal of Futures Markets,* Vol. 8 (February 1988), pp. 47–65.

APPENDIX 1: THE NORMAL AND STANDARDIZED NORMAL PROBABILITY DISTRIBUTIONS

The probability density function of a normally distributed random variable, which is depicted in Figure 19A-1, is described by a bell-shaped curve. It is symmetrical around the mean, and the mean, median, and mode are all equal. Regardless of the actual values of the mean and standard deviation, the probability that the variable will assume a value within one standard deviation of the mean is 68.3 percent; the probability that it will lie within two standard deviations of the mean is 95.4 percent; and the probability that it will lie within three standard deviations of the mean is 99.7 percent. Thus, the distribution is completely specified by its mean and standard deviation.

A standardized normal distribution has a mean of 0 and a standard deviation of 1.[1] Table 19A.1 shows the standard normal distribution table. The entries in the body of this table give the area under the curve between 0 and the indicated value of z_1. This table contains no negative values of z (i.e., z_2). This is

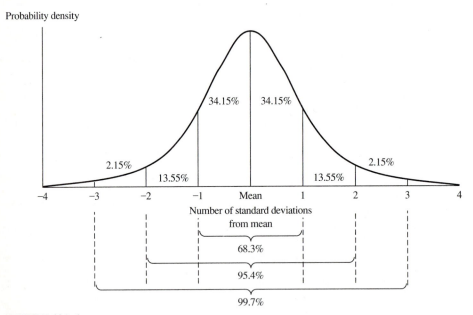

FIGURE 19A-1
Approximate areas under a normal curve.

---

[1] A variable with a nonstandard normal distribution can be transformed into a standard normal variable by subtracting the mean from each measurement and dividing by the standard deviation.

TABLE 19A.1
Standard normal distribution table

Entries in the body of the table give the area under the standard normal curve from 0 to z.

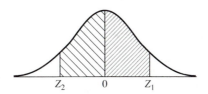

z	.00	.01	.02	.03	.04	.05	.06	.07	.08	.09
0.0	.0000	.0040	.0080	.0120	.0160	.0199	.0239	.0279	.0319	.0359
0.1	.0398	.0438	.0478	.0517	.0557	.0596	.0636	.0675	.0714	.0753
0.2	.0793	.0832	.0871	.0910	.0948	.0987	.1026	.1064	.1103	.1141
0.3	.1179	.1217	.1255	.1293	.1331	.1368	.1406	.1443	.1480	.1517
0.4	.1554	.1591	.1628	.1664	.1700	.1736	.1772	.1808	.1844	.1879
0.5	.1915	.1950	.1985	.2019	.2054	.2088	.2123	.2157	.2190	.2224
0.6	.2257	.2291	.2324	.2357	.2389	.2422	.2454	.2486	.2517	.2549
0.7	.2580	.2611	.2642	.2673	.2704	.2734	.2764	.2794	.2823	.2852
0.8	.2881	.2910	.2939	.2967	.2995	.3023	.3051	.3078	.3106	.3133
0.9	.3159	.3186	.3212	.3238	.3264	.3289	.3315	.3340	.3365	.3389
1.0	.3413	.3438	.3461	.3485	.3508	.3531	.3554	.3577	.3599	.3621
1.1	.3643	.3665	.3686	.3708	.3729	.3749	.3770	.3790	.3810	.3830
1.2	.3849	.3869	.3888	.3907	.3925	.3944	.3962	.3980	.3997	.4015
1.3	.4032	.4049	.4066	.4082	.4099	.4115	.4131	.4147	.4162	.4177
1.4	.4192	.4207	.4222	.4236	.4251	.4265	.4279	.4292	.4306	.4319
1.5	.4332	.4345	.4357	.4370	.4382	.4394	.4406	.4418	.4429	.4441
1.6	.4452	.4463	.4474	.4484	.4495	.4505	.4515	.4525	.4535	.4545
1.7	.4554	.4564	.4573	.4582	.4591	.4599	.4608	.4616	.4625	.4633
1.8	.4641	.4649	.4656	.4664	.4671	.4678	.4686	.4693	.4699	.4706
1.9	.4713	.4719	.4726	.4732	.4738	.4744	.4750	.4756	.4761	.4767
2.0	.4772	.4778	.4783	.4788	.4793	.4798	.4803	.4808	.4812	.4817
2.1	.4821	.4828	.4830	.4834	.4838	.4842	.4846	.4850	.4854	.4857
2.2	.4861	.4864	.4868	.4871	.4875	.4878	.4881	.4884	.4887	.4890
2.3	.4893	.4896	.4898	.4901	.4904	.4906	.4909	.4911	.4913	.4916
2.4	.4918	.4920	.4922	.4925	.4927	.4929	.4931	.4932	.4934	.4936
2.5	.4938	.4940	.4941	.4943	.4945	.4946	.4948	.4949	.4951	.4952
2.6	.4953	.4955	.4956	.4957	.4959	.4960	.4961	.4962	.4963	.4964
2.7	.4965	.4966	.4967	.4968	.4969	.4970	.4971	.4972	.4973	.4974
2.8	.4974	.4975	.4976	.4977	.4977	.4978	.4979	.4979	.4980	.4981
2.9	.4981	.4982	.4982	.4983	.4984	.4984	.4985	.4985	.4986	.4986
3.0	.4987	.4987	.4987	.4988	.4988	.4989	.4989	.4989	.4990	.4990

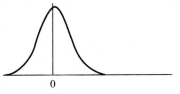

Normal density function

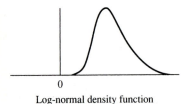

0

Log-normal density function

FIGURE 19A-2
Comparison of normal and log-normal probability
distributions.

not necessary since the area between 0 and any positive value of z is exactly
equal to the area between 0 and the corresponding negative value of z because of
the symmetry of the distribution. This is expressed symbolically as

$$P(0 < z < z_1) = P(-z_1 < z < 0)$$

The probability that a random variable falls between 0 and z_1 is the same as
between 0 and $-z_1$.

For example, if $z_1 = 0.7$, then z_1 is at 0.7 standard deviations above the
mean. A variable picked at random will have a 0.7580 probability that it will lie
below 0.7 (z_1). This probability is derived as follows:

- As shown in the normal probability distribution table in Table 19A.1, a z value
  of 0.7 has a corresponding probability of 0.2580 (i.e., the area under the curve
  between 0 and 0.7).
- Since the full area under the curve is 1 and the probability distribution is symmetrical around 0, there is a 0.5 probability that a random variable is above the
  mean and a 0.5 probability that it is below the mean. Thus, adding 0.5 (the
  area below the mean of 0) to 0.2580 yields a probability of 0.7580.

On the other hand, if $z_2 = -0.6$, then z_2 is at 0.6 standard deviations
below the mean of 0. The probability that a random variable will lie below -0.6
is 0.2743. This number is derived by first obtaining the relevant probability that
corresponds to a z value of 0.6, which is 0.2257, then subtracting this number
from 0.5, which yields the probability of 0.2743.

Figure 19A-2 graphically compares the normal distribution with the log-
normal distribution. A random variable is *log-normally distributed* if the natural
logarithm of the variable is normally distributed.

APPENDIX 2: THE BINOMIAL OPTION PRICING MODEL

The binomial option pricing model assumes that the asset price follows a multiplicative binomial process over discrete periods. The value of the asset underlying an option (S) is assumed to go up (u) or down (d) by a specific amount in the next period. In other words, the asset will take on a value in the next period of either uS or dS, where $u > 1$, and $0 < d < 1$.[2]

The One-Period Model

Assume that a stock with a current price of S will either increase to uS with probability q or decrease to dS with probability of $1 - q$. Assume also that a call option on the stock expires at the end of the next period.[3] The option value at expiration will depend on the value of the stock at expiration, and will be worth $C_u = \text{Max}(0, uS - K)$ if the stock rises to the uS, or $C_d = \text{Max}(0, dS - K)$ if the stock drops to dS, where K is the strike price.[4]

Period 0 value	Period 1 value	Probability
S (stock)	uS	q
	dS	$1 - q$
C (option)	$C_u = \text{Max}(0, uS - K)$	q
	$C_d = \text{Max}(0, dS - K)$	$1 - q$

Since the value of S at expiration is uncertain, the value of a call option with 1 period to expiration is obtained by discounting the expected terminal values of the option to period 0:

$$C = [pC_u + (1 - p)C_d]/R$$

---

[2]The binomial option pricing model was originally developed by Cox, Ross and Rubenstein. See J. Cox, S. Ross, and M. Rubenstein, "Option Pricing: A Simplified Approach," *Journal of Financial Economics*, 7: 229-63, 1979.

[3]The American feature of an option (i.e., early exercise) is handled by imposing on the model immediate exercise, whenever the option's exercisable value is higher than the expected fair option value.

[4]It is assumed that there are no taxes, no transaction costs, and individuals can sell short any security and receive the full proceeds.

where $R = 1$ plus the riskless interest rate (r), which is assumed to be a constant and positive

$$p = \frac{R-d}{u-d}$$

$$1 - p = \frac{u-R}{u-d}$$

Cox and Rubenstein show that p is always greater than 0 and less than 1, so that it has the properties of a probability. In addition, p is in fact the value that q would have in equilibrium if investors were risk neutral.[5]

The above valuation equation has several notable features. First, the probability q does not appear in the equation. Thus, knowing investors' subjective probabilities about upward or downward stock price moves is not critical to valuing call options. Second, the call option valuation formula does not depend on investors' attitudes toward risk. Lastly, the call option value depends on only one random variable: the stock price.

As an example, consider the following: If $S = 200, u = 1.1, d = 0.95$, $R = 1.05$, and $K = 200$, the option price can be determined as follows:

$$C_u = \text{Max}[0, (1.1 \times 200) - 200] = 20$$

$$C_d = \text{Max}[0, (0.95 \times 200) - 200] = 0$$

$$p = \frac{1.05 - 0.95}{1.10 - 0.95} = \frac{2}{3}$$

Therefore

$$C = \left[\frac{2}{3} \times 20 + \frac{1}{3} \times 0\right] \times \frac{1}{1.05} = 12.70$$

If the option is not priced at 12.70, an arbitrage profit is possible. If the option price is higher than 12.70, an investor can make a profit by writing calls and buying stock in the proper proportion (or the ratio HR) and financing the difference between the option premium and the price of the stock by borrowing at the riskless rate. If the price of the call is below 12.70, the reverse arbitrage can be done: buy calls and sell stock in the same ratio HR, investing the proceeds in a riskless asset. For the purpose of such arbitrage, the appropriate hedge ratio (HR) is

$$HR = \frac{C_u - C_d}{(u - d)S}$$

which in the context of the above example is equal to

$$HR = \frac{20 - 0}{(1.1 - 0.95) \times 200} = \frac{2}{3}$$

Thus, an arbitrager would write three calls against two shares of stock.

---

[5]See J. Cox and M. Rubenstein, *Options Markets*, New Jersey: Prentice-Hall, 1985, pp. 169–74.

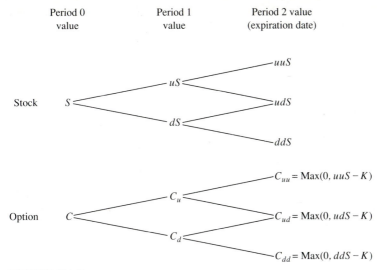

FIGURE 19A-3
Multi-period option values.

The Multi-Period Model

The one-period case is unrealistic. A stock price can move many times between a given date and the time that the option expires. The same pricing principles, nevertheless, can be applied to the multi-period case, although the computations are more tedious. To obtain the pricing formula for the multi-period case, we first extend the above pricing model to the two-period case and determine the pricing formula.

Assume that the stock price follows the same binomial process for price changes in each period (this is shown in Figure 19A-3). At the end of Period 1, the stock will be worth either uS or dS dollars. At the end of Period 2 (the option's expiration date), the stock price will be uuS (if it goes up by u in both periods), udS (if it goes up in one period and down in the next period), ddS (if it drops by d in both periods).[6] Thus, at the end of the first period, the option will have a price of C_u or C_d, depending on whether the stock goes up or down. At expiration, its price will be $C_{uu} = \text{Max}(0, u^2S - K)$ if the stock rises in both periods, $C_{ud} = \text{Max}(0, udS - K)$ if the stock goes up in one period and down in the other, or $C_{dd} = \text{Max}(0, d^2S - K)$ if the stock declines in both periods. The possible stock price outcomes and the related option prices are shown in Figure 19A-3.

---

[6]Note that $udS = duS$, so that the price of the stock at expiration will be the same regardless of in which period it goes up or down.

The value of the option (C) can now be derived by working backwards from the expiration date (Period 2) to Period 0, using the formula for the one-period case.

$$C_u = [pC_{uu} + (1 - p)C_{ud}]/R$$
$$C_d = [pC_{du} + (1 - p)C_{dd}]/R$$
$$C = [pC_u + (1 - p)C_d]/R$$

or

$$C = [p^2 C_{uu} + 2p(1 - p)C_{ud} + (1 - p)^2 C_{dd}]/R^2$$

Since the equation is expressed in terms of the known parameters, $S, K, R, u,$ and d, the possible values of the option at maturity can be determined exactly. The same procedure can be used to value an option in the multi-period case. We can express the general formula for n periods to maturity as

$$\left[\sum_{j=0}^{n} \frac{n!}{j!(n-j)!} p^j (1 - p)^{n-j} \text{Max}(0, u^j d^{n-j} S - K) \right] / R^n$$

Cox, Ross and Rubenstein have shown that this complicated expression can be written simply as[7]

$$C = S\Phi[a; n, p'] - KR^{-n}\Phi[a; n, p]$$

where
$$p = \frac{R-d}{u-d}$$
$$p' = (u/R)p$$
a = the minimum number of upward moves that a stock must make over the next n periods for the call option to finish in-the-money. Thus, a is the smallest non-negative integer such that $u^a d^{n-a} S > K$. By taking the natural logarithm of both sides of this inequality, a can be expressed as the smallest non-negative integer greater than $\ln(K/Sd^n)/\ln(u/d)$. Therefore, if $a > n, C = 0$ (i.e., the call will finish out-of-the-money even if the stock moves upward in every period, so that its current value must be 0.

$\Phi[a; n, p]$ = the complementary binomial distribution function.

The binomial pricing formula can be applied to various time periods: months, weeks, days, or even minutes. As the time period used becomes smaller, the number of periods to expiration (n) increases for an option with a given time to expiration. Thus, continuous-time option pricing formulas, such as the Black-Scholes model, are nothing more than the binomial pricing formula derived for an infinite number of arbitrarily small time periods.

---

[7]Cox and Rubenstein, 1985, pp. 176–78.

APPENDIX 3: A GENERALIZED
BLACK-SCHOLES OPTION PRICING MODEL

The equations below are generalized option pricing formulas applicable to securities (stocks and debt instruments), commodities, currencies, futures, and forward contracts.[8] In these formulas, alternative cost-of-carry terms are used to distinguish among the different underlying instruments.

The generalized pricing formulas for puts and calls are

$$C = \exp^{-rt}[U \exp^{ht} N(d_1) - KN(d_2)]$$

$$P = \exp^{-rt}[U \exp^{ht}(N(d_1) - 1) - K(N(d_2) - 1)]$$

$$d_1 = \frac{\ln(\frac{U \exp^{ht}}{K})}{\sigma \sqrt{t}} + 0.5\sigma \sqrt{t}$$

$$d_2 = d_1 - \sigma \sqrt{t}$$

where
C = call option premium
P = put option premium
U = underlying asset price: U can be stocks, debt instruments, foreign currencies, commodities, or futures contracts
K = strike price
t = time to expiration, in fraction of years
σ = annualized price volatility
r = annualized short-term risk-free interest rate
h = holding cost factor (explained below)
$N(\cdot)$ = cumulative normal distribution function

These formulas are similar to the Black-Scholes model and the Black model discussed in Sections 19.3 and 19.4, respectively, except that the holding cost factor, h, takes the following forms with respect to the following assets

- Stocks: $h = r - y$, where y = dividend yield
- Bonds: $h = r - y$, where y = coupon yield
- Currencies: $h = r - r_f$, where r_f = foreign short-term risk-free interest rate
- Commodities: $h = r + x$, where x = storage + insurance − convenience yield
- Futures: $h = 0$ (no carrying cost or income)

---

[8]This appendix is based on excerpts from J. Meisner and J. Richards, "Option Premium Dynamics: With Applications to Fixed Income Portfolio Analysis," in *Advances in Bond Analysis and Portfolio Strategies,* edited by F. Fabozzi and D. Garlicki, Chicago: Probus Publishing, 1987, pp. 395–415.

CHAPTER

20

SPECULATING AND HEDGING WITH OPTIONS

This chapter describes the various option trading strategies that are used by speculators and hedgers. In our discussion we also show how options can be used as a substitute for or complement to various futures trading strategies.

Options can be employed to create portfolios with unique features capable of achieving investment objectives not attainable with futures. For example, certain option positions will yield a profit even if there is no change in the price of the underlying asset. Others will yield a profit solely because of a change in the expected volatility of the underlying asset price.

Hedging with options also provides commercial firms with greater flexibility in managing risk. For example, commercial traders can use options as protection against an adverse movement in the underlying asset price without giving up the opportunity to profit from a favorable price move. In addition, option buyers are not subject to margin calls, as are hedgers using futures contracts.

The advantages of options over futures, however, are not free. Option premiums must be paid to those willing to bear the risks that buyers of options wish to avoid. These premiums can sometimes be so high as to make options unattractive.

20.1 SPECULATING ON PRICE CHANGES

Most option trading strategies are designed to yield a profit if a trader is correct in his expectations about the future price of the underlying asset. If a trader believes that asset prices will rise, he will adopt a *bullish* strategy; if he believes that prices will fall, he will adopt a *bearish* strategy. The difference among the alternative bullish and bearish option trading strategies is of one degree: some provide greater opportunity for profit but carry commensurately greater risk.[1]

20.1.1 Simple Call and Put Strategies

In Chapter 18 the payoff analyses for simple (or outright) long call and long put positions are provided (see Figures 18-3 and 18-5). It is clear from these analyses that a speculator who believes that asset prices will rise will adopt a long call position, and a speculator who believes that asset prices will fall will adopt a long put position. Further, the more bullish or bearish a trader is, the more attractive it will be to purchase an out-of-the-money call or put option. Such options are cheaper, and provide greater leverage with no additional downside risk.

Alternatively, a trader who believes that prices will either remain constant or fall can earn income from writing calls, and a trader who believes that prices will either remain constant or rise can earn income from selling puts. Speculators who strongly hold these beliefs will want to write in-the-money options. These short option strategies are directed at capturing the time value component of the option premium. It is important to recognize, however, that these income-enhancement strategies are speculative: they are speculations on future price movements, and as such are quite risky. If a trader's price expectations turn out to be incorrect, he can suffer substantial losses (see Figures 18-6 and 18-7).

In summary, the motivations behind outright long or short option positions can be summarized as follows:

	Call	Put
Buyer	Bullish	Bearish
Seller	Bearish to neutral	Bullish to neutral

---

[1]In our examples illustrating the various speculative option strategies, we use market prices on the S&P 500 futures options on November 1, 1990, to construct profit and loss profiles. Readers can refer to Tables 18.10b, 18.12, and 18.13 in Chapter 18 for the relevant price quotations and contract specifications.

20.2   COMBINING SIMPLE CALL AND PUT STRATEGIES WITH EXISTING SPECULATIVE POSITIONS

Traders can combine simple call and put strategies with existing speculative positions to create complex positions that alter the risk-return characteristics of the initial positions. This section discusses four basic complex option strategies: covered call and put options, and synthetic call and put options. These are defined, respectively, as

Covered call sale = short call + long futures
Covered put sale = short put + short futures
Synthetic call = long put + long futures
Synthetic put = long call + short futures

20.2.1   Covered Option Strategies

A *covered option strategy* involves the purchase or sale of an option in combination with an offsetting outright position in the underlying asset. Generally, covered option strategies are used to increase income. The additional income provides greater profits for the trader, which in the event of an adverse asset price move will mitigate losses.

COVERED CALL WRITING.   Selling a call option against (or to cover) a long futures (or asset) position is known as *covered call writing*.[2] This strategy permits the trader to receive the call option premium in return for giving up some or all of the upside profit potential due to an increase in the futures price. It is a desirable strategy if futures prices are expected to remain fairly stable, since under such a price scenario the long futures position will not be profitable. If futures prices decline, however, the trader may incur substantial losses. Figure 20-1 provides the payoff profile on a covered call sale.

COVERED PUT WRITING.   Selling a put against a short futures position is known as *covered put writing*. Similar to covered call writing, this is an income-augmenting strategy, since the trader receives the put premium. This strategy again is attractive if futures prices are expected to remain constant, since in this event the short futures position will not be profitable. But if futures prices rise, the trader may incur substantial losses. Figure 20-2 shows the payoff profile for a covered put sale.

---

[2]A *naked*, or *uncovered*, option position is the writing of an option when the writer does *not* hold an offsetting position in the underlying asset.

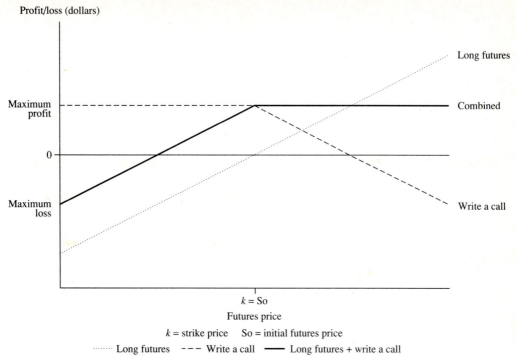

FIGURE 20-1
Covered call.

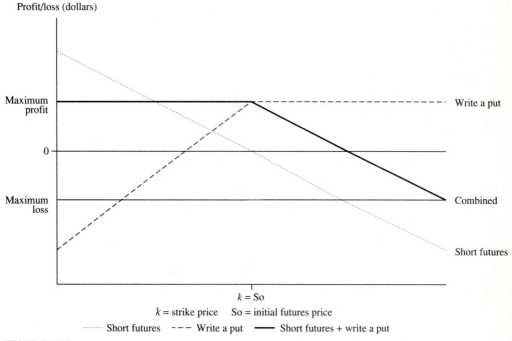

FIGURE 20-2
Covered put.

20.2.2 Synthetic Options

Synthetic options are created by combining the purchase of a call or a put option with an outright short or long futures position. Synthetic option positions are generally used either as an efficient way to alter the risk-return profile of an existing speculative position, perhaps because of a change in a speculator's price expectations, or as a way to lock in unrealized speculative profits.

SYNTHETIC CALLS. Combining a long put option with a long futures position creates a *synthetic long call option*. This strategy enables an investor to assume a position that has a risk and return profile similar to an outright long call position. A synthetic call strategy may be used by speculators who hold a long futures position and, while confident that futures prices will rise in the long or even intermediate term, fear an interim price decline. Buying the put protects them against potential losses associated with a large price decline. In effect, the trader is placing a *stop loss* order on his long futures position. Such a stop loss strategy can also be used to lock in an unrealized profit.

Figure 20-3 shows a synthetic call option. In this diagram, an investor has a long position in the December 90 S&P 500 futures, established at 290.00 on October 1, 1990. This diagram assumes that by November 1, the December S&P

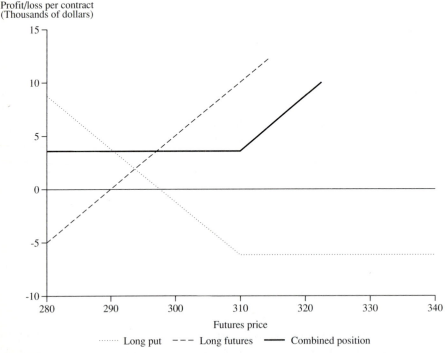

Profit/loss per contract
(Thousands of dollars)

Futures price

········ Long put   − − − Long futures   —— Combined position

FIGURE 20-3
Synthetic call option: Long put & long futures (Dec 90 S&P 500 futures and Dec 310 put).

500 index has moved to 310.00, so that the long position has a profit of $10,000. To protect this profit, the investor buys a December S&P 310 put at a premium of 12.95 ($6475), locking in a minimum profit of $3525 ($10, 000 − $6475). The purchase of the put guarantees, in effect, a selling price of 310.00 for the long S&P futures, insuring against a further decline in stock prices. Thus, the profit profile of the combined position is similar to that of a long call option (see Figure 18-3).

SYNTHETIC PUTS. A long call option can be combined with a short futures position to create a *synthetic long put option*, either to lock in an unrealized profit or to limit the loss on the short futures position. The profit profile for this position is similar to that of a long put (see Figure 18-5). This strategy insulates the speculator from losses due to a large price increase, but still permits him to profit from declining prices.

Suppose that on October 1, 1990, an investor sells a December 90 S&P 500 futures contract at 330.00, anticipating a drop in the stock market. By November 1, the December S&P futures price declines to 310.00, and the short futures position shows a profit of 20 points ($10,000). Instead of closing out this position, the investor can buy a Dec 310 S&P call at 11.40 ($5700), locking in an unrealized profit. This strategy guarantees him a profit of at least $4300 (subtracting the call premium of $5700 from the exercisable profit of $10,000). Further, if the S&P futures price continues to decline, profits will be higher. Figure 20-4 shows the payoff profile for a synthetic put, which is similar to that of a long put option (see Figure 18-5).

20.2.3 Summary

Covered call and covered put strategies are used when speculators expect underlying asset prices to remain relatively stable. Synthetic call and put strategies, which resemble outright long calls and long puts, are used when significant bullish or bearish price movements are expected.[3] To summarize:

Covered strategy	Resembles	Price outlook
Covered call sale	Short put	Neutral to slightly bullish
Covered put sale	Short call	Neutral to slightly bearish
Synthetic put	Long put	Bearish
Synthetic call	Long call	Bullish

---

[3] Simple covered strategies involve equal units of options and futures contracts. However, it is possible to employ options in combinations with futures positions in ratios other than one-for-one. These are usually referred to as *delta* or *ratio* strategies, and are discussed later in the chapter.

Profit/loss per contract
(Thousands of dollars)

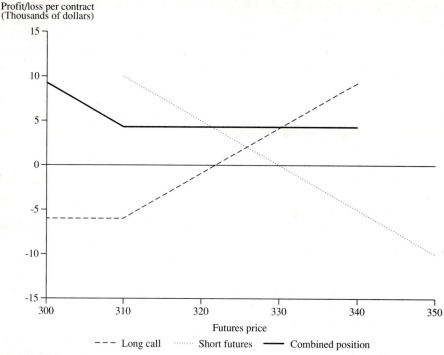

FIGURE 20-4
Synthetic put option: Long call & short futures (Dec 90 S&P 500 futures and Dec 310 call).

The pros and cons of using these combination or complex strategies instead of the analogous outright option positions depend on the speculator's objectives and expectations, as well as on relative transaction costs and market prices.[4]

20.3   OPTION SPREADS

Option spreads are a way to speculate on *relative* price changes. These strategies involve the simultaneous purchase and sale of different options, creating a price spread that widens or narrows according to what happens to underlying asset prices. An option spread in which the two legs of the spread have different strike prices but have the same expiration date is called a *vertical spread*. An option spread in which the two legs have different expiration dates but the same strike price is called a *horizontal spread* (or a *calendar* or *time spread*). The terms *vertical* and *horizontal* developed because options that differ only by their strike prices are listed vertically in published option quotation tables, while options that differ only by time to expiration are listed horizontally. A *diagonal* spread is

---

[4]Transaction costs, such as commissions, will usually be lower when executing an outright option transaction than when executing the above strategies. Investors often use the latter in situations where they already own long or short futures positions.

a hybrid: the legs of the spread have both different strike prices and different expiration dates.

The number and variety of option spreads are almost limitless. An option spread can be formed by going long and short any two options on the same instrument. This section describes the most commonly traded vertical and horizontal option spreads.

20.3.1 Bullish Option Spreads

Bullish option spreads are strategies that yield a profit when underlying asset prices *rise*. Such spreads are established by purchasing a low strike price and selling a high strike price option with the same expiration date.

VERTICAL CALL OPTION SPREADS. A *vertical call option spread* is created by simultaneously buying and selling call options with the same expiration date. A *bull vertical call spread* is created by buying a call option with a relatively low strike price and selling a call option with a relatively high strike price, both with the same expiration date. The premium income from selling the higher strike price call partially reduces the cost of buying the lower strike price call. However, to initiate this spread, the investor has to incur a cash investment equal to the difference between the low strike premium and the high strike premium (which is commonly known among option traders as the *net debit*).

If, when the options expire, the underlying futures (or asset) price is less than or equal to the lower of the two strike prices, both options will expire out-of-the-money. In this case the option trader will lose the difference between the premium paid for the lower strike call and the premium received for the sale of the higher strike call, or the net debit. The maximum loss that can occur on the position is

$$\text{Maximum loss} = \text{lower strike premium} - \text{higher strike premium}$$

If, on the other hand, prices rise prior to expiration, the lower strike call will gain in value faster than the higher strike call will incur losses, resulting in a net gain in the spread value. If the underlying futures price exceeds the higher of the two strike prices at expiration, both options will be in-the-money and will be exercised. In this case the maximum profit will be the difference between the two strike prices less the net premium paid:

$$\text{Maximum profit} = \text{higher strike price} - \text{lower strike price} - \text{net premium paid}$$

If at expiration the futures price lies between the two strike prices, so that the lower strike call is in-the-money but the higher strike call is out-of-the-money, there may or may not be a net profit, depending on the break-even price, which is

$$\text{Breakeven price} = \text{lower strike price} + \text{net premium paid}$$

Figure 20-5 provides the profit profile of a 310–320 bull call spread on the December 90 S&P 500 futures. On October 1, 1990, the cost of buying the Dec

Profit/loss per contract
(Thousands of dollars)

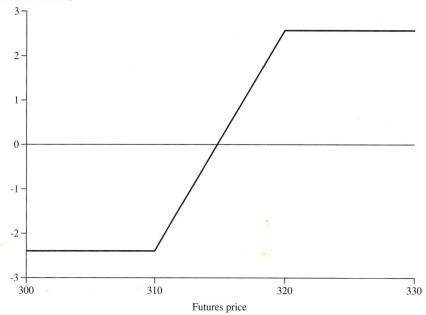

Futures price

FIGURE 20-5
310–320 bull call spread (Dec 90 S&P 500 futures options).

310 call is 11.40, or $5700 (11.40 × $500). The premium from selling the Dec 320 call is 6.55 ($3275). If, on the options' expiration dates, the December S&P 500 futures is at or below 310.00, the maximum loss will be the net premium cost of $2425 ($5700 − $3275). If, on the other hand, the futures price is at or above 320.00 at expiration, the maximum profit will be $2575: the difference between the two strike prices (10 index points, or $5000), less the net premium cost of $2425.

A bull vertical call spread is often preferred to the alternative strategy of buying a call option outright or going long the underlying futures because it is cheaper than the call and, in contrast to the futures strategy, has a maximum loss exposure.

VERTICAL PUT OPTION SPREADS. An alternative bull option spread is the *bull vertical put spread*, which is created by purchasing a put option with a low strike price and selling a put option with a higher strike price, both with the same expiration date. The premium paid to purchase the lower strike put option will always be less than the premium received from the sale of the higher strike put, so that the net option premium will generate a cash inflow (or a *net credit*). If, at expiration, the underlying futures price is greater than or equal to the higher of the two strike prices, both options will expire out-of-the-money and are not likely to be exercised. Thus, the investor's maximum profit will be the net premium income.

The maximum loss on this position will occur if the underlying futures price turns out to be less than or equal to the lower of the two strike prices at expiration. In this case both puts will be in-the-money and will be exercised. The break-even point occurs when the futures price falls between the two strike prices at expiration.

In summary, for a bull vertical put option spread, the following are true:

Maximum profit = net option premium income (or net credit)

Maximum loss = higher strike price − lower strike price − net option premium income

Break even price = higher strike price − net option premium income

Like a bull vertical call spread, bull vertical put spreads have limited profit and loss potential. The major distinction is that a call spread results in a net premium paid (or a net debit), while a put spread results in a net premium received (or a net credit). Some traders, therefore, prefer a bull put spread to a bull call spread because they receive a net credit rather than incur a net debit. A vertical put spread can be profitable even if asset prices do not rise, so long as they do not fall. (Readers should construct a profit profile graph for the bull vertical put spread and compare it with the bull vertical call spread shown in Figure 20-5.)

20.3.2 Bearish Option Spreads

Bearish option spreads yield a profit when there is a *decline* in the price of the underlying asset. A bearish spread entails the sale of an option with a relatively low strike price and the purchase of an option with a higher strike price, where both legs of the spread have a common expiration date.

VERTICAL CALL OPTION SPREADS. A *bear vertical call spread* is created by buying a call option with a high strike price and selling a call option with a lower strike price, both with the same expiration date. If asset prices decline to a level lower than the lower strike price, both options will expire out-of-the-money. The maximum profit on this position will be the net premium received (or the net credit), which is the premium income from selling the lower strike call minus the cost of buying the higher strike option. The maximum loss will be the difference between the strike prices of the two options less the net premium earned; and the break-even price will be equal to the higher of the two strike prices less the net premium per unit.

Figure 20-6 shows the profit profile for a bear vertical call spread on the December 90 S&P 500 futures options, where a 320 call is purchased and a 310 call is sold. The respective premiums are the same as those for the bull call spread shown in Figure 20-5.

VERTICAL PUT OPTION SPREADS. A *bear vertical put spread* is created by the purchase of a put option with a higher strike price and the sale of a put option with a lower strike price, both with the same expiration date. If underlying asset

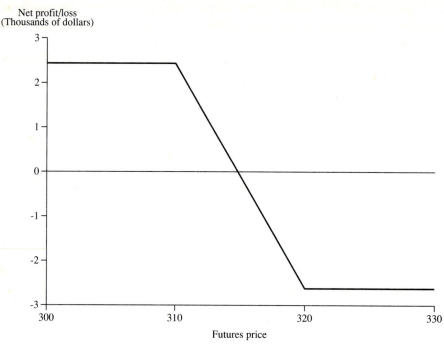

FIGURE 20-6
310–320 bear call spread (Dec 90 S&P 500 futures options).

prices rise to a level above the higher strike price, both options will expire out-of-the-money, and the maximum loss will be the net premium paid. The maximum profit on the position will be the difference between the strike prices less the net premium paid (or the net debit), which will occur if asset prices turn out to be equal to or lower than the lower strike price. The break-even price is equal to the higher strike price less the net premium paid per unit.

For example, on November 1, 1990, the December S&P 500 futures price is 310.00. In order to profit from an expected decline in stock prices, an investor pays a premium of 12.95 ($6475) to buy a Dec 310 put, and sells a Dec 300 put, receiving a premium of 9.25 ($4625). The net premium cost, therefore, is $1850. If the futures price at expiration is 300.00 or lower, the investor's profit will be $3150, which is the difference between the strike prices of the options (10 index points, or $5000) less the net premium cost of $1850 (i.e., net profit = $5000 − $1850 = $3150). The maximum loss the investor can incur is $1850, which will occur if the futures price at expiration is 310.00 or above, in which case both options will expire worthless. The break-even futures price is 306.30.[5] Figure 20-7 depicts the profit profile for this strategy.

The difference between bear vertical call and put spread strategies is that a vertical call spread will be profitable even if asset prices do not decline—just

---

[5] $306.30 = 310 − ($1850/$500).

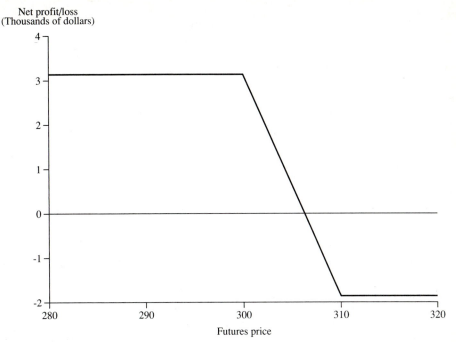

Net profit/loss
(Thousands of dollars)

FIGURE 20-7
310–300 bear put spread (Dec 90 S&P 500 futures options).

as long as prices do not rise. A vertical put spread will not be profitable unless prices actually decline.

20.3.3   Horizontal or Time Spreads

If an investor believes that underlying asset prices will be stable for a foreseeable period of time, he or she can attempt to profit from the declining time value of options by setting up a *horizontal option spread.* A horizontal spread is created by selling an option with a relatively short term to expiration and buying an option of the same type with a longer term to expiration, both with the same strike prices. In general, the time value (embedded in the premium) of a short-maturity option will decline at a faster rate than will the time value of a longer-maturity option. Thus, as long as the underlying asset price remains stable, or does not move significantly against the investor, he or she can profit from "riding down" the time value of the near-term option, since the loss on the long-term option will be less than the profit on the near-term option.

The relative rate of time-value decay on short-term versus longer-term options is shown in Table 20.1. As discussed in Chapter 19 (Section 19.6.4), the rate of time-value decay is measured by *theta,* which is the change in an option premium due to a 1-day passage of time. Table 20.1 contains the thetas for call options on the December 90 and March 91 S&P 500 futures, calculated using prevailing market prices on November 1, 1990. The table shows that the thetas

TABLE 20.1
Time-value decay for S&P 500 futures options: November 1, 1990

Strike price	December 90 call		March 91 call	
	Premium (points)*	Theta (points)*	Premium (points)*	Theta (points)*
305	14.35	0.1294	23.70	0.0685
310	11.40	0.1353	20.95	0.0699
315	8.80	0.1306	18.20	0.0708
320	6.55	0.1269	15.20	0.0710
325	4.70	0.1207	13.35	0.0705
Futures price		308.45		311.00
Time to maturity		49 days		140 days
Volatility		27%		27%

* S&P 500 futures and option contracts are quoted in index points, with each point equal to $500.

on the December 90 futures options are almost twice the size of those on the March 91 futures calls, for all strike prices.

For example, assume that an investor sells the Dec 310 S&P 500 call and buys the Mar 310 S&P 500 call, and that the underlying S&P 500 futures price remains constant. The Dec 310 call will lose 0.1353 index points (or $67.65) per day, while the Mar 310 call will lose only 0.0699 index points per day (or $34.95).[6] Since the investor is short the December call and long the March call, he will capture a net gain of $32.70 ($67.65-$34.95) per day (per option spread).

The risk associated with this type of spread, of course, is that either or both the underlying asset price or the expected price volatility will change significantly in an adverse way. If this occurs, the two legs of the spread will change in value by different amounts, since each has a different time to expiration and a different delta. The result may be a net loss.

20.4   CALL AND PUT COMBINATIONS

All of the trading strategies examined up to this point have employed puts and calls individually, or in combination either with underlying futures contracts or with other options of the same type. This section discusses trading strategies that combine both calls and puts to create *synthetic futures* and *straddle positions*.

20.4.1   Synthetic Futures

Synthetic futures are proxies for outright long or short futures positions: they have similar profit profiles to outright futures positions. Synthetic futures positions may be more attractive than outright futures positions because they are less costly or have margining advantages. As already discussed in Chapter 18 (Section 18.5.4 and Figures 18-8 and 18-9), *synthetic long futures* are created by combining a

---

[6]Since each index point is worth $500, 0.1353 is equal to $67.65 (0.1353 × 500).

long call option and a *short put* option with the same strike price. *Synthetic short futures* are created by combining a *long put* and a *short call* option with the same strike price.

20.4.2 Straddles

Straddles, like *spreads*, involve the simultaneous sale and purchase of options. Unlike spreads, however, straddles entail the *purchase* of a put *and* a call (a long straddle), or the *sale* of a put *and* a call (a short straddle). This strategy is often used by speculators who believe that asset prices either will move significantly in one direction or the other (but are uncertain as to which direction) or will remain fairly constant.

LONG A STRADDLE. A *long straddle* is formed by buying an equal number of calls and puts with the same strike price and with the same expiration date. This position will be profitable if underlying asset prices move significantly in either direction. If prices fall, the put option will become profitable. If prices rise, the call option will become profitable. To the extent that the gain on the profitable option exceeds the total premium cost of establishing the straddle, there will be a net profit. The potential profit on this position is unlimited: a substantial change in prices will result in large profits. The maximum loss is the cost of the straddle—the total premium paid, which will occur if the asset price at expiration is the same as the strike prices of the options. In that event, neither of the options will be exercised.

Suppose that a straddle is established in Dec 310 S&P 500 futures calls and puts on November 1, when the futures price is 310. The call option costs 11.40 index points (or $5700), and the put option costs 12.95 points ($6475), making the total cost 24.25 points (or $12,175). If S&P futures are at 310 on December 20, the expiration date, neither option will have any value and the investor will suffer a loss of $12,175. If, on the other hand, the futures price is 334.35 at expiration, the put option will expire worthless but the call will be in-the-money. The investor can exercise the call option and assume a long futures position at the 310 exercise price. Since the market price of the futures is 334.35, the investor will have a profit of 24.35 points ($12,175). This will exactly offset the premium paid, and the investor will have zero net profits.

If the futures price drops to 285.65, the call option will expire worthless, but the put option will be in-the-money. The investor can exercise the put at a profit of 24.35 points ($12,175), which again exactly offsets the cost of the straddle. Thus, the straddle will lose money if at expiration the futures price is between 285.65 and 334.35, but will make a profit if the futures price at or before expiration is outside of this range: either higher or lower. Figure 20-8 shows the payoff diagram for this long straddle.

SHORT A STRADDLE. If an investor expects prices to be stable, he can sell a straddle. A short straddle position profits from stable prices but loses if futures prices move substantially in either direction, just the opposite of a long straddle

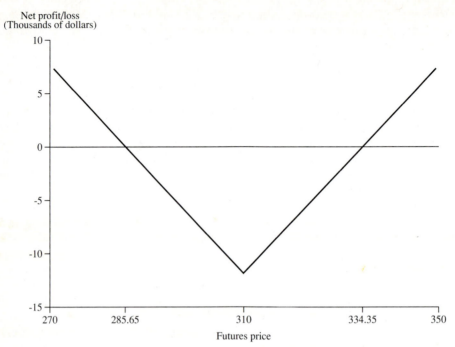

Net profit/loss
(Thousands of dollars)

FIGURE 20-8
Long a straddle: Dec 90 S&P 500 futures options (310 call and 310 put).

position. To go *short a straddle,* an investor sells both a call and a put with the same strike price and the same expiration date. If the futures price at expiration is the same as the options' strike prices, both options will expire worthless, and the investor will retain the total premium received from writing the options. Figure 20-9 shows the profit profile of a short December 310 S&P 500 futures option straddle.

20.4.3 Strangles

A *strangle* is a straddle in which the two legs do not share a common strike price. For example, a straddle in which both legs are out-of-the-money and have different strike prices is a strangle. A long (short) strangle strategy is used to profit from a volatile (stable) price scenario. Unlike the simple straddles shown above, however, the profit profile of a strangle is characterized by a broad, flat return between the two strike prices. In the case of a short strangle, this flat zone represents profits; in the case of a long strangle, this flat zone represent losses. Figure 20-10 provides the general profit profile of a long strangle position.

Short strangles are the more popular of the two strategies, and are employed to take advantage of the declining time value of options in markets where asset prices are expected to be constant.

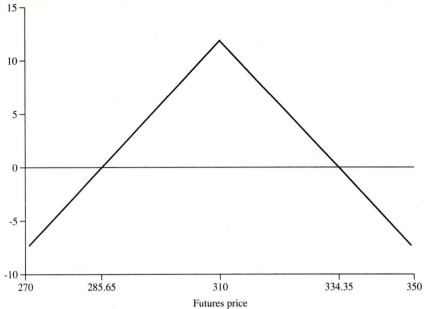

FIGURE 20-9
Short a straddle: Dec 90 S&P 500 futures options (310 call and 310 put).

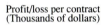

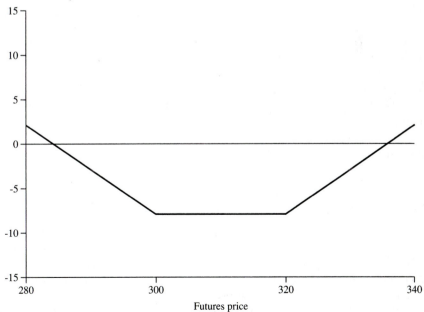

FIGURE 20-10
Long a strangle: Dec 90 S&P 500 futures options (320 call and 300 put).

20.4.4 Summary

The previous sections have described some of the more common option trading strategies employed by speculators. These include both simple option positions as well as more complex spread positions. Tables 20.2, 20.3, and 20.4 provide a summary of the various trading strategies discussed.[7]

Many other option trading strategies can be fashioned by putting together various combinations of these strategies. For example, *diagonal* spreads can be created by simultaneously buying and selling options of the same type (puts or calls) but with both different strike prices and different expiration dates. Or, traders can utilize various *ratio* spreads, selling (buying) more options that the number of options bought (sold). For example, to create a ratio call spread two high strike price calls might be sold for every low strike price call purchased. All of these strategies are variations on the basic option trading strategies, and have as their purpose the creation of specific risk-return configurations more appealing to a particular speculator.

While we have by no means discussed all of the possible option strategies, the strategies that we have covered provide a rich foundation upon which traders can construct and experiment with alternative trading strategies that more accurately reflect their particular price expectations and risk tolerances.

20.5 RISK MANAGEMENT WITH OPTIONS

Hedgers using futures basically attempt to lock in a specific price. In contrast, hedgers using options seek to set a specific floor or ceiling price. A futures hedger generally assumes a futures position opposite that of his cash position, hoping to offset any cash market loss and with a profit on the futures position. An option hedger, however, can establish a floor price (with a long put position), or a ceiling price (with a long call position), and still retain the possibility of profiting from favorable price movements.

This section examines the basic option hedging strategies. Most of these strategies, as we will see, involve trading strategies that have already been discussed in prior sections of the chapter. In the remaining sections of the chapter, therefore, we show how these trading strategies can be used by hedgers to manage their exposure to price risk.

20.5.1 Hedging against a Price Increase

THE PROBLEM. Suppose that on May 17, 1991, a gasoline distributor agrees to supply 4,200,000 gallons of gasoline to a transportation company, to be delivered on July 12, 1991, at a fixed price of 70.00 cents per gallon. Since the distributor's future sales price is fixed, he has a price exposure: if gasoline prices rise before he

---

[7]The column "Hedging implications" in these tables should be ignored until completion of the remaining sections of this chapter.

can acquire gasoline to meet his forward commitment, he may incur a substantial loss.

Table 20.5 provides price quotations for unleaded gasoline and heating oil in the cash, futures, and options markets on May 17, 1991. On May 17 the cash price for unleaded gasoline is 69.35 cents per gallon. Since the carrying cost for gasoline is approximately 1.25 cents per gallon per month, the distributor will incur a loss of 1.85 cents ($70.00 - 69.35 - 1.25 \times 2$) per gallon if he purchases gasoline in the cash market today, stores it until July 12, and delivers it in fulfillment of his contractual obligation. However, the gasoline market is in backwardation: nearby gasoline futures prices are higher than distant-month futures prices. Thus, anticipating lower prices in the future, the distributor decides to wait until July 12 to purchase the required gasoline in the cash market.

Table 20.6 shows the potential profits and losses of the distributor under two hypothetical market scenarios on July 12, 1991: 1) the cash gasoline price increases to 72 cents; and 2) the cash gasoline price decreases to 64 cents. Table 20.6 shows that the distributor will incur substantial losses if the first scenario occurs, but will make handsome profits if the second scenario occurs.

Because of the recent unpredictable volatility of energy prices, the distributor fears that gasoline prices may rise before he can fulfill his commitment in two months. Thus, he is considering using one of five possible hedging strategies: (1) buy futures, (2) buy calls, (3) buy a bull vertical call spread, (4) sell puts, and (5) buy calls and sell puts. In the following sections, the potential risk and return profiles for each of these hedging strategies is examined, using the prices existing on May 17, 1991 (see Table 20.5) and assuming no basis risk. In other words, we assume that the basis between the cash and spot month futures prices remains constant between May 17 and July 12.[8] On May 17 the cash gasoline price is 69.35 cents and the June gasoline futures price is 69 cents, resulting in a basis of 0.35 cents. Thus, if the cash gasoline price were to increase to 72 cents per gallon on July 12, we assume that the August 91 futures price would be 71.65 cents ($72 - 0.35$). Alternatively, if the cash gasoline price were to decrease to 64 cents per gallon, we assume that the August 91 futures price will be 63.65 cents ($64 - 0.35$). Table 20.7 provides the contract specifications for the relevant petroleum futures and option contracts used in the discussion below.

LONG FUTURES. A long futures strategy is the most straightforward. A long futures position can be used to offset the short cash (forward) market position. Since each gasoline futures contract covers 42,000 gallons, the distributor will have to purchase 100 August 91 gasoline futures contracts to fix his purchase price at 65.51 cents. Table 20.8 shows that if on July 12 the cash gasoline price is 72 cents, the profit on this futures position will more than offset the loss due to the increase in the cash gasoline price, and the distributor's effective purchase

---

[8]Petroleum product futures contracts cease trading on the last business day prior to the delivery month (see Table 12.7). Thus, in May the spot futures is the June contract. Similarly, on July 12, 1991, the spot futures is the August 91 contract.

TABLE 20.2
Summary of option trading and hedging strategies (market outlook: rising prices)

	Construction	Market outlook	Potential profit and loss	Hedging implications (long hedger)
Long futures	Buy futures; or Long call + short put (Synthetic futures)	• Strongly bullish price expectation. • Uncertain volatility.	• Profit is unlimited as prices rise. • Risk is unlimited as prices decline.	• Fixes the hedger's acquisition cost at the futures price. • Provides protection against rising prices, but has no potential to profit from favorable downward price movements.
Long call	Long call; or long futures + long put (Synthetic call)	• Bullish price expectation. • Rising volatility.	• Profit is unlimited as the underlying futures price rises beyond the strike price plus the premium paid. • Risk is strictly limited to the premium paid.	• If prices rise, the acquisition cost is protected by a ceiling price equal to the strike price plus the premium paid. • If prices decline below the strike price, the hedger participates fully in a declining market and the net acquisition cost equals the spot price plus the premium paid.

| Bull spread | Long call A + short call B (Vertical call spread); or Long put A + short put B (Vertical put spread) | • Mildly bullish price expectation. | • Profit is limited to the difference of the strike prices if futures price is at or above B at expiration.
• Risk is limited if futures price is at or less than A at expiration. | • Provides protection against limited price rise.
• If prices rise above B, protection is limited, but full profit participation if prices decline. |
| Short put | Short put; or Long futures + short call (Synthetic put) | • Neutral to mildly bullish price expectation.
• Declining volatility | • Profit is limited to the premium received.
• Risk is unlimited | • Premium received reduces the acquisition cost if futures prices remain stable or rise slightly.
• If prices rise sharply, the hedger is unprotected.
• If prices decline, the acquisition cost is fixed at the strike price minus the premium income. |

(A = strike price A; B = strike price B; A < B)

TABLE 20.3
Summary of option trading and hedging strategies (market outlook: declining prices)

	Construction	Market outlook	Potential profit and loss	Hedging implications (long hedger)
Short futures	Sell futures; or Long put + short call (Synthetic futures) 	• Strongly bearish price expectation. • Uncertain volatility.	• Profit is unlimited as prices fall. • Risk is unlimited as prices rise.	• Fixes the hedger's sales price at the futures price. • Provides full protection against falling prices, but with no participation in favorable upward price movements.
Long put	Long put; or long futures + long call (Synthetic put) 	• Bearish price expectation. • Rising volatility.	• Profit is unlimited as the underlying futures price falls beyond the strike price minus the premium paid. • Risk is strictly limited to the premium paid.	• If prices fall, the sales revenue is fully protected by a floor price equal to the strike price minus the premium paid. • If prices rise above the strike price, the hedger participates fully in a rising market and the net sales price equals the spot price minus the premium paid.

Strategy	Construction	Diagram	Outlook	Profit/Risk	Notes
Bear spread	Short call A + long call B (Vertical call spread); or Short put A + long put B (Vertical put spread)		• Mildly bearish price expectation.	• Profit is limited to the difference of the strike prices if futures price is at or below A at expiration. • Risk is limited if futures price is at or above B at expiration.	• Provides protection against moderate price declines. • If prices fall sharply below A, protection is limited, but full profit participation if prices rise.
Short call	Short call; or Short futures + short put (Synthetic call)		• Neutral to mildly bearish price expectation. • Declining volatility.	• Profit is limited to the premium received. • Risk is potentially unlimited.	• Premium income increases the revenue if futures prices remain stable or rise slightly. • If prices fall sharply, the hedger is unprotected. • If prices rise, the sales revenue is fixed at the strike price plus the premium income.

(A = strike price A; B = strike price B; A < B)

TABLE 20.4
Summary of option trading and hedging strategies (market outlook: stable prices)

	Construction	Market outlook	Potential profit and loss	Hedging implications
Long straddle	Long call A + long put A	• Uncertain price expectation • Increasing volatility • Typicallly entered when the underlying futures price is near the strike price and is likely to surge in either direction.	• Profit is unlimited if prices move up or down beyond either strike price. • Risk is limited to the premium paid if futures price is at either strike prices at expiration.	• Long hedge: The acquisition cost is fully protected by a ceiling price equal to the strike price plus the premium paid. Full profit participation if prices fall. If prices remain stable, the hedger loses the premium paid. • Short Hedge: Revenue is fully protected by a floor price equal to the strike price minus the premium paid. Full profit participation if prices rise. If prices remain stable, the hedger loses the premium paid.
Short straddle	Short call A + short put A	• Stable price expectation. • Declining volatility. • Typically entered when the underlying futures price is near the strike price and is unlikely to surge in either direction.	• Profit is limited to the net premium income if the futures price at expiration is at either strike price. • Risk is potentially unlimited as prices move up or down beyond the two strike prices.	• Long hedge: Premium income reduces the acquisition cost if prices remain between the strike prices. Limited protection if prices rise, and limited profit participation if prices fall. • Short Hedge: Premium income augments sales revenue if prices remain between the strike prices. Limited profit participation if prices rise, and limited protection if prices fall.

Strategy	Construction	Expectation	Profit/Risk	Hedge
Long strangle	Long put A + long call B; or Long call A + long put B.	• Uncertain price expectation. • Increasing volatility • Typically entered when the underlying futures price is between A and B and likely to surge in either direction.	• Profit is unlimited if prices move up or down. • Risk is limited to the premium paid if the futures price is between A and B at expiration.	• Long hedge: Acquisition cost is fully protected by a ceiling price, and with full profit participation if prices fall. • Short Hedge: The sales revenue is fully protected by a floor price, and with full profit participation if prises rise.
Short strangle	Short put A + short call B; or Short call A + short put B.	• Stable price expectation • Decreasing volatility • Typically entered when the underlying futures price is near A and B.	• Profit is limited to the premium received if the futures price is between A and B at expiration. • Risk is unlimited if prices move sharply up or down.	• Long hedge: Premium income reduces the acquisition cost if prices remain stable between the two strike prices. Limited protection if prices rise, and limited profit participation if prices fall. • Short hedge: Premium income augments the sales revenue if prices remain stable between the two strike prices. Limited profit participation if prices rise, and limited protection if prices fall.

(A = strike price A; B = strike price B; A < B)

TABLE 20.5
Oil prices

OIL PRICES

Friday, May 17, 1991.

CASH MARKET

CRUDE GRADES OFFSHORE-d

European "spot" or free market prices

	Fri	Thur	Yr. Ago
Arab lt.	hn15.75	16.05	14.90
Arab hvy.	hn12.75	13.05	13.55
Iran. lt.	hn15.55	15.85	14.80
Forties	hn18.55	18.85	17.00
Brent	hn18.60	18.90	17.40
Bonny lt.	hn18.90	19.20	17.35
Urals-Medit.	hn17.85	18.15	15.40

DOMESTIC-f
Spot market

W. Tex. Int Cush (1950-2000) (Jun)	h21.20	20.90	18.75
W.Tx.sour, Midl (1700-1840)	h19.50	18.75	15.90
La. sw. St.Ja (2000-2050)	h21.25	20.90	18.27
No. Slope del USGULF	hn18.30	17.75	15.60

Open-market crude oil values in Northwest Europe around 17:50 GMT in dlrs per barrel, for main loading ports in country of origin for prompt loading, except as indicated.

REFINED PRODUCTS

Fuel Oil, No. 2 NY gal.	g.5525	.5510	.5340
Gasoline, unlded, premium NY gal.	g.7600	.7525	.7485
Gasoline, unlded, reg. NY gal.	g.6935	.6910	.6650
Propane, Mont Belvieu, Texas, gal.	g.3325	.3375	.2250
Butane, normal, Mont Belvieu, Texas, gal.	g.3925	.3975	.2850

a-Asked. b-Bid. c-Corrected. d-as of 11 a.m. EST in Northwest Europe. f-As of 4 p.m. EST. Refiners' posted buying prices are in parentheses. g-Provided by Bloomberg News-Oil Buyers Guide. h-Dow Jones International Petroleum Report. n.a.-Not available. z-Not quoted. n-Nominal. r-Revised.

FUTURES MARKET

	Open	High	Low	Settle	Change	Lifetime High	Low	Open Interest
HEATING OIL NO. 2 (NYM) 42,000 gal.; $ per gal.								
June	.5555	.5620	.5555	.5591	+.0016	.8575	.4800	16,278
July	.5610	.5670	.5610	.5658	+.0017	.8500	.4800	21,435
Aug	.5710	.5760	.5705	.5735	+.0008	.8507	.4900	13,600
Sept	.5860	.5900	.5860	.5880	+.0003	.8428	.5025	7,071
Oct	.5970	.6005	.5970	.5988	+.0003	.8500	.5130	3,366
Nov	.6085	.6105	.6060	.6083	+.0003	.7800	.5230	3,595
Dec	.6160	.6200	.6160	.6173	+.0001	.8262	.5330	16,082
Ja92	.6180	.6210	.6170	.6178	−.0004	.8200	.5340	5,080
Feb	.6075	.6110	.6075	.6073	−.0004	.6115	.5225	3,403
Mar	.5845	.5895	.5840	.5848	+.0001	.5895	.5415	1,447
Apr	.5650	.5700	.5650	.5653	+.0001	.5700	.5000	446
May	....	....	....	.5503	+.0001	.5505	.4875	613
June	.5500	.5500	.5500	.5433	+.0001	.5500	.4800	418

Est vol 17,013; vol Thur 19,528; open int 92,909, +3,516.

	Open	High	Low	Settle	Change	Lifetime High	Low	Open Interest
GASOLINE, Unleaded (NYM) 42,000 gal.; $ per gal.								
June	.6830	.6960	.6790	.6900	+.0034	.9550	.5490	18,265
July	.6660	.6785	.6640	.6738	+.0036	.8270	.5525	18,096
Aug	.6500	.6590	.6475	.6551	+.0031	.9050	.5350	10,229
Sept	.6340	.6375	.6330	.6351	+.0031	.9025	.5160	5,119
Oct	.6050	.6130	.6040	.6090	+.0038	.8625	.4975	6,236
Nov	.5900	.5955	.5900	.5940	+.0039	.6675	.4860	2,239
Dec	.5790	.5830	.5780	.5795	+.0040	.7525	.4775	1,268
Ja92	.5715	.5760	.5715	.5710	+.0045	.6415	.4700	3,340
Feb	.5760	.5800	.5760	.5750	+.0038	.5755	.5070	5,681
Mar	....	....	....	.5890	+.0025	.5875	.5050	530
Apr	.6340	.6340	.6340	.6280	+.0025	.6340	.5500	592
May	....	....	....	.6240	+.0030	.6155	.5525	639
June	....	....	....	.6135	+.0035	.6020	.5500	1,159
Aug	....	....	....	.5875	+.0035	.5800	.5070	152

Est vol 24,445; vol Thur 19,557; open int 73,581, +369.

OPTIONS MARKET

HEATING OIL No.2 (NYM) 42,000 gal.; $ per gal.

Strike Price	Calls−Settle			Puts−Settle		
	Jly-c	Aug-c	Sp-c	Jly-p	Aug-p	Sep-p
52	.0463	.0553	....	.0005	.0018	.0025
54	.0283	.0380	.0535	.0025	.0045	.0055
56	.0143	.0235	.0380	.0085	.0100	.0100
58	.0055	.0135	.0260	.0197	....	.0180
60	.0020	.0070	.0170	.0362	....	....
62	.0088	....	.0110	.0550	....	....

Est. vol. 192; Thur vol. 66 calls; 120 puts
Open interest Thur; 11,925 calls; 9,781 puts

GASOLINE−Unleaded (NYM) 42,000 gal.; $ per gal.

Strike Price	Calls−Settle			Puts−Settle		
	Jly-c	Aug-c	Sp-c	Jly-p	Aug-p	Sep-p
64	.0393	.0341	.0290	.0055	.0190	.0339
66	.0243	.0240	.0215	.0105	.0289	....
68	.0150	.0170	.0160	.0212	.0419	....
70	.0085	.0125	.0120	.0347	....	....
72	.0045	.0085	.0090	....	....	....
74	.0030	.0060	....	....	....	....

Est. vol. 3,779; Thur vol. 829 calls; 376 puts
Open interest Thur; 15,096 calls; 8,835 puts

Source: The Wall Street Journal, May 20, 1991.

price will be 65.86.[9] However, as Table 20.8 also shows, if the cash price were to fall to 64 cents, the distributor's acquisition cost would still be 65.86 cents. Thus, by hedging with futures, the distributor has forfeited the opportunity to benefit from lower prices in order to lock in a certain and profitable acquisition cost.

---

[9]In this example the hedger is assumed not to hold the futures position until the last trading day (July 31). Hence, there is no convergence of the cash and futures prices (i.e., zero basis). Therefore, instead of locking in a fixed cost at 65.51 cents by going long August futures contracts, the distributor locks in a price of 65.86 cents (65.51 cents plus the basis of 0.35 cents).

TABLE 20.6
Gasoline distributor example: Potential profits and losses on unhedged position

Contractual obligation on May 17, 1991:

 Agrees to deliver 4,200,000 gallons of gasoline
 on July 12, 1991 at a fixed price of $0.70 per gallon

	Per gallon	Total profit/(loss)
Alternative scenarios on July 12, 1991:		
i) Cash gasoline price increases to 72 cents		
Loss on sales ($0.70−$0.72)	$(0.02)	$(84,000)
Effective purchase price	$ 0.72	
ii) Cash gasoline price decreases to 64 cents		
Gain on sales ($0.70−$0.64)	$ 0.06	$252,000
Effective purchase price	$ 0.64	

LONG CALLS. The long call option strategy is the simplest alternative to a long hedge with futures. By buying August 91 calls, the hedger guarantees that he will be able to purchase gasoline at a specified price at any time prior to expiration of the options, no matter what happens to cash prices. In return for this guarantee, the hedger pays a premium, which may be thought of as the cost of the price insurance he receives. The option premium is the maximum cost associated with this strategy.

As shown in Table 20.5, the distributor can purchase August 91 gasoline call options with a variety of strike prices, ranging from 64 cents to 74 cents.[10] Assume that on May 17 the distributor decides to purchase 100 August 66 calls, which entitle him to buy 100 August futures contracts at 66 cents per gallon during the next two months at a premium of 2.4 cents per gallon, or $1008 per contract ($0.024 × 42,000$).

Table 20.9 shows that if the cash gasoline price rises to 72 cents on July 12, the August 91 futures price will be 71.65 cents, and the August 66 call option will have an exercisable value of 5.65 cents (71.65 − 66). After deducting the option premium of 2.4 cents, the distributor will realize a net gain of 3.25 cents per gallon on his option position. This gain, of 3.25 cents, will reduce his actual purchase cost from 72 cents to 68.75 cents.

Alternatively, if, instead of rising, the price of gasoline were to fall to 64 cents on July 12, the distributor would allow the option to expire and buy gasoline at the lower cash price. In this case the effective purchase price will be 64 cents

---

[10]The August 91 options on gasoline futures expire on July 12, 1991. The August 91 futures contract expires on July 31, 1991.

TABLE 20.7
Contract specifications: Unleaded gasoline and heating oil futures and futures options

	Gasoline/heating oil futures	Futures options on gasoline/heating oil
Exchange	New York Mercantile Exchange (NYMEX).	New York Mercantile Exchange
Trading unit	42,000 gallons (1000 barrels).	One NYMEX unleaded gasoline or heating oil futures contract.
Trading hours	9:50 A.M. to 3:10 P.M. (New York time).	9:50 A.M. to 3:10 P.M. (New York time).
Contract months	Fifteen consecutive months commencing with the current calendar month.	Six consecutive months.
Price quotations	Cents per gallon.	Cents per gallon.
Minimum price fluctuation	0.01 cents per gallon.	0.01 cents per gallon.
Last trading day	Last business day of the month preceding the delivery month.	Second Friday of the month prior to the delivery month of the underlying futures contract.
Delivery and grade specifications	New York harbor ex-shore. Heating oil: industry standard for fungible No. 2 heating oil specifications. Gasoline: industry standard for fungible, northern grade, unleaded regular gasoline specifications.	—
Strike prices	—	Strike prices are in increments of 2 cents per gallon. At all times at least seven strike prices are available for puts and calls on the underlying futures contract.
Exercise	—	By 4:30 P.M. on any day up to and including the option's expiration.

plus 2.4 cents (the option premium paid), or 66.40 cents per gallon (see Table 20.9).

Thus, a long call strategy fixes a ceiling purchase price while still permitting the distributor to profit from a favorable downward price move. Further, the availability of a wide range of strike prices allows the distributor a choice of ceiling prices and profit potentials if prices decline. For example, in the case where the cash price rises to 72 cents, buying the in-the-money 64 cent call option, which costs 3.41 cents per gallon, establishes an effective purchase price of 67.76 cents per

TABLE 20.8
Hedging against a price increase in gasoline with a long futures position

May 17, 1991:

Go long 100 August 91 gasoline
futures at $0.6551 per gallon

	Per gallon	Total profit/(loss)
Alternative scenarios on July 12, 1991:		
i) Cash gasoline price increases to 72 cents		
Loss on forward sales ($0.70 − $0.72)	$(0.0200)	$(84,000)
Gain on futures ($0.7165 − $0.6551)*	0.0614	257,880
Net Profit	0.0414	173,880
Effective purchase price ($0.72 − $0.0614):	$0.6586	
ii) Cash gasoline price decreases to 64 cents		
Gain on forward sales ($0.70 − $0.64)	$0.0600	$252,000
Loss on futures ($0.6365 − $0.6551)*	(0.0186)	(78,120)
Net profit	0.0414	173,880
Effective purchase price ($0.64 + $0.0186):	$0.6586	

*Although the gasoline cash price rises to 72 cents, the gasoline futures price will be 71.65 cents because we have assumed that the basis remains constant at 0.35 cents. Similarly, as the gasoline cash price falls to 64 cents, the August gasoline futures price will be 63.65 cents.

TABLE 20.9
Hedging against a price increase in gasoline with long call options

May 17, 1991:

Buy 100 August 66 calls at a premium
of $0.024 per gallon

	Per gallon	Total profit/(loss)
Alternative scenarios on July 12, 1991:		
i) Cash gasoline price increases to 72 cents		
Loss on forward sales ($0.70 − $0.72)	$(0.0200)	$(84,000)
Gain on call option ($0.7165 − $0.66 − $0.024)	0.0325	136,500
Net Profit	0.0125	52,500
Effective purchase price ($0.72 − $0.0325):	$0.6875	
ii) Cash gasoline price decreases to 64 cents		
Gain on forward sales ($0.70 − $0.64)	$0.0600	$252,000
Loss on call options (i.e., the premium)	(0.0240)	(100,800)
Net profit	0.0360	151,200
Effective purchase price ($0.64 + $0.024):	$0.6640	

TABLE 20.10
Hedging against a price increase in gasoline with long bull call spread

May 17, 1991:

Buy 100 August 66 calls for $0.0240,
sell 100 August 70 calls for $0.0125,
establishing long bull call spreads at a net
premium cost of $0.0115 per gallon.

	Per gallon	Total profit/(loss)
Alternative scenarios on July 12, 1991:		
i) Cash gasoline price increases to 72 cents		
Loss on forward sales ($0.70 − $0.72)	$(0.0200)	$(84,000)
Gain on option spreads ($0.70 − $0.66 − $0.0115)	0.0285	119,700
Net Profit	0.0085	35,700
Effective purchase price ($0.72 − $0.0285):	$0.6915	
ii) Cash gasoline price decreases to 64 cents		
Gain on forward sales ($0.70 − $0.64)	$0.0600	$252,000
Loss on option spreads (the net premium cost)	(0.0115)	(48,300)
Net profit	0.0485	203,700
Effective purchase price ($0.64 + $0.0115):	$0.6515	

gallon [72 − (71.65 − 64 − 3.41)]. This ceiling price is the lowest attainable with the available options, and therefore yields the best protection against rising prices. However, the in-the-money 64 call has a large premium and entails the greatest hedging cost, and therefore provides the least amount of profit participation if cash prices were to decline.

LONG BULL CALL SPREADS. Some hedgers may consider the previous long call strategy to be an expensive form of price insurance because of the option premium. A less expensive alternative is a long bull vertical call spread. As discussed earlier, such a spread is created by purchasing a low-strike call coupled with the sale of a relatively high-strike call, where both legs of the spread share a common expiration date.

Table 20.10 shows the results of a hedging strategy of going long 100 August 66–70 bull call spreads. Buying the August 66 call at a premium of 2.4 cents per gallon and selling the August 70 call at 1.25 cents results in a net option premium cost of 1.15 cents per gallon. If gasoline prices were to rise to 72 cents, both the August 66 and 70 calls would be in-the-money and the distributor would have a net gain of 2.85 cents on this option spread.[11] This would reduce his actual

---

[11]Readers should verify how the 2.85 cents is derived by working through the calculations for both the long and short call option positions.

acquisition cost to 69.15 cents. However, should gasoline prices decline to 64 cents, the distributor would be able to purchase gasoline at a much lower cost in the cash market, so that his effective purchase price would be 65.15 cents (64 + 1.15, where 1.15 is the net cost of the bull call spread).

This strategy, while less expensive, provides protection against only a limited price increase. In the above example it provided full protection against the price increase that occurred. But if cash prices had risen above 72.85 cents, it would not have provided further protection. A bull call spread, therefore, does not provide "disaster" insurance, which explains why it is a cheaper strategy to implement.

SHORT PUTS. Hedgers can sell put options as protection against small price increases. The premium received from the put sales can be used to offset increased costs in the cash market due to a price increase. If, however, prices decline, the hedger will not benefit fully because the put options will be exercised against him.

Table 20.11 shows the gasoline distributor selling 100 August 66 put options at 2.89 cents per gallon (see Table 20.5), or for $1213.8 per contract ($0.0289 × 42,000). If gasoline prices were to rise to 72 cents, the distributor's effective acquisition price would be 69.11 cents per gallon: the 72 cent market price less the 2.89 cent premium received from the put sale. The distributor's upward price protection, however, is limited to the premium received from selling the put.

Conversely, should gasoline prices decline to 64 cents, the put option might be exercised and the distributor required to buy gasoline futures at the put strike

TABLE 20.11
Hedging against a price increase in gasoline with short put options

May 17, 1991:

Sell 100 August 66 puts at a premium
of $0.0289 per gallon.

	Per gallon	Total profit/(loss)
Alternative scenarios on July 12, 1991:		
i) Cash gasoline price increases to 72 cents		
Loss on forward sales ($0.70 − $0.72)	$(0.0200)	$(84,000)
Gain on Aug 66 puts (the premium)	0.0289	121,380
Net Profit	0.0089	37,380
Effective purchase price ($0.72 − $0.0289):	$0.6911	
ii) Cash gasoline price decreases to 64 cents		
Gain on forward sales ($0.70 − $0.64)	$0.0600	$252,000
Gain on Aug 66 puts ($0.6365 − $0.66 + $0.0289)	0.0054	22,680
Net profit	0.0654	274,680
Effective purchase price ($0.64 − $0.0054):	$0.6346	

price of 66 cents. The loss due to the exercise, however, would be reduced by the premium received. In the example in Table 20.11, the distributor would still have a net profit of 0.54 cents per gallon on his option hedge. Thus, his net acquisition cost would be 63.46 cents. However, the distributor's ability to benefit from further reductions in cash prices is limited, and is equal to the strike price (66 cents) less the put premium received (2.89 cents). If gasoline prices were to fall below 66 cents, the distributor could not reduce his acquisition cost to below 63.11 cents per gallon.

In summary, selling put options as a hedge against increases in cash prices is desirable if the underlying cash price remains stable or moves above the strike price by only a limited amount.

LONG MIN-MAX OPTION STRATEGY. The min-max option strategy involves buying calls and selling puts, and is commonly known as a *collar* or a *range-forward* contract. A long min-max option position used to hedge against increasing prices is created by purchasing calls and selling an equal number of puts with different strike prices but with the same expiration date. (A similar position to hedge against decreasing prices can be established by purchasing puts and selling an equal number of calls with different strike prices but with the same expiration date.)

This strategy establishes maximum and minimum buying prices as well as a range of prices over which hedgers will retain some risk but will be able to make some profits. More specifically, buying call options enables hedgers to fix a maximum buying price while still retaining the opportunity to acquire the asset at a lower cost should cash prices fall. By selling puts, however, the hedger fixes a minimum buying price even if cash prices move lower in the future. The cost of establishing this hedge is the call premium paid minus the put premium received.

The attractiveness of the min-max strategy is its low cost and the possibility of tailoring it to fit the hedger's desired risk exposure by selecting different call and put strike prices. For example, if the current August 91 gasoline futures price were 66 cents, the distributor could either buy the August 66 futures call option and sell the August 66 futures put option (at-the-money options) or buy the August 68 call and sell the August 64 put (out-of-the-money options with strike prices equidistant from the underlying futures price). In both cases the premium paid would exactly offset the premium received.

The respective call and put strike prices determine the hedger's risk exposure and profit potential.[12] If the call and put strike prices are equal to the underlying futures price (at-the-money options), the min-max strategy is equivalent to a synthetic futures, and the hedger has no risk exposure.[13] A difference between the call

---

[12]Depending on the strike prices of the calls and puts, the net cost to the hedger may be positive, negative, or zero.

[13]In Section 18.5.4, it is shown that a synthetic long futures position is created by combining a long call option with a short put option with the same strike price. Similarly, a synthetic short futures position is created by combining a long put option with a short call option with the same strike price.

and put strike prices establishes a price range within which the hedger participates in price movements, both up and down. Within this range the long hedger will benefit from lower prices, and the short hedger will benefit from higher prices. At prices outside the strike price range, the hedger is fully hedged, just as he would be with a futures position. The larger the range between the two strike prices, the greater the hedger's price participation.

Our gasoline distributor can use a min-max option hedging strategy to lock in a purchase price by buying 100 August 68 calls at a premium of 1.7 cents per gallon and simultaneously financing this purchase by selling 100 August 64 puts at 1.9 cents. Table 20.12 shows the range of net purchase prices resulting from this strategy under various price scenarios on July 12. The first column in the table shows hypothetical August 91 gasoline futures prices on July 12. Columns (2), (3) and (4) show the respective gains and losses on the long call and short put option positions as well as on the net option position. Column (5) shows the cash prices on July 12, 1991. Since the basis between the cash and the spot month futures prices is assumed to be constant, the cash price will always be 0.35 cents more than the respective futures price in Column (1). The last column is the effective net purchase price, which is obtained either by adding the net option loss to the cash price or by reducing the cash price by the net option gain. Table 20.12 clearly shows the floor and ceiling price effects of this hedging strategy. Figure 20-11 also provides a graphical presentation of these results.

Table 20.13 provides a specific example. If cash gasoline prices rise to 72 cents, the calls will be in-the-money and the puts will be out-of-the-money. The

TABLE 20.12
Hedging against a price increase in gasoline with a long min-max option strategy (Long call & short put on August 91 gasoline futures)

Premiums on May 17, 1991:

    August 68 call = 1.7 cents

    August 64 put = 1.9 cents

July 12, 1991:

	Profit (loss) on option positions				
Futures price	Long call	Short put	Net	Cash price	Net purchase price
		(Cents per gallon)			
60.00	−1.70	−2.10	−3.80	60.35	64.15
62.00	−1.70	−0.10	−1.80	62.35	64.15
64.00	−1.70	1.90	0.20	64.35	64.15
66.00	−1.70	1.90	0.20	66.35	66.15
68.00	−1.70	1.90	0.20	68.35	68.15
70.00	0.30	1.90	2.20	70.35	68.15
72.00	2.30	1.90	4.20	72.35	68.15
74.00	4.30	1.90	6.20	74.35	68.15

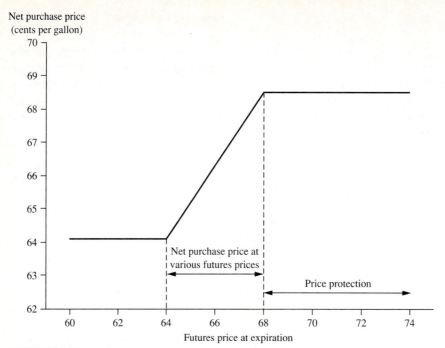

FIGURE 20-11
Min-max option hedging strategy: Gasoline (buy Aug 68 call, sell Aug 64 put).

TABLE 20.13
Hedging against a price increase in gasoline with a long min-max option strategy

May 17, 1991:

	Per gallon	Total profit/(loss)
Buy 100 August 68 calls at $0.017, sell 100 August 64 puts at $0.019.		

Alternative scenarios on July 12, 1991:

i) Cash gasoline price increases to 72 cents

		Per gallon	Total profit/(loss)
Loss on forward sales ($0.70 − $0.72)		$(0.0200)	$(84,000)
Gain on calls ($0.7165 − $0.68 − $0.017) = $0.0195			
Gain on puts (the option premium)　 = $0.0190			
Gain on options		0.0385	161,700
Net Profit		0.0185	77,700
Effective purchase price ($0.72 − $0.0385):		$0.6815	

ii) Cash gasoline price decreases to 64 cents

		Per gallon	Total profit/(loss)
Gain on forward sales ($0.70 − $0.64)		$0.0600	$252,000
Loss on calls (the option premium)　 = $(0.0170)			
Gain on puts ($0.6365 − $0.64 + $0.019) = $ 0.0155			
Loss on options		(0.0015)	(6,300)
Net profit		0.0585	245,700
Effective purchase price ($0.64 + $0.0015):		$0.6415	

distributor will realize a gain of 1.95 cents on his long call position and, in addition, will receive a put premium of 1.9 cents. This will reduce his purchase price to 68.15 cents. Alternatively, if gasoline prices decline to 64 cents, the calls will be out-of-the-money and the puts will be in-the-money, but the loss on the option position will be offset by lower prices in the cash market. In this case the effective purchase price will be 64.15 cents.

SUMMARY. The following table provides a summary of what the distributor's effective acquisition cost of gasoline would be on July 12 under each of the alternative hedging strategies discussed above:

Effective purchase prices under alternative hedging strategies

Alternative price scenarios on July 12	Unhedged	Alternative hedging strategies				
		Long futures	Buy call	Long bull call spread	Sell put	Min-max
($)	($)	($)	($)	($)	($)	($)
0.72	0.72	0.6586	0.6875	0.6915	0.6911	0.6815
0.64	0.64	0.6586	0.6640	0.6515	0.6346	0.6415

The costs and benefits of these strategies can be summarized as follows:

	Benefits	Costs
Buy futures	Locks in a specific purchase price	Does not benefit from price declines
Buy calls	Locks in a ceiling purchase price	Option premium
Bull call spread	Locks in a limited ceiling purchase price	Net option premium
Sell puts	Augments current income	Does not benefit from price declines
Min-max	Sets a collar price range at low cost	Limited participation in a price decline

20.5.2 Hedging against a Price Decline

THE PROBLEM. Similar option strategies can be used to hedge against price declines. Suppose that on May 17, 1991, an oil wholesaler purchases 4,200,000 gallons of heating oil from a refiner at the prevailing cash price of 55.25 cents a gallon. Since it is the summer season, the demand for heating oil is low. The wholesaler, consequently, enters into an agreement with an oil marketer to deliver the 4,200,000 gallons to him on August 9, at the cash price prevailing on that day. Thus, the wholesaler must carry the heating oil in his inventory, and incur

TABLE 20.14
Heating oil distributor example: Potential profits and losses on unhedged position

Contractual obligation on May 17, 1991:

> Agrees to deliver 4,200,000 gallons of
> heating oil on August 9, 1991, at the cash
> price prevailing on the delivery date.

		Per gallon	Total profit/(loss)
Alternative scenarios on August 9, 1991:			
i) Cash heating oil price increases to 60 cents			
Sales price		$0.6000	$2,520,000
Less: Cost	$(0.5525)		
Carrying cost	(0.0267)		
Total cost		(0.5792)	(2,432,640)
Net profit		0.0208	87,360
Effective sales price		$0.6000	
ii) Cash heating oil price decreases to 52 cents			
Sales price		$0.5200	$2,184,000
Less: Cost	$(0.5525)		
Carrying cost	(0.0267)		
Total cost		(0.5792)	(2,432,640)
Net loss		$(0.0592)	(248,640)
Effective sales price		$0.5200	

the risk that heating oil prices may decline before August 9. Table 20.14 shows how volatile the distributor's revenue can be if cash heating oil prices increase or decrease prior to August 9.

This section examines five basic futures and option hedging strategies that may be used to hedge against the risk of a price decline: 1) sell futures, 2) buy puts, 3) buy a vertical bear put spread, 4) sell calls, and 5) buy puts and sell calls. The remainder of this section examines each of these strategies using actual cash, futures, and option prices for heating oil on May 17, 1991 (see Table 20.5). In our examples, we make the following assumptions:

- On May 17, 1991, the cash heating oil price is 55.25 cents, and the June 91 heating oil futures price is 55.91 cents, resulting in a basis of −0.66 cents. This basis, between the cash price and the spot month futures price, is assumed to remain constant from May 17 through August 9.

- The cost of carrying heating oil is approximately 1 cent per gallon per month. Thus, the total carrying cost from May 17 to August 9, a period of about $2\frac{2}{3}$ months, amounts to 2.67 cents per gallon.

In addition, our examples utilize two price scenarios for the final day of our illustration period, August 9, 1991:

1. Cash heating oil prices increase to 60 cents per gallon, and the September 91 futures price is therefore 60.66 cents (60 + 0.66) per gallon.
2. Cash gasoline prices decrease to 52 cents per gallon, and the September 91 futures price is therefore 52.66 cents (52 + 0.66).

SHORT FUTURES. The oil wholesaler may hedge by going short 100 September 91 heating oil futures at 58.80 cents. As shown in Table 20.15, this strategy enables the wholesaler to lock in a net profit of 0.22 cents per gallon, whether cash heating oil prices increase to 60 cents or decline to 52 cents by August 9. In this case the wholesaler locks in a sales price of 58.14 cents per gallon.[14]

LONG PUTS. A second strategy is for the wholesaler to buy heating oil put options. That will guarantee a fixed sales price, no matter how far heating oil prices decline. If prices decline below the put strike price, he can exercise the put option to partially or fully offset cash market losses. At the same time, the wholesaler retains the ability to participate in an upward price advance: if prices advance, he will simply abandon the put. The cost of this strategy is the put premium paid.

In the example in Table 20.16 the wholesaler buys 100 September 58 puts on heating oil futures at a premium of 1.8 cents, giving the wholesaler the right to sell 100 September 91 heating oil futures at 58 cents per gallon on or before August 9, the last trading day of the September options. If, on August 9, the cash price were to rise to 60 cents, the wholesaler would simply let the options expire and sell his heating oil at the higher market price. Of course, his effective sales price would be reduced by the put option premium paid. Alternatively, if the cash price were to decline to 52 cents, the wholesaler would exercise his option at 58 cents, partially offsetting his losses in the cash market. This strategy fully protects the hedger against severe declines in cash prices.[15]

---

[14] In this example, there is no basis risk, and the hedger is assumed not to hold his futures hedge (the September 91 futures contracts) until the last trading day (August 30). Thus, we do not assume convergence of the cash and futures prices (i.e., zero basis). Therefore, instead of locking in a fixed sales price of 58.80 cents by going short the September futures contracts, the lock-in price is 58.14 cents (58.80 cents minus the basis of 0.66 cents assumed earlier).

[15] As indicated in Table 20.5, the September 60 put was not traded on May 17, 1991. Otherwise, it may have been more beneficial for the wholesaler to go long the September 60 put, which would have given him even greater downside protection.

TABLE 20.15
Hedging against a price decrease in heating oil with a short futures position

May 17, 1991:

Go short 100 September 91 heating oil futures
at $0.5880 per gallon

		Per gallon	Total profit/(loss)
Alternative scenarios on August 9, 1991:			
i)	Cash heating oil increases to 60 cents		
	Sales price	$0.6000	$2,520,000
	Less: Cost $(0.5525)		
	Carrying cost (0.0267)		
	Total Cost	(0.5792)	(2,432,640)
	Gain on forward sales	0.0208	87,360
	Loss on futures ($0.5880 − $0.6066)*	(0.0186)	(78,120)
	Net profit	0.0022	9,240
	Effective sales price ($0.60 − $0.0186)	$0.5814	
ii)	Cash heating oil price decreases to 52 cents		
	Sales price	$0.5200	$2,184,000
	Less: Cost $(0.5525)		
	Carrying cost (0.0267)		
	Total cost	(0.5792)	(2,432,640)
	Loss on forward sales	(0.0592)	(248,640)
	Gain on futures ($0.5880 − $0.5266)*	0.0614	257,880
	Net profit	$0.0022	9,240
	Effective sales price ($0.52 + $0.0614)	$0.5814	

* Although the heating oil cash price rises to 60 cents, the September heating oil futures price will be 60.66 cents because we have assumed that the basis remains constant at 0.66 cents. Similarly, as the heating oil cash price falls to 52 cents, the September heating oil futures price will be 52.66 cents.

LONG BEAR PUT SPREAD. A lower-cost hedging strategy is a long vertical bear put spread. While less costly, this strategy protects against only a limited downside price movement.

As discussed earlier, a vertical bear put spread is the purchase of a high strike price put coupled with the sale of a low strike price put, where both legs of the spread have a common expiration date. Table 20.17 provides the results of the wholesaler hedging with bear put spreads. The wholesaler will lose only the net option premium if prices increase. Should prices decline, however, a bear

TABLE 20.16
Hedging against a price decrease in heating oil with long put options

May 17, 1991:

Buy 100 September 58 puts at a premium
$0.018 per gallon

		Per gallon	Total profit/(loss)
Alternative scenarios on August 9, 1991:			
i) Cash heating oil increases to 60 cents			
Sales price		$0.6000	$2,520,000
Less: Cost	$(0.5525)		
Carrying cost	(0.0267)		
Total Cost		(0.5792)	(2,432,640)
Gain on forward sales		0.0208	87,360
Loss on options (the premium)		(0.0180)	(75,600)
Net profit		0.0028	11,760
Effective sales price ($0.60 − $0.018)		$0.5820	
ii) Cash heating oil price decreases to 52 cents			
Sales price		$0.5200	$2,184,000
Less: Cost	$(0.5525)		
Carrying cost	(0.0267)		
Total cost		(0.5792)	(2,432,640)
Loss on forward sales		(0.0592)	(248,640)
Gain on options ($0.5800 − $0.5266 − $0.018)		0.0354	148,680
Net loss		$(0.0238)	(99,960)
Effective sales price ($0.52 + $0.0354)		$0.5554	

put spread offers only limited protection against losses in the cash market. The maximum profit in a bear put spread is the difference between the strike prices less the net option premium. This amount, therefore, is the maximum protection provided in the event of a decline in cash prices.

SELL CALLS. A short call hedge is often referred to as a *covered call sale,* or as a *buy/write* strategy. In Table 20.18 the distributor sells 100 September 58 calls, receiving a premium of 2.6 cents per gallon. This strategy does not provide adequate downside protection if cash prices decline substantially. Such protection is limited to the 2.6 cents per gallon option premium received.

SHORT MIN-MAX OPTION STRATEGY. The heating oil wholesaler may also use a min-max option hedging strategy similar to that discussed earlier in Sec-

TABLE 20.17
Hedging against a price decrease in heating oil with long bear put spreads

May 17, 1991:

> Buy 100 September 58 puts for $0.018,
> sell 100 September 54 puts for $0.0055,
> establishing long bear put spreads at a
> net premium cost of $0.0125 per gallon.

		Per gallon	Total profit/(loss)
Alternative scenarios on August 9, 1991:			
i) Cash heating oil increases to 60 cents			
Sales price		$0.6000	$2,520,000
Less: Cost	$(0.5525)		
Carrying cost	(0.0267)		
Total Cost		(0.5792)	(2,432,640)
Gain on forward sales		0.0208	87,360
Loss on options (the net premium cost)		(0.0125)	(52,500)
Net profit		0.0083	34,860
Effective sales price ($0.60 − $0.0125):		$0.5875	
ii) Cash heating oil price decreases to 52 cents			
Sales price		$0.5200	$2,184,000
Less: Cost	$(0.5525)		
Carrying cost	(0.0267)		
Total cost		(0.5792)	(2,432,640)
Loss on forward sales		(0.0592)	(248,640)
Gain on options ($0.5800 − $0.5400 − $0.0125)		0.0275	115,500
Net loss		$(0.0317)	(133,140)
Effective sales price ($0.52 + $0.0275):		$0.5475	

tion 20.5.1. Specifically, the wholesaler can sell 100 September 62 calls at 1.10 cents per gallon and use the proceeds to purchase 100 September 56 puts at 1 cent per gallon, establishing a collar against a price decline. Table 20.19 shows the possible net sales prices that result from this strategy under hypothetical price scenarios. The first column shows hypothetical September 91 heating oil futures prices on August 9, 1991. Columns (2), (3), and (4) show the gains and losses on the respective long put and short call option positions, as well as on the net option position. Column (5) shows the cash prices on August 9. Since the basis between the cash and spot month futures prices is assumed to be constant, the cash price is always 0.66 cents less than the respective futures price in Column (1). The last

TABLE 20.18
Hedging against a price decrease in heating oil by shorting call options

May 17, 1991:

Sell 100 September 58 calls at a premium
of $0.026 per gallon

		Per gallon	Total profit/(loss)
Alternative scenarios on August 9, 1991:			
i) Cash heating oil price increases to 60 cents			
Sales price		$0.6000	$2,520,000
Less: Cost	$(0.5525)		
Carrying cost	(0.0267)		
Total Cost		(0.5792)	(2,432,640)
Gain on forward sales		0.0208	87,360
Loss on options ($0.58 − $0.6066 + $0.026)		(0.0006)	(2,520)
Net profit		0.0202	84,840
Effective sales price ($0.60 − $0.0006):		$0.5994	
ii) Cash heating oil price decreases to 52 cents			
Sales price		$0.5200	$2,184,000
Less: Cost	$(0.5525)		
Carrying cost	(0.0267)		
Total cost		(0.5792)	(2,432,640)
Loss on forward sales		(0.0592)	(248,640)
Gain on options (the premium)		0.0260	109,200
Net loss		$(0.0332)	(139,440)
Effective sales price ($0.52 + $0.0260):		$0.5460	

column is the effective net selling price, which is derived either by adding the net option gain to the cash price or by deducting the net option loss from the cash price. Figure 20-12 provides a graphical presentation of these results.

Table 20.20 provides a specific example. Since the September 91 heating oil futures price is 58.80 cents on May 17, both the September 56 put and the September 62 call are out-of-the-money. If, on August 9, cash heating oil prices rise to 60 cents, both the puts and calls will still be out-of-the-money. The wholesaler will lose the put premium but receive the call premium, resulting in a net gain of 0.10 cents, and an effective net purchase price of 60.10 cents. Alternatively, if heating oil prices fall to 52 cents, the puts will be in-the-money and the calls will be out-of-the-money. In this case the wholesaler will realize a net gain of 3.44 cents on his option position, resulting in an effective net sales price of 55.44 cents.

TABLE 20.19

Hedging against a price decrease in heating oil with a short min-max option strategy (Long put & short call on September 91 heating oil futures)

Premiums on May 17, 1991:

    September 56 put = 1.0 cents

    September 62 call = 1.1 cents

August 9, 1991:

Futures price	Profit (loss) on option positions			Cash price	Net sales price
	Long put	Short call	Net		
	(Cents per gallon)				
52.00	3.00	1.10	4.10	51.34	55.44
54.00	1.00	1.10	2.10	53.34	55.44
56.00	−1.00	1.10	0.10	55.34	55.44
58.00	−1.00	1.10	0.10	57.34	57.44
60.00	−1.00	1.10	0.10	59.34	59.44
62.00	−1.00	1.10	0.10	61.34	61.44
64.00	−1.00	−0.90	−1.90	63.34	61.44
66.00	−1.00	−2.90	−3.90	65.34	61.44

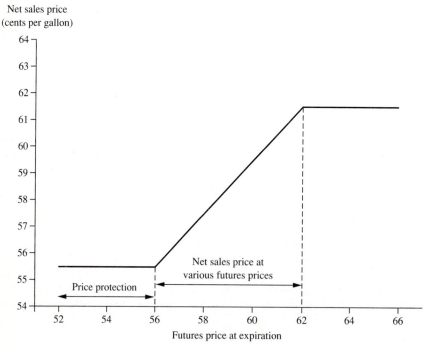

FIGURE 20-12

Min-max option hedging strategy: Heating oil (buy Sep 56 put, sell Sep 62 call).

612

TABLE 20.20
Hedging against a price decrease in heating oil with a short min-max option strategy

May 17, 1991:

  Buy 100 September 56 puts for $0.010,
  sell 100 September 62 calls for $0.011.

		Per gallon	Total profit/(loss)

Alternative scenarios on August 9, 1991:

i) Cash heating oil increases to 60 cents				
Sales price			$0.6000	$2,520,000
Less: Cost	$(0.5525)			
Carrying cost	(0.0267)			
Total Cost			(0.5792)	(2,432,640)
Gain on forward sales			0.0208	87,360
Loss on puts (the option premium)	(0.010)			
Gain on calls (the option premium)	0.011			
Gain on options			0.0010	4,200
Net profit			0.0218	91,560
Effective sales price ($0.60 + $0.0010)			$0.6010	
ii) Cash heating oil price decreases to 52 cents				
Sales price			$0.5200	$2,184,000
Less: Cost	$(0.5525)			
Carrying cost	(0.0267)			
Total cost			(0.5792)	(2,432,640)
Loss on forward sales			(0.0592)	(248,640)
Gain on puts ($0.5600 − $0.5266 − $0.010)	0.0234			
Gain on calls (the option premium)	0.0110			
Gain on options			0.0344	144,480
Net loss			$(0.0248)	(104,160)
Effective sales price ($0.52 + $0.0344)			$0.5544	

SUMMARY. The following table provides a summary of what the wholesaler's effective sales price would be on August 9, 1991, under each of the alternative hedging strategies discussed above:

Effective selling prices under alternative hedging strategies

Alternative price scenarios on August 9	Unhedged	Alternative hedging strategies				
		Short futures	Buy put	Long bear put spread	Sell call	Min-max
($)	($)	($)	($)	($)	($)	($)
0.60	0.60	0.5814	0.5820	0.5875	0.5994	0.6010
0.52	0.52	0.5814	0.5554	0.5475	0.5460	0.5544

613

The costs and benefits of these strategies can be summarized as follows:

	Benefits	Costs
Sell futures	Locks in a specific price	Does not benefit from price increases
Buy puts	Locks in a floor sales price	Option premium
Bear put spread	Locks in a limited floor sales price	Net option premium
Sell calls	Augments current income	Does not benefit from price increases
Min-max	Sets a collar price range at low cost	Limited participation in a price increase

20.6   DELTA HEDGING

Delta hedging is a strategy based on an option's delta. It is used to immunize portfolios from changes in underlying asset prices. The objective of this strategy is very much like that of a hedger using futures—to match cash market losses with futures market gains.

The delta of an option, as previously discussed in Section 19.6.1, is the expected change in the option premium for a given change in the price of the commodity underlying the option. A delta of 0.50 implies that the option premium will change by 50 cents for every one dollar change in the price of the underlying commodity (or by 50 percent of the change in the underlying asset price). Thus, if an option with a delta of 0.50 is used as a hedge, two options must be held for every unit of the commodity being hedged in order to equate value changes in both the option and asset portfolios. In other words, the minimum-variance hedge ratio is the reciprocal of the option's delta. A delta of 0.50, therefore, implies a minimum-variance hedge ratio of 2. As an option's delta changes, so too will the minimum-variance hedge ratio.

20.6.1   Variations in Delta: An Example

Option deltas are not constant, and it is important to recognize why they change. Long call and short put deltas are positive; short call and long put deltas are commonly shown as negatives. A delta of about 0.50, or −0.50, is characteristic of at- or near-the-money call and put options. As an option moves into-the-money, its delta approaches 1.0 in the case of long calls and −1.0 in the case of long puts. As an option moves out-of-the-money, both put and call deltas approach zero.

Table 20.21 shows how the value of delta changes as an option moves from at-the-money to deep in-the-money, using the May 89 crude oil futures call option with a $15 strike price, during the period December 1, 1988, to March 31, 1989. Column 2 shows the crude oil cash price, and column 3 provides the May 89 futures price. The option premium on the May 15 call is shown in column 4, and the corresponding implied price volatility is shown in column 5. The last column provides the daily delta on the May 15 call option.

TABLE 20.21
Daily Changes in May 89 Crude Oil Futures Call Options (strike price: $15.00): December 1, 1988, to May 31, 1989

Date	Cash price ($)	May 89 futures ($)	Option premuim ($)	Implied volatility (%)	Delta
881201	15.60	15.19	1.13	32.05	0.5381
881202	15.65	15.23	1.13	31.64	0.5433
881205	15.35	14.88	0.95	30.69	0.4941
881206	15.45	14.96	1.01	29.30	0.5037
881207	15.75	15.27	1.18	30.43	0.5493
881208	15.45	15.01	1.03	28.51	0.5103
881209	15.84	15.34	1.20	28.85	0.5607
881212	16.05	15.38	1.22	29.26	0.5668
881213	16.00	15.09	1.08	27.35	0.5224
881214	16.35	15.47	1.23	26.90	0.5841
881215	16.35	15.17	1.06	29.02	0.5358
881216	16.70	15.41	1.21	23.00	0.5825
881219	16.30	15.23	1.07	28.91	0.5446
881220	17.75	15.43	1.23	24.51	0.5831
881221	16.30	15.50	1.26	27.02	0.5901
881222	16.50	15.70	1.41	27.37	0.6210
881223	16.30	15.89	1.46	26.95	0.6518
881227	16.95	16.12	1.72	28.40	0.6811
881228	16.95	15.96	1.57	30.78	0.6507
881229	16.75	15.73	1.43	28.70	0.6254
881230	17.25	16.00	1.56	18.93	0.7286
890103	17.35	16.18	1.59	24.18	0.7206
890104	17.10	16.10	1.57	24.21	0.7090
890105	17.40	16.32	1.71	30.14	0.7069
890106	17.55	16.38	1.66	28.49	0.7245
890109	17.70	16.48	1.80	24.25	0.7706
890110	17.70	16.47	1.76	24.19	0.7710
890111	18.15	16.71	2.00	25.20	0.7950
890112	18.15	16.80	2.10	29.05	0.7787
890113	18.50	16.84	2.20	29.93	0.7787
890116	18.90	16.98	2.30	33.51	0.8063
890117	18.95	17.21	2.48	29.38	0.8250
890118	19.25	18.11	3.33	32.94	0.8704
890119	19.30	17.94	3.12	39.19	0.8276
890120	18.85	17.62	2.83	39.76	0.8038
890123	17.35	16.72	2.07	34.29	0.7540
890124	17.55	16.97	2.23	31.20	0.8001
890125	18.10	17.34	2.54	33.15	0.8244
890126	17.70	16.90	2.20	36.71	0.7650
890127	17.75	16.87	2.15	34.91	0.7727
890130	17.30	16.59	1.90	30.15	0.7732
890131	17.05	16.40	1.72	30.76	0.7462

(continued)

TABLE 20.21—cont'd.

Date	Cash price ($)	May 89 futures ($)	Option premuim ($)	Implied volatility (%)	Delta
890201	17.50	16.99	2.18	31.12	0.8160
890202	17.75	17.14	2.35	33.81	0.8159
890203	17.55	16.77	1.96	31.39	0.7938
890206	17.40	16.58	1.79	29.73	0.7870
890207	17.70	16.90	2.07	29.88	0.8261
890208	17.50	16.69	1.88	31.00	0.7962
890209	17.40	16.64	1.83	30.35	0.7963
890210	17.10	16.33	1.58	32.65	0.7425
890213	17.60	16.67	1.88	31.17	0.8030
890214	17.40	16.45	1.68	31.95	0.7712
890215	18.25	16.98	2.12	32.35	0.8352
890216	18.35	17.12	2.27	33.97	0.8415
890217	18.55	17.27	2.40	33.42	0.8610
890221	18.60	17.14	3.12	32.50	0.8646
890222	17.85	17.39	2.49	32.23	0.8901
890223	17.85	17.39	2.47	32.12	0.8932
890224	18.05	17.58	2.63	28.05	0.9306
890227	18.15	17.65	2.69	28.52	0.9379
890228	18.15	17.66	2.70	27.69	0.9441
890301	18.30	17.79	2.82	25.47	0.9586
890302	18.70	18.12	3.12	28.47	0.9595
890303	18.55	17.93	2.93	29.12	0.9540
890306	18.65	18.09	3.09	27.61	0.9664
890307	18.30	17.79	2.79	28.05	0.9601
890308	18.55	18.10	3.10	27.26	0.9696
890309	18.50	18.08	3.08	27.75	0.9697
890310	18.50	18.09	3.10	25.95	0.9735
890313	19.05	18.63	3.63	27.81	0.9775
890314	19.30	18.80	3.80	27.01	0.9787
890315	19.80	19.19	4.19	25.75	0.9796
890316	19.85	19.24	4.24	25.27	0.9800
890317	20.35	19.48	4.48	26.43	0.9805
890320	19.50	19.34	4.34	26.66	0.9802
890321	20.05	20.05	5.05	27.06	0.9806
890322	20.05	20.04	5.04	28.22	0.9812
890323	20.15	20.15	5.15	27.91	0.9818
890327	20.55	20.53	5.53	32.75	0.9844
890328	19.90	19.91	4.91	35.96	0.9851
890329	20.20	20.20	5.20	32.00	0.9861
890330	20.80	20.81	5.81	35.80	0.9869
890331	20.20	20.19	5.19	39.56	0.9878

On December 1, the cash price of crude oil was $15.60 per barrel, and the May 89 futures price was $15.19. Thus, on that day the May 15 call is basically at-the-money, has a premium of $1.13 per barrel, and a delta of 0.5381.

Between December 1, 1988, and March 31, 1989, crude oil cash prices increased from $15.60 to $20.20, and May 89 futures prices increased from $15.19 to $20.19. Consequently, the May 15 call became a deep in-the-money option, and its delta increased from 0.5381 to 0.9878.

Since option deltas change with both asset prices and the passage of time, it is necessary to adjust option hedge ratios that are based upon the delta. This process, known as *dynamic option hedging,* requires continuous hedge management. Below we provide two examples of such hedging.

20.6.2 Applying Delta Hedging

CASE 1: Assume that on December 1, 1988, a refiner enters into an agreement to purchase 300,000 barrels of crude oil each month for his refinery for the next five months at the spot month crude oil futures price prevailing at the time of delivery. In other words, the price that the refiner will pay for crude oil in January 1989 will be determined by the February 89 futures price on the delivery day in January, the price paid in February will depend on the March 89 futures price in February 1989, and so forth. To hedge his price exposure, the refiner could go long 300 crude oil futures contracts for each of the next five contract months.[16] However, the refiner decides instead to use a strip of crude oil futures call options: February 89, March 89, April 89, May 89, and June 89. Let us use the at-the-money futures call options on the May 89 futures contract discussed earlier to illustrate this delta hedging strategy. Table 20.22 provides the step-by-step procedure employed in delta hedging.

As shown in Table 20.21, on December 1, the May 15 call has a delta of 0.5381. Thus, the hedge ratio on that date is computed as

$$\frac{1}{0.5381} = 1.8584$$

and the total number of call options that the refiner must purchase is 558:[17]

$$300 \times 1.8584 = 557.52$$

Therefore, on December 1, the refiner buys 558 May 15 call options at a premium of $1.13 per barrel.

---

[16]In other words, the refiner could go long 300 February 89 futures, 300 March 89 futures, and so forth, since each crude oil futures contract calls for delivery of 1000 barrels (300,000 barrels/1000 barrels).

[17]The hedge ratio is the reciprocal of the option's delta and indicates the number of options that will equate changes in the value of the option position to changes in the value of the position being hedged.

TABLE 20.22
Delta hedging example

	Gain (loss)
December 1, 1988:	
i) Agrees to buy 300,000 barrels of crude oil in each of the next five months, the purchase price to be based on spot month crude oil futures prices on the delivery day.	
ii) Buy 558 crude oil May 89 futures options with $15 strike price at $1.13 per barrel to hedge the above price exposure for April 1989 (May 89 futures price is at $15.19).	
December 5, 1988:	
i) May 89 futures price drops to $14.88, a loss of $0.31 from Dec. 1. Total potential acquisition cost is reduced by: [$0.31 × 300,000 = $93,000]	$93,000
ii) May 15 call is at $0.95, a loss of $0.18 from Dec. 1. Total loss on option hedge position is [$0.18 × 1,000 × 558 = $100,440]	(100,440)
Net unrealized loss	(7,440)
iii) Buy additional 49 May 15 calls at $0.95 to rebalance the hedge.	
December 30,1988:	
i) May 89 futures price is at $16, a gain of $1.12 from Dec. 5. Potential acquisition cost is increased by: [$1.12 × 300,000 = $336,000]	(336,000)
ii) May 15 call is at 1.59, a gain of $0.64 from Dec. 5. Total gain on option position is: [$0.64 × 1,000 × 607 = $388,480]	388,480
Net unrealized gain	52,480
iii) Sell 195 May 15 calls at $1.59 to rebalance the hedge.	

Since the option's delta changes continuously, the refiner must monitor the call option hedge ratio closely and adjust it when necessary. More specifically, on December 5, the May 89 futures price drops to $14.88, reducing the refiner's potential acquisition cost by $0.31 per barrel, or a total of $93,000. The May 15 call option premium also declines on December 5 to $0.95, a loss of $0.18, which represents a total loss of $100,440 for all 558 contracts. The refiner, therefore, has an unrealized *net* loss of $7440. In addition, the delta associated with the long calls changes from 0.5381 to 0.4941, so that the hedger needs to adjust his hedge ratio. The new hedge ratio should be 2.0239 ($\frac{1}{0.4941}$), and 607 call option contracts are now required to maintain the hedge (300 × 2.0239). Thus, on December 5, the refiner buys an additional 49 May 15 calls (607 − 558). (See Table 20.22.)

If the refiner were to maintain this hedge ratio until December 30, he would have an unrealized net gain of $52,480. Between December 5 and December 30 the crude oil cash price increases from $15.35 to $17.25, and the May 89 futures price increases from $14.88 to $16. The refiner's potential cost, therefore, increases by $336,000. However, the May 15 call increases in value by $0.64 per barrel, giving him a profit of $388,480 on the option position. As a result, the refiner has a net unrealized gain of $52,480 (see Table 20-22).

The net gain of $52,480 occurred because of a change in the option's delta. As shown in Table 20-21, the value of the delta changed from 0.4941 to 0.7286 between December 5 and 30. The minimum-variance hedge ratio on December 30, therefore, is 1.3725 ($\frac{1}{0.7286}$), and the total option contracts required is 411.75 (300 × 1.3725). Thus, the refiner needs to sell 195 calls to bring his total position down to 412 long calls (607-195).

CASE 2: In our first example a refiner hedged a cash position with an option position, varying the option position in response to changes in the option delta. In this example a trader holds a call option position which she hedges with futures contracts.

In particular, using the data from the previous example (see Table 20.21), the option trader who sells the 558 May 15 calls to the refiner decides to hedge her price exposure on this short option position by going long May 89 crude oil futures. On December 1, the May 15 call has a delta of 0.5381. Since the parallel delta on a long futures contract is equal to 1, the option trader must go long 300 May 89 futures contracts to immunize her option position.[18] On December 2, since the option delta changes to 0.5433, she will have to go long an additional three May 89 futures contracts to maintain her neutral position (558 × 0.5433 − 300). The total long futures position, therefore, will be 303 contracts. On December 5 the delta declines to 0.4941, and the option trader will have to sell 27 futures contracts to maintain her neutral position (558 × 0.4941 − 303). Thus, to hedge her price exposure effectively, the option trader must continually adjust her futures position in response to changes in the option delta.

OTHER CONSIDERATIONS. When one employs delta hedging, several other factors must be taken into consideration. First, adjusting the hedge ratio can entail substantial transaction costs in a volatile market, since the hedge ratio will have to be adjusted frequently. Second, option values will also change because of changes in an option's gamma, theta, and lambda. A delta hedging strategy, therefore, is often used only for short periods of time during which changes in these factors are expected to be small.

---

[18]To obtain the requisite number of futures contracts, the option position is multiplied by the option delta, or 558 × 0.5381 = 300.

CONCLUSION

This chapter has examined the fundamental option strategies used by both speculators and hedgers. In discussing these strategies, the pros and cons of each are compared, and, where appropriate, are contrasted with strategies using futures to achieve the same investment or risk management objectives.

Among the speculative strategies discussed are simple put and call positions and various combinations of options and futures, such as covered calls and puts and synthetic calls and puts. In addition, various option spreads are examined. We show how vertical call and put option spreads can be used to profit from changes in underlying asset prices, and how horizontal option spreads can be used to profit from stable asset prices. Finally, we demonstrate how long and short straddles—the simultaneous purchase and sale of different combinations of puts and calls—can be used to profit from various movements in underlying asset prices. While the discussion in this chapter is by no means a complete analysis of all speculative option trading strategies, it provides a sufficient foundation on which traders can construct and experiment with more complex strategies that more accurately reflect their particular price expectations and risk preferences.

The second half of the chapter shows how the option trading strategies discussed in the first half of the chapter can be used to manage price risk. We show how the various option positions can be used to hedge against either an increase or decrease in the underlying asset price, and then compare these strategies with those using futures contracts. Numerical examples of each strategy are provided.

Tables 20.2, 20.3, and 20.4 contain what is fundamentally a complete summary of the pros and cons of the various option trading strategies discussed in the chapter, both with respect to their speculative and hedging applications.

The chapter concludes with a discussion and demonstration of delta hedging. We show how option hedges can be adjusted to maintain a fully hedged position over time, as both underlying asset prices change and the time to expiration of an option changes.

In conclusion, this chapter, together with Chapters 18 and 19, provides a comprehensive overview of the fundamentals of options and option markets, demonstrating how futures options can be used either to profit from changes in asset prices or to manage the risk exposure associated with such price changes.

QUESTIONS

1. If an investor has a substantial unrealized gain on a short futures position and does not want to liquidate the position, but still wants to lock in this profit and also be able to profit from further price declines, what kind of option position should he assume?
2. Why would an investor wish to write a covered call? What must be his implicit expectation about the price of the underlying asset in the near future?
3. What is the difference between a vertical and horizontal option spread?
4. What distinguishes a bull vertical spread from a bear vertical spread?
5. Construct a profit profile graph for a bull vertical put spread similar to the call spread shown in Figure 20-5.

6. Show how the maximum profit and loss shown in Figure 20-6 is calculated.

7. If an investor expects asset prices to rise, why would she want to use a vertical bull spread rather than simply buying a call option or going long futures?

8. What is the difference between a straddle and a spread?

9. What type of price expectations might cause an investor to assume a long straddle position?

10. If a commercial firm holding an inventory of heating oil believes that heating oil prices may fall significantly in the near future, what option hedging strategy would you recommend? Explain your answer. How would you compare the strategy you recommended with the alternative strategy of hedging with futures?

11. If you had decided to hedge with options, would you use the delta hedging approach to determine your hedge ratio? Why? How do you determine the hedge ratio? What are some disadvantages of using delta hedging?

12. Suppose that an investor strongly believes that asset prices will remain stable for at least the next three months. What option strategy might she use to profit from this belief?

SUGGESTED READING

Arnott, R. "Modeling Portfolios with Options: Risks and Returns." *Journal of Portfolio Management,* Vol. 7 (Fall 1980), pp.66-73.

Bookstaber, R. and R. Clark. "Options Can Alter Portfolio Return Distributions." *Journal of Portfolio Management,* Vol. 8 (Spring 1981), pp. 63–70.

Boyle, P. and D. Emanuel. "Discretely Adjusted Option Hedges." *Journal of Financial Economics,* Vol. 7 (September 1980), pp. 255–282.

Katz, R. "The Profitability of Put and Call Option Writing." *Industrial Management Review,* (Fall 1986), pp. 55–69.

Merton, R. M. Scholes, and M. Gladstein. "The Returns and Risks of Alternative Call-Option Portfolio Investment Strategies." *Journal of Business,* Vol. 51 (April 1978), pp. 183–242.

Morar, B. and A. Naciri. "Options and Investment Strategies." *The Journal of Futures Markets,* Vol. 10, No. 5 (Oct. 1990), pp. 505–518.

Murphy, A., and D. Gordon. "An Empirical Note on Hedging Mortgages with Puts." *The Journal of Futures Markets,* Vol. 10, No. 1 (1990), pp. 75–78.

Slivka, R. "Risk and Return for Option Investment Strategies." *Financial Analysts Journal,* Vol. 36 (September/October 1980), pp. 67–73.

Slivka, R. "Call Options Spreading." *Journal of Portfolio Management,* Vol. 8 (Spring 1981), pp. 71–76.

Yates, J. and R. Kopprasch. "Writing Covered Call Options: Profits and Risks." *Journal of Portfolio Management,* Vol. 7 (Fall 1980), pp. 74–79.

REFERENCES

Angrist, S. "Silver Prices Continue to Languish as Supply Outstrips Demand and Production is Maintained." *The Wall Street Journal*, January 14, 1991, p. 14, Col. 3.

Averch, H. and L. Johnson. "Behavior of the Firm Under Regulatory Constraint." *American Economic Review*, Vol. 51 (December 1962), pp. 1051–1069.

Barone-Adesi, G. and R. Whaley. "Efficient Analytic Approximation of American Option Values," *Journal of Finance*, Vol. 42, No. 2 (June 1987), pp. 301–320.

Barron's National Business and Financial Weeks. "Markets for Futures and Options," 1983.

Beja, A. and G. Goldman. "On the Dynamic Behavior of Prices in Disequilibrium," *Journal of Finance*, Vol. 35 (May 1980), pp. 235–248.

Black, F. "The Pricing of Commodity Contracts," *Journal of Financial Economics*, Vol. 3 (September 1976), pp. 167–79.

Black, F. and J. Cox. "Valuing Corporate Securities: Some Effects of Bond Indenture Provisions," *Journal of Finance*, Vol. 31 (May 1976), pp. 351–68.

Black, F. and M. Scholes. "The Pricing of Options and Corporate Liabilities," *Journal of Political Economy*, Vol. 81, No. 3 (1973), pp. 637–654.

Blanchard, O. "Bubbles, Rationale Expectations, and Financial Markets," *Crises in the Economic and Financial Structure*, ed. by Paul Wachtel, Lexington Books, Lexington, Mass. 1982, pp. 295–315.

Brennan, M. and E. Schwartz. "The Valuation of American Put Options," *Journal of Finance*, Vol. 32 (May 1977), pp. 449–462.

Brennan, M. and E. Schwartz. "Saving Bonds, Retractable Bonds and Callable Bonds," *Journal of Financial Economics*, Vol. 5 (August 1977), pp. 67–88.

Brennan, M. and E. Schwartz. "Convertible Bonds: Valuation and Optimal Strategies for Call and Conversion," *Journal of Finance*, Vol. 32 (December 1977), pp. 1699–1716.

Brennan, M. and E. Schwartz. "Alternative Methods for Valuing Debt Options," Working Paper 888, University of British Columbia, 1982.

Brorsen, B. W. and S. H. Irwin. "Public Futures Funds," *The Journal of Futures Markets*, Vol. 5, No. 2 (Summer 1985), pp. 149–171.

Brorsen, B. W. and S. H. Irwin. "Futures Funds and Price Volatility," *The Review of Futures Markets*, Vol. 6, No. 2 (1987), pp. 118–135.

Chang, E. "Return to Speculators and the Theory of Normal Backwardation," *Journal of Finance*, Vol. 40, No. 1 (March 1985), pp. 193–208.

Chicago Board of Trade. "Profile of U.S. Futures Markets," *Retail Traders 1983–84*, Part 1, 1983.

Chicago Mercantile Exchange. "SPAN Overview," July 1990.

Chicago Mercantile Exchange. "SPAN Technical Specifications," July 1990.

Chicago Mercantile Exchange. "Standard Portfolio Analysis of Risk," 1989.

Chiras, D. and S. Manaster. "The Information Content of Option Prices and a Test of Market Efficiency," *Journal of Financial Economics*, Vol. 6 (March 1978), pp. 213–234.

Commodity Futures Trading Commission. "Committment of Traders in Futures." 1989.

Constantinides, G. and R. Rosenthal. "Strategic Analysis of the Competitive Exercise of Certain Financial Options," *Journal of Economic Theory*, Vol. 32 (February 1984), pp. 128–38.

Cornell, B. and M. Reinganum. "Forward and Futures Prices: Evidence from the Foreign Exchange Markets," *Journal of Finance*, Vol 36 (1981), pp. 1035–1045.

Courtadon, G. "The Pricing of Options on Default-Free Bonds," *Journal of Financial and Quantitative Analysis*, Vol. 17 (March 1982), pp. 75–100.

Cox, J., J. Ingersoll, and S. Ross. "An Analysis of Variable Rate Loan Contracts," *Journal of Finance*, Vol. 35 (May 1980), pp. 389–404.

Cox, J., J. Ingersoll, and S. Ross. "The Relation between Forward and Futures Prices," *Journal of Financial Economics*, Vol. 9 (1981), pp. 321–346.

Cox, J. and S. Ross. "The Valuation of Options for Alternative Stochastic Processes," *Journal of Financial Economics*, Vol. 3 (January–March 1976), pp. 145–166.

Cox, J., S. Ross, and M. Rubinstein. "Option Pricing: A Simplified Approach," *Journal of Financial Economics*, Vol. 7 (September 1979), pp. 229–263.

Cox. J. and M. Rubinstein. *Options Markets*, Prentice-Hall, Englewood Cliffs, NJ, 1985.

Douglas, G. "Risk in the Equity Markets: An Empirical Appraisal of Market Efficiency," *Yale Economic Essays*, Spring 1969, pp. 3–45.

Draper, D. "The Small Public Trader in Futures Markets," *Futures Markets: Regulatory Issues*, ed. by A. Peck, American Enterprise Institute, Washington, D.C., 1985, pp. 211–269.

Dunn, K. and J. McConnell. "Valuation of GNMA Mortgage-Backed Securities," *Journal of Finance*, Vol. 36 (June 1981), pp. 599–616.

Eckards, W. and D. Rogoff. "100 Percent Margins Revisited," *Journal of Finance*, Vol. 31 (June 1976), pp. 995–1000.

Ederington, L. "The Hedging Performance of the New Futures Market," *Journal of Finance*, Vol. 34 (March 1979), pp. 157–170.

Edwards, F. "Managerial Objectives in Regulated Industries: Expense-Preference Behavior in Banking," *Journal of Political Economy*, Vol. 85 (January–February 1977), pp. 147–162.

Edwards, F. "Futures Trading and Cash Market Volatility: Stock Index and Interest Rate Futures," *The Journal of Futures Markets*, Vol. 8, No. 4 (1988), pp. 421–439.

Elliot, R. *Nature's Law: The Secret of the Universe*, Elliot, New York, 1946.

Elton, E., M. Gruber, and J. Rentzler. "The Performance of Publicly Offered Commodity Funds," *Financial Analysts Journal*, Vol 46 (July–August 1990), pp. 23–30.

Emanuel, D. "Warrant Valuation and Exercise Strategy," *Journal of Financial Economics*, Vol. 12 (August 1983), pp. 211–36.

Federal Reserve System, Board of Governors. "A Review and Evaluation of Federal Margin Regulations," December, 1984.

Financial Accounting Standard Board. Statement No. 80, "Accounting for Futures Contracts," August 1984.

Friedman, M. "The Case of Flexible Exchange Rates," *Essays in Positive Economics*, University of Chicago Press, Chicago, 1953.

"Futures Trading Act of 1978." Committee Print, Committee on Agriculture, Nutrition, and Forestry, U.S. Senate, 95th Congress, 2nd Session, Vol. 136 (January 1979).

Galai, D. "A Test of Market Efficiency of the Chicago Board Options Exchange," *Journal of Business*, Vol. 50 (April 1977), pp. 167–197.

Garman, M. and M. Klass. "On the Estimation of Security Price Volatilities from Historical Data," *Journal of Business*, Vol. 53 (January 1980), pp. 67–78.

Garman, M. and S. Kohlhagen. "Foreign Currency Option Values," *Journal of International Money and Finance*, Vol. 2 (December 1983), pp. 231–237.

Gay, G. and S. Manaster. "The Quality Option Implicit in Futures Contracts," *Journal of Financial Economics*, Vol. 13, No. 3 (September 1984), pp. 353–370.

Gay, G. and S. Manaster. "Implicit Delivery Options and Optimal Delivery Strategies for Financial Futures Contracts," *Journal of Financial Economics*, Vol. 16, No. 1 (May 1986), pp. 41–72.

Geske, R. and H. Johnson. "The Valuation of Corporate Liabilities as Compound Options: A Correction," *Journal of Financial and Quantitative Analysis*, Vol. 19 (June 1984), pp. 231–32.

Geske, R. and R. Roll. "On Valuing American Call Options with the Black-Scholes European Formula," *Journal of Finance*, Vol. 39 (June 1984), pp. 443–455.

Giddy, I. "Foreign Exchange Options," *The Journal of Futures Markets*, Vol. 3 (Summer 1983), pp. 143–166.

Gilberg, D. "Regulation of New Financial Instruments Under the Federal Securities and Committee Law," *Vanderbilt Law Review*, Vol. 39 (November 1986), pp. 1600–1640.

Grube, R., O. Joy, and D. Panton. "Market Responses to Federal Reserve Changes in the Initial Margin Requirements," *Journal of Finance*, Vol 34 (June 1979), pp. 659–675.

Hartzmark, M. "The Effects of Changing Margin Levels on Futures Market Activity, the Composition of Traders in the Market, and Price Performance," *Journal of Business*, Vol. 59 (1986), pp. S151–S180.

Hartzmark, M. "Returns to Individual Traders of Futures: Aggregate Results," *Journal of Political Economy*, Vol. 95, No. 6 (December 1987), pp. 1292–1306.

Hartzmark, M. "Luck versus Forecast Ability: Determinants of Trader Performance in Futures Markets," *Journal of Business*, 64 (1991), pp. 49–74.

Hedge, S. "On the Value of the Implicit Delivery Options," *The Journal of Futures Markets*, Vol. 9, No. 5 (October 1989), pp. 421–437.

Herbst, A. and J. McCormack. "An Examination of the Risk-Return Characteristics of Portfolio Combining Futures Contracts with Common Stocks," *The Review of Futures Markets*, Vol. 6, No. 3 (1987), pp. 416–425.

Hieronymus, T. *Economics of Futures Trading for Commercial and Personal Profit*, 2nd Edition, Commodity Research Bureau, New York, 1977.

Hoag, J. "The Valuation of Commodity Options." *Option Pricing*, ed. by Menachem Brenner, D.C. Heath, Lexington, MA, 1983, pp. 183–221.

Houthakker, H. "Can Speculators Forecast Prices?" *Review of Economics and Statistics*, Vol 38 (May 1957), pp. 143–51.

Indiana Farm Bureau, Commodity Futures Trading Commission Dock No. 75–14.

Irwin, S. H. and B. W. Brorsen. "Public Funds," *The Journal of Futures Markets*, Vol. 5 (1985), pp. 463–485.

Irwin, S. H., T. Krukemyer, and C. Zulauf. "Investment Performance of Public Commodity Pools: 1979–1989," Unpublished paper, January 1991.

Irwin, S. H. and J. Uhring. "Do Technical Analysts Have Holes in Their Shoes?" *The Review of Futures Markets*, Vol. 3 (1984), pp. 264–277.

Jarrow, R. and G. Oldfield. "Forward Contracts and Futures Contracts," *Journal of Financial Economics*, Vol. 11 (1981), pp. 373–382.

Johnson, H. "An Analytic Approximation to the American Put Price," *Journal of Financial and Quantitative Analysis*, Vol. 18 (March 1983), pp. 141–148.

Johnson, L. "The Theory of Hedging and Speculation in Commodity Futures," *Review of Economic Studies*, Vol. 27 (October 1960), pp. 139–151.

Jones, P. and S. Smith. "Applications of Option Pricing Analysis." *Handbook of Financial Economics*, ed. by J. Bicksler, North-Holland Publishing Company, New York, 1979, pp. 79–121.

Kahl, K. and S. Miller."Performance of Estimated Hedge Ratios Under Yield Uncertainty," *The Journal of Futures Markets*, Vol. 9 (August 1989), pp. 307–321.

Kane, A. and A. Marcus. "The Quality Option in the Treasury Bond Futures Markets: An Empirical Assessment," *The Journal of Futures Markets*, Vol. 6, No. 2 (Summer 1986b), pp. 231–248.

Largay, J. and R. West. "Margin Changes and Stock Price Behavior," *Journal of Political Economy*, Vol. 81 (March/April 1973), pp. 328–339.

Largay, J. "100 Percent Margins: Combatting Speculation in Individual Security Issues," *Journal of Finance*, Vol. 28 (September 1973), pp. 973–986.

London Metal Exchange. "Rules and Regulations." January 1991.

Lorie, L. and L. Fisher. "Some Studies of the Variability of Returns on Investment in Common Stocks," *Journal of Business*, Vol. 43 (April 1970), pp. 99–134.

Lukac, L. P., B. W. Brorsen, and S. H. Irwin. "Similarity of Computer Guided Technical Trading Systems," *The Journal of Futures Markets*, Vol. 8 (1988), pp. 1–14.

Lukac, L. P., B. W. Brorsen, and S. H. Irwin. "The Usefulness of Historical Data in Selecting Parameters for Technical Trading Systems," *The Journal of Futures Markets*, Vol. 9 (February 1989), pp. 55–66.

Ma, C. and L. Soenen. "Arbitrage Opportunities in Metal Futures Markets," *The Journal of Futures Markets*, Vol. 8 (1988), pp. 199–209.

Macaulay, F. *Some Theoretical Problems Suggested by the Movements of Interest Rates, Bond Yields, and Stock Prices in the United States since 1956*, National Bureau of Economic Research, New York, 1938.

Maddala, G. and J. Yoo. "Risk Premia and Price Volatility in Futures Markets," *The Journal of Futures Markets*, Vol. 11 (April 1991), pp. 165–178.

Markham, J. "Prohibited Floor Trading Activities Under the Commodity Exchange Act," *Fordham Law Review*, Vol. 58 (October 1989), pp. 1–52.

Mason, S. and R. Merton. "The Role of Contingent Claims Analysis in Corporate Finance," In *Recent Advances in Corporate Finance*, ed. by E. Altman and M. Subrahmanyam, Dow Jones-Irwin, Homewood, IL, 1985.

McConnell, J. and J. Schallheim. "Valuation of Asset Leasing Contracts," *Journal of Financial Economics*, Vol. 12 (August 1983), pp. 237–261.

Meisner, J. and J. Richards. "Option Premium Dynamics: With Applications to Fixed Income Portfolio Analysis," In *Advances in Bond Analysis and Portfolio Strategies*, ed. by F. Fabozzi and D. Garlicki, Probus Publishing, Chicago, 1987.

Merton, R. "Theory of Rational Option Pricing," *Bell Journal of Economics and Management Science*, Vol. 4, No. 1 (1973), pp. 141–183.

Merton, R. "On the Pricing of Corporate Debt: The Risk Structure of Interest Rates," *Journal of Finance*, Vol. 29 (May 1974), pp. 449–470.

Merton, R. "Option Pricing When Underlying Stock Returns are Discontinuous," *Journal of Financial Economics*, Vol. 3 (January–March 1976), pp. 125–144.

Moore, T. "Stock Market Margin Requirements," *Journal of Political Economy*, Vol. 74 (April 1966), pp. 158–167.

Neftci, S. and A. Policano. "Can Chartists Outperform the Market? Market Efficiency Tests for Technical Analysis," *The Journal of Futures Markets*, Vol 4 (1984), pp. 465–478.

Officer, R. "The Variability of the Market Factor of the New York Stock Exchange," *Journal of Business*, Vol. 46 (1973), pp. 434–453.

Parkison, M. "Option Pricing; The American Put," *Journal of Finance*, Vol. 32 (January 1977), pp. 21–36.

Parkison, M. "The Extreme Value Method for Estimating the Variance of the Rate of Return," *Journal of Business*, Vol. 53 (January 1980), pp. 61–65.

Peltzman, S. "Capital Investment in Commercial Banking and Its Relationship to Portfolio Regulation," *Journal of Political Economy*, pp. 78 (January 1970), pp. 1–26.

Peters, E. "Hedged Equity Portfolios: Components of Risk and Return," *Advances in Futures and Options Research*, Vol. 1B (1986), pp. 75–92.

Presidential Task Force on Market Mechanisms. "Report of the Presidential Task Force on Market Mechanisms," U.S. Government Printing Office, Washington, D.C., 1988.

Pruitt, S. and R. White. "The CRISMA Trading System: Who Says Technical Analysis Can't Beat the Market?" *The Journal of Portfolio Management*, Vol. 15 (Spring 1988), pp. 55–58.

Pruitt, S. and R. White. "Exchange-Traded Options and CRISMA Trading," *The Journal of Portfolio Management*, Vol. 16 (Spring 1989), pp. 55–56.

Rendleman R. and C. Carabini. "The Efficiency of the Treasury Bill Futures Market," *Journal of Finance*, Vol. 34 (1979), pp. 895–914.

Report by the Committee on Futures Regulation of the Association of the Bar of City of New York. "Large Order Execution in the Futures Markets," 1989.

Richard, S. and M. Sundaresan. "A Continuous Time Equilibrium Model of Forward Prices and Futures Prices in a Multigood Economy," *Journal of Financial Economics*, Vol. 9 (1981), pp. 347–372.

Rockwell, C. "Normal Backwardation, Forecasting and the Returns to Commodity Futures Traders," *Food Research Institute Studies*, Vol. 7 (1967), pp. 107–130.

Roll, R. "An Analytic Valuation Formula for Unprotected American Call Options on Stocks with Known Dividends," *Journal of Financial Economics*, Vol 4 (November 1977), pp. 251–258.

Roll, R. "Price Volatility, International Market Links, and Their Implications for Regulatory Policies," *Journal of Financial Services Research*, Vol. 3 (December 1989), pp. 211–246.

Ross, R. "Financial Consequences of Trading Commodity Futures Contracts," *Illinois Agricultural Economics*, Vol. 15, No. 2 (July 1975) pp. 27–31.

Rubenstein, M. and H. Leland. "Replicating Options with Positions in Stock and Cash," *Financial Analyst Journal*, Vol. 37 (1981), pp. 3–12.

Schwert, G. "Stock Market Volatility," *Financial Analysts Journal*, Vol. 46, No. 3 (May/June 1990), pp. 23–24.

SEC Staff Report. "The October 1987 Market Break," February 9, 1988, pp. 3–18.

Sharpe, W. and G. Cooper. "Risk-Return Classes of New York Exchange Common Stocks," *Financial Analyst Journal*, Vol. 28 (1972), pp. 46–54.

Silber, W. "Innovation, Competition, and New Contract Design in Futures Markets," *The Journal of Futures Markets*, Vol. 1 (Summer 1981), pp. 123–155.

Smith, C. "Option Pricing: A Review," *Journal of Financial Economics*, Vol. 3 (January–March 1976), pp. 3–51.

Smith, C. and J. Zimmerman. "Valuing Employee Stock Option Plans Using Option Pricing Models," *Journal of Accounting Research*, Vol. 14 (Autumn 1976), pp. 357–64.

Stassen, J. "How the Growth of Fundamental Economic Issues Has Been Done Through Legislation Rather than Research," Unpublished manuscript, January 1981.

Stein, J. "Speculative Price: Economic Welfare and the Idiot of Chance," *Review of Economic and Statistics*, Vol. 63 (May 1981), pp. 223–232.

Stewart, W. "An Analysis of Speculative Trading in Grain Futures," *Technical Bulletin No. 1001*, U.S. Department of Agriculture, Washington, D.C., 1949.

Stulz, R. "Options on the Minimum or the Maximum of Two Risky Assets: Analysis and Applications," *Journal of Financial Economics*, Vol. 10 (July 1982), pp. 161–185.

Teweles, R., C. Harlow, and H. Stone. *The Commodity Futures Games: Who Wins? Who Loses? Why?* McGraw-Hill, New York, 1977.

Tomek, W. and S. Querin. "Random Processes in Prices and Technical Analysis," *The Journal of Futures Markets*, Vol. 4 (1988), pp. 15–23.

Trippi, R. "A Test of Option Market Efficiency Using a Random-Walk Valuation Model," *Journal of Economics and Business*, Vol. 29 (1977), pp. 93–98.

U.S. Securities and Exchange Commission. "The October 1987 Market Break," February 1988.

Whaley, R. "On the Valuation of American Call Options on Stock with Known Dividends," *Journal of Financial Economics*, Vol. 9 (June 1981), pp. 207–212.

GLOSSARY

Alternative Delivery Procedure (ADP)   A delivery mechanism in which the long and the short agree to carry out physical delivery under terms or conditions that are different from the standardized contract rules prescribed by the exchange. The ADP is available only after the end of trading in a futures contract and after the longs and shorts have been matched by the clearinghouse.

American option   An option that can be exercised at any time prior to the contract's expiration date.

at-the-money option   An option with a strike price equal to the current market price of the underlying asset.

backwardation   A market in which the futures prices of distant contract months are lower than those of the nearby contract months.

basis   The difference between cash and futures prices for the same commodity. Specifically, the cash price minus the futures price of a specific futures contract.

basis point   A basis point equals 0.01%, or one-hundredth of a percentage point.

bear market   A market in which prices are declining.

beta   A statistical measure of the risk associated with an individual stock or stock portfolio. The beta of a stock or stock portfolio is the volatility of that stock's or stock portfolio's return relative to the volatility of the overall market return.

bull market   A market in which prices are rising.

cash settlement   A procedure whereby futures contracts are settled without physical delivery of the underlying asset. Instead, there is a final marking to market to the cash price prevailing at the close of futures trading, and gains and losses are paid.

call option   An option giving the buyer the right to purchase the underlying asset at a fixed strike price.

chart analysis   The use of graphs and charts to analyze prices and trading behavior and to anticipate future price movements.

clearinghouse   The organization which assures the financial integrity of futures and options markets by guaranteeing obligations among its clearing members. It registers, monitors, matches, and guarantees trades, and carries out the financial settlement of futures and options transactions. The clearinghouse can be part of an exchange or can be a separate corporate entity.

clearing member   A member of the clearinghouse. Each clearing member must be a member of an exchange, but not all members of an exchange are members of a clearinghouse. All trades made by a nonclearing member must be registered with, and eventually settled through, a clearing member.

Commodity Futures Trading Commission (CFTC)   The federal regulatory agency established by the Commodity Exchange Act of 1974 to regulate futures and commodity option trading in the United States.

commodity fund   An entity in which funds contributed by a number of people are pooled together to trade futures and option contracts under professional management.

contract market   A commodity futures market or an exchange that qualifies under the Commodity Futures Trading Commission Act.

contango market   A market in which futures prices are higher for distant contracts than for nearby delivery months—just the opposite of a backwardation market.

convenience yield   The implied yield or nonpecuniary return from holding a commodity. It is also a measure of the degree of backwardation in a market.

convergence   Refers to the tendency of cash and futures prices to come together (i.e., the basis shrinks) as a futures contract approaches expiration.

conversion   A trading strategy that locks in an arbitrage profit by combining a long put and a short call with the same strike price and expiration date with a long position in the underlying asset.

conversion factor   A pricing factor used to determine the prices of T-bonds or T-notes eligible for delivery on futures contracts. These factors are provided by exchanges.

cost-of-carry   The costs associated with holding (or carrying) a commodity or an asset. These include financing costs, storage costs, and insurance costs.

covered option   A written option that is covered by an offsetting cash or futures position in the underlying asset, or by an offsetting option position with specific characteristics. As such, it has little or no risk.

crack spread   The simultaneous purchase (or sale) of crude oil futures and sale (or purchase) of heating oil and gasoline futures.

cross hedging   Hedging a commodity by using a futures contract on a different but related commodity. A cross hedge is based on the premise that the price movements of the two commodities are related.

crush spread   The purchase (or sale) of soybean futures and the simultaneous sale (or purchase) of soybean oil and soymeal futures.

deliverable stock   The quantity of a commodity that meets exchange-specified quality standards and is available for delivery at exchange-specified locations (such as approved warehouses).

delivery month   The calendar month during which delivery on a futures contract must be made.

delta   A measure of how much an option's premium changes for a given unit change in the underlying asset price.

discount   The amount by which the price of one asset is less than the price of another asset.

duration   A measure of a bond's price sensitivity to interest rate changes. The duration of a bond is commonly defined as the weighted average of the maturities of the bond's coupon and principal repayment cash-flows, where the weights are the fractions of the bond's price that the cash flows in each time period represent.

Exchange of Futures for Physical (EFP)   An alternative delivery procedure for futures contracts where there is an exchange of a specified quantity of the cash instrument for the equivalent quantity of futures contracts at mutually agreed-upon terms and at a mutually agreed-upon price. Partners to an EFP must notify the clearinghouse of such transaction.

expiration date   The date on which an option or futures contract expires.

exercise   The action taken by the holder of an option contract either to acquire the underlying asset at the option's strike price or to sell the underlying asset at the option's strike price.

European option   An option that can be exercised only on the option's expiration date.

fair value   The theoretical value of an option or futures contract derived from a mathematical valuation model. It is also referred to as the no-arbitrage value.

floor broker   An exchange member who executes orders for other members and customers on the floor of an exchange.

floor trader   A member of an exchange who trades on the floor of the exchange.

forward contract   A deferred contract in which two parties agree to buy and sell an asset at some future time under conditions that are mutually agreeable. In contrast to futures contracts, forward contracts are not standardized, nor are they marked to market.

fundamental analysis   A method of analyzing and predicting price movements using information about supply and demand.

Futures Commission Merchant (FCM) An individual or organization legally authorized to solicit or accept orders to buy or sell futures and futures options contracts, subject to the rules of a contract market. An FCM also accepts payment from customers and holds the margin deposits of those whose orders are accepted. An FCM must be registered with the Commodity Futures Trading Commission.

futures contract An agreement to make or take delivery of a standardized amount of a commodity during a specific month, at a price established by open auction in a trading pit, under terms and conditions set by a designated contract market where trading is conducted.

gamma A measure of how much the delta of an option changes for a unit change in the price of the underlying asset.

hedging The technique of offsetting the price risk inherent in any cash market position by taking an opposite position in the futures or option market.

hedge ratio The number of futures or options contracts required to achieve a certain hedging objective.

horizontal option spread Buying and selling call or put options with the same strike price but different expiration dates.

implied volatility The future price volatility of an asset that the market currently expects, based on the current price of a particular option contract.

in-the-money option An option is "in-the-money" if it has intrinsic value. A call option is in-the-money if the current asset price is above the option's strike price; a put option is in-the-money if the current asset price is below the option's price.

initial margin The amount of money that customers must put up when establishing a futures or options position to guarantee their contract obligations.

intercommodity spread A spread between two futures contracts written on different but related commodities.

interest rate parity A theory stating that the forward premium or discount on one currency in terms of another currency is directly related to the short-term interest rate differential between the two countries.

intracommodity spread A spread between two futures contracts written on the same commodity but with different delivery months.

intrinsic value The amount by which an option is in-the-money (see in-the-money option.

invoice price The acutal price that a long pays to a short at delivery after all adjustments.

long hedge A futures or option position to protect against a possible increase in prices.

maintenance margin The minimum amount of funds that must be kept as margin at all times. If a customer's equity falls below this level, a broker must issue a margin call to restore the customer's equity to the initial margin level.

margin call   A demand made by a clearinghouse to a clearing member, or by a brokerage firm to a customer, for additional funds.

mark to market   The daily adjustment of an open futures contract to reflect profits and losses on the contract. All futures positions are marked to market using closing (or settlement) futures prices.

minimum-risk hedge ratio   The number of futures or option contracts that results in the maximum possible reduction in the variability of the value of the total hedged position.

nearby contract   A futures contract calling for delivery in a month that is nearby in time.

offset   The liquidation of a futures or option contract through the purchase or sale of an identical contract.

open interest   The total number of futures or options contracts on a given commodity that have not yet been offset by an opposite futures or option transaction, or fulfilled by delivery of the commodity, or by exercise of the option. Each open contract has both a buyer and a seller.

open outcry   The auction market system used on the floors of futures exchanges to establish prices. All bids and offers are made openly by public, competitive outcry in such manner as to be recognizable by others in the trading pit.

option contract   The right to buy or sell a specific quantity of a specific asset at a fixed price at or before a specified future date.

option premium   The price of an option, which the option buyer pays and the option seller receives.

option writer   The person who sells or grants an option in return for a premium, and who is obligated to perform if the option holder exercises his right under the option contract.

out-of-the-money option   An option that has no intrinsic value: a call option with a strike price above the current asset price, or a put option with a strike price below the current asset price.

par grade   The grade of a commodity that is used as the standard for making delivery on a futures contract.

position limit   The maximum number of futures or option contracts that a speculator can hold, which is determined by the Commodity Futures Trading Commission and/or the exchange upon which the contract is traded.

premium   The amount by which the price of one asset exceeds the price of another asset.

price limit   The maximum price advance or decline permitted on a contract during one day or trading session under the rules of the exchange.

put option   An option which gives its buyer the right to sell the underlying asset at a fixed price.

repurchase agreement (repo) An agreement between two parties under which one party agrees to sell a security and to buy it back on an agreed-upon date and at an agreed-upon price. The difference between the original sale price and the subsequent repurchase price is in effect the interest on a loan, which, when expressed as an interest rate, is commonly known as the repo rate.

reverse conversion A trading strategy that locks in an arbitrage profit by selling an asset short, writing a put, and buying a call on the asset with the same terms.

rho A measure of the change in an option premium with respect to a percentage-point change in the interest rate.

short hedge A futures or option position to protect against a possible decrease in prices.

speculator A trader whose objective is to make profits by successfully anticipating future price movements.

spread The price difference between two futures or option contracts.

strike price The price at which an option holder may buy or sell the underlying asset, which is specified in an option contract.

technical analysis An analysis of past prices and trading behavior in order to predict future price movements.

theta A measure of the change in an option premium with respect to a one-day change in time-to-maturity.

time value The amount of money that option buyers are willing to pay for an option in anticipation that, over time, a change in the underlying asset price will cause the option to increase in value. An option's premium is the sum of time value and intrinsic value. The amount by which an option's premium exceeds the option's intrinsic value is the option's time value.

uncovered option Writing a call or a put on an underlying asset not owned by the writer.

variation margin The gains or losses on open futures contracts calculated by marking the contracts to the market price at the end of each trading day (or session). These gains or losses are credited or debited by the clearinghouse to each clearing member's account, and by members to their respective customers' accounts.

vertical option spread Buying and selling call or put options with the same expiration date but different strike prices.

lambda A measure of the change in an option premium with respect to a unit change in the price volatility of the option's underlying asset.

volatility A measure of the amount by which an asset's price fluctuated over a given period. Normally, it is measured by the annualized standard deviation of daily returns on the asset.

volume The number of transactions that takes place during a specific trading session.

yield-to-maturity The rate of return earned by a debt instrument if held to maturity.

SOURCE
ACKNOWLEDGMENTS

CHAPTER 1

Figure 1-1: Volume of futures trading, 1960 through 1990. From Futures Industry Association, Inc.

Table 1.1: Futures contracts traded by commodity group. From Futures Industry Association, Inc.

Table 1.2: Ten most actively traded futures contracts. From Futures Industry Association, Inc.

Table 1.3: Futures exchanges in the United States. From Futures Industry Association, Inc.

Table 1.4: Commodity futures contracts traded in 1990. From Futures Industry Association, Inc.

Table 1.6: Crude oil, light 'sweet'—New York Mercantile Exchange commitments of traders in all futures combined and indicated futures, May 31, 1990. From Commodity Futures Trading Commission.

Table 1.9: Foreign futures and commodity options exchanges. From Futures Industry Association, Inc.

CHAPTER 4

Table 4.1: Price quotations for futures contracts. From *The Wall Street Journal,* April 12, 1989. Reprinted by permission of *The Wall Street Journal,* © 1989 Dow Jones & Company, Inc. All Rights Reserved Worldwide.

Table 4.2: Heating oil: Cash price quotations on April 11, 1989 (cents per gallon). From *Platt's Oilgram Price Report,* April 12, 1989.

Table 4.3: Cash prices for precious metals. From *The Wall Street Journal,* April 12, 1989. Reprinted by permission of *The Wall Street Journal,* © 1989 Dow Jones & Company, Inc. All Rights Reserved Worldwide.

Table 4.6: Copper futures prices: April 11, 1984. From *The Wall Street Journal,* April 12, 1984. Reprinted by permission of *The Wall Street Journal,* © 1984 Dow Jones & Company, Inc. All Rights Reserved Worldwide.

CHAPTER 9

Appendix: Commodity Futures Trading Commission's guideline 1, part 5 (amended). Issued in Washington, D.C. on October 28, 1982, by the CFTC.

633

CHAPTER 10

Figure 10-5: Seasonality of dividend yields for MMI index companies, 1987. From Chicago Board of Trade.

Table 10.2: Stock market indexes, November 22, 1989. From *The Wall Street Journal,* November 24, 1989. Reprinted by permission of *The Wall Street Journal,* © 1989 Dow Jones & Company, Inc. All Rights Reserved Worldwide.

Table 10.6: Foreign stock indexes: 1989. From *Financial Times,* November 24, 1989.

Table 10.13: Stock index futures: Price quotations, volume, and open interest for November 23, 1989. From *The Wall Street Journal,* November 24, 1989. Reprinted by permission of *The Wall Street Journal,* © 1989 Dow Jones & Company, Inc. All Rights Reserved Worldwide.

Table 10.16: Comparative quarterly annualized dividend yields on various stock indexes (percentages): 1984–1988. From Chicago Board of Trade.

Table 10.17: Expected dividends on MMI stocks during first quarter of 1989, as of January 1989. From Chicago Board of Trade.

Table 10.21: Selected sample of S&P 500 stocks: December 1988. From *Business Week,* 1989 special edition.

CHAPTER 11

Figure 11-1: S&P 500 cash and futures indexes, Monday, October 19, 1987. From Brady Commission Report, p. 31.

Figure 11-2: S&P 500 price differentials, Monday, October 19, 1987. From Brady Commission Report, pp. 31–37.

Figure 11-3: Volatility of daily returns to S&P 500, based on 15-minute returns within the day, and the ratio of S&P futures volume to NYSE share trading volume, February 1, 1983–October 19, 1989. From William Schwert, "Stock Market Volatility," *Financial Analyst Journal,* May/June 1990, pp. 23–34.

CHAPTER 12

Table 12.2: Price quotations for Treasury bills. From *The Wall Street Journal,* January 23, 1990. Reprinted by permission of *The Wall Street Journal,* © 1990 Dow Jones & Company, Inc. All Rights Reserved Worldwide.

Table 12.4: Prices of T-bill futures on January 22, 1990. From *The Wall Street Journal,* January 23, 1990. Reprinted by permission of *The Wall Street Journal,* © 1990 Dow Jones & Company, Inc. All Rights Reserved Worldwide.

Table 12.5: Short-term interest rates. From *The Wall Street Journal,* January 23, 1990. Reprinted by permission of *The Wall Street Journal,* © 1990 Dow Jones & Company, Inc. All Rights Reserved Worldwide.

Table 12.7: Prices of Eurodollar futures on January 22, 1990. From *The Wall Street Journal,* January 23, 1990. Reprinted by permission of *The Wall Street Journal,* © 1990 Dow Jones & Company, Inc. All Rights Reserved Worldwide.

CHAPTER 13

Table 13.3: Treasury bond cash quotations, as of December 13, 1989. From *The Wall Street Journal,* December 14, 1989. Reprinted by permission of *The Wall Street Journal,* © 1989 Dow Jones & Company, Inc. All Rights Reserved Worldwide.

Table 13.5: Conversion factors for outstanding T-bond futures contracts, September 15, 1989. From Chicago Board of Trade.

Table 13.6: Treasury bond futures prices, December 13, 1989. From *The Wall Street Journal,* December 14, 1989. Reprinted by permission of *The Wall Street Journal,* © 1989 Dow Jones & Company, Inc. All Rights Reserved Worldwide.

Table 13.7: U.S. Treasury bond futures conversion factor to yield 8.000%. From Financial Publishing Co.

CHAPTER 14

Table 14.2: Exchange rate quotations: August 9, 1990. From *The Wall Street Journal,* August 10, 1990. Reprinted by permission of *The Wall Street Journal,* © 1990 Dow Jones & Company, Inc. All Rights Reserved Worldwide.

Table 14.3: Key currency cross rates: August 9, 1990. From *The Wall Street Journal,* August 10, 1990. Reprinted by permission of *The Wall Street Journal,* © 1990 Dow Jones & Company, Inc. All Rights Reserved Worldwide.

Table 14.7: Currency futures price quotations: August 9, 1990. From *The Wall Street Journal,* August 10, 1990. Reprinted by permission of *The Wall Street Journal,* © 1990 Dow Jones & Company, Inc. All Rights Reserved Worldwide.

CHAPTER 15

Table 15.5: Cash price quotations: Agricultural and soft commodities (December 10, 1990). From *The Wall Street Journal,* December 11, 1990. Reprinted by permission of *The Wall Street Journal,* © 1990 Dow Jones & Company, Inc. All Rights Reserved Worldwide.

Table 15.6: Price quotations for agricultural and soft futures (December 10, 1990). From *The Wall Street Journal,* December 11, 1990. Reprinted by permission of *The Wall Street Journal,* © 1990 Dow Jones & Company, Inc. All Rights Reserved Worldwide.

Table 15.9: Cash price quotations for energy products (December 10, 1990). From *The Wall Street Journal,* December 11, 1990. Reprinted by permission of *The Wall Street Journal,* © 1990 Dow Jones & Company, Inc. All Rights Reserved Worldwide.

Table 15.10: Futures price quotations for crude oil, heating oil, and gasoline (December 10, 1990). From *The Wall Street Journal,* December 11, 1990. Reprinted by permission of *The Wall Street Journal,* © 1990 Dow Jones & Company, Inc. All Rights Reserved Worldwide.

Table 15.13: Futures price quotations for precious metals (December 10, 1990). From *The Wall Street Journal,* December 11, 1990. Reprinted by permission of *The Wall Street Journal,* © 1990 Dow Jones & Company, Inc. All Rights Reserved Worldwide.

Table 15.14: Cash price quotations for metals (December 10, 1990). From *The Wall Street Journal,* December 11, 1990. Reprinted by permission of *The Wall Street Journal,* © 1990 Dow Jones & Company, Inc. All Rights Reserved Worldwide.

Table 15.18: London Metal Exchange trading statistics: January 9, 1991. From International Commodities Clearing House.

Table 15.19: London Metal Exchange: Price quotations (December 10, 1990). From *The Wall Street Journal,* December 11, 1990. Reprinted by permission of *The Wall Street Journal,* © 1990 Dow Jones & Company, Inc. All Rights Reserved Worldwide.

Table 15.20: LME forward price quotations on February 27, 1991 (Broker–Dealer quotations). From Metallgesellschaft.

Table 15.21: Comparison of physical deliveries: NYMEX's crude oil versus LME base metals contracts, July 1988 to December 1990. From New York Mercantile Exchange for crude oil data, and International Commodity Clearing House for LME data.

CHAPTER 16

Figure 16-17: The CRISMA trading system for Pepsi stock, December 1989 to September 1990. From Knight-Ridder Trade Center.

Table 16.1: Economic statistics release schedule. From Indosuez Carr Futures Inc.

Table 16.2: Case study: A fundamental analysis of silver. From *The Wall Street Journal,* January 14, 1991. Reprinted by permission of *The Wall Street Journal,* © 1991 Dow Jones & Company, Inc. All Rights Reserved Worldwide.

CHAPTER 17

Figure 17-1: Total number of public futures funds. From Managed Accounts Reports.

Figure 17-2: Equity growth of public futures funds. From Managed Accounts Reports.

Table 17.1: Eurodollars (3-month)—International Monetary Market commitments of traders in all futures combined and indicated futures, November 30, 1990. From Commodity Futures Trading Commission.

Table 17.2: Volume of speculation in selected futures markets during 1989. From "Commitment of Traders in Futures," Commodity Futures Trading Commission, 1989.

Table 17.3: Reasons for initial decision to invest in futures: *Barron's* and CBT surveys, 1983 (percent). From *Barron's* National Business and Financial Weeks; Chicago Board of Trade survey; and D. Draper, "The Small Public Trader in Futures Markets."

Table 17.4: Primary investment objectives: *Barron's* survey, 1983. From *Barron's* National Business and Financial Weeks; and D. Draper, "The Small Public Trader in Futures Markets."

Table 17.5: Opinions about futures trading: *Barron's* survey, 1983. From *Barron's* National Business and Financial Weeks; and D. Draper, "The Small Public Trader in Futures Markets."

Table 17.6: Number of investment transactions in past 12 months: *Barron's* survey, 1983. From *Barron's* National Business and Financial Weeks; and D. Draper, "The Small Public Trader in Futures Markets."

Table 17.7: Performance measures by market and trader type (returns in millions of dollars). From Hartzmark, "Returns to Individual Traders of Futures."

Table 17.8: Annual rates of return of public commodity funds, 1984–1989. Data from Monthly Reports issued by Managed Accounts Reports, Inc.

Table 17.9: Returns on comparable investments, 1984–1989. Data from Managed Account Reports, and "Stock, Bonds, Bills, and Inflation: 1989 Yearbook" published by R.C. Ibbotson Associate, Inc.

Appendix: Estimating average operational and management fees. From Scott H. Irwin, Terry R. Krukemyer, and Carl R. Zulauf, "Investment Performance of Public Commodity Pools: 1979–1989," unpublished paper, January 1991.

CHAPTER 18

Table 18.3: Top 10 option contracts: U.S. and foreign. From Futures Industry Association, Inc. and *Futures and Options World*.

Table 18.4: Price quotations for stock options: November 1, 1990. From *The Wall Street Journal*, November 2, 1990. Reprinted by permission of *The Wall Street Journal*, © 1990 Dow Jones & Company, Inc. All Rights Reserved Worldwide.

Table 18.6: Price quotations for index options: November 1, 1990. From *The Wall Street Journal*, November 2, 1990. Reprinted by permission of *The Wall Street Journal*, © 1990 Dow Jones & Company, Inc. All Rights Reserved Worldwide.

Table 18.7: Price quotations for interest rate and currency options: November 1, 1990. From *The Wall Street Journal*, November 2, 1990. Reprinted by permission of *The Wall Street Journal*, © 1990 Dow Jones & Company, Inc. All Rights Reserved Worldwide.

Table 18.8: U.S. trading in futures options: 1985–90. From Futures Industry Association, Inc.

Table 18.9: Exchange-traded options on futures contracts. From Futures Industry Association, Inc.

Table 18.10a, b, and c: Price quotations for futures options: November 1, 1990. From *The Wall Street Journal*, November 2, 1990. Reprinted by permission of *The Wall Street Journal*, © 1990 Dow Jones & Company, Inc. All Rights Reserved Worldwide.

Table 18.13: S&P 500 futures prices: November 1, 1990. From *The Wall Street Journal*, November 2, 1990. Reprinted by permission of *The Wall Street Journal*, © 1990 Dow Jones & Company, Inc. All Rights Reserved Worldwide.

CHAPTER 20

Table 20.5: Oil prices. From *The Wall Street Journal*, May 20, 1991. Reprinted by permission of *The Wall Street Journal*, © 1991 Dow Jones & Company, Inc. All Rights Reserved Worldwide.

INDEX